THE CREATURE FROM FROM JEKYLL ISLAND

ADDITIONAL COPIES OF THIS BOOK

Single copy: Softcover $24.50; Hardbound $36.00*
For shipping in the US add $5.50*

2 to 11 copies: Softcover $19.60; Hardbound $28.80*
For shipping and insured US delivery add:
$6.85 for 2 copies*
$8.30 for 3 copies*
We pay shipping on 4 to 11 copies.*

Case purchases, 12 books per case:
Softcover $176.40 ($14.70 per book)*
Hardbound $259.20 ($21.60 per book)*
For shipping and insured US delivery add:
$30.00 per case of softcover.*
$34.00 per case of hardbound.*

California residents add 8.25 % sales tax to book price.*

Outside the US: Call for shipping charges.

Send your order to
American Media
P.O. Box 4646
Westlake Village, CA 91359-1646

For immediate service, order by phone
and charge to your credit card.
Call toll-free: (800) 595-6596

Orders may also be placed over the Internet at
www.realityzone.com

*These prices are good through April 2010.
After that date, please call for confirmation.

HOW TO READ
THIS BOOK

Thick books can be intimidating. We tend to put
off reading them until we have a suitably large
block of time—which is to say, often they are
never read. That is the reason a preview has been
placed at the beginning and a summary at the end
of each chapter. All of these together can be read
in about one hour. Although they will not contain
details nor documentation, they will cover the
major points and will provide an overview of the
complete story. The best way to read this book,
therefore, is to begin with the previews of each
section, followed by the chapter previews and
summaries. Even if the reader is not in a hurry,
this is still an excellent approach. A look at the
map before the journey makes it easier to grapple
with a topic such as this which spans so much
history.

THE CREATURE FROM JEKYLL ISLAND

A Second Look at the Federal Reserve

Fourth edition

by G. Edward Griffin

American Media

Dedicated to the next generation–especially my own brood:
James, Daniel, Ralph, and Kathleen.
May this effort help to build for them a better world.

27th printing: 2010 January
26th printing: 2009 October
25th printing: 2009 July
24th printing: 2009 May
23rd printing: 2009 February
22nd printing: 2008 November
21st printing: 2008 September
20th printing: 2008 February
19th printing: 2007 July
18th printing: 2006 September
17th printing: 2005 June
16th printing: 2004 September
15th printing: 2003 December
14th printing: 2003 February

13th printing: 2002 June
12th printing: 2001 July
11th printing: 2000 October
10th printing: 2000 January
9th printing: 1999 September
8th printing: 1999 February
7th printing: 1998 May
6th printing: 1997 September
5th printing: 1996 August
4th printing: 1995 September
3rd printing: 1995 April
2nd printing: 1994 November
1st printing: 1994 July

German edition: 2006 August
Japanese edition: 2005 February

Fourth edition: 2002 June
Third edition: 1998 May
Second edition: 1995 September
First edition: 1994 July

Published by American Media
P.O. Box 4646
Westlake Village, California 91359-1646

Library of Congress Catalog Card Number: 95–80322

Softcover ISBN 978–0–912986–39–5
Hardbound ISBN 978–0–912986–40–1
Manufactured in the United States

TABLE OF CONTENTS

I. WHAT CREATURE IS THIS?..................... 1

What is the Federal Reserve System? The answer may surprise you. It is not federal and there are no reserves. Furthermore, the Federal Reserve Banks are not even banks. The key to this riddle is to be found, not at the beginning of the story, but in the middle. Since this is not a textbook, we are not confined to a chronological structure. The subject matter is not a curriculum to be mastered but a mystery to be solved. So let us start where the action is.

II. A CRASH COURSE ON MONEY............... 133

The eight chapters contained in this and the following section deal with material that is organized by topic, not chronology. Several of them will jump ahead of events that are not covered until later. Furthermore, the scope is such that the reader may wonder what, if any, is the connection with the Federal Reserve System. Please be patient. The importance will eventually become clear. It is the author's intent to cover concepts and principles before looking at events. Without this background, the history of the Federal Reserve is boring. *With* it, the story emerges as an exciting drama which profoundly affects our lives today. So let us begin this adventure with a few discoveries about the nature of money itself.

III. THE NEW ALCHEMY........................ 215

The ancient alchemists sought in vain to convert lead into gold. Modern alchemists have succeeded in that quest. The lead bullets of war have yielded an endless source of gold for those magicians who control the Mandrake Mechanism. The startling fact emerges that, without the ability to create fiat money, most modern wars simply would not have occurred. As long as the Mechanism is allowed to function, future wars are inevitable. This is the story of how that came to pass.

IV. A TALE OF THREE BANKS.................... 307

It has been said that those who are ignorant of history are doomed to repeat its mistakes. It may come as a surprise to learn that the Federal Reserve System is America's fourth central bank, not its first. We have been through all this before and, each time, the result has been the same. Interested in what happened? Then let's set the coordinates of our time machine to the colony of Massachusetts and the year 1690. To activate, turn to chapter fifteen.

V. THE HARVEST 405

Monetary and political scientists continue to expound the theoretical merits of the Federal Reserve System. It has become a modern act of faith that economic life simply could not go on without it. But the time for theory is past. The Creature moved into its final lair in 1913 and has snorted and thrashed about the landscape ever since. If we wish to know if it is a creature of service or a beast of prey, we merely have to look at what it has done. And, after the test of all those years, we can be sure that what it has done, it will continue to do. Or, to use the Biblical axiom, a tree shall be known by the fruit it bears. Let us now examine the harvest.

VI. TIME TRAVEL INTO THE FUTURE

In the previous sections of this book, we have travelled through time. We began our journey by stepping into the past. As we crisscrossed the centuries, we observed wars, treachery, profiteering, and political deception. That has brought us to the present. Now we are prepared to ride our time machine into the future. It will be a hair-raising trip, and much of what lies ahead will be unpleasant. But it has not yet come to pass. It is merely the projection of present forces. If we do not like what we see, we still have an opportunity to change those forces. The future will be what we choose to make it.

PHOTOGRAPHS

APPENDIX

BIBLIOGRAPHY

INDEX

PREFACE

Does the world really need another book on the Federal Reserve System?

I have struggled with that question for several years. My own library is mute testimony to the fact that there has been no shortage of writers willing to set off into the dark forest to do battle with the evil dragon. But, for the most part, their books have been ignored by the mainstream, and the giant snorter remains undaunted in his lair. There seemed to be little reason to think that I could succeed where so many others have failed.

Yet, the idea was haunting. There was no doubt in my mind that the Federal Reserve is one of the most dangerous creatures ever to stalk our land. Furthermore, as my probing brought me into contact with more and more hard data, I came to realize that I was investigating one of the greatest "who-dunits" of history. And, to make matters worse, I discovered who did it.

Someone has to get this story through to the public. The problem, however, is that the public doesn't want to *hear* it. After all, this is bad news, and we certainly get enough of that as it is.

Another obstacle to communication is that this tale truly is incredible, which means *unbelievable*. The magnitude by which reality deviates from the accepted myth is so great that, for most people, it simply is beyond credibility. Anyone carrying this message is immediately suspected of paranoia. Who will listen to a madman?

And, finally, there is the subject matter itself. It can become pretty complex. Well, at least that's how it seems at first. Treatises on this topic often read like curriculum textbooks for banking and finance. It is easy to become ensnared in a sticky web of terminology and abstractions. Only monetary professionals are motivated to master the new language, and even they often find themselves in serious disagreement. For example, in a recent letter circulated by a group of monetary experts who, for years, have conducted an ongoing exchange of ideas regarding monetary reform, the editor said: "It is frustrating that we cannot find more agreement among ourselves on this vital issue. We seem to differ so much on definitions and on, really, an

i

unbiased, frank, honest, correct understanding of just how our current monetary system does function."

So why am I now making my own charge into the dragon's teeth? It's because I believe there is a definite change in the wind of public attitude. As the gathering economic storm draws nearer, more and more people will tune into the weather report—even if it *is* bad news. Furthermore, the evidence of the truth of this story is now so overpowering that I trust my readers will have no choice but to accept it, all questions of sanity aside. If the village idiot says the bell has fallen from the steeple and comes dragging the bell behind him, well,…

Lastly, I have discovered that this subject is not as complicated as it first appeared to be, and I am resolved to avoid the pitfall of trodding the usual convoluted path. What follows, therefore, will be the story of a crime, not a course on criminology.

It was intended that this book would be half its present size and be completed in about one year. From the beginning, however, it took on a life force of its own, and I became but a servant to its will. It refused to stay within the confines prescribed and, like the genie released from its bottle, grew to enormous size. When the job was done and it was possible to assess the entire manuscript, I was surprised to realize that *four* books had been written instead of one.

First, there is a crash course on money, the basics of banking and currency. Without that, it would be impossible to understand the fraud that now passes for acceptable practice within the banking system.

Second, there is a book on how the world's central banks—the Federal Reserve being one of them—are catalysts for war. That is what puts real fire into the subject, because it shows that we are dealing, not with mere money, but with blood, human suffering, and freedom itself.

Third, there is a history of central banking in America. That is essential to a realization that the *concept* behind the Federal Reserve was tried *three times* before in America. We need to know that and especially need to know why those institutions were eventually junked.

Finally, there is an analysis of the Federal Reserve itself and its dismal record since 1913. This is probably the least important part of all, but it is the reason we are here. It is the least important, not because the subject lacks significance, but because it has been written before by writers far more qualified and more skilled than I. As mentioned previously, however, those volumes generally have remained unread except by technical historians, and the Creature has continued to dine upon its hapless victims.

There are seven discernible threads that are woven throughout the fabric of this study. They represent the reasons for abolition of the Federal Reserve System. When stated in their purest form, without embellishment or explanation, they sound absurd to the casual observer. It is the purpose of this book, however, to show that these statements are all-too-easy to substantiate.

The Federal Reserve System should be abolished for the following reasons:

- It is incapable of accomplishing its stated objectives. (Chapter 1.)
- It is a cartel operating against the public interest. (Chapter 3.)
- It is the supreme instrument of usury. (Chapter 10.)
- It generates our most unfair tax. (Chapter 10.)
- It encourages war. (Chapter 14.)
- It destabilizes the economy. (Chapter 23.)
- It is an instrument of totalitarianism. (Chapters 5 and 26.)

This is a story about limitless money and hidden global power. The good news is that it is as fascinating as any work of fiction could be, and this, I trust, will add both pleasure and excitement to the learning process.

The bad news is that every detail of what follows is true.

G. Edward Griffin

ACKNOWLEDGMENTS

A writer who steals the work of another is called a plagiarist. One who takes from the works of *many* is called a researcher. That is a roundabout way of saying I am deeply indebted to the efforts of so many who have previously grappled this topic. It is impossible to acknowledge them except in footnote and bibliography. Without the cumulative product of their efforts, it would have taken a lifetime to pull together the material you are about to read.

In addition to the historical facts, however, there are numerous concepts which, to the best of my knowledge, are not to be found in prior literature. Primary among these are the formulation of certain "natural laws" which, it seemed to me, were too important to leave buried beneath the factual data. You will easily recognize these and other editorial expressions as the singular product of my own perceptions for which no one else can be held responsible.

I would like to give special thanks to Myril Creer and Jim Toft for having first invited me to give a lecture on this subject and, thus, forcing me to delve into it at some depth; and to Herb Joiner for encouraging me, after the speech, to "take it on the road." This book is the end result of a seven-year journey that began with those first steps. Wayne C. Rickert deserves a special medal for his financial support to get the project started and for his incredible patience while it crawled toward completion. Thanks to Bill Jasper for providing copies of numerous hard-to-locate documents. Thanks, also, to Linda Perlstein and Melinda Wiman for keeping my business enterprises functioning during my preoccupation with this project. And a very personal thanks to my wife, Patricia, for putting up with my periods of long absence while completing the manuscript, for meticulous proofreading, and for a most perceptive critique of its development along the way.

Finally, I would like to acknowledge those readers of the first three printings who have assisted in the refinement of this work. Because of their efforts most of the inevitable errata have been corrected for the second edition. Even so, it would be foolhardy to think that there are no more errors within the following pages. I have tried to be meticulous with even the smallest detail, but one cannot harvest such a huge crop without dropping a few seeds. Therefore, corrections and suggestions from new readers are sincerely invited. In my supreme optimism, I would like to think that they will be incorporated into *future* editions of this book.

INTRODUCTION

The following exchange was published in the British humor magazine, *Punch*, on April 3, 1957. It is reprinted here as an appropriate introduction and as a mental exercise to limber the mind for the material contained in this book.

Q. What are banks for?

A. To make money.

Q. For the customers?

A. For the banks.

Q. Why doesn't bank advertising mention this?

A. It would not be in good taste. But it is mentioned by implication in references to reserves of $249,000,000 or thereabouts. That is the money that they have made.

Q. Out of the customers?

A. I suppose so.

Q. They also mention Assets of $500,000,000 or thereabouts. Have they made that too?

A. Not exactly. That is the money they use to make money.

Q. I see. And they keep it in a safe somewhere?

A. Not at all. They lend it to customers.

Q. Then they haven't got it?

A. No.

Q. Then how is it Assets?

A. They maintain that it would be if they got it back.

Q. But they must have some money in a safe somewhere?

A. Yes, usually $500,000,000 or thereabouts. This is called Liabilities.

Q. But if they've got it, how can they be liable for it?

A. Because it isn't theirs.

Q. Then why do they have it?

A. It has been lent to them by customers.

Q. You mean customers lend banks money?

A. In effect. They put money into their accounts, so it is really lent to the banks.

Q. And what do the banks do with it?

A. Lend it to other customers.

Q. But you said that money they lent to other people was Assets?

A. Yes.

Q. Then Assets and Liabilities must be the same thing?

A. You can't really say that.

Q. But you've just said it. If I put $100 into my account the bank is liable to have to pay it back, so it's Liabilities. But they go and lend it to someone else, and he is liable to have to pay it back, so it's Assets. It's the same $100, isn't it?

A. Yes. But ...

Q. Then it cancels out. It means, doesn't it, that banks haven't really any money at all?

A. Theoretically....

Q. Never mind theoretically. And if they haven't any money, where do they get their Reserves of $249,000,000 or thereabouts?

A. I told you. That is the money they have made.

Q. How?

A. Well, when they lend your $100 to someone they charge him interest.

Q. How much?

A. It depends on the Bank Rate. Say five and a-half per cent. That's their profit.

Q. Why isn't it my profit? Isn't it my money?

A. It's the theory of banking practice that ...

Q. When I lend them my $100 why don't I charge them interest?

A. You do.

Q. You don't say. How much?

A. It depends on the Bank Rate. Say half a per cent.

Q. Grasping of me, rather?

A. But that's only if you're not going to draw the money out again.

Q. But of course, I'm going to draw it out again. If I hadn't wanted to draw it out again I could have buried it in the garden, couldn't I?

A. They wouldn't like you to draw it out again.

Q. Why not? If I keep it there you say it's a Liability. Wouldn't they be glad if I reduced their Liabilities by removing it?

A. No. Because if you remove it they can't lend it to anyone else.

Q. But if I wanted to remove it they'd have to let me?

A. Certainly.

Q. But suppose they've already lent it to another customer?

A. Then they'll let you have someone else's money.

Q. But suppose he wants his too ... and they've let me have it?

A. You're being purposely obtuse.

Q. I think I'm being acute. What if everyone wanted their money at once?

A. It's the theory of banking practice that they never would.

Q. So what banks bank on is not having to meet their commitments?

A. I wouldn't say that.

Q. Naturally. Well, if there's nothing else you think you can tell me ...?

A. Quite so. Now you can go off and open a banking account.

Q. Just one last question.

A. Of course.

Q. Wouldn't I do better to go off and open up a bank?

Section I

WHAT CREATURE IS THIS?

What is the Federal Reserve System? The answer may surprise you. It is not federal and there are no reserves. Furthermore, the Federal Reserve Banks are not even banks. The key to this riddle is to be found, not at the beginning of the story, but in the middle. Since this is not a textbook, we are not confined to a chronological structure. The subject matter is not a curriculum to be mastered but a mystery to be solved. So let us start where the action is.

Chapter One

THE JOURNEY TO JEKYLL ISLAND

The secret meeting on Jekyll Island in Georgia at which the Federal Reserve was conceived; the birth of a banking cartel to protect its members from competition; the strategy of how to convince Congress and the public that this cartel was an agency of the United States government.

The New Jersey railway station was bitterly cold that night. Flurries of the year's first snow swirled around street lights. November wind rattled roof panels above the track shed and gave a long, mournful sound among the rafters.

It was approaching ten P.M., and the station was nearly empty except for a few passengers scurrying to board the last Southbound of the day. The rail equipment was typical for that year of 1910, mostly chair cars that converted into sleepers with cramped upper and lower berths. For those with limited funds, coach cars were coupled to the front. They would take the brunt of the engine's noise and smoke that, somehow, always managed to seep through unseen cracks. A dining car was placed between the sections as a subtle barrier between the two classes of travelers. By today's standards, the environment was drab. Chairs and mattresses were hard. Surfaces were metal or scarred wood. Colors were dark green and gray.

In their hurry to board the train and escape the chill of the wind, few passengers noticed the activity at the far end of the platform. At a gate seldom used at this hour of the night was a spectacular sight. Nudged against the end-rail bumper was a long car that caused those few who saw it to stop and stare. Its gleaming black paint was accented with polished brass hand rails, knobs, frames, and filigrees. The shades were drawn, but through the open door, one could see mahogany paneling, velvet drapes, plush armchairs, and a well stocked bar. Porters with white serving coats were busying themselves with routine chores. And there was the distinct aroma of expensive cigars. Other cars in the station bore numbers on each end to distinguish them from their dull brothers. But numbers were not needed for this beauty. On the center of each side was a small plaque bearing but a single word: ALDRICH.

The name of Nelson Aldrich, senator from Rhode Island, was well known even in New Jersey. By 1910, he was one of the most powerful men in Washington, D.C., and his private railway car often was seen at the New York and New Jersey rail terminals during frequent trips to Wall Street. Aldrich was far more than a senator. He was considered to be the political spokesman for big business. As an investment associate of J.P. Morgan, he had extensive holdings in banking, manufacturing, and public utilities. His son-in-law was John D. Rockefeller, Jr. Sixty years later, his grandson, Nelson Aldrich Rockefeller, would become Vice-President of the United States.

When Aldrich arrived at the station, there was no doubt he was the commander of the private car. Wearing a long, fur-collared coat, a silk top hat, and carrying a silver-tipped walking stick, he strode briskly down the platform with his private secretary, Shelton, and a cluster of porters behind them hauling assorted trunks and cases.

No sooner had the Senator boarded his car when several more passengers arrived with similar collections of luggage. The last man appeared just moments before the final "aaall aboarrrd." He was carrying a shotgun case.

While Aldrich was easily recognized by most of the travelers who saw him stride through the station, the other faces were not familiar. These strangers had been instructed to arrive separately, to avoid reporters, and, should they meet inside the station, to pretend they did not know each other. After boarding the train, they had been told to use first names only so as not to reveal each other's identity. As a result of these precautions, not even the private-car porters and servants knew the names of these guests.

Back at the main gate, there was a double blast from the engine's whistle. Suddenly, the gentle sensation of motion; the excitement of a journey begun. But, no sooner had the train cleared the platform when it shuddered to a stop. Then, to everyone's surprise, it reversed direction and began moving toward the station again. Had they forgotten something? Was there a problem with the engine?

A sudden lurch and the slam of couplers gave the answer. They had picked up another car at the end of the train. Possibly the mail car? In an instant the forward motion was resumed, and all thoughts returned to the trip ahead and to the minimal comforts of the accommodations.

And so, as the passengers drifted off to sleep to the rhythmic clicking of steel wheels against rail, little did they dream that, riding in the car at the end of their train, were seven men who represented an estimated one-fourth of the total wealth of the entire world. This was the roster of the Aldrich car that night:

1. Nelson W. Aldrich, Republican "whip" in the Senate, Chairman of the National Monetary Commission, business associate of J.P. Morgan, father-in-law to John D. Rockefeller, Jr.;
2. Abraham Piatt Andrew, Assistant Secretary of the U.S. Treasury;
3. Frank A. Vanderlip, president of the National City Bank of New York, the most powerful of the banks at that time, representing William Rockefeller and the international investment banking house of Kuhn, Loeb & Company;
4. Henry P. Davison, senior partner of the J.P. Morgan Company;
5. Charles D. Norton, president of J.P. Morgan's First National Bank of New York;[1]
6. Benjamin Strong, head of J.P. Morgan's Bankers Trust Company;[2]
7. Paul M. Warburg, a partner in Kuhn, Loeb & Company, a representative of the Rothschild banking dynasty in England and France, and brother to Max Warburg who was head of the Warburg banking consortium in Germany and the Netherlands.

---

1. Norton is not mentioned in the memoirs of the other participants but, according to Tyler E. Bagwell, historian for the Jekyll Island Museum, he was present. See Bagwell's *Images of America; The Jekyll Island Club* (Charlston, SC, Arcadia, 1998), pp. 18, 19.
2. In private correspondence between the author and Andrew L. Gray, the Grand Nephew of Abraham P. Andrew, Mr. Gray claims that Strong was not in attendance. On the other hand, Frank Vanderlip—who was there—says in his memoirs that he was. How could Vanderlip be wrong? Gray's response: "He was in his late seventies when he wrote the book and the essay in question.... Perhaps the wish was father to the thought." If Vanderlip truly was in error, it was perhaps not so significant after all because, as Gray admits: "Strong would have been among those few to be let in on the secret." In the absence of further confirmation to the contrary, we are compelled to accept Vanderlip's account.

CONCENTRATION OF WEALTH

Centralization of control over financial resources was far advanced by 1910. In the United States, there were two main focal points of this control: the Morgan group and the Rockefeller group. Within each orbit was a maze of commercial banks, acceptance banks, and investment firms. In Europe, the same process had proceeded even further and had coalesced into the Rothschild group and the Warburg group. An article appeared in the *New York Times* on May 3, 1931, commenting on the death of George Baker, one of Morgan's closest associates. It said: "One-sixth of the total wealth of the world was represented by members of the Jekyll Island Club." The reference was only to those in the Morgan group, (members of the Jekyll Island Club). It did not include the Rockefeller group or the European financiers. When all of these are combined, the previous estimate that one-fourth of the world's wealth was represented by these groups is probably conservative.

In 1913, the year that the Federal Reserve Act became law, a subcommittee of the House Committee on Currency and Banking, under the chairmanship of Arsene Pujo of Louisiana, completed its investigation into the concentration of financial power in the United States. Pujo was considered to be a spokesman for the oil interests, part of the very group under investigation, and did everything possible to sabotage the hearings. In spite of his efforts, however, the final report of the committee at large was devastating:

> Your committee is satisfied from the proofs submitted ... that there is an established and well defined identity and community of interest between a few leaders of finance ... which has resulted in great and rapidly growing concentration of the control of money and credit in the hands of these few men....
>
> Under our system of issuing and distributing corporate securities the investing public does not buy directly from the corporation. The securities travel from the issuing house through middlemen to the investor. It is only the great banks or bankers with access to the mainsprings of the concentrated resources made up of other people's money, in the banks, trust companies, and life insurance companies, and with control of the machinery for creating markets and distributing securities, who have had the power to underwrite or guarantee the sale of large-scale security issues. The men who through their control over the funds of our railroad and industrial companies are able to direct where such funds shall be kept, and thus to create these great reservoirs of the people's money are the ones who are in a

position to tap those reservoirs for the ventures in which they are interested and to prevent their being tapped for purposes which they do *not* approve....

When we consider, also, in this connection that into these reservoirs of money and credit there flow a large part of the reserves of the banks of the country, that they are also the agents and correspondents of the out-of-town banks in the loaning of their surplus funds in the only public money market of the country, and that a small group of men and their partners and associates have now further strengthened their hold upon the resources of these institutions by acquiring large stock holdings therein, by representation on their boards and through valuable patronage, we begin to realize something of the extent to which this practical and effective domination and control over our greatest financial, railroad and industrial corporations has developed, largely within the past five years, and that it is fraught with peril to the welfare of the country.[1]

Such was the nature of the wealth and power represented by those seven men who gathered in secret that night and travelled in the luxury of Senator Aldrich's private car.

DESTINATION JEKYLL ISLAND

As the train neared its destination of Raleigh, North Carolina, the next afternoon, it slowed and then stopped in the switching yard just outside the station terminal. Quickly, the crew threw a switch, and the engine nudged the last car onto a siding where, just as quickly, it was uncoupled and left behind. When passengers stepped onto the platform at the terminal a few moments later, their train appeared exactly as it had been when they boarded. They could not know that their travelling companions for the night, at that very instant, were joining still another train which, within the hour, would depart Southbound once again.

The elite group of financiers was embarked on an eight hundred mile journey that led to Atlanta, then to Savannah and, finally, to the small town of Brunswick, Georgia. It would seem that Brunswick was an unlikely destination. Located on the Atlantic seaboard, it was primarily a fishing village with a small but lively port for cotton and lumber. It had a population of only a few thousand people. But, by that time, the Sea Islands that sheltered

---

1. Herman E. Krooss, ed., *Documentary History of Currency and Banking in the United States* (New York: Chelsea House, 1983), Vol. III, "Final Report from the Pujo Committee, February 28, 1913," pp. 222-24.

the coast from South Carolina to Florida already had become popular as winter resorts for the very wealthy. One such island, just off the coast of Brunswick, had recently been purchased by J.P. Morgan and several of his business associates, and it was here that they came in the fall and winter to hunt ducks or deer and to escape the rigors of cold weather in the North. It was called Jekyll Island.

When the Aldrich car was uncoupled onto a siding at the small Brunswick station, it was, indeed, conspicuous. Word travelled quickly to the office of the town's weekly newspaper. While the group was waiting to be transferred to the dock, several people from the paper approached and began asking questions. Who were Mr. Aldrich's guests? Why were they here? Was there anything special happening? Mr. Davison, who was one of the owners of Jekyll Island and who was well known to the local paper, told them that these were merely personal friends and that they had come for the simple amusement of duck hunting. Satisfied that there was no real news in the event, the reporters returned to their office.

Even after arrival at the remote island lodge, the secrecy continued. For nine days the rule for first-names-only remained in effect. Full-time caretakers and servants had been given vacation, and an entirely new, carefully screened staff was brought in for the occasion. This was done to make absolutely sure that none of the servants might recognize by sight the identities of these guests. It is difficult to imagine any event in history—including preparation for war—that was shielded from public view with greater mystery and secrecy.

The purpose of this meeting on Jekyll Island was not to hunt ducks. Simply stated, it was to come to an agreement on the structure and operation of a banking cartel. The goal of the cartel, as is true with all of them, was to maximize profits by minimizing competition between members, to make it difficult for new competitors to enter the field, and to utilize the police power of government to enforce the cartel agreement. In more specific terms, the purpose and, indeed, the actual outcome of this meeting was to create the blueprint for the Federal Reserve System.

THE STORY IS CONFIRMED

For many years after the event, educators, commentators, and historians denied that the Jekyll Island meeting ever took place. Even now, the accepted view is that the meeting was relatively unimportant, and only paranoid unsophisticates would try to make anything out of it. Ron Chernow writes: "The Jekyll Island meeting would be the fountain of a thousand conspiracy theories."[1] Little by little, however, the story has been pieced together in amazing detail, and it has come directly or indirectly from those who actually were there. Furthermore, if what they say about their own purposes and actions does not constitute a classic conspiracy, then there is little meaning to that word.

The first leak regarding this meeting found its way into print in 1916. It appeared in *Leslie's Weekly* and was written by a young financial reporter by the name of B.C. Forbes, who later founded *Forbes Magazine*. The article was primarily in praise of Paul Warburg, and it is likely that Warburg let the story out during conversations with the writer. At any rate, the opening paragraph contained a dramatic but highly accurate summary of both the nature and purpose of the meeting:

> Picture a party of the nation's greatest bankers stealing out of New York on a private railroad car under cover of darkness, stealthily hieing hundreds of miles South, embarking on a mysterious launch, sneaking on to an island deserted by all but a few servants, living there a full week under such rigid secrecy that the names of not one of them was once mentioned lest the servants learn the identity and disclose to the world this strangest, most secret expedition in the history of American finance.
>
> I am not romancing. I am giving to the world, for the first time, the real story of how the famous Aldrich currency report, the foundation of our new currency system, was written.[2]

In 1930, Paul Warburg wrote a massive book—1750 pages in all—entitled *The Federal Reserve System, Its Origin and Growth*. In this tome, he described the meeting and its purpose but did not mention either its location or the names of those who attended. But he did say: "The results of the conference were entirely confidential. Even the fact there had been a meeting was not permitted to become public." Then, in a footnote he added: "Though eighteen years have since gone by, I do not feel free to give a description of

---

1. Ron Chernow, *The House of Morgan: An American Banking Dynasty and the Rise of Modern Finance* (New York: Atlantic Monthly Press, 1990), p. 129.
2. "Men Who Are Making America," by B.C. Forbes, *Leslie's Weekly*, October 19, 1916, p. 423.

this most interesting conference concerning which Senator Aldrich pledged all participants to secrecy."[1]

An interesting insight to Paul Warburg's attendance at the Jekyll Island meeting came thirty-four years later, in a book written by his son, James. James had been appointed by F.D.R. as Director of the Budget and, during World War II, as head of the Office of War Information. In his book he described how his father, who didn't know one end of a gun from the other, borrowed a shotgun from a friend and carried it with him to the train to disguise himself as a duck hunter.[2]

This part of the story was corroborated in the official biography of Senator Aldrich, written by Nathaniel Wright Stephenson:

> In the autumn of 1910, six men [in addition to Aldrich] went out to shoot ducks. That is to say, they told the world that was their purpose. Mr. Warburg, who was of the number, gives an amusing account of his feelings when he boarded a private car in Jersey City, bringing with him all the accoutrements of a duck shooter. The joke was in the fact that he had never shot a duck in his life and had no intention of shooting any…. The duck shoot was a blind.[3]

Stephenson continues with a description of the encounter at Brunswick station. He tells us that, shortly after they arrived, the station master walked into the private car and shocked them by his apparent knowledge of the identities of everyone on board. To make matters even worse, he said that a group of reporters were waiting outside. Davison took charge. "Come outside, old man," he said, "and I will tell you a story." No one claims to know what story was told standing on the railroad ties that morning, but a few moments later Davison returned with a broad smile on his face. "It's all right," he said reassuringly. "They won't give us away."

Stephenson continues: "The rest is silence. The reporters dispersed, and the secret of the strange journey was not divulged. No one asked him how he managed it and he did not volunteer the information."[4]

---

1. Paul Warburg, *The Federal Reserve System: Its Origin and Growth* (New York: Macmillan, 1930), Vol. I, p. 58. It is apparent that Warburg wrote this line two years before the book was published.
2. James Warburg, *The Long Road Home* (New York: Doubleday, 1964), p. 29.
3. Nathaniel Wright Stephenson, *Nelson W. Aldrich in American Politics* (New York: Scribners, 1930; rpt. New York: Kennikat Press, 1971), p. 373.
4. Stephenson, p. 376.

In the February 9, 1935, issue of the *Saturday Evening Post,* an article appeared written by Frank Vanderlip. In it he said:

Despite my views about the value to society of greater publicity for the affairs of corporations, there was an occasion, near the close of 1910, when I was as secretive—indeed, as furtive—as any conspirator.... I do not feel it is any exaggeration to speak of our secret expedition to Jekyll Island as the occasion of the actual conception of what eventually became the Federal Reserve System....

We were told to leave our last names behind us. We were told, further, that we should avoid dining together on the night of our departure. We were instructed to come one at a time and as unobtrusively as possible to the railroad terminal on the New Jersey littoral of the Hudson, where Senator Aldrich's private car would be in readiness, attached to the rear end of a train for the South....

Once aboard the private car we began to observe the taboo that had been fixed on last names. We addressed one another as "Ben," "Paul," "Nelson," "Abe"—it is Abraham Piatt Andrew. Davison and I adopted even deeper disguises, abandoning our first names. On the theory that we were always right, he became Wilbur and I became Orville, after those two aviation pioneers, the Wright brothers....

The servants and train crew may have known the identities of one or two of us, but they did not know all, and it was the names of all printed together that would have made our mysterious journey significant in Washington, in Wall Street, even in London. Discovery, we knew, simply must not happen, or else all our time and effort would be wasted. If it were to be exposed publicly that our particular group had got together and written a banking bill, that bill would have no chance whatever of passage by Congress.[1]

THE STRUCTURE WAS PURE CARTEL

The composition of the Jekyll Island meeting was a classic example of cartel structure. A cartel is a group of independent businesses which join together to coordinate the production, pricing, or marketing of their members. The purpose of a cartel is to reduce competition and thereby increase profitability. This is accomplished through a shared monopoly over their industry which forces the public to pay higher prices for their goods or services than would be otherwise required under free-enterprise competition.

---

1. "From Farm Boy to Financier," by Frank A. Vanderlip, *The Saturday Evening Post,* Feb. 9, 1933, pp. 25, 70. The identical story was told two years later in Vanderlip's book bearing the same title as the article (New York: D. Appleton–Century Company, 1935), pp. 210–219.

Here were representatives of the world's leading banking consortia: Morgan, Rockefeller, Rothschild, Warburg, and Kuhn-Loeb. They were often competitors, and there is little doubt that there was considerable distrust between them and skillful maneuvering for favored position in any agreement. But they were driven together by one overriding desire to fight their common enemy. The enemy was competition.

In 1910, the number of banks in the United States was growing at a phenomenal rate. In fact, it had more than doubled to over twenty thousand in just the previous ten years. Furthermore, most of them were springing up in the South and West, causing the New York banks to suffer a steady decline of market share. Almost all banks in the 1880s were national banks, which means they were chartered by the federal government. Generally, they were located in the big cities, and were allowed by law to issue their own currency in the form of bank notes. Even as early as 1896, however, the number of non-national banks had grown to sixty-one per cent, and they already held fifty-four per cent of the country's total banking deposits. By 1913, when the Federal Reserve Act was passed, those numbers were seventy-one per cent non-national banks holding fifty-seven per cent of the deposits.[1] In the eyes of those duck hunters from New York, this was a trend that simply had to be reversed.

Competition also was coming from a new trend in industry to finance future growth out of profits rather than from borrowed capital. This was the outgrowth of free-market interest rates which set a realistic balance between debt and thrift. Rates were low enough to attract serious borrowers who were confident of the success of their business ventures and of their ability to repay, but they were high enough to discourage loans for frivolous ventures or those for which there were alternative sources of funding—for example, one's own capital. That balance between debt and thrift was the result of a limited money supply. Banks could create loans in excess of their actual deposits, as we shall see, but there was a *limit* to that process. And that limit was ultimately determined by the supply of gold they held. Consequently, between 1900 and 1910, seventy per cent of the funding for American corporate

---

1. See Gabriel Kolko, *The Triumph of Conservatism* (New York: The Free Press of Glencoe, a division of the Macmillan Co., 1963), p. 140.

growth was generated internally, making industry increasingly independent of the banks.[1] Even the federal government was becoming thrifty. It had a growing stockpile of gold, was systematically redeeming the Greenbacks—which had been issued during the Civil War—and was rapidly reducing the national debt.

Here was another trend that had to be halted. What the bankers wanted—and what many businessmen wanted also—was to intervene in the free market and tip the balance of interest rates downward, to favor debt over thrift. To accomplish this, the money supply simply had to be disconnected from gold and made more plentiful or, as they described it, more *elastic*.

THE SPECTER OF BANK FAILURE

The greatest threat, however, came, not from rivals or private capital formation, but from the public at large in the form of what bankers call a *run on the bank*. This is because, when banks accept a customer's deposit, they give in return a "balance" in his account. This is the equivalent of a promise to pay back the deposit anytime he wants. Likewise, when another customer *borrows* money from the bank, he *also* is given an account balance which usually is withdrawn immediately to satisfy the purpose of the loan. This creates a ticking time bomb because, at that point, the bank has issued more promises to "pay-on-demand" than it has money in the vault. Even though the depositing customer thinks he can get his money any time he wants, in reality it has been given to the *borrowing* customer and no longer is available at the bank.

The problem is compounded further by the fact that banks are allowed to lend even more money than they have received in deposit. The mechanism for accomplishing this seemingly impossible feat will be described in a later chapter, but it is a fact of modern banking that promises-to-pay often exceed savings deposits by a factor of ten-to-one. And, because only about three per cent of these accounts are actually retained in the vault in the form of cash—the rest having been put into even more loans and investments—the bank's promises exceed its ability to *keep* those promises by a factor of over three hundred-to-one.[2] As long as only a small percentage

---

1. William Greider, *Secrets of the Temple* (New York: Simon and Schuster, 1987), p. 274, 275. Also Kolko, p. 145.
2. Another way of putting it is that their reserves are underfunded by over 33,333% (10-to-1 divided by .03 = 333.333-to-1. That divided by .01 = 33,333%.)

of depositors request their money at one time, no one is the wiser. But if public confidence is shaken, and if more than a few per cent attempt to withdraw their funds, the scheme is finally exposed. The bank cannot keep all its promises and is forced to close its doors. Bankruptcy usually follows in due course.

CURRENCY DRAINS

The same result could happen—and, prior to the Federal Reserve System, often did happen—even without depositors making a run on the bank. Instead of withdrawing their funds at the teller's window, they simply wrote checks to purchase goods or services. People receiving those checks took them to a bank for deposit. If that bank happened to be the same one from which the check was drawn, then all was well, because it was not necessary to remove any real money from the vault. But if the holder of the check took it to *another* bank, it was quickly passed back to the issuing bank and settlement was demanded *between banks*.

This is not a one-way street, however. While the Downtown Bank is demanding payment from the Uptown Bank, the Uptown Bank is also clearing checks and demanding payment from the Downtown bank. As long as the money flow in both directions is equal, then everything can be handled with simple bookkeeping. But if the flow is not equal, then one of the banks will have to actually send money to the other to make up the difference. If the amount of money required exceeds a few percentage points of the bank's total deposits, the result is the same as a run on the bank *by depositors*. This demand of money by other banks rather than by depositors is called a *currency drain*.

In 1910, the most common cause of a bank having to declare bankruptcy due to a currency drain was that it followed a loan policy that was more reckless than that of its competitors. More money was demanded from it because more money was *loaned* by it. It was dangerous enough to lend ninety per cent of their customers' savings (keeping only one dollar in reserve out of every ten), but that had proven to be adequate *most* of the time. Some banks, however, were tempted to walk even closer to the precipice. They pushed the ratio to ninety-*two* per cent, ninety-*five* per cent, ninety-*nine* per cent. After all, the way a bank makes money is to collect interest, and the only way to do that is to make *loans*. The more loans, the better. And, so, there was a practice among some of the more reckless banks to "loan up," as they call it. Which was another way of saying to push *down* their reserve ratios.

A BANKERS' UTOPIA

If all banks could be forced to issue loans in the same ratio to their reserves as other banks did, then, regardless of how small that ratio was, the amount of checks to be cleared between them would balance in the long run. No major currency drains would ever occur. The entire banking industry might collapse under such a system, but not *individual* banks—at least not those that were part of the cartel. All would walk the same distance from the edge, regardless of how close it was. Under such uniformity, no individual bank could be blamed for failure to meet its obligations. The blame could be shifted, instead, to the "economy" or "government policy" or "interest rates" or "trade deficits" or the "exchange-value of the dollar" or even to the "capitalist system" itself.

But, in 1910, such a bankers' utopia had not yet been created. If the Downtown bank began to lend at a greater ratio to its reserves than its competitors, the amount of checks which would come back to it for payment also would be greater. Thus, the bank which pursued a more reckless lending policy had to draw *against* its reserves in order to make payments to the more conservative banks and, when those funds were exhausted, it usually was forced into bankruptcy.

Historian John Klein tells us that "The financial panics of 1873, 1884, 1893, and 1907 were in large part an outgrowth of ... reserve pyramiding and excessive deposit creation by reserve city ... banks. These panics were triggered by the currency drains that took place in periods of relative prosperity when banks were loaned up."[1] In other words, the "panics" and resulting bank failures were caused, not by negative factors in the economy, but by *currency drains* on the banks which were *loaned up* to the point where they had practically no reserves at all. The banks did not fail because the system was weak. The system failed because the banks were weak.

This was another common problem that brought these seven men over a thousand miles to a tiny island off the shore of Georgia. Each was a potentially fierce competitor, but uppermost in their minds were the so-called panics and the very real 1,748 bank

---

1. See Vera C. Smith, *The Rationale of Central Banking* (London: P.S. King & Son, 1936), p. 36.

failures of the preceding two decades. Somehow, they had to join forces. A method had to be devised to enable them to continue to make more promises to pay-on-demand than they could keep. To do this, they had to find a way to force all banks to walk the *same* distance from the edge, and, when the inevitable disasters happened, to shift public blame away from themselves. By making it appear to be a problem of the national economy rather than of private banking practice, the door then could be opened for the use of tax money rather than their own funds for paying off the losses.

Here, then, were the main challenges that faced that tiny but powerful group assembled on Jekyll Island:

1. How to stop the growing influence of small, rival banks and to insure that control over the nation's financial resources would remain in the hands of those present;
2. How to make the money supply more elastic in order to reverse the trend of private capital formation and to recapture the industrial loan market;
3. How to pool the meager reserves of the nation's banks into one large reserve so that all banks will be motivated to follow the same loan-to-deposit ratios. This would protect at least some of them from currency drains and bank runs;
4. Should this lead eventually to the collapse of the whole banking system, then how to shift the losses from the owners of the banks to the taxpayers.

THE CARTEL ADOPTS A NAME

Everyone knew that the solution to all these problems was a cartel mechanism that had been devised and already put into similar operation in Europe. As with all cartels, it had to be created by legislation and sustained by the power of government under the deception of protecting the consumer. The most important task before them, therefore, can be stated as objective number five:

5. How to convince Congress that the scheme was a measure to protect the public.

The task was a delicate one. The American people did not like the concept of a cartel. The idea of business enterprises joining together to fix prices and prevent competition was alien to the free-enterprise system. It could never be sold to the voters. But, if the word cartel was not used, if the venture could be described

with words which are emotionally neutral—perhaps even allur-
ing—then half the battle would be won.

The first decision, therefore, was to follow the practice adopted
in Europe. Henceforth, the cartel would operate as a *central bank*.
And even that was to be but a generic expression. For purposes of
public relations and legislation, they would devise a name that
would avoid the word *bank* altogether and which would conjure
the image of the federal government itself. Furthermore, to create
the impression that there would be no concentration of power, they
would establish regional branches of the cartel and make that a
main selling point. Stephenson tells us: "Aldrich entered this
discussion at Jekyll Island an ardent convert to the idea of a central
bank. His desire was to transplant the system of one of the great
European banks, say the Bank of England, bodily to America."[1] But
political expediency required that such plans be concealed from the
public. As John Kenneth Galbraith explained it: "It was his
[Aldrich's] thought to outflank the opposition by having not one
central bank but many. And the word bank would itself be
avoided."[2]

With the exception of Aldrich, all of those present were
bankers, but only one was an expert on the European model of a
central bank. Because of this knowledge, Paul Warburg became the
dominant and guiding mind throughout all of the discussions.
Even a casual perusal of the literature on the creation of the Federal
Reserve System is sufficient to find that he was, indeed, the cartel's
mastermind. Galbraith says "... Warburg has, with some justice,
been called the father of the system."[3] Professor Edwin Seligman, a
member of the international banking family of J. & W. Seligman,
and head of the Department of Economics at Columbia University,
writes that "... in its fundamental features, the Federal Reserve Act
is the work of Mr. Warburg more than any other man in the
country."[4]

---

1. Stephenson, p. 378.
2. John Kenneth Galbraith, *Money: Whence It Came, Where It Went* (Boston:
Houghton Mifflin, 1975), p. 122.
3. Galbraith, p. 123.
4. The Academy of Political Science, *Proceedings*, 1914, Vol. 4, No. 4, p. 387.

THE REAL DADDY WARBUCKS

Paul Moritz Warburg was a leading member of the investment banking firm of M.M. Warburg & Company of Hamburg, Germany, and Amsterdam, the Netherlands. He had come to the United States only nine years prior to the Jekyll Island meeting. Soon after arrival, however, and with funding provided mostly by the Rothschild group, he and his brother Felix had been able to buy partnerships in the New York investment banking firm of Kuhn, Loeb & Company, while continuing as partners in Warburg of Hamburg.[1] Within twenty years, Paul would become one of the wealthiest men in America with an unchallenged domination over the country's railroad system.

At this distance in history, it is difficult to appreciate the importance of this man. But some understanding may be had from the fact that the legendary character, Daddy Warbucks, in the comic strip *Little Orphan Annie*, was a contemporary commentary on the presumed benevolence of Paul Warburg, and his almost magic ability to accomplish good through the power of his unlimited wealth.

A third brother, Max Warburg, was the financial adviser of the Kaiser who became Director of the *Reichsbank* in Germany. This was, of course, a *central bank*, and it was one of the models used in the construction of the Federal Reserve System. Incidentally, a few years later, the *Reichsbank* would create the massive hyperinflation in Germany which wiped out the middle class and the entire economy as well.

Paul Warburg soon became well known on Wall Street as a persuasive advocate for a central bank in America. Three years before the Jekyll Island meeting, he had published several pamphlets. One was entitled *Defects and Needs of Our Banking System*, and the other was *A Plan for A Modified Central Bank*. These attracted wide attention in both financial and academic circles and set the intellectual climate for all future discussions regarding banking legislation. In these treatises, Warburg complained that the American monetary system was crippled by its dependency on gold and government bonds, both of which were in limited supply. What America needed, he argued, was an *elastic* money supply that

---

1. Antony Sutton, *Wall Street and FDR* (New Rochelle, New York: Arlington House, 1975), p. 92.

could be expanded and contracted to accommodate the fluctuating needs of commerce. The solution, he said, was to follow the German example whereby banks could create currency solely on the basis of "commercial paper," which is banker language for IOUs from corporations.

Warburg was tireless in his efforts. He was a featured speaker before scores of influential audiences and wrote a steady stream of published articles on the subject. In March of that year, for example, *The New York Times* published an eleven-part series written by Warburg explaining and expounding what he called the Reserve Bank of the United States.[1]

THE MESSAGE WAS PLAIN FOR THOSE WHO UNDERSTOOD

Most of Warburg's writing and lecturing on this topic was eyewash for the public. To cover the fact that a central bank is merely a cartel which has been legalized, its proponents had to lay down a thick smoke screen of technical jargon focusing always on how it would supposedly benefit commerce, the public, and the nation; how it would lower interest rates, provide funding for needed industrial projects, and prevent panics in the economy. There was not the slightest glimmer that, underneath it all, was a master plan which was designed from top to bottom to serve private interests at the expense of the public.

This was, nevertheless, the cold reality, and the more percep-tive bankers were well aware of it. In an address before the American Bankers Association the following year, Aldrich laid it out for anyone who was really listening to the meaning of his words. He said: "The organization proposed is not a bank, but a cooperative union of all the banks of the country for definite purposes."[2] Precisely. A *union* of banks.

Two years later, in a speech before that same group of bankers, A. Barton Hepburn of Chase National Bank was even more candid. He said: "The measure recognizes and adopts the principles of a central bank. Indeed, if it works out as the sponsors of the law hope, it will make all incorporated banks together joint owners of a

---

1. See J. Lawrence Laughlin, *The Federal Reserve Act: Its Origin and Problems* (New York: Macmillan, 1933), p. 9.
2. See Barry Siegel, *Money in Crisis: The Federal Reserve, The Economy, and Monetary Reform* (Massachusetts, Cambridge, Ballinger, 1984), p. 102.

central dominating power."[1] And that is about as good a definition of a cartel as one is likely to find.

In 1914, one year after the Federal Reserve Act was passed into law, Senator Aldrich could afford to be less guarded in his remarks. In an article published in July of that year in a magazine called *The Independent*, he boasted: "Before the passage of this Act, the New York bankers could only dominate the reserves of New York. Now we are able to dominate the bank reserves of the entire country."

MYTH ACCEPTED AS HISTORY

The accepted version of history is that the Federal Reserve was created to stabilize our economy. One of the most widely-used textbooks on this subject says: "It sprang from the panic of 1907, with its alarming epidemic of bank failures: the country was fed up once and for all with the anarchy of unstable private banking."[2] Even the most naive student must sense a grave contradiction between this cherished view and the System's actual performance. Since its inception, it has presided over the crashes of 1921 and 1929; the Great Depression of '29 to '39; recessions in '53, '57, '69, '75, and '81; a stock market "Black Monday" in '87; and a 1000% inflation which has destroyed 90% of the dollar's purchasing power.[3]

Let us be more specific on that last point. By 1990, an annual income of $10,000 was required to buy what took only $1,000 in 1914.[4] That incredible loss in value was quietly transferred to the federal government in the form of hidden taxation, and the Federal Reserve System was the mechanism by which it was accomplished.

Actions have consequences. The consequences of wealth confiscation by the Federal-Reserve mechanism are now upon us. In the current decade, corporate debt is soaring; personal debt is greater than ever; both business and personal bankruptcies are at an all-time high; banks and savings and loan associations are failing in

---

1. Quoted by Kolko, *Triumph*, p. 235.
2. Paul A. Samuelson, *Economics*, 8th ed. (New York: McGraw-Hill, 1970), p. 272.
3. See "Money, Banking, and Biblical Ethics," by Ronald H. Nash, *Durell Journal of Money and Banking*, February, 1990.
4. When one considers that the income tax had just been introduced in 1913 and that such low figures were completely exempt, an income at that time of $1,000 actually was the equivalent of earning $15,400 now, before paying 35% taxes. When the amount now taken by state and local governments is added to the total bite, the figure is close to $20,000.

larger numbers than ever before; interest on the national debt is consuming half of our tax dollars; heavy industry has been largely replaced by overseas competitors; we are facing an international trade deficit for the first time in our history; 75% of downtown Los Angeles and other metropolitan areas is now owned by foreigners; and over half of our nation is in a state of economic recession.

FIRST REASON TO ABOLISH THE SYSTEM

That is the scorecard eighty years after the Federal Reserve was created supposedly to stabilize our economy! There can be no argument that the System has failed in its stated objectives. Furthermore, after all this time, after repeated changes in personnel, after operating under both political parties, after numerous experiments in monetary philosophy, after almost a hundred revisions to its charter, and after the development of countless new formulas and techniques, there has been more than ample opportunity to work out mere procedural flaws. It is not unreasonable to conclude, therefore, that the System has failed, not because it needs a new set of rules or more intelligent directors, but because *it is incapable of achieving its stated objectives.*

If an institution is incapable of achieving its objectives, there is no reason to preserve it—unless it can be altered in some way to change its capability. That leads to the question: *why* is the System incapable of achieving its stated objectives? The painful answer is: *those were never its true objectives.* When one realizes the circumstances under which it was created, when one contemplates the identities of those who authored it, and when one studies its actual performance over the years, it becomes obvious that the System is merely a cartel with a government facade. There is no doubt that those who run it are motivated to maintain full employment, high productivity, low inflation, and a generally sound economy. They are not interested in killing the goose that lays such beautiful golden eggs. But, when there is a conflict between the public interest and the private needs of the cartel—a conflict that arises almost daily—the public will be sacrificed. That is the nature of the beast. It is foolish to expect a cartel to act in any other way.

This view is not encouraged by Establishment institutions and publishers. It has become their apparent mission to convince the American people that the system is not *intrinsically* flawed. It merely has been in the hands of bumbling oafs. For example,

William Greider was a former Assistant Managing Editor for *The Washington Post.* His book, *Secrets of The Temple*, was published in 1987 by Simon and Schuster. It was critical of the Federal Reserve because of its failures, but, according to Greider, these were not caused by any defect in the System itself, but were merely the result of economic factors which are "sooo complicated" that the good men who have struggled to make the System work just haven't been able to figure it all out. But, don't worry, folks, they're *working* on it! That is exactly the kind of powder-puff criticism which is acceptable in our mainstream media. Yet, Greider's own research points to an entirely different interpretation. Speaking of the System's origin, he says:

> As new companies prospered without Wall Street, so did the new regional banks that handled their funds. New York's concentrated share of bank deposits was still huge, about half the nation's total, but it was declining steadily. Wall Street was still "the biggest kid on the block," but less and less able to bully the others.
>
> This trend was a crucial fact of history, a misunderstood reality that completely alters the political meaning of the reform legislation that created the Federal Reserve. At the time, the conventional wisdom in Congress, widely shared and sincerely espoused by Progressive reformers, was that a government institution would finally harness the "money trust," disarm its powers, and establish broad democratic control over money and credit.... The results were nearly the opposite. The money reforms enacted in 1913, in fact, helped to preserve the status quo, to stabilize the old order. Money-center bankers would not only gain dominance over the new central bank, but would also enjoy new insulation against instability and their own decline. Once the Fed was in operation, the steady diffusion of financial power halted. Wall Street maintained its dominant position—and even enhanced it.[1]

Antony Sutton, former Research Fellow at the Hoover Institution for War, Revolution and Peace, and also former Professor of Economics at California State University, Los Angeles, provides a somewhat deeper analysis. He writes:

> Warburg's revolutionary plan to get American Society to go to work for Wall Street was astonishingly simple. Even today,... academic theoreticians cover their blackboards with meaningless equations, and the general public struggles in bewildered confusion with inflation and the coming credit collapse, while the quite simple explanation of

1. Greider, p. 275.

the problem goes undiscussed and almost entirely uncomprehended. The Federal Reserve System is a legal private monopoly of the money supply operated for the benefit of the few under the guise of protecting and promoting the public interest.[1]

The real significance of the journey to Jekyll Island and the creature that was hatched there was inadvertently summarized by the words of Paul Warburg's admiring biographer, Harold Kellock:

> Paul M. Warburg is probably the mildest-mannered man that ever personally conducted a revolution. It was a bloodless revolution: he did not attempt to rouse the populace to arms. He stepped forth armed simply with an idea. And he conquered. That's the amazing thing. A shy, sensitive man, he imposed his idea on a nation of a hundred million people.[2]

SUMMARY

The basic plan for the Federal Reserve System was drafted at a secret meeting held in November of 1910 at the private resort of J.P. Morgan on Jekyll Island off the coast of Georgia. Those who attended represented the great financial institutions of Wall Street and, indirectly, Europe as well. The reason for secrecy was simple. Had it been known that rival factions of the banking community had joined together, the public would have been alerted to the possibility that the bankers were plotting an agreement in restraint of trade—which, of course, is exactly what they were doing. What emerged was a cartel agreement with five objectives: stop the growing competition from the nation's newer banks; obtain a franchise to create money out of nothing for the purpose of lending; get control of the reserves of all banks so that the more reckless ones would not be exposed to currency drains and bank runs; get the taxpayer to pick up the cartel's inevitable losses; and convince Congress that the purpose was to protect the public. It was realized that the bankers would have to become partners with the politicians and that the structure of the cartel would have to be a central bank. The record shows that the Fed has failed to achieve its stated objectives. That is because those were never its true goals. As a banking cartel, and in terms of the five objectives stated above, it has been an unqualified success.

---

1. Sutton, *Wall Street and F.D.R.*, p. 94.
2. Harold Kellock, "Warburg, the Revolutionist," *The Century Magazine*, May 1915, p. 79.

Nelson W. Aldrich

Henry P. Davison (L) and Charles D. Norton (R)

Abraham Piatt Andrew

The seven men who attended the secret meeting on Jeky Island, where the Federal Reserve System was conceive represented an estimated one-fourth of the total wealth of entire world. They were:

1. Nelson W. Aldrich, Republican "whip" in the Senate, Chairman of the National Monetary Commission, father-in-law to John D. Rockefeller, Jr.;
2. Henry P. Davison, Sr. Partner of J.P. Morgan Compan
3. Charles D. Norton, Pres. of 1st National Bank of New
4. A. Piatt Andrew, Assistant Secretary of the Treasury;
5. Frank A. Vanderlip, President of the National City Ban New York, representing William Rockefeller.
6. Benjamin Strong, head of J.P. Morgan's Bankers Trus Company, later to become head of the System;
7. Paul M. Warburg, a partner in Kuhn, Loeb & Company representing the Rothschilds and Warburgs in Europe.

Frank A. Vanderlip

Benjamin Strong

Paul M. Warburg

Chapter Two

THE NAME OF THE GAME IS BAILOUT

The analogy of a spectator sporting event as a means of explaining the rules by which taxpayers are required to pick up the cost of bailing out the banks when their loans go sour.

It was stated in the previous chapter that the Jekyll Island group which conceived the Federal Reserve System actually created a national cartel which was dominated by the larger banks. It was also stated that a primary objective of that cartel was to involve the federal government as an agent for shifting the inevitable losses from the owners of those banks to the taxpayers. That, of course, is one of the more controversial assertions made in this book. Yet, there is little room for any other interpretation when one confronts the massive evidence of history since the System was created. Let us, therefore, take another leap through time. Having jumped to the year 1910 to begin this story, let us now return to the present era.

To understand how banking losses are shifted to the taxpayers, it is first necessary to know a little bit about how the scheme was designed to work. There are certain procedures and formulas which must be understood or else the entire process seems like chaos. It is as though we had been isolated all our lives on a South Sea island with no knowledge of the outside world. Imagine what it would then be like the first time we travelled to the mainland and witnessed a game of professional football. We would stare with incredulity at men dressed like aliens from another planet; throwing their bodies against each other; tossing a funny shaped object back and forth; fighting over it as though it were of great value, yet, occasionally kicking it out of the area as though it were worthless and despised; chasing each other, knocking each other to the ground and then walking away to regroup for another surge; all this with tens of thousand of spectators riotously shouting in unison for no apparent reason at all. Without a basic understanding that this was a game and without knowledge of the rules of that game, the event would appear as total chaos and universal madness.

The operation of our monetary system through the Federal Reserve has much in common with professional football. First, there are certain plays that are repeated over and over again with only minor variations to suit the special circumstances. Second, there are definite rules which the players follow with great precision. Third, there is a clear objective to the game which is uppermost in the minds of the players. And fourth, if the spectators are not familiar with that objective and if they do not understand the rules, they will never comprehend what is going on. Which, as far as monetary matters is concerned, is the common state of the vast majority of Americans today.

Let us, therefore, attempt to spell out in plain language what that objective is and how the players expect to achieve it. To demystify the process, we shall present an overview first. After the concepts are clarified, we then shall follow up with actual examples taken from the recent past.

The name of the game is *Bailout*. As stated previously, the objective of this game is to shift the inevitable losses from the owners of the larger banks to the taxpayers. The procedure by which this is accomplished is as follows:

RULES OF THE GAME

The game begins when the Federal Reserve System allows commercial banks to create checkbook money out of nothing. (Details regarding how this incredible feat is accomplished are given in chapter ten entitled The Mandrake Mechanism.) The banks derive profit from this easy money, not by spending it, but by lending it to others and collecting interest.

When such a loan is placed on the bank's books it is shown as an asset because it is earning interest and, presumably, someday will be paid back. At the same time an equal entry is made on the liability side of the ledger. That is because the newly created checkbook money now is in circulation, and most of it will end up in other banks which will return the canceled checks to the issuing bank for payment. Individuals may also bring some of this checkbook money back to the bank and request cash. The issuing bank, therefore, has a potential money pay-out liability equal to the amount of the loan asset.

When a borrower cannot repay and there are no assets which can be taken to compensate, the bank must write off that loan as a loss. However, since most of the money originally was created out of nothing and cost the bank nothing except bookkeeping overhead, there is little of tangible value that is actually lost. It is primarily a bookkeeping entry.

A bookkeeping loss can still be undesirable to a bank because it causes the loan to be removed from the ledger as an asset without a reduction in liabilities. The difference must come from the equity of those who own the bank. In other words, the loan asset is removed, but the money liability remains. The original checkbook money is still circulating out there even though the borrower cannot repay, and the issuing bank still has the obligation to redeem those checks. The only way to do this and balance the books once again is to draw upon the capital which was invested by the bank's stockholders or to deduct the loss from the bank's current profits. In either case, the owners of the bank lose an amount equal to the value of the defaulted loan. So, to *them*, the loss becomes very real. If the bank is forced to write off a large amount of bad loans, the amount could exceed the entire value of the owners' equity. When that happens, the game is over, and the bank is insolvent.

This concern would be sufficient to motivate most bankers to be very conservative in their loan policy, and in fact most of them do act with great caution when dealing with individuals and small businesses. But the Federal Reserve System, the Federal Deposit Insurance Corporation, and the Federal Deposit Loan Corporation now guarantee that massive loans made to large corporations and to other governments will not be allowed to fall entirely upon the bank's owners should those loans go into default. This is done under the argument that, if these corporations or banks are allowed to fail, the nation would suffer from vast unemployment and economic disruption. More on that in a moment.

THE PERPETUAL-DEBT PLAY

The end result of this policy is that the banks have little motive to be cautious and are protected against the effect of their own folly. The larger the loan, the better it is, because it will produce the greatest amount of profit with the least amount of effort. A single loan to a third-world country netting hundreds of millions of dollars in annual interest is just as easy to process—if not easier—than a loan for $50,000 to a local merchant on the shopping mall. If the interest is paid, it's gravy time. If the loan defaults, the federal government will "protect the public" and, through various mechanisms described shortly, will make sure that the banks continue to receive their interest.

The individual and the small businessman find it increasingly difficult to borrow money at reasonable rates, because the banks can make more money on loans to the corporate giants and to foreign governments. Also, the bigger loans are safer for the banks, because the government will make them good even if they default. There are no such guarantees for the small loans. The public will not swallow the line that bailing out the little guy is necessary to save the system. The dollar amounts are too small. Only when the figures become mind-boggling does the ploy become plausible.

It is important to remember that banks do not really want to have their loans repaid, except as evidence of the dependability of the borrower. They make a profit from interest *on* the loan, not repayment *of* the loan. If a loan is paid off, the bank merely has to find another borrower, and that can be an expensive nuisance. It is much better to have the existing borrower pay only the interest and *never* make payments on the loan itself. That process is called rolling over the debt. One of the reasons banks prefer to lend to governments is that they do not expect those loans ever to be repaid. When Walter Wriston was chairman of the Citicorp Bank in 1982, he extolled the virtue of the action this way:

> If we had a truth-in-Government act comparable to the truth-in-advertising law, every note issued by the Treasury would be obliged to include a sentence stating: "This note will be redeemed with the proceeds from an identical note which will be sold to the public when this one comes due."

When this activity is carried out in the United States, as it is weekly, it is described as a Treasury bill auction. But when basically the same process is conducted abroad in a foreign language, our news media usually speak of a country's "rolling over its debts." The perception remains that some form of disaster is inevitable. It is not.

To see why, it is only necessary to understand the basic facts of government borrowing. The first is that there are few recorded instances in history of government—any government—actually getting out of debt. Certainly in an era of $100-billion deficits, no one lending money to our Government by buying a Treasury bill expects that it will be paid at maturity in any way except by our Government's selling a new bill of like amount.[1]

THE DEBT ROLL-OVER PLAY

Since the system makes it profitable for banks to make large, unsound loans, that is the kind of loans which banks will make. Furthermore, it is predictable that most unsound loans eventually will go into default. When the borrower finally declares that he cannot pay, the bank responds by rolling over the loan. This often is stage managed to appear as a concession on the part of the bank but, in reality, it is a significant forward move toward the objective of perpetual interest.

Eventually the borrower comes to the point where he can no longer pay even the interest. Now the play becomes more complex. The bank does not want to lose the interest, because that is its stream of income. But it cannot afford to allow the borrower to go into default either, because that would require a write-off which, in turn, could wipe out the owners' equity and put the bank out of business. So the bank's next move is to create additional money out of nothing and lend *that* to the borrower so he will have enough to *continue paying the interest*, which by now must be paid on the original loan plus the additional loan as well. What looked like certain disaster suddenly is converted by a brilliant play into a major score. This not only maintains the old loan on the books as an asset, it actually increases the apparent size of that asset and also results in higher interest payments, thus, greater profit to the bank.

THE UP-THE-ANTE PLAY

Sooner or later, the borrower becomes restless. He is not interested in making interest payments with nothing left for himself. He comes to realize that he is merely working for the bank and, once again, interest payments stop. The opposing teams go into a huddle to plan the next move, then rush to the scrimmage

---

1. "Banking Against Disaster," by Walter B. Wriston, *The New York Times*, September 14, 1982.

line where they hurl threatening innuendoes at each other. The borrower simply cannot, will not pay. Collect if you can. The lender threatens to blackball the borrower, to see to it that he will never again be able to obtain a loan. Finally, a "compromise" is worked out. As before, the bank agrees to create still *more* money out of nothing and lend *that* to the borrower to cover the interest on both of the previous loans but, this time, they up the ante to provide still *additional* money for the borrower to spend on something *other* than interest. That is a perfect score. The borrower suddenly has a fresh supply of money for *his* purposes plus enough to keep making those bothersome interest payments. The bank, on the other hand, now has still *larger* assets, *higher* interest income, and *greater* profits. What an exciting game!

THE RESCHEDULING PLAY

The previous plays can be repeated several times until the reality finally dawns on the borrower that he is sinking deeper and deeper into the debt pit with no prospects of climbing out. This realization usually comes when the interest payments become so large they represent almost as much as the entire corporate earnings or the country's total tax base. This time around, roll-overs with larger loans are rejected, and default seems inevitable.

But wait. What's this? The players are back at the scrimmage line. There is a great confrontation. Referees are called in. Two shrill blasts from the horn tell us a score has been made for *both* sides. A voice over the public address system announces: "This loan has been *rescheduled*."

Rescheduling usually means a combination of a lower interest rate and a longer period for repayment. The effect is primarily cosmetic. It reduces the monthly payment but extends the period further into the future. This makes the current burden to the borrower a little easier to carry, but it also makes repayment of the capital even more unlikely. It postpones the day of reckoning but, in the meantime, you guessed it: The loan remains as an asset, and the interest payments continue.

THE PROTECT-THE-PUBLIC PLAY

Eventually the day of reckoning arrives. The borrower realizes he can *never* repay the capital and flatly refuses to pay interest on it. It is time for the Final Maneuver.

According to the *Banking Safety Digest*, which specializes in rating the safety of America's banks and S&Ls, most of the banks involved with "problem loans" are quite profitable businesses:

> Note that, *except for third-world loans*, most of the large banks in the country are operating quite profitably. In contrast with the continually-worsening S&L crisis, the banks' profitability has been the engine with which they have been working off (albeit slowly) their overseas debt.... At last year's profitability levels, the banking industry could, in theory, "buy out" the entirety of their own Latin American loans within two years.[1]

The banks *can* absorb the losses of their bad loans to multi-national corporations and foreign governments, but that is not according to the rules. It would be a major loss to the stockholders who would receive little or no dividends during the adjustment period, and any chief executive officer who embarked upon such a course would soon be looking for a new job. That this is not part of the game plan is evident by the fact that, while a small portion of the Latin American debt has been absorbed, the banks are continuing to make gigantic loans to governments in other parts of the world, particularly Africa, China, Russia, and Eastern European nations. For reasons which will be analyzed in chapter four, there is little hope that the performance of these loans will be different than those in Latin America. But the most important reason for not absorbing the losses is that there is a standard play that can still breathe life back into those dead loans and reactivate the bountiful income stream that flows from them.

Here's how it works. The captains of both teams approach the referee and the Game Commissioner to request that the game be extended. The reason given is that this is in the interest of the public, the spectators who are having such a wonderful time and who will be sad to see the game ended. They request also that, while the spectators are in the stadium enjoying themselves, the parking-lot attendants be ordered to quietly remove the hub caps from every car. These can be sold to provide money for additional salaries for all the players, including the referee and, of course, the Commissioner himself. That is only fair since they are now

---

1. "Overseas Lending ... Trigger for A Severe Depression?" *The Banking Safety Digest* (U.S. Business Publishing/Veribanc, Wakefield, Massachusetts), August, 1989, p. 3.

working overtime for the benefit of the spectators. When the deal is finally struck, the horn will blow three times, and a roar of joyous relief will sweep across the stadium.

In a somewhat less recognizable form, the same play may look like this: The president of the lending bank and the finance officer of the defaulting corporation or government will join together and approach Congress. They will explain that the borrower has exhausted his ability to service the loan and, without assistance from the federal government, there will be dire consequences for the American people. Not only will there be unemployment and hardship at home, there will be massive disruptions in world markets. And, since we are now so dependent on those markets, our exports will drop, foreign capital will dry up, and we will suffer greatly. What is needed, they will say, is for Congress to provide money to the borrower, either directly or indirectly, to allow him to continue to pay interest on the loan and to initiate new spending programs which will be so profitable he will soon be able to pay everyone back.

As part of the proposal, the borrower will agree to accept the direction of a third-party referee in adopting an austerity program to make sure that none of the new money is wasted. The bank also will agree to write off a small part of the loan as a gesture of its willingness to share the burden. This move, of course, will have been foreseen from the very beginning of the game, and is a small step backward to achieve a giant stride forward. After all, the amount to be lost through the write-off was created out of nothing in the first place and, without this Final Maneuver, the *entirety* would be written off. Furthermore, this modest write down is dwarfed by the amount to be gained through restoration of the income stream.

THE GUARANTEED-PAYMENT PLAY

One of the standard variations of the Final Maneuver is for the government, not always to directly provide the funds, but to provide the *credit* for the funds. That means to *guarantee* future payments should the borrower again default. Once Congress agrees to this, the government becomes a co-signer to the loan, and the inevitable losses are finally lifted from the ledger of the bank and placed onto the backs of the American taxpayer.

Money now begins to move into the banks through a complex system of federal agencies, international agencies, foreign aid, and direct subsidies. All of these mechanisms extract payments from the American people and channel them to the deadbeat borrowers who then send them to the banks to service their loans. Very little of this money actually comes from taxes. Almost all of it is generated by the Federal Reserve System. When this newly created money returns to the banks, it quickly moves out again into the economy where it mingles with and dilutes the value of the money already there. The result is the appearance of rising prices but which, in reality, is a lowering of the value of the dollar.

The American people have no idea they are paying the bill. They know that *someone* is stealing their hub caps, but they think it is the greedy businessman who raises prices or the selfish laborer who demands higher wages or the unworthy farmer who demands too much for his crop or the wealthy foreigner who bids up our prices. They do not realize that these groups *also* are victimized by a monetary system which is constantly being eroded in value by and through the Federal Reserve System.

Public ignorance of how the game is really played was dramatically displayed during a recent Phil Donahue TV show. The topic was the Savings and Loan crisis and the billions of dollars that it would cost the taxpayer. A man from the audience rose and asked angrily: "Why can't the government pay for these debts instead of the taxpayer?" And the audience of several hundred people actually cheered in enthusiastic approval!

PROSPERITY THROUGH INSOLVENCY

Since large, corporate loans are often guaranteed by the federal government, one would think that the banks which make those loans would never have a problem. Yet, many of them still manage to bungle themselves into insolvency. As we shall see in a later section of this study, insolvency actually is inherent in the system itself, a system called fractional-reserve banking.

Nevertheless, a bank can operate quite nicely in a state of insolvency so long as its customers don't know it. Money is brought into being and transmuted from one imaginary form to another by mere entries on a ledger, and creative bookkeeping can always make the bottom line appear to balance. The problem arises when depositors decide, for whatever reason, to withdraw their money. Lo and behold, there isn't enough to go around and, when that happens, the cat is finally out of the bag. The bank must close its doors, and the depositors still waiting in line outside are ... well, just that: still waiting.

The proper solution to this problem is to require the banks, like all other businesses, to honor their contracts. If they tell their customers that deposits are "payable upon demand," then they should hold enough cash to make good on that promise, regardless of when the customers want it or how many of them want it. In other words, they should keep cash in the vault equal to 100% of their depositors' accounts. When we give our hat to the hat-check girl and obtain a receipt for it, we don't expect her to rent it out while we eat dinner hoping she'll get it back—or one just like it—in time for our departure. We expect *all* the hats to remain there *all* the time so there will be no question of getting ours back precisely when we want it.

On the other hand, if the bank tells us it is going to lend our deposit to others so we can earn a little interest on it, then it should also tell us forthrightly that we *cannot* have our money back on demand. Why not? Because it is loaned out and not in the vault any longer. Customers who earn interest on their accounts should be told that they have *time* deposits, not *demand* deposits, because the bank will need a stated amount of time before it will be able to recover the money which was loaned out.

None of this is difficult to understand, yet bank customers are seldom informed of it. They are told they can have their money any time they want it *and* they are paid interest as well. Even if *they* do not receive interest, the *bank* does, and this is how so many customer services can be offered at little or no direct cost. Occasionally, a thirty-day or sixty-day delay will be mentioned as a possibility, but that is greatly inadequate for deposits which have been transformed into ten, twenty, or thirty-year loans. The banks are simply playing the odds that everything will work out *most of the time.*

We shall examine this issue in greater detail in a later section but, for now, it is sufficient to know that total disclosure is not how the banking game is played. The Federal Reserve System has legalized and institutionalized the dishonesty of issuing more hat checks than there are hats and it has devised complex methods of disguising this practice as a perfectly proper and normal feature of banking. Students of finance are told that there simply is no other way for the system to function. Once that premise is accepted, then all attention can be focused, not on the inherent fraud, but on ways and means to live with it and make it as painless as possible.

Based on the assumption that only a small percentage of the depositors will ever want to withdraw their money at the same time, the Federal Reserve allows the nation's commercial banks to operate with an incredibly thin layer of cash to cover their promises to pay "on demand." When a bank runs out of money and is unable to keep that promise, the System then acts as a lender of last resort. That is banker language meaning it stands ready to create money out of nothing and immediately lend it to any bank in trouble. (Details on how that is accomplished are in chapter eight.) But there are practical limits to just how far that process can work. Even the Fed will not support a bank that has gotten itself so deeply in the hole it has no realistic chance of digging out. When a bank's bookkeeping assets finally become less than its liabilities, the rules of the game call for transferring the losses to the depositors themselves. This means they pay *twice*: once as taxpayers and again as depositors. The mechanism by which this is accomplished is called the Federal Deposit Insurance Corporation.

THE FDIC PLAY

The FDIC guarantees that every insured deposit will be paid back regardless of the financial condition of the bank. The money to do this comes out of a special fund which is derived from assessments against participating banks. The banks, of course, do not pay this assessment. As with all other expenses, the bulk of the cost ultimately is passed on to their customers in the form of higher service fees and lower interest rates on deposits.

The FDIC is usually described as an insurance fund, but that is deceptive advertising at its worst. One of the primary conditions of insurance is that it must avoid what underwriters call "moral hazard." That is a situation in which the policyholder has little incentive to avoid or prevent that which is being insured against. When moral hazard is present, it is normal for people to become careless, and the likelihood increases that what is being insured against will actually happen. An example would be a government program forcing everyone to pay an equal amount into a fund to protect them from the expense of parking fines. One hesitates even to mention this absurd proposition lest some enterprising politician should decide to put it on the ballot. Therefore, let us hasten to point out that, if such a numb-skull plan were adopted, two things would happen: (1) just about everyone soon would be getting parking tickets and (2), since there now would be so many of them, the taxes to pay for those tickets would greatly exceed the previous cost of paying them *without* the so-called protection.

The FDIC operates exactly in this fashion. Depositors are told their insured accounts are protected in the event their bank should become insolvent. To pay for this protection, each bank is assessed a specified percentage of its total deposits. That percentage is the same for all banks regardless of their previous record or how risky their loans. Under such conditions, it does not pay to be cautious. The banks making reckless loans earn a higher rate of interest than those making conservative loans. They also are far more likely to collect from the fund, yet they pay not one cent more. Conservative banks are penalized and gradually become motivated to make more risky loans to keep up with their competitors and to get their "fair share" of the fund's protection. Moral hazard, therefore, is built right into the system. As with protection against parking tickets, the FDIC increases the likelihood that what is being insured against will actually happen. It is not a solution to the problem, it is *part* of the problem.

REAL INSURANCE WOULD BE A BLESSING

A true deposit-insurance program which was totally voluntary and which geared its rates to the actual risks would be a blessing. Banks with solid loans on their books would be able to obtain protection for their depositors at reasonable rates, because the chances of the insurance company having to pay would be small. Banks with unsound loans, however, would have to pay much higher rates or possibly would not be able to obtain coverage at any price. Depositors, therefore, would know instantly, without need to investigate further, that a bank without insurance is not a place where they want to put their money. In order to attract deposits, banks would have to have insurance. In order to have insurance at rates they could afford, they would have to demonstrate to the insurance company that their financial affairs are in good order. Consequently, banks which failed to meet the minimum standards of sound business practice would soon have no customers and would be forced out of business. A voluntary, private insurance program would act as a powerful regulator of the entire banking industry far more effectively and honestly than any political scheme ever could. Unfortunately, such is not the banking world of today.

The FDIC "protection" is not insurance in any sense of the word. It is merely part of a political scheme to bail out the most influential members of the banking cartel when they get into financial difficulty. As we have already seen, the first line of defense in this scheme is to have large, defaulted loans restored to life by a Congressional pledge of tax dollars. If that should fail and the bank can no longer conceal its insolvency through creative bookkeeping, it is almost certain that anxious depositors will soon line up to withdraw their money—which the bank does not have. The second line of defense, therefore, is to have the FDIC step in and make those payments for them.

Bankers, of course, do not want this to happen. It is a last resort. If the bank is rescued in this fashion, management is fired and what is left of the business usually is absorbed by another bank. Furthermore, the value of the stock will plummet, but this will affect the small stockholders only. Those with controlling interest and those in management know long in advance of the pending catastrophe and are able to sell the bulk of their shares while the price is still high. The people who create the problem seldom suffer the economic consequences of their actions.

THE FDIC WILL NEVER BE ADEQUATELY FUNDED

The FDIC never will have enough money to cover its potential liability for the entire banking system. If that amount were in existence, it could be held by the banks themselves, and an insurance fund would not even be necessary. Instead, the FDIC operates on the same assumption as the banks: that only a small percentage will ever need money at the same time. So the amount held in reserve is never more than a few percentage points of the total liability. Typically, the FDIC holds about $1.20 for every $100 of covered deposits. At the time of this writing, however, that figure had slipped to only 70 cents and was still dropping. That means that the financial exposure is about 99 times larger than the safety net which is supposed to catch it. The failure of just one or two large banks in the system could completely wipe out the entire fund.

And it gets even worse. Although the ledger may show that so many millions or billions are in the fund, that also is but creative bookkeeping. By law, the money collected from bank assessments must be invested in Treasury bonds, which means it is lent to the government and spent immediately by Congress. In the final stage of this process, therefore, the FDIC itself runs out of money and turns, first to the Treasury, then to Congress for help. This step, of course, is an act of final desperation, but it is usually presented in the media as though it were a sign of the system's great strength. *U.S. News & World Report* blandly describes it this way: "Should the agencies need more money yet, Congress has pledged the full faith and credit of the federal government."[1] Gosh, gee whiz. Isn't that wonderful? It sort of makes one feel rosy all over to know that the fund is so well secured.

Let's see what "full faith and credit of the federal government" actually means. Congress, already deeply in debt, has no money either. It doesn't dare openly raise taxes for the shortfall, so it applies for an additional loan by offering still more Treasury bonds for sale. The public picks up a portion of these I.O.U.s, and the Federal Reserve buys the rest. If there is a monetary crisis at hand and the size of the loan is great, the Fed will pick up the entire issue.

But the Fed has no money either. So it responds by creating out of nothing an amount of brand new money equal to the I.O.U.s and, through the magic of central banking, the FDIC is finally funded. This new money gushes into the banks where it is used to pay off the depositors. From there it floods through the economy diluting the value of *all* money and causing prices to rise. The old paycheck doesn't buy as much any more, so we learn to get along with a little bit less. But, see? The bank's doors are open again, and all the depositors are happy—until they return to their cars and discover the missing hub caps!

That is what is meant by "the full faith and credit of the federal government."

---

1. "How Safe Are Deposits in Ailing Banks, S&L's?" *U.S. News & World Report*, March 25, 1985, p. 73.

SUMMARY

Although national monetary events may appear mysterious and chaotic, they are governed by well-established rules which bankers and politicians rigidly follow. The central fact to understanding these events is that all the money in the banking system has been created out of nothing through the process of making loans. A defaulted loan, therefore, costs the bank little of tangible value, but it shows up on the ledger as a reduction in assets without a corresponding reduction in liabilities. If the bad loans exceed the size of the assets, the bank becomes technically insolvent and must close its doors. The first rule of survival, therefore, is to avoid writing off large, bad loans and, if possible, to at least continue receiving interest payments on them. To accomplish that, the endangered loans are rolled over and increased in size. This provides the borrower with money to continue paying interest plus fresh funds for new spending. The basic problem is not solved, but it is postponed for a little while and made worse.

The final solution on behalf of the banking cartel is to have the federal government guarantee payment of the loan should the borrower default in the future. This is accomplished by convincing Congress that not to do so would result in great damage to the economy and hardship for the people. From that point forward, the burden of the loan is removed from the bank's ledger and transferred to the taxpayer. Should this effort fail and the bank be forced into insolvency, the last resort is to use the FDIC to pay off the depositors. The FDIC is not insurance, because the presence of "moral hazard" makes the thing it supposedly protects against more likely to happen. A portion of the FDIC funds is derived from assessments against the banks. Ultimately, however, they are paid by the depositors themselves. When these funds run out, the balance is provided by the Federal Reserve System in the form of freshly created new money. This floods through the economy causing the appearance of rising prices but which, in reality, is the lowering of the value of the dollar. The final cost of the bailout, therefore, is passed to the public in the form of a hidden tax called inflation.

So much for the rules of the game. In the next chapter we shall look at the scorecard of the actual play itself.

Chapter Three

PROTECTORS OF THE PUBLIC

The Game-Called-Bailout as it actually has been applied to specific cases including Penn Central, Lockheed, New York City, Chrysler, Common-wealth Bank of Detroit, First Pennsylvania Bank, Continental Illinois, and others.

In the previous chapter, we offered the whimsical analogy of a sporting event to clarify the maneuvers of monetary and political scientists to bail out those commercial banks which comprise the Federal-Reserve cartel. The danger in such an approach is that it could leave the impression the topic is frivolous. So, let us abandon the analogy and turn to reality. Now that we have studied the hypothetical rules of the game, it is time to check the scorecard of the actual play itself, and it will become obvious that this is no trivial matter. A good place to start is with the rescue of a consortium of banks which were holding the endangered loans of Penn Central Railroad.

PENN CENTRAL

Penn Central was the nation's largest railroad with 96,000 employees and a payroll of $20 million a week. In 1970, it also became the nation's biggest bankruptcy. It was deeply in debt to just about every bank that was willing to lend it money, and that list included Chase Manhattan, Morgan Guaranty, Manufacturers Hanover, First National City, Chemical Bank, and Continental Illinois. Officers of the largest of those banks had been appointed to Penn Central's board of directors as a condition for obtaining funds, and they gradually had acquired control over the railroad's management. The banks also held large blocks of Penn Central stock in their trust departments.

The arrangement was convenient in many ways, not the least of which was that the bankers sitting on the board of directors were privy to information, long before the public received it, which would affect the market price of Penn Central's stock. Chris Welles, in *The Last Days of the Club*, describes what happened:

> On May 21, a month before the railroad went under, David Bevan, Penn Central's chief financial officer, privately informed representatives of the company's banking creditors that its financial condition was so weak it would have to postpone an attempt to raise $100 million in desperately needed operating funds through a bond issue. Instead, said Bevan, the railroad would seek some kind of government loan guarantee. In other words, unless the railroad could manage a federal bailout, it would have to close down. The following day, Chase Manhattan's trust department sold 134,300 shares of its Penn Central holdings. Before May 28, when the public was informed of the postponement of the bond issue, Chase sold another 128,000 shares. David Rockefeller, the bank's chairman, vigorously denied Chase had acted on the basis of inside information.[1]

More to the point of this study is the fact that virtually all of the major management decisions which led to Penn Central's demise were made by or with the concurrence of its board of directors, which is to say, by the banks that provided the loans. In other words, the bankers were not in trouble because of Penn Central's poor management, they *were* Penn Central's poor management. An investigation conducted in 1972 by Congressman Wright Patman, Chairman of the House Banking and Currency Committee, revealed the following: The banks provided large loans for disastrous expansion and diversification projects. Then they lent additional millions to the railroad so it could pay dividends to its stockholders. This created the false appearance of prosperity and artificially inflated the market price of its stock long enough to dump it on the unsuspecting public. Thus, the banker-managers were able to engineer a three-way bonanza for themselves. They (1) received dividends on essentially worthless stock, (2) earned interest on the loans which provided the money to pay those dividends, and (3) were able to unload 1.8 million shares of stock—*after* the dividends, of course—at unrealistically high prices.[2] Reports from the Securities and Exchange Commission

---

1. Chris Welles, *The Last Days of the Club* (New York: E.P. Dutton, 1975), pp. 398–99.
2. "Penn Central," *1971 Congressional Quarterly Almanac* (Washington, D.C.: Congressional Quarterly, 1971), p. 838.

showed that the company's top executives had disposed of their stock in this fashion at a personal savings of more than $1 million.[1]

Had the railroad been allowed to go into bankruptcy at that point and been forced to sell off its assets, the bankers still would have been protected. In any liquidation, creditors are paid off first, stockholders last; so the manipulators had dumped most of their stock while prices were relatively high. That is a common practice among corporate raiders who use borrowed funds to seize control of a company, bleed off its assets to other enterprises which they also control, and then toss the debt-ridden, dying carcass upon the remaining stockholders or, in this case, the taxpayers.

THE PUBLIC BE DAMNED

In his letter of transmittal accompanying the staff report, Congressman Patman provided this summary:

> It was as though everyone was a part of a close knit club in which Penn Central and its officers could obtain, with very few questions asked, loans for almost everything they desired both for the company and for their own personal interests, where the bankers sitting on the Board asked practically no questions as to what was going on, simply allowing management to destroy the company, to invest in questionable activities, and to engage in some cases in illegal activities. These banks in return obtained most of the company's lucrative banking business. The attitude of everyone seemed to be, while the game was going on, that all these dealings were of benefit to every member of the club, and the railroad and the public be damned.[2]

The banking cartel, commonly called the Federal Reserve System, was created for exactly this kind of bailout. Arthur Burns, who was the Fed's chairman, would have preferred to provide a direct infusion of newly created money, but that was contrary to the rules at that time. In his own words: "Everything fell through. We couldn't lend it to them ourselves under the law.... I worked on this thing in other ways."[3]

The company's cash crisis came to a head over a weekend and, in order to avoid having the corporation forced to file for bankruptcy on Monday morning, Burns called the homes of the heads of the Federal Reserve banks around the country and told them to get

---

1. "Penn Central: Bankruptcy Filed After Loan Bill Fails," 1970 *Congressional Quarterly Almanac* (Washington, D.C.: Congressional Quarterly, 1970), p. 811.
2. Quoted by Welles, pp. 404–05.
3. Quoted by Welles, p. 407.

the word out immediately that the System was anxious to help. On Sunday, William Treiber, who was the first vice-president of the New York branch of the Fed, contacted the chief executives of the ten largest banks in New York and told them that the Fed's Discount Window would be wide open the next morning. Translated, that means the Federal Reserve System was prepared to create money out of nothing and then immediately lend it to the commercial banks so they, in turn, could multiply and re-lend it to Penn Central and other corporations, such as Chrysler, which were in similar straits.[1] Furthermore, the rates at which the Fed would make these funds available would be low enough to compensate for the risk. Speaking of what transpired on the following Monday, Burns boasted: "I kept the Board in session practically all day to change regulation Q so that money could flow into CDs at the banks." Looking back at the event, Chris Welles approvingly describes it as "what is by common consent the Fed's finest hour."[2]

Finest hour or not, the banks were not that interested in the proposition unless they could be assured the taxpayer would co-sign the loans and guarantee payment. So the action inevitably shifted back to Congress. Penn Central's executives, bankers, and union representatives came in droves to explain how the railroad's continued existence was in the best interest of the public, of the working man, of the economic system itself. The Navy Department spoke of protecting the nation's "defense resources." Congress, of course, could not callously ignore these pressing needs of the nation. It responded by ordering a retroactive, 13 ½ per cent pay raise for all union employees. After having added that burden to the railroad's cash drain and putting it even deeper into the hole, it then passed the Emergency Rail Services Act of 1970 authorizing $125 million in federal loan guarantees.[3]

None of this, of course, solved the basic problem, nor was it really intended to. Almost everyone knew that, eventually, the railroad would be "nationalized," which is a euphemism for becoming a black hole into which tax dollars disappear. This came

---

1. For an explanation of the multiplier effect, see chapter eight, The Mandrake Mechanism.
2. Welles, pp. 407–08.
3. "Congress Clears Railroad Aid Bill, Acts on Strike," *1970 Congressional Almanac* (Washington, D.C.: 1970), pp. 810–16.

to pass with the creation of AMTRAK in 1971 and CONRAIL in 1973. AMTRAK took over the passenger services of Penn Central, and CONRAIL assumed operation of freight services. CONRAIL is a private corporation. When it was created, 85% of its stock was held by the government. The rest was held by employees. Fortunately, the government's stock was sold in a public offering in 1987.

AMTRAK continues under political control and operates at a loss. It is sustained by government subsidies—which is to say by taxpayers. By 1998, Congress had dutifully given it $21 billion. In 2002, it was consuming more than $200 million of taxes per year. By 2005, it requested an increase in subsidy to $1.8 billion per year. Between 1990 and 2009, it had lost another $23 billion. CONRAIL, on the other hand, since it was returned to the private sector, has experienced an impressive turnaround and has been running at a profit—paying taxes instead of consuming them.

LOCKHEED

In 1970, the Lockheed Corporation, the nation's largest defense contractor, was teetering on the verge of bankruptcy. The Bank of America and several smaller banks had lent $400 million to the Goliath and they were not anxious to lose the bountiful income stream that flowed from that; nor did they wish to lose such a large asset from their ledgers. In due course, the banks joined forces with Lockheed's management, stockholders, and labor unions, and descended on Washington. Sympathetic politicians were told that, if Lockheed were allowed to fail, 31,000 jobs would be lost, hundreds of sub contractors would go down, thousands of suppliers would be forced into bankruptcy, and national security would be seriously jeopardized. What the company needed was to borrow more money and lots of it. But, because of its current financial predicament, no one was willing to lend. The answer? In the interest of protecting the economy and defending the nation, the government simply had to provide either the money or the credit.

A bailout plan was quickly engineered by Treasury Secretary John B. Connally which provided the credit. The government agreed to guarantee payment on an additional $250 million in loans—an amount which would put Lockheed 60% deeper into the debt hole than it had been before. But that made no difference now. Once the taxpayer had been made a co-signer to the account, the banks had no qualms about advancing the funds.

The not-so-obvious part of this story is that the government now had a powerful motivation to make sure Lockheed would be awarded as many defense contracts as possible and that those contracts would be as profitable as possible. This would be an indirect method of paying off the banks with tax dollars, but doing so in such a way as not to arouse public indignation. Other defense contractors which had operated more efficiently would lose business, but that could not be proven. Furthermore, a slight increase in defenses expenditures would hardly be noticed.

By 1977, Lockheed had, indeed, paid back this loan, and that fact was widely advertised as proof of the wisdom and skill of all the players, including the referee and the game commissioner. A deeper analysis, however, must include two facts. First, there is no evidence that Lockheed's operation became more cost efficient during these years. Second, every bit of the money used to pay back the loans came from defense contracts which were awarded by the same government which was guaranteeing those loans. Under such an arrangement, it makes little difference if the loans were paid back or not. Taxpayers were doomed to pay the bill either way.

NEW YORK CITY

Although the government of New York City is not a corporation in the usual sense, it functions as one in many respects, particularly regarding debt.

In 1975, New York had reached the end of its credit rope and was unable even to make payroll. The cause was not mysterious. New York had long been a welfare state within itself, and success in city politics was traditionally achieved by lavish promises of benefits and subsidies for "the poor." Not surprisingly, the city also was notorious for political corruption and bureaucratic fraud. Whereas the average large city employed thirty-one people per one-thousand residents, New York had forty nine. That's an excess of fifty-eight per cent. The salaries of these employees far outstripped those in private industry. While an X-ray technician in a private hospital earned $187 per week, a porter working for the city earned $203. The average bank teller earned $154 per week, but a change maker on the city subway received $212. And municipal fringe benefits were fully twice as generous as those in private industry within the state. On top of this mountainous overhead were heaped additional costs for free college educations, subsidized housing, free medical care, and endless varieties of welfare programs.

City taxes were greatly inadequate to cover the cost of this utopia. Even after transfer payments from Albany and Washington added state and federal taxes to the take, the outflow continued to exceed the inflow. There were now only three options: increase city taxes, reduce expenses, or go into debt. The choice was never in serious doubt. By 1975, New York had floated so many bonds it had saturated the market and could find no more lenders. Two billion dollars of this debt was held by a small group of banks, dominated by Chase Manhattan and Citicorp.

When the payment of interest on these loans finally came to a halt, it was time for serious action. The bankers and the city fathers traveled down the coast to Washington and put their case before Congress. The largest city in the world could not be allowed to go bankrupt, they said. Essential services would be halted and millions of people would be without garbage removal, without transportation, even without police protection. Starvation, disease, and crime would run rampant through the city. It would be a disgrace to America. David Rockefeller at Chase Manhattan persuaded his friend Helmut Schmidt, Chancellor of West Germany, to make a statement to the media that the disastrous situation in New York could trigger an international financial crisis.

Congress, understandably, did not want to turn New York into a zone of anarchy, nor to disgrace America, nor to trigger a world-wide financial panic. So, in December of 1975, it passed a bill authorizing the Treasury to make direct loans to the city up to $2.3 billion, an amount which would more than *double* the size of its current debt to the banks. Interest payments on the old debt resumed immediately. All of this money, of course, would first have to be borrowed by Congress which was, itself, deeply in debt. And most of it would be created, directly or indirectly, by the Federal Reserve System. That money would be taken from the taxpayer through the loss of purchasing power called inflation, but at least the banks could be repaid, which is the object of the game.

There were several restrictions attached to this loan, including an austerity program and a systematic repayment schedule. None of these conditions was honored. New York City has continued to be a welfare utopia, and it is unlikely that it will *ever* get out of debt.

CHRYSLER

By 1978, the Chrysler Corporation was on the verge of bank-ruptcy. It had rolled over its debt to the banks many times, and the game was nearing an end. In spite of an OPEC oil embargo which had pushed up the cost of gasoline and in spite of the increasing popularity of small-automobile imports, the company had contin-ued to build the traditional gas hog. It was now saddled with a mammoth inventory of unsaleable cars and with a staggering debt which it had acquired to build those cars.

The timing was doubly bad. America was also experiencing high interest rates which, coupled with fears of U.S. military involvement in Cambodia, had led to a slump in the stock market. Banks felt the credit crunch keenly and, in one of those rare instances in modern history, the money makers themselves were scouring for money.

Chrysler needed additional cash to stay in business. It was not interested in borrowing just enough to pay the interest on its existing loans. To make the game worth playing, it wanted over a *billion* dollars in new capital. But, in the prevailing economic environment, the banks were hard pressed to create anything close to that kind of money.

Managers, bankers, and union leaders found common cause in Washington. If one of the largest corporations in America was allowed to fold, think of the hardship to thousands of employees and their families; consider the damage to the economy as shock waves of unemployment move across the country; tremble at the thought of lost competition in the automobile market, of only two major brands from which to choose instead of three.

Well, could anyone blame Congress for not wanting to plunge innocent families into poverty nor to upend the national economy nor to deny anyone their Constitutional right to freedom-of-choice? So a bill was passed directing the Treasury to guarantee up to $1.5 billion in new loans to Chrysler. The banks agreed to write down $600 million of their old loans and to exchange an additional $700 million for preferred stock. Both of these moves were advertised as evidence the banks were taking a terrible loss but were willing to yield in order to save the nation. It should be noted, however, that the value of the stock which was exchanged for previously uncol-lectable debt rose drastically after the settlement was announced to the public. Furthermore, not only did interest payments resume on the balance of the old loans, but the banks now replaced the written down portion with fresh loans, and these were far superior in quality because they were fully guaranteed by the taxpayers. So valuable was this guarantee that Chrysler, in spite of its previously poor debt performance, was able to obtain loans at 10.35% interest while its more solvent competitor, Ford, had to pay 13.5%. Applying the difference of 3.15% to one and-a-half billion dollars, with a declining balance continuing for only six years, produces a savings in excess of $165 million. That is a modest estimate of the size of the federal subsidy. The real value was far greater because, without it, the corporation would have ceased to exist, and the banks would have taken a loss of almost their entire loan exposure.

FEDERAL DEPOSIT INSURANCE CORPORATION

It will be recalled from the previous chapter that the FDIC is not a true insurance program and, because it has been politicized, it embodies the principle of moral hazard and it actually increases the likelihood that bank failures will occur.

The FDIC has three options when bailing out an insolvent bank. The first is called a *payoff*. It involves simply paying off the insured depositors and then letting the bank fall to the mercy of the liquidators. This is the option usually chosen for small banks with no political clout. The second possibility is called a *sell off*, and it involves making arrangements for a larger bank to assume all the real assets and liabilities of the failing bank. Banking services are uninterrupted and, aside from a change in name, most customers are unaware of the transaction. This option is generally selected for small and medium banks. In both a payoff and a sell off, the FDIC takes over the bad loans of the failed bank and supplies the money to pay back the insured depositors.

The third option is called *bailout*, and this is the one which deserves our special attention. Irvine Sprague, a former director of the FDIC, explains: "In a bailout, the bank does not close, and everyone—insured or not—is fully protected.... Such privileged treatment is accorded by FDIC only rarely to an elect few."[1]

That's right, he said everyone—insured *or not*—is fully protected. The banks which comprise the elect few generally are the

---

1. Irvine H. Sprague, *Bailout: An Insider's Account of Bank Failures and Rescues* (New York: Basic Books, 1986), p. 23.

large ones. It is only when the number of dollars at risk becomes mind numbing that a bailout can be camouflaged as protection of the public. Sprague says:

> The FDI Act gives the FDIC board sole discretion to prevent a bank from failing, at whatever cost. The board need only make the finding that the insured bank is in danger of failing and "is essential to provide adequate banking service in its community."... FDIC boards have been reluctant to make an essentiality finding unless they perceive a clear and present danger to the nation's financial system.[1]

Favoritism toward the large banks is obvious at many levels. One of them is the fact that, in a bailout, the FDIC covers *all* deposits, whether insured or not. That is significant, because the banks pay an assessment based only on their *insured* deposits. So, if *un*insured deposits are covered also, that coverage is free—more precisely, paid by someone else. What deposits are *un*insured? Those in excess of $100,000 and those held outside the United States. Which banks hold the vast majority of such deposits? The *large* ones, of course, particularly those with extensive overseas operations.[2] The bottom line is that the large banks get a whopping free ride when they are bailed out. Their uninsured accounts are paid by FDIC, and the cost of that benefit is passed to the smaller banks and to the taxpayer. This is not an oversight. Part of the plan at Jekyll Island was to give a competitive edge to the large banks.

UNITY BANK

The first application of the FDIC essentiality rule was, in fact, an exception. In 1971, Unity Bank and Trust Company in the Roxbury section of Boston found itself hopelessly insolvent, and the federal agency moved in. This is what was found: Unity's capital was depleted; most of its loans were bad; its loan collection practices were weak; and its personnel represented the worst of two worlds: overstaffing and inexperience. The examiners reported that there were two persons for every job, and neither one had been taught the job.

With only $11.4 million on its books, the bank was small by current standards. Normally, the depositors would have been paid back, and the stockholders—like the owners of any other failed

---

1. Sprague, pp. 27–29.
2. The Bank of America is the exception. Despite its size, it has not acquired foreign deposits to the same degree as its competitors.

business venture—would have lost their investment. As Sprague, himself, admitted: "If market discipline means anything, stockholders should be wiped out when a bank fails. Our assistance would have the side effect ... of keeping the stockholders alive at government expense."[1] But Unity Bank was different. It was located in a black neighborhood and was minority owned. As is often the case when government agencies are given discretionary powers, decisions are determined more by political pressures than by logic or merit, and Unity was a perfect example. In 1971, the specter of rioting in black communities still haunted the halls of Congress. Would the FDIC allow this bank to fail and assume the awesome responsibility for new riots and bloodshed? Sprague answers:

> Neither Wille [another director] nor I had any trouble viewing the problem in its broader social context. We were willing to look for a creative solution.... My vote to make the "essentiality" finding and thus save the little bank was probably foreordained, an inevitable legacy of Watts.... The Watts riots ultimately triggered the essentiality doctrine.[2]

On July 22, 1971, the FDIC declared that the continued operation of Unity Bank was, indeed, essential and authorized a direct infusion of $1.5 million. Although appearing on the agency's ledger as a loan, no one really expected repayment. In 1976, in spite of the FDIC's own staff report that the bank's operations continued "as slipshod and haphazard as ever," the agency rolled over the "loan" for another five years. Operations did not improve and, on June 30, 1982, the Massachusetts Banking Commissioner finally revoked Unity's charter. There were no riots in the streets, and the FDIC quietly wrote off the sum of $4,463,000 as the final cost of the bailout.

COMMONWEALTH BANK OF DETROIT

The bailout of the Unity Bank of Boston was the exception to the rule that small banks are dispensable while the giants must be saved at all costs. From that point forward, however, the FDIC game plan was strictly according to Hoyle. The next bailout occurred in 1972 involving the $1.5 billion Bank of the Commonwealth of Detroit. Commonwealth had funded most of its

---

1. Sprague, pp. 41–42.
2. *Ibid.*, p. 48.

phenomenal growth through loans from another bank, Chase Manhattan in New York. When Commonwealth went belly up, largely due to securities speculation and self dealing on the part of its management, Chase seized 39% of its common stock and actually took control of the bank in an attempt to find a way to get its money back. FDIC director Sprague describes the inevitable sequel:

> Chase officers ... suggested that Commonwealth was a public interest problem that the government agencies should resolve. That unsubtle hint was the way Chase phrased its request for a bailout by the government.... Their proposal would come down to bailing out the shareholders, the largest of which was Chase.[1]

The bankers argued that Commonwealth must not be allowed to fold because it provided "essential" banking services to the community. That was justified on two counts: (1) it served many minority neighborhoods and, (2) there were not enough other banks in the city to absorb its operation without creating an unhealthy concentration of banking power in the hands of a few. It was unclear what the minority issue had to do with it inasmuch as every neighborhood in which Commonwealth had a branch was served by other banks as well. Furthermore, if Commonwealth were to be liquidated, many of those branches undoubtedly would have been purchased by competitors, and service to the communities would have continued. Judging by the absence of attention given to this issue during discussions, it is apparent that it was merely thrown in for good measure, and no one took it very seriously.

In any event, the FDIC did not want to be accused of being indifferent to the needs of Detroit's minorities and it certainly did not want to be a destroyer of free-enterprise competition. So, on January 17, 1972, Commonwealth was bailed out with a $60 million loan plus numerous federal guarantees. Chase absorbed some losses, primarily as a result of Commonwealth's weak bond portfolio, but those were minor compared to what would have been lost without FDIC intervention.

Since continuation of the bank was necessary to prevent concentration of financial power, FDIC engineered its sale to the First Arabian Corporation, a Luxembourg firm funded by Saudi

---

1. Sprague, p. 68.

princes. Better to have financial power concentrated in Saudi Arabia than in Detroit. The bank continued to flounder and, in 1983, what was left of it was resold to the former Detroit Bank & Trust Company, now called Comerica. Thus the dreaded concentration of local power was realized after all, but not until Chase Manhattan was able to walk away from the deal with most of its losses covered.

FIRST PENNSYLVANIA BANK

The 1980 bailout of the First Pennsylvania Bank of Philadelphia was next. First Penn was the nation's twenty-third largest bank with assets in excess of $9 billion. It was six times the size of Commonwealth; nine hundred times larger than Unity. It was also the nation's oldest bank, dating back to the Bank of North America which was created by the Continental Congress in 1781.

The bank had experienced rapid growth and handsome profits largely due to the aggressive leadership of its chief executive officer, John Bunting, who had previously been an economist with the Federal Reserve Bank of Philadelphia. Bunting was the epitome of the era's go-go bankers. He vastly increased earnings ratios by reducing safety margins, taking on risky loans, and speculating in the bond market. As long as the economy expanded, these gambles were profitable, and the stockholders loved him dearly. When his gamble in the bond market turned sour, however, the bank plunged into a negative cash flow. By 1979, First Penn was forced to sell off several of its profitable subsidiaries in order to obtain operating funds, and it was carrying $328 million in questionable loans. That was $16 million more than the entire stockholder investment. The bank was insolvent, and the time had arrived to hit up the taxpayer for the loss.

The bankers went to Washington and presented their case. They were joined by spokesmen from the nation's top three: Bank of America, Citibank, and of course the ever-present Chase Manhattan. They argued that, not only was the bailout of First Penn "essential" for the continuation of banking services in Philadelphia, it was also critical to the preservation of *world* economic stability. The bank was so large, they said, if it were allowed to fall, it would act as the first domino leading to an international financial crisis. At first, the directors of the FDIC resisted that theory and earned the angry impatience of the Federal Reserve. Sprague recalls:

We were far from a decision on how to proceed. There was strong pressure from the beginning not to let the bank fail. Besides hearing from the bank itself, the other large banks, and the comptroller, we heard frequently from the Fed. I recall at one session, Fred Schultz, the Fed deputy chairman, argued in an ever rising voice, that there were no alternatives—we had to save the bank. He said, "Quit wasting time talking about anything else!"...

The Fed's role as lender of last resort first generated contention between the Fed and FDIC during this period. The Fed was lending heavily to First Pennsylvania, fully secured, and Fed Chairman Paul Volcker said he planned to continue funding indefinitely until we could work out a merger or a bailout to save the bank.[1]

The directors of the FDIC did not want to cross swords with the Federal Reserve System, and they most assuredly did not want to be blamed for tumbling the entire world economic system by allowing the first domino to fall. "The theory had never been tested," said Sprague. "I was not sure I wanted it to be just then."[2] So, in due course, a bailout package was put together which featured a $325 million loan from FDIC, interest free for the first year and at a subsidized rate thereafter; about half the market rate. Several other banks which were financially tied to First Penn, and which would have suffered great losses if it had folded, lent an additional $175 million and offered a $1 billion line of credit. FDIC insisted on this move to demonstrate that the banking industry itself was helping and that it had faith in the venture. To bolster that faith, the Federal Reserve opened its Discount Window offering low-interest funds for that purpose.

The outcome of this particular bailout was somewhat happier than with the others, at least as far as the bank is concerned. At the end of the five-year taxpayer subsidy, the FDIC loan was fully repaid. The bank has remained on shaky ground, however, and the final page of this episode has not yet been written.

CONTINENTAL ILLINOIS

Everything up to this point was but mere practice for the big event which was yet to come. In the early 1980s, Chicago's Continental Illinois was the nation's seventh largest bank. With assets of $42 billion and with 12,000 employees working in offices

---

1. Sprague, pp. 88–89.
2. *Ibid.*, p. 89.

in almost every major country in the world, its loan portfolio had undergone spectacular growth. Its net income on loans had literally doubled in just five years and by 1981 had rocketed to an annual figure of $254 million. It had become the darling of the market analysts and even had been named by *Dun's Review* as one of the five best managed companies in the country. These opinion leaders failed to perceive that the spectacular performance was due, not to an expertise in banking or investment, but to the financing of shaky business enterprises and foreign governments which could not obtain loans anywhere else. But the public didn't know that and wanted in on the action. For awhile, the bank's common stock actually sold at a premium over others which were more prudently managed.

The gaudy fabric began to unravel during the Fourth of July weekend of 1982 with the failure of the Penn Square Bank in Oklahoma. That was the notorious shopping-center bank that had booked a billion dollars in oil and gas loans and resold them to Continental just before the collapse of the energy market. Other loans also began to sour at the same time. The Mexican and Argentine debt crisis was coming to a head, and a series of major corporate bankruptcies were receiving almost daily headlines. Continental had placed large chunks of its easy money with all of them. When these events caused the bank's credit rating to drop, cautious depositors began to withdraw their funds, and new funding dwindled to a trickle. The bank became desperate for cash to meet its daily expenses. In an effort to attract new money, it began to offer unrealistically high rates of interest on its CDs. Loan officers were sent to scour the European and Japanese markets and to conduct a public relations campaign aimed at convincing market managers that the bank was calm and steady. David Taylor, the bank's chairman at that time, said: "We had the Continental Illinois Reassurance Brigade and we fanned out all over the world."[1]

In the fantasy land of modern finance, glitter is often more important than substance, image more valuable than reality. The bank paid the usual quarterly dividend in August, in spite of the fact that this intensified its cash crunch. As with the Penn Central Railroad twelve years earlier, that move was calculated to project an image of business-as-usual prosperity. And the ploy worked—

---

1. Quoted by Chernow, p. 657.

for a while, at least. By November, the public's confidence had been restored, and the bank's stock recovered to its pre-Penn Square level. By March of 1983, it had risen even higher. But the worst was yet to come.

By the end of 1983, the bank's burden of non-performing loans had reached unbearable proportions and was growing at an alarming rate. By 1984, it was $2.7 billion. That same year, the bank sold off its profitable credit-card operation to make up for the loss of income and to obtain money for paying stockholders their expected quarterly dividend. The internal structure was near collapse, but the external facade continued to look like business as usual.

The first crack in that facade appeared at 11:39 A.M. On Tuesday, May 8, Reuters, the British news agency, moved a story on its wire service stating that banks in the Netherlands, West Germany, Switzerland, and Japan had increased their interest rate on loans to Continental and that some of them had begun to withdraw their funds. The story also quoted the bank's official statement that rumors of pending bankruptcy were "totally preposterous." Within hours, another wire, the Commodity News Service, reported a second rumor: that a Japanese bank was interested in buying Continental.

WORLD'S FIRST ELECTRONIC BANK RUN

As the sun rose the following morning, foreign investors began to withdraw their deposits. A billion dollars in Asian money moved out that first day. The next day—a little more than twenty-four hours following Continental's assurance that bankruptcy was totally preposterous, its long-standing customer, the Board of Trade Clearing Corporation, located just down the street—withdrew $50 million. Word of the defection spread through the financial wire services, and the panic was on. It became the world's first global electronic bank run.

By Friday, the bank had been forced to borrow $3.6 billion from the Federal Reserve in order to cover its escaping deposits. A consortium of sixteen banks, led by Morgan Guaranty, offered a generous thirty-day line of credit, but all of this was far short of the need. Within seven more days, the outflow surged to over $6 billion.

In the beginning, almost all of this action was at the institutional level: other banks and professionally managed funds which closely monitor every minuscule detail of the financial markets. The general public had no inkling of the catastrophe, even as it unfolded. Chernow says: "The Continental run was like some modernistic fantasy: there were no throngs of hysterical depositors, just cool nightmare flashes on computer screens."[1] Sprague writes: "Inside the bank, all was calm, the teller lines moved as always, and bank officials recall no visible sign of trouble—except in the wire room. Here the employees knew what was happening as withdrawal order after order moved on the wire, bleeding Continental to death. Some cried."[2]

This was the golden moment for which the Federal Reserve and the FDIC were created. Without government intervention, Continental would have collapsed, its stockholders would have been wiped out, depositors would have been badly damaged, and the financial world would have learned that banks, not only have to *talk* about prudent management, they actually have to *adopt* it. Future banking practices would have been severely altered, and the long-term economic benefit to the nation would have been enormous. But *with* government intervention, the discipline of a free market is suspended, and the cost of failure or fraud is politically passed to the taxpayers. Depositors continue to live in a dream world of false security, and banks can operate recklessly and fraudulently with the knowledge that their political partners in government will come to their rescue when they get into trouble.

FDIC GENEROSITY WITH TAX DOLLARS

One of the challenges at Continental was that, while only four per cent of its liability was covered by FDIC "insurance," the regulators felt compelled to cover the entire exposure. Which means that the bank paid insurance premiums into the fund based on only four per cent of its total coverage, and the taxpayers now would pick up the other ninety-six per cent. FDIC director Sprague explains:

> Although Continental Illinois had over $30 billion in deposits, 90 percent were uninsured foreign deposits or large certificates substantially exceeding the $100,000 insurance limit. Off-book

---

1. Chernow, p. 658.
2. Sprague, p. 153.

liabilities swelled Continental's real size to $69 billion. In this massive liability structure only some $3 billion within the insured limit was scattered among 850,000 deposit accounts. So it was in our power and entirely legal simply to pay off the insured depositors, let everything else collapse, and stand back to watch the carnage.[1]

That course was never seriously considered by any of the players. From the beginning, there were only two questions: how to come to Continental's rescue by covering its *total* liabilities and, equally important, how to politically justify such a fleecing of the taxpayer. As pointed out in the previous chapter, the rules of the game require that the scam must always be described as a heroic effort to protect the public. In the case of Continental, the sheer size of the numbers made the ploy relatively easy. There were so many depositors involved, so many billions at risk, so many other banks interlocked, it could be claimed that the economic fabric of the entire nation—of the world itself—was at stake. And who could say that it was not so. Sprague argues the case in familiar terms:

> An early morning meeting was scheduled for Tuesday, May 15, at the Fed.... We talked over the alternatives. They were few—none really.... [Treasury Secretary] Regan and [Fed Chairman] Volcker raised the familiar concern about a national banking collapse, that is, a chain reaction if Continental should fail. Volcker was worried about an international crisis. We all were acutely aware that never before had a bank even remotely approaching Continental's size closed. No one knew what might happen in the nation and in the world. It was no time to find out just for the purpose of intellectual curiosity.[2]

THE FINAL BAILOUT PACKAGE

The bailout was predictable from the start. There would be some preliminary lip service given to the necessity of allowing the banks themselves to work out their own problem. That would be followed by a plan to have the banks and the government *share* the burden. And that finally would collapse into a mere public-relations illusion. In the end, almost the entire cost of the bailout would be assumed by the government and passed on to the taxpayer.

At the May 15 meeting, Treasury Secretary Regan spoke eloquently about the value of a free market and the necessity of having the banks mount their own rescue plan, at least for a part of

---

1. Sprague, p. 184.
2. *Ibid.*, pp. 154–55, 183.

the money. To work out that plan, a summit meeting was arranged the next morning among the chairmen of the seven largest banks: Morgan Guaranty, Chase Manhattan, Citibank, Bank of America, Chemical Bank, Bankers Trust, and Manufacturers Hanover. The meeting was perfunctory at best. The bankers knew full well that the Reagan Administration would not risk the political embarrassment of a major bank failure. That would make the President and the Congress look bad at re-election time. But, still, some kind of tokenism was called for to preserve the Administration's conservative image. So, with urging from the Fed and the Treasury, the consortium agreed to put up the sum of $500 million—an average of only $71 million for each, far short of the actual need. Chernow describes the plan as "make-believe" and says "they pretended to mount a rescue."[1] Sprague supplies the details:

> The bankers said they wanted to be in on any deal, but they did not want to lose any money. They kept asking for guarantees. They wanted it to look as though they were putting money in but, at the same time, wanted to be absolutely sure they were not risking anything.... By 7:30 A.M. we had made little progress. We were certain the situation would be totally out of control in a few hours. Continental would soon be exposing itself to a new business day, and the stock market would open at ten o'clock. Isaac [another FDIC director] and I held a hallway conversation. We agreed to go ahead without the banks. We told Conover [the third FDIC director] the plan and he concurred....
>
> [Later], we got word from Bernie McKeon, our regional director in New York, that the bankers had agreed to be at risk. Actually, the risk was remote since our announcement had promised 100 percent insurance.[2]

The final bailout package was a whopper. Basically, the government took over Continental Illinois and assumed all of its losses. Specifically, the FDIC took $4.5 billion in bad loans and paid Continental $3.5 billion for them. The difference was then made up by the infusion of $1 billion in fresh capital in the form of stock purchase. The bank, therefore, now had the federal government as a stockholder controlling 80 per cent of its shares, and its bad loans had been dumped onto the taxpayer. In effect, even though

---

1. Chernow, p. 659.
2. Sprague, pp. 159–60.

Continental retained the appearance of a private institution, it had been nationalized.

LENDER OF LAST RESORT

Perhaps the most important part of the bailout, however, was that the money to make it possible was created—directly or indirectly—by the Federal Reserve System. If the bank had been allowed to fail, and the FDIC had been required to cover the losses, the drain would have emptied the entire fund with nothing left to cover the liabilities of thousands of other banks. In other words, this one failure alone, if it were allowed to happen, would have wiped out the entire FDIC! That's one reason the bank had to be kept operating, losses or no losses, and that's why the Fed had to be involved in the bail out. In fact, that was precisely the reason the System was created at Jekyll Island: to manufacture whatever amount of money might be necessary to cover the losses of the cartel. The scam could never work unless the Fed was able to create money out of nothing and pump it into the banks along with "credit" and "liquidity" guarantees. Which means, if the loans go sour, the money is eventually extracted from the American people through the hidden tax called inflation. That's the meaning of the phrase "lender of last resort."

FDIC director Irvine Sprague, while discussing the press release which announced the Continental bail-out package, describes the Fed's role this way:

> The third paragraph ... granted 100 percent insurance to all depositors, including the uninsured, and all general creditors.... The next paragraph ... set forth the conditions under which the Fed, as lender of last resort, would make its loans.... The Fed would lend to Continental to meet "any extraordinary liquidity requirements." That would include another run. All agreed that Continental could not be saved without 100 percent insurance by FDIC and unlimited liquidity support by the Federal Reserve. No plan would work without these two elements.[1]

By 1984, "unlimited liquidity support" had translated into the staggering sum of $8 billion. By early 1986, the figure had climbed to $9.24 billion and was still rising. While explaining this fleecing of the taxpayer to the Senate Banking Committee, Fed Chairman Paul Volcker said: "The operation is the most basic function of the

---

1. Sprague, pp. 162–63.

Federal Reserve. It was why it was founded."[1] With those words, he has confirmed one of the more controversial assertions of this book.

SMALL BANKS BE DAMNED

It has been mentioned previously that the large banks receive a free ride on their FDIC coverage at the expense of the small banks. There could be no better example of this than the bail out of Continental Illinois. In 1983, the bank paid a premium into the fund of only $6.5 million to protect its insured deposits of $3 billion. The actual liability, however—including its institutional and overseas deposits—was ten times that figure, and the FDIC guaranteed payment on the whole amount. As Sprague admitted, "Small banks pay proportionately far more for their insurance and have far less chance of a Continental-style bailout."[2]

How true. Within the same week that the FDIC and the Fed were providing billions in payments, stock purchases, loans, and guarantees for Continental Illinois, it closed down the tiny Bledsoe County Bank of Pikeville, Tennessee, and the Planters Trust and Savings Bank of Opelousas, Louisiana. During the first half of that year, forty-three smaller banks failed without FDIC bailout. In most cases, a merger was arranged with a larger bank. The impact of this inequity upon the banking system is enormous. It sends a message to bankers and depositors alike that small banks, if they get into trouble, will be allowed to fold, whereas large banks are safe regardless of how poorly or fraudulently they are managed. As a New York investment analyst stated to news reporters, Continental Illinois, even though it had just failed, was "obviously the safest bank in the country to have your money in."[3] Nothing could be better calculated to drive the small independent banks out of business or to force them to sell out to the giants. And that is exactly what has been happening. Since 1984, while hundreds of small banks have been forced out of business, the average size of the banks that remain has more than doubled. It will be recalled that this advantage of the big banks over their smaller competitors was also one of the objectives of the Jekyll Island plan.

---

1. Quoted by Greider, p. 628.
2. Sprague, p. 250.
3. "New Continental Illinois Facing Uncertain Future," by Keith E. Leighty, Associated Press, Thousand Oaks, Calif., *News Chronicle*, May 13, 1985, p. 18.

Perhaps the most interesting—and depressing—aspect of the Continental Illinois bailout was the lack of public indignation over the principle of using taxes and inflation to protect the banking industry. Smaller banks have complained of the unfair advantage given to the larger banks, but not on the basis that the government should have let the giant fall. Their lament was that it should now protect *them* in the same paternalistic fashion. Voters and politicians were silent on the issue, apparently awed by the sheer size of the numbers and the specter of economic chaos. Decades of public education had left their mark. After all, wasn't this exactly what government schools have taught is the proper function of government? Wasn't this the American way? Even Ronald Reagan, viewed as the national champion of economic conservatism, praised the action. From aboard Air Force One on the way to California, the President said: "It was a thing that we should do and we did it. It was in the best interest of all concerned."[1]

The Reagan endorsement brought into focus one of the most amazing phenomena of the 20th century: the process by which America has moved toward statism while marching behind the banner of those who speak the language of *opposing* statism. William Greider, a former writer for the liberal *Washington Post* and *The Rolling Stone*, complains:

> The nationalization of Continental was, in fact, a quintessential act of modern liberalism—the state intervening in behalf of private interests and a broad public purpose. In this supposedly conservative era, federal authorities were setting aside the harsh verdict of market competition (and grossly expanding their own involvement in the private economy)....
>
> In the past, conservative scholars and pundits had objected loudly at any federal intervention in the private economy, particularly emergency assistance for failing companies. Now, they hardly seemed to notice. Perhaps they would have been more vocal if the deed had been done by someone other than the conservative champion, Ronald Reagan.[2]

Four years after the bailout of Continental Illinois, the same play was used in the rescue of BankOklahoma, which was a bank holding company. The FDIC pumped $130 million into its main banking unit and took warrants for 55% ownership. The pattern

1. "Reagan Calls Rescue of Bank No Bailout," *New York Times,* July 29, 1984.
2. Greider, p. 631.

had been set. By accepting stock in a failing bank in return for bailing it out, the government had devised an ingenious way to nationalize banks without calling it that. Issuing stock sounds like a *business* transaction in the private sector. And the public didn't seem to notice the reality that Uncle Sam was going into banking.

THE SUBPRIME MELTDOWN

By 2008, the engine of destruction was running at full throttle. Decades of low interest rates had lured homeowners, speculators, and lending institutions into the real estate market where fortunes could be made by what appeared to be perpetually rising values. Knowing that they would be bailed out by the Fed if they got into trouble, large banks threw caution to the wind and offered loans to just about anyone who would sign the documents, regardless of ability to make payments. Many of them crafted fraudulent documents overstating the value of underlying properties and the incomes of borrowers, and then made loans that were greater than the value of the property. The game was simple: Make as many subprime loans as possible, package them into large blocks of similar loans, give the packages impressive names such as "Prime Diversified Fund," and then sell them to unsuspecting investors. Two of the largest conduits for this scam are Fannie Mae and Freddie Mac, loan re-packagers sponsored by the government.

The scheme worked for a while, because the Fed's artifically low interest rates created a real estate boom with rising home prices. Those who had been enticed into loans they could not afford were able to sell their properties at a profit and come out ahead even if they could not afford payments. Foreclosures were rare, and the investment packages appeared to be solid. However, as with all booms caused by manipulation of market forces, the real estate boom came to an end. When it did, it was compounded by rampant inflation, high taxes, crippling regulation, and loss of jobs to other countries, all of which combined to create an economic recession.

As foreclosure rates began to climb, Fannie Mae, Freddie Mac, large banks and loan brokers were in trouble. Not only were their loans not performing, they became defendents in hundreds of law suits from institutional buyers of their fraudulent investment packages. It was time, once again, for the Federal Reserve to bail them out, which it did with over a trillion dollars of newly created money. Ambrose Evans-Prichard with the *London Telegraph* reports:

The emergency bail-out gives the US Treasury sweeping authority to inject capital into the giant mortgage lenders Fannie Mae and Freddie Mac, which together own or guarantee half the country's $12 trillion stock of home loans. The ceiling on the US national debt has been lifted by a further $800bn, giving the Treasury almost unlimited resources to prop up the two lenders. In parallel, the Federal Housing Authority (FHA) is to guarantee up to $300bn of fresh mortgages for struggling homeowners trapped with soaring loan costs, often the result of "honeytrap" contracts.

The scheme aims to avoid an avalanche of fresh defaults as the housing market continues to deteriorate. Over 740,000 homes fell into foreclosure in the second quarter. ... The share prices of Fannie and Freddie, the world's two biggest financial institutions, have dropped by almost 85pc.[1]

The trillion dollars for this bailout will not come from the Federal Reserve or the government. It will come from American consumers in the form of inflation.

SECOND REASON TO ABOLISH THE FEDERAL RESERVE

A sober evaluation of this long and continuing record leads to the second reason for abolishing the Federal Reserve: Far from being a protector of the public, *it is a cartel operating against the public interest.*

SUMMARY

The game called bailout is not a whimsical figment of the imagination, it is real. Here are some of the big games of the past and their final scores.

In 1970, Penn Central railroad became bankrupt. The banks which lent the money had taken over its board of directors and had driven it further into the hole, all the while extending bigger and bigger loans to cover the losses. Directors concealed reality from the stockholders and made additional loans so the company could pay dividends to keep up the false front. During this time, the directors and their banks unloaded their stock at unrealistically high prices. When the truth became public, the stockholders were left holding the empty bag. The bailout, which was engineered by the Federal Reserve, involved government subsidies to other banks to grant additional loans. Then Congress was told that the collapse

---

1. "Fannie Mae and Freddie Mac: Congress backs rescue package," by Ambrose Evans-Prichard, *Telegraph.co.uk*, Jul7 28, 2008.

of Penn Central would be devastating to the public interest. Congress responded by granting $125 million in loan guarantees so that banks would not be at risk. The railroad eventually failed anyway, but the bank loans were covered. Penn Central was nationalized into AMTRAK and continues to operate at a loss.

In 1970, as Lockheed faced bankruptcy, Congress heard essentially the same story. Thousands would be unemployed, subcontractors would go out of business, and the public would suffer greatly. So Congress agreed to guarantee $250 million in new loans, which put Lockheed 60% deeper into debt than before. Now that government was guaranteeing the loans, it had to make sure Lockheed became profitable. This was accomplished by granting lucrative defense contracts at non-competitive bids. The banks were paid back.

In 1975, New York City had reached the end of its credit rope. It had borrowed heavily to maintain an extravagant bureaucracy and a miniature welfare state. Congress was told that the public would be jeopardized if city services were curtailed and that America would be disgraced in the eyes of the world. So Congress authorized additional direct loans up to $2.3 billion, which more than doubled the size of the current debt. The banks continued to receive their interest.

In 1978, Chrysler was on the verge of bankruptcy. Congress was informed that the public would suffer greatly if the company folded, and that it would be a blow to the American way if freedom-of-choice were reduced from three to two makes of automobiles. So Congress guaranteed up to $1.5 billion in new loans. The banks reduced part of their loans and exchanged another portion for preferred stock. News of the deal pushed up the market value of that stock and largely offset the loan write-off. The banks' previously uncollectable debt was converted into a government-backed, interest-bearing asset.

In 1972, the Commonwealth Bank of Detroit—with $1.5 billion in assets, became insolvent. It had borrowed heavily from the Chase Manhattan Bank in New York to invest in high-risk and potentially high-profit ventures. Now that it was in trouble, so was Chase. The bankers went to Washington and told the FDIC the public must be protected from the great financial hardship that would follow if Commonwealth were allowed to close. So the FDIC pumped in a $60 million loan plus federal guarantees of repayment. Commonwealth was sold to an Arab consortium. Chase took a minor write down but converted most of its potential loss into government-backed assets.

In 1979, the First Pennsylvania Bank of Philadelphia became insolvent. With assets in excess of $9 billion, it was six-times the size of Commonwealth. It, too, had been an aggressive player in the '70s. Now the bankers and the Federal Reserve told the FDIC that the public must be protected from the calamity of a bank failure of this size, that the national economy was at stake, perhaps even the entire world. So the FDIC gave a $325 million loan—interest-free for the first year, and at half the market rate thereafter. The Federal Reserve offered money to other banks at a subsidized rate for the specific purpose of relending to First Penn. With that enticement, they advanced $175 million in immediate loans plus a $1 billion line of credit.

In 1982, Chicago's Continental Illinois became insolvent. It was the nation's seventh largest bank with $42 billion in assets. The previous year, its profits had soared as a result of loans to high-risk business ventures and foreign governments. Although it had been the darling of market analysts, it quickly unraveled when its cash flow turned negative, and overseas banks began to withdraw deposits. It was the world's first electronic bank run. Federal Reserve Chairman Volcker told the FDIC that it would be unthinkable to allow the world economy to be ruined by a bank failure of this magnitude. So, the FDIC assumed $4.5 billion in bad loans and, in return for the bailout, took 80% ownership of the bank in the form of stock. In effect, the bank was nationalized, but no one called it that. The United States government was now in the banking business.

All of the bail outs of previous years pale by comparison to the trillions of dollars pumped into the banks beginning in 2008 in response to the subprime meltdown. This huge amount of money will not come from the government or The Federal Reserve. It will come from American consumers in the form of higher prices.

All of the money to accomplish these bailouts was made possible by the Federal Reserve System acting as the "lender of last resort." That was one of the purposes for which it had been created. We must not forget that the phrase "lender of last resort" means that the money is created out of nothing, resulting in the confiscation of our nation's wealth through the hidden tax called inflation.

Chapter Four

HOME, SWEET LOAN

The history of increasing government intervention in the housing industry; the stifling of free-market forces in residential real estate; the resulting crisis in the S&L industry; the bailout of that industry with money taken from the taxpayer.

As we have seen in previous chapters, the damage done by the banking cartel is made possible by the fact that money can be created out of nothing. It also destroys our purchasing power through the hidden tax called inflation. The mechanism by which it works is hidden and subtle.

Let us turn, now, from the arcane world of central banking to the giddy world of savings-and-loan institutions. By comparison, the problem in the savings-and-loan industry is easy to comprehend. It is simply that vast amounts of money are disappearing into the black hole of government mismanagement, and the losses must eventually be paid by us. The end result is the same in both cases.

SOCIALISM TAKES ROOT IN AMERICA

It all began with a concept. The concept took root in America largely as a result of the Great Depression of the 1930s. American politicians were impressed at how radical Marxists were able to attract popular support by blaming the capitalist system for the country's woes and by promising a socialist utopia. They admired and feared these radicals; admired them for their skill at mass psychology; feared them lest they become so popular as to win a plurality at the ballot box. It was not long before many political figures began to mimic the soap-box orators, and the voters enthusiastically put them into office.

While the extreme and violent aspects of Communism generally were rejected, the more genteel theories of socialism became popular among the educated elite. It was they who would naturally become the leaders in an American socialist system. Someone had to look after the masses and tell them what to do for their own good, and many with college degrees and those with great wealth became enamored by the thought of playing that role. And so, the concept became widely accepted at all levels of American life—the "downtrodden masses" as well as the educated elite—that it was desirable for the government to take care of its citizens and to protect them in their economic affairs.

And so, when more than 1900 S&Ls went belly-up in the Great Depression, Herbert Hoover—and a most willing Congress—created the Federal Home Loan Bank Board to protect depositors in the future. It began to issue charters to institutions that would submit to its regulations, and the public was led to believe that government regulators would be more wise, prudent, and honest than private managers. A federal charter became a kind of government seal of approval. The public, at last, was being protected.

Hoover was succeeded by FDR in the White House who became the epitome of the new breed. Earlier in his political career, he had been the paragon of free enterprise and individualism. He spoke out against big government and for the free market, but in mid life he reset his sail to catch the shifting political wind. He went down in history as a pioneer of socialism in America.

It was FDR who took the next step toward government paternalism in the S&L industry—as well as the banking industry—by establishing the Federal Deposit Insurance Corporation (FDIC) and the Federal Saving and Loan Insurance Corporation (FSLIC). From that point forward, neither the public nor the managers of the thrifts needed to worry about losses. Everything would be reimbursed by the government.

A HOUSE ON EVERY LOT

At about the same time, loans on private homes became subsidized through the Federal Housing Authority (FHA) which allowed S&Ls to make loans at rates lower than would have been possible without the subsidy. This was to make it easier for everyone to realize the dream of having their own home. While the Marxists were promising a chicken in every pot, the New Dealers were winning elections by pushing for a house on every lot.

In the beginning, many people were able to purchase a home who, otherwise, might not have been able to do so or who would have had to wait longer to accumulate a higher down payment. On the other hand, the FHA-induced easy credit began to push up the price of houses for the middle class, and that quickly offset any real advantage of the subsidy. The voters, however, were not perceptive enough to understand this canceling effect and continued to vote for politicians who promised to expand the system.

The next step was for the Federal Reserve Board to require banks to offer interest rates lower than those offered by S&Ls. The result was that funds moved from the banks into the S&Ls and became abundantly available for home loans. This was a deliberate national policy to favor the home industry at the expense of other industries that were competing for the same investment dollars. It may not have been good for the economy as a whole but it was good politics.

ABANDONMENT OF THE FREE MARKET

These measures effectively removed real estate loans from the free market and placed them into the political arena, where they have remained ever since. The damage to the public as a result of this intervention would be delayed a long time in coming, but when it came, it would be cataclysmic.

The reality of government disruption of the free market cannot be overemphasized, for it is at the heart of our present and future crisis. We have savings institutions that are controlled by government at every step of the way. Federal agencies provide protection against losses and lay down rigid guidelines for capitalization levels, number of branches, territories covered, management policies, services rendered, and interest rates charged. The additional cost to S&Ls of compliance with this regulation has been estimated by the American Bankers Association at about $11 billion per year, which represents a whopping 60% of all their profits.

On top of that, the healthy component of the industry must spend over a billion dollars each year for extra premiums into the so-called insurance fund to make up for the failures of the unhealthy component, a form of penalty for success. When some of the healthy institutions attempted to convert to banks to escape this penalty, the regulators said no. Their cash flow was needed to support the bailout fund.

INSURANCE FOR THE COMMON MAN?

The average private savings deposit is about $6,000. Yet, under the Carter administration, the level of FDIC insurance was raised from $40,000 to $100,000 for each account. Those with more than that merely had to open several accounts, so, in reality, the sky was the limit. Clearly this had nothing to do with protecting the common man. The purpose was to prepare the way for brokerage houses to reinvest huge blocks of capital at high rates of interest virtually without risk. It was, after all, insured by the federal government.

In 1979, Federal Reserve policy had pushed up interest rates, and the S&Ls had to keep pace to attract deposits. By December of 1980, they were paying 15.8% interest on their money-market certificates. Yet, the average rate they were charging for new mortgages was only 12.9%. Many of their older loans were still crunching away at 7 or 8% and, to compound the problem, some of those were in default, which means they were really paying 0%. The thrifts were operating deep in the red and had to make up the difference somewhere.

The weakest S&Ls paid the highest interest rates to attract depositors and they are the ones which obtained the large blocks of brokered funds. Brokers no longer cared how weak the operation was, because the funds were fully insured. They just cared about the interest rate.

On the other hand, the S&L managers reasoned that they had to make those funds work miracles for the short period they had them. It was their only chance to dig out, and they were willing to take big risks. For them also, the government's insurance program had removed any chance of loss to their depositors, so many of them plunged into high-profit, high-risk real-estate developments.

Deals began to go sour, and 1979 was the first year since the Great Depression of the 1930s that the total net worth of federally insured S&Ls became negative. And that was despite expansion almost everywhere else in the economy. The public began to worry.

FULL FAITH AND CREDIT

The protectors in Washington responded in 1982 with a joint resolution of Congress declaring that the full faith & credit of the United States government stood behind the FSLIC. That was a reassuring phrase, but many people had the gnawing feeling that, somehow, we were going to pay for it ourselves. And they were right. *Consumer Reports* explained:

Behind the troubled banks and the increasingly troubled insurance agencies stands "the full faith and credit" of the Government—in effect, a promise, sure to be honored by Congress, that all citizens will chip in through taxes or through inflation to make all depositors whole.[1]

The plight of the S&Ls was dramatically brought to light in Ohio in 1985 when the Home State Savings Bank of Cincinnati collapsed as a result of a potential $150 million loss in a Florida securities firm. This triggered a run, not only on the thirty-three branches of Home State, but on many of the other S&Ls as well. The news impacted international markets where overseas speculators dumped paper dollars for other currencies, and some rushed to buy gold.

Within a few days, depositors demanding their money caused $60 million to flow out of the state's $130 million "insurance" fund which, true to form for all government protection schemes, was terribly inadequate. If the run had been allowed to continue, the fund likely would have been obliterated the next day. It was time for a political fix.

On March 15, Ohio Governor Richard Celeste declared one of the few "bank holidays" since the Great Depression and closed all seventy-one of the state-insured thrifts. He assured the public there was nothing to worry about. He said this was merely a "cooling-off period ... until we can convincingly demonstrate the soundness of our system." Then he flew to Washington and met with Paul Volcker, chairman of the Federal Reserve Board, and with Edwin Gray, chairman of the Federal Home Loan Bank Board, to request federal assistance. They assured him it was available.

A few days later, depositors were authorized to withdraw up to $750 from their accounts. On March 21, President Reagan calmed the world money markets with assurances that the crisis was over. Furthermore, he said, the problem was "limited to Ohio."[2]

This was not the first time there had been a failure of state-sponsored insurance funds. The one in Nebraska was pulled down in 1983 when the Commonwealth Savings Company of Lincoln failed. It had over $60 million in deposits, but the insurance fund

---

1. "How Safe Are Your Deposits?", *Consumer Reports*, August, 1988, p. 503.
2. "Ohio Bank Crisis That Ruffled World," *U.S. News & World Report*, April 1, 1985, p. 11.

had less than $2 million to cover, not just Commonwealth, but the whole system. Depositors were lucky to get 65 cents on the dollar, and even that was expected to take up to 10 years.[1]

AN INVITATION TO FRAUD

In the early days of the Reagan administration, government regulations were changed so that the S&Ls were no longer restricted to the issuance of home mortgages, the sole reason for their creation in the first place. In fact, they no longer even were required to obtain a down payment on their loans. They could now finance 100% of a deal—or even *more*. Office buildings and shopping centers sprang up everywhere regardless of the need. Developers, builders, managers, and appraisers made millions. The field soon became overbuilt and riddled with fraud. Billions of dollars disappeared into defunct projects. In at least twenty-two of the failed S&Ls, there is evidence that the Mafia and CIA were involved.

Fraud is not necessarily against the law. In fact, most of the fraud in the S&L saga was, not only legal, it was encouraged by the government. The Garn-St. Germain Act allowed the thrifts to lend an amount of money equal to the *appraised* value of real estate rather than the *market* value. It wasn't long before appraisers were receiving handsome fees for appraisals that were, to say the least, unrealistic. But that was not fraud, it was the *intent* of the regulators. The amount by which the appraisal exceeded the market value was defined as "appraised equity" and was counted the same as capital. Since the S&Ls were required to have $1 in capital for every $33 held in deposits, an appraisal that exceeded market value by $1 million could be used to pyramid $33 million in deposits from Wall Street brokerage houses. And the anticipated profits from those funds was one of the ways in which the S&Ls were supposed to recoup their losses without the government having to cough up the money—which it didn't have. In effect the government was saying: "We can't make good on our protection scheme, so go get the money yourself by putting the investors at risk. Not only will we back you up if you fail, we'll show you exactly how to do it."

---

1. "How Safe Are Deposits in Ailing Banks, S&Ls?," *U.S. News & World Report*, March 25, 1985, p. 74.

THE FALLOUT BEGINS

In spite of the accounting gimmicks which were created to make the walking-dead S&Ls look healthy, by 1984 the fallout began. The FSLIC closed one institution that year and arranged for the merger of twenty-six others which were insolvent. In order to persuade healthy firms to absorb insolvent ones, the government provides cash settlements to compensate for the liabilities. By 1984, these subsidized mergers were costing the FDIC over $1 billion per year. Yet, that was just the small beginning.

Between 1980 and 1986, a total of 664 insured S&Ls failed. Government regulators had promised to protect the public in the event of losses, but the losses were already far beyond what they could handle. They could not afford to close down all the insolvent thrifts because they simply didn't have enough money to cover the pay out. In March of 1986, the FSLIC had only 3 cents for every dollar of deposits. By the end of that year, the figure had dropped to two-tenths of a penny for each dollar "insured." Obviously, they had to keep those thrifts in business, which meant they had to invent even more accounting gimmicks to conceal the reality.

Postponement of the inevitable made matters even worse. Keeping the S&Ls in business was costing the FSLIC $6 million per day.[1] By 1988, two years later, the thrift industry as a whole was losing $9.8 million per day, and the unprofitable ones—the corpses which were propped up by the FSLIC—were losing $35.6 million per day. And, still, the game continued.

By 1989, the FSLIC no longer had even two-tenths of a penny for each dollar insured. Its reserves had vanished altogether. Like the thrifts it supposedly protected, it was, itself, insolvent and looking for loans. It had tried offering bond issues, but these fell far short of its needs. Congress had discussed the problem but had failed to provide new funding. The collapse of Lincoln Savings brought the crisis to a head. There was no money, period.

THE FED USURPS THE ROLE OF CONGRESS

In February, an agreement was reached between Alan Greenspan, Chairman of the Federal Reserve Board, and M. Danny Wall, Chairman of the Federal Home Loan Bank Board, to have

---

1. "Fizzling FSLIC," by Shirley Hobbs Scheibla, *Barron's*, Feb. 9, 1987, p. 16.

$70 million of bailout funding for Lincoln Savings come directly from the Federal Reserve.

This was a major break in precedent. Historically, the Fed has served to create money only for the government or for banks. If it were the will of the people to bail out a savings institution, then it is up to Congress to approve the funding. If Congress does not have the money or cannot borrow it from the public, then the Fed can create it (out of nothing, of course) and give it to the government. But, in this instance, the Fed was usurping the role of Congress and making political decisions entirely on its own. There is no basis in the Federal Reserve Act for this action. Yet, Congress remained silent, apparently out of collective guilt for its own paralysis.

Finally, in August of that year, Congress was visited by the ghost of FDR and sprang into action. It passed the Financial Institutions Reform and Recovery Act (FIRREA) and allocated a minimum of $66 billion for the following ten years, $300 billion over thirty years. Of this amount, $225 billion was to come from taxes or inflation, and $75 billion was to come from the healthy S&Ls. It was the biggest bailout ever, bigger than the *combined* cost for Lockheed, Chrysler, Penn Central, and New York City.

In the process, the FSLIC was eliminated because it was hopelessly insolvent and replaced by the Savings Association Insurance Fund. Also created was the Banking Insurance Fund for the protection of commercial banks, and both are now administered by the FDIC.

As is often the case when previous government control fails to produce the desired result, the response of Congress is to *increase* the controls. Four entirely new layers of bureaucracy were added to the existing tangled mess: the Resolution Trust Oversight Board, to establish strategies for the RTC; the Resolution Funding Corporation, to raise money to operate the RTC; The Office of Thrift Supervision, to supervise thrift institutions even more than they had been; and the Oversight Board for the Home Loan Banks, the purpose of which remains vague but probably is to make sure that the S&Ls continue to serve the political directive of subsidizing the home industry. When President Bush signed the bill, he said:

> This legislation will safeguard and stabilize America's financial system and put in place permanent reforms so these problems will never happen again. Moreover, it says to tens of millions of savings-and-loan depositors, "You will not be the victim of others'

mistakes. We will see—guarantee—that your insured deposits are secure."[1]

THE ESTIMATES ARE SLIGHTLY WRONG

By the middle of the following year, it was clear that the $66 billion funding would be greatly inadequate. Treasury spokesmen were now quoting $130 billion, about twice the original estimate. How much is $130 billion? In 1990, it was 30% more than the salaries of all the schoolteachers in America. It was more than the combined profits of all the Fortune-500 industrial companies. It would send 1.6 million students through the best four-year colleges, including room and board. And the figure did not even include the cost of liquidating the huge backlog of thrifts already seized nor the interest that had to be paid on borrowed funds. Within only a few days of the announced increase, the Treasury again revised the figure upward from $130 billion to $150 billion. As Treasury Secretary Nicholas Brady told the press, "No one should assume that the estimates won't change. They will."

Indeed, the estimates continued to change with each passing week. The government had sold or merged 223 insolvent thrifts during 1988 and had given grossly inadequate estimates of the cost. Financiers such as Ronald Perelman and the Texas investment partnership called Temple-Inland, Inc., picked up many of these at fantastic bargains, especially considering that they were given cash subsidies and tax advantages to sweeten the deal. At the time, Danny Wall, who was then Chairman of the Federal Home Loan Bank Board, announced that these deals "took care" of the worst thrift problems. He said the cost of the bailout was $39 billion. The *Wall Street Journal* replied:

> Wrong again. The new study, a compilation of audits prepared by the Federal Deposit Insurance Corporation, indicates that the total cost of the so-called Class of '88 will be $90 billion to $95 billion, including tax benefits granted the buyers and a huge amount of interest on government debt to help finance this assistance....
>
> But the 1988 thrift rescues' most expensive flaw doesn't appear to be the enrichment of tycoons. Rather it's that none of the deals ended or even limited the government's exposure to mismanagement by the new owners, hidden losses on real estate in the past, or the vicissitudes of the real-estate markets in the future.... And some of the deals

---

1. "Review of the News," *The New American*, Sept. 11, 1989, p. 15.

appear to be sham transactions, in which failing thrifts were sold to failing thrifts, which are failing all over again....

Although the thrifts proved to be in far worse shape than the Bank Board estimated, Mr. Wall defends his strategy for rescuing them with open-ended assistance. "We didn't have the money to liquidate," he says.[1]

When Congress passed FIRREA the previous year to "safeguard and stabilize America's financial system," the staggering sum of $300 billion dollars was authorized to be taken from taxes and inflation over the following thirty years to do the job. Now, Federal Reserve Chairman Alan Greenspan was saying that the true long-term cost would stand at $500 billion, an amount even greater than the default of loans to all the Third-World countries combined. The figure was *still* too low. A non-biased private study released by Veribank, Inc. showed that, when all the hidden costs are included, the bill presented to the American people will be about $532 billion.[2] The problems that President Bush promised would "never happen again" were happening again.

BOOKKEEPING SLEIGHT OF HAND

Long before this point, the real estate market had begun to contract, and many mortgages exceeded the actual price for which the property could be sold. Furthermore, market interest rates had risen far above the rates that were locked into most of the S&L loans, and that decreased the value of those mortgages. The true value of a $50,000 mortgage that is paying 7% interest is only half of a $50,000 mortgage that is earning 14%. So the protectors of the public devised a scheme whereby the S&Ls were allowed to value their assets according to the original loan value rather than their true market value. That helped, but much more was still needed.

The next step was to create bookkeeping assets out of thin air. This was accomplished by authorizing the S&Ls to place a monetary value on community "good will"! With the mere stroke of a pen, the referees created $2.5 billion in such assets, and the players continued the game.

---

1. "Audit Report by FDIC Shows Wall's Estimates for Thrift Bailouts in 1988 Were Wildly Low," by Charles McCoy and Todd Mason, The *Wall Street Journal*, Sept. 14, 1990, p. A-12.
2. "S&L Industry Rebuilds As Bailout Reaches Final Phase," *Veribanc News Release*, Veribanc, Inc. (Wakefield, Massachusetts), January 12, 1994, p. 2.

Then the FSLIC began to issue "certificates of net worth," which were basically promises to bail out the ailing S&Ls should they need it. The government had already promised to do that but, by printing it on pieces of paper and calling them "certificates of net worth," the S&Ls were allowed to count them as assets on their books. Such promises *are* assets but, since the thrifts would be obligated to pay back any money it received in a bailout, those pay-back obligations should also have been put on the books as liabilities. The *net* position would not change. The only way they could count the certificates as assets without adding the offsetting liabilities would be for the bailout promises to be outright gifts with no obligation to ever repay. That may be the eventual result, but it is not the way the plan was set up. In any event, the thrifts were told they could count these pieces of paper as capital, the same as if the owners had put up their own cash. And the game continued.

The moment of truth arrives when the S&Ls have to liquidate some of their holdings, such as in the sale of their mortgages or foreclosed homes to other S&Ls, commercial banks, or private parties. That is when the inflated bookkeeping value is converted into the true market value, and the difference has to be entered into the ledger as a loss. But not in the never-never land of socialism where government is the great protector. Dennis Turner explains:

> The FSLIC permits the S&L which sold the mortgage to take the loss over a 40-year period. Most companies selling an asset at a loss must take the loss immediately: only S&Ls can engage in this patent fraud. Two failing S&Ls could conceivably sell their lowest-yielding mortgages to one another, and both would raise their net worth! *This dishonest accounting in the banking system is approved by the highest regulatory authorities.*[1]

U.S. News & World Report continues the commentary:

> Today, scores of savings-and-loan associations, kept alive mainly by accounting gimmicks, continue to post big losses.... Only a fraction of the industry's aggregate net worth comprises hard assets such as mortgage notes. Intangible assets, which include bookkeeping entries such as good will, make up nearly all of the industry's estimated net worth of 37.6 billion dollars.[2]

1. Dennis Turner, *When Your Bank Fails* (Princeton, New Jersey: Amwell Publishing, Inc., 1983), p. 141.
2. "It's Touch And Go for Troubled S&Ls," by Patricia M. Scherschel, *U.S. News & World Report*, March 4, 1985, p. 92.

ACCOUNTING GIMMICKS ARE NOT FRAUD

We must keep in mind that a well managed institution would never assume these kinds of risks or resort to fraudulent accounting if it wanted to stay in business for the long haul. But with Washington setting guidelines and standing by to make up losses, a manager would be fired if he didn't take advantage of the opportunity. After all, Congress specifically said it was OK when it passed the laws. These were loopholes deliberately put there to be used. Dr. Edward Kane explains:

> Deception itself doesn't constitute illegal fraud when it's authorized by an accounting system such as the Generally Accepted Accounting Principles (GAAP) system which allows institutions to forego recording assets at their true worth, maintaining them instead at their inflated value. The regulatory accounting principles system in 1982 added even new options to overstate capital.... Intense speculation, such as we observed in these firms, is not necessarily bad management at all. In most of these cases, it was clever management. There were clever gambles that exploited, not depositors or savers, but taxpayers.[1]

The press has greatly exaggerated the role of illegal fraud in these matters with much time spent excoriating the likes of Donald Dixon at Vernon S&L and Charles Keating at Lincoln Savings. True, these flops cost the taxpayer well over $3 billion dollars, but all the illegal fraud put together amounts to only about one-half of one per cent of the total losses so far.[2] Focusing on that minuscule component serves only to distract from the fact that the real problem is government regulation itself.

JUNK BONDS ARE NOT JUNK

Another part of the distraction has been to make it appear that the thrifts got into trouble because they were heavily invested in "junk bonds."

Wait a minute! What are junk bonds, anyway? This may come as a surprise, but those held by the S&Ls were anything but junk. In fact, in terms of risk-return ratios, most of them were superior-grade investments to bonds from the Fortune-500 companies.

---

1. "FIRREA: Financial Malpractice," by Edward J. Kane, *Durell Journal of Money and Banking*, May, 1990, p. 5.
2. "Banking on Government," by Jane H. Ingraham, *The New American*, August 24, 1992, p. 24.

So-called junk bonds are merely those that are offered by smaller companies which are not large enough to be counted among the nation's giants. The large reinvestors, such as managers of mutual funds and retirement funds, prefer to stay with well-known names like General Motors and IBM. They need to invest truly huge blocks of money every day, and the smaller companies don't have enough to offer to satisfy their needs. Consequently, bonds from most smaller companies are not traded by the large brokerage houses or the Bonds Division of the New York Stock Exchange. They are traded in smaller exchanges or directly between brokers in what is called "over the counter." Because they do not have the advantage of being traded in the larger markets, they have to pay a higher interest rate to attract investors, and for that reason, they are commonly called high-yield bonds.

Bonds offered by these companies are derided by some brokers as not being "investment grade," yet, many of them are excellent performers. In fact, they have become an important part of the American economy because they are the backbone of new industry. The most successful companies of the future will be found among their ranks. During the last decade, while the Fortune-500 companies were shrinking and eliminating 3.6 million jobs, this segment of new industry has been growing and has created 18 million new jobs.

Not all new companies are good investments—the same is true of older companies—but the small-company sector generally provides more jobs, has greater profit margins, and pays more dividends than the so-called "investment-grade" companies. From 1981 to 1991, the average return on ten-year Treasury bills was 10.4 per cent; the Dow Jones Industrial Average was 12.9 per cent; and the average return on so-called junk bonds was 14.1 per cent. Because of this higher yield, they attracted more than $180 billion from savvy investors, some of whom were S&Ls. It was basically a new market which was orchestrated by an upstart, Michael Milken, at the California-based Drexel Burnham Lambert brokerage house.

CAPITAL GROWTH WITHOUT BANK LOANS OR INFLATION

One of the major concerns at Jekyll Island in 1910 was the trend to obtain business-growth capital from sources other than bank loans. Here, seventy years later, the same trend was developing again in a slightly different form. Capital, especially for small companies, was now coming from bonds which Drexel had found a way to mass market. In fact, Drexel was even able to use those bonds to engineer corporate takeovers, an activity that previously had been reserved for the mega-investment houses. By 1986, Drexel had become the most profitable investment bank in the country.

Here was $180 billion that no longer was being channeled through Wall Street. Here was $180 billion that was coming from people's savings instead of being created out of nothing by the banks. In other words, here was growth built upon real investment, not inflation. Certain people were not happy about it.

Glenn Yago, Director of the Economic Research Bureau and Associate Professor of Management at the State University of New York at Stony Brook, explains the problem:

> It was not until high yield securities were applied to restructuring through deconglomeration and takeovers that hostilities against the junk bond market broke out.... The high yield market grew at the expense of bank debt, and high yield companies grew at the expense of the hegemony of many established firms. As Peter Passell noted in *The New York Times*, the impact was first felt on Wall Street, "where sharp elbows and a working knowledge of computer spreadsheets suddenly counted more than a nose for dry sherry or membership in Skull and Bones."[1]

The first line of attack on this new market of high-yield bonds was to call them "junk." The word itself was powerful. The financial media picked it up and many investors were frightened away.

The next step was for compliant politicians to pass a law requiring S&Ls to get rid of their "junk," supposedly to protect the public. That this was a hoax is evident by the fact that only 5% ever held any of these bonds, and their holdings represented only 1.2% of the total S&Ls assets. Furthermore, the bonds were performing satisfactorily and were a source of much needed revenue. Nevertheless, The Financial Institutions Reform and Recovery Act, which was discussed previously, was passed in 1989. It forced S&Ls to liquidate *at once* their "junk" bond holdings. That caused their

---

1. Glenn Yago, *Junk Bonds: How High Yield Securities Restructured Corporate America* (New York: Oxford University Press, 1991), p. 5.

prices to plummet, and the thrifts were even further weakened as they took a loss on the sale. Jane Ingraham comments:

> Overnight, profitable S&Ls were turned into government-owned basket cases in the hands of the Resolution Trust Corporation (RTC). To add to the disaster, the RTC itself, which became the country's largest owner of junk bonds ... flooded the market again with $1.6 billion of its holdings at the market's bottom in 1990....
>
> So it was government itself that crashed the junk bond market, not Michael Milken, although the jailed Milken and other former officials of Drexel Burnham Lambert have just agreed to a $1.3 billion settlement of the hundreds of lawsuits brought against them by government regulators, aggrieved investors, and others demanding "justice."[1]

Incidentally, these bonds have since recovered and, had the S&Ls been allowed to keep them, they would be in better financial condition today. And so would be the RTC.

With the California upstarts out of the way, it was a simple matter to buy up the detested bonds at bargain prices and to bring control of the new market back to Wall Street. The New York firm of Salomon Brothers, for example, one of Drexel's most severe critics during the 1980s, went on to become a leading trader in the market Drexel created.

REAL PROBLEM IS GOVERNMENT REGULATION

So the real problem within the savings-and-loan industry is government regulation which has insulated it from the free market and encouraged it to embark upon unsound business practices. As the *Wall Street Journal* stated on March 10, 1992:

> If you're going to wreck a business the size of the U.S. Thrift industry, you need a lot more power than Michael Milken ever had. You need the power of national political authority, the kind of power possessed only by regulators and Congress. Whatever "hold" Milken or junk bonds may have had on the S&Ls, it was nothing compared with the interventions of Congress.[2]

At the time this book went to press, the number of S&Ls that operated during the 1980s had dropped to less than half. As failures, mergers, and conversion into banks continue, the number will decline further. Those that remain fall into two groups: those

---

1. "Banking on Government," pp. 24, 25.
2. Quoted in "Banking on Government," p. 26.

that have been taken over by the RTC and those that have not. Most of those that remain under private control—and that is a relative term in view of the regulations they endure—are slowly returning to a healthy state as a result of improved profitability, asset quality, and capitalization. The RTC-run organizations, on the other hand, continue to hemorrhage due to failure by Congress to provide funding to close them down and pay them off. Losses from this group are adding $6 billion per year to the ultimate cost of bailout. President Clinton was asking Congress for an additional $45 billion and hinting that this should be the last bailout—but no promises.

The game continues.

CONGRESS IS PARALYZED, WITH GOOD REASON

Congress seems disinterested and paralyzed with inaction. One would normally expect dozens of politicians to be calling for a large-scale investigation of the ongoing disaster, but there is hardly a peep. The reason becomes obvious when one realizes that savings-and-loan associations, banks, and other federally regulated institutions are heavy contributors to the election campaigns of those who write the regulatory laws. A thorough, public investigation would undoubtedly turn up some cozy relationships that the legislators would just as soon keep confidential.

The second reason is that any honest inquiry would soon reveal the shocking truth that Congress itself is the primary cause of the problem. By following the socialist path and presuming to protect or benefit their constituency, they have suspended and violated the natural laws that drive a free-market economy. In so doing, they created a Frankenstein monster they could not control. The more they tried to tame the thing, the more destructive it became. As economist Hans Sennholz has observed:

> The real cause of the disaster is the very financial structure that was fashioned by legislators and guided by regulators; they together created a cartel that, like all other monopolistic concoctions, is playing mischief with its victims.[1]

A CARTEL WITHIN A CARTEL

Sennholz has chosen exactly the right word: *cartel*. The savings-and-loan industry, is really a cartel *within* a cartel. It could not

---

1. "The Great Banking Scandal," by Hans F. Sennholz, *The Freeman*, Nov., 1990, p. 405.

function without Congress standing by to push unlimited amounts of money into it. And Congress could not do that without the banking cartel called the Federal Reserve System standing by as the "lender of last resort" to create money out of nothing for Congress to borrow. This comfortable arrangement between political scientists and monetary scientists permits Congress to vote for any scheme it wants, regardless of the cost. If politicians tried to raise that money through taxes, they would be thrown out of office. But being able to "borrow" it from the Federal Reserve System upon demand, allows them to collect it through the hidden mechanism of inflation, and not one voter in a hundred will complain.

The thrifts have become the illegitimate half-breed children of the Creature. And that is why the savings-and-loan story is included in this study.

If America is to survive as a free nation, her citizens must become far more politically educated than they are at present. As a people, we must learn not to reach for every political carrot dangled in front of us. As desirable as it may be for everyone to afford a home, we must understand that government programs pretending to make that possible actually wreak havoc with our system and bring about just the opposite of what they promise. After 60 years of subsidizing and regulating the housing industry, how many young people today can afford a home? Tinkering with the laws of supply and demand, plus the hidden tax called inflation to pay for the tinkering, has driven prices beyond the reach of many and has wiped out the down payments of others. Without such costs, common people would have much more money and purchasing power than they do today, and homes would be well within their reach.

SUMMARY

Our present-day problems within the savings-and-loan industry can be traced back to the Great Depression of the 1930s. Americans were becoming impressed by the theories of socialism and soon embraced the concept that it was proper for government to provide benefits for its citizens and to protect them against economic hardship.

Under the Hoover and Roosevelt administrations, new government agencies were established which purported to protect deposits in the S&Ls and to subsidize home mortgages for the middle class. These measures distorted the laws of supply and demand and, from that point forward, the housing industry was moved out of the free market and into the political arena.

Once the pattern of government intervention had been established, there began a long, unbroken series of federal rules and regulations that were the source of windfall profits for managers, appraisers, brokers, developers, and builders. They also weakened the industry by encouraging unsound business practices and high-risk investments.

When these ventures failed, and when the value of real estate began to drop, many S&Ls became insolvent. The federal insurance fund was soon depleted, and the government was confronted with its own promise to bail out these companies but not having any money to do so.

The response of the regulators was to create accounting gimmicks whereby insolvent thrifts could be made to appear solvent and, thus, continue in business. This postponed the inevitable and made matters considerably worse. The failed S&Ls continued to lose billions of dollars each month and added greatly to the ultimate cost of bailout, all of which would eventually have to be paid by the common man out of taxes and inflation. The ultimate cost is estimated at over one trillion dollars.

Congress appears to be unable to act and is strangely silent. This is understandable. Many representatives and senators are the beneficiaries of generous donations from the S&Ls. But perhaps the main reason is that Congress, itself, is the main culprit in this crime. In either case, the politicians would like to talk about something else.

In the larger view, the S&L industry is a cartel within a cartel. The fiasco could never have happened without the cartel called the Federal Reserve System standing by to create the vast amounts of bailout money pledged by Congress.

Chapter Five

NEARER TO THE HEART'S DESIRE

The 1944 meeting in Bretton Woods, New Hampshire, at which the world's most prominent socialists established the International Monetary Fund and the World Bank as mechanisms for eliminating gold from world finance; the hidden agenda behind the IMF/World Bank revealed as the building of world socialism; the role of the Federal Reserve in bringing that about.

As we have seen, the game called Bailout has been played over and over again in the rescue of large corporations, domestic banks, and savings-and-loan institutions. The pretense has been that these measures were necessary to protect the public. The result, however, has been just the opposite. The public has been exploited as billions of dollars have been expropriated through taxes and inflation. The money has been used to make up losses that should have been paid by the failing banks and corporations as the penalty for mismanagement and fraud.

While this was happening in our home-town stadium, the same game was being played in the international arena. There are two primary differences. One is that the amount of money at stake in the international game is much larger. Through a complex tangle of bank loans, subsidies, and grants, the Federal Reserve is becoming the "lender of last resort" for virtually the entire planet. The other difference is that, instead of claiming to be Protectors of the Public, the players have emblazoned across the backs of their uniforms: *Saviors of the World.*

BRETTON WOODS: AN ATTACK ON GOLD

The game began at an international meeting of financiers, politicians, and theoreticians held in July of 1944 at the Mount Washington Hotel in Bretton Woods, New Hampshire. Officially, it was called the United Nations Monetary and Financial Conference, but is generally referred to today as simply the Bretton Woods Conference. Two international agencies were created at that meeting: the International Monetary Fund and its sister organization, the International Bank for Reconstruction and Development— commonly called the World Bank.

The announced purposes of these organizations were admirable. The World Bank was to make loans to war-torn and underdeveloped nations so they could build stronger economies. The International Monetary Fund (IMF) was to promote monetary cooperation between nations by maintaining fixed exchange rates between their currencies. But the method by which these goals were to be achieved was less admirable. It was to terminate the use of gold as the basis of international currency exchange and replace it with a politically manipulated paper standard. In other words, it was to allow governments to escape the discipline of gold so they could create money out of nothing without paying the penalty of having their currencies drop in value on world markets.

Prior to this conference, currencies were exchanged in terms of their gold value, and the arrangement was called the "gold-exchange standard." This is not the same as a "gold-standard" in which a currency is backed by gold. It was merely that the exchange ratios of the various currencies—most of which were *not* backed by gold—were determined by how much gold they could buy in the open market. Their values, therefore, were set by supply and demand. Politicians and bankers hated the arrangement, because it was beyond their ability to manipulate. In the past, it had served as a remarkably efficient mechanism but it was a strict disciplinarian. As John Kenneth Galbraith observed:

> The Bretton Woods arrangements sought to recapture the advantages of the gold standard—currencies that were exchangeable at stable and predictable rates into gold and thus at stable and predictable rates into each other. And this it sought to accomplish while minimizing the pain imposed by the gold standard on countries that were buying too much, selling too little and thus losing gold.[1]

The method by which this was to be accomplished was exactly the method devised on Jekyll Island to allow American banks to

---

1. John Kenneth Galbraith, *Money: Whence It Came, Where It Went* (Boston: Houghton Mifflin, 1975), pp. 258, 259.

create money out of nothing without paying the penalty of having their currencies devalued by other banks. It was the establishment of a *world* central bank which would create a common fiat money for all nations and then require them to inflate together at the same rate. There was to be a kind of international insurance fund which would rush that fiat money to any nation that temporarily needed it to face down a "run" on its currency. It wasn't born with all these features fully developed, just as the Federal Reserve wasn't fully developed when it was born. That, nevertheless, was the plan, and it was launched with all the structures in place.

The theoreticians who drafted this plan were the well-known Fabian Socialist from England, John Maynard Keynes,[1] and the Assistant Secretary of the U.S. Treasury, Harry Dexter White.

THE FABIAN SOCIETY

The Fabians originally were an elite group of intellectuals who formed a semi-secret society for the purpose of bringing socialism to the world. Whereas Communists wanted to establish socialism quickly through violence and revolution, the Fabians preferred to do it slowly through propaganda and legislation. The word social-ism was not to be emphasized. Instead, they would speak of benefits for the people such as welfare, medical care, higher wages, and better working conditions. In this way, they planned to accomplish their objective without bloodshed and even without serious opposition. They scorned the Communists, not because they disliked their goals, but because they disagreed with their methods. To emphasize the importance of gradualism, they adopted the turtle as the symbol of their movement. The three most prominent leaders in the early days were Sidney and Beatrice Webb and George Bernard Shaw. A stained-glass window in the Beatrice Webb House in Surrey, England is especially enlightening. Across the top appears the last line from Omar Khayyam:

Dear love, couldst thou and I with fate conspire
To grasp this sorry scheme of things entire,
Would we not shatter it to bits, and then
Remould it nearer to the heart's desire!

---

1. Keynes often is portrayed as having been merely a liberal. But, for his lifelong involvement with Fabians and their work, see Rose Martin, *Fabian Freeway; High Road to Socialism in the U.S.A.* (Boston: Western Islands, 1966).

Beneath the line *Remould it nearer to the heart's desire,* the mural depicts Shaw and Webb striking the earth with hammers. Across the bottom, the masses kneel in worship of a stack of books advocating the theories of socialism. Thumbing his nose at the docile masses is H.G. Wells who, after quitting the Fabians, denounced them as "the new machiavellians." The most revealing component, however, is the Fabian crest which appears Between Shaw and Webb. It is a wolf in sheep's clothing![1]

COMMUNIST MOLES

Harry Dexter White was America's chief technical expert and the dominant force at the conference. He eventually became the first Executive Director for the United States at the IMF. An interesting footnote to this story is that White was simultaneously a member of the Council on Foreign Relations (CFR) and a member of a Communist espionage ring in Washington while he served as Assistant Secretary of the Treasury. And even more interesting is that the White House was informed of that fact when President Truman appointed him to his post. The FBI had transmitted to the White House detailed proof of White's activities on at least two separate occasions.[2] Serving as the technical secretary at the Bretton Woods conference was Virginius Frank Coe, a member of the same espionage ring to which White belonged. Coe later became the first Secretary of the IMF.

Thus, completely hidden from public view, there was a complex drama taking place in which the intellectual guiding lights at the Bretton Woods conference were Fabian Socialists and Communists. Although they were in disagreement over method, they were in perfect harmony on goal: international socialism.

There were undoubtedly other reasons for Communists to be enthusiastic about the IMF and the World Bank, despite the fact

---

1. See Zygmund Dobbs, *The Great Deceit: Social Pseudo-Sciences* (West Sayville, New York: Veritas Foundation, 1964), opposite p. 1. Also Rose L. Martin, *Fabian Freeway: High Road to Socialism in the U.S.A.* (Boston: Western Islands, 1966), pp. 30, 31.

2. See: David Rees, *Harry Dexter White: A Study in Paradox* (New York: Coward, McCann & Geoghegan, 1973); Whittaker Chambers, *Witness* (New York: Random House, 1952); Allen Weinstein, *Perjury: The Hiss-Chambers Case* (New York: Vintage Books, 1978); James Burnham, *The Web of Subversion: Underground Networks in the U.S. Government* (New York: The John Day Co., 1954); Elizabeth Bentley, *Out of Bondage* (New York: Devin-Adair, 1951)

that the Soviet Union elected at the time not to become a member. The goal of the organizations was to create a world currency, a world central bank, and a mechanism to control the economies of all nations. In order for these things to happen, the United States would of necessity have to surrender its dominant position. In fact, it would have to be reduced to just one part of the collective whole. That fit in quite nicely with the Soviet plan. Furthermore, the World Bank was seen as a vehicle for moving capital from the United States and other industrialized nations to the underdeveloped nations, the very ones over which Marxists have always had the greatest control. They looked forward to the day when we would pay their bills. It has all come to pass.

IMF STRUCTURE AND FUNDING

The International Monetary Fund appears to be a part of the United Nations, much as the Federal Reserve System appears to be a part of the United States government, but it is entirely independent. It is funded on a quota basis by its member nations, almost two hundred in number. The greatest share of capital, however, comes from the more highly industrialized nations such as Great Britain, Japan, France, and Germany. The United States contributes the most, at about twenty per cent of the total. In reality, that twenty per cent represents about twice as much as the number indicates, because most of the other nations contribute worthless currencies which no one wants. The world prefers dollars.

One of the routine operations at the IMF is to exchange worthless currencies for dollars so the weaker countries can pay their international bills. This is supposed to cover temporary "cash-flow" problems. It is a kind of international FDIC which rushes money to a country that has gone bankrupt so it can avoid devaluing its currency. The transactions are seldom paid back.

Although escape from the gold-exchange standard was the long-range goal of the IMF, the only way to convince nations to participate at the outset was to use gold itself as a backing for its own money supply—at least as a temporary expedient. As Keynes explained it:

> I felt that the leading central banks would never voluntarily relinquish the then existing forms of the gold standard; and I did not desire a catastrophe sufficiently violent to shake them off

involuntarily. The only practical hope lay, therefore, in a gradual evolution in the forms of a managed world currency, taking the existing gold standard as a starting point.[1]

It was illegal for American citizens to own gold at that time, but everyone else in the world could exchange their paper dollars for gold at a fixed price of $35 per ounce. That made it the *de facto* international currency because, unlike any other at the time, its value was guaranteed. So, at the outset, the IMF adopted the dollar as its own international monetary unit.

PAPER GOLD

But the Fabian turtle was crawling inexorably toward its destination. In 1970, the IMF created a new monetary unit called the SDR, or Special Drawing Right. The media optimistically described it as "paper gold," but it was pure bookkeeping wizardry with no relationship to gold or anything else of tangible value. SDRs are based on "credits" which are provided by the member nations. These credits are not money. They are merely promises that the governments will *get* the money by taxing their own citizens should the need arise. The IMF considers these to be "assets" which then become the "reserves" from which loans are made to other governments. As we shall see in chapter ten, this is almost identical to the bookkeeping sleight-of-hand that is used to create money out of nothing at the Federal Reserve System.

Dennis Turner cuts through the garbage:

> SDRs are turned into loans to Third-World nations by the creation of checking accounts in the commercial or central banks of the member nations in the name of the debtor governments. These bank accounts are created out of thin air. The IMF creates dollars, francs, pounds, or other hard currencies and gives them to a Third-World dictator, with inflation resulting in the country where the currency originated.... Inflation is caused in the industrialized nations while wealth is transferred from the general public to the debtor country. And the debtor doesn't repay.[2]

When the IMF was created, it was the vision of Fabian Socialist John Maynard Keynes that there be a world central bank issuing a

---

1. John Maynard Keynes, *The Collected Writings of*, Vol V (1930 rpt. New York: Macmillan, 1971), p. xx.
2. Dennis Turner, *When Your Bank Fails* (Princeton, New Jersey: Amwell Publishing, 1983), p. 32.

reserve currency called the "bancor" to free all governments from the discipline of gold. With the creation of SDRs, the IMF had finally begun to fulfill that dream.

GOLD IS FINALLY ABANDONED

But there was still an obstacle. As long as the dollar was the primary currency used by the IMF and as long as it was redeemable in gold at $35 per ounce, the amount of international money that could be created would be limited. If the IMF were to function as a true world central bank with *unlimited* issue, the dollar had to be broken away from its gold backing as a first step toward replacing it completely with a bancor, an SDR or something else equally free from restraint.

On August 15, 1971, President Nixon signed an executive order declaring that the United States would no longer redeem its paper dollars for gold. So ended the first phase of the IMF's metamorphosis. It was not yet a true central bank, because it could not create its own world currency. It had to depend on the central banks of its member nations to provide cash and so-called credits; but since these banks, themselves, could create as much money as they wished, from now on, there would be no limit.

The original purpose had been to maintain fixed rates of exchange between currencies; but the IMF has presided over more than two hundred currency devaluations. In private industry, a failure of that magnitude might be cause for going out of business, but not in the world of politics. The greater the failure, the greater the pressure to *expand* the program. So, when the dollar broke loose from gold and there was no longer a ready standard for measuring currency values, the IMF merely changed its goal and continued to expand its operation. The new goal was to "overcome trade deficits."

TRADE DEFICITS

The topic of trade deficits is a favorite among politicians, economists, and talk-show hosts. Everyone agrees they are bad, but there is much disagreement over what causes them. Let's have a try at it.

A trade deficit is a condition that exists when a country imports a greater value of goods than it exports. In other words, it spends more than it earns in international trade. This is similar to the situation of an individual who spends more than he earns. In both cases, the process cannot be sustained unless: (1) earnings are increased; (2) money is taken out of savings; (3) assets are sold; (4) money is counterfeited; or (5) money is borrowed. Unless one of these occurs, the individual or the country has no choice but to decrease spending.

Increasing one's earnings is the best solution. In fact, it is the *only* solution for the long haul. All else is temporary at best. An individual can increase his income by working harder or smarter or longer. A country does it the same way. But it cannot happen unless private industry is allowed to flourish in a system of free-enterprise. The problem with this option is that few politicians respect the dynamic power of the free-enterprise system. Their world is built upon political programs in which the laws of the free market are manipulated to achieve politically popular goals. They may desire the option of increasing the nation's income by increasing its productivity, but their political agenda prevents that from happening.[1]

The second option is to obtain extra money out of savings. But there are virtually no governments in the world today that have any savings. Their debts and liabilities exceed assets by a large margin. Likewise, most of their industries and their citizens are in a similar position. Their savings already have been consumed by government.

The third option, the selling of assets, also is not available for most countries. By assets, we mean tangible items other than merchandise which is normally for sale. Although these, too, are assets in the broad meaning, in accounting methodology, they are classified as inventory. The only *government* asset that is readily marketable is gold, and few countries today have a stockpile from which to draw. Even in those cases, what little they have is already

---

1. It is the author's opinion that it's time to get the politicians wearing Uncle-Sam suits off our backs. Which is easier said than done, because Americans still like their protectionist subsidies: tariffs to protect the business man, minimum wages and compulsory unionism to protect the worker, ethnic quotas in hiring to protect the underdog, cradle-to-the-grave insurance programs, unemployment benefits, disability compensation, extreme environmental and safety measures—regardless of cost. Free enterprise can and will produce all of these benefits in order to compete for buyers and employees alike. But, as long as these measures are *compulsory* and chosen on the basis of political popularity without regard to economic consequences, American industry will never be able to recover. And then *none* of the illusory benefits will remain.

owed to another government or a bank. As for *private* assets, nations can, for a while, sell these to foreign buyers and offset their negative trade balances. That is what has been happening in the United States for many years as office buildings, stocks, factories, and entire companies have been sold to foreign investors. But the fact remains that the nation is *still* spending more than it earns, and that process cannot continue indefinitely. Foreign ownership and control over industry and commerce also create sociological and political problems. Underdeveloped countries do not have to worry about any of that, however, because they have few private assets to sell.

THE COUNTERFEIT OPTION

The counterfeit option is available only if a country happens to be in the unique position of having its currency accepted as the medium of international trade, as has been the case for the United States. In that event, it is possible to create money out of nothing, and other nations have no choice but to accept it. Thus, for years, the United States has been able to spend more money than it earned in trade by having the Federal Reserve create whatever it needed.

When the dollar was separated entirely from gold in 1971, it ceased being the official IMF world currency and finally had to compete with other currencies—primarily the mark and the yen— on the basis of its relative merit. From that point forward, its value increasingly became discounted. Nevertheless, it was still the preferred medium of exchange. Also, the U.S. was one of the safest places in the world to invest one's money. But, to do so, one first had to convert his native currency into dollars. These facts gave the U.S. dollar greater value on international markets than it otherwise would have merited. So, in spite of the fact that the Federal Reserve was creating huge amounts of money during this time, the demand for it by foreigners was seemingly limitless. The result is that America has continued to finance its trade deficit with fiat money— counterfeit, if you will—a feat which no other nation in the world could hope to accomplish.

We have been told that our nation's trade deficit is a terrible thing, and that it would be better to "weaken the dollar" to bring it to an end. Weakening the dollar is a euphemism for increasing inflation. In truth, America is not hurt by a trade deficit at all. In fact, we are the benefactors while our trading partners are the victims. We get the cars and TV sets while they get the funny money. We get the hardware. They get the paperware.

There is a dark side to the exchange, however. As long as the dollar remains in high esteem as a trade currency, America can continue to spend more than it earns. But when the day arrives—as it certainly must—when the dollar tumbles and foreigners no longer want it, the free ride will be over. When that happens, *hundreds of billions* of dollars that are now resting in foreign countries will quickly come back to our shores as people everywhere in the world attempt to convert them into yet more real estate, factories, and tangible products, and to do so as quickly as possible before they become even more worthless. As this flood of dollars bids up prices, we will finally experience the inflation that should have been caused in years past but which was postponed because foreigners were kind enough to take the dollars out of our economy in exchange for their products.

The chickens *will* come home to roost. But, when they do, it will not be because of the trade deficit. It will be because we were able to *finance* the trade deficit with fiat money created by the Federal Reserve. If it were not for that, the trade deficit could not have happened.

Back to the main topic, which is the five methods by which a trade deficit can be paid. Through the process of elimination, the fourth option of *borrowing* is where the action is today for most of the world, and that is where the IMF positioned itself in 1970. Its new mission was to provide loans so countries can continue to spend more than they earn, but to do so in the name of "overcoming trade deficits."

IMF LOANS: DOOMED BUT SWEET

These loans do not go into private enterprises where they have a chance of being turned for a profit. They go into state-owned and state-operated industries which are constipated by bureaucracy and poisoned by corruption. Doomed to economic failure from the start, they consume the loans with no possibility of repayment. Even the interest quickly becomes too much to handle. Which means the IMF must fall back to the "reserves," back to the "assets," back to the "credits," and eventually back to the taxpayers to bail them out.

Whereas the International Monetary Fund is evolving into a world central bank which eventually will issue a world currency based on nothing, its sister organization, the World Bank, has become its lending agency. Acting as *Savior of the World*, it seeks to aid the underdeveloped nations, to feed the hungry, and to bring a better life to all mankind. In pursuit of these humanitarian goals, it provides loans to governments at favorable terms, usually at rates below market, for terms as long as fifty years, and often with no payments due until after ten years.

Funding for these loans comes from member states in the form of a small amount of cash, plus promises to deliver about ten-times more if the Bank gets into trouble. The promises, described as "callable capital," constitute a kind of FDIC insurance program but with no pretense at maintaining a reserve fund. (In that sense it is more honest than the real FDIC which does maintain the pretense but, in reality, is based on nothing more than a similar promise.)

Based upon the small amount of seed money plus the far greater amount of "credits" and "promises" from governments of the industrialized countries, the World Bank is able to go into the commercial loan markets and borrow larger sums at extremely low interest rates. After all, the loans are backed by the most powerful governments in the world which have promised to force their taxpayers to make the payments if the Bank should get into trouble. It then takes these funds and relends them to the underdeveloped countries at slightly higher rates, making a profit on the arbitrage.

The unseen aspect of this operation is that the money it processes is money which, otherwise, would have been available for investment in the private sector or as loans to consumers. It siphons off much-needed development capital for private industry, prevents new jobs from being created, causes interest rates to rise, and retards the economy at large.

THE HIDDEN AGENDA: WORLD SOCIALISM

Although most of the policy statements of the World Bank deal with economic issues, a close monitoring of its activities reveal a preoccupation with social and political issues. This should not be surprising considering that the Bank was perceived by its founders as an instrument for social and political change. The change which it was designed to bring about was the building of world socialism, and that is exactly what it is accomplishing today.

This hidden agenda becomes crystal clear in the nature of what the Bank calls Sectoral Loans and Structural-Adjustment Loans. In the first category, only part of the money is to be used for the costs of specific projects while the rest goes to support policy changes in the economic sector. In the second group, *all* of the money is for policy changes and *none* of it is for projects. In recent years, almost half of the loans to underdeveloped countries have been in that category. What are the policy changes that are the object of these loans? They add up to one thing: *the building of world socialism.*

As the Fabians had planned it, the word socialism is not to be used. Instead, the loans are issued for government hydro-electric projects, government oil refineries, government lumber mills, government mining companies, and government steel plants. It is delivered from the hands of politicians and bureaucrats into the hands of other politicians and bureaucrats. When the money comes from government, goes to government, and is administered by government, the result will be the expansion of government.

Here is an example. One of the policy changes often required by the World Bank as a condition of granting a loan is that the recipient country must hold down its wages. The assumption is that the government has the power—and rightfully *should* have the power—to set wages! In other words, one of the conditions of its loan is that the state must be omnipotent.

Paul Roberts holds the William E. Simon Chair of Political Economy at the Center for Strategic and International Studies in Washington. Writing in *Business Week*, he says:

> The entire "development process" has been guided by the belief that reliance on private enterprise and equity investment is incompatible with economic and social progress. In place of such proven avenues of success, development planning substituted loans and foreign aid so that governments of the LDCs [Less Developed Countries] could control economic activity in keeping with plans drawn up by experts.
>
> Consequently, economic life in the LDCs was politicized from the start. By endowing governments with extensive control over their economies, the U.S. set up conditions exactly opposite to those required for economic growth.[1]

---

1. "How 'Experts' Caused the Third World Debt Crisis," by Paul Craig Roberts, *Business Week*, November 2, 1987.

Ken Ewert explains further that the conditions imposed by the Fund are seldom free-market oriented. He says:

The Fund concentrates on "macro-policies," such as fiscal and monetary policies or exchange rates, and pays little attention to fundamental issues like private property rights and freedom of enterprise. Implicit ... is the belief that with proper "macro-management" any economic system is viable....

Even more important, it has allowed governments the world over to expropriate the wealth of their citizens more efficiently (through the hidden tax of inflation) while at the same time aggrandizing their own power. There is little doubt that the IMF is an influence for world-wide socialism.[1]

An important feature of the Structural-Adjustment Loans is that the money need not be applied to any specific development project. It can be spent for anything the recipient wishes. That includes interest payments on overdue bank loans. Thus, the World Bank becomes yet one more conduit from the pockets of taxpayers to the assets of commercial banks which have made risky loans to Third-World countries.

AUSTERITY MEASURES AND SCAPEGOATS

Not every measure advocated by the IMF and World Bank is socialistic. Some of them even appear to be in support of the private sector, such as the reduction of government subsidies and welfare. They may include tax increases to reduce budget deficits. These policy changes are often described in the press as "austerity measures," and they are seen as hard-nosed business decisions to salvage the failing economies of underdeveloped countries. But, as the wolf (in sheep's clothing) said to Little Red-Riding-Hood, "All the better to fool you with, my dear." These austerity measures are mostly rhetoric. The borrowing nations usually ignore the conditions with impunity, and the World Bank keeps the money coming anyway. It's all part of the game.

Nevertheless, the "structural-adjustment" conditions provide a scapegoat for local politicians who can now place the blame for their nation's misery on big, bad "capitalists" from America and the IMF. People who have been taught that it is government's role to provide for their welfare, their health care, their food and housing,

---

1. "The International Monetary Fund," by Ken S. Ewert, *The Freeman*, April, 1989, pp. 157, 158.

their jobs and retirement—such people will not be happy when they hear that these "rights" are being threatened. So they demonstrate in the streets in protest, they riot in the commercial sections of town so they can steal goods from stores, and they throng to the banner of politicians who promise to restore or increase their benefits. As described by *Insight* magazine:

> National strikes, riots, political upheavals and social unrest in Argentina, Bolivia, Brazil, Ecuador, Egypt, Haiti, Liberia, Peru, Sudan and elsewhere have at various times been attributed to IMF austerity programs....
> Some came to the fund with domestic trouble already brewing and seized on the fund as a convenient scapegoat.[1]

Quite true. An honest reading of the record shows that the IMF, far from being a force for austerity in these countries, has been an engine of socialist waste and a fountain of abundance for the corrupt leaders who rule.

FINANCING CORRUPTION AND DESPOTISM

Nowhere is this pattern more blatant than in Africa. Julius Nyerere, the dictator of Tanzania, is notorious for his "villagization" program in which the army has driven the peasants from their land, burned their huts, and loaded them like cattle into trucks for relocation into government villages. The purpose is to eliminate opposition by bringing everyone into compounds where they can be watched and controlled. Meanwhile the economy staggers, farms have gone to weed, and hunger is commonplace. Yet, Tanzania has received more aid per capita from the World Bank than any other nation.

In Uganda, government security forces have engaged in mass detentions, torture, and killing of prisoners. The same is true under the terrorist government in Zimbabwe. Yet, both regimes continue to be the recipients of millions of dollars in World Bank funding.

Zimbabwe (formerly Rhodesia) is a classic case. After its independence, the leftist government nationalized (confiscated) many of the farms previously owned by white settlers. The most desirable of these lands became occupied by the government's senior ruling-party officials, and the rest were turned into state-run collectives. They were such miserable failures that the workers on

---

1. "IMF Hands Out Prescription for Sour Economic Medicine," *Insight*, February 9, 1987, p. 14.

these farmlands were, themselves, soon begging for food. Not daunted by these failures, the socialist politicians announced in 1991 that they were going to nationalize half of the remaining farms as well. And they barred the courts from inquiring into how much compensation would be paid to their owners.

The IMF was represented in Zimbabwe at the time by Michel Camdessus, the Governor of the central Bank of France, and a former finance minister in Francois Mitterrand's Socialist government. After being informed of Zimbabwe's plan to confiscate additional land and to resettle people to work on those lands, Camdessus agreed to a loan valued at 42 billion rands with full knowledge that much of it would be used for the resettlement project.

Perhaps the worst violations of human rights have occurred in Ethiopia under the Marxist regime of Mengistu Haile Mariam. The famine of 1984–85, which threatened the lives of millions of people, was the result of government nationalization and disruption of agriculture. Massive resettlement programs have torn hundreds of thousands of people from their privately owned land in the north and deported them to concentration-camp "villages" in the south, complete with guard towers. A report by a French voluntary medical-assistance group, Doctors without Borders, reveals that the forced resettlement program may have killed as many people as the famine itself.[1] Dr. Rony Brauman, director of the organization, describes their experience:

> Armed militiamen burst into our compounds, seized our equipment and menaced our volunteers. Some of our employees were beaten, and our trucks, medicines and food stores confiscated. We left Ethiopia branded as enemies of the revolution. The regime spoke the truth. The atrocities committed in the name of Mengistu's master plan *did* make us enemies of the revolution.[2]

FINANCING FAMINE AND GENOCIDE

In the 1980s, the world was saddened by photographs of starving children in Ethiopia, but what the West did not realize was that this was a *planned* famine. It was modelled after Stalin's

---

1. "Ethiopia Bars Relief Team," by Blaine Harden, *Washington Post*, December 3, 1985, p. A-21.
2. "Famine Aid: Were we Duped?" by Dr. Rony Brauman, *Reader's Digest*, October 1986, p. 71.

starvation program in the Ukraine in the 1930s and Mao's starvation of the peasants in the '40s. Its purpose was to starve the population into total submission to the government, for it is the government which decides who will eat and who will not. Yet, right up to the time Mengistu was overthrown, the World Bank continued to send him hundreds of millions of dollars, with much of it going specifically to the Ministry of Agriculture, the very agency in charge of the resettlement program.[1]

In the late 1970s the same story unfolded in Communist Vietnam. There were resettlement programs, forced collectivization, concentration camps, atrocities, and tens of thousands of dissidents escaping to the sea only to drown in overcrowded, leaky boats. Throughout it all, the regime was generously funded by the World Bank.

Laos has jailed thousands of political prisoners; Syria has massacred 20,000 members of its opposition; Indonesia has uprooted several million people from their homelands in Java; the Sandinistas in Nicaragua murdered their opposition and terrorized the nation into submission; Poland, while a puppet state of the Soviet Union, brutally suppressed its trade-union movement; China massacred its dissident students and imprisoned its religious leaders; and the former Soviets slaughtered civilians in Afghanistan while conducting a relentless espionage war against the entire free world. Yet, these regimes have been the recipient of literally billions of dollars from the World Bank.

How can the Bank's managers continue in conscience to fund such genocidal regimes? Part of the answer is that they are not permitted to have a conscience. David Dunn, head of the Bank's Ethiopia Desk explained: "Political distinctions are not something our charter allows us to take into account."[2] The greater part of the answer, however, is that all socialist regimes have the potential for genocide, and the Bank is committed to socialism. The brutalities of these countries are all in a day's work for serious socialists who view them as merely unfortunate necessities for the building of their utopia. Lenin said you cannot make an omelet without

1.   James Bovard, *The World Bank vs. The World's Poor*, Cato Policy Analysis (Washington, D.C.: Cato Institute, 1987), pp. 4–6.
2.   "Harnessing World Bank to the West," *Insight*, February 9, 1987, p. 8.

cracking a few eggs. George Bernard Shaw, one of the early leaders of the Fabian Socialist movement, expressed it this way:

> Under Socialism, you would not be allowed to be poor. You would be forcibly fed, clothed, lodged, taught, and employed whether you liked it or not. If it were discovered that you had not character and industry enough to be worth all this trouble, you might possibly be executed in a kindly manner; but whilst you were permitted to live, you would have to live well.[1]

REASON TO ABOLISH THE FEDERAL RESERVE

The top echelon at the World Bank are brothers under the skin to the socialist dictators with whom they do daily business. Under the right circumstances, they could easily switch roles. What we have seen is merely a preview of what can be expected for the entire world if the envisioned *New World Order* becomes operational.

The IMF/World Bank is the protégé of the Federal Reserve. It would not exist without the flow of American dollars and the benevolence of American leadership. The Fed has become an accomplice in the support of totalitarian regimes throughout the world. As stated at the beginning of this study, that is one of the reasons it should be abolished: *It is an instrument of totalitarianism.*

GETTING RICH FIGHTING POVERTY

While the top leaders and theoreticians at the IMF and World Bank dream of world socialism, the middle managers and political rulers have more immediate goals in mind. The bureaucracy enjoys a plush life administering the process, and the politicians on the receiving end obtain wealth and power. Ideology is not their concern. Socialism, capitalism, fascism, it makes no difference to them as long as the money flows.

Graham Hancock has been an astute observer of the international-aid "industry" and has attended their plush conferences. He knows many of the leading players personally. In his book, *Lords of Poverty*, he speaks of the IMF's Structural-Adjustment loans:

> Corrupt Ministers of Finance and dictatorial Presidents from Asia, Africa, and Latin America are tripping over their own expensive footwear in their unseemly haste to "get adjusted." For such people, money has probably never been easier to obtain than it is today; with

---

1. George Bernard Shaw, *The Intelligent Woman's Guide to Socialism and Capitalism* (1928; rpt. New Brunswick, New Jersey: Transaction Books, 1984), p. 470.

no complicated projects to administer and no messy accounts to keep, the venal, the cruel and the ugly are laughing literally all the way to the bank. For them structural adjustment is like a dream come true. No sacrifices are demanded of them personally. All they have to do—amazing but true—is *screw the poor*, and they've already had plenty of practice at that.[1]

In India, the World Bank funded the construction of a dam that displaced two million people, flooded 360 square miles, and wiped out 81,000 acres of forest cover. In Brazil, it spent a billion dollars to "develop" a part of the Amazon basin and to fund a series of hydroelectric projects. It resulted in the deforestation of an area half the size of Great Britain and has caused great human suffering because of resettlement. In Kenya, the Bura irrigation scheme caused such desolation that a fifth of the native population abandoned the land. The cost was $50,000 *per family* served. In Indonesia, the transmigration program mentioned previously has devastated tropical forests—at the same time that the World Bank is funding reforestation projects. The cost of resettling one family is $7,000, which is about ten-times the Indonesian per-capita income.

Livestock projects in Botswana led to the destruction of grazing land and the death of thousands of migratory animals. This resulted in the inability of the natives to obtain food by hunting, forcing them into dependence on the government for survival. While Nigeria and Argentina are drowning in debt, billions from the World Bank have gone into building lavish new capital cities to house government agencies and the ruling elite. In Zaire, Mexico, and the Philippines, political leaders became billionaires while receiving World Bank loans on behalf of their nations. In the Central African Republic, IMF and World Bank loans were used to stage a coronation for its emperor.

The record of corruption and waste is endless. But the real eye-opener is in the failure of socialist ventures, those magnificent projects which were to bring prosperity to the underdeveloped countries. Here are just a few examples.

CONVERTING MONEY INTO FAILURE

Before receiving loans from the World Bank, Tanzania was not wealthy, but it fed its own people, and it had economic growth.

---

1. Graham Hancock, *Lords of Poverty: The Power, Prestige, and Corruption of the International Aid Business* (New York: Atlantic Monthly Press, 1989), pp. 59,60.

After receiving more than 3 billion dollars in loans, it nationalized the nation's farms and industries and converted every business into a government agency. It built a truck assembly plant, a tire factory, electronic factories, highways, ports, railways, and dams. Tanzania's industrial production and agricultural output fell by almost one-third. Food was the main export in 1966. Under socialism, food had to be imported—paid for by foreign aid and more loans from the World Bank. The country is hopelessly in debt with no way to repay.

Argentina once had one of the highest standards of living in Latin America. But then it became the recipient of massive loans from the World Bank as well as commercial banks in the United States. Since the money was given to politicians, it was used to build the only system politicians know how to build: socialism. By 1982, the Gross National Product was in a nose dive, manufacturing had fallen to less than half of capacity, thousands of privately owned companies had been forced into bankruptcy, unemployment was soaring, and so was welfare. By 1989, inflation was running at an average of 5,000% and, in the summer of that year, topped at 1,000,000%! Banks were offering interest rates of 600% per month in hopes of keeping deposits from being moved out of the country. People were rioting in the streets for food, and the government was blaming greedy shop owners for raising prices. The nation was hopelessly in debt with no way to repay.

Brazil is run by the military, and the state controls the economy. Government-owned companies consume 65% of all industrial investment, which means that the private sector is limited to 35% and is shrinking. The government used loans from U.S. banks to create an oil company, Petroleo Brasileiro S.A., which became Latin America's largest corporation. Despite huge oil deposits and record-high oil prices, the company operated at a loss and was not even able to produce enough gasoline for its own citizens. By 1990, inflation was running at 5,000%. Since 1960, its prices had risen to 164,000 times their original level. A new crime was invented called "hedging against inflation," and people were arrested for charging the free-market price for their goods and for using dollars or gold as money. Led by Communist organizers, mobs roamed the streets shouting "We're hungry. Steal what you will!" The nation was hopelessly in debt with no way to repay.

The experience in Mexico was a carbon copy of that in Brazil, except that the amount of money was larger. When the world's fourth largest oil reserves were discovered, Mexican politicians reached for the brass ring. With billions borrowed from U.S. banks, they launched Petroleos Mexicanos (PEMEX) and soon became the world's fifth largest oil producer. They also built chemical plants and railroads, and launched many other industrial projects. These were run as welfare agencies instead of businesses: too many people on the payroll, too many managers, excessive salaries, too many holidays, and unrealistic benefits. The ventures floundered and lost money. Private businesses failed by the thousands, and unemployment rose. The government increased the minimum wage causing more businesses to fail and more unemployment. That led to more welfare and unemployment benefits. To pay for that, the government borrowed even more and began creating its own fiat money. Inflation destroyed what was left of the economy.

Price controls were next, along with rent and food subsidies, and doubling the minimum wage. By 1982, Mexicans were trading their pesos for dollars and sending their savings out of the country, as the peso became all but worthless in commerce.[1] In 1981, the average wage for Mexican workers was 31% of the average wage for Americans. By 1989, it had fallen to 10%. Mexico, once one of the major food exporters in the world, was now required to import millions of dollars worth of food grains. This required still more money and more loans. All this occurred while oil prices were high and production was booming. A few years later, when oil prices fell, the failures and shortfalls became even more dramatic.

In 1995, Mexico's bank loans were once again on the brink of default, and, once again, U.S. taxpayers were thrown into the breach by Congress to cover more than $30 billion at risk. Although this loan was eventually repaid, the money to do so was extracted from the Mexican people through another round of massive inflation, which plunged their standard of living even lower. The nation is now hopelessly mired in socialism. The Communist Party, promising "reform" and still more socialism, is attracting a large following and could become a potent political force.

---

1. The same American banks that were making the loans were soliciting this flight capital and ended up getting deposits of the same money they had lent. It was nice business both ways.

Thus, the saga continues. After pouring billions of dollars into underdeveloped countries around the globe, no development has taken place. In fact, we have seen just the opposite. Most countries are worse off than before the Saviors of the World got to them.

SUMMARY

The IMF and the World Bank were created at a meeting of global financiers and politicians held at Bretton Woods, New Hampshire, in 1944. Their announced goals were to facilitate international trade and to stabilize the exchange rates of national currencies. The *un*announced goals were quite different. They were the elimination of the gold-exchange standard as the basis of currency valuation and the establishment of world socialism.

The method by which gold was to be eliminated in international trade was to replace it with a world currency which the IMF, acting as a world central bank, would create out of nothing. The method by which world socialism was to be established was to use the World Bank to transfer money—disguised as loans—to the governments of the underdeveloped countries and to do so in such a way as to insure the demise of free enterprise. The money was to be delivered from the hands of politicians and bureaucrats into the hands of other politicians and bureaucrats. When the money comes from government, goes to government, and is administered by government, the result will be the expansion of government.

The theoreticians who dominated the conference at Bretton Woods were the well-known Fabian Socialist from England, John Maynard Keynes, and the Assistant Secretary of the U.S. Treasury, Harry Dexter White. White became the first Executive Director for the United States at the IMF.

The Fabians are an elite group of intellectuals who agree with Communists as to the goal of socialism but disagreed over tactics. Whereas Communists advocate revolution by force and violence, Fabians advocate gradualism and the transformation of society through legislation.

It was learned in later years that Harry Dexter White was a member of a Communist espionage ring. Thus, hidden from view, there was a complex drama taking place in which the two intellectual founders of the Bretton-Woods accords were a Fabian Socialist and a Communist, working together to bring about their mutual goal: world socialism.

Capital for the IMF and the World Bank comes from the industrialized nations, with the United States putting up the most. Currencies, such as the dollar, yen, mark, and franc, are augmented by many times that amount in the form of "credits." These are merely promises by the member governments to get the money from their taxpayers if the Bank gets into trouble with its loans.

The IMF gradually is evolving into a central bank for the world with the World Bank as its lending arm. It has become the engine for transfer of wealth to underdeveloped countries. This has lowered the economic level of the donating countries but it has not raised the level of the recipients. The money has simply disappeared down the drain of political corruption and waste.

REMOULD IT NEARER TO THE HEARTS DESIRE

This is an accurate rendering of the stained-glass window in the Beatrice Webb House in Surrey, England, former headquarters of the Fabian Society. It depicts Sidney Webb and George Bernard Shaw striking the Earth with hammers to "*Remould it nearer to the hearts desire.*" Note the wolf in sheep's clothing in the Fabian crest above the globe. The window is now on display at the London School of Economics. See a color photo at www.freedom-force.org/redir_fabianwindow.cfm.

Chapter Six

BUILDING THE NEW WORLD ORDER

The Game-Called-Bailout reexamined and shown to be far more than merely a means of getting taxpayers to foot the cost of bad loans; the final play revealed as the merger of all nations into world government; the unfolding of that strategy as applied to Panama, Mexico, Brazil, Argentina, China, Eastern Europe, and Russia.

Let us return now to the game called bailout. Everything in the previous chapter has been merely background information to understand the game as it is played in the international arena. Here, finally, are the rules:

1. Commercial banks in the industrialized nations, backed by their respective central banks, create money out of nothing and lend it to the governments of underdeveloped nations. They know that these are risky loans, so they charge an interest rate that is high enough to compensate. It is more than what they expect to receive in the long run.

2. When the underdeveloped nations cannot pay the interest on their loans, the IMF and World Bank enter the game as both players and referees. Using additional money created out of nothing by the central banks of their member nations, they advance "development" loans to the governments which now have enough to pay the interest on the original loans with enough left over for their own political purposes.

3. The recipient country quickly exhausts the new supply of money, and the play returns to point number two. This time, however, the new loans are guaranteed by the World Bank and the central banks of the industrialized nations. Now that the risk of default is removed, the commercial banks agree to reduce the interest to

the point anticipated at the beginning. The debtor governments resume payments.

4. The final play is — well, in this version of the game there appears to be no final play, because the plan is to keep the game going *forever*. To make that possible, certain things must happen that are very final, indeed. They include the conversion of the IMF into a world central bank as Keynes had planned, which then issues an international fiat money. Once that "Bank of Issue" is in place, the IMF can collect unlimited resources from the citizens of the world through the hidden tax called inflation. The money stream then can be sustained indefinitely—with or without the approval of the separate nations—because they will no longer have money of their own.

Since this game results in a hemorrhage of wealth from the industrialized nations, their economies are doomed to be brought down further and further, a process that has been going on since Bretton Woods. The result will be a severe lowering of their living standards and their demise as independent nations. The hidden reality behind so-called development loans is that America and other industrialized nations are being subverted by that process. *That is not an accident; it is the essence of the plan.* A strong nation is not likely to surrender its sovereignty. Americans would not agree to turn over their monetary system, their military, or their courts to a world body made up of governments which have been despotic to their own people, especially since most of those regimes have already revealed anti-American hostility. But if Americans can be brought to the point where they are suffering from a collapse of their economy and from a breakdown in civil order, things will be different. When they stand in bread lines and face anarchy in their streets, they will be more willing to give up sovereignty in return for "assistance" from the World Bank and the UN "peacekeeping" forces. This will become even more acceptable if a structured demise of Communism can be arranged ahead of time to make it appear that the world's major political systems have converged into the common denominator of "social democracy."

THE FINAL PLAY

The underdeveloped nations, on the other hand, are *not* being raised up. What *is* happening to them is that their political leaders are becoming addicted to the IMF cash flow and will be unable to break the habit. These countries are being conquered by money instead of arms. Soon they will no longer be truly independent nations. They are becoming mere components in the system of world socialism planned by Harry Dexter White and John Maynard Keynes. Their leaders are being groomed to become potentates in a new, high-tech feudalism, paying homage to their Lords in New York. And they are eager to do it in return for privilege and power within the "New World Order." *That* is the final play.

The essence of socialism is redistribution of the wealth. The goal is equality, and that means taking from the rich and giving to the poor. At least that's the theory. Unfortunately, the poor are never benefited by this maneuver. They either do not get the money in the first place—too much is siphoned off by the bureaucracies which administer the programs—or, if they do get any of it, they don't know what to do with it. They merely spend it until it is gone, and then *no one* has any money— except, of course, those who administer the government programs. Nevertheless, politicians know that promises to redistribute the wealth are popular among two groups: the voters who naively believe it will help the poor, and the socialist managers who see it as job security. Supported by these two voting blocs, election to office is assured.

One of the early American advocates of socialism on a global scale—including the draining of wealth away from the "rich" United States—was John F. Kennedy. He undoubtedly learned the concept while attending the Fabian London School of Economics in 1935–36 just prior to his father's appointment as Ambassador to England.[1] When JFK became President, his political views continued to carry the imprint of that training. In September of 1963, he addressed the finance ministers and central-bank governors from 102 nations at the annual meeting of the IMF/World Bank. He explained the concept of world socialism in glowing terms:

> Twenty years ago, when the architects of these institutions met to design an international banking structure, the economic life of the world was polarized in overwhelming, and even alarming, measure on the United States.... Sixty per cent of the gold reserves of the world were here in the United States.... There was a need for redistribution of the financial resources of the world.... And there was an equal need to organize a flow of capital to the impoverished countries of the

---

1. Martin, p. 25.

world. All this has come about. It did not come about by chance but by conscious and deliberate and responsible planning.[1]

CFR SETS STRATEGY

The brain trust for implementing the Fabian plan in America is called the Council on Foreign Relations (CFR). We shall look at it closely in future chapters, but it is important to know at this point that almost all of America's leadership has come from this small group. That includes our presidents and their advisers, cabinet members, ambassadors, board members of the Federal Reserve System, directors of the largest banks and investment houses, presidents of universities, and heads of metropolitan newspapers, news services, and TV networks.[2] It is not an exaggeration to describe this group as the hidden government of the United States.

CFR members have never been shy about calling for the weakening of America as a necessary step toward the greater good of building world government. One of the CFR founders was John Foster Dulles, who later was appointed Secretary-of-State by CFR member Dwight Eisenhower. In 1939, Dulles said:

> Some dilution or leveling off of the sovereignty system as it prevails in the world today must take place ... to the immediate disadvantage of those nations which now possess the preponderance of power.... The establishment of a common money ... would deprive our government of exclusive control over a national money.... The United States must be prepared to make sacrifices afterward in setting up a world politico-economic order which would level off inequalities of economic opportunity with respect to nations.[3]

CFR member Zbigniew Brzezinski was the National Security Adviser to CFR member Jimmy Carter. In 1970, Brzezinski wrote:

> ... some international cooperation has already been achieved, but further progress will require greater American sacrifices. More intensive efforts to shape a new world monetary structure will have to be undertaken, with some consequent risk to the present relatively favorable American position.[4]

---

1. "Text of Kennedy Speech to World Monetary Parley," *New York Times*, October 1, 1963, p. 16.
2. For an in-depth analysis of the CFR, including a comprehensive list of members, see James Perloff, *Shadows of Power* (Appleton, Wisconsin: Western Islands, 1988).
3. "Dulles Outlines World Peace Plan," *New York Times*, October 28, 1939.
4. Zbigniew Brzezinski, *Between Two Ages: America's Role in the Technetronic Era* (Westport, Connecticut: Greenwood Press, 1970), p. 300.

At the Spring, 1983, Economic Summit in Williamsburg, Virginia, President Ronald Reagan declared:

> National economies need monetary coordination mechanisms, and that is why an integrated world economy needs a common monetary standard.... But, no national currency will do—only a world currency will work.

The CFR strategy for convergence of the world's monetary systems was spelled out by Harvard Professor Richard N. Cooper, a CFR member who had been the Under Secretary of State for Economic Affairs in the Carter Administration:

> I suggest a radical alternative scheme for the next century: *the creation of a common currency for all of the industrial democracies, with a common monetary policy and a joint Bank of Issue to determine that monetary policy....* How can independent states accomplish that? They need to turn over the determination of monetary policy to a supranational body. [Emphasis in original]...
>
> It is highly doubtful whether the American public, to take just one example, could ever accept that countries with oppressive autocratic regimes should vote on the monetary policy that would affect monetary conditions in the United States.... For such a bold step to work at all, it presupposes a certain convergence of political values....[1]

Phrases such as, *monetary coordination mechanisms, modern world economic order, convergence of political values,* or *new world order* are not very specific. To the average person, they sound pleasant and harmless. Yet, to the insiders of the club, they are code phrases which have a specific meaning: the termination of national sovereignty and the creation of world government. CFR member, Richard Gardner—another adviser to President Carter—explains the meaning of these phrases and also calls for the Fabian strategy of deception and gradualism:

> In short, the "house of world order" will have to be built from the bottom up.... An end run around national sovereignty, eroding it piece by piece, will accomplish much more than the old-fashioned frontal assault.[2]

As for the programmed decline of the American economy, CFR member Samuel Huntington argues that, if higher education is

---

1. "A Monetary System for the Future," by Richard N. Cooper, *Foreign Affairs*, Fall, 1984, pp. 166, 177, 184.
2. "The Hard Road to World Order," by Richard Gardner, *Foreign Affairs*, April, 1974, p. 558.

considered to be desirable for the general population, "a program is then necessary to lower the job expectations of those who receive a college education."[1] CFR member Paul Volcker, former Chairman of the Federal Reserve, says: "The standard of living of the average American has to decline.... I don't think you can escape that."[2]

By 1993, Volcker had become the U.S. Chairman of the Trilateral Commission. The TLC was created by David Rockefeller to coordinate the building of The New World Order in accordance with the Gardner strategy: "An end run around national sovereignty, eroding it piece by piece." The objective is to draw the United States, Mexico, Canada, Japan, and Western Europe into political and economic union. Under slogans such as free trade and environmental protection, each nation is to surrender its sovereignty "piece by piece" until a full-blown regional government emerges from the process. The new government will control each nation's working conditions, wages, and taxes. Once that has happened, it will be a relatively simple step to merge the regionals into global government. That is the reality behind the so-called trade treaties within the European Union (EU), the North American Free Trade Agreement (NAFTA), the Asia-Pacific Economic Cooperation agreement (APEC), and the General Agreement on Tariffs and Trade (GATT). They have little to do with trade. In the Trilateral Commission's annual report for 1993, Volcker explains:

> Interdependence is driving our countries toward convergence in areas once considered fully within the domestic purview. Some of these areas involve government regulatory policy, such as environmental standards, the fair treatment of workers, and taxation.[3]

In 1992, the Trilateral Commission released a report co-authored by Toyoo Gyohten, Chairman of the Board of the Bank of Tokyo and formerly Japan's Minister of Finance for International Affairs. Gyohten had been a Fulbright Scholar who was trained at Princeton and taught at Harvard Business School. He also had been in charge of the Japan Desk of the International Monetary Fund. In short, he represents the Japanese monetary interests within The

---

1. Michael Crozier, Samuel P. Huntington, and Joji Watanuki, *The Crisis of Democracy* (New York: New York University Press, 1975), pp. 183–84.
2. "Volcker Asserts U.S. Must Trim Living Standard," *New York Times*, October 18, 1979, p. 1.
3. *Washington 1993: The Annual Meeting of the Trilateral Commission*, Trialogue 46 (New York: Trilateral Commission, 1993), p. 77.

New World Order. In this report, Gyohten explains that the real importance of "trade" agreements is not trade but the building of global government:

> Regional trade arrangements should not be regarded as ends in themselves, but as supplements to global liberalization.... Regional arrangements provide models or building blocks for increased or strengthened globalism.... Western Europe [the EU] represents regionalism in its truest form.... The steps toward deepening [increasing the number of agreements] are dramatic and designed to be irreversible.... A common currency.... central bank.... court and parliament—will have expanded powers.... After the Maastricht summit [the Dutch town where the meeting was held], an *Economist* editorial pronounced the verdict: "Call it what you will: by any other name it is federal government."... In sum, the regional integration process in Europe can be seen as akin to an exercise in nation-building.[1]

Applying this same perspective to the NAFTA treaty, former Secretary-of-State, Henry Kissinger (CFR), said it "is not a conventional trade agreement but the architecture of a new international system.... the vital first step for a new kind of community of nations." The newspaper article that contained this statement was appropriately entitled: "With NAFTA, U.S. Finally Creates a New World Order."[2] David Rockefeller (CFR) was even more emphatic. He said that it would be "criminal" not to pass the treaty because: "Everything is in place—after 500 years—to build a true 'new world' in the Western Hemisphere."[3]

By early 1994, the drift toward the New World Order had become a rush. On April 15, the government of Morocco placed a full-page ad in the *New York Times* celebrating the creation of the World Trade Organization which was formed by the signing of the General Agreement on Tariffs and Trade (GATT) which took place in the Moroccan city of Marrakech. While Americans were still being told that GATT was merely a "trade" agreement, the internationalists were celebrating a much larger concept. The ad spelled it out in unmistakable terms:

---

1. Toyoo Gyohten and Charles E. Morrison, *Regionalism in A Converging World* (New York: Trilateral Commission, 1992), pp. 4, 7-9, 11.
2. "With NAFTA, U.S. Finally Creates a New World Order," by Henry Kissinger, *Los Angeles Times*, July 18, 1993, pp. M-2, 6.
3. "A Hemisphere in the Balance," by David Rockefeller, *Wall Street Journal*, October 1, 1993, p. A-10.

1944, Bretton Woods: The IMF and the World Bank
1945, San Francisco: The United Nations
1994, Marrakech: The World Trade Organization
History knows where it is going.... The World Trade Organization,
the third pillar of the New World Order, along with the United
Nations and the International Monetary Fund.[1]

A RARE GLIMPSE INTO THE INNER WORKINGS

So much for the *final play*. Let us return, now, to the game called
bailout as it is actually played today on the international scene. Let
us begin with a glimpse into the inner workings of the Presidential
Cabinet. James Watt was the Secretary of the Interior in the Reagan
Administration. In his memoirs, he described an incident at a
Cabinet meeting in the spring of 1982. The first items on the agenda
were reports by Treasury Secretary Donald Regan and Budget
Director David Stockman concerning problems the less-developed
countries were having with their bank loans. Watt said:

> Secretary Regan was explaining the inability of those destitute
> countries to pay even the interest on the loans that individual banks
> such as Bank of America, Chase Manhattan and Citibank had made.
> The President was being told what actions the United States "must"
> take to salvage the situation.
>
> After the Regan and Stockman briefings, there were several
> minutes of discussion before I asked, "Does anyone believe that these
> less developed countries will ever be able to pay back the principal on
> these loans?" When no one spoke up, I asked, "If the loans are never
> going to be repaid, why should we again bail out the countries and
> arrange payment for their interest?"
>
> The answer came from several voices at once, "If we don't arrange
> for their interest payments, the loans will go into default, and it could
> put our American banks in jeopardy." Would the customers lose their
> money? No, came the answer, but the stockholders might lose
> dividends.
>
> In amazement, I leaned back in my large, leather chair, only two
> seats from the President of the United States. I realized that nothing in
> the world could keep these high government officials from scrambling
> to protect and bail out a few very large and sorely troubled American
> banks.[2]

---

1. *New York Times*, April 15, 1994, p. A9.
2. James G. Watt, *The Courage of A Conservative* (New York: Simon and Schuster, 1985), pp. 124–25.

PANAMA

The first major score in the game had been made under the Carter Administration when Panama fell in arrears on the payment of its loans. A consortium of banks including Chase Manhattan, First National of Chicago, and Citibank brought pressure to bear on Washington to give the Canal to the Panamanian government so it could use the revenue to pay interest on its loans. Although there was massive opposition to this move among the American people, the Senate yielded to insider pressure and passed the give-away treaty. The Panamanian government inherited $120 million in annual revenue, and the interest payments to the banks were restored. As Congressman Philip Crane observed:

> At the time of the Torrijos-backed coup in 1968, Panama's total official overseas debt stood at a manageable and, by world standards, modest $167 million. Under Torrijos, indebtedness has skyrocketed nearly *one thousand percent* to a massive $1.5 billion. Debt-service ratio now consumes an estimated 39 percent of the entire Panamanian budget.... What it appears we really have here is not just aid to a tinhorn dictator in the form of new subsidies and canal revenues the treaties would give to the Torrijos regime, but a bailout of a number of banks which should have known better than to invest in Panama and, in any event, should not escape responsibility for having done so.[1]

The Panama bailout was a unique play. In no other country did we have an income-producing property to give away, so from that point forward the bailout would have to be done with mere money. To pave the way for that, Congress passed the Monetary Control Act of 1980 which authorized the Federal Reserve to "monetize foreign debt." That is banker language meaning that the Fed was now authorized to create money out of nothing for the purpose of lending to foreign governments. It classifies those loans as "assets" and then uses them as collateral for the creation of even more money here in the United States. That was truly a revolutionary expansion of the Fed's power to inflate. Until then, it was permitted to make money only for the *American* government. Now, it was able to do it for *any* government. Since then it has been functioning as a central bank for the entire world.

---

1. Philip M. Crane, *Surrender in Panama* (Ottawa, Illinois: Caroline House Books, 1978), pp. 64, 68.

MEXICO

By 1982, almost every Third-World government was running behind in payments. Mexico led the way by announcing it could not send any more money that year on its $85 billion debt. Federal Reserve Governor Henry Wallich rushed to Switzerland to negotiate an IMF loan of $4.5 billion through the Bank of International Settlements. The central banks of Europe and Japan provided $1.85 billion (about 40%); the rest came from the Federal Reserve. Commercial banks postponed payments on the principal for two years; but, with the infusion of new loans, payment on the interest was resumed. That did not solve the problem. Within a few years, Mexico was in arrears again and, in 1985, the banks agreed to postpone $29 billion in payments and rolled over another $20 billion, which means they issued new loans to pay off the old.

In that same year, Secretary of the Treasury James Baker announced the government's plan to solve the world's debt crisis. It was a formal statement encouraging banks to continue lending to Third-World governments provided they promised to enact economic reforms favoring a free market. It was more of a philosophy than a plan, because there was no hope that it would be implemented by any of the socialist governments receiving the loans. Behind the announcement was the implication that the federal government, acting through the Federal Reserve System, could be counted on to assist if the loans went sour. Baker called for funneling $29 billion over three years primarily to Latin American countries, of which Mexico was a prime recipient.

CURRENCY SWAP

Shortly after the Mexican government had loaned $55 million to Fidel Castro, it announced to the banks: "We will pay only what we have, and no more." Whereupon Paul Volcker, head of the Federal Reserve, rushed to meet with Mexico's finance minister, Jesus Silva Herzog, and offered to put the American taxpayer into the breach. A $600 million short-term loan was extended to get Mexico past its election date of July 4. It was called a "currency swap" because Mexico exchanged an equal number of pesos which it promised to redeem in U.S. dollars. Pesos, of course, were worthless in international markets—which is the reason Mexico wanted the dollars.

The importance of this loan was not its size nor even the question of repayment. It was the manner in which it was made.

First, it was made by the Federal Reserve *directly*, acting as a central bank for Mexico, not the U.S.; and secondly, it was done almost in total secrecy. William Greider gives the details:

> The currency swaps had another advantage: they could be done secretly. Volcker discreetly informed both the Administration and the key congressional chairmen, and none objected. But the public reporting of currency swaps was required only every quarter, so the emergency loan from the Fed would not be disclosed for three or four months.... By that time, Volcker hoped, Mexico would be arranging more substantial new financing from the IMF.... The foreign assistance was done as discreetly as possible to avoid setting off a panic, but also to avoid domestic political controversy.... Bailing out Mexico, it seemed, was too grave to be controversial.[1]

DEBT SWAP

The currency swap did not solve the problem. So, in March of 1988, the players and referees agreed to introduce a new maneuver in the game: an accounting trick called a "debt swap." A debt swap is similar to a currency swap in that the United States exchanges something of real value in return for something that is worthless. But, instead of currencies, they exchange government bonds. The transaction is complicated by the time-value of those bonds. Currencies are valued by their *immediate* worth, what they will buy today, but bonds are valued by their *future* worth, what they will buy in the future. After that differential factor is calculated, the process is essentially the same. Here is how it worked.

Mexico, using U.S. dollars, purchased $492 million worth of American Treasury Bonds that pay no interest but which will pay $3.67 billion when they mature in twenty years. (Technically, these are called zero-coupon bonds.) Then Mexico issued its own bonds with the U.S. securities tied to them as collateral. This meant that the future value of Mexico's bonds, previously considered worthless, were now guaranteed by the United States government. The banks eagerly swapped their old loans for these new Mexican bonds at a ratio of about 1.4 to 1. In other words, they accepted $100 million in bonds in return for canceling $140 million in old debt. That reduced their interest income, but they were happy to do it, because they had swapped worthless loans for fully-guaranteed bonds.

---

1. Greider, pp. 485–6.

This maneuver was hailed in the press as true monetary magic. It would save the Mexican government more than $200 million in annual interest charges; it would restore cash flow to the banks; and—miracle of miracles—it would cost nothing to American taxpayers.[1] The reasoning was that the Treasury bonds were sold at normal market rates. The Mexican government paid as much for them as anyone else. That part was true, but what the commentators failed to notice was where Mexico got the American dollars with which to buy the bonds. They came through the IMF in the form of "foreign-currency exchange reserves." In other words, they were subsidies from the industrialized nations, primarily the United States. So, the U.S. Treasury put up the lion's share of the money to buy its own bonds. It went a half-billion dollars *deeper* in debt and agreed to pay $3.7 billion *more* in future payments so the Mexican government could continue paying interest to the banks. That is called bailout, and it *does* fall on the American taxpayer.

IMF BECOMES FINAL GUARANTOR

The following year, Secretary of State, James Baker (CFR), and Treasury Secretary, Nicholas Brady (CFR), flew to Mexico to work out a new debt agreement that would begin to phase in the IMF as final guarantor. The IMF gave Mexico a new loan of $3.5 billion (later increased to $7.5 billion), the World Bank gave another $1.5 billion, and the banks reduced their previous loan values by about a third. The private banks were quite willing to extend new loans and reschedule the old. Why not? Interest payments would now be guaranteed by the taxpayers of the United States and Japan.

That did not permanently solve the problem, either, because the Mexican economy was suffering from massive inflation caused by internal debt, which was in addition to the *external* debt owed to the banks. The phrases "internal debt" and "domestic borrowing" are code for the fact that government has inflated its money supply by selling bonds. The interest it must pay to entice people to purchase those bonds can be staggering and, in fact, interest on Mexico's domestic borrowing was draining three times as much from the economy as the foreign debt service had been siphoning off.[2]

---

1. "U.S. Bond Issue Will Aid Mexico in Paying Debts," by Tom Redburn, *Los Angeles Times*, December 30, 1987.
2. "With Foreign IOUs Massaged, Interest Turns to Internal Debt," *Insight*, October 2, 1989, p. 34.

Notwithstanding this reality, Citicorp chairman, John S. Reed (CFR), whose bank is one of Mexico's largest lenders, said they were prepared to lend even more now. Why? Did it have anything to do with the fact that the Federal Reserve and the IMF would guarantee payments? Not so. "Because we believe the Mexican economy is doing well," he said. [1]

At the end of 1994, the game was still going, and the play was the same. On December 21, the Mexican government announced that it could no longer pay the fixed exchange rate between the peso and the dollar and that the peso would now have to float in the free market to find its true value. The next day it plummeted 39 per cent, and the Mexican stock market tumbled. Once again, Mexico could not pay the interest on its loans. On January 11, President Clinton (CFR) urged Congress to approve U.S. guarantees for new loans up to $40 billion. Secretary of the Treasury Robert Rubin (CFR) explained: "It is the judgment of all, including Chairman Alan Greenspan [CFR], that the probability of the debts being paid [by Mexico] is exceedingly high." But, while Congress debated the issue, the loan clock was ticking. Payment of $17 billion in Mexican bonds was due within 60 days, and $4 billion of that was due on the first of February! *Who* was going to pay the banks?

This matter could not wait. On January 31, acting independently of Congress, President Clinton announced a bailout package of over $50 billion in loan guarantees to Mexico; $20 billion from the U.S. Exchange Stabilization Fund, $17.8 billion from the IMF, $10 billion from the Bank of International Settlements, and $3 billion from commercial banks.

BRAZIL

Brazil became a major player in 1982 when it announced that it too was unable to make payments on its debt. In response, the U.S. Treasury made a direct loan of $1.23 billion to keep those checks going to the banks while negotiations were under way for a more permanent solution through the IMF. Twenty days later, it gave another $1.5 billion; the Bank of International Settlements advanced $1.2 billion. The following month, the IMF provided $5.5 billion; Western banks extended $10 billion in trade credits; old loans were rescheduled; and $4.4 billion in new loans were made by a Morgan

---

1. *Ibid.*, p. 35.

Bank syndication. The "temporary" loans from the U.S. Treasury were extended with no repayment date established. Ron Chernow comments:

> The plan set a fateful precedent of "curing" the debt crisis by heaping on more debt. In this charade, bankers would lend more to Brazil with one hand, then take it back with the other. This preserved the fictitious book value of loans on bank balance sheets. Approaching the rescue as a grand new syndication, the bankers piled on high interest rates and rescheduling fees.[1]

By 1983, Third-World governments owed $300 billion to banks and $400 billion to the industrialized governments. Twenty-five nations were behind in their payments. Brazil was in default a second time and asked for rescheduling, as did Rumania, Cuba, and Zambia. The IMF stepped in and made additional billions of dollars available to the delinquent countries. The Department of Agriculture, through its Commodity Credit Corporation, paid $431 million to American banks to cover payments on loans from Brazil, Morocco, Peru, and Rumania. At the conclusion of these agreements, the April 20, 1983, *Wall Street Journal* editorialized that "the international debt crisis ... is, for all practical purposes, over."

Not quite. By 1987, Brazil was again in default on its monstrous $121 billion debt, this time for one and a-half years. In spite of the torrent of money that had passed through its hands, it was now so broke, it couldn't even buy gasoline for its police cars. In 1989, as a new round of bailout was being organized, President Bush, Sr. (CFR) announced that the only real solution to the Third-World debt problem was debt forgiveness. Thirteen years later, President Bush, Jr., was continuing the tradition and calling for another $30 billion IMF loan to Brazil, backed by the U.S taxpayer.

At the risk of running this history into the ground through repetition, here are just a few more examples before moving along.

ARGENTINA

By 1982, Argentina was unable to make a $2.3 billion payment that was due in July and August. The banks extended their loans while the IMF prepared a new infusion in the amount of $2.15 billion. This restored the interest payments and gave the Argentinian politicians a little extra spending money. Seven

---

1. Chernow, p. 644.

months later, Argentina announced it could not make any more payments until the fall of 1983. The banks immediately began negotiations for rollovers, guarantees, and new IMF loans.

Argentina then signed an agreement with 350 creditor banks to stretch out payments on nearly a fourth of its $13.4 billion debt, and the banks agreed to lend an extra $4.2 billion to cover interest payments and political incentives. The IMF gave $1.7 billion. The United States government gave an additional $500 million directly. Argentina then paid $850 million in overdue interest charges to the banks.

By 1988, Argentina had again stopped payment on its loans and was falling hopelessly behind as bankers and politicians went into a huddle to call the next bailout play. They came out of the huddle with yet another package of new loans, rollovers, and guarantees. As summarized by Larry A. Sjaastad at the University of Chicago:

> There isn't a U.S. bank that would not sell its entire Latin American portfolio for 40 cents on the dollar were it not for the possibility that skillful political lobbying might turn up a sucker willing to pay 50 or 60 or even 90 cents on the dollar. And that sucker is the U.S. Taxpayer.[1]

The IMF bailed out Argentina again for $40 billion in 2001 and another $8 billion in 2002.

This history can become repetitious and boring. It would be counterproductive to cover the same sordid story as it has unfolded in each country. Suffice it to say that the identical game has been played with teams from Bolivia, Peru, Venezuela, Costa Rica, Morocco, the Philippines, the Dominican Republic, and almost every other less-developed country in the world.

THE NEED FOR CONVERGENCE

This sets the stage for understanding the next phase of the game which is unfolding as these words are being written. It is the inclusion of China and the former Soviet bloc into the Grand Design for global government. As with all the other countries in the world, the primary *mechanism* being used to accomplish this goal—at least in the field of economics—is the IMF/World Bank.[2] The *process* is: (1) the transfer of money from the industrialized

---

1. "Another Plan to Mop Up the Mess," *Insight*, April 10, 1989, p. 31.
2. Other mechanisms which involve culture, education, political sovereignty, and military power are embodied in agencies of the United Nations.

nations—which drags them down economically to a suitable common denominator—and (2) the acquisition of effective control over the political leaders of the recipient countries as they become dependent upon the money stream. The thing that is new and which sets this stage apart from previous developments is that the apparent crumbling of Communism has created an acceptable rationale for the industrialized nations to now allow their lifeblood to flow into the veins of their former enemies. It also creates the appearance of global, political "convergence," a condition which CFR theoretician, Richard Cooper, said was necessary before Americans would accept having their own destinies determined by governments other than their own.

CHINA

Red China joined the IMF/World Bank in 1980 and immediately began to receive billions of dollars in loans, although it was well known that she was devoting a huge portion of her resources to military development. By 1987, China was the IMF's second largest borrower, next to India, and the transfusions have grown at a steady pace ever since.

The Bank has asserted that loans will encourage economic reforms in favor of the private sector. Yet, none of the money has gone to the private sector. All of it is funneled into the government bureaucracy which, in turn, wages war against the free market. In 1989, after small businesses and farms in the private sector had begun to flourish and surpass the performance of similar government enterprises, Red China's leaders clamped down on them with harsh controls and increased taxes. Vice Premier Yao Yilin announced that there was too much needless construction, too many private loans, and too much spending on "luxuries" such as cars and banquets. To stop these excesses, he said, it would be necessary to increase government controls over wages, prices, and business activities.

Then there is the question of why China needs the money in the first place. Is it to develop her industry or natural resources? Is it to fight poverty and improve the living standard of her citizens? James Bovard answers:

> The Bank's defense of its China Policy is especially puzzling because China itself is going on a foreign investment binge. The World Bank gives China money at zero interest, and then China buys

property in Hong Kong, the United States, Australia, and elsewhere. An economist with Citibank estimated that China's "direct investment in property, manufacturing and services [in Hong Kong alone] topped $6 billion." In 1984, China had a net outflow of capital of $1 billion. Moreover, China has its own foreign aid program, which has given more than $6 billion in recent decades, largely to leftist governments.[1]

THE GREAT DECEPTION

It is the author's contention that the much heralded demise of Communism in the Soviet bloc is a mixture of fact and fantasy. It is fact at the bottom level of Communist society where the people, in truth, rejected it long ago. The only reason they appeared to embrace it for so many years was that they had no choice. As long as the Soviets held control of the weapons and the means of communication, the people had to accept their fate.

But at the tip of the pyramid of state power, it is a different story. The top Communist leaders have never been as hostile to their counterparts in the West as the rhetoric suggests. They are quite friendly to the world's leading financiers and have worked closely with them when it suits their purposes. As we shall see in the following section, the Bolshevik revolution actually was financed by wealthy financiers in London and New York. Lenin and Trotsky were on the closest of terms with these moneyed interests—both before and after the Revolution. Those hidden liaisons have continued to this day and occasionally pop to the surface when we discover a David Rockefeller holding confidential meetings with a Mikhail Gorbachev in the absence of government sponsorship or diplomatic purpose.

It is not unreasonable to imagine a scenario in which the leaders of the Communist bloc come to realize they cannot hold themselves in power much longer. There comes a point where even physical force is not enough, especially when the loyalties of those who hold the weapons also begin to falter. With economic gangrene creeping up the legs of their socialist systems, they realize they must obtain outside financial assistance or perish.

In such a scenario, quiet agreements can be worked out to the mutual advantage of all negotiators. The plan could be as simple as a statue-of-liberty play in a college football game: the appearance of doing one thing as a cover for accomplishing something else. While

---

1. Bovard, pp. 18–19.

Americans are prepared to accept such deception on a football field, they cannot believe that world financiers and politicians are capable of it. The concept is rejected out of hand as a "conspiracy theory."

Nevertheless, in this scenario, we theorize it is agreed among the negotiators that the Soviet Bloc needs financial support. It is agreed that the Western nations have the capacity to provide it. It is agreed that the best way to move money from the industrialized nations into the Soviet bloc is through international agencies such as the IMF/World Bank. It is agreed this cannot happen until hostility between world systems is replaced by political convergence. It is agreed that future conflict is wasteful and dangerous to all parties. Therefore, it is finally agreed that the Soviet bloc must abandon its posture of global aggression while the Western nations continue to move toward socialism, necessary steps for the long-range goal of merger into a world government. But, in doing so, it must be insured that the existing Communist leaders retain control over their respective states.

COMMUNISTS BECOME SOCIAL DEMOCRATS

To that end, they change their public identities to "Social Democrats." They speak out against the brutal excesses of their predecessors and they offer greater freedom of expression in the media. A few dispensable individuals among their ranks are publicly purged as examples of the demise of the old order. States that once were held captive by the Soviet Union are allowed to break away and then return on a voluntary basis. If any leaders of the newly emancipated states prefer true independence instead of alignment with Russia, they are replaced.

No other changes are required. Socialism remains the economic system of choice and, although lip service may be given to free-market concepts, the economy and all means of production remain under state control. The old Communists are now Social Democrats and, without exception, they become the leaders in the new system.

The West rejoices, and the money starts to move. As an extra bonus, the former Bolsheviks are now hailed by the world as great statesmen who put an end to the Cold War, brought freedom to their people, and helped to forge a New World Order.

When did Communism depart? We are not quite sure. All we know is that one day we opened our newspapers and it was accomplished. Social Democrats were everywhere. No one could find any Communists. Russian leaders spoke as long-time enemies of the old regime. Peristroika was here. Communism was dead. It was not killed by an enemy. It voted itself out of existence. It committed suicide!

Does it not seem strange that Communism fell without a struggle? Is it not curious that the system which was born out of class conflict and revolution and which maintained itself by force and violence for almost a century just went away on its own? Communism was not overthrown by people rising up with clubs and pitchforks to throw off their yoke of tyranny. There was no revolution or counterrevolution, no long period of fragmentation, no bloody surges between opposing forces. Poof! It just happened. True, there was blood in the streets in those areas where opposing groups vied for power, but that was *after* Communism had departed, not before. Such an event had never occurred in history. Until then, it had been contrary to the way governments act; contrary to the very nature of power which never surrenders without a life-and-death struggle. This, indeed, is a great curiosity—which should cause people to think.

Our premise is that the so-called demise of Communism is a Great Deception—not awfully different from many of the others that are the focus of this volume. We see it as having been stage managed for the purposes outlined previously: the transition to world government. In our view, *that* scenario is the only one that makes sense in terms of today's geopolitical realities and the only one consistent with the lessons of history.

We realize, of course, that such a view runs contrary to popular opinion and conventional wisdom. For many, it is shocking just to hear it spelled out. It would not be possible to convince anyone of its truth without extensive evidence. Certainly, such evidence abounds, but it is not within the scope of this study. So, now that we have stated it, we shall leave it behind merely as a clarification of the author's point of view so the reader can step around it if he wishes.

EASTERN EUROPE

American aid to Eastern European governments, while they were still puppet states of the Soviet Union, has been justified by the same theory advanced on behalf of China: it would improve their economies, show their people a better way of life, and wean them from Communism. Advocates of that theory now point to the demise of Communism as evidence of the soundness of their plan. The truth, however, is that the money did *not* improve the economy and did *not* show the people a better way of life. In fact, it did not help the people in any way. It went directly to their *governments* and was used for *government* priorities. It strengthened the ruling parties and enabled them to solidify their control.

It is well known that one of the reasons Poland's economy was weak is that much of her productive output was shipped to the Soviet Union at concessionary prices, primarily to support the military. Polish-built tanks fought in the Vietnam war; 20% of the Soviet merchant marine was built in Poland; 70% of Poland's computer and locomotive production and 80% of her communications equipment was shipped to the Soviets; American grain purchased by Poland with money borrowed from American banks was sent to Cuba. Poland was merely a middle man, a conduit to Russia and her satellites. The banks were really funding Russia.

It was in 1982 that Poland first defaulted on bank loans which had been guaranteed by the U.S. government through the Commodity Credit Corporation. Under the terms of the guarantee, taxpayers would make payments on any bank loan that went into default. That was what the banks were counting on when they made those loans, but to classify them as "in default" would require the banks to remove them from their books as assets. That was unacceptable, because it would make their balance sheets look as bad as they really were. So the Treasury agreed to bend the rules and make payments *without* requiring the loans to be in default. That was eventually stopped by an irate Congress, but not until the Reagan Administration had stalled long enough to pay $400 million directly to the banks on behalf of Poland.

In November, 1988, the World Bank made its first loan to Poland in the amount of $17.9 million. Three years later, in a dramatic demonstration of what the President had meant when he advocated "debt forgiveness," the Bush Administration canceled a full 70% of the $3.8 billion owed to the United States. Taxpayers picked up the bill.

The same story has been unfolding in all the former Soviet-bloc countries. In 1980, for example, just before Hungary was brought into the IMF/World Bank, her annual per-capita GNP was $4,180. This was a problem, because the policy of the World Bank was to make development loans only to countries that had per-capita GNPs of less than $2,650. Not to worry. In 1981, the Hungarian government simply revised its statistics downward from $4,180 to $2,100.[1] That was a drop of 50% in one year, surely one of the sharpest depressions in world history. Everyone knew it was a lie, but no one raised an eyebrow. It was all part of the game. By 1989, the Bush Administration had granted "most favored nation" trade status to the Hungarian government and established on its behalf a special $25 million development fund.

RUSSIA

American banks had always been willing to make loans to the Soviet Union, except for short periods of expediency during the Cuban Missile Crisis, the Vietnam War, the Soviet invasion of Afghanistan, and other minor business interruptions. In 1985, after the public had lost interest in Afghanistan, banks of the "free world" reopened their loan windows to the Soviets. A $400 million package was put together by a consortium of First National of Chicago, Morgan Guaranty, Bankers Trust, and Irving Trust—plus a London subsidiary of the Royal Bank of Canada. The loan was offered at unusually low interest rates "to buy American and Canadian grain."

Public indignation is easily disarmed when the announced purpose of a loan to a totalitarian government is to purchase commodities from the country where the loan originates—especially if the commodity is grain for the assumed purpose of making bread or feeding livestock. Who could possibly object to having the money come right back to our own farmers and merchants in the form of profits? And who could fault a project that provided food for the hungry?

The deception is subtly appealing. It is true that the money will be used—in part at least—to buy grain or other locally produced

---

1. "World Bank Courts Eastern Europe," by Jerry Lewis, *Wall Street Journal*, August 30, 1984.

commodities. But the borrowing nations are like a homeowner who increases the mortgage on his house "to enlarge his living room." He probably will make the addition, but he borrows twice as much as he needs so he can also buy a new car. Since the government allows a tax deduction on mortgage interest, in effect he now gets a tax deduction for the interest paid on his car as well. Likewise, the borrowing nations usually borrow more than they need for the announced purchase, but they receive *all* the money at favorable rates.

Yet, this is not the most serious fault in the transaction. In the case of Russia, the grain was no small item on her list of needs. After repeated failures of her socialist agriculture, she was not able to feed her population. Hungry people are dangerous to a government. Russia needed grain to head off internal revolt far more than the homeowner needed to increase the size of his living room. In other words, Russia *had* to have the grain, with or without the loan. Without it, she would have had to curtail spending somewhere else to obtain the money, most likely in her military. By giving her the money "to buy grain," we actually allowed her to spend more money on armaments.

But even that is not the primary flaw in making loans to Russia. The bottom line is that most of those loans *will never be repaid!* As we have seen, the name of the game is *bailout*, and it is as certain as the setting sun that, somewhere down the line, Russia will not be able to make her payments, and the taxpayers of the industrialized nations will be put through the IMF wringer one more time to squeeze out the transferred purchasing power.

BUSINESS VENTURES IN RUSSIA INSURED BY U.S.

In 1990, the U.S. Export-Import Bank announced it would begin making direct loans to Russia. Meanwhile, the U.S. Overseas Private Investment Corporation was providing free "insurance" to private companies that were willing to invest in the ex-Soviet state. In other words, it was now doing for industrial corporations what it had been doing all along for banks: guaranteeing that, if their investments turned sour, the government—make that taxpayers— would compensate them for their losses. The limit on that insurance had been $100 million, a generous figure, indeed. But, to encourage an even greater flow of private capital into Russia, the

Bush Administration authorized *unlimited* protection for "sound American corporate investments."

If these truly were sound investments, they would not need foreign-aid subsidies or government guarantees. What is really happening in this play is a triple score:

1. International lending agencies provide the Social Democrats with money to purchase goods and services from American firms. No one really expects them to repay. It is merely a clever method of redistributing wealth from those who have it to those who don't—without those who have it catching on.
2. American firms do not need money to participate. Since their ventures are guaranteed, banks are anxious to loan whatever amount of money is required. Efficiency or competitiveness are not important factors. Contracts are awarded on the basis of political influence. Profits are generous and without risk.
3. When the Social Democrats eventually default in their contracts to the American firms or when the joint venture loses money because of socialist mismanagement, the federal government provides funds to cover corporate profits and repayment of bank loans.

There you have it: The Social Democrats get the goodies; the corporations get the profits, and the banks get the interest on money created out of nothing. You *know* what the taxpayers get!

By 1992, the wearisome pattern was clearly visible. Writing in the *New York Times*, columnist Leslie H. Gelb gave the numbers:

> The ex-Soviet states are now meeting only 30 percent of their interest payments (and almost no principal) on debts to the West of $70 billion.... Various forms of Western aid to the ex-Soviet states totaled about $50 billion in the last 20 months, and the money has virtually disappeared without a trace or a dent on the economic picture.[1]

The interesting thing about this report is that Leslie Gelb has been a member of the CFR since 1973. Why would a CFR spokesman blow the whistle on one of their most important maneuvers toward The New World Order? The answer is that he is doing just the opposite. Actually he is making a plea for *more* loans

---

1. "The Russian Sinkhole," by Leslie H. Gelb, *New York Times*, March 30, 1992, p. L-A17.

and *more* outright aid on the basis that the need is so great! He advocates the prioritizing of funding with first attention to aiding Russia's nuclear-power facilities, agriculture, and industrial capacity. At the end of his article, he writes: "The stakes could not be higher. All the more reason for substantial, practical and immediate aid—not for grand illusions."

The excuse for all of this is that, if we do not keep the money flowing, Russia may fall back into the hands of those "bad Communists" who are just waiting to unleash nuclear war against us. Congress hears and obeys. In spite of the fact that all the preceding billions have "disappeared without a trace or a dent," the transfusion continues. In 1993 the World Bank advanced another half-billion-dollar loan to Russia; before leaving office, President Bush arranged for another $2 billion loan through the Export-Import Bank; and Congress authorized hitting the voters with another $2.5 billion in foreign aid specifically for Russia. In July of that year, at the meeting of the Group-of-Seven industrialized nations, another $24 billion was promised, half of which was to come from the IMF. In 1998, Russia defaulted on several billions of its debt, so the IMF restructured the old loans and issued new ones. In 1999, it was discovered that Russian officials had "laundered" (stolen) about $20 billion of this funding. The IMF publicly expressed shock and dismay; but soon resumed negotiations to issue new loans. As this book goes to print, there is no end in sight.

THE CONSPIRACY THEORY

A moment's reflection on these events leads us to a crossroads of conscience. We must choose between two paths. Either we conclude that Americans have lost control over their government, or we reject this information as a mere distortion of history. In the first case, we become advocates of the conspiratorial view of history. In the latter, we endorse the accidental view. It is a difficult choice because we have been conditioned to laugh at conspiracy theories, and few people will risk public ridicule by advocating them. On the other hand, to endorse the accidental view is absurd. Almost all of history is an unbroken trail of one conspiracy after another. Conspiracies are the norm, not the exception.

The industrialized nations of the world are being bled to death in a global transfer of their wealth to the less developed countries. Furthermore, it is not being done *to* them by their enemies. It is being done *by their own leaders*. The process is well coordinated across national lines and perfectly dovetails with the actions of other leaders who are doing the same thing in their respective countries, and these leaders regularly meet together to better coordinate their activities. This could not happen without planning.

A spokesman from the IMF would answer, yes, there *is* a plan, and it is to aid the less developed countries. But, after forty years and hundreds of billions of dollars, they have totally failed to accomplish that goal. Would intelligent people believe that pursuing the same plan will produce different results in the future? Then why do they follow a plan that cannot work? The answer is they are *not* following that plan. They are following a *different* one: one that has been very successful from their point of view. Otherwise, we must conclude that the leaders of the industrialized nations are, to a man, just plain stupid. We do not believe it.

These men and women are following a higher loyalty than to their respective countries. In their hearts they may honestly believe that, in the long run, the world will be better for it, including their fellow countrymen. But, for the present, their goals are not shared by those who have placed them in office, which is why they must conceal their plan from public view. If their fellow citizens knew what they were really doing, they would be thrown out of office and, in some cases, might even be shot as traitors.

If all of this is accidental, then there is no plan, no cooperation, no goal, and no deceit, just the blind forces of history following the path of least resistance. For some it is easier and more comfortable to accept that model. But the evidence speaks against it; not just the evidence in the previous chapters, but everything that follows in this book. By contrast, the evidence for the accidental theory of history is — a blank page.

SUMMARY

The international version of the game called Bailout is similar to the domestic version in that the overall objective is to have the taxpayers cover the defaulted loans so that interest payments can continue going to the banks. The differences are: (1) instead of justifying this as protecting the American public, the pretense is that it is to save the world from poverty; and (2) the main money pipeline goes from the Federal Reserve through the IMF/World Bank. Otherwise, the rules are basically the same.

There is another dimension to the game, however, that involves more than mere profits and scam. It is the conscious and deliberate evolution of the IMF/World Bank into a world central bank with the power to issue a world fiat currency. And that is an important step in an even larger plan to build a true world government within the framework of the United Nations.

Economically strong nations are not candidates for surrendering their sovereignty to a world government. Therefore, through "loans" that will never be paid back, the IMF/World Bank directs the massive transfer of wealth from the industrialized nations to the less developed nations. This ongoing process eventually drains their economies to the point where they also will be in need of assistance. No longer capable of independent action, they will accept the loss of sovereignty in return for international aid.

The less developed countries, on the other hand, are being brought into The New World Order along an entirely different route. Many of these countries are ruled by petty tyrants who care little for their people except how to extract more taxes from them without causing a revolt. Loans from the IMF/World Bank are used primarily to perpetuate themselves and their ruling parties in power—and that is exactly what the IMF/World Bank intends. Rhetoric about helping the poor notwithstanding, the true goal of the transfer of wealth disguised as loans is to get control over the leaders of the less developed countries. After these despots get used to the taste of such an unlimited supply of sweet cash, they will never be able to break the habit. They will be content—already *are* content—to become little gold-plated cogs in the giant machinery of world government. Ideology means nothing to them: capitalist, communist, socialist, fascist, what does it matter so long as the money keeps coming. The IMF/World Bank literally is *buying* these countries and using our money to do it.

The recent inclusion of Red China and the former Soviet bloc on the list of IMF/World Bank recipient countries signals the final phase of the game. Now that Latin America and Africa have been "purchased" into the New World Order, this is the final frontier. In a relatively short time span, China, Russia, and the Eastern European countries have now become the biggest borrowers and, already, they are in arrears on their payments. This is where the action will lie in the months ahead.

Section II

A CRASH COURSE
ON MONEY

The eight chapters contained in this and the following section deal with material that is organized by topic, not chronology. Several of them will jump ahead of events that are not covered until later. Furthermore, the scope is such that the reader may wonder what, if any, is the connection with the Federal Reserve System. Please be patient. The importance will eventually become clear. It is the author's intent to cover concepts and principles before looking at events. Without this background, the history of the Federal Reserve is boring. *With* it, the story emerges as an exciting drama which profoundly affects our lives today. So let us begin this adventure with a few discoveries about the nature of money itself.

Chapter Seven

THE BARBARIC METAL

The history and evolution of money; the emergence of gold as the universal money supply; the attempts by governments to cheat their subjects by clipping or debasing gold coins; the reality that any quantity of gold will suffice for a monetary system and that "more money" does not require more gold.

There is a great mystique surrounding the nature of money. It is generally regarded as beyond the understanding of mere mortals. Questions of the origin of money or the mechanism of its creation are seldom matters of public debate. We accept them as facts of life which are beyond our sphere of control. Thus, in a nation which is founded on the principle of government by the people, and which assumes a high level of understanding among the electorate, the people themselves have blocked out one of the most important factors affecting, not only their government, but their personal lives as well.

This attitude is not accidental, nor was it always so. There was a time in the fairly recent past when the humble voter—even without formal education—was well informed on money matters and vitally concerned about their political implementation. In fact, as we shall see in a later chapter, major elections were won or lost depending on how candidates stood on the issue of a central bank. It has been in the interest of the money mandarins, however, to convince the public that, now, these issues are too complicated for novices. Through the use of technical jargon and by hiding simple reality inside a maze of bewildering procedures, they have caused an understanding of the *nature* of money to fade from the public consciousness.

WHAT IS MONEY?

The first step in this maneuver was to scramble the definition of money itself. For example, the July 20, 1975 issue of the *New York*

Times, in an article entitled "Money Supply: A Growing Muddle," begins with the question: "What is money nowadays?" The *Wall Street Journal* of August 29, 1975, comments: "The men and women involved in this arcane exercise [of watching the money supply] ... aren't exactly sure what the money supply consists of." And, in its September 24, 1971 issue, the same paper said: "A pro-International Monetary Fund Seminar of eminent economists couldn't agree on what money is or how banks create it."

Even the government cannot define money. Some years ago, a Mr. A.F. Davis mailed a ten-dollar Federal Reserve Note to the Treasury Department. In his letter of transmittal, he called attention to the inscription on the bill which said that it was redeemable in "lawful money," and then requested that such money be sent to him. In reply, the Treasury merely sent two five-dollar bills from a different printing series bearing a similar promise to pay. Mr. Davis responded:

> Dear Sir:
> Receipt is hereby acknowledged of two $5.00 United States notes, which we interpret from your letter are to be considered as lawful money. Are we to infer from this that the Federal Reserve notes are not lawful money?
> I am enclosing one of the $5.00 notes which you sent to me. I note that it states on the face, "The United States of America will pay to the bearer on demand five dollars." I am hereby demanding five dollars.

One week later, Mr. Davis received the following reply from Acting Treasurer, M.E. Slindee:

> Dear Mr. Davis:
> Receipt is acknowledged of your letter of December 23rd, transmitting one $5. United States Note with a demand for payment of five dollars. You are advised that the term "lawful money" has not been defined in federal legislation.... The term "lawful currency" no longer has such special significance. The $5. United States Note received with your letter of December 23rd is returned herewith.[1]

The phrases "...will pay to the bearer on demand" and "... is redeemable in lawful money" were deleted from our currency altogether in 1964.

---

1. As quoted by C.V. Myers, *Money and Energy: Weathering the Storm* (Darien, Connecticut: Soundview Books, 1980), pp. 161, 163. Also by Lawrence S. Ritter, ed., *Money and Economic Activity* (Boston: Houghton Mifflin, 1967), p. 33.

Is money really so mysterious that it cannot be defined? Is it the coin and currency we have in our pockets? Is it numbers in a checking account or electronic impulses in a computer? Does it include the balance in a savings account or the available credit on a charge card? Does it include the value of stocks and bonds, houses, land, or personal possessions? Or is money nothing more than purchasing power?

The main function of the Federal Reserve is to regulate the supply of money. Yet, if no one is able to define what money is, how can we have an opinion about how the System is performing? The answer, of course, is that we cannot, and that is exactly the way the cartel wants it.

The reason the Federal Reserve appears to be a complicated subject is because most discussions start somewhere in the *middle*. By the time we get into it, definitions have been scrambled and basic concepts have been assumed. Under such conditions, intellectual chaos is inevitable. If we start at the beginning, however, and deal with each concept in sequence from the general to the specific, and if we agree on definitions as we go, we shall find to our amazement that the issues are really quite simple. Furthermore, the process is not only painless, it is—believe it or not—intensely interesting.

The purpose of this and the next three chapters, therefore, is to provide what could be called a crash course on money. It will *not* be complicated. In fact, you already know much of what follows. All we shall attempt to do is tie it all together so that it will have continuity and relativity to our subject. When you are through with these next few pages, you *will* understand money. That's a promise.

So, let's get started with the basics. What is money?

A WORKING DEFINITION

The dictionary is of little help. If economists cannot agree on what money is, it is partly due to the fact that there are so many definitions available that it is difficult to insist that any of them is the obvious choice. For the purpose of our analysis, however, it will be necessary to establish *one* definition so we can at least know what is meant when the word is used within this text. To that end, we shall introduce our own definition which has been assembled from bits and dabs taken from numerous sources. The structure is designed, not to reflect what we think money *ought* to be or to support the view of any particular school of economics, but simply to reduce the concept to its most fundamental essence and to reflect the reality of today's world. It is not necessary to agree or disagree with this definition. It is introduced solely for the purpose of providing an understanding of the word *as it is used within these pages*. This, then, shall be our working definition:

Money is anything which is accepted as a medium of exchange and it may be classified into the following forms:

1. Commodity money
2. Receipt money
3. Fiat money
4. Fractional money

Understanding the difference between these forms of money is practically all we need to know to fully comprehend the Federal Reserve System and to come to a judgment regarding its value to our economy and to our nation. Let us, therefore, examine each of them in some detail.

BARTER (PRE-MONEY)

Before there was any kind of money, however, there was barter, and it is important first to understand the link between the two. Barter is defined as that which is directly exchanged for something of like value. Mr. Jones swaps his restored Model-T Ford for a Steinway grand piano.[1] This exchange is not monetary in nature because both items are valued for themselves rather than held as a *medium* of exchange to be used later for something else. Note, however, that both items have intrinsic value or they would not be accepted by the other parties. Labor also may be exchanged as barter when it, too, is perceived to have intrinsic value to the person for whom the labor is performed. The concept of *intrinsic value* is the key to an understanding of the various forms of money that evolved from the process of barter.

COMMODITY MONEY

In the natural evolution of every society, there always have been one or two items which became more commonly used in

---

1. Strictly speaking, each party holds the value of what he is receiving to be more than what he is giving. Otherwise he would not make the trade. In the mind of the traders, therefore, the items have *unequal* value. That opinion is shared *equally* by them both. The shorter explanation, however, is less unwieldy.

barter than all others. This was because they had certain characteristics which made them useful or attractive to almost everyone. Eventually, they were traded, not for themselves, but because they represented a storehouse of value which could be exchanged at a later time for something else. At that point, they ceased being barter and became true money. They were, according to our working definition, a *medium* of exchange. And, since that medium was a commodity of intrinsic value, it may be described as *commodity money*.

Among primitive people, the most usual item to become commodity money was some form of food, either produce or livestock. Lingering testimony to this fact is our word *pecuniary*, which means pertaining to money. It is derived from the word *pecunia*, which is the Latin word for cow.

But, as society progressed beyond the level of bare existence, items other than food came into general demand. Ornaments were occasionally prized when the food supply was ample, and there is evidence of some societies using colored sea shells and unusual stones for this purpose. But these never seriously challenged the use of cattle, or sheep, or corn, or wheat, because these staples possessed greater intrinsic value for themselves even if they were not used as money.

METALS AS MONEY

Eventually, when man learned how to refine crude ores and to craft them into tools or weapons, the metals themselves became of value. This was the dawning of the Bronze Age in which iron, copper, tin, and bronze were traded between craftsmen and merchants along trade routes and at major sea ports.

The value of metal ingots was originally determined by weight. Then, as it became customary for the merchants who cast them to stamp the uniform weights on the top, they eventually were valued simply by counting their number. Although they were too large to carry in a pouch, they were still small enough to be transported easily and, in this form, they became, in effect, primitive but functional coins.

The primary reason metals became widely used as commodity money is that they meet all of the requirements for convenient trading. In addition to being of intrinsic value for uses *other* than money, they are not perishable, which is more than one can say for cows; by melting and reforming they can be divided into smaller units and conveniently used for purchases of minor items, which is not possible with diamonds, for example; and, because they are not in great abundance, small quantities carry high value, which means they are more portable than such items as timber, for example.

Perhaps the most important monetary attribute of metals, however, is their ability to be precisely measured. It is important to keep in mind that, in its fundamental form and function, money is both a storehouse and a *measure* of value. It is the reference by which all other things in the economy can be compared. It is essential, therefore, that the monetary unit itself be both measurable and constant. The ability to precisely assay metals in both purity and weight makes them ideally suited for this function. Experts may haggle over the precise quality of a gemstone, but an ingot of metal is either 99% pure or it isn't, and it either weighs 100 ounces or it doesn't. One's opinion has little to do with it. It is not without reason, therefore, that, on every continent and throughout history, man has chosen metals as the ideal storehouse and measure of value.

THE SUPREMACY OF GOLD

There is one metal, of course, that has been selected by centuries of trial and error above all others. Even today, in a world where money can no longer be defined, the common man instinctively knows that gold will do just fine until something better comes along. We shall leave it to the sociologists to debate *why* gold has been chosen as the universal money. For our purposes, it is only important to know that it *has* been. But we should not overlook the possibility that it was an excellent choice. As for quantity, there seems to be just the right amount to keep its value high enough for useful coinage. It is less plentiful than silver —which, incidentally, has run a close second in the monetary contest—and more abundant than platinum. Either could have served the purpose quite well, but gold has provided what appears to be the perfect compromise. Furthermore, it is a commodity in great demand for purposes other than money. It is sought for both industry and ornament, thus assuring its intrinsic value under all conditions. And, of course, its purity and weight can be precisely measured.

THE MISLEADING THEORY OF QUANTITY

It often is argued that gold is inappropriate as money because it is too limited in supply to satisfy the needs of modern commerce. On the surface, that may sound logical—after all, we *do* need a lot of money out there to keep the wheels of the economy turning—but, upon examination, this turns out to be one of the most childish ideas imaginable.

First of all, it is estimated that approximately 45% of all the gold mined throughout the world since the discovery of America is now in government or banking stockpiles.[1] There undoubtedly is at least an additional 30% in jewelry, ornaments, and private hoards. Any commodity which exists to the extent of 75% of its total world production since Columbus discovered America can hardly be described as in short supply.

The deeper reality, however, is that the supply is not even important. Remember that the primary function of money is to *measure* the value of the items for which it is exchanged. In this sense, it serves as a yardstick or ruler of value. It really makes no difference if we measure the length of our rug in inches, feet, yards, or meters. We could even manage it quite well in *miles* if we used decimals and expressed the result in *millimiles*. We could even use multiple rulers, but no matter what measurement we use, the reality of what we are measuring does not change. Our rug does not become larger just because we have increased the quantity of measurement units by painting additional markers onto our rulers.

If the supply of gold in relation to the supply of available goods is so small that a one-ounce coin would be too valuable for minor transactions, people simply would use half-ounce coins or tenth-ounce coins. The amount of gold in the world does not affect its ability to serve as money, it only affects the *quantity* that will be used to measure any given transaction.

Let us illustrate the point by imagining that we are playing a game of Monopoly. Each person has been given a starting supply of play money with which to transact business. It doesn't take long before we all begin to feel the shortage of cash. If we just had more *money*, we could really wheel and deal. Let us suppose further that someone discovers another game-box of Monopoly sitting in the

---

1. See Elgin Groseclose, *Money and Man: A survey of Monetary Experience*, 4th ed. (Oklahoma: University of Oklahoma Press, 1976), p. 259.

closet and proposes that the currency from that be added to the game under progress. By general agreement, the little bills are distributed equally among all players. What would happen?

The money supply has now been doubled. We all have twice as much money as we did a moment before. But would we be any better off? There is no corresponding increase in the quantity of property, so everyone would bid up the prices of existing pieces until they became twice as expensive. In other words, the law of supply and demand would rapidly seek exactly the same equilibrium as existed with the more limited money supply. When the quantity of money expands without a corresponding increase in goods, the effect is a reduction in the purchasing power of each monetary unit. In other words, nothing really changes except that the quoted price of everything goes up. But that is merely the *quoted* price, the price as expressed in terms of the monetary unit. In truth, the *real* price, in terms of its relationship to all other prices, remains the same. It's merely that the relative value of the money supply has gone down. This, of course, is the classic mechanism of inflation. Prices do not go up. The value of the money goes down.

If Santa Claus were to visit everyone on Earth next Christmas and leave in our stockings an amount of money exactly equal to the amount we already had, there is no doubt that many would rejoice over the sudden increase in wealth. By New Year's day, however, prices would have doubled for everything, and the net result on the world's standard of living would be exactly zero.[1]

The reason so many people fall for the appealing argument that the economy needs a larger money supply is that they zero in only on the need to increase *their* supply. If they paused for a moment to reflect on the consequences of the *total* supply increasing, the nonsense of the proposal becomes immediately apparent.

Murray Rothbard, professor of economics at the University of Nevada at Las Vegas, says:

> We come to the startling truth that *it doesn't matter what the supply of money is.* Any supply will do as well as any other supply. The free market will simply adjust by changing the purchasing power, or effectiveness, of its gold-unit. There is no need whatever for any planned increase in the money supply, for the supply to rise to offset

---

1. Those who rushed to market first, however, would benefit temporarily from the old prices. Under inflation, those who save are punished.

any condition, or to follow any artificial criteria. More money does not supply more capital, is not more productive, does not permit "economic growth."[1]

GOLD GUARANTEES PRICE STABILITY

The Federal Reserve claims that one of its primary objectives is to stabilize prices. In this, of course, it has failed miserably. The irony, however, is that maintaining stable prices is the easiest thing in the world. All we have to do is stop tinkering with the money supply and let the free market do its job. Prices become *automatically* stable under a commodity money system, and this is particularly true under a gold standard.

Economists like to illustrate the workings of the marketplace by creating hypothetical micro and macro economies in which everything is reduced to only a few factors and a few people. In that spirit, therefore, let us create a hypothetical economy consisting of only two classes of people: gold miners and tailors. Let us suppose that the law of supply and demand has settled on the value of one ounce of gold to be equal to a fine, custom-tailored suit of clothes. That means that the labor, tools, materials, and talent required to mine and refine one ounce of gold are equally traded for the labor, tools, and talent required to weave and tailor the suit. Up until now, the number of ounces of gold produced each year have been roughly equal to the number of fine suits made each year, so prices have remained stable. The price of a suit is one ounce of gold, and the value of one ounce of gold is equal to one finely-tailored suit.

Let us now suppose that the miners, in their quest for a better standard of living, work extra hours and produce more gold this year than previously—or that they discover a new lode of gold which greatly increases the available supply with little extra effort. Now things are no longer in balance. There are more ounces of gold than there are suits. The result of this expansion of the money supply over and above the supply of available goods is the same as in our game of Monopoly. The quoted prices of the suits go up because the relative value of the gold has gone down.

The process does not end there, however. When the miners see that they are no better off than before in spite of the extra work, and especially when they see the tailors making a greater profit for no

---

1. Murray Rothbard, *What Has Government Done to Our Money?* (Larkspur, Colorado: Pine Tree Press, 1964), p. 13.

increase in labor, some of them decide to put down their picks and turn to the trade of tailoring. In other words, they are responding to the law of supply and demand in labor. When this happens, the annual production of gold goes down while the production of suits goes up, and an equilibrium is reached once again in which suits and gold are traded as before. The free market, if unfettered by politicians and money mechanics, will always maintain a stable price structure which is automatically regulated by the underlying factor of human effort. The human effort required to extract one ounce of gold from the earth will always be approximately equal to the amount of human effort required to provide the goods and services for which it is freely exchanged.

CIGARETTES AS MONEY

A perfect example of how commodities tend to self-regulate their value occurred in Germany at the end of World War II. The German mark had become useless, and barter was common. But one item of exchange, namely cigarettes, actually became a commodity money, and they served quite well. Some cigarettes were smuggled into the country, but most of them were brought in by U.S. servicemen. In either case, the quantity was limited and the demand was high. A single cigarette was considered small change. A package of twenty and a carton of two hundred served as larger units of currency. If the exchange rate began to fall too low—in other words, if the quantity of cigarettes tended to expand at a rate faster than the expansion of other goods—the holders of the currency, more than likely, would smoke some of it rather than spend it. The supply would diminish and the value would return to its previous equilibrium. That is not theory, it actually happened.[1]

With gold as the monetary base, we would expect that improvements in manufacturing technology would gradually reduce the cost of production, causing, not *stability*, but a *downward* movement of all prices. That downward pressure, however, is partially offset by an increase in the cost of the more sophisticated tools that are required. Furthermore, similar technological efficiencies are being applied in the field of mining, so everything tends to balance out. History has shown that changes in this natural equilibrium are minimal and occur only gradually over a long

---

1. See Galbraith, p. 250.

period of time. For example, in 1913, the year the Federal Reserve was enacted into law, the average annual wage in America was $633. The exchange value of gold that year was $20.67. That means that the average worker earned the equivalent of 30.6 ounces of gold per year.

In 1990, the average annual wage had risen to $20,468. That is a whopping increase of 3,233 per cent, an average rise of 42 per cent each year for 77 years. But the exchange value of gold in 1990 had also risen. It was at $386.90 per ounce. The average worker, therefore, was earning the equivalent of 52.9 ounces of gold per year. That is an increase of only 73 per cent, a rise of less than 1 per cent per year over that same period. It is obvious that the dramatic increase in the size of the paycheck was meaningless to the average American. The reality has been a small but steady increase in purchasing power (about 1 per cent per year) that has resulted from the gradual improvement in technology. This and only this has improved the standard of living and brought down real prices—as revealed by the relative value of gold.

In areas where personal service is the primary factor and where technology is less important, the stability of gold as a measure of value is even more striking. At the Savoy Hotel in London, one gold sovereign will still buy dinner for three, exactly as it did in 1913. And, in ancient Rome, the cost of a finely made toga, belt, and pair of sandals was one ounce of gold. That is almost exactly the same cost today, two-thousand years later, for a hand-crafted suit, belt, and a pair of dress shoes. There are no central banks or other human institutions which could even come close to providing that kind of price stability. And, yet, it is totally automatic under a gold standard.

In any event, before leaving the subject of gold, we should acknowledge that there is nothing mystical about it. It is merely a commodity which, because it has intrinsic value and possesses certain qualities, has become accepted throughout history as a medium of exchange. Hitler waged a campaign against gold as a tool of the Jewish bankers. But the Nazis traded heavily in gold and largely financed their war machine with it. Lenin claimed that gold was used only to keep the workers in bondage and that, after the revolution, it would be used to cover the floors of public lavatories. The Soviet Union under Communism became one of the world's biggest producers and users of gold. Economist John Maynard

Keynes once dismissed gold as a "barbaric metal." Many followers of Keynes today are heavily invested in gold. It is entirely possible, of course, that something other than gold *would* be better as the basis for money. It's just that, in over two thousand years, no one has been able to find it.

NATURAL LAW NO. 1

The amazing stability of gold as a measure of value is simply the result of human nature reacting to the forces of supply and demand. The process, therefore, may be stated as a natural law of human behavior:

LESSON: When gold (or silver) is used as money and when the forces of supply and demand are not thwarted by government intervention, the amount of new metal added to the money supply will always be closely proportional to the expanding services and goods which can be purchased with it. Long-term stability of prices is the dependable result of these forces. This process is automatic and impartial. Any attempt by politicians to intervene will destroy the benefit for all. Therefore,

LAW: Long-term price stability is possible only when the money supply is based upon the gold (or silver) supply without government interference.

As the concept of money was slowly developing in the mind of ancient man, it became obvious that one of the advantages of using gold or silver as the medium of exchange was that, because of their rarity as compared to copper or iron, great value could be represented by small size. Tiny ingots could be carried in a pouch or fastened to a belt for ease of transportation. And, of course, they could be more readily hidden for safekeeping. Goldsmiths then began to fashion them into round discs and to put their stamps on them to attest to purity and weight. In this way, the world's first coins began to make their appearance.

It is believed that the first precious metal coins were minted by the Lydians in Asia Minor (now Northwest Turkey), in about 600 B.C. The Chinese used gold cubes as early as 2100 B.C. But it wasn't until the kings stepped into the picture that true coinage became a reality. It was only when the *state* certified the tiny discs that they became widely accepted, and it is to the Greeks more than anyone that we owe this development. Groseclose describes the result:

These light, shining discs, adorned with curious new emblems and a variety of vigorous, striking images, made a deep impression on both Greek and barbarian. And to the more practical minded, the abundance of uniform pieces of metal, each of a standard weight, certified by the authority of the state, meant a release from the cumbersomeness of barter and new and dazzling opportunities in every direction....

All classes of men succumbed to money, and those who had formerly been content to produce only for their needs and the necessities of the household, found themselves going to the market place with their handicraft, or the fruits of their toil, to exchange them for the coins they might obtain.[1]

EXPANDING THE MONEY SUPPLY BY COIN CLIPPING

From the very beginning, the desire for a *larger* money supply led to practices which were destructive to the economy. Unscrupulous merchants began to shave off a tiny portion of each coin they handled—a process known as coin clipping—and then having the shavings melted down into new coins. Before long, the king's treasury began to do the same thing to the coins it received in taxes. In this way, the money supply was increased, but the supply of gold was not. The result was exactly what we now know always happens when the money supply is artificially expanded. There was inflation. Whereas one coin previously would buy twelve sheep, now it would only be accepted for ten. The total amount of gold needed for twelve sheep never really changed. It's just that everyone knew that one coin no longer contained it.

As governments became more brazen in their debasement of the currency, even to the extent of diluting the gold or silver content, the population adapted quite well by simply "discounting" the new coins. That is to say, they accepted them at a realistic value, which was lower than what the government had intended. This was, as always, reflected in a general rise in prices quoted in terms of those coins. *Real* prices, in terms of labor or other goods or even of gold itself remained unchanged.

Governments do not like to be thwarted in their plans to exploit their subjects. So a way had to be found to *force* people to accept these slugs as real money. This led to the first legal-tender laws. By royal decree, the "coin of the realm," was declared legal for the

---

1. Groseclose, *Money and Man*, p. 13.

settlement of all debts. Anyone who refused it *at face value* was subject to fine, imprisonment, or, in some cases, even death. The result was that the good coins disappeared from circulation and went into private hoards. After all, if the government forces you to accept junk at the same rate of exchange as gold, wouldn't you keep the gold and spend the junk? That is what happened in America in the '60s when the mint began to issue cheap metal tokens to replace the silver dimes, quarters, and half-dollars. Within a few months, the silver coins were in dresser drawers and safe-deposit boxes. The same thing has happened repeatedly throughout antiquity. In economics, that is called Gresham's Law: "Bad money drives out good."

The final move in this game of legal plunder was for the government to fix prices so that, even if everyone is using only junk as money, they can no longer compensate for the continually expanding supply of it. Now the people were caught. They had no escape except to become criminals, which most of them, incidentally, chose to do. The history of artificially expanding money is the history of great dissatisfaction with government, much lawlessness, and a massive underground economy.

GOLD IS THE ENEMY OF THE WELFARE STATE

In more modern times, rulers of nations have become more sophisticated in the methods by which they debase the currency. Instead of clipping coins, it is done through the banking system. The *consequences* of that process were summarized in 1966 by Alan Greenspan who, a few years later, would become Chairman of the Board of Governors of the Federal Reserve. Greenspan wrote:

> The abandonment of the gold standard made it possible for the welfare statists *to use the banking system* as a means to an unlimited expansion of credit....
>
> The law of supply and demand is not to be conned. As the supply of money (of claims) increases relative to the supply of tangible assets in the economy, prices must eventually rise. Thus the earnings saved by the productive members of the society lose value in terms of goods. When the economy's books are finally balanced, one finds that this loss in value represents the goods purchased by the government for welfare or other purposes....
>
> In the absence of the gold standard, there is no way to protect savings from confiscation through inflation. There is no safe store of value. If there were, the government would have to make its holding illegal, as was done in the case of gold.... The financial policy of the

welfare state requires that there be no way for the owners of wealth to protect themselves.

This is the shabby secret of the welfare statists' tirades against gold. Deficit spending is simply a scheme for the "hidden" confiscation of wealth. Gold stands in the way of this insidious process. It stands as a protector of property rights.[1]

Unfortunately, when Greenspan was appointed as Chairman of the Federal Reserve System, he became silent on the issue of gold. Once he was seated at the control panel which holds the levers of power, he served the statists well as they continued to confiscate the people's wealth through the hidden tax of inflation. Even the wisest of men can be corrupted by power and wealth.

REAL COMMODITY MONEY IN HISTORY

Returning to the topic of debasing the currency in ancient times, it must be stated that such practices were by no means universal. There are many examples throughout history of regents and kingdoms which used great restraint in money creation. Ancient Greece, where coinage was first developed, is one of them. The *drachma* became the defacto monetary unit of the civilized world because of the dependability of its gold content. Within its borders, cities flourished and trade abounded. Even after the fall of Athens in the Peloponnesian War, her coinage remained, for centuries, as *the* standard by which all others were measured.[2]

Perhaps the greatest example of a nation with sound money, however, was the Byzantine Empire. Building on the sound monetary tradition of Greece, the emperor Constantine ordered the creation of a new gold piece called the *solidus* and a silver piece called the *miliarense*. The gold weight of the *solidus* soon became fixed at 65 grains and was minted at that standard for the next eight-hundred years. Its quality was so dependable that it was freely accepted, under the name *bezant*, from China to Brittany, from the Baltic Sea to Ethiopia.

Byzantine laws regarding money were strict. Before being admitted to the profession of banking, the candidate had to have sponsors who would attest to his character, that he would not file

---

1. Alan Greenspan, "Gold and Economic Freedom," in *Capitalism: The Unknown Ideal*, ed. Ayn Rand (New York: Signet Books, 1967), p. 101.
2. Even the Greeks, under Solon, had one, brief experience with a debased currency. But it was short lived, and never repeated. See Groseclose, *Money and Man*, pp. 14, 20–54.

or chip either the *solidi* or the *miliarensia,* and that he would not issue false coin. Violation of these rules called for cutting off a hand.[1]

It is an amazing fact of history that the Byzantine Empire flourished as the center of world commerce for eight-hundred years without falling into bankruptcy nor, for that matter, even into debt. Not once during this period did it devalue its money. "Neither the ancient nor the modern world," says Heinrich Gelzer, "can offer a complete parallel to this phenomenon. This prodigious stability...secured the *bezant* as universal currency. On account of its full weight, it passed with all the neighboring nations as a valid medium of exchange. By her money, Byzantium controlled both the civilized and the barbarian worlds."[2]

BAD COMMODITY MONEY IN HISTORY

The experience of the Romans was quite different. Basically a militaristic people, they had little patience for the niceties of monetary restraint. Especially in the later Empire, debasement of the coinage became a deliberate state policy. Every imaginable means for plundering the people was devised. In addition to taxation, coins were clipped, reduced, diluted, and plated. Favored groups were given franchises for state-endorsed monopolies, the origin of our present-day corporation. And, amidst constantly rising prices in terms of constantly expanding money, speculation and dishonesty became rampant.

By the year 301 A.D., mutiny was developing in the army, remote regions were displaying disloyalty, the treasury was empty, agriculture depressed, and trade almost at a standstill. It was then that Diocletian issued his famous price-fixing proclamation as the last measure of a desperate emperor. We are struck by the similarity to such proclamations in our own time. Most of the chaos can be traced directly to government policy. Yet, the politicians point the accusing finger at everyone else for their "greed" and "disregard for the common good." Diocletian declared:

---

1. *Le livre du préfet ou l'empereur Léon le Sage sur les corporations de Constantinople,* French translation from the Geneva text by Jules Nicole, p. 38. Cited by Groseclose, *Money and Man,* p. 52.
2. Byzantininsche Kulturgeschichte (Tübingen, 1909), p. 78. As quoted by Groseclose, *Money and Man,* p. 54.

Who is of so hardened a heart and so untouched by a feeling of humanity that he can be unaware, nay that he has not noticed, that in the sale of wares which are exchanged in the market, or dealt with in the daily business of the cities, an exorbitant tendency in prices has spread to such an extent that the unbridled desire of plundering is held in check neither by abundance nor by seasons of plenty.... Inasmuch as there is seen only a mad desire without control, to pay no heed to the needs of the many,...it seems good to us, as we look into the future, to us who are the fathers of the people, that justice intervene to settle matters impartially.[1]

What followed was an incredibly detailed list of mandated prices for everything from a serving of beer or a bunch of watercress to a lawyer's fee and a bar of gold. The result? Conditions became even worse, and the royal decree was rescinded five years later.

The Roman Empire never recovered from the crisis. By the fourth century, all coins were weighed, and the economy was slipping back into barter again. By the seventh century, the weights themselves had been so frequently changed that it was no longer possible to effect an exchange in money at all. For all practical purposes, money became extinct, and the Roman Empire was no more.

RECEIPT MONEY

When new civilizations rose from the ruins of Rome, they reclaimed the lost discovery of money and used it to great advantage. The invention was truly a giant step forward for mankind, but there were many problems yet to be solved and much experimentation lay ahead. The development of paper money was a case in point. When a man accumulated more coins than he required for daily purchases, he needed a safe place to store them. The goldsmiths, who handled large amounts of precious metals in their trades, had already built sturdy vaults to protect their own inventory, so it was natural for them to offer vault space to their customers for a fee. The goldsmith could be trusted to guard the coins well because he also would be guarding his own wealth.

When the coins were placed into the vault, the warehouseman would give the owner a written receipt which entitled him to

---

1. As quoted by Groseclose, *Money and Man*, pp. 43–44.

withdraw at any time. At first, the only way the coins could be taken from the vault was for the owner to personally present the receipt. Eventually, however, it became customary for the owner to merely endorse his receipt to a third party who, upon presentation, could make the withdrawal. These endorsed receipts were the forerunners of today's checks.

The final stage in this development was the custom of issuing, not just one receipt for the entire deposit, but a series of smaller receipts, adding up to the same total, and each having printed across the top: PAY TO THE BEARER ON DEMAND. As the population learned from experience that these paper receipts were truly backed by good coin in the goldsmith's warehouse and that the coin really would be given out in exchange for the receipts, it became increasingly common to use the paper instead of the coin.

Thus, *receipt money* came into existence. The paper itself was useless, but what it represented was quite valuable. As long as the coin was held in safe keeping as promised, there was no difference in value between the receipt and the coin which backed it. And, as we shall see in the next chapter, there were notable examples of the honest use of receipt money at the very beginning of the development of banking. When the receipt was scrupulously honored, the economy moved forward. When it was used as a gimmick for the artificial expansion of the money supply, the economy convulsed and stagnated.

NATURAL LAW NO. 2

This is not a textbook on the history of money, so we cannot afford the luxury of lingering among the fascinating details. For our purposes, it is sufficient to recognize that human behavior in these matters is predictable and, because of that predictability, it is possible to formulate another principle that is so universal that it, too, may be considered a natural law. Drawing from the vast experience of this early period, it can be stated as follows:

LESSON: Whenever government sets out to manipulate the money supply, regardless of the intelligence or good intentions of those who attempt to direct the process, the result is inflation, economic chaos, and political upheaval. By contrast, whenever government is limited in its monetary power to only the maintenance of honest weights and measures of precious metals, the result is price stability, economic prosperity, and political tranquility. Therefore,

LAW: For a nation to enjoy economic prosperity and political tranquility, the monetary power of its politicians must be limited solely to the maintenance of honest weights and measures of precious metals.

As we shall see in the following chapters, the centuries of monetary upheaval that followed that early period contain no evidence that this law has been repealed by modern man.

SUMMARY

Knowledge of the nature of money is essential to an understanding of the Federal Reserve. Contrary to common belief, the topic is neither mysterious nor complicated. For the purposes of this study, money is defined as anything which is accepted as a medium of exchange. Building on that, we find there are four kinds of money: commodity, receipt, fiat, and fractional. Precious metals were the first commodity money to appear in history and ever since have been proven by actual experience to be the only reliable base for an honest monetary system. Gold, as the basis of money, can take several forms: bullion, coins, and fully backed paper receipts. Man has been plagued throughout history with the false theory that the quantity of money is important, specifically that more money is better than less. This has led to perpetual manipulation and expansion of the money supply through such practices as coin clipping, debasement of the coin content, and, in later centuries, the issuance of more paper receipts than there was gold to back them. In every case, these practices have led to economic and political disaster. In those rare instances where man has refrained from manipulating the money supply and has allowed it to be determined by free-market production of the gold supply, the result has been prosperity and tranquility.

Chapter Eight

FOOL'S GOLD

The history of paper money without precious-metal backing forced on the public by government decree; the emergence of our present-day fractional-reserve banking system based on the issuance of a greater amount of receipts for gold than the bank has in gold to back them up.

We previously have broken down the concept of money into four categories: commodity, receipt, fiat, and fractional. In the last chapter we examined commodity and receipt money in some detail. In doing so, we also established certain monetary principles which apply regardless of their form. We shall now turn to the remaining two categories, both of which are represented by paper and which are at the root of almost all of modern man's economic woes.

FIAT MONEY

The *American Heritage Dictionary* defines fiat money as "paper money decreed legal tender, not backed by gold or silver." The two characteristics of fiat money, therefore, are (1) it does not represent anything of intrinsic value and (2) it is decreed legal tender. Legal tender simply means that there is a law requiring everyone to accept the currency in commerce. The two always go together because, since the money really is worthless, it soon would be rejected by the public in favor of a more reliable medium of exchange, such as gold or silver coin. Thus, when governments issue fiat money, they always declare it to be legal tender under pain of fine or imprisonment. The only way a government can exchange its worthless paper money for tangible goods and services is to give its citizens no choice.

The first notable use of this practice was recorded by Marco Polo during his travels to China in the thirteenth century. The famous explorer gives us this account:

The Emperor's mint then is in this same City of Cambaluc, and the way it is wrought is such that you might say he hath the Secret of Alchemy in perfection, and you would be right!...

What they take is a certain fine white bast or skin which lies between the wood of the tree and the thick outer bark, and this they make into something resembling sheets of paper, but black. When these sheets have been prepared they are cut up into pieces of different sizes. The smallest of these sizes is worth a half tornesel.... There is also a kind worth one Bezant of gold, and others of three Bezants, and so up to ten.

All these pieces of paper are issued with as much solemnity and authority as if they were of pure gold or silver; and on every piece, a variety of officials, whose duty it is, have to write their names and to put their seals. And when all is prepared duly, the chief officer deputed by the Kaan smears the Seal entrusted to him with vermilion and impresses it on the paper, so that the form of the Seal remains stamped upon it in red; the money is then authentic. Any one forging it would be punished with death. And the Kaan causes every year to be made such a vast quantity of this money, which costs him nothing, that it must equal in amount all the treasures in the world.

With these pieces of paper, made as I have described, he causes all payments on his own account to be made, and he makes them to pass current universally over all his Kingdoms.... And nobody, however important he may think himself, dares to refuse them on pain of death. And indeed everybody takes them readily.[1]

One is tempted to marvel at the Kaan's audacious power and the subservience of his subjects who endured such an outrage; but our smugness rapidly vanishes when we consider the similarity to our own Federal Reserve Notes. They are adorned with signatures and seals; counterfeiters are severely punished; the government pays its expenses with them; the population is forced to accept them; they—and the "invisible" checkbook money into which they can be converted—are made in such vast quantity that it must equal in amount all the treasures of the world. And yet they cost nothing to make. In truth, our present monetary system is an almost exact replica of that which supported the warlords of seven centuries ago.

---

1. Original from Henry Thule's edition of *Marco Polo's Travels*, reprinted in W. Vissering, *On Chinese Currency: Coin and Paper Money* (Leiden: E.J. Brill, 1877), reprinted 1968 by Ch'eng-wen Publishing Co., Taiwan, as cited by Anthony Sutton, *The War on Gold* (Seal Beach, California: '76 Press, 1977), pp. 26–28.

THE COLONIAL EXPERIENCE

Unfortunately, the present situation is not unique to our history. In fact, after China, the next place in the world to adopt the use of fiat money was America; specifically, the Massachusetts Bay Colony. This event has been described as "not only the origin of paper money in America, but also in the British Empire, and almost in the Christian world."[1]

In 1690, Massachusetts launched a military raid against the French colony in Quebec. She had done this before and, each time, had brought back sufficient plunder to more than pay for the expedition. This time, however, the foray was a dismal failure, and the men returned empty handed. When the soldiers demanded their pay, Massachusetts found its coffers empty. Disgruntled soldiers have a way of becoming unruly, so the officials scrambled for some way to raise the funds. Additional taxes would have been extremely unpopular, so they decided simply to print paper money. In order to convince the soldiers and the citizenry to accept it, the government made two solemn promises: (1) it would redeem the paper for gold or silver coin just as soon as there was sufficient tax revenue to do so, and (2) absolutely no additional paper notes would ever be issued. Both pledges were promptly broken. Only a few months later, it was announced that the original issue was insufficient to discharge the government's debt, and a new issue almost six times greater was put into circulation. The currency wasn't redeemed for nearly forty years, long after those who had made the pledge had faded from the scene.

A CLASSIC PATTERN

Most of the other colonies were quick to learn the magic of the printing press, and the history that followed is a classic example of cause and effect: Governments artificially expanded the money supply through the issuance of fiat currency. This was followed by legal tender laws to force its acceptance. Next came the disappearance of gold or silver coins which went, instead, into private hoards or to foreign traders who insisted on the real thing for their wares. Many of the colonies repudiated their previous money by issuing new bills valued at multiples of the old. Then came political

---

1. Ernest Ludlow Bogart, *Economic History of the American People* (New York: Longmans, Green and Co., 1930), p. 172.

discontent and civil disobedience. And at the end of each cycle there was rampant inflation and economic chaos.

In 1703, South Carolina declared that its money was "a good payment and tender in law" and then added that, should anyone refuse to honor it as such, they would be fined an amount equal to "double the value of the bills so refused." By 1716, the penalty had been increased to "treble the value."[1]

THE PRINTING PRESS AND INFLATION

Benjamin Franklin was an ardent proponent of fiat money during those years and used his great influence to sell the idea to the public. We can get some idea of the ferment of the times by noting that, in 1736, writing in his *Pennsylvania Gazette*, Franklin apologized for its irregular publication, and explained that the printer was "with the Press, labouring for the publick Good, to make Money more plentiful."[2] The printing of money was apparently a major, time-consuming operation.

In 1737, Massachusetts devalued its fiat currency by 66%, offering one dollar of new currency for three of the old. The promise was made that, after five years, the new money would be fully redeemed in silver or gold. The promise was not kept.[3]

By the late 1750s, Connecticut had prices inflated by 800%. The Carolinas had inflated 900%. Massachusetts 1000%. Rhode Island 2300%.[4] Naturally, these inflations all had to come to an end and, when they did, they turned into equally massive deflations and depressions. It has been shown that, even in colonial times, the classic booms and busts which modern economists are fond of blaming on an "unbridled free market" actually were direct manifestations of the expansion and contraction of fiat money which no longer was governed by the laws of supply and demand.[5]

---

1. Statutes at Large of South Carolina, II. 211,665, as cited by George Bancroft, *A Plea for the Constitution* (Originally published by Harpers in 1886. Reprinted in Sewanee, Tennessee: Spencer Judd Publishers, 1982), p. 7.
2. Leonard W. Labaree, ed., *The Papers of Benjamin Franklin* (New Haven: Yale University Press, 1960), Vol. 2, p. 159.
3. Province Laws, II. 826, cited by Bancroft, p. 14.
4. Ron Paul and Lewis Lehrman, *The Case for Gold* (Washington, D.C.: Cato Institute, 1982), p. 22. Also Sutton, *The War on Gold*, p. 44.
5. See Donald L. Kemmerer, "Paper Money in New Jersey, 1668–1775," New Jersey Historical Society, *Proceedings* 74 (April 1956): pp. 107–144, as cited by Paul and Lehrman, *The Case for Gold*, p. 22.

By this time, coins had completely disappeared from the scene. Some were in private hoards, but most of them had been exported to other countries, leaving the colonies with little choice but to use fiat money or barter. Merchants from abroad were interested in neither of those, however, and international trade ground almost to a halt.

A BLESSING IN DISGUISE

The experiment with fiat money was a calamity to the colonists, but it was also a thorn in the side of the Bank of England. The bank had used its influence with the Crown to forbid the colonies to mint their own coins or to establish local banks. This meant that, if the colonists wanted the convenience of paper money, they would be forced to use the notes issued by the Bank of England. No one had anticipated that the colonial governments would be so inventive as to create their own *paper* money. So, in 1751, Great Britain began to pressure the colonies to redeem all of their currency and withdraw it from circulation. This they eventually did, and at bargain prices. By then, their fiat money was heavily discounted in the market place and the governments were able to buy back their own currency for pennies on the dollar.

The decree from the British Parliament, although heavily resented by the colonists, turned out to be a blessing in disguise. The paper notes of the Bank of England never did become a primary medium of exchange. Probably because of their recent bad experience with paper money, the colonists merely brought what few gold and silver coins they had out of hiding and returned to a true commodity-money system. At first, the doomsdayers predicted this would spell further ruin for the colonial economy. "There isn't enough money" was the all-too-familiar cry. But there was, indeed, quite enough for, as we have already seen, *any* amount is sufficient.

TOBACCO BECOMES MONEY

There was, in fact, a period in which other commodities became accepted as a secondary medium of exchange. Such items as nails, lumber, rice, and whisky filled the monetary void, but tobacco was the most common. Here was a commodity which was in great demand both within the colonies and for overseas commerce. It had intrinsic value; it could not be counterfeited; it could be divided into almost any denominational quantity; and its supply could not be increased except by the exertion of labor. In other words, it was regulated by the law of supply and demand, which gave it great stability in value. In many ways, it was an ideal money. It was officially adopted as such by Virginia in 1642 and a few years later by Maryland, but it was used *unofficially* in all the other colonies, as well. So close was the identity of tobacco with money that the previous fiat currency of New Jersey, not a tobacco growing state, displayed a picture of a tobacco leaf on its face. It also carried the inscription: "To counterfeit is *Death*." Tobacco was used in early America as a secondary medium of exchange for about two-hundred years, until the new Constitution declared that money was, henceforth, the sole prerogative of the federal government.[1]

The primary currency at that juncture, however, was still gold and silver coin, or *specie*, as it is called. And the immediate result of returning to a sound monetary unit was a rapid recovery from the economic stagnation previously inflicted by the booms and busts of fiat money. Trade and production rose dramatically, and this, in turn, attracted an inflow of gold and silver coin from around the world, filling the void that had been created by years of worthless paper. The law of supply and demand was visibly at work. For a while, Massachusetts had returned to specie while Rhode Island remained on fiat money. The result was that Newport, which had been the trade center for the West Indies, lost its trade to Boston and became an empty port.[2] After the colonies had returned to coin, prices quickly found their natural equilibrium and then *stayed* at that point, even during the Seven Years War and the disruption of trade that occurred immediately prior to the Revolution.[3] There is no better example of the fact that economic systems in distress can and do recover rapidly if government does not interfere with the natural healing process.

WAR BRINGS A RETURN OF FIAT MONEY

The War for Independence brought all of this to a sudden halt. Wars are seldom funded out of the existing treasury, nor are they even done so out of increased taxes. If governments were to levy

1. Galbraith, pp. 48–50.
2. Paul and Lehrman, pp. 22–23.
3. "The Colonial Monetary Standard of Massachusetts," by Roger W. Weiss, *Economic History Review*, No. 27, November, 1974, p. 589.

taxes on their citizens fully adequate to finance the conflict, the amount would be so great that many of even its most ardent supporters would lose enthusiasm. By artificially increasing the money supply, however, the real cost is hidden from view. It is still paid, of course, but through inflation, a process that few people understand.

The American Revolution was no exception. In order to pay the bill for independence, both the Confederation and the individual states went heavily into the printing business. At the beginning of the war in 1775, the total money supply stood at $12 million. In June of that year, the Continental Congress issued another $2 million. Before the notes were even put into circulation, another $1 million was authorized. By the end of the year, another $3 million. In 1776, another $19 million. $13 million in 1777. $64 million in 1778. $125 million in 1779. And still more: the Continental Army issued its own "certificates" for the purchase of supplies totalling $200 million. A total of $425 million in five years on top of a base of $12 million is an increase of over 3500%. And, in addition to this massive expansion of the money supply on the part of the central government, it must be remembered that the states were doing exactly the same thing. It is estimated that, in just five years from 1775 to the end of 1779, the total money supply expanded by 5000%. By contrast, the amount raised in taxes over the five-year period was inconsequential, amounting to only a few million dollars.

AND A MASSIVE INFLATION

The first exhilarating effect of this flood of new money was the flush of apparent prosperity, but that was quickly followed by inflation as the self-destruct mechanism began to operate. In 1775, paper Continentals were traded for one dollar in gold. In 1777, they were exchanged for twenty-five cents. By 1779, just four years from their issue, they were worth less than a penny. The phrase "Not worth a Continental" has its origin in this dismal period. Shoes sold for $5,000 a pair. A suit of clothes cost a million.

It was in that year that George Washington wrote, "A wagon load of money will scarcely purchase a wagon load of provisions."[1]

---

1. Quoted by Albert S. Bolles, *The Financial History of the United States* (New York: D. Appleton, 1896, 4th ed.), Vol. I, p. 132.

Even Benjamin Franklin began to see the light. In a mood of sarcasm, he wrote:

> This Currency, as we manage it, is a wonderful machine. It performs its Office when we issue it; it pays and clothes Troops and provides Victuals and Ammunition; and when we are obliged to issue a Quantity excessive, it pays itself off by Depreciation.[1]

When speaking of deficit spending, it is common to hear the complaint that we are saddling future generations with the bill for what we enjoy today. Why *not* let those in the future help pay for what will benefit them also? Don't be deceived. That is a misconception encouraged by politicians to calm the public. When money is fiat, as the colonists discovered, every government building, public work, and cannon of war is paid out of current labor and current wealth. These things must be built *today* with *today's* labor, and the man who performs that labor must also be paid *today*. It is true that *interest* payments fall partly to future generations, but the *initial cost* is paid by those in the present. It is paid by loss of value in the monetary unit and loss of purchasing power for one's wages.

INFLATION IS A HIDDEN TAX

Fiat money is the means by which governments obtain instant purchasing power without taxation. But where does that purchasing power come from? Since fiat money has nothing of tangible value to offset it, government's fiat purchasing power can be obtained only by subtracting it from somewhere else. It is, in fact, "collected" from us all through a decline in *our* purchasing power. It is, therefore, exactly the same as a tax, but one that is hidden from view, silent in operation, and little understood by the taxpayer.

In 1786, Thomas Jefferson provided a clear explanation of this process when he wrote:

> Every one, through whose hands a bill passed, lost on that bill what it lost in value during the time it was in his hands. This was a real tax on him; and in this way the people of the United States actually contributed those... millions of dollars during the war, and by a mode of taxation the most oppressive of all because the most unequal of all.[2]

---

1. Letter to Samuel Cooper, April 22, 1779, quoted by Albert Henry Smyth, ed., *The Writings of Benjamin Franklin*, (New York: Macmillan, 1906), Vol. VII, p. 294.
2. Thomas Jefferson, *Observations on the Article Etats-Unis Prepared for the Encyclopedia*, June 22, 1786, from *Writings* (New York: G.P. Putnam's Sons, 1894), Vol. IV, p. 165.

ENTER PRICE CONTROLS AND LEGAL TENDER LAWS

As prices skyrocketed, the colonies enacted wage and price controls, which was like plugging up the whistle on a tea kettle in hopes of keeping the steam from escaping. When that failed, there followed a series of harsh legal tender laws. One law even invoked the specter of treason. It said: "If any person shall hereafter be so lost to all virtue and regard for his Country as to refuse to receive said bills in payment...he shall be deemed, published, and treated as an enemy in this Country and precluded from all trade or intercourse with the inhabitants of these colonies."[1]

Rhode Island not only levied a heavy fine for non-acceptance of its notes but, upon a *second* offense, an individual was stripped of citizenship. When a court declared the act unconstitutional, the legislature called the judges before it and summarily dismissed the offenders from office.[2]

ENTER ECONOMIC CHAOS AND INSURRECTION

If the ravages of war were a harsh burden for the colonies to bear, the havoc of fiat money was equally so. After the war, inflation was followed by deflation as reality returned to the market place. Prices fell drastically, which was wonderful for those who were buying. But, for the merchants who were *selling* or the farmers who had borrowed heavily to acquire property at inflated wartime prices, it was a disaster. The new, lower prices were not adequate to sustain their fixed, inflated mortgages, and many hard-working families were ruined by foreclosure. Furthermore, most people still did not understand the inflation process, and there were many who continued to advocate the "paper money cure." Several of the states were receptive to the pressure, and their printing presses continued to roll.

Historian Andrew McLaughlin recalls a typical scene in Rhode Island at that time as witnessed by a visiting Frenchman:

> A French traveler who passed through Newport about this time gives a dismal picture of the place: idle men standing with folded arms at the corners of the streets; houses falling to ruins; miserable shops offering for sale nothing but a few coarse stuffs;...grass growing in the streets; windows stuffed with rags; everywhere announcing misery,

---

1. David Ramsay, *History of the American Revolution* (London: Johnson and Stockdale, 1791), Vol. II, pp. 134–36.
2. Merrill Jensen, *The New Nation* (New York: Vintage Books, 1950), p. 324.

the triumph of paper money and the influence of bad government. The merchants had closed their stores rather than take payment in paper; farmers from neighboring states did not care to bring their produce.[1]

Idleness and economic depression also led to outbursts of rebellion and insurrection. In 1786, George Washington wrote to James Warren: "The wheels of government are clogged and ... we are descending into the vale of confusion and darkness."[2] Two years later, in a letter to Henry Knox, he said: "If ... any person had told me that there would have been such formidable rebellion as exists, I would have thought him a bedlamite, a fit subject for a madhouse."[3]

Fortunately, there is a happy ending to that part of the story. As we shall see in a subsequent chapter, when the state delegates assembled to draft the Constitution, the effects of fiat money were so fresh in their minds they decided to put an end to it once and for all. Then, the new republic not only rapidly recovered but went on to become the economic envy of the world—for a while, at least—until the lesson had been forgotten by following generations. But that is getting ahead of our story. For now, we are dealing with the topic of fiat money; and the experience of the American colonies is a classic example of what *always* happens when men succumb to its siren call.

NATURAL LAW NO. 3

Let us pause at this point and observe another of those lessons derived from centuries of experience. That lesson is so clear and so universal and so widely seen throughout history that it may be stated as a natural law of human behavior:

> LESSON: Fiat money is paper money without precious-metal backing and which people are required by law to accept. It allows politicians to increase spending without raising taxes. Fiat money is the cause of inflation, and the amount which people lose in purchasing power is exactly the amount which was taken from them and transferred to their government by this process. Inflation, therefore, is a hidden tax.

---

1. Andrew C. McLaughlin, *The Confederation and the Constitution* (New York: Collier Books, 1962), pp. 107–08.
2. Harry Atwood, *The Constitution Explained* (Merrimac, Massachusetts: Destiny Publishers, 1927; 2nd ed. 1962), p. 3.
3. *Ibid.*, p. 4.

This tax is the most unfair of all because it falls most heavily on those who are least able to pay: the small wage earner and those on fixed incomes. It also punishes the thrifty by eroding the value of their savings. This creates resentment among the people, leading always to political unrest and national disunity. Therefore,

LAW: A nation that resorts to the use of fiat money has doomed itself to economic hardship and political disunity.

FRACTIONAL MONEY

Let us turn, now, to the fourth and final possible form of money: a most intriguing concept called *fractional money*. And, to understand how this functions, we must return to Europe and the practice of the early goldsmiths who stored the precious metal coins of their customers for a fee.

In addition to the goldsmiths who *stored* coins, there was another class of merchants, called "scriveners," who *lent* coins. The goldsmiths reasoned that they, too, could act as scriveners, but do so with *other* people's money. They said it was a pity for all that coin to just sit idle in their vaults. Why not lend it out and earn a profit which then could be split between themselves and their depositors? Put it to *work*, instead of merely gathering dust. They had learned from experience that very few of their depositors ever wanted to remove their coins at the same time. In fact, net withdrawals seldom exceeded ten or fifteen per cent of their stockpile. It seemed perfectly safe to lend up to eighty or even eighty-five per cent of their coins. And so the warehousemen began to act as loan brokers on behalf of their depositors, and the concept of banking, as we know it today, was born.

That's the way many history books describe it, but there is more involved here than merely putting idle money to work. First of all, sharing the interest income with the owners of the deposits was not part of the original concept. That only became general practice many years later after the depositors became outraged and needed to be reassured that these loans were in their interest as well. In the beginning, they didn't even know that their coins were being lent out. They naively thought that the goldsmiths were lending their *own* money.

DEPOSITS ARE NOT AVAILABLE FOR LENDING

In the second place, we need to consider whether the coin in the vault was even *available* for lending—regardless of whether or not the depositors received a part of the profit. Let us suppose that we are playing a game of poker at the home of Charlie Smith. Each of us has given $20 to Charlie who, acting as the banker, has put our money into a shoe box and given us, in return, twenty poker chips. It is the understanding that, anytime we want to go home, we can get back a dollar for each chip we have at that time. Now let us suppose that Charlie's brother-in-law, Larry, shows up, not to play poker, but to borrow some money. Since six of us are playing and each has put in $20, there is a total of $120 in the shoe box, and that turns out to be perfect for Larry's needs. You can imagine what would happen if Charlie decided to lend out the "idle" money. It is not *available* for lending.

Neither Charlie nor any of the players have the right to lend *those* dollars, because they are being held in escrow, so to speak, pending completion of the contract between Charlie and his guests. Those dollars no longer even exist as money. They have been replaced—in concept at least—by the poker chips. If any of us are so touched by Larry's story that we decide to lend him the money ourselves, we would have to do it with *other* dollars or cash in our chips for the dollars in the shoe box. In that case, of course, we could no longer stay in the game. *We cannot spend, lend, or give away the deposit and also consider the chips to be worth anything.*

If you are a member of an organization and have given your proxy to a friend to vote in your absence at the annual meeting, you cannot then show up and cast your own vote *in addition* to your proxy. Likewise, in the beginning of banking, the certificates which were circulated as money were, in effect, *proxies* for the coins. Consequently, those coins were not *available* for lending. Their monetary value had been assigned to the certificates. If the certificate holders had wanted to lend out their coins, they should have retired the certificates first. They were not entitled to hold spendable paper money and *also* authorize their banker to lend that same money as coins. *One cannot spend, lend, or give away the coins and also consider the certificates to be worth anything.*

All of this is just common sense. But there is another dimension to the problem which has to do with honesty in business contracts.

When the bankers used those coins as the basis for loans, they were putting themselves in a position of not having enough coin in the vault to make good on their contracts when it came time for depositors to take their money home. In other words, the new contracts were made with the full knowledge that, under certain circumstances, they would have to be broken. But the bankers never bothered to explain that. The general public was led to believe that, if they approved of putting these supposedly idle funds to work, they would be helping the economy and earning a little profit besides. It was an appealing proposal, and the idea caught on like wildfire.

FRACTIONAL-RESERVE BANKING

Most borrowers wanted paper money, of course, not bulky coins, so, when they received their loans, they usually put the coins right back into the vault for safekeeping. They were then given *receipts* for these deposits which, as we have observed, were readily accepted in commerce as money. At this point, things began to get complicated. The original depositors had been given receipts for all of the bank's coins. But the bank now issued loans in the amount of eighty-five per cent of its deposits, and the borrowers were given receipts for that same amount. These were *in addition to* the original receipts. That made 85% *more* receipts than *coins*. Thus, the banks *created* 85% more money and placed it into circulation through their borrowers. In other words, by issuing phony receipts, they artificially expanded the money supply. At this point, the certificates were no longer 100% backed by gold. They now had a backing of only 54%,[1] but they were accepted by the unsuspecting public as equal in value to the old receipts. The gold behind all of them, however, now represented only a fraction of their face value. Thus, the receipts became what may be called *fractional money*, and the process by which they were created is called *fractional-reserve banking*.

None of this shortfall, unfortunately, was ever explained. The bankers decided that it would be better not to discuss reality where the public could hear. These facts became the arcane secrets of the profession. The depositors were never encouraged to question how the banks could lend out their money and still have it on hand to

---

1.   100 units of gold divided by 185 certificates equals .54

pay back on an instant's notice. Instead, bankers put on great airs of respectability, stability, and accountability; dressed and acted serious if not stern; erected great edifices resembling government buildings and temples, all to bolster the false image of being able to honor their contracts to pay *on demand*.

It was John Maynard Keynes who observed:

> A "sound" banker, alas! is not one who foresees danger, and avoids it, but one who, when he is ruined, is ruined in a conventional and orthodox way along with his fellows, so that no one can readily blame him. It is necessarily part of the business of a banker to maintain appearances, and to confess a conventional respectability, which is more than human. Life-long practices of this kind make them the most romantic and the least realistic of men.[1]

CREATING MONEY OUT OF DEBT

Let us step back for a moment and analyze. In the beginning, banks served as warehouses for the safe keeping of their customers' coins. When they issued paper receipts for those coins, they converted commodity money into receipt money. This was a great convenience, but it did not alter the money supply. People had a choice of using either coin or paper but they could not use both. If they used coin, the receipt was never issued. If they used the receipt, the coin remained in the vault and did not circulate.

When the banks abandoned this practice and began to issue receipts to *borrowers*, they became magicians. Some have said they created money out of nothing, but that is not quite true. What they did was even more amazing. They created money out of *debt*.

Obviously, it is easier for people to go into debt than to mine gold. Consequently, money no longer was limited by the natural forces of supply and demand. From that point in history forward, it was to be limited only by the degree to which bankers have been able to push down the gold-reserve fraction of their deposits.

From this perspective, we can now look back on fractional money and recognize that it really is a transitional form between receipt money and fiat money. It has some of the characteristics of both. As the fraction becomes smaller, the less it resembles receipt money and the more closely it comes to fiat money. When the fraction finally reaches zero, then it has made the complete

---

1. As quoted by Lever and Huhne, *Debt and Danger: The World Financial Crisis* (New York: The Atlantic Monthly, 1986), p. 42.

transition and becomes pure fiat. Furthermore, there is no example in history where men, once they had accepted the concept of fractional money, didn't reduce the fraction lower and lower until, eventually, it became zero.

No bank can stay in business for very long with a zero reserve. The only way to make people accept such a worthless currency is by government force. That's what legal-tender laws are all about. The transition from fractional-reserve money to fiat money, therefore, requires the participation of government through a mechanism which is called a central bank. Most of the balance of this book will be devoted to a study of that Creature, but, for now, suffice it to say that the euphoria of being able to create money without human effort is so great that, once such a narcotic is taken, there is no politician or banker who can kick the habit. As William Sumner observed: "A man might as well jump off a precipice intending to stop half way down."[1]

NATURAL LAW NO. 4

And so, once again, we come to one of those natural laws that emerge from centuries of human experience. It can be stated as follows:

> LESSON: Fractional money is paper money which is backed by precious metals up to only a portion of the face amount. It is a hybrid, being part receipt money and part fiat money. Generally, the public is unaware of this fact and believes that fractional money can be redeemed in full at any time. When the truth is discovered, as periodically happens, there are runs on the bank, and only the first few depositors in line can be paid. Since fractional money earns just as much interest for the bankers as does gold or silver, the temptation is great for them to create as much of it as possible. As this happens, the fraction which represents the reserve becomes smaller and smaller until, eventually, it is reduced to zero. Therefore,
>
> LAW: Fractional money will always degenerate into fiat money. It is but fiat money in transition.

So much for the overview and generalities. In the next chapter we shall see what history has to say on this process. And what a history it is!

---

1. William Graham Sumner, *A History of American Currency* (New York: Holt, 1884), p. 214.

SUMMARY

Fiat money is paper money without precious-metal backing which people are required by law to accept. The first recorded appearance of fiat money was in thirteenth century China, but its use on a major scale did not occur until colonial America. The experience was disastrous, leading to massive inflation, unemployment, loss of property, and political unrest. During one period when the Bank of England forced the colonies to abandon their fiat money, general prosperity quickly returned. The Revolutionary War brought fiat money back to the colonies with a vengeance. The economic chaos that resulted led the colonial governments to impose price controls and harsh legal tender laws, neither of which was effective.

Fractional money is defined as paper money with precious-metal backing for part, not all, of its stated value. It was introduced in Europe when goldsmiths began to issue receipts for gold which they did not have, thus only a fraction of their receipts was redeemable. Fractional money always degenerates into pure fiat money.

Chapter Nine

THE SECRET SCIENCE

The condensed history of fractional-reserve bank-
ing; the unbroken record of fraud, booms, busts,
and economic chaos; the formation of the Bank of
England, the world's first central bank, which
became the model for the Federal Reserve System.

Banks of deposit first appeared in early Greece, concurrent with the development of coinage itself. They were known in India at the time of Alexander the Great. They also operated in Egypt as part of the public granary system. They appeared in Damascus in 1200 and in Barcelona in 1401. It was the city-state of Venice, however, which is considered the cradle of banking as we know it today.

THE BANK OF VENICE

By the year 1361, there already had been sufficient abuse in banking that the Venetian Senate passed a law forbidding bankers to engage in any other commercial pursuit, thus removing the temptation to use their depositors' funds to finance their own enterprises. They were also required to open their books for public inspection and to keep their stockpile of coins available for viewing at all reasonable times. In 1524, a board of bank examiners was created and, two years later, all bankers were required to settle accounts between themselves in coin rather than by check.

In spite of these precautions, however, the largest bank at that time, the house of Pisano and Tiepolo, had been active in lending against its reserves and, in 1584, was forced to close its doors because of inability to refund depositors. The government picked up the pieces at that point and a state bank was established, the *Banco della Piazza del Rialto*. Having learned from the recent experience with bankruptcy, the new bank was not allowed to make any loans. There could be no profit from the issuance of credit. The bank was required to sustain itself solely from fees for coin storage, exchanging currencies, handling the transfer of payments between customers, and notary services.

The formula for honest banking had been found. The bank prospered and soon became the center of Venetian commerce. Its paper receipts were widely accepted far beyond the country's borders and, in fact, instead of being discounted in exchange for gold coin as was the usual practice, they actually carried a *premium* over coins. This was because there were so many kinds of coin in circulation and such a wide variance of quality within the same type of coin that one had to be an expert to evaluate their worth. The bank performed this service automatically when it took the coins into its vault. Each was evaluated, and the receipt given for it was an accurate reflection of its intrinsic worth. The public, therefore, was far more certain of the value of the paper receipts than of many of the coins and, consequently, was willing to exchange a little bit more for them.

Unfortunately, with the passage of time and the fading from memory of previous banking abuses, the Venetian Senate eventually succumbed to the temptation of credit. Strapped for funds and not willing to face the voters with a tax increase, the politicians decided they would authorize a new bank without restrictions against loans, have the bank create the money they needed, and then "borrow" it. So, in 1619, the *Banco del Giro* was formed, which, like its bankrupt predecessor, began immediately to create money out of nothing for the purpose of lending it to the government. Eighteen years later, the *Banco della Piazza del Rialto* was absorbed into the new bank, and history's first tiny flame of sound banking sputtered and died.

Throughout the fifteenth and sixteenth centuries, banks had been springing up all over Europe. Almost without exception, however, they followed the lucrative practice of lending money which was not truly available for loan. They created excess obligations against their reserves and, as a result, every one of them failed. That is not to say that their owners and directors did not prosper. It merely means that their depositors lost all or a part of their assets entrusted for safekeeping.

THE BANK OF AMSTERDAM

It wasn't until the Bank of Amsterdam was founded in 1609 that we find a second example of sound banking practices, and the results were virtually the same as previously experienced by the *Banco della Piazza del Rialto*. The bank only accepted deposits and steadfastly refused to make loans. Its income was derived solely from service fees. All payments in and around Amsterdam soon came to be made in paper currency issued by the bank and, in fact, that currency carried a premium over coin itself. The burgomasters and the city council were required to take an annual oath swearing that the coin reserve of the bank was intact. Galbraith reminds us:

> For a century after its founding it functioned usefully and with notably strict rectitude. Deposits were deposits, and initially the metal remained in storage for the man who owned it until he transferred it to another. None was loaned out. In 1672, when the armies of Louis XIV approached Amsterdam, there was grave alarm. Merchants besieged the bank, some in the suspicion that their wealth might not be there. All who sought their money were paid, and when they found this to be so, they did not want payment. As was often to be observed in the future, however desperately people want their money from a bank, when they are assured they can get it, they no longer want it.[1]

The principles of honesty and restraint were not to be long lived, however. The temptation of easy profit from money creation was simply too great. As early as 1657, individuals had been permitted to overdraw their accounts which means, of course, that the bank created new money out of their debt. In later years enormous loans were made to the Dutch East Indies Company. The truth finally became known to the public in January of 1790, and demands for a return of deposits were steady from that date forward. Ten months later, the bank was declared insolvent and was taken over by the City of Amsterdam.

THE BANK OF HAMBURG

The third and last experience with honest banking occurred in Germany with the Bank of Hamburg. For over two centuries it faithfully adhered to the principle of safe deposit. So scrupulous was its administration that, when Napoleon took possession of the bank in 1813, he found 7,506,956 *marks* in silver held against liabilities of 7,489,343. That was 17,613 *more* than was actually needed. Most of the bank's treasure that Napoleon hauled away was restored a few years later by the French government in the form of securities. It is not clear if the securities were of much value but, even if they were, they were not the same as silver. Because of foreign invasion, the bank's currency was no longer fully convert-

---

1. Galbraith, p. 16.

ible into coin as receipt money. It was now *fractional* money, and the self-destruct mechanism had been set in motion. The bank lasted another fifty-five years until 1871 when it was ordered to liquidate all of its accounts.

That is the end of the short story of honest banking. From that point forward, fractional-reserve banking became the universal practice. But there were to be many interesting twists and turns in its development before it would be ready for something as sophisticated as the Federal Reserve System.

EARLY BANKING IN ENGLAND

In England, the first paper money was the exchequer order of Charles II. It was pure fiat and, although it was decreed legal tender, it was not widely used. It was replaced in 1696 by the exchequer *bill*. The bill was redeemable in gold, and the government went to great lengths to make sure that there was enough actual coin or bullion to make good on the pledge. In other words, it was true receipt money, and it became widely accepted as the medium of exchange. Furthermore, the bills were considered as short-term loans to the government and actually paid interest to the holders.

In 1707, the recently created Bank of England was given the responsibility of managing this currency, but the bank found more profit in the circulation of its own banknotes, which were in the form of *fractional* money and which provided for the *collection* of interest, not the payment of it. Consequently, the government bills gradually passed out of use and were replaced by banknotes which, by the middle of the eighteenth century, became England's only paper money.

It must be understood that, at this time, the Bank of England was not yet fully developed as a central bank. It had been given a monopoly over the issue of banknotes within London and other prime geographic areas, but they were not yet decreed as legal tender. No one was forced to use them. They were merely private fractional receipts for gold coin issued by a private bank which the public could accept, reject, or discount at its pleasure. Legal tender status was not conferred upon the bank's money until 1833.

Meanwhile, Parliament had granted charters to numerous other banks throughout the empire and, without exception, the issuance of fractional money led to their ultimate demise and the ruin of their depositors. "Disaster after disaster had to come upon the country," says Shaw, because "of the indifference of the state to these mere private paper tokens."[1] The Bank of England, however, was favored by the government above all others and, time after time, it was saved from insolvency by Parliament. How it came to be that way is an interesting story.

THE BANK OF ENGLAND

England was financially exhausted after half a century of war against France and numerous civil wars fought largely over excessive taxation. By the time of the War of the League of Augsberg in 1693, King William was in serious need for new revenue. Twenty years previously, King Charles II had flat out repudiated a debt of over a million pounds which had been lent to him by scores of goldsmiths, with the result that ten-thousand depositors lost their savings. This was still fresh in everyone's memory, and, needless to say, the government was no longer considered a good investment risk. Unable to increase taxes and unable to borrow, Parliament became desperate for some other way to obtain the money. The objective, says Groseclose, was not to bring "the money mechanism under more intelligent control, but to provide means outside the onerous sources of taxes and public loans for the financial requirements of an impecunious government."[2]

There were two groups of men who saw a unique opportunity arise out of this necessity. The first group consisted of the *political scientists* within the government. The second was comprised of the *monetary scientists* from the emerging business of banking. The organizer and spokesman of this group was William Paterson from Scotland. Paterson had been to America and came back with a grandiose scheme to obtain a British charter for a commercial company to colonize the Isthmus of Panama, then known as Darien. The government was not interested in that, so Paterson turned his attention to a scheme that *did* interest it very much, the creation of money.

The two groups came together and formed an alliance. No, that is too soft a word. The *American Heritage Dictionary* defines a *cabal*

---

1. W.A. Shaw, *Theory and Principles of Central Banking* (London & New York: Sir I. Pitman & Sons, Ltd., 1930), pp. 32–32.
2. Groseclose, *Money and Man*, p. 175.

as "A conspiratorial group of plotters or intriguers." There is no other word that could so accurately describe this group. With much of the same secrecy and mystery that surrounded the meeting on Jekyll Island, the Cabal met in Mercer's Chapel in London and hammered out a seven-point plan which would serve their mutual purposes:

1. The government would grant a charter to the monetary scientists to form a bank;
2. The bank would be given a monopoly to issue banknotes which would circulate as England's paper currency;
3. The bank would create money out of nothing with only a fraction of its total currency backed by coin;
4. The monetary scientists then would lend the government all the money it needed;
5. The money created for government loans would be backed primarily by government I.O.U.s;
6. Although this money was to be created out of nothing and would cost nothing to create, the government would pay "interest" on it at the rate of 8%;
7. Government I.O.U.s would also be considered as "reserves" for creating additional loan money for private commerce. These loans also would earn interest. Thus, the monetary scientists would collect *double* interest on the same nothing.[1]

The circular which was distributed to attract subscribers to the Bank's initial stock offering explained: "The Bank hath benefit of interest on all the moneys which it, the Bank, creates out of nothing."[2] The charter was issued in 1694, and a strange creature took its initial breath of life. It was the world's first central bank. Rothbard writes:

---

1. For an overview of these agreements, see Murray Rothbard, *The Mystery of Banking* (New York: Richardson & Snyder, 1983), p. 180. Also Martin Mayer, *The Bankers* (New York: Weybright & Talley, 1974), pp. 24–25.
2. Quoted by Caroll Quigley, *Tragedy and Hope: A History of the World in Our Time* (New York: Macmillan, 1966), p. 49. Paterson did not benefit from his own creation. He withdrew from the Bank over a policy disagreement within a few months after its formation and then returned to Scotland where he succeeded in selling his Darien scheme. Frugal Scots thronged to buy stock and to book passage to the fever-ridden land. The stock became worthless and almost all the 1200 colonists lost their lives.

In short, since there were not enough private savers willing to finance the deficit, Paterson and his group were graciously willing to buy government bonds, provided they could do so with newly-created out-of-thin-air bank notes carrying a raft of special privileges with them. This was a splendid deal for Paterson and company, and the government benefited from the flimflam of a seemingly legitimate bank's financing their debts.... As soon as the Bank of England was chartered in 1694, King William himself and various members of Parliament rushed to become shareholders of the new money factory they had just created.[1]

THE SECRET SCIENCE OF MONEY

Both groups within the Cabal were handsomely rewarded for their efforts. The political scientists had been seeking about £500,000 to finance the current war. The Bank promptly gave them more than twice what they originally sought. The monetary scientists started with a pledged capital investment of £1,200,000. Textbooks tell us that this was lent to the government at 8% interest, but what is usually omitted is the fact that, at the time the loan was made, only £720,000 had been invested, which means the Bank "lent" 66% more than it had on hand.[2] Furthermore, the Bank was given the privilege of creating at least an equal amount of money in the form of loans to the public. So, after lending their capital to the government, they still had it available to lend out a second time.

An honest loan of their £720,000 at 8% would have yielded £57,600 interest. But, with the new secret science, they were able to earn 8% on £1,200,000 given to the government plus an estimated 9% on £720,000 lent to the public. That adds up to £160,800, more than 22% on their investment. The real point, however, is that, under these circumstances, it is meaningless to talk about a rate of interest. When money is created out of nothing, the true interest rate is not 8% or 9% or even 22%. It is *infinity*.

In this first official act of the world's first central bank can be seen the grand pretense that has characterized all those which have followed. The Bank *pretended* to make a loan but what it really did was to *manufacture* the money for government's use. If the government had done this directly, the fiat nature of the currency would

---

1. Rothbard, *Mystery*, p. 180.
2. See R.D. Richards, Ph.D., *The Early History of Banking in England* (New York: Augustus M. Kelley, original edition 1929, reprinted 1965), pp. 148–50.

have been immediately recognized, and it probably would not have been accepted at full face value in payment for the expenses of war. By creating money through the banking system, however, the process became mystifying to the general public. The newly created bills and notes were indistinguishable from those previously backed by coin, and the public was none the wiser.

The reality of central banks, therefore—and we must not forget that the Federal Reserve System is such a creature—is that, under the guise of purchasing government bonds, they act as hidden money machines which can be activated any time the politicians want. This is a godsend to the political scientists who no longer must depend on taxes or the good credit of their treasury to raise money. It is even easier than printing and, because the process is not understood by the public, it is politically safe.

The monetary scientists, of course, are amply paid for this service. To preserve the pretense of banking, it is said they collect *interest*, but this is a misnomer. They didn't lend money, they created it. Their compensation, therefore, should be called what it is: a professional fee, or commission, or royalty, or kickback, depending on your perspective, but *not* interest.

FROM INFLATION TO BANK RUNS

The new money created by the Bank of England splashed through the economy like rain in April. The country banks outside of the London area were authorized to create money on their own, but they had to hold a certain percentage of either coin *or* Bank of England certificates in reserve. Consequently, when these plentiful banknotes landed in their hands, they quickly put them into the vaults and then issued their own certificates in even greater amounts. As a result of this pyramiding effect, prices rose 100% in just two years. Then, the inevitable happened: There was a run on the bank, and the Bank of England could not produce the coin.

When banks cannot honor their contracts to deliver coin in return for their receipts, they are, in fact, bankrupt. They should be allowed to go out of business and liquidate their assets to satisfy their creditors just like any other business. This, in fact, is what always had happened to banks which lent out their deposits and created fractional money. Had this practice been allowed to continue, there is little doubt that people eventually would have understood that they simply do not want to do business with those kinds of banks. Through the painful but highly effective process of trial and error, mankind would have learned to distinguish real money from fool's gold. And the world would be a lot better because of it today.

That, of course, was not allowed to happen. The Cabal is a *partnership*, and each of the two groups is committed to protect each other, not out of loyalty, but out of mutual self interest. They know that, if one falls, so does the other. It is not surprising, therefore, that, when there was a run on the Bank of England, Parliament intervened. In May of 1696, just two years after the Bank was formed, a law was passed authorizing it to "suspend payment in specie." By force of law, the Bank was now exempted from having to honor its contract to return the gold.

THE PATTERN OF PROTECTION WAS SET

This was a fateful event in the history of money, because the precedent has been followed ever since. In Europe and America, the banks have always operated with the assumption that their partners in government will come to their aid when they get into trouble. Politicians may speak about "protecting the public," but the underlining reality is that the government *needs* the fiat money produced by the banks. The banks, therefore—at least the big ones— must not be allowed to fail. Only a cartel with government protection can enjoy such insulation from the workings of a free market.

It is commonly observed in modern times that criminals often are treated lightly when they rob their neighbor. But if they steal from the government or a bank, the penalties are harsh. This is merely another manifestation of the Cabal's partnership. In the eyes of government, banks are *special*, and it has been that way even from the beginning of their brotherhood. For example, Galbraith tells us:

> In 1780, when Lord George Gordon led his mob through London in protest against the Catholic Relief Acts, the Bank was a principal target. It signified the Establishment. For so long as the Catholic districts of London were being pillaged, the authorities were slow to react. When the siege of the Bank began, things were thought more serious. Troops intervened, and ever since soldiers have been sent to guard the Bank by night.[1]

---
1. Galbraith, p. 34.

BOOMS AND BUSTS NOW GUARANTEED

Once the Bank of England had been legally protected from the consequences of converting debt into money, the British economy was doomed to a nauseating roller-coaster ride of inflation, booms, and busts. The natural and immediate result was the granting of *massive* loans for just about any wild scheme imaginable. Why not? The money cost nothing to make, and the potential profits could be enormous. So the Bank of England, and the country banks which pyramided their own money supply on top of the Bank's supply, pumped a steady stream of new money into the economy. Great stock companies were formed and financed by this money. One was for the purpose of draining the Red Sea to recover the gold supposedly lost by the Egyptians when pursuing the Israelites. £150,000,000 were siphoned into vague and fruitless ventures in South America and Mexico.

The result of this flood of new money—how many times must history repeat it?—was even more inflation. In 1810, the House of Commons created a special committee, called the Select Committee on the High Price of Gold Bullion, to explore the problem and to find a solution. The verdict handed down in the final report was a model of clarity. Prices were not going up, it said. The value of the currency was going down, and that was due to the fact that it was being created at a faster rate than the creation of goods to be purchased with it. The solution? The committee recommended that the notes of the Bank of England be made fully convertible into gold coin, thus putting a brake on the supply of money that could be created.

IN DEFENSE OF THE GOLD STANDARD

One of the most outspoken proponents of a true gold standard was a Jewish London stockbroker by the name of David Ricardo. Ricardo argued that an ideal currency "should be absolutely invariable in value."[1] He conceded that precious metals were not perfect in this regard because they do shift in purchasing power to a small degree. Then he said: "They are, however, the best with which we are acquainted."[2]

---

1. David Ricardo, *The Works and Correspondence of David Ricardo: Pamphlets 1815–1823*, Piero Sraffa, ed. (Cambridge: Cambridge University Press, 1951), Vol. IV, p. 58.
2. *Ibid.*, p. 62.

Almost everyone in government agreed with Ricardo's assessment, but, as is often the case, theoretical truth was fighting a losing battle against practical necessity. Men's opinions on the best form of money were one thing. The war with Napoleon was another, and it demanded a constant inflow of funding. England continued to use the central-bank mechanism to extract that revenue from the populace.

DEPRESSION AND REFORM

By 1815, prices had doubled again and then fell sharply. The Corn Act was passed that year to protect local growers from lower-priced imports. Then, when corn and wheat prices began to climb once more in spite of the fact that wages and other prices were falling, there was widespread discontent and rebellion. "By 1816," notes Roy Jastram, "England was in deep depression. There was stagnation of industry and trade generally; the iron and coal industries were paralyzed.... Riots occurred spasmodically from May through December."[1]

In 1821, after the war had ended and there was no longer a need to fund military campaigns, the political pressure for a gold standard became too strong to resist, and the Bank of England returned to a convertibility of its notes into gold coin. The basic central-bank mechanism was not dismantled, however. It was merely limited by a new formula regarding the allowable fraction of reserves. The Bank continued to create money out of nothing for the purpose of lending and, within a year, the flower of a new business boom unfolded. Then, in November of 1825, the flower matured into its predestined fruit. The crisis began with the collapse of Sir Peter Cole and Company and was soon followed by the failure of sixty-three other banks. Fortunes were wiped out and the economy plunged back into depression.

When a similar crisis with still more bank failures struck again in 1839, Parliament attempted to come to grips with the problem. After five more years of analysis and debate, Sir Robert Peel succeeded in passing a banking reform act. It squarely faced the cause of England's booms and busts: an *elastic* money supply. What Peel's Bank Act of 1844 attempted to do was to limit the amount of money the banks could create to roughly the same as it would be if

---

1. Roy W. Jastram, *The Golden Constant* (New York: Wiley, 1977), p. 113.

their banknotes were backed by gold or silver. It was a good try, but it ultimately failed because it fell short on three counts: (1) It was a political compromise and was not strict enough, allowing the banks to still create lending money out of nothing to the extent of £14,000,000; in other words, a "fractional" amount thought to be safe at the time; (2) The limitation applied only to paper currency issued by the Bank. It did not apply to checkbook money, and that was then becoming the preferred *form* of exchange. Consequently, the so-called reform did not even apply to the area where the greatest amount of abuse was taking place; and (3) The basic concept was allowed to remain unchallenged that *man*, in his infinite political wisdom, can determine what the money supply should be more effectively than an unmanaged system of gold or silver responding to the law of supply and demand.

THE ROLLER COASTER CONTINUES

Within three years of the "reform," England faced another crisis with still more bank failures and more losses to depositors. But when the Bank of England tottered on the edge of insolvency, once again the government intervened. In 1847, the Bank was exempted from the legal reserve requirements of the Peel Act. Such is the rock-steady dependability of man-made limits to the money supply.

Groseclose continues the story:

> Ten years later, in 1857, another crisis occurred, due to excessive and unwise lending as a result of over-optimism regarding foreign trade prospects. The bank found itself in the same position as in 1847, and similar measures were taken. On this occasion the bank was forced to use the authority to increase its fiduciary [debt-based money] issue beyond the limit imposed by the Bank Charter Act....
>
> Again in 1866, the growth of banking without sufficient attention to liquidity, and the use of bank credit to support a speculative craze...prepared the way for a crash which was finally precipitated by the failure of the famous house of Overend, Gurney and Co. The Act of 1844 was once more suspended....
>
> In 1890, the Bank of England once again faced crisis, again the result of widespread and excessive speculation in foreign securities, particularly American and Argentine. This time it was the failure of Baring Brothers that precipitated the crash.[1]

---

1. Groseclose, *Money and Man*, pp. 195–96.

THE MECHANISM SPREADS TO OTHER COUNTRIES
It is an incredible fact of history that, in spite of the general and recurring failures of the Bank of England during these years, the central-bank mechanism was so attractive to the political and monetary scientists that it became the model for all of Europe. The Bank of Prussia became the Reichsbank. Napoleon established the Banque de France. A few decades later, the concept became the venerated model for the Federal Reserve System. Who cares if the scheme is destructive? Here is the perfect tool for obtaining unlimited funding for politicians and endless profits for bankers. And, best of all, the little people who pay the bills for both groups have practically no idea what is being done to them.

Leaders of the Leninist block of countries are no exception. They have been the most outspoken critics of the banking system of Western Countries. John Maynard Keynes writes:

> Lenin is said to have delared that the best way to destroy the Capitalist System was to debauch the currency. By a continuing process of inflation, governments can confiscate, secretly and unobserved, an important part of the wealth of their citizens. By this method, they not only confiscate, but they confiscate *arbitrarily*; and while the process impoverishes many, it actually enriches some. ... As the inflation proceeds and the real value of the currency fluctuates wildly and from month to month, all permanent relations between debtors and creditors, which form the ultimate foundation of capitalism, become so uterly disordered as to be almost meaningless; and the process of wealth-getting degenerates into a gamble and a lottery.
>
> Lenin was right. There is no subtler, no surer means of overturning the existing basis of society than to debauch the currency. The process engages all the hidden forces of economic law on the side of destruction, and does it in a manner which not one man in a million is able to diagnose.[1]

From this we may reasonably assume that the Leninists (and their Fabian counterparts) are well informed on this phenomenon. Yet, after all the words of wisdom have been written, wherever Leninists and their socialist counterparts come to power, they invariably form partnerships with banks and unleash all the hidden forces of inflation to plunder their own people.

---

1. John Maynard Keynes, *The Economic Consequences of the Peace* (New York, Harcourt, Brace, and Howe, 1919) p. 235 *ff.*

SUMMARY

The business of banking began in Europe in the fourteenth century. Its function was to evaluate, exchange, and safeguard people's coins. In the beginning, there were notable examples of totally honest banks which operated with remarkable efficiency considering the vast variety of coinage they handled. They also issued paper receipts which were so dependable they freely circulated as money and cheated no one in the process. But there was a great demand for more money and more loans, and the temptation soon caused the bankers to seek easier paths. They began lending out pieces of paper that *said* they were receipts, but which in fact were counterfeit. The public could not tell one from the other and accepted both of them as money. From that point forward, the receipts in circulation exceeded the gold held in reserve, and the age of fractional-reserve banking had dawned. This led immediately to what would become an almost unbroken record from then to the present: a record of inflation, booms and busts, suspension of payments, bank failures, repudiation of currencies, and recurring spasms of economic chaos.

The Bank of England was formed in 1694 to institutionalize fractional-reserve banking. As the world's first central bank, it introduced the concept of a partnership between bankers and politicians. The politicians would receive spendable money (created out of nothing by the bankers) without having to raise taxes. In return, the bankers would receive a commission on the transaction—deceptively called interest—which would continue in perpetuity. Since it all seemed to be wrapped up in the mysterious rituals of banking, which the common man was not expected to understand, there was practically no opposition to the scheme. The arrangement proved so profitable to the participants that it soon spread to many other countries in Europe and, eventually, to the United States.

Chapter Ten

THE MANDRAKE
MECHANISM

*The method by which the Federal Reserve creates
money out of nothing; the concept of usury as the
payment of interest on pretended loans; the true
cause of the hidden tax called inflation; the way in
which the Fed creates boom-bust cycles.*

In the 1940s, there was a comic strip character called Mandrake
the Magician. His specialty was creating things out of nothing and,
when appropriate, to make them disappear back into that same
void. It is fitting, therefore, that the process to be described in this
section should be named in his honor.

In the previous chapters, we examined the technique developed
by the political and monetary scientists to create money out of nothing for the purpose of lending. This is not an entirely accurate
description because it implies that money is created first and then
waits for someone to borrow it. On the other hand, textbooks on
banking often state that money is created out of debt. This also is
misleading because it implies that debt exists first and then is
converted into money. In truth, money is not created until the
instant it is borrowed. It is the act of borrowing which causes it to
spring into existence. And, incidentally, it is the act of paying off the
debt that causes it to vanish.[1] There is no short phrase that perfectly
describes that process. So, until one is invented along the way, we
shall continue using the phrase "create money out of nothing" and
occasionally add "for the purpose of lending" where necessary to
further clarify the meaning.

---

1. Printed Federal Reserve Notes that sit in the Treasury's vault do not become
money until they are released into circulation in exchange for checkbook money
that was created by a bank loan. As long as the bills are in the vault with no
debt-based money to replace them, they technically are just paper, not money.

So, let us now leave the historical figures of the past and jump into *their* "future," in other words, into our present, and see just how far this money/debt-creation process has been carried—and how it works.

The first fact that needs to be considered is that our money today has no gold or silver behind it whatsoever. The fraction is not 54% nor 15%. It is 0%. It has travelled the path of all previous fractional money in history and already has degenerated into pure fiat money. The fact that most of it is in the form of checkbook balances rather than paper currency is a mere technicality; and the fact that bankers speak about "reserve ratios" is eye wash. The so-called reserves to which they refer are, in fact, Treasury bonds and other certificates of *debt*. Our money is pure fiat through and through.

The second fact that needs to be clearly understood is that, in spite of the technical jargon and seemingly complicated procedures, the actual mechanism by which the Federal Reserve creates money is quite simple. They do it exactly the same way the goldsmiths of old did except, of course, the goldsmiths were limited by the need to hold *some* precious metal in reserve, whereas the Fed has no such restriction.

THE FEDERAL RESERVE IS CANDID

The Federal Reserve itself is amazingly frank about this process. A booklet published by the Federal Reserve Bank of New York tells us: "Currency cannot be redeemed, or exchanged, for Treasury gold or any other asset used as backing. The question of just what assets 'back' Federal Reserve notes has little but bookkeeping significance."[1]

Elsewhere in the same publication we are told: "Banks are creating money based on a borrower's promise to pay (the IOU)... Banks create money by 'monetizing' the private debts of businesses and individuals."[2]

In a booklet entitled *Modern Money Mechanics*, the Federal Reserve Bank of Chicago says:

> In the United States neither paper currency nor deposits have value as commodities. Intrinsically, a dollar bill is just a piece of paper. Deposits are merely book entries. Coins do have some intrinsic value as metal, but generally far less than their face amount.

---

1. *I Bet You Thought*, Federal Reserve Bank of New York, p. 11.
2. *Ibid.*, p. 19.

What, then, makes these instruments—checks, paper money, and coins—acceptable at face value in payment of all debts and for other monetary uses? Mainly, it is the confidence people have that they will be able to exchange such money for other financial assets and real goods and services whenever they choose to do so. This partly is a matter of law; currency has been designated "legal tender" by the government—that is, it must be accepted.[1]

In the fine print of a footnote in a bulletin of the Federal Reserve Bank of St. Louis, we find this surprisingly candid explanation:

Modern monetary systems have a fiat base—literally money by decree—with depository institutions, acting as fiduciaries, creating obligations against themselves with the fiat base acting in part as reserves. The decree appears on the currency notes: "This note is legal tender for all debts, public and private." While no individual could refuse to accept such money for debt repayment, exchange contracts could easily be composed to thwart its use in everyday commerce. However, a forceful explanation as to why money is accepted is that the federal government requires it as payment for tax liabilities. Anticipation of the need to clear this debt creates a demand for the pure fiat dollar.[2]

MONEY WOULD VANISH WITHOUT DEBT

It is difficult for Americans to come to grips with the fact that their total money supply is backed by nothing but debt, and it is even more mind boggling to visualize that, if everyone paid back all that was borrowed, *there would be no money left in existence.* That's right, there would be not one penny in circulation—all coins and all paper currency would be returned to bank vaults—and there would be not one dollar in any one's checking account. In short, all money would disappear.

Marriner Eccles was the Governor of the Federal Reserve System in 1941. On September 30 of that year, Eccles was asked to give testimony before the House Committee on Banking and Currency. The purpose of the hearing was to obtain information regarding the role of the Federal Reserve in creating conditions that led to the depression of the 1930s. Congressman Wright Patman, who was Chairman of that committee, asked how the Fed got the money to

---

1. *Modern Money Mechanics,* Federal Reserve Bank of Chicago, revised October 1982, p. 3.
2. "Money, Credit and Velocity," *Review,* May, 1982, Vol. 64, No. 5, Federal Reserve Bank of St. Louis, p. 25.

purchase two billion dollars worth of government bonds in 1933. This is the exchange that followed.

ECCLES: We created it.
PATMAN: Out of what?
ECCLES: Out of the right to issue credit money.
PATMAN: And there is nothing behind it, is there, except our government's credit?
ECCLES: That is what our money system is. If there were no debts in our money system, there wouldn't be any money.

It must be realized that, while money may represent an asset to selected individuals, when it is considered as an aggregate of the total money supply, it is not an asset at all. A man who borrows $1,000 may think that he has increased his financial position by that amount but he has not. His $1,000 cash asset is offset by his $1,000 loan liability, and his net position is zero. Bank accounts are exactly the same on a larger scale. Add up all the bank accounts in the nation, and it would be easy to assume that all that money represents a gigantic pool of assets which support the economy. Yet, every bit of this money is owed by someone. Some will owe nothing. Others will owe many times what they possess. All added together, the national balance is zero. What we think is money is but a grand illusion. The reality is debt.

Robert Hemphill was the Credit Manager of the Federal Reserve Bank in Atlanta. In the foreword to a book by Irving Fisher, entitled *100% Money*, Hemphill said this:

> If all the bank loans were paid, no one could have a bank deposit, and there would not be a dollar of coin or currency in circulation. This is a staggering thought. We are completely dependent on the commercial banks. Someone has to borrow every dollar we have in circulation, cash, or credit. If the banks create ample synthetic money we are prosperous; if not, we starve. We are absolutely without a permanent money system. When one gets a complete grasp of the picture, the tragic absurdity of our hopeless situation is almost incredible—but there it is.[1]

With the knowledge that money in America is based on debt, it should not come as a surprise to learn that the Federal Reserve System is not the least interested in seeing a reduction in debt in this

---

1.   Irving Fisher, *100% Money* (New York: Adelphi, 1936), p. xxii.

country, regardless of public utterances to the contrary. Here is the bottom line from the System's own publications. The Federal Reserve Bank of Philadelphia says: "A large and growing number of analysts, on the other hand, now regard the national debt as something useful, if not an actual blessing.... [They believe] the national debt need not be reduced at all."[1]

The Federal Reserve Bank of Chicago adds: "Debt—public and private—is here to stay. It plays an essential role in economic processes.... What is required is not the abolition of debt, but its prudent use and intelligent management."[2]

WHAT'S WRONG WITH A LITTLE DEBT?

There is a kind of fascinating appeal to this theory. It gives those who expound it an aura of intellectualism, the appearance of being able to grasp a complex economic principle that is beyond the comprehension of mere mortals. And, for the less academically minded, it offers the comfort of at least *sounding* moderate. After all, what's *wrong* with a little debt, prudently used and intelligently managed? The answer is nothing, *provided* the debt is based on an honest transaction. There is plenty wrong with it if it is based upon fraud.

An honest transaction is one in which a borrower pays an agreed upon sum in return for the temporary use of a lender's asset. That asset could be anything of tangible value. If it were an automobile, for example, then the borrower would pay "rent." If it is money, then the rent is called "interest." Either way, the concept is the same.

When we go to a lender—either a bank or a private party—and receive a loan of money, we are willing to pay interest on the loan in recognition of the fact that the money we are borrowing is an asset which we want to use. It seems only fair to pay a rental fee for that asset to the person who owns it. It is not easy to acquire an automobile, and it is not easy to acquire money—*real* money, that is. If the money we are borrowing was earned by someone's labor and talent, they are fully entitled to receive interest on it. But what are we to think of money that is created by the mere stroke of a pen or the click of a computer key? Why should anyone collect a rental fee on *that*?

---

1. *The National Debt*, Federal Reserve Bank of Philadelphia, pp. 2, 11.
2. *Two Faces of Debt*, Federal Reserve Bank of Chicago, p. 33.

When banks place credits into your checking account, they are merely *pretending* to lend you money. In reality, they have nothing to lend. Even the money that non-indebted depositors have placed with them was originally created out of nothing in response to someone else's loan. So what entitles the banks to collect rent on *nothing*? It is immaterial that men everywhere are forced by law to accept these nothing certificates in exchange for real goods and services. We are talking here, not about what is legal, but what is *moral*. As Thomas Jefferson observed at the time of his protracted battle against central banking in the United States, "No one has a natural right to the trade of money lender, but he who has money to lend."[1]

THIRD REASON TO ABOLISH THE SYSTEM

Centuries ago, *usury* was defined as any interest charged for a loan. Modern usage has redefined it as *excessive* interest. Certainly, any amount of interest charged for a *pretended* loan is excessive. The dictionary, therefore, needs a new definition. *Usury: The charging of any interest on a loan of fiat money.*

Let us, therefore, look at debt and interest in this light. Thomas Edison summed up the immorality of the system when he said:

> People who will not turn a shovel full of dirt on the project nor contribute a pound of materials will collect more money...than will the people who will supply all the materials and do all the work.[2]

Is that an exaggeration? Let us consider the purchase of a $100,000 home in which $30,000 represents the cost of the land, architect's fee, sales commissions, building permits, and that sort of thing and $70,000 is the cost of labor and building materials. If the home buyer puts up $30,000 as a down payment, then $70,000 must be borrowed. If the loan is issued at 11% over a 30-year period, the amount of interest paid will be $167,806. That means the amount paid to those who lend the money is about 2 ½ times greater than

---

1. *The Writings of Thomas Jefferson*, Library Edition (Washington: Jefferson Memorial Association, 1903), Vol XIII, p. 277–78.
2. As quoted by Brian L. Bex, *The Hidden Hand* (Spencer, Indiana: Owen Litho, 1975), p. 161. Unfortunately, Edison did not understand the whole problem. He was correctly opposed to paying interest to banks for their fiat money, but he was not opposed to *government* fiat money. It was only the interest to which he objected. He did not see the larger picture of how fiat money, even when issued solely by the government and without interest, has always been destructive of the economy through the creation of inflation, booms, and busts.

paid to those who provide all the labor and all the materials. It is true that this figure represents the time-value of that money over thirty years and easily could be justified on the basis that a lender deserves to be compensated for surrendering the use of his capital for half a lifetime. But that assumes the lender actually had something to surrender, that he had earned the capital, saved it, and then lent it for construction of someone else's house. What are we to think, however, about a lender who did nothing to earn the money, had not saved it, and, in fact, simply created it out of thin air? What is the time-value of nothing?

As we have already shown, every dollar that exists today, either in the form of currency, checkbook money, or even credit card money—in other words, our *entire* money supply—exists only because it was borrowed by someone; perhaps not you, but *someone*. That means all the American dollars in the entire world are earning daily and compounded interest for the banks which created them. A portion of every business venture, every investment, every profit, every transaction which involves money—and that even includes *losses* and the payment of *taxes*—a portion of all that is earmarked as payment to a bank. And what did the banks do to earn this perpetually flowing river of wealth? Did they lend out their own capital obtained through the investment of stockholders? Did they lend out the hard-earned savings of their depositors? No, neither of these was their major source of income. They simply waved the magic wand called fiat money.

The flow of such unearned wealth under the guise of interest can only be viewed as usury of the highest magnitude. Even if there were no other reasons to abolish the Fed, the fact that *it is the supreme instrument of usury* would be more than sufficient by itself.

WHO CREATES THE MONEY TO PAY THE INTEREST?

One of the most perplexing questions associated with this process is "Where does the money come from to pay the interest?" If you borrow $10,000 from a bank at 9%, you owe $10,900. But the bank only manufactures $10,000 for the loan. It would seem, therefore, that there is no way that you—and all others with similar loans—can possibly pay off your indebtedness. The amount of money put into circulation just isn't enough to cover the total debt, including interest. This has led some to the conclusion that it is necessary for you to *borrow* the $900 for the interest, and that, in turn, leads to still *more* interest. The assumption is that, the more we borrow, the more we *have* to borrow, and that debt based on fiat money is a never-ending spiral leading inexorably to more and more debt.

This is a partial truth. It is true that there is not enough money created to include the interest, but it is a fallacy that the only way to pay it back is to borrow still more. The assumption fails to take into account the exchange value of *labor*. Let us assume that you pay back your $10,000 loan at the rate of approximately $900 per month and that about $80 of that represents interest. You realize you are hard pressed to make your payments so you decide to take on a part-time job. The bank, on the other hand, is now making $80 profit each month on your loan. Since this amount is classified as "interest," it is not extinguished as is the larger portion which is a return of the loan itself. So this remains as spendable money in the account of the bank. The decision then is made to have the bank's floors waxed once a week. You respond to the ad in the paper and are hired at $80 per month to do the job. The result is that you *earn* the money to pay the interest on your loan, and—this is the point—the money you receive is the *same* money which you previously had paid. As long as you perform labor for the bank each month, the same dollars go into the bank as interest, then out the revolving door as your wages, and then back into the bank as loan repayment.

It is not necessary that you work directly for the bank. No matter where you earn the money, its *origin* was a bank and its ultimate *destination* is a bank. The loop through which it travels can be large or small, but the fact remains all interest is paid eventually by human effort. And the significance of that fact is even more startling than the assumption that not enough money is created to pay back the interest. It is that the total of this human effort ultimately is for the benefit of those who create fiat money. It is a form of modern serfdom in which the great mass of society works as indentured servants to a ruling class of financial nobility.

UNDERSTANDING THE ILLUSION

That's really all one needs to know about the operation of the banking cartel under the protection of the Federal Reserve. But it would be a shame to stop here without taking a look at the actual cogs, mirrors, and pulleys that make the magical mechanism work. It is a truly fascinating engine of mystery and deception. Let us, therefore, turn our attention to the actual process by which the magicians create the illusion of modern money. First we shall stand back for a general view to see the overall action. Then we shall move in closer and examine each component in detail.

THE MANDRAKE MECHANISM: AN OVERVIEW

DEBT

The entire function of this machine is to convert debt into money. It's just that simple. First, the Fed takes all the government bonds which the public does not buy and writes a check to Congress in exchange for them. (It acquires other debt obligations as well, but government bonds comprise most of its inventory.) There is no money to back up this check. These fiat dollars are created on the spot for that purpose. By calling those bonds "reserves," the Fed then uses them as the base for creating 9 additional dollars for every dollar created for the bonds themselves. The money created for the bonds is spent by the government, whereas the money created on top of those bonds is the source of all the bank loans made to the nation's businesses and individuals. The result of this process is the same as creating money on a printing press, but the illusion is based on an accounting trick rather than a printing trick. The bottom line is that Congress and the banking cartel have entered into a partnership in which the cartel has the privilege of collecting interest on money which it creates out of nothing, a perpetual override on every American dollar that exists in the world. Congress, on the other hand, has access to unlimited funding without having to tell the voters their taxes are being raised through the process of inflation. If you understand this paragraph, you understand the Federal Reserve System.

MONEY

Now for a more detailed view. There are three general ways in which the Federal Reserve creates fiat money out of debt. One is by making loans to the member banks through what is called the *Discount Window*. The second is by purchasing Treasury bonds and other certificates of debt through what is called the *Open Market Committee*. The third is by changing the so-called *reserve ratio* that member banks are required to hold. Each method is merely a different path to the same objective: taking in IOUs and converting them into spendable money.

THE DISCOUNT WINDOW

The Discount Window is merely bankers' language for the *loan* window. When banks run short of money, the Federal Reserve stands ready as the "bankers' bank" to lend it. There are many reasons for them to need loans. Since they hold "reserves" of only about one or two per cent of their deposits in vault cash and eight or nine per cent in securities, their operating margin is extremely thin. It is common for them to experience temporary negative balances caused by unusual customer demand for cash or unusually large clusters of checks all clearing through other banks at the same time. Sometimes they make bad loans and, when these former "assets" are removed from their books, their "reserves" are also decreased and may, in fact, become negative. Finally, there is the profit motive. When banks borrow from the Federal Reserve at one interest rate and lend it out at a higher rate, there is an obvious advantage. But that is merely the beginning. When a bank borrows a dollar from the Fed, it becomes a one-dollar *reserve*. Since the banks are required to keep reserves of only about ten per cent, they actually can lend up to *nine* dollars for each dollar borrowed.[1]

Let's take a look at the math. Assume the bank receives $1 million from the Fed at a rate of 8%. The total annual cost, therefore, is $80,000 (.08 X $1,000,000). The bank treats the loan as a cash deposit, which means it becomes the basis for manufacturing an additional $9 million to be lent to its customers. If we assume that it lends that money at 11% interest, its gross return would be $990,000 (.11 X $9,000,000). Subtract from this the bank's cost of $80,000 plus an appropriate share of its overhead, and we have a net return of about $900,000. In other words, the bank borrows a million and can almost

---

1. This 10% figure (ten-to-one ratio) is based on averages. The Federal Reserve requires a minimum reserve of 10% on deposits over $47.6 million but only 3% on deposits from $7 million up to that amount and no reserves whatsoever below that amount. Reserves consist of vault cash and deposits at the Federal Reserve. See Federal Reserve Press Release: "Annual adjustments for reserve calculations, Reg D" October 6, 2004.

double it in one year.[1] That's *leverage!* But don't forget the *source* of that leverage: the manufacture of another $9 million which is added to the nation's money supply.

THE OPEN MARKET OPERATION

The most important method used by the Federal Reserve for the creation of fiat money is the purchase and sale of securities on the open market. But, before jumping into this, a word of warning. Don't expect what follows to make any sense. Just be prepared to know that this is how they do it.

The trick lies in the use of words and phrases which have technical meanings quite different from what they imply to the average citizen. So keep your eye on the words. They are not meant to explain but to deceive. In spite of first appearances, the process is *not* complicated. It is just absurd.

THE MANDRAKE MECHANISM: A DETAILED VIEW

Start with...

GOVERNMENT DEBT

The federal government adds ink to a piece of paper, creates impressive designs around the edges, and calls it a bond or Treasury note. It is merely a promise to pay a specified sum at a specified interest on a specified date. As we shall see in the following steps, this debt eventually becomes the foundation for almost the entire nation's money supply.[2] In reality, the government has created cash, but it doesn't yet *look* like cash. To convert these IOUs into paper bills and checkbook money is the function of The Federal Reserve System. To bring about that transformation, the bond is given to the Fed where it is then classified as a ...

(Continued on next page)

---

1. The banks must cover these loans with bonds or other interest-bearing assets which it possesses, but that does not diminish the money-multiplier effect of the new deposit.
2. Debt obligations from the private sector and from other governments also are used in the same way, but government bonds are the primary instruments.

(Continued from previous page)

SECURITIES ASSET

An instrument of government debt is considered an asset because it is assumed the government will keep its promise to pay. This is based upon its ability to obtain whatever money it needs through taxation. Thus, the strength of this asset is the power to take back that which it gives. So the Federal Reserve now has an "asset" which can be used to offset a liability. It then creates this liability by adding ink to yet another piece of paper and exchanging that with the government in return for the asset. That second piece of paper is a ...

FEDERAL RESERVE CHECK

There is no money in any account to cover this check. Anyone else doing that would be sent to prison. It is legal for the Fed, however, because Congress wants the money, and this is the easiest way to get it. (To raise taxes would be political suicide; to depend on the public to buy all the bonds would not be realistic, especially if interest rates are set artificially low; and to print very large quantities of currency would be obvious and controversial.) This way, the process is mysteriously wrapped up in the banking system. The end result, however, is the same as turning on government printing presses and simply manufacturing fiat money (money created by the order of government with nothing of tangible value backing it) to pay government expenses. Yet, in accounting terms, the books are said to be "balanced" because the liability of the money is offset by the "asset" of the IOU. The Federal Reserve check received by the government then is endorsed and sent back to one of the Federal Reserve banks where it now becomes a ...

(Continued from previous page)

GOVERNMENT DEPOSIT

Once the Federal Reserve check has been deposited into the government's account, it is used to pay government expenses and, thus, is transformed into many ...

GOVERNMENT CHECKS

These checks become the means by which the first wave of fiat money floods into the economy. Recipients now deposit them into their own bank accounts where they become ...

COMMERCIAL BANK DEPOSITS

Commercial bank deposits immediately take on a split personality. On the one hand, they are liabilities to the bank because they are owed back to the depositors. But, as long as they remain in the bank, they also are considered as assets because they are on hand. Once again, the books are balanced: the assets offset the liabilities. But the process does not stop there. Through the magic of fractional-reserve banking, the deposits are made to serve an additional and more lucrative purpose. To accomplish this, the on-hand deposits now become reclassified in the books and called ...

BANK RESERVES

Reserves for what? Are these for paying off depositors should they want to close out their accounts? No. That's the lowly function they served when they were classified as mere assets. Now that they have been given the name of "reserves," they become the magic wand to materialize even larger amounts of fiat money. This is where the real action is: at the level of the commercial banks. Here's how it works. The banks are permitted by the Fed to hold as little as 10% of their deposits in "reserve." That means, if they receive deposits of $1 million from the first wave of fiat money created by the Fed, they have

$900,000 more than they are required to keep on hand ($1 million less 10% reserve). In bankers' language, that $900,000 is called ...

EXCESS RESERVES

The word "excess" is a tipoff that these so-called reserves have a special destiny. Now that they have been transmuted into an excess, they are considered as available for lending. And so in due course these excess reserves are converted into ...

BANK LOANS

But wait a minute. How can this money be lent out when it is owned by the original depositors who are still free to write checks and spend it any time they wish? Isn't that a double claim against the same money? The answer is that, when the new loans are made, they are *not* made with the same money at all. They are made with brand *new* money created out of thin air for that purpose. The nation's money supply simply increases by ninety per cent of the bank's deposits. Furthermore, this new money is far more interesting to the banks than the old. The old money, which they received from depositors, requires them to pay out interest or perform services for the privilege of using it. But, with the *new* money, the banks *collect* interest, instead, which is not too bad considering it cost them nothing to make. Nor is that the end of the process. When this *second* wave of fiat money moves into the economy, it comes right back into the banking system, just as the first wave did, in the form of ...

MORE COMMERCIAL BANK DEPOSITS

The process now repeats but with slightly smaller numbers each time around. What was a "loan" on Friday comes back into the bank as a "deposit" on Monday. The deposit then is reclassified as a "reserve" and ninety per cent of that becomes an "excess" reserve which, once again, is available for a new "loan." Thus, the $1 million of *first* wave fiat money gives birth to $900,000 in the *second* wave, and that gives birth to $810,000 in the *third* wave ($900,000 less 10% reserve). It takes about twenty-eight times through the revolving door of deposits becoming loans becoming deposits becoming more loans until the process plays itself out to the maximum effect, which is ...

BANK FIAT MONEY = UP TO 9 TIMES NATIONAL DEBT

The amount of fiat money created by the banking cartel is approximately nine times the amount of the original government debt which made the entire process possible.[1] When the original debt itself is added to that figure, we finally have ...

TOTAL FIAT MONEY=UP TO 10 TIMES NATIONAL DEBT

The total amount of fiat money created by the Federal Reserve and the commercial banks together is approximately ten times the amount of the underlying government debt. To the degree that this newly created money floods into the economy in excess of goods and services, it causes the purchasing power of all money, both old and new, to decline. Prices go up because the relative value of the money has gone down. The result is the same as if that purchasing power had been taken from us in taxes. The reality of this process, therefore, is that it is a ...

HIDDEN TAX = UP TO 10 TIMES THE NATIONAL DEBT

Without realizing it, Americans have paid over the years, in *addition* to their federal income taxes and excise taxes, a completely hidden tax equal to many times the national debt! And that still is not the end of the process. Since our money supply is purely an arbitrary entity with nothing behind it except debt, its quantity can go

---

1. That is a theoretical maximum. In actual practice, the banks can seldom lend out all of the money they are allowed to create, and the numbers fall short of the maximum.

down as well as up. When people are going deeper into debt, the nation's money supply expands and prices go up, but when they pay off their debts and refuse to renew, the money supply contracts and prices tumble. That is exactly what happens in times of economic or political uncertainty. This alternation between periods of expansion and contraction of the money supply is the underlying cause of ...

BOOMS, BUSTS, AND DEPRESSIONS

Who benefits from all of this? Certainly not the average citizen. The only beneficiaries are the political scientists in Congress who enjoy the effect of unlimited revenue to perpetuate their power, and the monetary scientists within the banking cartel called the Federal Reserve System who have been able to harness the American people, without their knowing it, to the yoke of modern feudalism.

RESERVE RATIOS

The previous figures are based on a "reserve" ratio of 10% (a money-expansion ratio of 10-to-1). It must be remembered, however, that this is purely arbitrary. Since the money is fiat with no precious-metal backing, there is no *real* limitation except what the politicians and money managers decide is expedient for the moment. Altering this ratio is the third way in which the Federal Reserve can influence the nation's supply of money. The numbers, therefore, must be considered as transient. At any time there is a "need" for more money, the ratio can be increased to 20-to-1 or 50-to-1, or the pretense of a reserve can be dropped altogether. There is virtually *no* limit to the amount of fiat money that can be manufactured under the present system.

NATIONAL DEBT NOT NECESSARY FOR INFLATION

Because the Federal Reserve can be counted on to "monetize" (convert into money) virtually any amount of government debt, and because this process of expanding the money supply is the primary cause of inflation, it is tempting to jump to the conclusion that federal debt and inflation are but two aspects of the same phenomenon. This, however, is not necessarily true. It is quite possible to have either one without the other.

The banking cartel holds a monopoly in the manufacture of money. Consequently, money is created only when IOUs are "monetized" by the Fed or by commercial banks. When private individuals, corporations, or institutions purchase government bonds, they must use money they have previously earned and saved. In other words, no new money is created, because they are using funds that are already in existence. Therefore, the sale of government bonds to the banking system *is* inflationary, but when sold to the private sector, it is *not*. That is the primary reason the United States avoided massive inflation during the 1980s when the federal government was going into debt at a greater rate than ever before in its history. By keeping interest rates high, these bonds became attractive to *private* investors, including those in other countries.[1] Very little new money was created, because most of the bonds were purchased with American dollars already in existence. This, of course, was a temporary fix at best. Today, those bonds are continually maturing and are being replaced by still *more* bonds to include the original debt plus accumulated interest. Eventually this process must come to an end and, when it does, the Fed will have no choice but to literally buy back all the debt of the '80s—that is, to replace all of the formerly invested private money with newly manufactured fiat money—plus a great deal more to cover the interest. *Then* we will understand the meaning of inflation.

On the other side of the coin, the Federal Reserve has the option of manufacturing money even if the federal government does *not* go deeper into debt. For example, the huge expansion of the money supply leading up to the stock market crash in 1929 occurred at a time when the national debt was being paid off. In every year from 1920 through 1930, federal revenue exceeded expenses, and there were relatively few government bonds being offered. The massive inflation of the money supply was made possible by converting commercial bank loans into "reserves" at the Fed's discount window and by the Fed's purchase of banker's acceptances, which are commercial contracts for the purchase of goods.[2]

Now the options are even greater. The Monetary Control Act of 1980 has made it possible for the Creature to monetize virtually *any*

---

1. Only about 11 to 15 per cent of the federal debt at that time was held by the Federal Reserve System.
2. See chapter twenty-three.

debt instrument, including IOUs from foreign governments. The apparent purpose of this legislation is to make it possible to bail out those governments which are having trouble paying the interest on their loans from American banks. When the Fed creates fiat American dollars to give foreign governments in exchange for their worthless bonds, the money path is slightly longer and more twisted, but the effect is similar to the purchase of U.S. Treasury Bonds. The newly created dollars go to the foreign governments, then to the American banks where they become cash reserves. Finally, they flow back into the U.S. money pool (multiplied by nine) in the form of additional loans. The cost of the operation once again is borne by the American citizen through the loss of purchasing power. Expansion of the money supply, therefore, and the inflation that follows, no longer even require federal deficits. As long as *someone* is willing to borrow American dollars, the cartel will have the option of creating those dollars specifically to purchase their bonds and, by so doing, continue to expand the money supply.

We must not forget, however, that one of the reasons the Fed was created in the first place was to make it possible for Congress to spend without the public knowing it was being taxed. Americans have shown an amazing indifference to this fleecing, explained undoubtedly by their lack of understanding of how the Mandrake Mechanism works. Consequently, at the present time, this cozy contract between the banking cartel and the politicians is in little danger of being altered. As a practical matter, therefore, even though the Fed may also create fiat money in exchange for commercial debt and for bonds of foreign governments, its *major* concern likely will be to continue supplying Congress.

The implications of this fact are mind boggling. Since our money supply, at present at least, is tied to the national debt, to pay off that debt would cause money to disappear. Even to seriously *reduce* it would cripple the economy.[1] Therefore, as long as the Federal Reserve exists, America will be, *must* be, in debt.

The purchase of bonds from other governments is accelerating in the present political climate of internationalism. Our own money

---

1. With the Fed holding only 7% of the national debt, the effect would still be devastating. Since the money supply is pyramided ten times on top of the underlying government bonds, each $1 eliminated from the federal debt would cause the money supply to shrink by 70¢ (1.00 X .07 X 10 = .70).

supply increasingly is based upon *their* debt as well as ours, and they, too, will not be allowed to pay it off even if they are able.

TAXES NOT EVEN NECESSARY

It is a sobering thought that the federal government now could operate—even at its current level of spending—without levying any taxes whatsoever. All it has to do is create the required money through the Federal Reserve System by monetizing its own bonds. In fact, most of the money it *now* spends is obtained that way.

If the idea of eliminating the IRS sounds like good news, remember that the inflation that results from monetizing the debt is just as much a tax as any other; but, because it is hidden and so few Americans understand how it works, it is more politically popular than a tax that is out in the open.

Inflation can be likened to a game of Monopoly in which the game's banker has no limit to the amount of money he can distribute. With each throw of the dice he reaches under the table and brings up another stack of those paper tokens which all the players must use as money. If the banker is also one of the players—and in our real world that is exactly the case—obviously he is going to end up owning all the property. But, in the meantime, the increasing flood of money swirls out from the banker and engulfs the players. As the quantity of money becomes greater, the relative worth of each token becomes less, and the prices bid for the properties goes up. The game is called *monopoly* for a reason. In the end, one person holds all the property and everyone else is bankrupt. But what does it matter. It's only a game.

Unfortunately, it is *not* a game in the real world. It is our livelihood, our food, our shelter. It *does* make a difference if there is only one winner, and it makes a *big* difference if that winner obtained his monopoly simply by manufacturing everyone's money.

FOURTH REASON TO ABOLISH THE SYSTEM

Make no mistake about it, inflation is a tax. Furthermore, it is the most unfair tax of them all because it falls most heavily upon those who are thrifty, those on fixed incomes, and those in the middle and lower income brackets. The important point here is that this hidden tax would be impossible without fiat money. Fiat money in America is created solely as a result of the Federal Reserve System. Therefore, it is totally accurate to say that *the Federal Reserve System generates our most unfair tax.* Both the tax and the System that makes it possible should be abolished.

The political scientists who authorize this process of monetizing the national debt, and the monetary scientists who carry it out, know that it is not true debt. It is not true debt, because no one in Washington really expects to repay it—*ever.* The dual purpose of this magic show is simply to create free spending money for the politicians, without the inconvenience of raising direct taxes, and also to generate a perpetual river of gold flowing into the banking cartel. The partnership is merely looking out for itself.

Why, then, does the federal government bother with taxes at all? Why not just operate on monetized debt? The answer is twofold. First, if it did, people would begin to wonder about the *source* of the money, and that might cause them to wake up to the reality that inflation is a tax. Thus, open taxes at *some* level serve to perpetuate public ignorance which is essential to the success of the scheme. The second reason is that taxes, particularly *progressive* taxes, are weapons by which elitist social planners can wage war on the middle class.

A TOOL FOR SOCIAL PLANNING

The January 1946 issue of *American Affairs* carried an article written by Beardsley Ruml who, at that time, was Chairman of the Federal Reserve Bank of New York. Ruml had devised the system of automatic withholding during World War II, so he was well qualified to speak on the nature and purpose of the federal income tax. His theme was spelled out in the title of his article: "Taxes for Revenue Are Obsolete."

In an introduction to the article, the magazine's editor summarized Ruml's views as follows:

> His thesis is that, given control of a central banking system and an inconvertible currency [a currency not backed by gold], a sovereign national government is finally free of money worries and needs no longer levy taxes for the purpose of providing itself with revenue. All taxation, therefore, should be regarded from the point of view of social and economic consequences.[1]

Ruml explained that, since the Federal Reserve now can create out of nothing all the money the government could ever want, there

---

1. "Taxes for Revenue Are Obsolete," by Beardsley Ruml, *American Affairs*, January, 1946, p. 35.

remain only two reasons to have taxes at all. The first of these is to combat a rise in the general level of prices. His argument was that, when people have money in their pockets, they will spend it for goods and services, and this will bid up the prices. The solution, he says, is to take the money away from them through taxation and let the government spend it instead. This, too, will bid up prices, but Ruml chose not to go into that. He explained his theory this way:

> The dollars the government spends become purchasing power in the hands of the people who have received them. The dollars the government takes by taxes cannot be spent by the people, and therefore, these dollars can no longer be used to acquire the things which are available for sale. Taxation is, therefore, an instrument of the first importance in the administration of any fiscal and monetary policy.[1]

REDISTRIBUTION OF WEALTH

The other purpose of taxation, according to Ruml, is to redistribute the wealth from one class of citizens to another. This must always be done in the name of social justice or equality, but the real objective is to override the free market and bring society under the control of the master planners. Ruml said:

> The second principal purpose of federal taxes is to attain more equality of wealth and of income than would result from economic forces working alone. The taxes which are effective for this purpose are the progressive individual income tax, the progressive estate tax, and the gift tax. What these taxes should be depends on public policy with respect to the distribution of wealth and of income. These taxes should be defended and attacked in terms of their effect on the character of American life, not as revenue measures.[2]

As we have seen, Senator Nelson Aldrich was one of the creators of the Federal Reserve System. That is not surprising in light of the cartel nature of the System and the financial interests which he represented. Aldrich also was one of the prime sponsors of the federal income tax. The two creations work together as a far more delicate mechanism for control over the economic and social life of society than either one alone.

In more recent years, there has been hopeful evidence that the master planners were about to abandon Ruml's blueprint. We have

---

1. Ruml, p. 36.
2. *Ibid.*, p. 36.

heard a great deal both in Congress and at the Federal Reserve about the necessity of reducing expenses so as to diminish the growth of federal debt and inflation. But it has been lip service only. The great bulk of federal funding continues to be created by the Mandrake Mechanism, the cost of government continues to outpace tax revenues, and the Ruml formula reigns supreme.

EXPANSION LEADS TO CONTRACTION

While it is true that the Mandrake Mechanism is responsible for the expansion of the money supply, the process also works in reverse. Just as money is created when the Federal Reserve *purchases* bonds or other debt instruments, it is extinguished by the *sale* of those same items. When they are sold, the money is given back to the System and disappears into the inkwell or computer chip from which it came. Then, the same secondary ripple effect that *created* money through the commercial banking system causes it to be *withdrawn* from the economy. Furthermore, even if the Federal Reserve does not deliberately contract the money supply, the same result can and often does occur when the public decides to resist the availability of credit and reduce its debt. A man can only be tempted to borrow, he cannot be forced to do so.

There are many psychological factors involved in a decision to go into debt that can offset the easy availability of money and a low interest rate: A downturn in the economy, the threat of civil disorder, the fear of pending war, an uncertain political climate, to name just a few. Even though the Fed may try to pump money into the economy by making it abundantly available, the public can thwart that move simply by saying no, thank you. When this happens, the old debts that are being paid off are not replaced by new ones to take their place, and the entire amount of consumer and business debt will shrink. That means the money supply also will shrink, because, in modern America, debt *is* money. And it is this very expansion and contraction of the monetary pool—a phenomenon that could not occur if based upon the laws of supply and demand—that is at the very core of practically every boom and bust that has plagued mankind throughout history.

In conclusion, it can be said that modern money is a grand illusion conjured by the magicians of finance and politics. We are living in an age of fiat money, and it is sobering to realize that every previous nation in history that has adopted such money eventually was economically destroyed by it. Furthermore, there is nothing in our present monetary structure that offers any assurance that we may be exempted from that morbid roll call.

SUMMARY

The American dollar has no intrinsic value. It is a classic example of fiat money with no limit to the quantity that can be produced. Its primary value lies in the willingness of people to accept it and, to that end, legal tender laws require them to do so. It is true that our money is created out of nothing, but it is more accurate to say that it is based upon debt. In one sense, therefore, our money is created out of *less* than nothing. The entire money supply would vanish into bank vaults and computer chips if all debts were repaid. Under the present System, therefore, our leaders cannot allow a serious reduction in either the national or consumer debt. Charging interest on pretended loans is usury, and that has become institutionalized under the Federal Reserve System. The Mandrake Mechanism by which the Fed converts debt into money may seem complicated at first, but it is simple if one remembers that the process is not intended to be logical but to confuse and deceive. The end product of the Mechanism is artificial expansion of the money supply, which is the root cause of the hidden tax called inflation. This expansion then leads to contraction and, together, they produce the destructive boom-bust cycle that has plagued mankind throughout history wherever fiat money has existed.

ADDENDUM: DEBT-CANCELLATION PROGRAMS

Because banks lend money that does not exist prior to the transaction, many debtors have concluded they are not obligated to repay. This is a compelling concept in view of the fact that bank and credit-card loan contracts typically lead customers to think they are borrowing someone else's money, which is why they are willing to pay interest. When challenged in court, these contracts often are judged to be fraudulent, and there now are companies offering "debt-cancellation" services to challenge these contracts with the end in mind that debts will be canceled. A discussion of the pros and cons of these programs is beyond the scope of this work, but interested parties are invited to read or view a video of the author's analysis at the following web site:

www.freedom-force.org/freedom.cfm?fuseaction=issues.

Cecil Rhodes made one of the world's greatest fortunes of the 19th century. Financed by Nathan Rothschild and the Bank of England, he established a monopoly over the diamond output of South Africa and most of the gold as well. He formed a secret society which included many of the top leaders of British government. Their elitist goal was nothing less than world domination and the establishment of a modern feudalist society controlled by themselves through the world's central banks. In America, the Council on Foreign Relations (CFR) was an outgrowth of that group.

August Belmont came to New Yo▮ in 1837 as the financial agent of th▮ Rothschilds. He funneled vast amounts of capital into American investments, often without anyone knowing whose money he was spending. The purpose of concealment was to blunt the growing anti-Rothschild resentme▮ that was then prevalent in Europe as well as America. When his affiliation became commonly know▮ his usefulness came to an end an▮ he was replaced by J.P. Morgan.

208

P. Morgan, Sr. (left) was brought into banking by his father, Junius Morgan, in ngland. The Morgans were friendly competitors with the Rothschilds and became cially close to them. Morgan's London-based firm was saved from financial ruin in 57 by the Bank of England over which the Rothschilds held great influence. ereafter, Morgan appears to have served as a Rothschild financial agent and went great length to appear totally American.

hn D. Rockefeller (right) made his initial fortune in oil but soon gravitated into nking and finance. His entry into the field was not welcomed by Morgan, and they came fierce competitors. Eventually, they decided to minimize their competition by tering into joint ventures. In the end, they worked together to create a national nking cartel called the Federal Reserve System.

Above is the clubhouse for the private resort on Jekyll Island in Georgia where the Federal Reserve System was conceived in great secrecy in 1910. It is shown here shortly after completion.

Jacob Schiff (right) was head of the New York investment firm, Kuhn, Loeb & Co. He was one of the principal backers of the Bolshevik revolution and personally financed Trotsky's trip from New York to Russia. He was a major contributor to Woodrow Wilson's presidential campaign and an advocate for passage of the Federal Reserve Act.

"DEE·LIGHTED!"

This cartoon by Robert Minor appeared in the St. Louis Post-Dispatch in 1911. It shows Karl Marx surrounded by enthusiastic Wall Street financiers: Morgan partner George Perkins; J.P. Morgan; John Ryan of National City Bank; John D. Rockefeller; and Andrew Carnegie. Immediately behind Marx is Teddy Roosevelt, leader of the Progressive Party.

211

Harry Dexter White (left) and John Maynard Keynes (right) were the theoreticians who guided the 1944 Bretton Woods Monetary Conference at which the IMF/World Bank was created. White was a member of the Communist Party. Keynes was a member of the Fabian Society. They shared the same goal of international socialism. The IMF/World Bank has furthered that goal ever since.

Macm

Raymond Robins is shown here as the Chairman of the Progressive Pa convention in Chicago in 1912. He later became head of the American Red Cross Mission in Russia after th Bolshevik revolution. Although he represented Wall Street interests, he was a disciple of Cecil Rhodes and was anti-capitalist in his beliefs. He held great influence over Lenin.

Edward Mandell House was the man who secured Woodrow Wilson's nomination for President and who, thereafter, became the hidden power at the White House. He negotiated a secret agreement to draw the U.S. into World War I at the very time Wilson was campaigning on the promise to keep America out of the war. On behalf of Wall Street, House lobbied Congress to pass the Federal Reserve Act.

National Archives

Carroll Quigley was a professor of history at Georgetown University. His book, *Tragedy and Hope*, revealed that the Council on Foreign Relations (CFR) is an outgrowth of the secret society formed by Cecil Rhodes. He wrote the history of how an international network of financiers has created a system of financial control able to dominate the political systems of all countries through their central banks. He named names and provided meticulous documentation. His book was suppressed.

Georgetown University

Winston Churchill was the First Lord of
Admiralty in World War I. As the *Lusita*
entered into an area where a German
U-Boat was known to be operating, he
called off the destroyer escort that had
assigned to protect her. He calculated
the destruction of a British ship with U.
passengers aboard would inflame Ame
passions against Germany and help cr
political climate for coming into the war

Hulton Deutsch

U.S. Army Pictoral Service

Lord Mersey (right) was put in charge of
an official inquiry into the sinking of the
Lusitania. It was not an investigation but a
coverup. He was instructed by the
Admiralty to place the entire blame on the
Captain of the ship. Mersey obeyed his
orders but refused payment for his
services and declined to accept further
judicial assignments. In later years, he
said the affair "was a damn dirty business."

214

Section III

THE NEW ALCHEMY

The ancient alchemists sought in vain to convert lead into gold. Modern alchemists have succeeded in that quest. The lead bullets of war have yielded an endless source of gold for those magicians who control the Mandrake Mechanism. The startling fact emerges that, without the ability to create fiat money, most modern wars simply would not have occurred. As long as the Mechanism is allowed to function, future wars are inevitable. This is the story of how that came to pass.

Chapter Eleven

THE ROTHSCHILD FORMULA

The rise of the House of Rothschild in Europe; the tradition among financiers of profiting from both sides of armed conflict; the formula by which war is converted into debt and debt converted back into war.

So far we have adhered closely to the subject of money and the history of its manipulation by political and monetary scientists. Now we are going to take a short detour along a parallel path and view some of the same historical scenery from a different perspective. As we progress, it may seem that we have lost our way, and you may wonder what connection any of this can possibly have with the Federal Reserve System. Please be assured, however, it has *everything* to do with it, and, when we finally return to that topic, the connection will have become painfully clear.

THE PROFITS OF WAR

The focus of this chapter is on the profits of war and, more specifically, the tendency of those who reap those profits to manipulate governments into military conflicts, not for national or patriotic reasons, but for private gain. The mechanism by which this was accomplished in the past was more complex than simply lending money to warring governments and then collecting interest, although that was part of it. The real payoff has always been in the form of political favoritism in the market place. Writing in the year 1937, French historian Richard Lewinsohn explains:

> Although often called bankers, those who financed wars in the pre-capitalist period ... were not bankers in the modern sense of the word. Unlike modern bankers who operate with money deposited with them by their clients [or, in more recent times, created out of nothing by a central bank—E.G.], they generally worked with the fortune which they themselves had amassed or inherited, and which

they lent at a high rate of interest. Thus those who risked the financing of a war were for the most part already very rich, and this was the case down to the seventeenth century.

When they agreed to finance a war, these rich lenders did not, however, always attach great importance to the rate of interest. In this respect they often showed the greatest compliance to their august clients. But in return they secured for themselves privileges which could be turned into industrial or commercial profit, such as mining concessions, monopolies of sale or importation, etc. Sometimes even they were given the right to appropriate certain taxes as a guarantee of their loans. So though the loan itself carried a very real risk and often did not bring in much interest, the indirect profits were very considerable, and the lenders' leniency well rewarded.[1]

THE ROTHSCHILD DYNASTY

No discussion of banking as a mechanism for financing wars would be complete without turning eventually to the name Rothschild. It was Mayer Amschel Rothschild who is quoted as saying: "Let me issue and control a nation's money and I care not who writes the laws."[2] Biographer Frederic Morton concluded that the Rothschild dynasty had: "... conquered the world more thoroughly, more cunningly, and much more lastingly than all the Caesars before or all the Hitlers after them."[3] The dynasty was begun in Frankfurt, Germany, in the middle of the eighteenth century by Mayer Amschel Bauer, the son of a goldsmith. Mayer became a clerk in the Oppenheimer Bank in Hanover and was eventually promoted to junior partner. After his father's death, he returned to his home in Frankfurt to continue the family business. Over the door hung a red shield with an eagle as a sign to identify the establishment. The German words for red shield are *roth schild*, so he changed his name from Bauer to Rothschild and added five gold arrows held in the talons of the eagle to represent his five sons.

---

1.   Richard Lewinsohn, *The Profits of War through the Ages* (New York: E.P. Dutton, 1937), pp. 55–56.
2.   Quoted by Senator Robert L. Owen, former Chairman of the Senate Committee on Banking and Currency and one of the sponsors of the Federal Reserve Act, *National Economy and the Banking System*, (Washington, D.C.: U.S. Government Printing Office, 1939), p. 99. This quotation could not be verified in a primary reference work. However, when one considers the life and accomplishments of the elder Rothschild, there can be little doubt that this sentiment was, in fact, his outlook and guiding principle.
3.   Frederic Morton, *The Rothschilds: A Family Portrait* (New York: Atheneum, 1962), p. 14.

The Rothschild fortune began when Mayer adopted the practice of fractional-reserve banking. As we have seen, he was not alone in this, but the House of Rothschild greatly surpassed the competition. That was due to his sharp business acumen and also because of his five most unusual sons, all of whom became financial power centers of their own. As they matured and learned the magic of converting debt into money, they moved beyond the confines of Frankfurt and established additional operations in the financial centers, not only of Europe, but of much of the civilized world.

Throughout the first half of the nineteenth century, the brothers conducted important transactions on behalf of the governments of England, France, Prussia, Austria, Belgium, Spain, Naples, Portugal, Brazil, various German states, and other smaller countries. They were the personal bankers of many of the crowned heads of Europe. They made large investments, through agents, in markets as distant as the United States, India, Cuba, and Australia. They were financiers to Cecil Rhodes, making it possible for him to establish a monopoly over the diamond fields of South Africa. They are still connected with the de Beers.[1]

Biographer Derek Wilson writes:

> Those who lampooned or vilified the Rothschilds for their "sinister" influence had a considerable amount of justification for their anger and anxiety. The banking community had always constituted a "fifth estate" whose members were able, by their control of royal purse strings, to affect important events. But the house of Rothschild was immensely more powerful than any financial empire that had ever preceded it. It commanded vast wealth. It was international. It was independent. Royal governments were nervous of it because they could not control it. Popular movements hated it because it was not answerable to the people. Constitutionalists resented it because its influence was exercised behind the scenes—secretly.[2]

Secrecy, of course, is essential for the success of a cabal, and the Rothschilds perfected the art. By remaining behind the scenes, they were able to avoid the brunt of public anger which was directed, instead, at the political figures which they largely controlled. This is a technique which has been practiced by financial manipulators

---

1. Morton, pp. 145, 219.
2. Derek Wilson, *Rothschild: The Wealth and Power of A Dynasty* (New York: Charles Scribner's Sons, 1988), pp. 79, 98–99.

ever since, and it is fully utilized by those who operate the Federal Reserve System today. Wilson continues:

Clandestinity was and remained a feature of Rothschild political activity. Seldom were they to be seen engaging in open public debate on important issues. Never did they seek government office. Even when, in later years, some of them entered parliament, they did not feature prominently in the assembly chambers of London, Paris or Berlin. Yet all the while they were helping to shape the major events of the day: by granting or withholding funds; by providing statesmen with an official diplomatic service; by influencing appointments to high office; and by an almost daily intercourse with the great decision makers.[1]

A FORTUNE IN SMUGGLING

Continual war in Europe created excellent opportunities for profit from smuggling scarce consumer goods past military blockades. Since the Rothschilds often financed both sides in a conflict and were known to have great political influence, the mere sight of the red shield on a leather pouch, a carriage, or a ship's flag was sufficient to insure that the messenger or his cargo could pass through check points in either direction. This immunity allowed them to deal in a thriving black market for cotton goods, yarn, tobacco, coffee, sugar, and indigo; and they moved freely through the borders of Germany, Scandinavia, Holland, Spain, England, and France.[2] This government protection was one of those indirect benefits that generated commercial profits far in excess of the interest received on the underlying government loans.

It is generally true that, one man's loss is another man's gain. And even the friendliest of biographers admit that, for more than two centuries, the House of Rothschild profited handsomely from wars and economic collapses, the very occasions on which others sustained the greatest losses.

NAPOLEON VS THE BANKERS

If one picture is worth a thousand words, then one example surely must be worth a dozen explanations. There is no better example than the economic war waged by the financiers of nineteenth-century Europe against Napoleon Bonaparte. It is an easily forgotten fact of history that Napoleon had restored law and

---

1. Derek Wilson, p. 99.
2. Morton, pp. 40–41.

order to a chaotic, post-revolutionary France and had turned his attention, not to war, but to establishing peace and improving economic conditions at home. He was particularly anxious to get his country and his people out of debt and out of the control of bankers. R. McNair Wilson, in *Monarchy or Money Power*, says:

> It was ordained by him that money should not be exported from France on any pretext whatever except with the consent of the Government, and that in no circumstance should loans be employed to meet current expenditure whether civil or military.... "One has only to consider," Napoleon remarked, "what loans can lead to in order to realize their danger. Therefore, I would never have anything to do with them and have always striven against them."...
>
> The object was to withhold from finance the power to embarrass the Government as it had embarrassed the Government of Louis XVI. When a Government, Bonaparte declared, is dependent for money upon bankers, they and not the leaders of that Government control the situation, since "the hand that gives is above the hand that takes."...
>
> "Money," he declared, "has no motherland; financiers are without patriotism and without decency: their sole object is gain."[1]

One of Napoleon's first blows against the bankers was to establish an independent Bank of France with himself as president. But even this bank was not trusted, and government funds were never placed into it. It was his refusal to borrow, however, that caused the most concern among the financiers. Actually, to them this was a mixture of both bad and good news. The bad news was that they were denied the benefit of royalty payments on fractional money. The good news was that, without resorting to debt, they were confident Napoleon could not militarily defend himself. Thus, he easily could be toppled and replaced by Louis XVI of the old monarchic dynasty who was receptive to banker influence. Wilson continues:

> They had good hope of compassing his downfall. None believed that he could finance war on a great scale now that the resource of paper money had been denied him by the destruction of the Assignat.[2] Where would he obtain the indispensable gold and silver to feed and equip a great army? Pitt [the Prime Minister of England] counted already on a coalition of England, Austria, Prussia, Russia, Spain,

---

1. R. McNair Wilson, *Monarchy or Money Power* (London: Eyre and Spottiswoode, Ltd., 1933), pp. 68, 72.
2. The Assignat was pure fiat money which rapidly became totally worthless in commerce and which all but destroyed the French economy.

Sweden, and numerous small states. Some 600,000 men would be put into the field. All the resources of England's wealth—that is to say, of the world's wealth—would be placed at the disposal of this overwhelming force. Could the Corsican muster 200,000? Could he arm them? Could he feed them? If the lead bullets did not destroy him, the gold bullets would soon make an end. He would be forced, like his neighbors, to come, hat in hand, for loans and, like them, to accept the banker's terms....

He could not put his hands on £2,000,000, so empty was the Treasury and so depleted the nation's stock of metallic money. London waited with interest to see how the puzzle would be solved.[1]

Napoleon solved the puzzle quite simply by selling off some real estate. Those crazy Americans gave him £3,000,000 for a vast swamp called Louisiana.

A PLAN TO DESTROY THE UNITED STATES

Napoleon did not want war, but he knew that Europe's financial rulers would not settle for peace—unless, of course, they were forced into it by the defeat of their puppet regimes or unless, somehow, it would be to their monetary advantage. It was in pursuit of the latter tactic that he threatened to take direct possession of Holland, which then was ruled by his brother, King Louis. Napoleon knew that the Dutch were heavily in debt to the English bankers. If Holland were to be annexed by France, this debt would never be repaid. So Napoleon made a proposal to England's bankers that, if they would convince the English government to accept peace with France, he would agree to leave Holland alone.

The negotiations were handled by the banker, Pierre-Cesar Labouchere, who was sent by the Dutch, and the English banker, Sir Francis Baring who was Labouchere's father-in-law. Although this was an attractive proposal to the bankers, at least on a short-term basis, it was still against their nature to forego the immense profits of war and mercantilism. They revised the proposal, therefore, to include a plan whereby both England and France would combine forces to destroy the newly independent United States and bring at least half of it—the industrial half—back under the domination of England. The incredible plan, conceived by the French banker, Ouvrard, called for military invasion and conquest followed by division of the spoils. England would receive

---

1. R. McNair Wilson, pp. 71–72.

the northern states, united with Canada, while the southern states would fall to France. Napoleon was to be tempted by offering him the awesome title of "King of America." McNair Wilson tells us:

> Labouchere wrote to Baring on March 21, and enclosed a note for [British Foreign Secretary] Wellesley dictated by Ouvrard which ran:
> "From a conqueror he (Napoleon) is becoming a preserver; the first result of his marriage with Marie Louise will be that he will make an offer of peace to England. It is to this nation's (*i.e.*, England's) interest to make peace, for it has the command of the sea; on the contrary, it is really in the interest of France to continue war, which allows her to expand indefinitely and make a fresh fleet, which cannot be done once peace is established. Why does not the English Cabinet make a proposal to France to destroy the United States of America, and by making them again dependent on England, persuade Napoleon to lend his aid to destroy the life-work of Louis XVI?... It is to her (England's) interest to conclude peace and to flatter Napoleon's vanity by recognizing his work and his imperial title."...
> The Cabinet discussed the proposals and approved them. Wellesley at once hurried to Baring's house to give him the good news.... The Dutch would be able to pay and would be compelled to pay in gold.
> Unhappily Napoleon found out what was afoot and took somewhat strong objections to the plan of a joint attack on the United States. He arrested Ouvrard, dismissed and exiled Fouche, and published the whole story, to the grave distress of Wellesley and Baring.[1]

It must not be concluded from this that Napoleon was a paragon of virtue or a champion of honest money. His objection to the bankers was that their monetary power was able to threaten the sovereignty of his own political power. He allowed them a free hand while they served the purpose of the state. Then, when the need for military financing subsided, he would condemn them for making "unholy profits" and simply take it from them in the name of the people. If the bankers protested, they were sent to prison.

And so the battle lines were drawn. Napoleon had to be destroyed at all costs. To make this possible, the Bank of England created vast new amounts of fiat money to "lend" to the government so it could finance an overpowering army. A steady stream of gold flowed out of the country to finance the armies of Russia, Prussia, and Austria. The economy staggered once again under the

---

1. R. McNair Wilson, pp. 81–82.

load of war debt, and the little people paid the bill with hardly a grumble because they hadn't the slightest knowledge it was being charged to their account. Wilson concludes the story:

> The bankers won. Louis XVIII was restored by British arms and British diplomacy to the throne of his ancestors. Loans were placed at his disposal, though Napoleon had left a France which enjoyed a credit balance.
>
> A year later the man whom every King and every banker in Europe called "usurper" won back his throne with 800 men and without the firing of a single shot. On this occasion he had no option but to raise a loan for the defense of France. The City of London [banking district] accommodated him with £5,000,000. With this sum he equipped the army which Wellington defeated at Waterloo.[1]

GOLD FOR THE DUKE OF WELLINGTON

One of the most fascinating and revealing episodes to be recorded by Rothschild biographers concerns the smuggling of a large shipment of gold to finance the Duke of Wellington who was attempting to feed and equip an army in Portugal and in the Pyrenees mountains between Spain and France.

It was not at all certain that Wellington would be able to defeat Napoleon in the coming battle, and the Duke was hard pressed to convince bankers and merchants in Portugal and Spain to accept his written promises-to-pay, even though they were officially guaranteed by the British government. These notes were deeply discounted, and Wellington was desperate for gold coin. It was at this point that Nathan Rothschild offered the services of himself and his brothers. With an efficient smuggling apparatus already functioning throughout Europe, he was able to offer Wellington much better terms while still making a magnificent profit. But, to accomplish this, the gold had to pass right under Napoleon's nose. Frederic Morton describes the scene:

> There was only one way to route the cash: through the very France England's army was fighting. Of course, the Rothschild blockade-running machine already had superb cogs whirring all over Germany, Scandinavia and England, even in Spain and Southern France. But a very foxy new wheel was needed in Napoleon's capital itself. Enter Jacob—henceforth called James—the youngest of Mayer's sons.[2]

---

1. R. McNair Wilson, p. 83.
2. Morton, p. 46.

James was only nineteen years old but was well trained by his father in the art of deception. He arrived in Paris with a dual mission. First, he was to provide the French authorities with a false report about the British gold movement, with just enough truth in it to sound convincing. He presented the government with falsified letters indicating that the English were desperate to *halt* the flow of their gold into France. The ploy paid off when the French authorities then actually *encouraged* the financial community to accept British gold and to convert it into commercially sound banknotes. Second, James was to serve as a vital link in a financial chain stretching between London and the Pyrenees. He was to coordinate the receipt of the gold into France, the conversion of that gold into Spanish banknotes, and the movement of those notes out of the country on their way to Wellington. All of this he did with amazing dexterity, especially considering his youth. Morton concludes:

> In the space of a few hundred hours Mayer's youngest had not only gotten the English gold rolling through France, but conjured a fiscal mirage that took in Napoleon himself. A teen-age Rothschild tricked the imperial government into sanctioning the very process that helped to ruin it....
>
> The family machine began to hum. Nathan sent big shipments of British guineas, Portuguese gold ounces, French napoleons d'or (often freshly minted in London) across the Channel. From the coast James saw them to Paris and secretly transmuted the metal into bills on certain Spanish bankers. South of the capital, Kalmann [another of Mayer's sons] materialized, took over the bills, blurred into a thousand shadowed canyons along the Pyrenees—and reappeared, with Wellington's receipts in hand. Salomon [another son] was everywhere, trouble-shooting, making sure the transit points were diffuse and obscure enough not to disturb either the French delusion or the British guinea rate. Amschel stayed in Frankfurt and helped father Mayer to staff headquarters.
>
> The French did catch a few whiffs of the truth. Sometimes the suspicious could be prosperously purged of their suspicion. The police chief of Calais, for example, suddenly was able to live in such distracting luxury that he found it difficult to patrol the shoreline thoroughly....
>
> While Napoleon struggled his might away in the Russian Winter, there passed through France itself a gold vein to the army staving in the Empire's back door.[1]

---

1. Morton, p. 47.

At a dinner party in later years, Nathan casually summed up the episode as though it were merely a good piece of routine business. He said:

> The East India Company had £800,000 worth of gold to sell. I went to the sale and bought it all. I knew the Duke of Wellington must have it. The government sent for me and said they must have the gold. I sold the gold to them, but they didn't know how to get it to the Duke in Portugal. I undertook all that and sent it through France. It was the best business I have ever done.[1]

THE BATTLE OF WATERLOO

The final outcome of the battle at Waterloo between Wellington and Napoleon was crucial to Europe both politically and economically. If Napoleon had been victorious, England would have been in even greater economic trouble than before. Not only would she have lost international power and prestige, but even at home, her subjects would have been further disgruntled over such great personal and financial wartime sacrifices. Her defeat almost surely would have resulted in not being able to repay the great amounts she had borrowed to conduct the war. In the London stock exchange, therefore, where British government bonds were traded along with other securities, everyone waited anxiously for news of the outcome.

It was well known that the Rothschilds had developed a private courier service that was used, not only to transport gold and other tangible cargo, but to rapidly move *information* that could be useful in making investment decisions. It was expected, therefore, that Nathan in London would be the first to know the name of the victor after the cannon smoke had cleared from the battlefield. And they were not to be disappointed. The first news of Wellington's victory arrived in Brussels around midnight on June 18, 1815, where a Rothschild agent named Rothworth was waiting in readiness. He immediately mounted a fresh horse and set off for the port of Ostend where a boat was standing by to speed him across the channel to London. In the early hours of June 20, the exhausted messenger was pounding on Nathan's door, a full twenty-four hours before Wellington's own courier, Major Henry Percy, arrived.

---

1. Morton, p. 45.

At least one friendly biographer claims that Nathan's first act was to deliver the news to the Prime Minister, but that government officials were hesitant at first to believe it, because it ran contrary to reports they had received previously telling of serious British setbacks. At any rate, there is no doubt that Nathan's *second* act of the morning was to set off for the stock exchange to take up a position at his usual pillar.

All eyes were upon him as he slumped dejectedly, staring at the floor. Then, he raised his gaze and, with pained expression, began to *sell*. The whisper went through the crowded room, "Nathan is selling?" "Nathan is *selling!*" "Wellington must have lost." "Our government bonds will *never* be repaid." "Sell them now. Sell. Sell!"

Prices tumbled, and Nathan sold again. Prices plummeted, and still Nathan sold. Finally, prices collapsed altogether and, in one quick move, Nathan reversed his call and purchased the entire market in government bonds. In a matter of just a few hours, he had acquired the dominant holding of England's entire debt at but a tiny fraction of its worth. [1]

SIDONIA

Benjamin Disraeli, the Prime Minister of England, wrote a book in 1844 called *Coningsby*. It was a political novel in which the author expressed his views about contemporary issues. One of the strong characters in the book was a financier named Sidonia, but every detail of Sidonia's actions was an exact replica of the real Lord Rothschild, whom Disraeli greatly admired. In the guise of a novel, we read about Rothschild's emigration from Germany, his family and banking ties throughout Europe, his handling of the gold for Wellington, and his financial coup after Waterloo. Then Disraeli wrote:

> Europe did require money, and Sidonia was ready to lend it to Europe. France wanted some; Austria more; Prussia a little; Russia a few millions. Sidonia could furnish them all....
>
> It is not difficult to conceive that, after having pursued the career we have intimated for about ten years, Sidonia had become one of the

---

1. *The New York Times*, in its April 1, 1915, edition, reported that Baron Nathan Mayer de Rothschild had attempted to secure a court order to suppress a book written by Ignatious Balla entitled *The Romance of the Rothschilds* on the grounds that the Waterloo story about his grandfather was untrue and libelous. The court ruled that the story was true, dismissed the suit, and ordered Rothschild to pay all court costs.

most considerable personages in Europe. He had established a brother, or a near relative, in whom he could confide, in most of the principal capitals. He was lord and master of the money market of the world, and of course virtually lord and master of everything else. He literally held the revenues of Southern Italy in pawn; and monarchs and ministers of all countries courted his advice and were guided by his suggestions.[1]

That Disraeli was not exaggerating was made clear by the boast of James Rothschild himself. When U.S. Treasury agents approached him in Paris in 1842 with a request for a loan to the American government, he said to them: "You have seen the man who is at the head of the finances of Europe."[2]

There have always been men who were in a position to make private fortunes out of cooperating with both sides in a war. The Rothschilds were not unique in this, but they no doubt perfected the art and became the personification of that breed. They were not necessarily evil in a moral sense. What preoccupied their minds were not questions of right or wrong but of profit and loss. This analytical indifference to human suffering was aptly described by one Rothschild when he said: "When the streets of Paris are running with blood, I buy."[3] They may have held citizenship in the country of their residence, but patriotism was beyond their comprehension. They were also very bright, if not cunning, and these combined traits made them the role model of the cool pragmatists who dominate the political and financial world of today. Disraeli well described this type when he wrote of Sidonia:

> He was a man without affections. It would be harsh to say he had no heart, for he was susceptible of deep emotions, but not for individuals.... The individual never touched him. Woman was to him a toy, man a machine.[4]

It would seem that an absence of patriotism and a cold, analytical outlook would lead financiers to avoid making loans to governments, particularly foreign ones. Private borrowers can be hauled into court and their assets confiscated to make good on their

---

1. Benjamin Disraeli, *Coningsby* (New York: Alfred A. Knopf, originally published in England in 1844), p. 225.
2. Stephen Birmingham, *"Our Crowd": The Great Jewish Families of New York* (New York: Harper & Row, 1986), p. 73.
3. Quoted in *The New York Times*, October 21, 1987, cited by Chernow, p. 13.
4. Disraeli, p. 229.

debts. But governments control the legalized use of force. They *are* the courts. They *are* the police. Who will seize their assets? The answer is *another* government. Speaking of a relatively modern example of this principle, Ron Chernow explains:

> The new alliance [between the monetary and political scientists] was mutually advantageous. Washington wanted to harness the new financial power to coerce foreign governments into opening their markets to American goods or adopting pro-American policies. The banks, in turn, needed levers to force debt repayment and welcomed the government's police powers in distant places. The threat of military intervention was an excellent means by which to speed loan repayment. When Kuhn, Loeb considered a loan to the Dominican Republic, backed by customs receipts, Jacob Schiff inquired of his London associate Sir Ernest Cassel, "If they do not pay, who will collect these customs duties?" Cassel replied, "Your marines and ours."[1]

One of the great puzzles of history is why governments always go into debt and seldom attempt to put themselves on a "pay-as-you-go" basis. A partial answer is that kings and politicians lack the courage to tax their subjects the enormous sums that would be required under such an arrangement. There is also the deeper question of *why* the expenditures are so high in the first place.

Given the mentality of the world's financial lords and masters, as Disraeli described them, it is conceivable that a coldly calculated strategy has been developed over the years to insure this result. In fact, the historical evidence strongly suggests that just such a plan *was* developed in eighteenth-century Europe and perfected in twentieth-century America. For the purposes of hypothetical analysis, let us identify this strategy as *The Rothschild Formula*.

THE FORMULA

Let us imagine a man who is totally pragmatic. He is smarter and more cunning than most men and, in fact, holds them in thinly disguised contempt. He may respect the talents of a few, but has little concern over the condition of mankind. He has observed that kings and politicians are always fighting over something or other and has concluded that wars are inevitable. He also has learned that wars can be profitable, not only by lending or creating the

---

1. Quoted by Jacques Attali, translated by Barbara Ellis, *A Man of Influence: Sir Siegmund Warburg, 1902–82* (London: Weidenfeld, & Nicolson, 1986), p. 57.

money to finance them, but from government favoritism in the granting of commercial subsidies or monopolies. He is not capable of such a primitive feeling as patriotism, so he is free to participate in the funding of any side in any conflict, limited only by factors of self interest. If such a man were to survey the world around him, it is not difficult to imagine that he would come to the following conclusions which would become the prime directives of his career:

1. War is the ultimate discipline to any government. If it can successfully meet the challenge of war, it will survive. If it cannot, it will perish. All else is secondary. The sanctity of its laws, the prosperity of its citizens, and the solvency of its treasury will be quickly sacrificed by any government in its primal act of self-survival.

2. All that is necessary, therefore, to insure that a government will maintain or expand its debt is to involve it in war or the threat of war. The greater the threat and the more destructive the war, the greater the need for debt.

3. To involve a country in war or the threat of war, it will be necessary for it to have enemies with credible military might. If such enemies already exist, all the better. If they exist but lack military strength, it will be necessary to provide them the money to build their war machine. If an enemy does not exist at all, then it will be necessary to *create* one by financing the rise of a hostile regime.

4. The ultimate obstacle is a government which declines to finance its wars through debt. Although this seldom happens, when it does, it will be necessary to encourage internal political opposition, insurrection, or revolution to replace that government with one that is more compliant to our will. The assassination of heads of state could play an important role in this process.

5. No nation can be allowed to remain militarily stronger than its adversaries, for that could lead to peace and a reduction of debt. To accomplish this balance of power, it may be necessary to finance both sides of the conflict. Unless one of the combatants is hostile to our interests and, therefore, must be destroyed, neither side should be allowed a decisive victory or defeat. While we must always proclaim the virtues of peace, the unspoken objective is perpetual war.

Whether anyone actually put this strategy into words or passed it along from generation to generation is not important. In fact, it is doubtful it has ever worked that way. Whether it is the product of conscious planning or merely the consequence of men responding to the profit opportunities inherent in fiat money, the world's financial lords have *acted* as though they were following such a plan, and this has become especially apparent since the creation of the central-bank Mandrake Mechanism three centuries ago.

The "balance-of-power" question is particularly intriguing. Most history texts present the concept as though it were some kind of natural, social phenomenon which, somehow, has worked to the benefit of mankind. The implication is that it's just wonderful how, after all those European wars, no nation was strong enough to completely dominate the others. When the United States emerged from World War II with exactly such power, it was widely deplored, and massive political/financial mechanisms such as foreign aid and disarmament were set in motion to restore the balance. This has become almost a revered doctrine of international democracy. But the overlooked consequence of this sentimental notion is that wars "between equals" have become the permanent landscape of history.

This does not mean that every war-like group that comes along will find easy financing from the lords and masters. It depends on whom they threaten and how likely they are to succeed. In 1830, for example, the Dutch were facing an uprising of their subjects in Belgium. Both the ruling government and the revolutionaries were dependent upon the Rothschilds for financing their conflict. The Dutch rulers were reliable customers for loans and, just as important, they were reliable in their payment of interest on those loans. It would have been foolhardy to provide more than token assistance to the rebels who, if they came to power, quite likely would have refused to honor the debts of the former puppet regime. Salomon Rothschild explained:

> These gentlemen should not count on us unless they decide to follow a line of prudence and moderation.... Our goodwill does not yet extend to the point of putting clubs into the hands that would beat us, that is, lending money to make war and ruin the credit that we sustain with all our efforts and all our means.[1]

---

1. As quoted by Derek Wilson, p. 100.

After the revolution was resolved by negotiation rather than by arms, the new government in Brussels was a natural target for financial takeover. James Rothschild laid out the strategy that has become the model of such operations ever since:

> Now is the moment of which we should take advantage to make ourselves absolute masters of that country's finances. The first step will be to establish ourselves on an intimate footing with Belgium's new Finance Minister, to gain his confidence ... and to take all the treasury bonds he may offer us.[1]

PERPETUAL WAR IN EIGHTEENTH CENTURY ENGLAND

Wars, great and small, have always been a plague to Europe, but it was not until they were easy to finance through central banking and fiat money that they became virtually perpetual. For example, the following war chronicle begins immediately following the formation of the Bank of England which, as you recall, was created for the specific purpose of financing a war:

1689–1697 The War of the League of Augsberg
1702–1713 The War of Spanish Succession
1739–1742 The War of Jenkin's Ear
1744–1748 The War of Austrian Succession
1754–1763 The French and Indian War
1793–1801 The War against Revolutionary France
1803–1815 The Napoleonic Wars

In addition to these European conflicts, there also were two wars with America: the War for Independence and the War of 1812. In the 126 years between 1689 and 1815, England was at war 63 of them. That is one out of every two years in combat. The others were spent *preparing* for combat.

The mark of the Rothschild Formula is unmistakable in these conflicts. The monetary scientists often were seen financing both sides. Whether ending in victory or defeat, the outcome merely preserved or restored the European "balance of power." And the most permanent result of any of these wars was expanded government debt for all parties.

SUMMARY

By the end of the eighteenth century, the House of Rothschild had become one of the most successful financial institutions the

---

1. Derek Wilson, p. 100.

world has ever known. Its meteoric rise can be attributed to the great industry and shrewdness of the five brothers who established themselves in various capitals of Europe and forged the world's first international financial network. As pioneers in the practice of lending money to governments, they soon learned that this provided unique opportunities to parlay wealth into political power as well. Before long, most of the princes and kings of Europe had come within their influence.

The Rothschilds also had mastered the art of smuggling on a grand scale, often with the tacit approval of the governments whose laws they violated. This was perceived by all parties as an unofficial bonus for providing needed funding to those same governments, particularly in time of war. The fact that different branches of the Rothschild network also might be providing funds for the enemy was pragmatically ignored. Thus, a time-honored practice among financiers was born: profiting from both sides.

The Rothschilds operated a highly efficient intelligence gathering system which provided them with advance knowledge of important events, knowledge which was invaluable for investment decisions. When an exhausted Rothschild courier delivered the first news of the Battle of Waterloo, Nathan was able to deceive the London bond traders into a selling panic, and that allowed him to acquire the dominant holding of England's entire debt at but a tiny fraction of its worth.

A study of these and similar events reveals a personality profile, not just of the Rothschilds, but of that special breed of international financiers whose success typically is built upon certain character traits. Those include cold objectivity, immunity to patriotism, and indifference to the human condition. That profile is the basis for proposing a theoretical strategy, called the Rothschild Formula, which motivates such men to propel governments into war for the profits they yield. This formula most likely has never been consciously phrased as it appears here, but subconscious motivations and personality traits work together to implement it nevertheless. As long as the mechanism of central banking exists, it will be to such men an irresistible temptation to convert debt into perpetual war and war into perpetual debt.

In the following chapters we shall track the distinctive footprint of the Rothschild Formula as it leads up to our own doorstep in the present day.

Verlag von J. B. Simon in Frankfurt ⅗m.

Historisches Museum, Frankfurt, Germany

A satirical cartoon of 1848 depicts "Rothschild" pondering over which of Europe's rulers to favor with loans, while revolutionaries challenge the ancient order he is supporting.

A caricature of Nathan Rothschild, showing him in his habitual position before one of the pillars in the Exchange. It was here that he capitalized on his advance knowledge of Wellington's defeat of Napoleon at Waterloo and was able to acquire the dominant holding of England's entire debt at but a small fraction of its worth.

British Museum Print Room

Chapter Twelve

SINK THE LUSITANIA!

The role of J.P. Morgan in providing loans to England and France in World War I; the souring of those loans as it became apparent that Germany would win; the betrayal of a British ship and the sacrifice of American passengers as a stratagem to bring America into the war; the use of American taxes to pay off the loans.

The origin of World War I usually is attributed to the assassination of Archduke Francis Ferdinand of Austria-Hungary by a Serbian nationalist in 1914. This was a serious affront to Austria but hardly sufficient reason to plunge the world into a mortal conflict that would claim over ten million lives and twenty million wounded. American schoolchildren are taught that Uncle Sam came into the war "to make the world safe for democracy." But, as we shall see, the American war drums were pounded by men with far less idealistic objectives.

Since the latter part of the eighteenth century, the Rothschild Formula had controlled the political climate of Europe. Nations had increasingly confronted each other over border disputes, colonial territories, and trade routes. An arms race had been in progress for many years; large, standing armies had been recruited and trained; military alliances had been hammered together; all in preparation for war. The assassination of Ferdinand was not the cause but the trigger. It was merely the spark that lit the fuse that fired the first loaded cannon.

AN INVESTMENT IN WAR

The exigencies of war in Europe required England and France to go heavily into debt. When their respective central banks and local merchant banks could no longer meet that need, the beleaguered governments turned to the Americans and selected the House of Morgan—acting as partners of the Rothschilds—to act as sales agent for their bonds. Most of the money raised in this fashion was quickly returned to the United States to acquire war-sensitive materials, and Morgan was selected as the U.S. purchase agent for those as well. A commission was paid on all transactions in both directions: once when the money was borrowed and again when it was spent. Furthermore, many of the companies receiving production contracts were either owned outright by Morgan holding companies or were securely within his orbit of bank control. Under such an arrangement, it will not be surprising to learn, as we shall in a moment, that Morgan was not overly anxious to see hostilities come to a close. Even the most honorable of men can be corrupted by the temptation of such gigantic flows of cash.

Writing in the year 1919, just a few months after the end of the war, John Moody says:

> Not only did England and France pay for their supplies with money furnished by Wall Street, but they made their purchases through the same medium.... Inevitably the house of Morgan was selected for this important task. Thus the war had given Wall Street an entirely new role. Hitherto it has been exclusively the headquarters of finance; now it became the greatest industrial mart the world had ever known. In addition to selling stocks and bonds, financing railroads, and performing the other tasks of a great banking center, Wall Street began to deal in shells, cannon, submarines, blankets, clothing, shoes, canned meats, wheat, and the thousands of other articles needed for the prosecution of a great war.[1]

The money began to flow in January of 1915 when the House of Morgan signed a contract with the British Army Council and the Admiralty. The first purchase, curiously, was for horses, and the amount tendered was $12 million. But that was but the first drop of rain before the deluge. Total purchases would eventually climb to an astronomical $3 billion. The firm became the largest consumer on earth, spending up to $10 million per day. Morgan offices at 23 Wall Street were mobbed by brokers and manufacturers seeking to cut a deal. The bank had to post guards at every door and at the partners' homes as well. Each month, Morgan presided over purchases which were equal to the gross national product of the entire world just one generation before.[2]

1. John Moody, *The Masters of Capital* (New Haven: Yale University Press, 1919), pp. 164–165.
2. Chernow, pp. 187–89.

Throughout all this, Morgan vigorously claimed to be a pacifist. "Nobody could hate war more than I do," he told the Senate Munitions Committee. But such professions of righteousness were difficult to accept. Lewinsohn comments:

> The 500 million dollar loan contracted in autumn 1915 brought to the group of bankers, at whose head Morgan was, a net profit of 9 million dollars.... Again, in 1917, the French government paid to Morgan's and other banks a commission of 1,500,000 dollars, and a further million in 1918.
>
> Besides the issue of loans there was another source of profit: the purchase and sale of American stock which the Allies surrendered so that they could buy munitions in the States. It is estimated that in the course of the war some 2000 million [two billion] dollars passed in this way through Morgan's hands. Even if the commission was very small, transactions of such dimensions would give him an influence on the stock market which would carry very real advantages....
>
> His hatred against war did not prevent him, citizen of a neutral country, from furnishing belligerent powers with 4,400,000 rifles for a matter of $194,000,000.... The profits were such as to compensate to some degree his hatred of warfare. According to his own account, he received, as agent of the English and French governments, a commission of 1% on orders totalling $3,000,000,000. That is, he received some $30,000,000.... Besides these two chief principals, Morgan, however, also acted for Russia (for whom he did business amounting to $412,000,000) and for Italy and Canada (figures for his business with the last two not having been published)....
>
> J.P. Morgan, and some of his partners in the bank, were at the time shareholders in companies that were ... concerns which made substantial profits from the orders he placed with them.... It is really astonishing that a central buying organization should have been confided to one who was buyer and seller at the same time.[1]

GERMANY'S U-BOATS ALMOST WON THE WAR

But there were dark clouds gathering above Wall Street as the war began to go badly for the Allies. With the passage of time and the condensing of history, it is easy to forget that Germany and the Central Powers almost won the war prior to U.S. entry. Employing a small fleet of newly developed submarines, Germany was well on her way to cutting off England and her allies from all outside help. It was an amazing feat and it changed forever the concept of naval warfare. Germany had a total of twenty-one U-boats, but, because

---

1. Lewinsohn, pp. 103–4, 222–24.

they constantly had to be repaired and serviced, the maximum number at sea was only seven at any one time. Yet, between 1914 and 1918, German submarines had sunk over 5,700 surface ships. Three-hundred thousand tons of Allied shipping were sent to the bottom every week. One out of every four steamers leaving the British Isles never returned. In later years, British Foreign Secretary, Arthur Balfour, wrote: "At that time, it certainly looked as though we were going to lose the war."[1] Robert Ferrell, in his *Woodrow Wilson and World War I*, concluded: "The Allies approached the brink of disaster, with no recourse other than to ask Germany for terms."[2] William McAdoo, who was Secretary of the Treasury at the time (and also Wilson's son-in-law), says in his memoirs:

> Across the sea came the dismay of the British—a dismay that carried a deepening note of disaster. There was a fear, and a well-grounded one, that England might be starved into abject surrender.... On April 27, 1917, Ambassador Walter H. Page reported confidentially to the President that the food in the British Isles was not more than enough to feed the civil population for six weeks or two months.[3]

Under these circumstances, it became impossible for Morgan to find new buyers for the Allied war bonds, neither for fresh funding nor to replenish the old bonds which were coming due and facing default. This was serious on several counts. If bond sales came to a halt, there would be no money to continue purchasing war materials. Commissions would be lost at both ends. Furthermore, if the previously sold bonds were to go into default, as they certainly would if Britain and France were forced to accept peace on Germany's terms, the investors would sustain gigantic losses. *Something* had to be done. But what? Robert Ferrell hints at the answer:

> In the mid thirties a Senate committee headed by Gerald P. Nye of North Dakota investigated the pre-1917 munitions trade and raised a possibility that the Wilson administration went to war because American bankers needed to protect their Allied loans.[4]

---

1. Balfour MSS, FO/800/208, British Foreign Office records, Public Record Office, London, as cited by Robert H. Ferrell, *Woodrow Wilson and World War I* (New York: Harper & Row, 1985), p. 35.
2. Ferrell, p. 12.
3. William G. McAdoo, *Crowded Years* (New York: Houghton Mifflin, 1931; rpt. New York: Kennikat Press, 1971), p. 392.
4. Ferrell, p. 88.

As previously mentioned by William McAdoo, the American ambassador to England at that time was Walter Hines Page, a trustee of Rockefeller's social-engineering foundation called the General Education Board. It was learned by the Nye committee that, in addition to his government salary, which he complained was not high enough, Page also received an allowance of $25,000 a year (an enormous amount in 1917) from Cleveland Dodge, president of Rockefeller's National City Bank. On March 15, 1917, Ambassador Page sent a telegram to the State Department outlining the financial crisis in England. Since sources of new capital had dried up, the only way to keep the war going, he said, was to make direct grants from the U.S. Treasury. But, since this would be a violation of neutrality treaties, the United States would have to abandon its neutrality and enter the war. He said:

> I think that the pressure of this approaching crisis has gone beyond the ability of the Morgan Financial Agency for the British and French Governments.... The greatest help we could give the Allies would be such a credit.... Unless we go to war with Germany, our Government, of course, cannot make such a direct grant of credit.[1]

The Morgan group had floated one-and-a-half billion dollars in loans to Britain and France. With the fortunes of war turning against them, investors were facing the threat of a total loss. As Ferdinand Lundberg observed: "The declaration of war by the United States, in addition to extricating the wealthiest American families from a dangerous situation, also opened new vistas of profits."[2]

COLONEL HOUSE

One of the most influential men behind the scenes at this time was Colonel Edward Mandell House, personal adviser to Woodrow Wilson and, later, to F.D.R. House had close contacts with both J.P. Morgan and the old banking families of Europe. He had received several years of his schooling in England and, in later years, surrounded himself with prominent members of the Fabian Society. Furthermore, he was a man of great personal wealth, most of it acquired during the War Between the States. His father, Thomas William House, had acted as the confidential American agent of

---

1. Quoted by Ferdinand Lundberg, *America's Sixty Families* (New York: Vanguard Press, 1937), p. 141. Also see Link *et al.*, eds., *The Papers of Woodrow Wilson*, Vol. 41 (1983), pp. 336–37, cited by Ferrell, p. 90.
2. Lundberg, pp. 141–42.

unknown banking interests in London. It was commonly believed he represented the Rothschilds. Although settled in Houston, Texas, the elder often remarked that he wanted his sons to "know and serve England." He was one of the few residents of a Confederate state who emerged from the War with a great fortune.

It is widely acknowledged that Colonel House was the man who selected Wilson as a presidential candidate and who secured his nomination.[1] He became Wilson's constant companion, and the President admitted publicly that he depended on him greatly for instruction and guidance. Many of Wilson's important appointive posts in government were hand selected by House. He and Wilson even went so far as to develop a private code so they could communicate freely over the telephone.[2] The President himself had written: "Mr. House is my second personality. He is my independent self. His thoughts and mine are one."[3]

George Viereck, an admiring biographer of House, tells us:

> House had the Texas delegation in his pocket.... Always moving quietly in the background, he made and unmade several governors of Texas.... House selected Wilson because he regarded him as the best available candidate....
>
> For seven long years Colonel House was Woodrow Wilson's other self. For six long years he shared with him all but the title of the Chief Magistracy of the Republic. For six years two rooms were at his disposal in the North Wing of the White House.... It was House who made the slate for the Cabinet, formulated the first policies of the Administration and practically directed the foreign affairs of the United States. We had, indeed, two Presidents for one!... Super-ambassador, he talked to emperors and kings as an equal. He was the spiritual generalissimo of the Administration. He was the pilot who guided the ship.[4]

A SECRET AGREEMENT TO GET THE U.S. INTO WAR

As the presidential election neared for Wilson's second term, Colonel House entered into a series of confidential talks with Sir

1. *The Columbia Encyclopedia* (Third Edition, 1962, p. 2334) says the Democratic Party nomination went to Wilson when William Jennings Bryan switched his support to him "prompted by Edward M. House." For details, see Martin, p. 155.
2. Charles Seymour, *The Intimate Papers of Colonel House* (New York: Houghton Mifflin Co., 1926), Vol. I, pp. 114–15.
3. Seymour, Vol. I, p. 114.
4. George Sylvester Viereck, *The Strangest Friendship in History: Woodrow Wilson and Colonel House* (New York: Liveright Publishers, 1932), pp. 4, 18–19, 33, 35.

William Wiseman, who was attached to the British embassy in Washington and who acted as a secret intermediary between House and the British Foreign Office. Charles Seymour writes: "Between House and Wiseman there were soon to be few political secrets."[1] This was upsetting to the Secretary of State, William Jennings Bryan. Mrs. Bryan, as co-author of her husband's memoirs, writes:

> While Secretary Bryan was bearing the heavy responsibility of the Department of State, there arose the curious conditions surrounding Mr. E.M. House's unofficial connection with the President and his voyages abroad on affairs of State, which were not communicated to Secretary Bryan.... The President was unofficially dealing with foreign governments.[2]

What was the purpose of those dealings? It was nothing less than to work out the means whereby the United States could be brought into the war. Viereck explains:

> Ten months before the election which returned Wilson to the White House in 1916 "because he kept us out of war," Colonel House negotiated a secret agreement with England and France on behalf of Wilson which pledged the United States to intervene on behalf of the Allies.
> On March 9, 1916, Woodrow Wilson formally sanctioned the undertaking. If an inkling of the conversations between Colonel House and the leaders of England and France had reached the American people before the election, it might have caused incalculable revulsions of public opinion....
> From this conversation and various conferences with Sir Edward Grey grew the Secret Treaty, made without the knowledge and consent of the United States Senate, by which Woodrow Wilson and House chained the United States to the chariot of the Entente.... After the War the text of the agreement leaked out. Grey was the first to tattle. Page discussed it at length. Colonel House tells its history. C. Hartley Grattan discusses it at length in his book, *Why We Fought*. But for some incomprehensible reason the enormous significance of the revelation never penetrated the consciousness of the American people.[3]

---

1. Seymour, Vol. II, p. 399.
2. William Jennings Bryan and Mary Baird Bryan, *The Memoirs of William Jennings Bryan* (New York: Kennikat Press, 1925), Vol. II, pp. 404–5.
3. Viereck, pp. 106–08. This matter, along with the complete text of Sir Edward's memorandum, is discussed in *The Memoirs of William Jennings Bryan* Vol. II, pp. 404–6.

The basic terms of the agreement were that the United States government would offer to negotiate a peaceful settlement between Germany and the Allies and would then put forth a specific proposal for the terms of that settlement. If either side refused to accept the proposal, then the United States would come into the war as an ally of the other side. The catch was that the terms of the proposal were carefully drafted so that Germany could not possibly accept them. Thus, to the world, it would look as though Germany was at fault and the United States was humanitarian. As Ambassador Page observed in a memorandum dated February 9, 1916:

> House arrived from Berlin-Havre-Paris full of the idea of American intervention. First his plan was that he and I and a group of the British Cabinet (Grey, Asquith, Lloyd George, Reading, etc.) should at once work out a minimum programme of peace—the least that the Allies would accept, *which, he assumed, would be unacceptable to the Germans*; and that the President would take this programme and present it to both sides; the side that declined would be responsible for continuing the war.... Of course, the fatal moral weakness of the foregoing scheme is that we should plunge into the War, not on the merits of the cause, but by a carefully sprung trick.[1]

On the surface it is a paradox that Wilson, who had always been a pacifist, should now enter into a secret agreement with foreign powers to involve the United States in a war which she could easily avoid. The key that unlocks this mystery is the fact that Wilson also was an internationalist. One of the strongest bonds between House and himself was their common dream of a world government. They both recognized that the American people would never accept such a concept unless there were extenuating circumstances. They reasoned that a long and bloody war was probably the only event that could condition the American mind to accept the loss of national sovereignty, especially if it were packaged with the promise of putting an end to all wars in the future. Wilson knew, also, that, if the United States came into the war early enough to make a real difference on the battlefield and if large amounts of American dollars could be lent to the Allied powers, he would be in a position after the war to dictate the terms of peace. He wrote to Colonel House: "England and France have not the same views with regard to peace as we have by any means. When the war is over, we can force them

---

1. Quoted by Viereck, pp. 112–13.

to our way of thinking, because by that time they will among other things be financially in our hands."[1] And so Wilson tolerated the agony of mixed emotions as he plotted for war as a necessary evil to bring about what he perceived as the ultimate good of world government.

With the arrival of 1917, the President was planting hints of both war and world government in almost every public utterance. In a typical statement made in March of that year, he said: "The tragic events of the thirty months of vital turmoil through which we have just passed have made us citizens of the world. There can be no turning back. Our own fortunes as a nation are involved, whether we would have it so or not."[2]

It was about this same time that Wilson called together the Democratic leaders of Congress to a special breakfast meeting at the White House. He told them that, in spite of public sentiment, there were many sound reasons for the country to enter the war and he asked them to help him sell this plan to Congress and the voters. Harry Elmer Barnes tells us:

> These men were opposed to war and, hence, rejected his proposals somewhat heatedly. Wilson knew that it was a poor time to split the party just before an election, so he dropped the matter at once and, with Col. House, mapped out a pacifist platform for the coming campaign. Governor Martin Glynn of New York and Senator Ollie James of Kentucky were sent to the St. Louis convention to make keynote speeches, which were based on the slogan: "He kept us out of war!"... Before he had been inaugurated a second time, the Germans played directly into his hands by announcing the resumption of submarine warfare.... It was fortunate for Britain and the bankers that the Germans made this timely blunder, as Great Britain had overdrawn her American credit by some $450,000,000 and the bankers were having trouble in floating more large private loans. It was necessary now to pass on the burden of financing the Entente to the Federal Treasury.[3]

---

1. Quoted by Ferrell, p. 88.
2. Ferrell, p. 12.
3. Harry Elmer Barnes, *In Quest of Truth and Justice: De-Bunking the War Guilt Myth* (Chicago: National Historical Society, 1928; rpt. New York: Arno Press & The New York Times, 1972), p. 104. For an additional account of this meeting, see Viereck, pp. 180–83.

SELLING WAR TO THE AMERICAN PEOPLE

Through secret agreements and trickery, America had been committed to war, but the political and monetary scientists realized that something still had to be done to change public sentiment. How could that be accomplished?

Wall Street control over important segments of the media was considerable. George Wheeler tells us: "Around this time the Morgan firm was choosing the top executives for the old and troubled Harper & Brothers publishing house.... In the newspaper field, Pierpont Morgan at this period was in effective control of the New York *Sun*,... the Boston News Bureau, *Barron's* magazine, and the *Wall Street Journal*."[1]

On February 9, 1917, Representative Callaway from Texas took the floor of Congress and provided further insight. He said:

> In March, 1915, the J.P. Morgan interests, the steel, shipbuilding, and powder interests, and their subsidiary organizations, got together 12 men high up in the newspaper world and employed them to select the most influential newspapers in the United States and sufficient number of them to control generally the policy of the daily press.... They found it was only necessary to purchase the control of 25 of the greatest papers.... An agreement was reached; the policy of the papers was bought, to be paid for by the month; an editor was furnished for each paper to properly supervise and edit information regarding the questions of preparedness, militarism, financial policies, and other things of national and international nature considered vital to the interests of the purchasers.[2]

Charles S. Mellen of the New Haven Railroad testified before Congress that his Morgan-owned railroad had over one-thousand New England newspaper editors on the payroll, costing about $400,000 annually. The railroad also held almost a half-million dollars in bonds issued by the *Boston Herald*.[3] This web of control was multiplied by hundreds of additional companies which also were controlled by Morgan and other investment-banking houses.

In addition, the Morgan trust exercised media control by its power of advertising. Writing in 1937, Lundberg says: "More advertising is controlled by the J.P. Morgan junta than by any single

---

1. George Wheeler, *Pierpont Morgan and Friends: The Anatomy of a Myth* (Englewood Cliffs, New Jersey: Prentice Hall, 1973), pp. 283–84.
2. *Congressional Record*, Vol. 54, Feb. 9, 1917, p. 2947.
3. Lundberg, p. 257. [A $400,000 "payroll" in 1915 was equal to $4,400,000 today.]

financial group, a factor which immediately gives the banking house the respectful attention of all alert independent publishers."[1] Morgan control over the media at that time is well documented, but he was by no means alone in this. During the 1912 hearings held by the Senate Privileges and Elections Committee, it was revealed that Representative Joseph Sibley from Pennsylvania was acting as a funnel for Rockefeller money to various cooperative Congressmen. A letter was introduced to the Committee written by Sibley in 1905 to John D. Archbold, the man at Rockefeller's Standard Oil Company who provided the money. In that letter Sibley said: "An efficient literary bureau is needed, not for a day or a crisis but a permanent healthy control of the Associated Press and kindred avenues. It will cost money but will be the cheapest in the end."[2]

Lundberg comments further:

> So far as can be learned, the Rockefellers have given up their old policy of owning newspapers and magazines outright, relying now upon the publications of all camps to serve their best interests in return for the vast volume of petroleum and allied advertising under Rockefeller control. After the J.P. Morgan bloc, the Rockefellers have the most advertising of any group to dispose of. And when advertising alone is not sufficient to insure the fealty of a newspaper, the Rockefeller companies have been known to make direct payments in return for a friendly editorial attitude.[3]

It is not surprising, therefore, that a large part of the nation's press, particularly in the East, began to editorially denounce Germany. The cry spread across the land to take up arms against "the enemy of western civilization." Editors became eloquent on the patriotic duty of all Americans to defend world democracy. Massive "preparedness" demonstrations and parades were organized.

But it was not enough. In spite of this massive sales campaign, the American people still were not buying. Polls conducted at the time showed popular sentiment continuing to run ten-to-one in favor of staying out of Europe's war. Clearly, what was needed was something both drastic and dramatic to change public opinion.

---

1. Lundberg, p. 252.
2. *Ibid.*, pp. 97, 249.
3. *Ibid.*, p. 247.

MORGAN CONTROL OVER SHIPPING

Banking was not the only business in which Morgan had a strong financial interest. Using his control over the nation's railroads as financial leverage, he had created an international shipping trust which included Germany's two largest lines plus one of the two in England, the White Star Lines. Morgan had attempted in 1902 to take over the remaining British line, the Cunard Company, but was blocked by the British Admiralty which wanted to keep Cunard out of foreign control so her ships could be pressed into military service, if necessary, in time of war. The *Lusitania* and the *Mauretania* were built by Cunard and became major competitors of the Morgan cartel. It is an interesting footnote of history, therefore, that, from the Morgan perspective, the *Lusitania* was quite dispensable. Ron Chernow explains:

> Pierpont assembled a plan for an American-owned shipping trust that would transpose his "community of interest" principle—cooperation among competitors in a given industry—to a global plane. He created ... the world's largest [fleet] under private ownership.... An important architect of the shipping trust was Albert Ballin, whose Hamburg-Amerika Steamship Line, with hundreds of vessels, was the world's largest shipping company.... Pierpont had to contend with a single holdout, Britain's Cunard Line.... After the Boer War, the Morgan combine and Cunard exhausted each other in debilitating rate wars."[1]

As stated previously, Morgan had been retained as the official trade agent for Britain. He handled the purchasing of all war materials in the United States and coordinated their shipping as well. Following in the footsteps of the Rothschilds of centuries past, he quickly learned the profitable skills of war-time smuggling. Colin Simpson, author of *The Lusitania*, describes the operation:

> Throughout the period of America's neutrality, British servicemen in civilian clothes worked at Morgan's. This great banking combine rapidly established such a labyrinthine network of false shippers, bank accounts and all the paraphernalia of smuggling that, although they fooled the Germans, there were also some very serious occasions when they flummoxed the Admiralty and Cunard, not to speak of the unfortunate passengers on the liners which carried the contraband.[2]

---

1. Chernow, pp. 100–01.
2. Colin Simpson, *The Lusitania* (Boston: Little, Brown & Co., 1972), p. 50.

THE LUSITANIA

The *Lusitania* was a British passenger liner that sailed regularly between Liverpool and New York. She was owned by the Cunard Company, which, as previously mentioned, was the only major ship line which was a competitor of the Morgan cartel. She left New York harbor on May 1, 1915, and was sunk by a German submarine off the coast of Ireland six days later. Of the 1,195 persons who lost their lives, 195 were Americans. It was this event, more than any other, that provided the advocates of war with a convincing platform for their views, and it became the turning point where Americans reluctantly began to accept, if not the necessity of war, at least its inevitability.

The fact that the *Lusitania* was a passenger ship is misleading. Although she was built as a luxury liner, her construction specifications were drawn up by the British Admiralty so that she could be converted, if necessary, into a ship of war. Everything from the horsepower of her engines and the shape of her hull to the placement of ammunition storage areas were, in fact, military designs. She was built specifically to carry twelve six-inch guns. The construction costs for these features were paid for by the British government. Even in times of peace, it was required that her crew include officers and seamen from the Royal Navy Reserve.

In May of 1913, she was brought back into dry dock and outfitted with extra armor, revolving gun rings on her decks, and shell racks in the hold for ammunition. Handling elevators to lift the shells to the guns were also installed. Twelve high-explosive cannons were delivered to the dry dock. All this is a matter of public record at the National Maritime Museum in Greenwich, England, but whether the guns were actually installed at that time is still hotly debated. There is no evidence that they were. In any event, on September 17, the *Lusitania* returned to sea ready for the rigors of war, and she was entered into the Admiralty fleet register, not as a passenger liner, but an *armed auxiliary cruiser!* From then on, she was listed in *Jane's Fighting Ships* as an auxiliary cruiser and in the British publication, *The Naval Annual*, as an armed merchant man.[1]

Part of the dry dock modification was to remove all the passenger accommodations in the lower deck to make room for more

---

1. Simpson, pp. 17–28, 70.

military cargo. Thus, the *Lusitania* became one of the most important carriers of war materials—including munitions—from the United States to England. On March 8, 1915, after several close calls with German submarines, the captain of the *Lusitania* turned in his resignation. He was willing to face the U-boats, he said, but he was no longer willing "to carry the responsibility of mixing passengers with munitions or contraband."[1]

CHURCHILL SETS A TRAP

From England's point of view, the handwriting on the wall was clear. Unless the United States could be brought into the war as her ally, she soon would have to sue for peace. The challenge was how to push Americans off their position of stubborn neutrality. How that was accomplished is one of the more controversial aspects of the war. It is inconceivable to many that English leaders might have deliberately plotted the destruction of one of their own vessels with American citizens aboard as a means of drawing the United States into the war as an ally. Surely, any such idea is merely German propaganda. Robert Ballard, writing in *National Geographic,* says: "Within days of the sinking, German sympathizers in New York came up with a conspiracy theory. The British Admiralty, they said, had deliberately exposed *Lusitania* to harm, hoping she would be attacked and thus draw the U.S. into the war."[2]

Let's take a closer look at this conspiracy theory. Winston Churchill, who was First Lord of the Admiralty at that time, said:

> There are many kinds of maneuvers in war.... There are maneuvers in time, in diplomacy, in mechanics, in psychology; all of which are removed from the battlefield, but react often decisively upon it.... The maneuver which brings an ally into the field is as serviceable as that which wins a great battle. The maneuver which gains an important strategic point may be less valuable than that which placates or overawes a dangerous neutral.[3]

The maneuver chosen by Churchill was particularly ruthless. Under what was called the Cruiser Rules, warships of both England and Germany gave the crews of unarmed enemy merchant ships a

---

1. Simpson, p. 87.
2. "Riddle of the Lusitania," by Robert Ballard, *National Geographic,* April, 1994, p. 74.
3. Winston Churchill, *The World Crisis* (New York: Scribner's Sons, 1949), p. 300. This appears on p. 464 of the Barnes & Noble 1993 reprint.

chance to take to the lifeboats before sinking them. But, in October of 1914, Churchill issued orders that British merchant ships must no longer obey a U-boat order to halt and be searched. If they had armament, they were to engage the enemy. If they did not, they were to attempt to ram the sub. The immediate result of this change was to force German U-boats to remain submerged for protection and to simply sink the ships without warning.

Why would the British want to do such a stupid thing that would cost the lives of thousands of their own seamen? The answer is that it was *not* an act of stupidity. It was *cold blooded strategy.* Churchill boasted:

> The first British countermove, made on my responsibility,... was to deter the Germans from surface attack. The submerged U-boat had to rely increasingly on underwater attack and thus ran the greater risk of mistaking neutral for British ships and of drowning neutral crews and thus embroiling Germany with other Great Powers.[1]

To increase the likelihood of accidentally sinking a ship from a neutral "Great Power," Churchill ordered British ships to remove their names from their hulls and, when in port, to fly the flag of a neutral power, preferably that of the United States. As further provocation, the British navy was ordered to treat captured U-boat crew members not as prisoners of war but as felons. "Survivors," wrote Churchill, "should be taken prisoner or shot—whichever is the most convenient."[2] Other orders, which now are an embarrassing part of official navy archives, were even more ruthless: "In all actions, white flags should be fired upon with promptitude."[3]

The trap was carefully laid. The German navy was goaded into a position of shoot-first and ask questions later and, under those conditions, it was inevitable that American lives would be lost.

A FLOATING MUNITIONS DEPOT

After many years of investigation, it is now possible to identify the cargo that was loaded aboard the *Lusitania* on her last voyage. It included 600 tons of pyroxyline (commonly called gun cotton),[4]

---

1. Churchill, pp. 274–75.
2. Taken from the Diaries of Admiral Sir Hubert Richmond, Feb. 27, 1915, National Maritime Museum, Greenwich, as quoted by Simpson, p. 37.
3. P.R.O., ADM/116/1359, Dec. 23, 1914, quoted by Simpson, p. 37.
4. Gun cotton explodes with three-times the force of gunpowder in a confined space and can be ignited at a much lower flash point. See Eissler, Manuel, *Modern High Explosives* (New York: John Wiley & Sons, 1914), pp. 110, 112, 372.

six-million rounds of ammunition, 1,248 cases of shrapnel shells (which may not have included explosive charges), plus an unknown quantity of munitions that completely filled the holds on the lowest deck and the trunkways and passageways of F deck. In addition, there were many tons of "cheese," "lard," "furs" and other items which were shown later to be falsely labelled. What they were is not now known, but it is certain they were at least contraband if not outright weapons of war. They were all consigned through the J.P. Morgan Company. But none of this was suspected by the public, least of all those hapless Americans who unknowingly booked a passage to death for themselves and their families as human decoys in a global game of high finance and low politics.

The German embassy in Washington was well aware of the nature of the cargo being loaded aboard the *Lusitania* and filed a formal complaint to the United States government, because almost all of it was in direct violation of international neutrality treaties. The response was a flat denial of any knowledge of such cargo. Seeing that the Wilson Administration was tacitly approving the shipment, the German embassy made one final effort to avert disaster. It placed an ad in fifty East Coast newspapers, including those in New York City, warning Americans not to take passage on the *Lusitania*. The ad was prepaid and requested to be placed on the paper's travel page a full week before the sailing date. It read as follows:

NOTICE!

TRAVELLERS intending to embark on the Atlantic voyage are reminded that a state of war exists between Germany and her allies and Great Britain and her allies; that the zone of war includes the waters adjacent to the British Isles; that, in accordance with formal notice given by the Imperial German Government, vessels flying the flag of Great Britain, or of any of her allies, are liable to destruction in those waters and that travelers sailing in the war zone on ships of Great Britain or her allies do so at their own risk.

IMPERIAL GERMAN EMBASSY
Washington, D.C., April 22, 1915.

Although the ad was in the hands of newspapers in time for the requested deadline, the State Department intervened and, raising the specter of possible libel suits, frightened the publishers into not printing it without prior clearance from State Department attorneys. Of the fifty newspapers, only the *Des Moines Register* carried the ad on the requested date. What happened next is described by Simpson:

> George Viereck [who was the editor of a German-owned newspaper at that time and who had placed the ads on behalf of the embassy] spent April 26 asking the State Department why his advertisement had not been published. Eventually he managed to obtain an interview with [Secretary of State, William Jennings] Bryan and pointed out to him that on all but one of her wartime voyages the *Lusitania* had carried munitions. He produced copies of her supplementary manifests, which were open to public inspection at the collector's office. More important, he informed Bryan, no fewer than six million rounds of ammunition were due to be shipped on the *Lusitania* the following Friday and could be seen at that moment being loaded on pier 54. Bryan picked up the telephone and cleared the publication of the advertisement. He promised Viereck that he would endeavor to persuade the President publicly to warn Americans not to travel. No such warning was issued by the President, but there can be no doubt that President Wilson was told of the character of the cargo destined for the *Lusitania*. He did nothing, but was to concede on the day he was told of her sinking that his foreknowledge had given him many sleepless hours.[1]

It is probably true that Wilson was a pacifist at heart, but it is equally certain that he was not entirely the master of his own destiny. He was a transplanted college professor from the ivy-covered walls of Princeton, an internationalist at heart who dreamed of helping to create a world government and to usher in a millennium of peace. But he found himself surrounded by and dependent upon men of strong wills, astute political aptitudes, and powerful financial resources. Against these forces, he was all but powerless to act on his own, and there is good reason to believe that he inwardly suffered over many of the events in which he was compelled to participate. We shall leave it to others to moralize about a man who, by his deliberate refusal to warn his countrymen of their mortal peril, sends 195 of them to their watery graves. We may wonder, also,

---

1. Simpson, p. 97.

about how such a man can commit the ultimate hypocrisy of condemning the Germans for this act and then doing everything possible to prevent the American public from learning the truth. It would be surprising if the extent of his private remorse was not greater than merely a few sleepless hours.

THE FINAL VOYAGE

But we are getting slightly ahead of the story. While Morgan and Wilson were setting the deadly stage on the American side of the Atlantic, Churchill was playing his part on the European side. When the *Lusitania* left New York Harbor on May 1, her orders were to rendezvous with a British destroyer, the *Juno*, just off the coast of Ireland so she would have naval protection as she entered hostile waters. When the *Lusitania* reached the rendezvous point, however, she was alone, and the captain assumed they had missed each other in the fog. In truth, the *Juno* had been called *out* of the area at the last minute and ordered to return to Queenstown. And this was done with the full knowledge that the *Lusitania* was on a direct course into an area where a German submarine was known to be operating. To make matters worse, the *Lusitania* had been ordered to cut back on the use of coal, not because of shortages, but because it would be less expensive. Slow targets, of course, are much easier to hit. Yet, she was required to shut down one of her four boilers and, consequently, was now entering submarine-infested waters at only 75% of her potential speed.

As the *Lusitania* drew closer to hostile waters, almost everyone knew she was in grave danger. Newspapers in London were alive with the story of German warnings and recent sinkings. In the map room of the British Admiralty, Churchill watched the play unfold and coldly called the shots. Small disks marked the places where two ships had been torpedoed the day before. A circle indicated the area within which the U-boat must still be operating. A larger disk represented the *Lusitania* travelling at nineteen knots *directly into the circle*. Yet, nothing was done to help her. Admiral Coke at Queenstown was given perfunctory instructions to protect her as best he could, but he had no means to do so and, in fact, no one even bothered to notify the captain of the *Lusitania* that the rendezvous with the *Juno* had been canceled.

One of the officers present in the high-command map room on that fateful day was Commander Joseph Kenworthy, who previously had been called upon by Churchill to submit a paper on what would be the political results of an ocean liner being sunk with American passengers aboard. He left the room in disgust at the cynicism of his superiors. In 1927, in his book, *The Freedom of the Seas*, he wrote without further comment: "The *Lusitania* was sent at considerably reduced speed into an area where a U-boat was known to be waiting and with her escorts withdrawn."[1] Further comment is not needed.

Colonel House was in England at that time and, on the day of the sinking, was scheduled to have an audience with King George V. He was accompanied by Sir Edward Grey and, on the way, Sir Edward asked him: "What will America do if the Germans sink an ocean liner with American passengers on board?" As recorded in House's diaries, he replied: "I told him if this were done, a flame of indignation would sweep America, which would in itself probably carry us into the war."[2] Once at Buckingham Palace, King George also brought up the subject and was even more specific about the possible target. He asked, "Suppose they should sink the *Lusitania* with American passengers on board...."[3]

A MIGHTY EXPLOSION, A WATERY GRAVE

Four hours after this conversation, the black smoke of the *Lusitania* was spotted on the horizon through the periscope of the German submarine, *U-20*. The ship came directly toward the U-boat, allowing it to full-throttle out of her path and swing around for a ninety-degree shot at her bow as she passed only 750 yards away. The torpedo struck nine feet below the water line on the starboard side slightly forward of the bridge. A second torpedo was readied but not needed. Quickly after the explosion of the impact, there was a *second and much larger* explosion that literally blew the side off of cargo hold number two and started the great ship immediately toward the bottom. And what a hole it must have been. The *Lusitania*, one of the largest ships ever built, sank in less than eighteen minutes!

---

1. Joseph M. Kenworthy and George Young, *The Freedom of the Seas* (New York: Ayer Company, 1929), p. 211.
2. Seymour, Vol I, p. 432
3. *Ibid.*, p. 432.

Survivors among the crew who were working in the boiler rooms during the attack have attested that the boilers did not blow at that time. Simpson tells us:

> The G torpedo had failed to blow in the inner bulkhead of No. 1 boiler room, but just further forward *something* blew out most of the bottom of the bow of the ship. It may have been the Bethlehem Company's 3-inch shells, the six million rounds of rifle ammunition, or the highly dubious contents of the bales of furs or the small forty-pound boxes of cheese. Divers who have been down to the wreck unanimously testify that the bow was blasted by a massive internal explosion, and large pieces of the bow plating, buckled from the inside, are to be found some distance from the hull.[1]

When a search team from the Woods Hole Oceanographic Institute surveyed the wreckage in 1993, they reported: "When our cameras swept across the hold, we got a big surprise: There was no hole.... We found no evidence that U-20's torpedo had detonated an explosion, undermining one theory of why the liner sank."[2]

It is difficult to share the team's surprise. Photographs show that the wreck is resting on its starboard (right) side. Since that is where the torpedo struck, it is logical that the hole would not be visible. It would be on the side buried in the ocean floor. Failure to see the hole does *not* undermine the theory of internal explosion. It is exactly what one would *expect*.

In any event, it is obvious that the *Lusitania* would not have gone to the bottom in eighteen minutes without a hole *somewhere*. Even the search team had to acknowledge that fact indirectly when it addressed the question of what might have caused the second explosion. In an effort to avoid giving support to a "conspiracy theory," the report concluded that the explosion probably was caused, not by munitions, but by coal dust.

The controversy over the ships cargo was finally resolved in 2008 when divers moved inside the Lusitania's hull and found millions of rounds of military ammunition. Sam Greenhill, witing for *Mail Online*, reported:

> Divers have revealed a dark secret about the cargo carried by the Lusitania on its final journey in May 1915. Munitions they found in the hold suggest that the Germans had been right all along in claiming the

---

1. Simpson, p. 157.
2. Ballard, "Riddle of the Lusitania," pp. 74, 76.

ship was carrying war materials and was a legitimate military target.... The diving team estimates that around four million rounds of U.S.-manufactured Remington .303 bullets lie in the Lusitania's hold at a depth of 300 ft.[1]

A HURRIED COVER-UP

An official inquiry, under the direction of Lord Mersey, was held to determine the facts of the sinking and to place the blame. It was a rigged affair from the beginning. All evidence and testimony was carefully pre-screened to make sure that nothing was admitted into the record that would reveal duplicity on the part of British or American officials. Among the papers submitted to Lord Mersey prior to the hearings was one from Captain Richard Webb, one of the men chosen by the navy to assist in the cover up. It read: "I am directed by the board of Admiralty to inform you that it is considered politically expedient that Captain Turner, the master of the Lusitania, be most prominently blamed for the disaster."[2]

And so he was. Anyone reading the the final report without knowledge of the facts would conclude that Captain William Turner certainly was to blame. Even so, Mersey attempted to soften the blow. He wrote: "...blame ought not to be imputed to the captain.... His omission to follow the advice in all respects cannot fairly be attributed either to negligence or incompetence." And then he added a final paragraph which, on the surface, appears to be a condemnation of the Germans but which, if read with understanding of the background, was an indictment of Churchill, Wilson, House and Morgan. He wrote:

> The whole blame for the cruel destruction of life in this catastrophe must rest solely with those who plotted and with those who committed the crime.[3]

Two days after delivering his judgment, Mersey wrote to Prime Minister Asquith and turned down his fee for services. He added: "I must request that henceforth I be excused from administering His Majesty's Justice." In later years, his only comment on the event was: "The Lusitania case was a damn dirty business."[4]

---

1. "Secret of the Lusitania: Arms find challenges Allied claims it was solely a passenger ship," by Sam Greenhill, Mail Online, Dec. 20, 2008, posted to Internet.
2. The Papers of Lord Mersey, Bignor Park, Sussex, as quoted by Simpson, p. 190.
3. Simpson, p. 241.
4. Ibid., p. 241.

THE CRY FOR WAR

The purposes of the Cabal would have been better served had
an *American* ship been sunk by the Germans, but a British ship with
195 Americans drowned was sufficient to do the job. The players
wasted no time in whipping up public sentiment. Wilson sent a note
of outraged indignation to the Imperial German Government, and
this was widely quoted in the press.

By that time, Bryan had become completely disillusioned by the
duplicity of his own government. On May 9, he sent a dour note to
Wilson:

> Germany has a right to prevent contraband going to the Allies,
> and a ship carrying contraband should not rely upon passengers to
> protect her from attack—it would be like putting women and children
> in front of an army.[1]

This did not deter Wilson from his commitment. The first note
was followed by an even stronger one with threatening overtones,
which was intensely discussed at the Cabinet meeting on the first of
June. McAdoo, who was present at the meeting, says:

> I remember that Bryan had little to say at this meeting; he sat
> throughout the proceedings with his eyes half closed most of the time.
> After the meeting he told the President, as I learned later, that he could
> not sign the note.... Bryan went on to say that he thought his
> usefulness as Secretary of State was over, and he proposed to resign.[2]

At the request of Wilson, McAdoo was dispatched to the Bryans'
home to persuade the Secretary to change his mind, lest his resignation be taken as a sign of disunity within the President's Cabinet.
Bryan agreed to think it over one more day but, the following morning, his decision remained firm. In his memoirs, annotated by his
wife, Mrs. Bryan reveals that her husband could not sleep that night.
"He was so restless I suggested that he read a little till he should
become drowsy. He had in his handbag a copy of an old book
printed in 1829 and called 'A Wreath of Appreciation of Andrew
Jackson.' He found it very interesting."[3]

What irony. In chapter seventeen we shall review the total war
waged by President Jackson against the Bank of the United States,

---

1. Bryan, Vol II, pp. 398–9.
2. McAdoo, p. 333.
3. Bryan, Vol. II, p. 424.

the predecessor of the Federal Reserve System, and we shall be reminded that it was Jackson who prophesied:

> Is there no danger to our liberty and independence in a bank that in its nature has so little to bind it to our country?... [Is there not] cause to tremble for the purity of our elections in peace and for the independence of our country in war?... Controlling our currency, receiving our public monies, and holding thousands of our citizens in dependence, it would be more formidable and dangerous than a naval and military power of the enemy.[1]

One can only wonder what thoughts went through Bryan's mind as he recalled Jackson's warning and applied it to the artificially created war hysteria that, at that very moment, was being generated by the financial powers on Wall Street and at the newly created Federal Reserve.

From England, Colonel House sent a telegram to President Wilson which he, in turn, read to his Cabinet. It became the genesis of thousands of newspaper editorials across the land. He said piously:

> America has come to the parting of the ways, when she must determine whether she stands for civilized or uncivilized warfare. We can no longer remain neutral spectators. Our action in this crisis will determine the part we will play when peace is made, and how far we may influence a settlement for the lasting good of humanity. We are being weighed in the balance, and our position amongst nations is being assessed by mankind.[2]

In another telegram two days later, House reveals himself as the master psycho-politician playing on Wilson's ego like a violinist stroking the strings of a Stradivarius. He wrote:

> If, unhappily, it is necessary to go to war, I hope you will give the world an exhibition of American efficiency that will be a lesson for a century or more. It is generally believed throughout Europe that we are so unprepared and that it would take so long to put our resources into action, that our entering would make but little difference.
> In the event of war, we should accelerate the manufacture of munitions to such an extent that we could supply not only ourselves but the Allies, and so quickly that the world would be astounded.[3]

---

1. Herman E. Krooss, ed. *Documentary History og Banking and Currency in the United States* (New York: Chelsea House, 1983), Vol. III, pp. 26–27.
2. Seymour, p. 434.
3. *Ibid.*, p. 435.

Congress could not resist the combined pressure of the press and the President. On April 16, 1917, the United States officially declared war on the Axis powers. Eight days later, Congress dutifully passed the War Loan Act which extended $1 billion in credit to the Allies. The first advance of $200 million went to the British the next day and was immediately applied as payment on the debt to Morgan. A few days later, $100 million went to France for the same purpose. But the drain continued. Within three months the British had run up their overdraft with Morgan to $400 million dollars, and the firm presented it to the government for payment. The Treasury, however, was unable to put its hands on that amount of money without jeopardizing its own spendable funds and, at first, refused to pay. The problem was quickly solved, however, through a maneuver described at some length in chapter ten. The Federal Reserve System under Benjamin Strong simply created the needed money through the Mandrake Mechanism. "The Wilson Administration found itself in an extremely awkward position, having to bail out J.P. Morgan," wrote Ferrell, but Benjamin Strong "offered to help [Treasury-Secretary] McAdoo out of the difficulty. Over the following months in 1917-18, the Treasury quietly paid Morgan piecemeal for the overdraft."[1] By the time the war was over, the Treasury had lent a total of $9,466,000,000 including $2,170,000,000 given after the Armistice.

That was the cash flow they had long awaited. In addition to saving the Morgan loans, even larger profits were to be made from war production. The government had been secretly preparing for war for six months prior to the actual declaration. According to Franklin D. Roosevelt, then Assistant Secretary of the Navy, the Navy Department began extensive purchasing of war supplies in the Fall of 1916.[2] Ferdinand Lundberg adds this perspective:

> By no accident all the strategic government posts, notably those concerned with buying, were reserved for the Wall Street patriots. On the most vital appointments, Wilson consulted with Dodge [President of Rockefeller's National City Bank], who ... recommended the hitherto unknown [Bernard] Baruch, speculator in copper stocks, as chairman of the all-powerful War Industries Board....

1. Ferrell, p. 89, 90.
2. Clarence W. Barron, *They Told Barron*; Notes of Clarence Walker Barron, edited by Arthur Pound and Samuel Taylor Moore (New York: Harper and Brothers, 1930), p. 51.

As head of the War Industries Board, Baruch spent government funds at the rate of $10,000,000,000 annually.... Baruch packed the War Industries Board and its committees with past and future Wall Street manipulators, industrialists, financiers, and their agents ... who fixed prices on a cost-plus basis and, as subsequent investigations revealed, saw to it that costs were grossly padded so as to yield hidden profits....

The American soldiers fighting in the trenches, the people working at home,the entire nation under arms, were fighting, not only to subdue Germany, but to subdue themselves. That there is nothing metaphysical about this interpretation becomes clear when we observe that the total wartime expenditure of the United States government from April 6, 1917, to October 31, 1919, when the last contingent of troops returned from Europe, was $35,413,000,000. Net corporation profits for the period January 1, 1916, to July, 1921, when wartime industrial activity was finally liquidated, were $38,000,000,000, or approximately the amount of the war expenditures. More than two-thirds of these corporation profits were taken by precisely those enterprises which the Pujo Committee had found to be under the control of the "Money Trust."[1]

The banking cartel was able, through the operation of the Federal Reserve System, to *create* the money to give to England and France so they, in turn, could pay back the American banks— exactly as was to be done again in World War II and again in the Big Bailout of the 1980s and '90s. It is true that, in 1917, the recently enacted income tax was useful for raising a sizable amount of revenue to conduct the war and also, as Beardsley Ruml pointed out a few years later, to take purchasing power away from the middle class. But the greatest source of funding came, as it always does in wartime, not from direct taxes, but from the hidden tax called inflation. Between 1915 and 1920, the money supply doubled from $20.6 billion to $39.8 billion.[2] Conversely, during World War I, the purchasing power of the currency fell by almost 50%. That means Americans unknowingly paid to the government approximately one-half of every dollar that existed. And that was in *addition* to their taxes. This massive infusion of money was the product of the Mandrake Mechanism and cost nothing to create. Yet, the banks were able to collect interest on it all. The ancient partnership

---

1. Lundberg, pp. 134, 144–45.
2. "Deposits and Currency—Adjusted Deposits of All Banks and Currency Outside Banks, 1892–1941," *Banking and Monetary Statistics, 1914–1942* (Washington, D.C.: Board of Governors of the Federal Reserve System, 1976), p. 34.

between the political and monetary scientists had performed its mission well.

SUMMARY

To finance the early stages of World War I, England and France had borrowed heavily from investors in America and had selected the House of Morgan as sales agent for their bonds. Morgan also acted as their U.S. purchasing agent for war materials, thus profiting from both ends of the cash flow: once when the money was borrowed and again when it was spent. Further profits were derived from production contracts placed with companies within the Morgan orbit. But the war began to go badly for the Allies when Germany's submarines took virtual control of the Atlantic shipping lanes. As England and France moved closer to defeat or a negotiated peace on Germany's terms, it became increasingly difficult to sell their bonds. No bonds meant no purchases, and the Morgan cash flow was threatened. Furthermore, if the previously sold bonds should go into default, as they certainly would in the wake of defeat, the Morgan consortium would suffer gigantic losses.

The only way to save the British Empire, to restore the value of the bonds, and to sustain the Morgan cash flow was for the United States government to provide the money. But, since neutral nations were prohibited from doing that by treaty, America would have to be brought into the war. A secret agreement to that effect was made between British officials and Colonel House, with the concurrence of the President. From that point forward, Wilson began to pressure Congress for a declaration of war. This was done at the very time he was campaigning for reelection on the slogan "He kept us out of war." Meanwhile, Morgan purchased control over major segments of the news media and engineered a nation-wide editorial blitz against Germany, calling for war as an act of American patriotism.

Morgan had created an international shipping cartel, including Germany's merchant fleet, which maintained a near monopoly on the high seas. Only the British Cunard Lines remained aloof. The *Lusitania* was owned by Cunard and operated in competition with Morgan's cartel. The *Lusitania* was built to military specifications and was registered with the British Admiralty as an armed auxiliary cruiser. She carried passengers as a cover to conceal her real mission, which was to bring contraband war materials from the United States. This fact was known to Wilson and others in his administration, but they did nothing to stop it. When the German embassy tried to publish a warning to American passengers, the State Department intervened and prevented newspapers from printing it. When the *Lusitania* left New York harbor on her final voyage, she was virtually a floating ammunition depot.

The British knew that to draw the United States into the war would mean the difference between defeat and victory, and *anything* that could accomplish that was proper—even the coldly calculated sacrifice of one of her great ships with Englishmen aboard. But the trick was to have *Americans* on board also in order to create the proper emotional climate in the United States. As the *Lusitania* moved into hostile waters, where a German U-boat was known to be operating, First Lord of the Admiralty, Winston Churchill, ordered her destroyer protection to abandon her. This, plus the fact that she had been ordered to travel at reduced speed, made her an easy target. After the impact of one well placed torpedo, a mighty second explosion *from within* ripped her apart, and the ship that many believed could not be sunk, gurgled to the bottom in less than eighteen minutes.

The deed had been done, and it set in motion great waves of revulsion against the Germans. These waves eventually flooded through Washington and swept the United States into war. Within days of the declaration, Congress voted $1 billion in credit for England and France. $200 million was sent to England immediately and was applied to the Morgan account. The vast quantity of money needed to finance the war was created by the Federal Reserve System, which means it was collected from Americans through that hidden tax called inflation. Within just five years, this tax had taken fully one-half of all they had saved. The infinitely higher cost in American blood was added to the bill.

Thus it was that the separate motives of such diverse personalities as Winston Churchill, J.P. Morgan, Colonel House, and Woodrow Wilson all found common cause in bringing America into World War I. Churchill maneuvered for military advantage, Morgan sought the profits of war, House schemed for political power, and Wilson dreamed of a chance to dominate a post-war League of Nations.

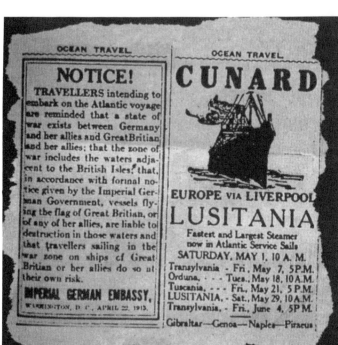

The German Embassy attempted to place ads in 50 newspapers warning that the *Lusitania* was a target of war, but the U.S. government prevented them from being printed except for this one which was run in the *Des Moines Register*. When the ship was sunk off the coast of Ireland with 195 Americans aboard, it became the center of a national campaign to generate emotional support for coming into the war.

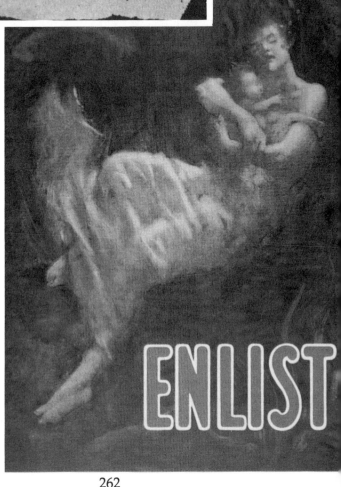

ENLIST

Chapter Thirteen

MASQUERADE IN MOSCOW

The secret society founded by Cecil Rhodes for the purpose of world dominion; the establishment in America of a branch of that group called the Council on Foreign Relations; the role played by financiers within these groups in financing the Russian revolution; the use of the Red Cross mission in Moscow as a cover for that maneuver.

One of the greatest myths of contemporary history is that the Bolshevik Revolution in Russia was a popular uprising of the downtrodden masses against the hated ruling class of the Tsars. As we shall see, however, the planning, the leadership, and especially the financing came entirely from outside Russia, mostly from financiers in Germany, Britain, and the United States. Furthermore, we shall see that the Rothschild Formula played a major role in shaping these events.

This amazing story begins with the war between Russia and Japan in 1904. Jacob Schiff, who was head of the New York investment firm of Kuhn, Loeb, and Company, had raised the capital for large war loans to Japan. It was due to this funding that the Japanese were able to launch a stunning attack against the Russians at Port Arthur and, the following year, to virtually decimate the Russian fleet. In 1905, the Mikado awarded Jacob Schiff a medal, the *Second Order of the Treasure of Japan*, in recognition of his important role in that campaign.

During the two years of hostilities, thousands of Russian soldiers and sailors were taken as prisoners. Sources outside of Russia which were hostile to the Tsarist regime paid for the printing of Marxist propaganda and had it delivered to the prison camps. Russian-speaking revolutionaries were trained in New York and sent to distribute the pamphlets among the prisoners and to indoctrinate them into rebellion against their own government. When the war was ended, these officers and enlisted men returned home to become virtual seeds of treason against the Tsar. They were to play a major role a few years later in creating mutiny among the military during the Communist takeover of Russia.

TROTSKY WAS A MULTIPLE AGENT

One of the best known Russian revolutionaries at that time was Leon Trotsky. In January of 1916, Trotsky was expelled from France and came to the United States. It has been claimed that his expenses were paid by Jacob Schiff. There is no documentation to substantiate that claim but the circumstantial evidence does point to a wealthy donor in New York. He remained for several months while writing for a Russian socialist paper, the *Novy Mir* (New World), and giving revolutionary speeches at mass meetings in New York City. According to Trotsky himself, on many occasions a chauffeured limousine was placed at his service by a wealthy friend identified as Dr. M. In his book, *My Life*, Trotsky wrote:

> The doctor's wife took my wife and the boys out driving and was very kind to them. But she was a mere mortal, whereas the chauffeur was a magician, a titan, a superman! With the wave of his hand, he made the machine obey his slightest command. To sit beside him was the supreme delight. When they went into a tea-room, the boys would anxiously demand of their mother, "Why doesn't the chauffeur come in?"[1]

It must have been a curious sight to see the family of the great socialist radical, defender of the working class, enemy of capitalism, enjoying the pleasures of tea rooms and chauffeurs, the very symbols of capitalist luxury.

On March 23, 1917, a mass meeting was held at Carnegie Hall to celebrate the abdication of Nicholas II, which meant the overthrow of Tsarist rule in Russia. Thousands of socialists, Marxists, nihilists, and anarchists attended to cheer the event. The following day there was published on page two of the *New York Times*, a telegram from Jacob Schiff which had been read to this audience. He expressed regrets that he could not attend and then described the successful Russian revolution as "... what we had hoped and striven for these long years."[2]

---

1. Leon Trotsky, *My Life* (New York: Scribner's, 1930), p. 277.
2. "Mayor Calls Pacifists Traitors," *The New York Times*, March 24, 1917, p. 2.

In the February 3, 1949, issue of the *New York Journal American*, Schiff's grandson, John, was quoted by columnist Cholly Knicker-bocker as saying that his grandfather had given about $20 million for the triumph of Communism in Russia.[1]

When Trotsky returned to Petrograd in May of 1917 to organize the Bolshevik phase of the Russian Revolution, he carried $10,000 for travel expenses, a generously ample fund considering the value of the dollar at that time. The amount is known with certainty because Trotsky was arrested by Canadian and British naval personnel when the ship on which he was travelling, the *S.S. Kristianiafjord*, put in at Halifax. The money in his possession is now a matter of official record. The source of that money has been the focus of much speculation, but the evidence strongly suggests that its origin was the German government. It was a sound investment.

Trotsky was not arrested on a whim. He was recognized as a threat to the best interests of England, Canada's mother country in the British Commonwealth. Russia was an ally of England in the First World War which then was raging in Europe. Anything that would weaken Russia—and that certainly included internal revolution—would be, in effect, to strengthen Germany and weaken England. In New York, on the night before his departure, Trotsky had given a speech in which he said: "I am going back to Russia to overthrow the provisional government and stop the war with Germany."[2] Trotsky, therefore, represented a real threat to England's war effort. He was arrested as a German agent and taken as a prisoner of war.

With this in mind, we can appreciate the great strength of those mysterious forces, both in England and the United States, that intervened on Trotsky's behalf. Immediately, telegrams began to

---

1. To appraise Schiff's motives for supporting the Bolsheviks, we must remember that he was a Jew and that Russian Jews had been persecuted under the Tsarist regime. Consequently, the Jewish community in America was inclined to support any movement which sought to topple the Russian government, and the Bolsheviks were excellent candidates for the task. As we shall see further along, however, there were also strong financial incentives for Wall Street firms such as Kuhn, Loeb & Company— of which Schiff was a senior partner—to see the old regime fall into the hands of revolutionaries who would agree to grant lucrative business concessions in the future in return for financial support today.

2. A full report on this meeting had been submitted to the U.S. Military Intelligence. See Senate Document No. 62, 66th Congress, *Report and Hearings of the Subcommittee on the Judiciary, United States Senate*, 1919, Vol. II, p. 2680.

come into Halifax from such divergent sources as an obscure attorney in New York City, from the Canadian Deputy Postmaster-General, and even from a high-ranking British military officer, all inquiring into Trotsky's situation and urging his immediate release. The head of the British Secret Service in America at the time was Sir William Wiseman who, as fate would have it, occupied the apartment directly above the apartment of Edward Mandell House and who had become fast friends with him. House advised Wiseman that President Wilson wished to have Trotsky released, Wiseman advised his government, and the British Admiralty issued orders on April 21st that Trotsky was to be sent on his way.[1] It was a fateful decision that would affect, not only the outcome of war, but the future of the entire world.

It would be a mistake to conclude that Jacob Schiff and Germany were the only players in this drama. Trotsky could not have gone even as far as Halifax without having been granted an American passport, and this was accomplished by the personal intervention of President Wilson. Professor Antony Sutton says:

> President Woodrow Wilson was the fairy godmother who provided Trotsky with a passport to return to Russia to "carry forward" the revolution.... At the same time careful State Department bureaucrats, concerned about such revolutionaries entering Russia, were unilaterally attempting to tighten up passport procedures.[2]

And there were others, as well. In 1911, the *St. Louis Dispatch* published a cartoon by a Bolshevik named Robert Minor. Minor was later to be arrested in Tsarist Russia for revolutionary activities and, in fact, was himself bankrolled by famous Wall Street financiers. Since we may safely assume that he knew his topic well, his cartoon is of great historical importance. It portrays Karl Marx, with a book entitled *Socialism* under his arm, standing amid a cheering crowd on Wall Street. Gathered around and greeting him with enthusiastic handshakes are characters in silk hats identified as John D. Rockefeller, J.P. Morgan, John D. Ryan of National City Bank, Morgan partner George W. Perkins, and Teddy Roosevelt, leader of the Progressive Party.

---

1. "Why Did We Let Trotsky Go? How Canada Lost an Opportunity to Shorten the War," *MacLeans* magazine, Canada, June, 1919. Also see Martin, pp. 163–64.
2. Antony C. Sutton, Ph.D., *Wall Street and the Bolshevik Revolution* (New Rochelle, New York: Arlington House, 1974), p. 25.

What emerges from this sampling of events is a clear pattern of strong support for Bolshevism coming from the highest financial and political power centers in the United States; from men who, supposedly, were "capitalists" and who, according to conventional wisdom, should have been the mortal enemies of socialism and communism.

Nor was this phenomenon confined to the United States. Trotsky, in his book, *My Life*, tells of a British financier who, in 1907, gave him a "large loan" to be repaid after the overthrow of the Tsar. Arsene de Goulevitch, who witnessed the Bolshevik Revolution first hand, has identified both the name of the financier and the amount of the loan. "In private interviews," he said, "I have been told that over 21 million roubles were spent by Lord [Alfred] Milner in financing the Russian Revolution.... The financier just mentioned was by no means alone among the British to support the Russian revolution with large financial donations." Another name specifically mentioned by de Goulevitch was that of Sir George Buchanan, the British Ambassador to Russia at the time.[1]

It was one thing for Americans to undermine Tsarist Russia and, thus, indirectly help Germany in the war, because Americans were not then into it, but for British citizens to do so was tantamount to treason. To understand what higher loyalty compelled these men to betray their battlefield ally and to sacrifice the blood of their own countrymen, we must take a look at the unique organization to which they belonged.

THE SECRET SOCIETY

Lord Alfred Milner was a key figure in organizing a secret society which, at the time of these events, was about sixteen years old. It was dedicated to nothing less than the quiet domination of the world. The conquest of Russia was seen as but the first phase of that plan. Since the organization is still in existence today and continues to make progress toward its goal, it is important to have its history included in this narrative.

One of the most authoritative reference works on the history of this group is *Tragedy and Hope* by Dr. Carroll Quigley. Dr. Quigley was a professor of history at Georgetown University where President Clinton had been one of his students. He was the author of the

---

1. See Arsene de Goulevitch, *Czarism and Revolution* (Hawthorne, California: Omni Publications, n.d., rpt. from 1962 French edition), pp. 224, 230.

widely used textbook, *Evolution of Civilization;* he was a member of the editorial board of the monthly periodical, *Current History;* and he was a frequent lecturer and consultant for such groups as the Industrial College of the Armed Forces, the Brookings Institution, the U.S. Naval Weapons Laboratory, the Naval College, the Smithsonian Institute, and the State Department. But Dr. Quigley was no mere academic. He also had been closely associated with many of the family dynasties of the super-rich. He was, by his own boast, an insider with a front row view of the world's money power structure.

When Dr. Quigley wrote his scholarly, 1300-page book of dry history, it was not intended for the masses. It was to be read by the intellectual elite, and to that select readership he cautiously exposed one of the best-kept secrets of all time. He also made it clear, however, that he was a friendly apologist for this group and that he supported its goals and purposes. Dr. Quigley said:

> I know of the operation of this network because I have studied it for twenty years and was permitted for two years, in the 1960s, to examine its papers and secret records. I have no aversion to it or to most of its aims and have, for much of my life, been close to it and to many of its instruments.... In general, my chief difference of opinion is that it wishes to remain unknown.[1]

As mentioned, Quigley's book was intended for an elite readership composed of scholars and network insiders. But, unexpectedly, it began to be quoted in the journals of the John Birch Society, which correctly had perceived that his work provided a valuable insight to the inner workings of a hidden power structure. That exposure triggered a large demand for the book by people who were *opposed* to the network and curious to see what an insider had to say about it. That was not according to the original plan. What happened next is best described by Quigley, himself. In a personal letter dated December 9, 1975, he wrote:

> Thank you for your praise of *Tragedy and Hope*, a book which has brought me headaches as it apparently says something which powerful people do not want known. My publisher stopped selling it in 1968 and told me he would reprint (but in 1971 he told my lawyer that they had destroyed the plates in 1968). The rare-book price went

---

1.   Carroll Quigley, *Tragedy and Hope: A History of the World in Our Time*, (New York: Macmillan, 1966), p. 950.

up to $135 and parts were reprinted in violation of copyright, but I could do nothing because I believed the publisher, and he would not take action even when a pirate copy of the book appeared. Only when I hired a lawyer in 1974 did I get any answers to my questions....

In another personal letter, Quigley commented further on the duplicity of his publisher:

They lied to me for six years, telling me that they would reprint when they got 2,000 orders, which could never happen because they told anyone who asked that it was out of print and would not be reprinted. They denied this to me until I sent them Xerox copies of such replies in libraries, at which they told me it was a clerk's error. In other words, they lied to me but prevented me from regaining publication rights.... I am now quite sure that *Tragedy and Hope* was suppressed....[1]

To understand why "powerful people" would want to suppress this book, note carefully what follows. Dr. Quigley describes the goal of this network of world financiers as:

... nothing less than to create a world system of financial control in private hands able to dominate the political system of each country and the economy of the world as a whole. This system was to be controlled in a feudalist fashion by the central banks of the world acting in concert, by secret agreements arrived at in frequent private meetings and conferences....

Each central bank, in the hands of men like Montagu Norman of the Bank of England, Benjamin Strong of the New York Federal Reserve Bank, Charles Rist of the Bank of France, and Hjalmar Schacht of the Reichsbank, sought to dominate its government by its ability to control treasury loans, to manipulate foreign exchanges, to influence the level of economic activity in the country, and to influence cooperative politicians by subsequent economic rewards in the business world.[2]

---

1. These letters were first published in the Summer, 1976, issue of *Conspiracy Digest*, published by Peter McAlpine (Alpine Press, Dearborn, Michigan). The originals cannot now be located. However, the author was able to locate the attorney, Mr. Paul Wolff (with the firm of Williams & Connolly in Washington, D.C.) who represented Quigley in his legal action against the publisher. Mr. Wolff cannot vouch for the authenticity of the letters themselves, but has confirmed in phone conversations and later in writing that the essential details are correct. He writes: "It is my recollection that they withheld from me and the Professor for some time the information that they had in fact destroyed 'the plates.'"
2. Quigley, *Tragedy*, p. 324.

That is the information that "powerful people" do not want the common man to know.

Notice that Quigley refers to this group as a "network." That is a precise choice of words, and it is important to an understanding of the forces of international finance. The network to which he refers is *not* the secret society. It is no doubt *directed by* it, and there are society members in key positions within the network, but we can be sure that there are many in the network who have little or no knowledge of hidden control. To explain how this can be possible, let us turn to the origin and growth of the secret society itself.

RUSKIN, RHODES, AND MILNER

In 1870, a wealthy British socialist by the name of John Ruskin was appointed as professor of fine arts at Oxford University in London. He taught that the state must take control of the means of production and organize them for the good of the community as a whole. He advocated placing control of the state into the hands of a small ruling class, perhaps even a single dictator. He said: "My continual aim has been to show the eternal superiority of some men to others, sometimes even of one man to all others."[1]

This, of course, is the same intellectual appeal of Communism. Lenin taught that the masses could not be trusted to handle their own affairs and that a special group of disciplined intellectuals must assume this role for them. That is the function of the Communist Party, which never comprises more than about three per cent of the population. Even when the charade of free elections is allowed, only members of the Party—or those over whom the KGB has total control—are permitted to run for office. The concept that a ruling party or class is the ideal structure for society is at the heart of all collectivist schemes, regardless of whether they are called Socialism, Communism, Nazism, Fascism, or any other "ism" which may yet be invented to disguise it. It is easy, therefore, for adherents of this elitist mentality to be comfortable in almost any of these collectivist camps, a fact to which Dr. Quigley alluded when he wrote: "This network, which we may identify as the Round Table Groups, has no aversion to cooperating with the Communists, or any other groups, and frequently does so."[2]

---

1. See Kenneth Clark, *Ruskin Today* (New York: Holt, Reinhart & Winston, 1964), p. 267.
2. Quigley, *Tragedy*, p. 950.

Returning to the subject of the origins of this group, however, Dr. Quigley tells us:

> Ruskin spoke to the Oxford undergraduates as members of the privileged ruling class. He told them that they were the possessors of a magnificent tradition of education, beauty, rule of law, freedom, decency, and self-discipline, but that this tradition could not be saved, and did not deserve to be saved, unless it could be extended to the lower classes in England itself and to the non-English masses throughout the world.
>
> Ruskin's message had a sensational impact. His inaugural lecture was copied out in long-hand by one undergraduate, Cecil Rhodes, who kept it with him for thirty years.[1]

Cecil Rhodes made one of the world's greatest fortunes. With the cooperation of the Bank of England and financiers like Rothschild, he was able to establish a virtual monopoly over the diamond output of South Africa and most of the country's gold as well. The major portion of this vast income was spent to advance the ruling-class ideas of John Ruskin.

Dr. Quigley explains:

> The Rhodes Scholarships, established by the terms of Cecil Rhodes' seventh will, are known to everyone. What is not so widely known is that Rhodes in five previous wills left his fortune to form a secret society, which was to devote itself to the preservation and expansion of the British Empire. And what does not seem to be known to anyone is that this secret society was created by Rhodes and his principal trustee, Lord Milner, and continues to exist to this day.... In his book on Rhodes' wills, he [Stead, who was a member of the inner circle] wrote in one place: "Mr. Rhodes was more than the founder of a dynasty. He aspired to be the creator of one of those vast semi-religious, quasi-political associations which, like the Society of Jesus, have played so large a part in the history of the world. To be more strictly accurate, he wished to found an Order as the instrument of the will of the Dynasty."[2]...
>
> In this secret society Rhodes was to be leader; Stead, Brett (Lord Esher), and Milner were to form an executive committee; Arthur (Lord) Balfour, (Sir) Harry Johnston, Lord Rothschild, Albert (Lord) Grey, and others were listed as potential members of a "Circle of Initiates;" while there was to be an outer circle known as the

---

1. Quigley, *Tragedy*, p. 130.
2. Carroll Quigley, *The Anglo-American Establishment: From Rhodes to Cliveden* (New York: Books in Focus, 1981), pp. *ix*, 36.

"Association of Helpers" (later organized by Milner as the Round Table organization).[1]

THE PATTERN OF CONSPIRACY

Here, then, was the classical pattern of political conspiracy. This was the structure that made it possible for Quigley to differentiate between an international "network" and the secret society *within* that network. At the center, there is always a tiny group in complete control, with one man as the undisputed leader. Next is a circle of secondary leadership that, for the most part, is unaware of an inner core. They are led to believe that *they* are the inner-most ring.

In time, as these conspiracies are built from the center out, they form additional rings of organization. Those in the outer echelons usually are idealists with an honest desire to improve the world. They never suspect an inner control for other purposes, and only those few who demonstrate a ruthless capacity for higher leadership are ever allowed to see it.

After the death of Cecil Rhodes, the inner core of his secret society fell under the control of Lord Alfred Milner, Governor-General and High Commissioner of South Africa. As director of a number of public banks and as corporate precursor of England's Midland Bank, he became one of the greatest political and financial powers in the world. Milner recruited into his secret society a group of young men chiefly from Oxford and Toynbee Hall and, according to Quigley:

> Through his influence these men were able to win influential posts in government and international finance and became the dominant influence in British imperial and foreign affairs up to 1939.... In 1909–1913 they organized semi-secret groups, known as Round Table Groups, in the chief British dependencies and the United States....
>
> Money for the widely ramified activities of this organization came ... chiefly from the Rhodes Trust itself, and from wealthy associates such as the Beit brothers, from Sir Abe Bailey, and (after 1915) from the Astor family ... and from foundations and firms associated with the international banking fraternity, especially the Carnegie United Kingdom Trust, and other organizations associated with J.P. Morgan, the Rockefeller and Whitney families, and the associates of Lazard Brothers and of Morgan, Grenfell, and Company....

---

1. Quigley, *Tragedy*, p. 131.

At the end of the war of 1914, it became clear that the organization of this system had to be greatly extended. Once again the task was entrusted to Lionel Curtis who established, in England and each dominion, a front organization to the existing local Round Table Group. This front organization, called the Royal Institute of International Affairs, had as its nucleus in each area the existing submerged Round Table Group. In New York it was known as the Council on Foreign Relations, and was a front for J.P. Morgan and Company in association with the very small American Round Table Group.[1]

The Council on Foreign Relations was a spin-off from the failure of the world's leaders at the end of World War I to embrace the League of Nations as a true world government. It became clear to the master planners that they had been unrealistic in their expectations for rapid acceptance. If their plan were to be carried forward, it would have to be done on the basis of patient gradualism symbolized by the Fabian turtle. Rose Martin says:

> Colonel House was only one man, where a multitude was needed. He had set the pattern and outlined goals for the future, and he still had a scheme or two in mind. In particular, he foresaw it would be necessary for the Fabians to develop a top level Anglo-American planning group in the field of foreign relations which could secretly influence policy on the one hand and gradually "educate" public opinion on the other....
>
> To the ambitious young Fabians, British and American, who had flocked to the peace conference as economists and junior officials, it soon became evident that a New World Order was not about to be produced at Paris.... For them, Colonel House arranged a dinner meeting at the Hotel Majestic on May 19, 1919, together with a select group of Fabian-certified Englishmen—notably, Arnold Toynbee, R.H. Tawney and John Maynard Keynes. All were equally disillusioned, for various reasons, by the consequences of the peace. They made a gentlemen's agreement to set up an organization, with branches in England and America, "to facilitate the *scientific* study of international questions." As a result two potent and closely related opinion-making bodies were founded.... The English branch was called the Royal Institute of International Affairs. The American branch, first known as the Institute of International Affairs, was reorganized in 1921 as the Council on Foreign Relations.[2]

---

1. Quigley, *Tragedy*, pp. 132, 951–52.
2. Martin, pp. 174–5.

It is through this front group, called the Council on Foreign Relations, and its influence over the media, tax-exempt foundations, universities, and government agencies that the international financiers have been able to dominate the domestic and foreign policies of the United States ever since.

We shall have more to say about the CFR, but our focal point for now is Great Britain and, in particular, the help given to Communism in Russia by Lord Alfred Milner and his web of secret societies.

ROUND TABLE AGENTS IN RUSSIA

In Russia, prior to and during the revolution, there were many local observers, tourists, and newsmen who reported that British and American agents were everywhere, particularly in Petrograd, providing money for insurrection. One report said, for example, that British agents were seen handing out 25-rouble notes to the men at the Pavlovski regiment just a few hours before it mutinied against its officers and sided with the revolution. The subsequent publication of various memoirs and documents made it clear that this funding was provided by Milner and channeled through Sir George Buchanan who was the British Ambassador to Russia at that time.[1] It was a repeat of the ploy that had worked so well for the cabal many times in the past. Round Table members were once again working *both* sides of the conflict to weaken and topple a target government. Tsar Nicholas had every reason to believe that, since the British were Russia's allies in the war against Germany, British officials would be the last persons on Earth to conspire against him. Yet, the British Ambassador himself represented the hidden group which was financing the regime's downfall.

The Round Table agents from America did not have the advantage of using the diplomatic service as a cover and, therefore, had to be considerably more ingenious. They came, not as diplomats or even as interested businessmen, but disguised as Red Cross officials on a humanitarian mission. The group consisted almost entirely of financiers, lawyers, and accountants from New York banks and investment houses. They simply had overpowered the American Red Cross organization with large contributions and, in

---

1. See de Goulevitch, p. 230.

effect, purchased a franchise to operate in its name. Professor Sutton tells us:

> The 1910 [Red Cross] fund-raising campaign for $2 million, for example, was successful only because it was supported by these wealthy residents of New York City. J.P. Morgan himself contributed $100,000.... Henry P. Davison [a Morgan partner] was chairman of the 1910 New York Fund-Raising Committee and later became chairman of the War Council of the American Red Cross.... The Red Cross was unable to cope with the demands of World War I and in effect was taken over by these New York bankers.[1]

For the duration of the war, the Red Cross had been made, nominally, a part of the armed forces and subject to orders from the proper military authorities. It was not clear who these authorities were and, in fact, there were never any orders, but the arrangement made it possible for the participants to receive military commissions and wear the uniform of American army officers. The entire expense of the Red Cross Mission in Russia, including the purchase of uniforms, was paid for by the man who was appointed by President Wilson to become its head, "Colonel" William Boyce Thompson.

Thompson was a classical specimen of the Round Table network. Having begun his career as a speculator in copper mines, he soon moved into the world of high finance. He refinanced the American Woolen Company and the Tobacco Products Company; launched the Cuban Cane Sugar Company; purchased controlling interest in the Pierce Arrow Motor Car Company; organized the Submarine Boat Corporation and the Wright-Martin Aeroplane Company; became a director of the Chicago Rock Island & Pacific Railway, the Magma Arizona Railroad, and the Metropolitan Life Insurance Company; was one of the heaviest stockholders in the Chase National Bank; was the agent for J.P. Morgan's British securities operation; became the first full-time director of the Federal Reserve Bank of New York, the most important bank in the Federal Reserve System; and, of course, contributed a quarter-million dollars to the Red Cross.

When Thompson arrived in Russia, he made it clear that he was not your typical Red Cross representative. According to Hermann Hagedorn, Thompson's biographer:

---

1. Sutton, *Revolution*, p. 72.

He deliberately created the kind of setting which would be expected of an American magnate: established himself in a suite in the Hotel de l'Europe, bought a French limousine, went dutifully to receptions and teas and evinced an interest in objects of art. Society and the diplomats, noting that here was a man of parts and power, began to flock about him. He was entertained at the embassies, at the houses of Kerensky's ministers. It was discovered that he was a collector, and those with antiques to sell fluttered around him, offering him miniatures, Dresden china, tapestries, even a palace or two.[1]

When Thompson attended the opera, he was given the imperial box. People on the street called him the American Tsar. And it is not surprising that, according to George Kennan, "He was viewed by the Kerensky authorities as the 'real' ambassador of the United States."[2]

It is now a matter of record that Thompson syndicated the purchase on Wall Street of Russian bonds in the amount of ten-million roubles.[3] In addition, he gave over two-million roubles to Aleksandr Kerensky for propaganda purposes inside Russia and, with J.P. Morgan, gave the rouble equivalent of one-million dollars to the Bolsheviks for the spreading of revolutionary propaganda outside of Russia, particularly in Germany and Austria.[4] A photograph of the cablegram from Morgan to Thompson advising that the money had been transferred to the National City Bank branch in Petrograd is included in this book.

AN OBJECT LESSON IN SOUTH AFRICA

At first it may seem incongruous that the Morgan group would provide funding for both Kerensky and Lenin. These men may have both been socialist revolutionaries, but they were miles apart in their plans for the future and, in fact, were bitter competitors for control of the new government. But the tactic of funding *both* sides in a political contest by then had been refined by members of the

---

1. Hermann Hagedorn, *The Magnate: William Boyce Thompson and His Time* (New York: Reynal & Hitchcock, 1935), pp. 192–93.
2. George F. Kennan, *Russia Leaves the War: Soviet-American Relations, 1917–1920* (Princeton, New Jersey: Princeton University Press, 1956), p. 60.
3. Hagedorn, p. 192.
4. Sutton, *Revolution*, pp. 83, 91. It was the agitation made possible by this funding that led to the abortive German Sparticus Revolt of 1918. See "W.B. Thompson, Red Cross Donor, Believes Party Misrepresented," *Washington Post*, Feb. 2, 1918.

Round Table into a fine art. A stunning example of this occurred in South Africa during the outset of Boer War in 1899.

The British and Dutch had been active in the settlement of Southern Africa for decades. The Dutch had developed the provinces of Transvaal and the Orange Free State, while the British had colonized such areas as Rhodesia, Cape Hope, Basutoland, Swaziland, and Bechuanaland. Conflict was inevitable between these two groups of settlers whenever they found themselves in competition for the resources of the same territory, but it was the discovery of gold in the Whitewater area of the Transvaal that provided the motive for war.

Politically, the Transvaal was in the hands of the Boers, who were the descendants of the Dutch settlers. But, after the discovery of gold in that area, the mine fields had been developed primarily by the British and became solidly under their control. Not surprisingly, one of the largest players in that game was Cecil Rhodes who already had monopolized the diamond fields under British control to the South. Historian Henry Pike tells us:

> With the discovery of gold in the Transvaal, Rhodes' greed became passionate. His hatred of Paul Kruger, the Afrikaner President of the Transvaal, knew no limits. He was bitterly opposed to Kruger's independent Transvaal, and viewed this as the main obstacle to his efforts to sweep all Southern Africa under British rule.[1]

In 1895, Rhodes set in motion a plan to overthrow Kruger's government by organizing an uprising among the British inhabitants in Johannesburg. The uprising was financed by himself and was to be led by his brother, Frank, and other loyal supporters. This was to be followed by a military invasion of the Transvaal by British troops from Bechuanaland and Rhodesia led by Sir Leander Jameson. The uprising fizzled and ended in Jameson's arrest and public disgrace.

But Rhodes was determined to have the Transvaal, and began immediately to prepare a second, more patient ploy. Through Rhodes' influence, Lord Alfred Milner was appointed as the British High Commissioner of South Africa. In London, Lord Esher—another member of the secret society—became the chief political adviser to King Edward and was in daily contact with him

---

1. Henry R. Pike, Ph.D., *A History of Communism in South Africa* (Germiston, South Africa: Christian Mission International of South Africa, 1985), p. 39.

throughout this period. That took care of the *British* side of this contest. With regard to the *Boers'* side, Professor Quigley tells the amazing story:

> By a process whose details are still obscure, a brilliant young graduate of Cambridge, Jan Smuts, who had been a vigorous supporter of Rhodes and acted as his agent in Kimberly [South Africa's largest diamond mine] as late as 1895 and who was one of the most important members of the Rhodes-Milner group in the period 1908–1950, went to the Transvaal and, by violent anti-British agitation, became state secretary of that country (although a British subject) and chief political adviser to President Kruger; Milner made provocative troop movements on the Boer frontiers in spite of the vigorous protests of his commanding general in South Africa, who had to be removed; and, finally, war was precipitated when Smuts drew up an ultimatum insisting that the British troop movements cease and when this was rejected by Milner.[1]

And so, as a result of careful engineering by Round Table members on *both* sides—one making outrageous demands and the other responding to those demands in pretended indignation—the war finally began with a British invasion in October of 1899. After 2 ½ years of fierce fighting, the Boers were forced to surrender, and Milner administered the former republic as a militarily occupied territory. Round Table members, known to the public as "Milner's Kindergarten," were placed into all key government posts, and the gold fields were finally secured.

PLACING BETS ON ALL HORSES

On the other side of the world, in New York City, the same tactic of playing both sides against each other was being applied with brilliant precision by Round Table member J.P. Morgan. Professor Quigley tells us:

> To Morgan all political parties were simply organizations to be used, and the firm always was careful to keep a foot in all camps. Morgan himself, Dwight Morrow, and other partners were allied with Republicans; Russell C. Leffingwell was allied with the Democrats; Grayson Murphy was allied with the extreme Right; and Thomas W. Lamont was allied with the Left.[2]

---

1. Quigley, *Tragedy*, pp. 137–38.
2. *Ibid.*, p. 945.

Although it is true that Thomas Lamont was the father of Corliss Lamont, a well-known Communist, and was himself widely regarded as a man of leftist persuasions, it must also be remembered that he felt equally at home among the Fascists and, in fact, served as an unofficial business consultant for Mussolini in the 1920s.[1]

At the same time that Morgan was funding pro-Bolshevik groups, he founded what was probably the most virulent anti-Bolshevik organization ever to exist in America. It was called United Americans and it set about to frighten everyone into believing that a Red mob was at that very moment poised to capture New York City. It issued shocking reports warning about a pending financial collapse, widespread starvation, and a desperate working class being maneuvered into accepting Communist slogans and rhetoric as a last resort. Ironically, the officers of this organization were Allen Walker of the Guarantee Trust Company, which was then acting as the Soviet's fiscal agent in the U.S.; Daniel Willard, president of the Baltimore & Ohio Railway, which was then active in the development of Soviet railways; H.H. Westinghouse of Westinghouse Air Brake Company which was then operating a major plant in Russia; and Otto H. Kahn of Kuhn, Loeb & Company, which was one of the principal financial backers of the fledgling Soviet regime.[2]

Even inside Russia itself, the Round Table was spreading its bets. In addition to the funding, previously mentioned, which was given to the Bolsheviks *and* to their opponents, the Mensheviks, Morgan also financed the military forces of Admiral Kolchak who was fighting *against* the Bolsheviks in Siberia. Not surprisingly, Kolchak also received funding from a consortium of British financiers, including Alfred Milner.[3]

It is commonly stated that the original intent of the Red Cross mission to Moscow was to prevent the Russian government from making a separate peace with Germany which would release German troops to fight against England and France. According to that version of the story—which portrays the actors as patriots

1. See John P. Diggins, *Mussolini and Fascism: The View from America* (Princeton, New Jersey: Princeton University Press, 1972).
2. Sutton, *Revolution*, pp. 163–68.
3. *Ibid.*, pp. 102, 146, 166–67.

merely doing what was best for the war effort—the first goal was to support the Tsar. When the Tsar was overthrown, they supported the Mensheviks because they had pledged to stay in the war. When the Mensheviks were ousted, they continued to support the Bolsheviks in order to gain sufficient influence to convince them not to give aid to Germany. It takes a great deal of gullibility to swallow that line. A far more plausible reading is that the Morgan interests were merely doing what they had always done: placing bets on all horses so that, no matter which one crossed the finish line, the winner would be obligated to them.

BRITISH AGENT OF THE ROUND TABLE

After the Bolsheviks had seized power in Russia, Sir George Buchanan was recalled as the British Ambassador and replaced by a member of Milner's Kindergarten, a young man by the name of Bruce Lockhart. In his book, *British Agent*, Lockhart describes the circumstances of his assignment. Speaking of a meeting with Prime Minister Lloyd George, he wrote:

> I saw that his own mind was made up. He had been greatly impressed, as Lord Milner told me afterwards, by an interview with Colonel Thompson of the American Red Cross, who had just returned from Russia and who had denounced in blunt language the folly of the Allies in not opening up negotiations with the Bolsheviks....
>
> Three days later all my doubts were put at rest. I was to go to Russia as head of a special mission to establish unofficial relations with the Bolsheviks.... I had been selected for this Russian mission not by the Foreign Secretary but by the War Cabinet—actually by Lord Milner and Mr. Lloyd George....
>
> Lord Milner I saw almost daily. Five days before my departure I dined alone with him at Brook's. He was in his most inspiring mood. He talked to me with a charming frankness about the war, about the future of England, about his own career, and about the opportunities of youth.... He was, too, very far from being the Jingo and the Conservative reactionary whom popular opinion at one time represented him to be. On the contrary, many of his views on society were startling modern. He believed in the highly organized state, in which service, efficiency, and hard work were more important than titles or money-bags.[1]

---

1.   R.H. Bruce Lockhart, *British Agent* (New York and London: G.P. Putnam's Sons, 1933), pp. 198–99, 204, 206–07.

AMERICAN AGENT OF THE ROUND TABLE

When Thompson returned to the United States, the man he selected to replace himself as head of the American Red Cross Mission was his second-in-command, Raymond Robins. Not much is known about Robins except that he was the protégé of Col. Edward Mandell House, and he might have remained an obscure player in this drama had it not been for the fact that he became one of the central characters in Bruce Lockhart's book. It is there that we get this inside view:

> Another new acquaintance of these first days in the Bolshevized St. Petersburg was Raymond Robins, the head of the American Red Cross Mission.... He had been a leading figure in Roosevelt's "Bull Moose" campaign for the American Presidency in 1912. Although a rich man himself, he was an anti-capitalist.... Hitherto, his two heroes had been Roosevelt and Cecil Rhodes. Now Lenin had captured his imagination.... Robins was the only man whom Lenin was always willing to see and who ever succeeded in imposing his own personality on the unemotional Bolshevik leader.
>
> In a less official sense Robins had a similar mission to my own. He was the intermediary between the Bolsheviks and the American Government and had set himself the task of persuading President Wilson to recognize the Soviet regime.[1]

What an amazing revelation is contained in those words. First, we learn that Robins was a leader in the team effort that threw the election of 1912 to Woodrow Wilson. Then we learn that he was an anti-capitalist. Third, we discover that an anti-capitalist can hero-worship Cecil Rhodes. Then we see the tremendous power he wielded over Lenin. And finally, we are told that, although he was part of a private group financed by Wall Street bankers, he was in reality the intermediary between the Bolsheviks and the American Government. One will look in vain for a better summary.

The fact that Cecil Rhodes was one of Robins' great heroes has special significance for this story. It was not merely an intellectual infatuation from college days. On the night before he left Russia, Robins dined with Lockhart. Describing the occasion, Lockhart says: "He had been reading Rhodes' life and after dinner he gave us a wonderful exposition of Rhodes' character."[2] Thus, both Lockhart

---

1. Lockhart, p. 220.
2. *Ibid.*, p. 270.

and Robins were dedicated disciples of Cecil Rhodes and both were undoubtedly part of the international network to which Professor Quigley alluded—possibly even members of the Round Table. Lockhart reported to the British group while Robins reported to the American group, but both were clearly working for identical objectives and doing the work of the unseen hand.

The Bolsheviks were well aware of the power these men represented, and there was no door closed to them. They were allowed to attend meetings of the Central Executive Committee[1], and were consulted regarding important decisions.[2] But perhaps the best way to appraise the extent of the influence these "capitalists" had over the "anti-capitalists" is to let Lockhart tell his own story. In his memoirs, he wrote:

> I returned from our interview to our flat to find an urgent message from Robins requesting me to come to see him at once. I found him in a state of great agitation. He had been in conflict with Saalkind, a nephew of Trotsky and then Assistant Commissar for Foreign Affairs. Saalkind had been rude, and the American, who had a promise from Lenin that, whatever happened, a train would always be ready for him at an hour's notice, was determined to exact an apology or to leave the country. When I arrived, he had just finished telephoning to Lenin. He had delivered his ultimatum, and Lenin had promised to give a reply within ten minutes. I waited, while Robins fumed. Then the telephone rang and Robins picked up the receiver. Lenin had capitulated. Saalkind was dismissed from his post. But he was an old member of the Party. Would Robins have any objection if Lenin sent him as a Bolshevik emissary to Berne? Robins smiled grimly. "Thank you, Mr. Lenin," he said. "As I can't send the son of a bitch to hell, 'burn' is the next best thing you can do with him."[3]

Such was the raw power over the leaders of Communism that was concealed behind the innocent facade of the American Red Cross Mission. And yet, the world—even today—has no inkling of its reality. It has been a carefully guarded secret, and even many of those who were close to it were unable to see it. The assistant to William Thompson in Russia was Cornelius Kelleher. In later years, reflecting on the naiveté of Dr. Franklin Billings, who was head of the mission's medical team, Kelleher wrote:

---

1. *Ibid.*, p. 253.
2. U.S. State Dept. Decimal File, 861.00/3449.
3. Lockhart, pp. 225–26.

Poor Mr. Billings believed he was in charge of a scientific mission for the relief of Russia.... He was in reality nothing but a mask—the Red Cross complexion of the mission was nothing but a mask.[1]

The purpose of a mask, of course, is to *conceal*. And so we are led to ask the question, what was *behind* that mask? What were the true motives and goals of the masqueraders?

We shall turn to that subject next.

SUMMARY

The Bolshevik revolution was not a spontaneous uprising of the masses. It was planned, financed, and orchestrated by outsiders. Some of the financing came from Germany which hoped that internal problems would force Russia out of the war against her. But most of the money and leadership came from financiers in England and the United States. It was a perfect example of the Rothschild formula in action.

This group centered mainly around a secret society created by Cecil Rhodes, one of the world's wealthiest men at the time. The purpose of that group was nothing less than world dominion and the establishment of a modern feudalist society controlled by the world's central banks. Headquartered in England, the Rhodes inner-most directorate was called the Round Table. In other countries, there were established subordinate structures called Round-Table Groups. The Round-Table Group in the United States became known as the Council on Foreign Relations. The CFR, which was initially dominated by J.P. Morgan and later by the Rockefellers, is the most powerful group in America today. It is even more powerful than the federal government, because almost all of the key positions in government are held by its members. In other words, it *is* the United States government.

Agents of these two groups cooperated closely in pre-revolutionary Russia and particularly after the Tsar was overthrown. The American contingent in Russia disguised itself as a Red Cross mission allegedly doing humanitarian work. Cashing in on their close friendship with Trotsky and Lenin, they obtained profitable business concessions from the new government which returned their initial investment many times over.

---

1. Kennan, *Russia*, p. 59.

Above is the "Red Cross Mission" in Moscow shortly after the Bolshevik Revolution. (L-R) J.W. Andrews, Raymond Robins, Allen Wardell, D. Heywood Hardy. Under the pretense of humanitarianism, the Misson's key personnel were Wall Street financiers following their own agenda for acquiring profitable commercial concessions from the new government. They heavily financed all factions of the revolutionary movement to be sure of gaining influence with whatever group should come out on top.

Below is a cablegram from J.P. Morgan to William Boyce Thompson—head of the Red Cross Mission prior to Robins—advising that one million dollars had been transferred to Thompson via the National City Bank. There were many such infusions of "Capitalist" money into the new Communist regime. The process continues to this day.

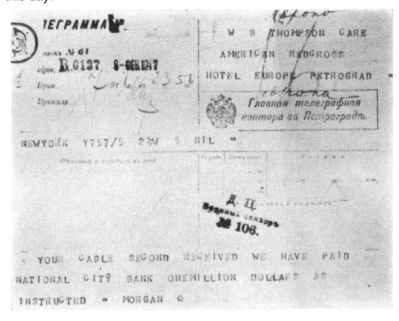

Chapter Fourteen

THE BEST ENEMY
MONEY CAN BUY

The coup d'etat in Russia in which the Bolshevik minority seized control from the revolutionary majority; the role played by New York financiers, masquerading as Red Cross officials, in supporting the Bolsheviks; the unbroken record since then of American assistance in building Russia's war-making potential; the emergence of a "credible enemy" in accordance with the Rothschild Formula.

In the previous section we saw that the Red Cross Mission in revolutionary Russia was, in the words of its own personnel, "nothing but a mask." This leads to the logical question, what were the true motives and goals that were hidden behind that mask.

In later years, it would be explained by the participants themselves that they simply were engaged in a humanitarian effort to keep Russia in the war against Germany and, thus, to help the cause of freedom for England and her allies. For Jacob Schiff and other Jewish financiers in New York, there was the additional explanation that they opposed the Tsar because of his anti-Semitism. These, of course, are admirable motives, and they have been uncritically accepted by mainstream historians ever since. Unfortunately, the official explanations do not square with the facts.

RUSSIA'S TWO REVOLUTIONS

The facts are that there were two revolutions in Russia that year, not one. The first, called the February Revolution, resulted in the establishment of a provisional socialist government under the leadership of Aleksandr Kerensky. It was relatively moderate in its policies and attempted to accommodate all revolutionary factions including the Bolsheviks who were the smallest minority. When the February Revolution occurred, Lenin and Trotsky were not even in Russia. Lenin was in Switzerland and didn't arrive until April. Trotsky was still in New York writing propaganda and giving speeches.

The second revolution, called the October Revolution, was the one through which the Bolsheviks came to power. It was, in fact, no revolution at all. It was a *coup d'etat*. The Bolsheviks simply took advantage of the confusion and indecisiveness that existed among the various groups that comprised the new government and caught them by surprise with a lightening strike of force. With a combination of bribes and propaganda, they recruited several regiments of soldiers and sailors and, in the early morning darkness of October 25, methodically took military possession of all government buildings and communication centers. No one was prepared for such audacity, and resistance was almost non-existent. By dawn, without the Russian people even knowing what had happened—much less having any *voice* in that action, their country had been captured by a minority faction and became the world's first so-called "people's republic." Within two days, Kerensky had fled for his life, and all Provisional Government ministers had been arrested. That is how the Communists seized Russia and that is how they held it afterward. Contrary to the Marxian myth, they have never represented the people. They simply have the guns.

The basic facts of this so-called revolution are described by Professor Leonard Schapiro in his authoritative work, *The Russian Revolutions of 1917*:

> All the evidence suggests that when the crisis came the great majority of units of the Petrograd Garrison did not support the government but simply remained neutral.... The Cossack units rejected its call for support, leaving the government with only a few hundred women soldiers and around two thousand military cadets on its side. The Bolsheviks, on the other hand, could count on several regiments to carry out their orders. Units of the Baltic Fleet also supported them....
>
> In the event, the Bolshevik take-over was almost bloodless: in contrast with what had happened in February, nothing could have been less like a city in the throes of revolution than Petrograd on 25 October. Crowds of well-dressed people thronged the streets in the evening. Theaters and restaurants were open, and at the opera, Shaliapin sang in *Boris Godunov*. The principal stations and services

had all been taken over by the morning of 25 October without a shot being fired....

A battleship and several cruisers, including the *Aurora*, had reached Petrograd from Kronstadt and were anchored with their guns trained on targets in the city....

The Provisional Government inside the Winter Palace...received an ultimatum calling for surrender of its members, under threat of bombardment of the palace by *Aurora* and by the guns of the Peter and Paul Fortress.... It was only at 9:40 P.M. that the *Aurora* was ordered to fire—and discharged one blank shell. The main effect of this was to accelerate the thinning out of the cadet defenders of the palace, who had already begun to dwindle. The women soldiers, who had formed part of its defense force, also left before the palace was invaded. At 11 P.M. some live shells were fired, and the palace was slightly damaged....

The story of the dramatic storming of the Winter Palace, popular with Soviet historians and in the cinema, is a myth. At around 2 A.M. on 26 October, a small detachment of troops, followed by an unruly crowd and led by two members of the MRC [Military Revolutionary Committee], entered the palace. The remaining officer cadets were, apparently, prepared to resist, but were ordered to surrender by the ministers. In the end, the total casualties were three officer cadets wounded.[1]

POPULAR SUPPORT WAS NOT NECESSARY

Eugene Lyons had been a correspondent for United Press in revolutionary Russia. He began his career as highly sympathetic to the Bolsheviks and their new regime, but six years of actual living inside the new socialist utopia shattered his illusions. In his acclaimed book, *Workers' Paradise Lost*, he summarizes the true meaning of the October Revolution:

> Lenin, Trotsky, and their cohorts did not overthrow the monarchy. They overthrew the first democratic society in Russian history, set up through a truly popular revolution in March, 1917.... They represented the smallest of the Russian radical movements.... But theirs was a movement that scoffed at numbers and frankly mistrusted the multitudes. The workers could be educated for their role *after* the revolution; they would not be led but driven to their terrestrial heaven. Lenin always sneered at the obsession of competing socialist groups with their "mass base." "Give us an organization of

1. Leonard Shapiro, *The Russian Revolutions of 1917* (New York: Basic Books, 1984), pp. 135–36.

professional revolutionaries," he used to say, "and we will turn Russia upside down."...

Even these contingents were pathetically duped, having not the remotest notion of the real purposes for which they were being used. They were striking out, they thought, for the multi-party Soviets, for freedom, equality, and other goals which their organizers regarded as emotional garbage....

On the brink of the dictatorship, Lenin dared to promise that the state will fade away, since "all need of force will vanish." Not at some remote future, but at once: "The proletarian state begins to wither immediately after its triumph, for in a classless society a state is unnecessary and impossible.... Soviet power is a new kind of state, in which there is no bureaucracy, no police, no standing army." Also: "So long as the state exists, there is no freedom. When there is freedom, there will be no state."

Within a few months after they attained power, most of the tsarist practices the Leninists had condemned were revived, usually in more ominous forms: political prisoners, convictions without trial and without the formality of charges, savage persecution of dissenting views, death penalties for more varieties of crime than in any other modern nation. The rest were put into effect in the following years, including the suppression of all other parties, restoration of the internal passport, a state monopoly of the press, along with repressive practices the monarchy had outlived for a century or more.[1]

All of this, of course, is a departure from the main narrative, but it has been necessary to illustrate a fact that has been obscured by the passage of time and the acceptance of myth by mainstream historians. The fact is that Lenin and Trotsky were not sent to Russia to overthrow the anti-Semitic Tsar. Their assignment from Wall Street was to overthrow the *revolution*.

NOTES FROM LINCOLN STEFFENS' DIARY

That this was the prevailing motive of the New York money powers was clearly brought to light in the diary of Lincoln Steffens, one of America's best-known leftist writers of that time. Steffens was on board the *S.S. Kristianiafjord* when Trotsky was taken off and arrested in Halifax. He carefully wrote down the conversations he had with other passengers who also were headed to strife-torn Russia. One of these was Charles Crane, vice president of the Crane Company. Crane was a backer of Woodrow Wilson and former

---

1. Eugene Lyons, *Workers' Paradise Lost* (New York: Funk & Wagnalls, 1967) pp. 13–29.

chairman of the Democratic Party's finance committee. He also had organized the Westinghouse Company in Russia and had made no fewer than twenty-three prior visits. His son, Richard Crane, was the confidential assistant to then Secretary of State, Robert Lansing. It is instructive, therefore, to read Steffens' notes regarding the views of these traveling companions. He wrote: "... all agree that the revolution is in its first phase only, that it must grow. Crane and the Russian Radicals on the ship think we shall be in Petrograd for the re-revolution."[1]

Precisely. *Re*-revolution was the expectation and the goal, not the elimination of anti-Semitism.

With regard to Thompson's claim that he was merely trying to keep Russia in the war against Germany, here again, the logic of actual events speak against it. Kerensky and the provisional government were *for* the war effort. Yet, the Red Cross masquerad-ers eventually threw their strongest support to the Bolsheviks who were *against* it. Their excuse was that it was obvious the Bolsheviks would soon control the new government and they were merely looking to the future. They did not like the Bolsheviks, they said, but had to deal with them pragmatically. So they became staunch supporters merely to gain influence with the inevitable victors and, hopefully, to persuade them to *change* their position on the war.

Alas, it didn't work out that way. Influence they had, as we have seen, but the Bolsheviks never wavered in their views. After seizing control in the October *coup d'etat*, they did exactly what they claimed all along they would do. They signed a peace treaty with Germany and confiscated private property. They also began one of the world's greatest bloodbaths to eliminate their opposition. None of this could be blamed on the masqueraders, you understand. It was all the fault of Wilson and the other politicians at home who, by not following Thompson's recommendation to send U.S. tax dollars to the Bolsheviks, forced them into such drastic action. That, at least, is the accepted view.

In reality, a Bolshevik victory at that time was anything but certain, and there was little reason—beyond the support given by the New York financiers themselves—to believe they would become the dominant voice of Russia. But, even if we grant the

---

1. Lincoln Steffens, *The Letters of Lincoln Steffens* (New York: Harcourt, Brace, 1941), p. 396.

assumption that these men were unusually astute political observers who were truly able to foresee the future course, we are still faced with serious obstacles, not the least of which are the thoughts and words of the masqueraders themselves. For example, in February of 1918, Arthur Bullard was in Russia as head of the Russian branch of the Committee on Public Information, which was the war-propaganda arm of the U.S. government. Bullard was aptly described by historian George Kennan as a "liberal socialist, free lance writer, and private eye of Colonel House."[1] In his official capacity he had many occasions to consult with Raymond Robins and, in a report describing one of these conversations, Bullard wrote:

> He [Robins] had one or two reservations—in particular, that recognition of the Bolsheviks was long overdue, that it should have been effected immediately, and that had the U.S. so recognized the Bolsheviks, "I believe that we would now be in control of the surplus resources of Russia and have control officers at all points on the frontier."[2]

WOLVES BEHIND THE MASK

The following year, the U.S. Senate conducted an investigation into the role played by prominent American citizens in supporting the Bolshevik's rise to power. One of the documents entered into the record was an early communique from Robins to Bruce Lockhart. In it Robins said:

> You will hear it said that I am an agent of Wall Street; that I am the servant of William B. Thompson to get Altai Copper for him; that I have already got 500,000 acres of the best timber land in Russia for myself; that I have already copped off the Trans-Siberian Railway; that they have given me a monopoly of the platinum in Russia; that this explains my working for the soviet.... You will hear that talk. Now, I do not think it is true, Commissioner, but let us assume it is true. Let us assume that I am here to capture Russia for Wall Street and American business men. Let us assume that you are a British wolf and I am an American wolf, and that when this war is over we are going to eat each other up for the Russian market; let us do so in perfectly frank, man fashion, but let us assume at the same time that we are fairly intelligent

---

1. George F. Kennan, *The Decision to Intervene: Soviet-American Relations, 1917–1920* (Princeton, New Jersey: Princeton University Press, 1958), pp. 190, 235.
2. Bullard ms., U.S. State Dept. Decimal File, 316–11-1265, March 19, 1918.

wolves, and that we know that if we do not hunt together in this hour the German wolf will eat us both up.[1]

Professor Sutton has placed all this into perspective. In the following passage, he is speaking specifically about William Thompson, but his remarks apply with equal force to Robins and all of the other financiers who were part of the Red Cross Mission in Russia.

> Thompson's motives were primarily financial and commercial. Specifically, Thompson was interested in the Russian market, and how this market could be influenced, diverted, and captured for postwar exploitation by a Wall Street syndicate, or syndicates. Certainly Thompson viewed Germany as an enemy, but less a political enemy than an economic or a commercial enemy. German industry and German banking were the real enemy. To outwit Germany, Thompson was willing to place seed money on any political power vehicle that would achieve his objective. In other words, Thompson was an American imperialist fighting against German imperialism, and this struggle was shrewdly recognized and exploited by Lenin and Trotsky....
>
> Thompson was not a Bolshevik; he was not even pro-Bolshevik. Neither was he pro-Kerensky. Nor was he even pro-American. *The overriding motivation was the capturing of the postwar Russian market.* This was a commercial objective. Ideology could sway revolutionary operators like Kerensky, Trotsky, Lenin et al., but not financiers.[2]

Did the wolves of the Round Table actually succeed in their goal? Did they, in fact, capture the surplus resources of Russia? The answer to that question will not be found in our history books. It must be tracked down along the trail of subsequent events, and what we must look for is this. If the plan had *not* been successful, we would expect to find a decline of interest on the part of high finance, if not outright hostility. On the other hand, if it *did* succeed, we would expect to see, not only continued support, but some evidence of profit taking by the investors, a payback for their efforts and their risk. With those footprints as our guide, let us turn now to an overview of what has actually happened since the Bolsheviks were assisted to power by the Round Table network.

---

1. U.S. Cong., Senate, *Bolshevik Propaganda*, Subcommittee of the Committee on the Judiciary, 65th Cong., 1919, p. 802.
2. Sutton, *Revolution*, pp. 97–98.

ITEM: After the October Revolution, all the banks in Russia were taken over and "nationalized" by the Bolsheviks—except one: the Petrograd branch of Rockefeller's National City Bank.

ITEM: Heavy industry in Russia was also nationalized— except the Westinghouse plant, which had been established by Charles Crane, one of the dignitaries aboard the *S.S. Kristianiafjord* who had traveled to Russia with Trotsky to witness the *re*-revolution.

ITEM: In 1922, the Soviets formed their first international bank. It was not owned and run by the state as would be dictated by Communist theory, but was put together by a syndicate of private bankers. These included, not only former Tsarist bankers, but representatives of German, Swedish, and American banks. Most of the foreign capital came from England, including the British government itself.[1] The man appointed as Director of the Foreign Division of the new bank was Max May, Vice President of Morgan's Guaranty Trust Company in New York.

ITEM: In the years immediately following the October Revolution, there was a steady stream of large and lucrative (read non-competitive) contracts issued by the Soviets to British and American businesses which were directly or indirectly run by the Round Table network. The largest of these, for example, was a contract for fifty million pounds of food products to Morris & Company, Chicago meat packers. Edward Morris was married to Helen Swift, whose brother was Harold Swift. Harold Swift had been a "Major" at the Red Cross Mission in Russia.

ITEM: In payment for these contracts and to return the "loans" of the financiers, the Bolsheviks all but drained their country of its gold—which included the Tsarist government's sizable reserve—and shipped it primarily to American and British banks. In 1920 alone, one shipment came to the U.S. through Stockholm valued at 39,000,000 Swedish kroner; three shipments came direct involving 540 boxes of gold valued at 97,200,000 gold roubles; plus at least one other direct shipment bringing the total to about $20 million. (Remember, these are *1920* values!) The arrival of these shipments was coordinated by Jacob Schiff's Kuhn, Loeb & Company and deposited by Morgan's Guaranty Trust.[2]

---

1. U.S. State Dept. Decimal File, 861.516/129, August 28, 1922.
2. U.S. State Dept., Decimal File, 861.51/815, 836, 837, October, 1920. Also Sutton, *Revolution*, pp. 159–60, 165.

ITEM: It was at about this time that the Wilson Administration sent 700,000 tons of food to the Soviet Union which, not only saved the regime from certain collapse, but gave Lenin the power to consolidate his control over all of Russia.[1] The U.S. Food Administration, which handled this giant operation, was handsomely profitable for those commercial enterprises that participated. It was headed by Herbert Hoover and directed by Lewis Lichtenstein Strauss, married to Alice Hanauer, daughter of one of the partners of Kuhn, Loeb & Company.

ITEM: U.S., British, and German wolves soon found a bonanza of profit in selling to the new Soviet regime. Standard Oil and General Electric supplied $37 million worth of machinery from 1921 to 1925, and that was just the beginning. Junkers Aircraft in Germany literally created Soviet air power. At least three million slave laborers perished in the icy mines of Siberia digging ore for Britain's Lena Goldfields, Ltd. W. Averell Harriman—a railroad magnate and banker from the United States who later was to become Ambassador to Russia—acquired a twenty-year monopoly over all Soviet manganese production. Armand Hammer—close personal friend of Lenin—made one of the world's greatest fortunes by mining Russian asbestos.

ADDITIONAL BACKGROUND: THE DEAF MUTE BLINDMEN

In those early years, the Bolsheviks were desperate for foreign goods, services, and capital investment. They knew that they would be gouged by their "capitalist" associates, but what of it? It wasn't *their* money. All they cared about was staying in power. And that was not as easy as it may have seemed. Even after the *coup d'etat* in which they seized control of the mechanism of government, they still did not control the country at large. In fact, in 1919, Lenin had almost given up hope of expanding beyond Petrograd and a part of Moscow. Except for Odessa, all of Southern Russia and the Crimea were in the hands of General Deniken who was strongly anti-Communist. Speaking before the Tenth Congress of the Russian Communist Party, Lenin laid it out plainly:

---

1. See George F. Kennan, *Russia and the West under Lenin and Stalin* (Boston: Little, Brown and Company, 1961), p. 180.

> Without the assistance of capital it will be impossible for us to retain proletarian power in an incredibly ruined country in which the peasantry, also ruined, constitutes the overwhelming majority—and, of course, for this assistance capital will squeeze hundreds per cent out of us. This is what we have to understand. Hence, either this type of economic relations or nothing....[1]

On another occasion Lenin further explained his rationale for accepting Wall Street's terms. He said:

> The Capitalists of the world and their governments, in pursuit of conquest of the Soviet market, will close their eyes to the indicated higher reality and thus will turn into deaf mute blindmen. They will extend credits, which will strengthen for us the Communist Party in their countries; and giving us the materials and technology we lack, they will restore our military industry, indispensable for our future victorious attack on our suppliers. In other words, they will labor for the preparation of their own suicide.[2]

Arthur Bullard, mentioned previously as the representative in Russia of the U.S. Committee on Public Information, apparently understood the Bolshevik strategy well. Even as early as March of 1918, he sent a cablegram to Washington warning that, while it is true we ought to be ready to help any honest government in need, nevertheless, he said, "men or money sent to the present rulers of Russia will be used against Russians at least as much as against Germans.... I strongly advise against giving material help to the present Russian government. Sinister elements in Soviets seem to be gaining control."[3]

Unfortunately, Mr. Bullard was a minor player in this game, and his opinion was filtered by others along the way. This cablegram was sent to his superior, none other than Col. Edward Mandell House, in hopes that it would be relayed to the President. The message did not get through.

A SIDE TRIP THROUGH WORLD WAR II

Returning to the trail of actual events since that time, let us pause briefly to take a short side trip through World War II.

---

1. V.I. Lenin, Report to the Tenth Congress of the Russian Communist Party, March 15, 1921. Quoted by Sutton, *Revolution*, p. 157.
2. Quoted by Joseph Finder, *Red Carpet* (New York: Holt, Rinehart and Winston, 1983), p. 8.
3. Arthur Bullard papers, Princeton University, cited by Sutton, *Revolution*, p. 46.

Financing and profiting from both sides in a conflict has never been more blatant.

ITEM: From the beginning of Hitler's rise to power, German industry was heavily financed by American and British bankers. Most of the largest U.S. Corporations were knowingly invested *in war industries*. I.G. Farben was the largest of the industrial cartels and was a primary source of political funding for Hitler. It was Farben that staffed and directed Hitler's intelligence section and ran the Nazi slave labor camps as a supplemental source of manpower for Germany's factories. Farben even hired the New York public relations firm of Ivy Lee, who was John D. Rockefeller's PR specialist, to help improve Hitler's public image in America. Lee, incidentally, had also been used to help sell the Soviet regime to the American public in the late 1920s.[1]

ITEM: Much of the capital for the expansion of I.G. Farben came from Wall Street, primarily Rockefeller's National City Bank; Dillon, Read & Company, also a Rockefeller firm; Morgan's Equitable Trust Company; Harris Forbes & Company; and, yes, the predominantly Jewish firm of Kuhn, Loeb & Company.[2]

ITEM: During the Allied bombing raids over Germany, the factories and administrative buildings of I.G. Farben were spared. The U.S. War Department, which determined bombing priorities, was liberally staffed with men, who in civilian life, had been associates of the investment firms previously mentioned. For example, Under Secretary of War at that time was Robert P. Patterson. James Forrestal was Secretary of the Navy and later became Secretary of Defense. Both men had come from Dillon Read and, in fact, Forrestal had been president of that firm.

ITEM: During World War II, under the Lend-Lease program, the United States sent to the Soviets more than $11 billion in aid, including 14,000 aircraft, nearly half a million tanks and other military vehicles, more than 400 combat ships, and even half of the entire U.S. supply of uranium which then was critically needed for the development of the atomic bomb. But fully one-third of all the Lend-Lease shipments during this period comprised industrial equipment and supplies to be used for the development of the

---

1. Antony Sutton, *Wall Street and the Rise of Hitler* (Seal Beach, California: '76 Press, 1976),. 15–18, 33–43, 67–97, 99–113. Also *Revolution*, p. 174.
2. Sutton, *Hitler*, pp. 23–61.

Russian economy *after* the war. And when the war did end, the Lend-Lease program continued to flow into the Soviet Union for over a year. As late as the end of 1946, Russia was still receiving twenty-year credit terms at $2\frac{3}{8}$ per cent interest, a far lower rate than returning GIs could obtain.[1]

THE TRANSFUSION MECHANISM

With the termination of the Lend-Lease program, it was necessary to invent new mechanisms for the support of Soviet Russia and her satellites. One of these was the sale of much-needed commodities at prices below the world market and, in fact, below the prices that Americans themselves had to pay for the same items. This meant, of course—as it did in the case of Lend Lease—that the American taxpayer had to make up the difference. The Soviets were not even required to have the money to buy these goods. American financial institutions, the federal government, and international agencies, which are largely *funded* by the federal government, such as the International Monetary Fund and the World Bank—*lent* the money to them. Furthermore, the interest rates on these loans also are below the market requiring still additional subsidy by American citizens. And that is not all. Almost all of these loans have been guaranteed by the United States government, which means that if—no, make that *when*—these countries default in their payments, the gullible American public is once again called upon to make them good. In other words, the new mechanism, innocently and deceptively referred to as "trade," is little more than a thinly disguised means by which members of the Round Table who direct our national policies have bled *billions* of dollars from American citizens for an ongoing economic transfusion into the Soviet bloc—and continue to do so now that the word Soviet has been changed to the less offensive *Democratic Socialism*. This enables those regimes to enter into contracts with American businessmen to provide essential services. And the circle is complete: *From the American taxpayer to the American government to the "socialist" regime to the American businessman and, ultimately, to the American financier who funded the project and provided the political influence to make it all possible.*

---

1. Antony C. Sutton, *National Suicide: Military Aid to the Soviet Union* (New Rochelle. New York: Arlington House, 1973), p. 24.

This is the key to understanding the transfusion mechanism. Many Americans have looked at this process and have jumped to the conclusion that there must be a nest of Communist agents within our government. In an exam on reality politics, they would receive half credit for that answer. Yes, there undoubtedly have been, and continue to be, Red agents and sympathizers burrowed deep into our government woodwork, and they are all too happy to help the process along. But the main motive force has always come from the non-Communist, non-Democratic Socialist, non-American, non-*anything* members of the Round Table network who, as Lenin said, in the pursuit of profit are laboring for the preparation of their own suicide.

These men are incapable of genuine patriotism. They think of themselves, not as citizens of any particular country, but as citizens of the world. They can do business just as easily with bloodthirsty dictatorships as with any other government—especially since they are assured by the transfer mechanism that the American taxpayer is going to make good on the deal.

When David Rockefeller was asked about the propriety of providing funding for Marxist and Communist countries which are openly hostile to the United States, he responded: "I don't think an international bank such as ours ought to try to set itself as a judge about what kind of government a country wishes to have."

Wishes to have? He was talking about Angola where the Marxist dictatorship was *forced* upon the people with Cuban soldiers and Soviet weapons!

Thomas Theobald, Vice President of Citicorp, was asked in 1981 about his bank's loans to Poland. Was he embarrassed by making loans to a Communist country, especially following the regime's brutal repression of free-trade unions? Not at all. "Who knows which political system works?" he replied. "The only test we care about is, can they pay their bills." What he meant, of course, was can the *American taxpayer* pay Poland's bills.

ITEM: The following item, taken directly from the *Los Angeles Times* just a few months after Theobald's statement, tells the story:

WASHINGTON—For months, the Reagan Administration has been using federal funds to repay Polish loans owed to U.S. banks, and the bill for this fiscal year may amount to $400 million, Deputy Secretary of Agriculture Richard E. Lyng said Monday.... "They (the Polish authorities) have not been making payments for at least the last half of the last year," Lyng said. "When they don't make a payment, the U.S. Department of Agriculture makes a payment."...

Lyng said the U.S. Government paid $60 million to $70 million a month on guaranteed Polish loans in October, November, December, and January—and "we will continue to pay them."[1]

This, remember, was precisely at the time the Polish government had declared martial law and was using military force to crush workers' demonstrations for political reform. The Polish default on this $1.6 billion loan was by no means an isolated event. Communist Rumania and a multitude of Latin American countries were soon to follow.

The hard fact is that American taxpayers unknowingly have been making monthly bank payments on behalf of Communist, socialist, and so-called Third-World countries for many years. And, with the more recent staging of apparent reform within the former Soviet bloc, Congress has tripped all over itself to greatly accelerate that trend.

Americans, of course, *want* to believe that the Evil Empire is crumbling, and the Soviets-turned-Democrats play directly to that desire. Since the end of World War II, their primary objectives have been (1) to disarm us and (2) to get our money. The facade of *Perestroika* and *Glasnost* has been merely a ploy to accomplish both objectives at once. All they have had to do is get rid of a few of the old hard-liners, replace them with less well-known personalities who are essentially the same (*all* of the new leaders come from the ranks of the *old* leadership), change their labels from "Communists" to "Social Democrats," and then sit back while we happily tear down our military defenses and rush billions of dollars to their failing economies. There undoubtedly will be some progress allowed in the area of free speech, but the military and security organizations continue in full readiness. The iron fist beneath the velvet glove remains ready to strike when the time comes that the facade is no longer necessary.

Even if the entire ploy were genuine, there is no reason to believe that these Social Democracies will ever become better investment risks. The primary thing that has held them back economically in the past is their socialist system, and that most

---

1. "U.S. Repaying Loans Owed by Poland to American Banks," by William J. Eaton, *Los Angeles Times*, February 2, 1982.

definitely will not be changed. All of the new "anti-Communist Social Democrats" have pledged their loyalty to the principles of Marx and have said in plain language that they will use our money to *develop*, not abandon socialism. These countries will continue to be unproductive and will continue to be unable to pay their loans. The American taxpayers will continue to be forced by the Cabal to pay the bill.

ITEM: Before the Bolshevik *coup d'etat*, Russia was one of the most productive agricultural nations in the world. The great wheat fields in Ukraine justly earned her the title of the Bread Basket of Europe. But when the people's utopia arrived, agriculture came to a standstill, and famine stalked the land. Even after Stalin, when the regime is said to have adopted more humane and productive policies, Russia *never* produced enough food for itself. A nation that cannot feed its citizens cannot develop its industry and it certainly cannot build a potent military force. It is not surprising, therefore, that for decades, the United States has annually "sold" tens of millions of tons of wheat—and other food stuffs—to Russia. The quote marks are to emphasize the underlying transfusion mechanism previously described.

ITEM: The American government-industrial complex provided the Soviets with the money, technology, and the actual construction of two of the world's largest and most modern truck plants. The Kama River plant and the Zil plant produce over 150,000 heavy-duty trucks per year—including armored personnel carriers and missile launchers—plus 250,000 diesel engines, many of which are used to power Soviet tanks. Forty-five per cent of the cost of this project came from the U.S. Export-Import Bank, an agency of the federal government, and an equal amount from David Rockefeller's Chase Manhattan Bank. The Soviets put up only ten per cent. The loan, of course, was taxpayer-guaranteed by the U.S. Export-Import Bank which, at the time, was under the direction of William Casey. Casey later was appointed as head of the C.I.A. to protect America from global Communism.[1] (Are you beginning to get the picture?)

ITEM: Almost every important facet of Eastern-Bloc heavy industry could well be stamped "Made in the U.S.A." With the

---

1. "U.S. Builds Soviet War Machine," *Industrial Research & Development*, July, 1980, pp. 51–54.

specific approval of each successive president, we have provided the latest oil-drilling equipment, chemical processing plants, air-traffic radar systems, equipment to produce precision bearings, large-craft helicopter engines, laser technology, highly advanced computer systems, and nuclear power plants. We have trained hundreds of their technicians in American institutions and factories and have provided their astronauts with the space suits developed by NASA. We have even trained their pilots at U.S. Air Force bases and paid for their military officers to attend our War College. All of this has been used by the Russian government—as Lenin predicted it would—to build their military industry in preparation for an attack on their suppliers. The great pretense of crumbling Communism has not altered that strategy. It is the brilliant implementation of it.

ITEM: When Boris Yeltsin seized control of the former Soviet government, one of his first official acts was to decree that foreign businesses had the right to take their profits out of the country. From a purely business perspective, that was a sound move because it would provide incentive for foreign investment. But there was more to it than that. Recall from a previous chapter that the lion's share of that investment was to be funded by American taxpayers in the form of direct aid, bank-loan bailouts, and government insurance through the Overseas Private Investment Corporation. Jane Ingraham provides the details:

> During 1992 Yeltsin wheeled and dealed with Royal Dutch/Shell, British Petroleum, Amoco, Texaco, and Exxon. The Chevron joint venture to develop the Tengiz oil field was signed. McDermott International, Marathon Oil, and Mitsui signed a contract with the Russian government to develop oil and natural gas off Sakhalin Island. Chevron and Oman formed a consortium to build a huge pipeline to carry crude oil from Kazakhstan to the Black Sea, Mediterranean, and Persian Gulf. Occidental Petroleum signed a joint venture with Russia to modernize two oil fields in Siberia.... Newmont mining signed a joint venture to extract gold in Uzbekistan. Merrill Lynch's chairman, William Schreyer (CFR), signed up as financial adviser to "aid in privatizing" the Ukrainian State Property Fund. AT&T CEO Robert Allen (CFR, TC[1]) signed a huge contract to supply switching systems for all of Kazakhstan....

---

1. Trilateral Commission.

US West joined with the Hungarian government to own and operate a national cellular telephone system; GM Vice President Marina Whitman (CFR, TC) joined the governments of Hungary and Yugoslavia to make cars; GE CEO John Welch (CFR) and vice chairman of the board, Lawrence Bossidy (TC), bought a majority stake in Hungary's lighting industry; Ralston-Purina, Dow Chemical, Eastman Kodak, SC Johnson & Son, Xerox, American Express, Procter & Gamble, Woolworth, Philip Morris, Ford, Compaq Computer—hardly a single American brand name was missing.[1]

ITEM: In February of 1996, the Clinton Administration made a $1 billion loan of US taxpayers' money to Russia's state-controlled Aeroflot company so it could more effectively compete with American companies such as Boeing in the building of jumbo jets. By the end of that year, the former Soviet Bloc countries had received transfusions from the World Bank of over $3 billion. By mid 2000, it was clear that Russian officials had laundered an additional $7 billion from IMF loans through the Bank of New York. Yet, new "loans" continue to flow.

ITEM: Now the action has spread to China. American banks and businessmen—with taxpayers standing by with guarantees—have provided power-generating equipment, steel mills, and military hardware including anti-submarine torpedoes and high-tech electronic gear to update Russian-made jet fighters. All of this is explained as a means of weaning the Red Chinese away from mother Russia and encouraging them to move closer to free-enterprise capitalism. Yet, in 1985, at the height of the frenzy over building trade bridges to China, the regime signed a $14 billion trade pact with Russia and, in 1986, sent a $20 million interest-free loan to the Communist Sandinistas in Nicaragua. Even after the 1989 Tiananmen Square massacre in Beijing, when U.S. officials were publicly condemning China for human-rights violations, business quietly continued as usual. "The United States cannot condone the violent attacks and cannot ignore the consequence for our relationship with China," said President Bush. Yet, within only a few weeks of the bloodshed, and at the very time that student leaders were being executed, the Administration approved a $200 million, low-interest loan for delivery of four of Boeing's newest jumbo-jet aircraft. In 1993, forty-seven more jetliners were sold with

---

1. "The Payoff," by Jane H. Ingraham, *The New American*, June 28, 1993, pp. 25–26.

a projected sale of 800 more over the next fifteen years. Amoco is spending $1.5 billion to develop oil fields in the China Sea. A joint venture between the Chinese government and Chrysler is building military jeeps. A similar joint project is upgrading their F-8 fighter planes. Three communications satellites were cleared for delivery. AT&T contracted a $30 million cellular communications network.

China's interest in military technology is revealing. In addition to the advanced hardware purchased from the United States, the Chinese have bought MIG-31 and SU-27 jet fighters from Russia and an aircraft carrier constructed in Ukraine. In May of 1992, China set off its biggest underground nuclear blast. In 1997, the purchase list was extended to include self-propelled gun-mortar systems and Russia's most advanced diesel-electric submarines.

Although it is known that China maintains a slave-labor work force in excess of a million people—they call them "convicts"—and although the Tariff Act of 1930 prohibits the United States from importing any goods made even in part by convicts or other forced labor, every administration starting with Nixon has renewed the "most-favored-nation" trade status for China.

How is China expected to pay for all this "trade"? Very simple. By 1996, China had become the largest single recipient of guaranteed loans and subsidies from the World Bank.

ITEM: In *addition* to these decades of global trade, credit, and taxpayer guarantees, the United States has transferred tens of billions of dollars in *direct foreign-aid grants* with no pretense at all regarding expectation of repayment. Why is this done? In June of 2000, President Clinton spoke before the Russian Parliament and provided the answer. He said "The United States wants a strong Russia." The next day, he announced that the U.S. would give $78 million to improve the Chernobyl atomic power plant in Kiev.

The trail leads to Wall Street, and the tracks are *fresh*. The Round Table network did succeed in exploiting the markets of Eastern Europe and continues to do so today. The cast of characters has changed, but the play remains the same. In the beginning, the Council on Foreign Relations was dominated by J.P. Morgan. It is still controlled by international financiers. The Morgan group gradually has been replaced by the Rockefeller consortium, and the roll call of participating businesses now reads like the Fortune 500. The operation no longer pretends to be a Red Cross mission; it now masquerades under the cover of "East-West Trade."

Politicians are fond of talking about the necessity of preserving world peace, and trade, we are told, is one of the best ways to do it. The implication is that this *is* a time of peace. In truth, we live in one of the most war-torn eras the world has ever seen. No continent today, except Antarctica, is free from war. There are from 25 to 40 military struggles going on somewhere every day of the year. There have been more than 150 armed conflicts since the end of World War II with the death count already in excess of 20 million and rising.[1] We cannot help noticing that this *also* has been a period of rising government debt and the global creation of fiat money.

THE NEW ALCHEMY

The alchemists of ancient times vainly sought the philosophers' stone which they believed would turn lead into gold. Is it possible that such a stone actually has been found? Can it be that the money alchemists of our own time have learned how to transmute war into debt, and debt into war, and *both* into gold for themselves?

In a previous section, we theorized a strategy, dubbed the Rothschild Formula, in which the world's money cabal deliberately encourages war as a means of stimulating the profitable production of armaments and of keeping nations perpetually in debt. This is not profit seeking, it is *genocide*. It is not a trivial matter, therefore, to inquire into the possibility that our elected and non-elected leaders are, in fact, implementing the Rothschild Formula today.

ITEM: In his address to the graduating class at Annapolis in 1983, Secretary of the Navy, John Lehman, said: "Within weeks, many of you will be looking across just hundreds of feet of water at some of the most modern technology ever invented in America. Unfortunately, it is on Soviet ships."

As Professor Sutton observed in his book, *The Best Enemy Money Can Buy*, the guns, the ammunition, the weapons, and the transportation systems that killed Americans in Korea and Vietnam came from the American-subsidized economy of the Soviet Union. The trucks that carried these weapons down the Ho Chi Minh Trail were manufactured in American-built plants. The ships that carried the supplies to Sihanoukville and Haiphong and later to Angola

---

1. These figures are taken from United Nations publication E/CN.5/1985/Rev.1, *1985 Report on the World Social Situation*, p. 14. More recent editions of that document do not give cumulative figures but show that the number of conflicts has been accelerating. So the current numbers, whatever they may be, are even worse.

and Nicaragua came from NATO allies and used propulsion systems that our State Department could have kept out of Soviet hands. Sutton concludes: "The technical capability to wage the Korean and Vietnamese wars originated *on both sides* in Western, mainly American, technology, and the political illusion of "peaceful trade" promoted by the deaf mute blindmen was the carrier for this war-making technology."[1]

ITEM: That leads us to the more recent wars in the Middle East and the rise of "Islamic Fundamentalism." Iran, Iraq, Syria, Algeria, the PLO, the Muslim Brotherhood, and similar anti-American groupings have all received weapons, funding, and clandestine support from the U.S. government. In the Gulf War, every effort was made to insure that Hussein's regime was contained but not destroyed (shades of the Korean and Vietnam wars). His military infrastructure and most of his weapons were spared. After the cease fire, he was allowed to keep his fleet of helicopter gunships, which he promptly used to put down a large-scale internal revolt.

The big pill to swallow is that, for many years, Hussein was an asset to the global planners in the West, and they did everything possible to keep him in power. It was only when he refused to allow U.S. companies to dominate Iraqi oil production that he was seriously targeted. Prior to that, he was untouchable precisely because he was widely percieved as a perfect, despicable enemy.

As mentioned previously, the talent pool for the implementation of this strategy has been the Council on Foreign Relations. In 1996, the Managing Editor of the CFR's journal, *Foreign Affairs*, was Fareed Zakaria, who offered the following rationalization:

> Yes, it's tempting to get rid of Saddam. But his bad behavior actually serves America's purposes in the region.... If Saddam Hussein did not exist, we would have to invent him.... The end of Saddam Hussein would be the end of the anti-Saddam coalition. Nothing destroys an alliance like the disappearance of the enemy.... Maintaining a long-term American presence in the gulf would be difficult in the absence of a regional threat.[2]

That is about as clear a statement of the Rothschild Formula as one is apt to find. Yet, many people cannot believe it is real, even

---

1. Antony Sutton, *The Best Enemy Money Can Buy* (Billings, Montana: Liberty House Press, 1986), p. 191.
2. "Thank Goodness for a Villain," *Newsweek*, Sept. 16, 1996, p. 43.

Congressmen. For example, Representative James Traficant from Ohio, speaking before the House on April 29, 1997, exclaimed:

> America gives billions to Russia. With American cash, Russia builds missiles. Russia then sells those missiles to China. And China, who gets about $45 billion in trade giveaways from Uncle Sam, then sells those Russian-made missiles to Iran. Now Iran, with those Russian-made missiles sold to them by China, threatens the Mideast. So Uncle Sam ... sends more troops and sends more dollars.... Mr. Speaker, this is not foreign policy. This is foreign stupidity.[1]

Traficant was on target seeing the problem, but he missed the bull's eye with the cause. CFR policy makers are *not* stupid. They are implementing the Rothschild Formula. To justify world government, there must be wars. Wars require enemies with frightful weapons. Iran is one of the best enemies money can buy.

ITEM: The latest act in this play is the buildup of North Korea. Its nuclear capabilities come from China and Russia., both of which receive U.S. trade, investments, and technology. While President Bush was saying that North Korea was part of the "Axis of Evil" his administration was sending it so-called humanitarian shipments of food, which the regime used to strengthen its control.

We must assume that Western leaders have considered Lenin's prediction that, by funding their enemies, they are preparing their own suicide—ours, also, by the way. We must also conclude they are confident of avoiding that fate. Whether they are right or wrong is not the issue here. The point is they *believe* they are correct and they are building a world order which they think they can. How they plan to do that is the subject of a later section, but perpetual war is an important part of it.

FIFTH REASON TO ABOLISH THE SYSTEM

There are few historians who would challenge the fact that the funding of World War I, World War II, the Korean War, and the Vietnam War was accomplished by the Mandrake Mechanism through the Federal Reserve System. An overview of all wars since the establishment of the Bank of England in 1694 suggests that most of them would have been greatly reduced in severity, or perhaps not even fought at all, without fiat money. It is the ability of governments to acquire money without direct taxation that makes

---

1. *Congressional Record,* April 29, 1997.

modern warfare possible, and a central bank has become the preferred method of accomplishing that.

One can argue the necessity, or at least the inevitability, of fiat money in time of war as a means of raw survival. That is the primal instinct of both individuals and governments, all other considerations aside. We shall leave that for the philosophers. But there can be no debate over the fact that fiat money *in time of peace* has no such justification. Furthermore, the ability of governments and banking institutions to use fiat money to fund the wars of *other* nations is a powerful temptation for them to become embroiled in those wars for personal profit, political advancement, or other reasons which fall far short of a moral justification for bloodshed.

The Federal Reserve System has always served that function. The on-going strategy of building up the military capabilities of America's potential enemies leaves us no reason to believe we have seen the last of war. Therefore, it is not an exaggeration to say that *the Federal Reserve System encourages war.* There can be no better reason for the Creature to be put to sleep.

SUMMARY

The Bolshevik Revolution was a *coup d'etat* in which a radical minority captured the Russian government from the moderate revolutionary majority. The Red Cross Mission of New York financiers threw support to the Bolsheviks and, in return, received economic rewards in the form of rights to Russia's natural resources plus contracts for construction and supplies. The continued participation in the economic development of Russia and Eastern Europe since that time indicates that this relationship has survived to the present day. These financiers are not pro-Communist. Their motivation is profit and power. They are now working to bring both Russia and the United States into a world government which they expect to control. War and threats of war are tools to prod the masses toward the acceptance of that goal. It is essential, therefore, that the United States and the industrialized nations of the world have credible enemies. As these words are being written, Russia is wearing the mask of peace and cooperation. But we have seen that before. We may yet see a return of the Evil Empire when the timing is right. U.S. government and megabank funding, first of Russian, and now of Chinese and Middle-East military capabilities, cannot be understood without this insight.

Section IV

A TALE OF THREE BANKS

It has been said that those who are ignorant of history are doomed to repeat its mistakes. It may come as a surprise to learn that the Federal Reserve System is America's fourth central bank, not its first. We have been through all this before and, each time, the result has been the same. Interested in what happened? Then let's set the coordinates of our time machine to the colony of Massachusetts and the year 1690. To activate, turn the page.

Chapter Fifteen

THE LOST TREASURE MAP

The bitter experience of the American colonies with fiat money; the resolve of the founding fathers to prohibit the new nation from resorting to paper money without backing; the drafting of the Constitution to that end; the creation of a true American dollar; the prosperity that followed.

In the golden days of radio, on the Edgar Bergen Show, the ventriloquist would ask his dummy, Mortimer Snerd, "How can you be so stupid?" And the answer was always the same. After a moment of deep thought on the part of Mortimer, he would drawl his reply, "Well, it ain't easy!"

When we look at the monetary chaos around us today—the evaporating value of the dollar and the collapsing financial institutions—we are compelled to ask: How did we get into this fix? And, unfortunately, Mortimer's response would be quite appropriate.

To find out how we got to where we are, it will be necessary to know where we started, and a good place to begin that inquiry is with the Constitution of the United States. Article I, Sections 8 and 10 say:

Congress shall have the power —
To borrow money ... to coin money, regulate the value thereof, and of foreign coin, and fix the standard of weights and measures;... [and] to provide for the punishment of counterfeiting....
No state shall ... coin money; emit bills of credit; [or] make anything but gold and silver coin a tender in payment of debts.

The delegates were precise in their use of these words. Congress was given the power to "coin money," not to print it. Thomas M. Cooley's *Principles of Constitutional Law* explains that "to coin money is to stamp pieces of metal for use as a medium of exchange in commerce according to fixed standards of value."

What was *prohibited* was to "emit bills of credit" which, according to the speeches and writings of those who drafted the document, meant the printing of paper IOUs which were intended to be circulated as money—in other words, the printing of fiat money not backed by gold or silver.

At first, it would seem that nothing could be more clear. Yet, these two simple clauses have become the basis for literally thousands of pages of conflicting interpretation. The crux of the problem is that, while the Constitution clearly prohibits the *states* from issuing fiat money, it does not specifically prevent the *federal* government from doing so. That was truly an unfortunate oversight on the part of the document's framers, but they probably never dreamed in their wildest nightmares that their descendants "could be so stupid" as to not understand their intent.

Furthermore, "it ain't easy" to *miss* their intent. All one has to do is look at the monetary history that led up to the Constitutional Convention and to read the published letters and debates of the men who affixed their signatures to that founding document.

As one reads through the debates on the floor of the convention, one is struck by the passion that these delegates held on the subject of money. Every one of them could remember from his personal experience the utter chaos in the colonies caused by the issuance of fiat money. They spoke out against it in no uncertain terms, and they were adamant that it should never be tolerated again in America—at either the state *or* federal level.

PAPER MONEY IN THE COLONIES

The first colonial experience with fiat money was in the period from 1690 to 1764. Massachusetts was the first to use it as a means of financing its military raids against the French colony in Quebec. The other colonies were quick to follow suit and, within a few years, were engaging in a virtual orgy of printing "bills of credit." There was no central bank involved. The process was simple and direct, as was the reasoning behind it. As one colonial legislator explained it:

> Do you think, gentlemen, that I will consent to load my constituents with taxes when we can send to our printer and get a wagon load of money, one quire of which will pay for the whole?[1]

---

1. See William M. Gouge, *A Short History of Paper Money and Banking in the United States* (Philadelphia: T.W. Ustick, 1833), Part II, p. 27.

The consequences of this enlightened statesmanship were classic. Prices skyrocketed, legal tender laws were enacted to *force* the colonists to accept the worthless paper, and the common man endured great personal losses and hardship. By the late 1750s, Connecticut had price inflated by 800%, the Carolinas had inflated 900%, Massachusetts 1000%, Rhode Island 2300%.[1]

The situation was so out of hand that, beginning in 1751, the British Parliament stepped in and, in one of those rare instances where interference from the mother country actually benefited the colonies, it forced them to cease the production of fiat money. Henceforth, the Bank of England would be the only source.

What followed was unforeseen by the promoters of fiat money. Amid great gloom about "insufficient money," a miracle boom of prosperity occurred. The forced use of fiat money had compelled everyone to hoard their *real* money and use the worthless paper instead. Now that the paper was in disgrace, the colonists began to use their English and French and Dutch gold coins once again, prices rapidly adjusted to reality, and commerce returned to a solid footing. It remained so even during the economic strain of the Seven-Years War (1756–1763) and during the period immediately prior to the Revolution. Here was a perfect example of how an economic system in distress can recover if government does not interfere with the healing process.[2]

WARTIME INFLATION

But all of this came to a halt with the onset of colonial rebellion. Not only did open hostilities throw England deeper into the cogs and wheels of the central-bank mechanism, it also was the compelling motive for the colonies to return to their printing presses. The following figures speak eloquently for themselves:

- At the beginning of the war in 1775, the total money supply for the federated colonies stood at $12 million.

- In June of that year, the Continental Congress issued another $2 million. Before the notes were printed, another $1 million was authorized.

- By the end of the year, another $3 million.

---

1. Paul and Lehrman, p. 23.
2. Roger W. Weiss, "The Colonial Monetary Standard of Massachusetts," *Economic History Review* 27 (November 1974), p. 589.

- $19 million in 1776.
- $13 million in 1777.
- $64 million in 1778.
- $125 million in 1779.
- A total of $227 million in five years on top of a base of $12 million is an increase of about 2000%.
- On top of this "federal" money, the states were doing the same in an approximately equal amount.
- And still more: the Continental Army, unable to get enough money from Congress, issued "certificates" for the purchase of supplies totalling $200 million.
- $650 million created in five years on top of a base of $12 million is an expansion of the money supply of over 5000%.[1]

Although the economy was devastated by this flood of fiat money, most victims were totally unaware of the cause. In 1777, the sentiment of a large segment of the population was expressed by the words of one patriotic old lady who said: "What a shame it is that Congress should let the poor soldiers suffer when they have power to make just as much money as they choose."[2]

The immediate result of this money infusion was the appearance of prosperity. After all, everyone had *more money* and that was perceived as a very good thing. But this was quickly followed by inflation as the self-destruct mechanism began to roll. In 1775, the colonial monetary unit, called the Continental, was valued at one-dollar in gold. In 1778, it was exchanged for twenty-five cents. By 1779, just four years from its issue, it was worth less than a penny and ceased to circulate as money at all. It was in that year that George Washington wrote: "A wagon-load of money will scarcely purchase a wagon-load of provisions."[3]

The saying "Not worth a Continental" has its origin in this gloomy period.

---

1. For an overview of expenditures, see Paul and Lehrman, pp. 26–27.
2. Gouge, p. 28. The naivité of this lady may be humorous, but are Americans any more enlightened today? Would she not feel at home among our modern-day electorate who clamor for legislation to pump Federal-Reserve fiat money into projects to alleviate hardship among the poor and unemployed?
3. Quoted by Bolles, Vol. I, p. 132.

The true nature of the inflation effect has never been more accurately perceived or more vividly described than it was by Thomas Jefferson:

> It will be asked how will the two masses of Continental and of State money have cost the people of the United States seventy-two millions of dollars, when they are to be redeemed now with about six million? I answer that the difference, being sixty-six millions, has been lost on the paper bills separately by the successive holders of them. Every one, through whose hands a bill passed, lost on that bill what it lost in value during the time it was in his hands. This was a real tax on him; and in this way the people of the United States actually contributed those sixty-six millions of dollars during the war, and by a mode of taxation the most oppressive of all because the most unequal of all.[1]

PRICE CONTROLS AND LEGAL-TENDER LAWS

It was natural that people struggled to find ways to escape the destruction of their savings, and the two most obvious methods were (1) to regularly adjust prices upward as the value of the money went downward or (2) exchange their goods and services only for gold coins. In response, the colonial legislatures and the Continental Congress did what governments *always* do to prevent it. They resorted to wage and price controls and to legal-tender laws with harsh penalties for non-compliance. Under one such law, those who refused to accept worthless money were even described as *traitors*. It declared:

> If any person shall hereafter be so lost to all virtue and regard for his Country as to refuse to accept its notes, such person shall be deemed an enemy of his Country.[2]

Rhode Island not only levied a substantial fine for non-acceptance of its notes but, upon a second offense, an individual lost his citizenship. When this was declared unlawful by a panel of judges, the legislature reacted by dismissing the judges from office.[3]

---

1. Thomas Jefferson, *Observations on the Article Etats-Unis Prepared for the Encyclopedia,* June 22, 1786, *Writings,* Vol. IV, p. 165.
2. F. Tupper Saussy, *The Miracle on Mainstreet* (Sewanee, Tennessee: Spencer Judd, 1980), p. 12. Also see Anthony Sutton, *The War on Gold* (Seal Beach, Calif.: '76 Press, 1977), pp. 47, 48.
3. Jensen, p. 324.

Then, as now, those who suffered the most from fiat money were those who held the most trust in government. In 1777 these were mostly the Whigs, for it was they who patriotically held paper money and, as a result, lost their livelihoods and their life savings. The Tories, on the other hand, mistrusting both government and its paper money, passed the bills as quickly as possible in trade for real assets, especially gold. Consequently, as a group, they weathered the storm fairly well. But they often were derided by their less prudent neighbors as "Torie speculators," "hoarders," and even "traitors."

All of this was painfully fresh in the memories of the delegates to the Constitutional Convention and, as the opening session convened in Philadelphia in 1787, there were angry mobs in the streets threatening the legislators. Looting was rampant. Businesses were bankrupt. Drunkenness and lawlessness were everywhere to be seen. The fruit of fiat money had ripened, and the delegates did not enjoy its taste.

In October of 1785, George Washington wrote: "The wheels of government are clogged, and ... we are descending into the vale of confusion and darkness."[1] A year later, in a letter to James Madison, he said: "No day was ever more clouded than the present. We are fast verging to anarchy."[2]

In February of 1787, Washington wrote to Henry Knox: "If any person had told me that there would have been such formidable rebellion as exists, I would have thought him fit for a madhouse."[3]

Just three months prior to the opening of the convention, Washington voiced his reasons for rejecting the notion of fiat money. In answer to the complaint that there was not enough gold coin (specie) to satisfy the needs of commerce, he replied:

> The necessity arising from a want of specie is represented as greater than it really is. I contend that it is by the substance, not the shadow of a thing, we are to be benefited. The wisdom of man, in my humble opinion, cannot at this time devise a plan by which the credit of paper money would be long supported; consequently, depreciation keeps pace with the quantity of the emission, and articles for which it is exchanged rise in a greater ratio than the sinking value of the money. Wherein, then, is the farmer, the planter, the artisan benefited?

---

1. Quoted by Atwood, p. 3.
2. *Ibid.*, p. 4.
3. *Ibid.*, p. 4.

An evil equally great is the door it immediately opens for speculation, by which the least designing and perhaps most valuable part of the community are preyed upon by the more knowing and crafty speculators.[1]

THE CONSTITUTIONAL CONVENTION

This was the prevailing view held by the great majority of delegates to the Convention. They were adamant in their resolve to create a constitution which would prevent any state, and *especially* the federal government itself, from ever again issuing fiat money. And they said so in unmistakable terms.

Oliver Ellsworth from Connecticut, who later was to become our third Chief Justice of the Supreme Court, said:

This is a favorable moment to shut and bar the door against paper money. The mischief of the various experiments which have been made are now fresh in the public mind and have excited the disgust of all the respectable parts of America.[2]

George Mason from Virginia told the delegates he had a "mortal hatred to paper money." Previously he had written to George Washington: "They may pass a law to issue paper money, but twenty laws will not make the people receive it. Paper money is founded upon fraud and knavery."

James Wilson from Pennsylvania said: "It will have the most salutary influence on the credit of the United States to remove the possibility of paper money."

John Langdon from New Hampshire warned that he would rather reject the whole plan of federation than to grant the new government the right to issue fiat money.

George Reed from Delaware declared that a provision in the Constitution granting the new government the right to issue fiat money "would be as alarming as the mark of the beast in Revelation."

Thomas Paine, although not a delegate to the Convention, had written the previous year that he was strongly opposed to fiat money, which he called counterfeiting by the state, and he especially abhorred legal tender laws which force people to accept the

---

1. Washington to Stone, 16 February, 1787. Quoted by Bancroft, pp. 231–32.
2. For the context of this and the following statements expressing a similar sentiment, see Bancroft, pp. 30, 43–44, 82; also Paul and Lehrman, p. 168.

counterfeit. He said: "The punishment of a member [of a legislature] who should move for such a law ought to be *death*."
An interesting thought.

If any further evidence is needed that the Founding Fathers intended to prohibit the federal government from issuing "bills of credit," consider this. The first draft of the Constitution was copied in large measure from the original Articles of Confederation. When it was taken up for consideration by the delegates, therefore, it contained the old provision that had caused so much chaos. It stated: "The legislature of the United States shall have the power to borrow money and emit bills of credit." But, after a lively discussion on the matter, the offending provision was voted to be *removed* from the Constitution by an overwhelming margin.[1] Voicing the sentiment of the majority of the delegates, Alexander Hamilton said: "To emit an unfunded paper as the sign of value ought not to continue a formal part of the Constitution, nor ever hereafter to be employed; being, in its nature, repugnant with abuses and liable to be made the engine of imposition and fraud."[2]

The journal of the Convention for August 16 contains this notation:

> It was moved and seconded to strike out the words "and emit bills of credit," and the motion ... passed in the affirmative. [The vote cleared by a margin of better than four to one.][3]

The Tenth Amendment states: "The powers not delegated to the United States by the Constitution, nor prohibited by it to the States, are reserved to the States respectively, or to the people." The power to issue bills of credit is definitely not delegated to the United States, and it is specifically prohibited to the States. Therefore, if any power to issue fiat money legally exists at all, it is reserved for the *people*. In other words, individuals and private institutions, such as banks, have the right to issue IOUs and hope that the public will use them as money, but *government, at any level, is clearly prohibited by the Constitution from doing so.*

---

1. For an excellent summary of the interplay of ideas between the delegates, see Edwin Vieira, Jr., *Pieces of Eight: The Monetary Powers and Disabilities of the United States Constitution* (New Jersey: Sound Dollar Committee, 1983), pp. 71–76.
2. Alexander Hamilton, *Works*, Part II, p. 271, as cited by Bancroft, p. 26.
3. Quoted by Bancroft, pp. 39, 40.

A SUGGESTION FOR YOUR CONGRESSMAN

Incidentally, the Constitution has never been amended on this point, nor has the provision that only silver and gold can be used as lawful money. It would be interesting if each reader of this book would send copies to his or her elected representatives in Washington, or at least a photocopy of this section. Every member of Congress has sworn to uphold the Constitution, and you might attach a short note asking them when they intend to begin.

Do not be disappointed if your reply is less than satisfactory. Politicians have a similar problem to that which judges have. It is permissible to rock the boat from time to time, but they are not supposed to *sink* it. Suits against the government challenging the constitutionality of our monetary system seldom get to court. It is safer for the justices to decline to accept these cases or to dismiss them as supposedly "frivolous." Otherwise they would face a difficult choice. Either they would have to mutilate logic in order to uphold the present inconsistencies—thus, opening themselves to possible ridicule—or they would have to declare in favor of the Constitution and literally cause the collapse of the entire deficit-spending, central-bank mechanism. Such an act would take a considerable amount of courage. Not only would they suffer the wrath of the Establishment that is *nourished* by that mechanism, they also would have to face a bewildered public which, because of lack of knowledge about the Constitution or the nature of money, could easily be convinced that the judges had lost their minds. Likewise, it is safer for politicians to respond to inquiries of this kind merely by quoting some self-serving government document which makes our fiat monetary system sound quite legal and marvelously constitutional.

Unfortunately, that is reality. Until the public becomes considerably better informed than it is at present, we cannot expect too much from the courts or from Congress. Bringing this matter to the attention of your elected representatives, however, is still well worth the effort, because the process of education has to start somewhere, and Washington is an excellent place to begin.

Returning to the point of this digression, however, it is important to know that the federal government was given a precisely limited monetary function: "to coin money" and to "regulate the value thereof." In view of the fact that gold and silver coin was specifically defined as the only kind of money to be allowed, there can be no doubt of what was meant by the first half of that power. To coin money meant to mint precious-metal coins. Period.

The second half is equally clear. Both in the Constitution and in the discussions among the delegates, the power to regulate the value of gold and silver coin was closely tied to the power to determine weights and measures. They are, in fact, one and the same. To regulate the value of coin is exactly the same as to set the nationally accepted value of a mile or a pound or a quart. It is to create a standard against which a thing may be measured. The wording of this section of the Constitution can be traced to the original Articles of Confederation which further clarifies the meaning that was generally understood at that time:

> The United States in congress assembled shall ... have the sole and exclusive right and power of regulating the alloy and value of coin struck by their own authority, or by that of the respective states—fixing the Standard of Weights and Measures throughout the United States.

The intent, therefore, was simply for Congress to determine the exact weight of a precious metal that would constitute the national monetary unit.

THE ORIGIN OF THE DOLLAR

At the time of these deliberations, Spanish silver coins, called pieces of eight, had already become the *de facto* monetary unit. An official commission had been established by the Continental Congress to sample the circulating coins in the country and determine their average value by weight and purity. Charts were published, and all coins of various origin were listed by comparative value. Congress was already "regulating the value of" the nation's money by the time the Constitution was drafted. How these coins became dollars is an interesting story. Edwin Vieira tells us:

> Monetary historians generally first associate the dollar with one Count Schlick, who began striking such silver coins in 1519 in Joachim's Thal, Bavaria. Then called *"Schlicktenthalers"* o r *"Joachimsthalers,"* the coins became known simply as *"thalers,"* which transliterated into "dollars." Interestingly, the American colonies did not adopt the dollar from England, but from Spain. Under that country's monetary reform of 1497, the silver *real* became the Spanish money-unit, or unit of account. A new coin consisting of eight *reales* also appeared. Variously known as *pesos, duros, piezas de ocho* ("pieces

of eight"), or Spanish dollars (because of their similarity in weight and fineness to the *thaler*), the coins quickly achieved predominance in financial markets of the New World because of Spain's then-important commercial and political position.[1]

In 1785, Thomas Jefferson urged the adoption of the Spanish silver dollar as the nation's official monetary unit. In a pamphlet submitted to the delegates of the Continental Congress, he said:

> Taking into our view all money transactions, great and small, I question if a common measure, of more convenient size than the dollar, could be proposed.... The unit or dollar is a known coin, and the most familiar of all to the minds of people. It is already adopted from south to north; has identified our currency, and therefore happily offers itself as an unit already introduced.[2]

On July 6, 1785, Congress unanimously voted to adopt the Spanish dollar as the official monetary unit of the United States. Jefferson realized, however, that this was not sufficient. Although the coin had been one of the most dependable in terms of weight and quality, it still varied in content between issues, and a way had to be found to rate one coin in value against another. That was, after all, the service that Congress was required to render when it was given the power to "regulate the value" of money. Jefferson came directly to the point when he said: "If we determine that a dollar shall be our unit, we must then say with precision what a dollar is. This coin as struck at different times, of different weight and fineness, is of different values."[3]

The logic voiced by Jefferson could not be ignored. Two years later, after carefully examining the actual weight and fineness of the Spanish dollars currently in circulation, Congress *defined* the dollar. After ratification of the Constitution, a dollar would contain 371.25 grains of fine silver, and all items in commerce, including other coins, were to be measured in value against that standard.

As the Spaniards continued to reduce the silver content of their coins, the pressure for the minting of an *American* dollar of predictable value began to mount. Secretary of the Treasury, Alexander Hamilton, in his 1791 report to Congress, urged the

---

1. Vieira, p. 66.
2. *Propositions Respecting the Coinage of Gold, Silver, and Copper* (printed pamphlet presented to the Continental Congress on May 13, 1785), pp. 9–10. Cited by Vieira, p. 68.
3. *Ibid.*, p. 11.

establishment of a federal mint and also presented a powerful case for maintaining an inviolable standard for the coins to be produced by that mint. He said:

> The dollar originally contemplated in the money transactions of this country, by successive diminutions of its weight and fineness, has sustained a depreciation of five per cent, and yet the new dollar has a currency in all payments in place of the old, with scarcely any attention to the difference between them. The operation of this in depreciating the value of property depending upon past contracts, and ... of all other property is apparent. Nor can it require argument to prove that a nation ought not to suffer the value of the property of its citizens to fluctuate with the fluctuations of a foreign mint, or to change with the changes in the regulations of a foreign sovereign....
>
> The quantity of gold and silver in the national coins, corresponding with a given sum, cannot be made less than heretofore without disturbing the balance of intrinsic value, and making every acre of land, as well as every bushel of wheat, of less actual worth than in time past.... [This] could not fail to distract the ideas of the community, and would be apt to breed discontent as well among those who live on the income of their money as among the poorer classes of the people to whom the necessities of life would ... become dearer.[1]

BIMETALLISM

Note in the preceding quotation that Hamilton referred to both gold *and* silver coins, not merely silver. That is because it was precisely at this time that Congress began to consider a *bimetallic* coinage. In retrospect, this was a mistake for, throughout history, bimetallism has never worked well very long. It always has led to confusion and, ultimately, the disappearance *as money* of one of the metals. This is because there is always a subtle shifting of the relative values between gold and silver—or any other two metals for that matter—depending on constantly changing supply and demand. We may set a value ratio of one to the other that is quite acceptable today but, eventually, that ratio will no longer reflect reality. The metal which grows in value over the other will be hoarded or possibly even melted down because it will bring a higher price *as metal* than it will as money.

That is precisely what happened in the early days of our Republic. It was determined after careful analysis of the free-

---

1. *The Debates and Proceedings in the Congress of the United States* (J. Gales, compil. 1834), Appendix, pp. 2059, 2071–73. Cited by Vieira, pp. 95, 97.

market that the value of gold *at that time* was approximately fifteen times the value of silver. The Coinage Act of 1792 accordingly set the relative value of gold-to-silver at fifteen-to-one. It then authorized the federal government to mint gold coins called *Eagles*, and it specified that their value was ten dollars. In other words, the gold coins would be equal in value to ten silver coins. Ten silver coins, each of 371.25 grains of fine silver, would contain a total of 3,712.5 grains. The content of the *Eagle*, therefore, was one-fifteenth that amount, or 247.5 grains of fine gold.

Contrary to popular misconception, Congress did *not* create a "gold dollar." (It didn't do that until fifty-seven years later in The Coinage Act of 1849.) In fact it reaffirmed that "the money of account of the United States shall be expressed in dollars or units" and again *defined* those units as coins containing 371.25 grains of pure silver. What Congress *did* do was authorize the minting of a gold coin and arbitrarily fix the value of the gold in that coin at fifteen times the value of the dollar. And it also stated that all silver and gold coins produced in the federal mint were to be legal tender in accordance with their value, based on weight and purity, relative to the standard of the silver dollar.

Oh yes, another thing. It set the death penalty for anyone who debases the nation's coinage; a law which, if enforced today, would wipe out the House of Representatives, the Senate, the managerial level of the Treasury Department, and the Presidency as well.

FREE COINAGE

Perhaps the most important provision of this Act, however, was the establishment of what is called *free coinage*. Under free coinage, any citizen may take raw silver or gold to the mint and, for a nominal fee, have it converted into coins for personal use. The government merely performs a technical function of creating the coin and stamping it with its insignia to certify the correct weight and purity. The state's role in this is exactly the same as inspecting the scales in a grocery store or the meter on a gasoline pump. It is merely fulfilling the Constitutional requirement to set standards and verify the accuracy of weights and measures.

Free coinage was to become an important part of the American success story, and it lasted until the Gold Reserve Act of 1934 which, not only terminated it, but even made it illegal for citizens to *possess* gold. We shall take a closer look at that dismal period in a later section but, for now, it is important to recall the greatness of our monetary system as it once was. Elgin Groseclose explains:

> The principle of free coinage has proved its practical worth as a deterrent to debasement and depreciation. Where coinage is on private account there is no profit to the state in tampering with the standard, and there is no opportunity for such practice by the individual. The circulation of coins of similar appearance and denomination but of uncertain standard, the arbitrary and unpredictable modifications in the standard by autocratic government, the temptations to profit which were constantly dangled before despotic rulers—these were evils which had perplexed and harassed society and hindered the natural growth of economy since the days when coined money first appeared. By a stroke they were swept away. At the same time, the institution of free coinage, by giving stability and character to one of the chief instruments of organized economy, made possible a more vigorous and healthy commercial life and gave prestige and increased substance to the government adopting it.[1]

SOUND MONEY AND ECONOMIC PROSPERITY

This was, indeed, an auspicious beginning for the new nation, and the result was immediately observable in an upsurge in prosperity. The December 16, 1789 edition of the *Pennsylvania Gazette* declared: "Since the federal constitution has removed all danger of our having a paper tender, our trade is advanced fifty per cent."[2] But that was just the beginning. Historian Douglass North says that "the years 1793–1808, were years of unparalleled prosperity."[3] Louis Hacker describes the period as one "of unexampled business expansion, one of the greatest, in fact, the United States has had.... The exports of the country mounted from $19 millions in 1791 to $93 millions in 1801."[4] Furthermore, the federal deficit, which amounted to twenty-eight per cent of expenditures in 1792, dropped to twenty-one per cent in 1795. By 1802, the deficit had disappeared altogether and had been replaced by a surplus that was almost as large as the government's total spending.

George Washington watched this economic miracle with great satisfaction and, in correspondence to his friend, LaFayette, the

---

1. Groseclose, *Money and Man*, p. 167.
2. Quoted by Saussy, p. 36.
3. Douglass C. North, *The Economic Growth of the United States* (New York: W.W. Norton, 1966), p. 53.
4. Louis M. Hacker, *American Capitalism* (New York: Anvil, 1957), p. 39.

French statesman and former General in the Continental Army, Washington commented: "Our country, my dear sir,... is fast progressing in its political importance and social happiness." In a letter to Catherine Macaulay Graham, he said: "The United States enjoys a sense of prosperity and tranquility under the new government that could hardly have been hoped for." And in a letter to the American poet and diplomat, David Humphreys, Washington exclaimed: "Our public credit stands on that high ground which three years ago it would have been considered as a species of madness to have foretold."[1]

On the specific subject of paper money without backing by gold or silver, Washington wrote:

> We may one day become a great commercial and flourishing nation. But if in the pursuit of the means we should unfortunately stumble again on unfunded paper money or any similar species of fraud, we shall assuredly give a fatal stab to our national credit in its infancy.[2]

This, then, was the monetary blueprint laid down by the men who drafted our Constitution. In retrospect, about the only flaw one can find was the attempt to set a fixed ratio between the value of gold and silver. Rather than placing a *dollar* value on a gold coin, the mint should have imprinted the *gold* value in terms of weight and fineness. The free market then would have assigned it an *exchange* value in terms of goods and services, and that automatically would have determined its correct *monetary* value as a ratio to the silver dollars which were bidding for the purchase of the same items. It was inevitable, therefore, that soon after the "ten-dollar" *Eagle* was created, the value of gold over silver began to climb higher than the prescribed ratio of fifteen-to-one, and the *Eagles* ceased to circulate. In later years, with the discovery of the great gold fields in California and Australia, the process reversed itself, and silver dollars disappeared from commerce. But, even though this bimetallism led to a discrepancy between the actual conversion ratio and that which the government had prescribed, nevertheless, it took place in the open market and no one was greatly injured by the inconvenience. Throughout it all, there was just one standard:

---

1. These letters were written in 1790 and 1791, quoted by Atwood, pp. 5–6.
2. Written in 1789, quoted by Louis Basso, *A Treatise on Monetary Reform* (St. Louis, Missouri: Monetary Realist Society, 1982), p. 5.

the defined silver content of a dollar. Furthermore, *both* the silver *and* gold coins were of intrinsic value and totally honest in their measure. No nation could do more for the prosperity of its citizens than that.

SUMMARY

The Constitution prohibits both the states and the federal government from issuing fiat money. This was the deliberate intent of the Founding Fathers who had bitter experience with fiat money before and especially during the Revolutionary War. In response to the need to have a precisely defined national monetary unit, Congress adopted the Spanish dollar then currently in use and defined the content of that dollar to be 371.25 grains of pure silver. With the establishment of a federal mint, American silver dollars were issued in accordance with that standard, and gold *Eagles* also were produced which were then equal in value to ten silver dollars. Most importantly, free coinage was established wherein Americans were able to convert their raw silver and gold into national coins officially certified by the government as to their intrinsic value. The product of these measures was a period of sound money and great economic prosperity, a period that would come to an end only when the next generation of Americans forgot to read their history and returned to the use of paper money and "bills of credit."

The monetary plan laid down by the Founding Fathers was the product of collective genius. Nowhere in history can one find so many men in one legislative body who understood the fraud inherent in fiat money and the hidden-taxation nature of inflation. There was never such an assembly of scholars and statesmen determined to set a safe course for the nation of their own creation. Literally, they handed us a *treasure map*. All we had to do was follow it to economic security and national prosperity. But, as we shall see in the following sections, that map was discarded when the lessons of history died out with those who had lived it.

Chapter Sixteen

THE CREATURE
COMES TO AMERICA

*The story of the Bank of North America, the
nation's first central bank, which was formed even
before the Constitution was drafted; the story of
the First Bank of the United States, the nation's
second central bank, which was formed in 1791;
the massive inflation caused by both banks; the
causes of their demise.*

It is a surprising fact that the United States had its first central
bank even before the Constitution was drafted. It was chartered by
the Continental Congress in the Spring of 1781 and opened its
doors the following year. There were great expectations at that time
that the province of Canada would soon join the rebel colonies to
form a union extending across the entire North American continent. In anticipation of that, the new financial institution was called
the Bank of North America.

The Bank was organized by Robert Morris, a member of
Congress, who was a leader of a group of politicians and merchants
who wanted the new nation to imitate the mercantilism of England.
They wanted high taxes to support a powerful, centralized government, high tariffs to subsidize domestic industry, a large army and
navy, and the acquisition of colonial outposts to expand into
foreign lands and markets. He was a wealthy Philadelphia merchant who had profited greatly from war contracts during the
Revolution. He had carefully studied the secret science of money
and, by 1781, was widely considered to be the financial wizard of
Congress.

The Bank of North America was modeled closely after the Bank
of England. Following the practice of fractional reserve, it was
allowed to issue paper promissory notes in excess of actual
deposits, but, since *some* gold and silver had to be held in the vault,

there were definite limits to how far that process could go. Bank notes were not forced on the people as legal tender for all debts, public and private, but the government did agree to accept them *at their face value* in payment of all taxes and duties, which made them as good as gold for that specific purpose. Furthermore, unlike the central banks of today, the Bank of North America was not given the power to directly issue the nation's money.

FUNCTIONED AS A CENTRAL BANK

On the other hand, the Bank was given the right of monopoly in its field, which means there were no other bank notes allowed to circulate in competition. This, plus the fact that they were accepted at face value in payment of all federal and state taxes, plus the further fact that the federal government did not at that time have a functioning money of its own, made these bank notes attractive for use as a circulating medium of exchange. The intended result was that the Bank's paper would be accepted as money, which for a while, it was. Furthermore, the Bank was made the official depository for all federal funds and it almost immediately lent $1.2 million to the government, much of which was created out of nothing for that purpose. So, in spite of the limitations placed upon the Bank, and in spite of the fact that it was essentially a private institution, it was intended to be and, in fact, did function as a central bank.

The Bank of North America was fraudulent from the very start. The charter required that private investors provide $400,000 for the initial subscription. When Morris was unable to raise that money, he used his political influence to make up the shortfall out of government funds. In a maneuver that was nothing less than legalized embezzlement, he took the gold that had been lent to the United States from France and had it deposited in the Bank. Then, using this as a fractional-reserve base, he simply created the money that was needed for the subscription and lent it to himself and his associates. Such is the power of the secret science.[1]

It is hard to reconcile the fact that the same men who adopted the brilliant monetary restraints of the Constitution a few years later would have allowed the Bank of North America to exist. It must be remembered, however, that the war was still in progress

---

1. See Murray N. Rothbard, *Conceived in Liberty: The Revolutionary War, 1775–1784* (New Rochelle, New York: Arlington House, 1979), Vol. IV, p. 392.

when the charter was issued, and even the wisest of statesmen are often obliged to follow expediency in such times. One also must conclude that, while the founding fathers were wise on the nature of fiat money created by the government's printing press, they had not yet had extensive experience with the same mechanism hidden behind the obscurities of fractional-reserve banking.

In any event, the Bank was not to have its charter renewed by Congress and it did not survive beyond the end of the war. Murray Rothbard details its demise:

> Despite the monopoly privileges conferred upon the Bank of North America and its nominal redeemability in specie, the market's lack of confidence in the inflated notes led to their depreciation outside the Bank's home base in Philadelphia. The Bank even tried to bolster the value of its notes by hiring people to urge redeemers of its notes not to insist on specie—a move scarcely calculated to improve the long-run confidence in the Bank.
>
> After a year of operation, Morris's political power slipped, and he moved quickly to shift the Bank of North America from a central bank to a purely commercial bank chartered by the state of Pennsylvania. By the end of 1783,... the first experiment with a central bank in the United States had ended.[1]

A fitting epilogue to this story was written two hundred years later when, in 1980, the First Pennsylvania Bank of Philadelphia, the "oldest bank in the nation," was bailed out by the FDIC.

AN END RUN AROUND THE CONSTITUTION

It will be recalled that, after the Bank of North America was terminated and after the Constitutional Convention "closed the door on paper money," the United States enjoyed a period of unparalleled economic growth and prosperity. But, while the door may have been closed, the window was still open. Congress was denied the power to *print* money, but it was not denied the power to *borrow* it.

In the vocabulary of the common man, to borrow is to accept a loan of something that already exists. He is confused, therefore, when the banker issues money out of nothing and then says he is *lending* it. He *appears* to be lending but, in reality, he is *creating*.

Then, as now, the mysteries of banking vocabulary were not revealed to the average man, and it was difficult to understand

---

1. Rothbard, *Mystery*, pp. 194–95.

how privately-issued bank notes could serve precisely the same purpose as printing-press money—with precisely the same disastrous results. That being the case, the monetary and political scientists decided to end run the Constitution. Their plan was to establish a bank, to give that bank the power to create money, to *lend* most of that money to the government, and then to make sure the IOUs are accepted as money by the public. Congress, therefore, would not be emitting bills of credit. The *bank* would do that.

Thus, the First Bank of the United States was conceived.

The proposal was submitted to Congress in 1790 by Alexander Hamilton who, at that time, was Secretary of the Treasury. Hamilton, incidentally, was a former aide to Robert Morris, founder of the Bank of North America, so in that sense his role in this matter is not surprising. What is surprising is the fact that Hamilton had been a staunch supporter of a sound currency during the Constitutional Convention. This is hard to reconcile, and one must suspect that, even the most well intentioned of men can become corrupted by the temptations of wealth and power. It is possible that Hamilton, Morris, and other Federalist leaders had hoped to keep the government out of the money-making business, not because it was the constitutional thing to do, but because that would leave the field clear for a central-bank mechanism which, because it was further from public view and political control, could become their own private engine of profit. It would appear that the only other explanation is that these men were fickle in their views and did not really understand the implications of their acts. In view of their brilliance in all other matters, however, it is difficult to muster enthusiasm for that interpretation.

THE HAMILTON-JEFFERSON CONFLICT

Hamilton's proposal was strongly opposed by Thomas Jefferson, then Secretary of State, and this was the beginning of a heated political debate that would preoccupy Congress for many decades to come. In fact, it was one of the central issues that led to the creation of our first political parties. The Federalists gathered around the ideas of Hamilton. The anti-Federalists, later called the Republicans, were attracted to the ideas of Jefferson.[1]

---

1. Curiously, the present Democratic Party traces its origin to Jefferson's Republicans.

Jefferson pointed out that the Constitution did not grant to Congress the power to create a bank or anything similar. That means such power is reserved to the states or to the people. In a rebuttal to Hamilton's proposal, he said: "To take a single step beyond the boundaries thus specially drawn around the powers of Congress, is to take possession of a boundless field of power, no longer susceptible of any definition."[1] Furthermore, he said, even if the Constitution *had* granted such power, it would be an extremely unwise thing to do, because allowing banks to create money could only lead to national ruin.

Hamilton, on the other hand, argued that debt was a good thing, if kept within reason, and that the nation needed more money in circulation to keep up with expanding commerce. Only the Bank, he said, would be able to provide that. Furthermore, while it is true the Constitution did not *specifically* grant the power to create such a bank, it was, nevertheless, an *implied* power, because it was needed to accomplish *other* functions which *were* granted in the Constitution.

That was the end run.

Nothing could be more polarized than the opposing ideas of these two men:

JEFFERSON: "A private central bank issuing the public currency is a greater menace to the liberties of the people than a standing army."[2] "We must not let our rulers load us with perpetual debt."[3]

HAMILTON: "No society could succeed which did not unite the interest and credit of rich individuals with those of the state."[4] "A national debt, if it is not excessive, will be to us a national blessing."[5]

AMERICA'S SECOND CENTRAL BANK IS CREATED

After a year of intense debate, Hamilton's views prevailed and, in 1791, Congress granted a twenty-year charter to the Bank of the

---

1. "Opinion of Thomas Jefferson, Secretary of State," February 15, 1791, quoted by Krooss, pp. 147–48.
2. The comparison between private banks and standing armies can be found in many of Jefferson's letters and public utterances. For example, see *The Writings of Thomas Jefferson* (New York: G.P. Putnam & Sons, 1899), Vol. X, p. 31.
3. *The Basic Writings of Thomas Jefferson* (Willey Book Company, 1944), p. 749.
4. Quoted by Arthur M. Schlesinger, Jr., *The Age of Jackson* (New York: Mentor Books, 1945), pp. 6–7.
5. Written on April 30, 1781, to his mentor, Robert Morris. Quoted by John H. Makin, *The Global Debt Crisis: America's Growing Involvement* (New York: Basic Books, 1984), p. 246.

United States. It was modelled closely after the Bank of England, which means it was almost an exact replica of the previous Bank of North America. In fact, as evidence of continuity with the past, the president of the new bank was Thomas Willing, the same man who had been a partner of Robert Morris and president of the old bank.[1]

As before, the new Bank was given a monopoly in the issuance of bank notes. Once again, these notes were not forced on the people as legal tender for *private* debts and contracts, but they *were* legal tender at face value for all debts to the *government* in the form of taxes and duties, which made them attractive for use as common money. And once again, the Bank was made the official depository of all federal funds.

The charter specified that the Bank was required at all times to redeem its notes in gold or silver specie upon demand by the depositor. That was an admirable provision but, since the Bank was not also required to keep specie in its vaults in the full amount of its note obligations, it was a mathematical impossibility to uphold.

As with the old Bank of North America, the new Bank of the United States was to have eighty per cent of its capital provided by private investors with the federal government putting up only twenty per cent. That was a mere bookkeeping sleight-of-hand, however, because it had been prearranged for the Bank to immediately lend back to the federal government exactly that same amount. Reminiscent of the Morris scheme in capitalizing the Bank of North America, this federal "investment" was essentially a means whereby federal funds could be used to make up the short-fall of the private investors. "Call it by what name you please," said Jefferson, this was not a loan or an investment but an outright gift. And he was certainly right. The Bank was able to open its doors with less than nine per cent of the private capital required by its charter. The total capitalization was specified at $10 million, which means that $8 million was to come from private stockholders. However, as John Kenneth Galbraith wryly observed: "Numerous thrifty participants confined themselves to a modest down payment, and the bank began operations on around $675,000 in hard cash."[2]

---

1. It is interesting to note that, as a member of the Continental Congress, Willing had been one of those who voted against the Declaration of Independence.
2. Galbraith, p. 72

THE CREATURE COMES FROM EUROPE

Who were these private investors? Their names do not appear in the published literature, but we can be certain they included the Congressmen and Senators—and their associates—who engineered the charter. But there is an interesting line in Galbraith's text that hints at another dimension to the composition of this group. On page 72 of *Money: Whence It Came, Where It Went*, he states matter-of-factly: "Foreigners could own shares but not vote them."

What a story is hidden behind that innocuous statement. The blunt reality is that the Rothschild banking dynasty in Europe was the dominant force, both financially and politically, in the formation of the Bank of the United States. Biographer, Derek Wilson, explains:

> Over the years since N.M. [Rothschild], the Manchester textile manufacturer, had bought cotton from the Southern states, Rothschilds had developed heavy American commitments. Nathan ... had made loans to various states of the Union, had been, for a time, the official European banker for the US government and was a pledged supporter of the Bank of the United States.[1]

Gustavus Myers, in his *History of the Great American Fortunes*, is more pointed. He says:

> Under the surface, the Rothschilds long had a powerful influence in dictating American financial laws. The law records show that they were the power in the old Bank of the United States.[2]

The Rothschilds, therefore, were not merely investors nor just an important power. They were *the* power behind the Bank of the United States! The significance of the Rothschild power in American finance and politics was the subject of extensive comment in a previous section, so there is no need to cover that ground again. It is important here, however, to at least make a mental note of the fact that the Creature from Jekyll Island is descended from a species that is *not* native to this land.

INFLATION ALL OVER AGAIN

From the beginning, the primary purpose of the Bank was to create money for the federal government. Money for the private

---

1. Derek Wilson, p. 178.
2. Gustavus Myers, *History of the Great American Fortunes* (New York: Random House, 1936), p. 556.

sector was strictly secondary. That was made clear by the fact that the maximum rate of interest it was allowed to charge was six per cent. That made it impractical to make loans to anyone except the federal government and a few large, prime-rate borrowers. And the government wasted no time putting its new central-bank mechanism to work. Having "invested" $2 million at the start, it converted that into $8.2 million borrowed within the next five years. Which means that $6.2 million was created specifically for its use.

Anyone familiar with the history of money as outlined in the previous section could easily write the following paragraph.

The creation of millions of new fractional-reserve dollars, which the government pushed into the economy through spending programs, caused an imbalance between the supply of money and the supply of goods and services. Prices appeared to go up as the relative value of the dollar went down. In that same five-year period, wholesale prices rose by 72%, which is another way of saying that 42% of everything people had saved in the form of money was quietly confiscated by the government through the hidden tax called inflation.

The same inflation effect that previously had plagued the colonies now returned to plague the new generation. This time, instead of being caused by printing-press money, it was fractional-reserve money. The cog that linked the two mechanisms together and caused them to function as one was federal debt. It was federal debt that allowed the political and monetary scientists to violate the intent of the founding fathers, and it was this same federal debt that prompted Jefferson to exclaim:

> I wish it were possible to obtain a single amendment to our Constitution. I would be willing to depend on that alone for the reduction of the administration of our government to the general principle of the Constitution; I mean an additional article, taking from the federal government their power of borrowing.[1]

Like so many things in the real world, the Bank of the United States was a mixture of evil with some good. It certainly was not all bad. In colonial times, the state governments printed as much paper money as they pleased, and the loss of purchasing power was, in many cases, total. The Bank, on the other hand, was

---

1. Letter to John Taylor, November 26, 1789. Quoted by Martin A. Larson, *The Continuing Tax Rebellion* (Old Greenwich, Connecticut: Devin-Adair, 1979), p. xii.

required to maintain *some* gold and specie as a base for its pyramid of money. Even though it was an *inverted* pyramid with reserves being smaller than the quantity of bank notes, it still represented a boundary to just how far the money supply could be expanded. And that was good.

Furthermore, it is apparent that the bank's directors were imbued with a certain amount of enlightened self interest in that they actually *wanted* to keep the creation of new money within some kind of control. They could profit from the central-bank mechanism only so long as the economy as a whole was productive enough to support it. They did not want to kill the goose that laid the golden egg. So, like their counterparts in the Federal Reserve System of our modern day, they spoke the language of restraint and, in a few instances, even acted with restraint as well.

WILDCAT BANKS

For example, it was during this period that "wildcat banks" began to flourish. They were given that name not because they were untamed—although that would have been another good reason to do so—but because they were located in areas so remote in the frontier that it was said their only customers were wildcats.

Wildcat banks were not noted for meticulous accounting or business practices. Like all banks at that time, they were required to keep a certain portion of their deposits on hand in the form of gold or silver coin. To engender public confidence in their faithfulness to that obligation, it was common practice to keep the vault door open so a keg or two of gold coins could be viewed during business hours—not altogether different from the modern practice of financial institutions advertising how many billions in assets they hold but never mentioning the size of their liabilities. The wildcatters, however, were not reluctant to sprinkle a few precious-metal coins over the top of *nails* and let *that* take care of public relations. In some cases, as state examiners went from bank to bank to check the reserves, the gold would arrive only a few minutes ahead of them, having been rushed from the vault of the bank previously audited.

The point is that the Bank of the United States was able to place considerable restraint upon the practices of all banks, both wildcat and urban. It did this simply by refusing to accept the notes of any other bank unless it had a reputation for redeeming those notes in specie on demand. The public reacted accordingly. If the notes were not good enough for the Bank of the United States, they were not good enough for them either. This served as an indirect force of moderation that affected all banks of that time. And that, too, was good.

Some historians have said that the Bank was a positive force in yet another way. Galbraith, for example, writes admiringly:

> On occasion, the Bank of the United States came to the assistance of good state banks that were being besieged by their note holders or other creditors. So, besides enforcing restraint, it served also as the lender of last resort. Thus in its short span of life it went far to perceive and develop the basic regulatory functions of a central bank.[1]

One who is less enamored with the idea of a central bank would be tempted to ask: If those state banks were so "good," why did they need assistance in keeping faith with their depositors? The whole idea of a "lender of last resort," which is accepted as sacred dogma today, is based on the assumption that it is perfectly acceptable for the entire banking system to be fraudulent. It is assumed that any single bank or cluster of banks could at any time become "besieged by their note holders or other creditors." Therefore, it is prudent to have a central bank to take what meager reserves there are within the system and rush them from bank to bank, if not minutes before the examiner arrives, at least before the customers do.

As for the much talked about restraint exercised over other banks, it is not unreasonable to think that this same effect would have developed even without the presence of a government bank. If the free market had been left to operate, it is certain that, before long, one or more banks would gain a deserved reputation for honesty and full faith with their depositors. They would become the most popular banks and, therefore, the most prosperous. In order to accomplish this, however, they would *have* to reject the worthless notes of other banks. The public would react as expected, and even the most unscrupulous banks would have to toe the line if they wanted to survive. Moderation would be forced on the entire banking system as a result of open competition within a free market. To assume that only a federally-chartered central bank could have brought moderation into the monetary system is to

---

1. Galbraith, p. 73.

believe that only politicians, bureaucrats, and agencies of government can act with integrity, a shaky notion at best.

AN INSTRUMENT OF PLUTOCRACY

In any event, there is no denying the fact that the Bank of the United States did provide some braking force to the runaway tendencies of many of the nation's private banks. So it could have been worse. The inflation that it caused by its own activities could have been enlarged even further by the activities of the other banks as well. But, that it could have been worse does not make it good. As it was, the Bank was the means by which the American people lost forty-two per cent of the value of all the money they earned or possessed during just those five years. We must not forget, either, that this confiscation of property was *selective*. It did *not* work against the *wealthy* classes which were able to ride the wave of inflation aboard the raft of tangible property which they owned. And it especially did not work against those elite few, the political and monetary scientists, who were making huge profits from the enterprise. The Bank had done precisely what Hamilton had advocated: "... unite the interest and credit of rich individuals with those of the state."

The development of this plutocracy was well described by Governeur Morris, the former delegate from New York who had helped to draft the Constitution into its final form. He had been an assistant to Robert Morris (not related) and was a champion of the concept of a natural aristocracy. So he knew his subject well when he warned:

> The rich will strive to establish their dominion and enslave the rest. They always did. They always will.... They will have the same effect here as elsewhere, if we do not, by such a government, keep them within their proper spheres. We should remember that the people never act from reason alone. The rich will take advantage of their passions, and make these the instruments for oppressing them. The result of the contest will be a violent aristocracy, or a more violent despotism.[1]

The tide of political pressure against the Bank was steadily rising during these years. It is tempting for critics of the central-bank mechanism to attribute that to the awakening common sense

---

1. Written on July 2, 1787, in a letter to James Madison. Quoted in "Prosperity Economics," by W. Cleon Skousen, *Freeman Digest*, February, 1985, p. 9.

of the American public. Unfortunately, the picture is not that pleasing. It is true that the Jeffersonian Republicans were eloquently holding forth against the Creature's progenitor, and their influence was substantial. But there was another group that joined with them which had almost exactly opposite ideas and goals. The Jeffersonians opposed the Bank because they believed it was unconstitutional and because they wanted a monetary system based only upon gold and silver coin. The other group was made up of the wildcatters, the land speculators, and the empire-building industrialists. They opposed the Bank because they wanted a monetary system with no restraints at all, not even those associated with fractional reserve. They wanted every local bank to be free to create as much paper money as the public would swallow, because they would then use that money for their own projects and profit. Indeed, politics *does* produce strange bedfellows.

As the time approached for renewal of the Bank's charter, the battle lines inched toward each other. They were of equal force. The halls of Congress echoed with the cannon roar of angry debate. The vote was deadlocked. Another attack and counter attack. Again a deadlock. Into the night the forces clashed.

When the smoke of battle lifted, the bill for charter renewal had been defeated by *one* vote in the House and *one* vote, cast by Vice-President George Clinton to break the tie, in the Senate. And so, on January 24, 1811, the Bank of the United States closed its doors.

The battle may have been decided, but the war was far from over. The losers, bitter with defeat, merely regrouped their forces and began to prepare for the next encounter. Unfortunately, the events that followed were ideally suited for their plans.

With the moderating effect of the Bank now removed from the scene, the nation's banking system passed wholly into the hands of the state-chartered corporations, many of which were imbued with the wildcat mentality. Their numbers grew rapidly, and so did the money supply which they created. Inflation followed in their footsteps. Public dissatisfaction began to rise.

If the free market had been allowed to operate, it is likely that competition soon would have weeded out the wildcatters and restored balance to the system, but it was never given a chance. The War of 1812 saw to that.

THE WAR OF 1812

The War of 1812 was one of the most senseless wars in history. The primary cause, we are told, was the British impressment into their navy of American sailors on the high seas to assist in the war against Napoleonic France. But the French had done exactly the same thing to assist in the war against England, yet their acts were ignored. Furthermore, the British had already rescinded their policy regarding American seamen *before* the war was underway, which means that the *cause* of the war had been removed, and peace could have been restored in honor if Congress had so wanted. One must conclude that the pro-banking interests in the United States actually *wanted* the conflict because of the profits that could be realized from it. As evidence of this is the fact that the New England states, which were home to the seamen who had been impressed into service, were firmly against the war, while the Western and inland Southern states, which were home to the myriad of wildcat banks, howled loudly for a clash of arms.

In any event, the war was unpopular with the average citizen, and it was out of the question for Congress to obtain funding for armaments through an increase in taxes. So the government *needed* the state banks to create that money *outside* the tax structure and came to their rescue to protect them from the discipline of the free market. It was a classic case of the unholy alliance, the *cabal*, that always develops between political and monetary scientists. Professor Rothbard gives the details:

> The U.S. government encouraged an enormous expansion in the number of banks and in bank notes and deposits to purchase the growing war debt. These new and recklessly inflationary banks in the Middle Atlantic, Southern, and Western states, printed enormous quantities of new notes to purchase government bonds. The federal government then used these notes to purchase arms and manufactured goods in New England....
>
> By August 1814, it became clear that the banks of the nation apart from New England could not pay [in specie], that they were insolvent. Rather than allow the banks of the nation to fail, the governments, state and federal, decided in August 1814 to allow the banks to continue in business while refusing to redeem their obligations in specie. In other words, the banks were allowed to refuse to pay their solemn contractual obligations....
>
> This general suspension was not only highly inflationary at the time; it set a precedent for all financial crises from then on. Whether

the U.S. had a central bank or not, the banks were assured that if they inflated together and then got in trouble, government would bail them out.[1]

The state banks had created enough instant money for the federal government to raise the debt from $45 million to $127 million, a staggering sum for the fledgling nation. Tripling the money supply, with no appreciable increase in goods, means the value of the dollar shrank to about one-third its former purchasing power. By 1814, when the depositors began to awake to the scam and demanded their gold instead of paper, the banks closed their doors and had to hire extra guards to protect officials and employees from the angry crowds. Once again, the monetary and political scientists had succeeded in fleecing the American public of approximately 66% of all the money they held during that period, and that was on *top* of the 42% fleecing they got a few years earlier by the Bank of the United States.

JUGGLING TRICKS AND BANKING DREAMS

Leaning against the storm of paper money all this time was Thomas Jefferson, by now, past-President of the United States. Trying to bring the nation to its senses, he never ceased speaking out against the evil of dishonest money and debt:

> Although all the nations of Europe have tried and trodden every path of force and folly in a fruitless quest of the same object, yet *we* still expect to find in juggling tricks and banking dreams, that money can be made out of nothing, and in sufficient quantity to meet the expense of heavy war.[2]...
>
> The toleration of banks of paper discount costs the United States one-half of their war taxes; or, in other words, doubles the expenses of every war.[3]...
>
> The crisis, then, of the abuses of banking is arrived. The banks have pronounced their own sentence of death. Between two and three hundred millions of dollars of their promissory notes are in the hands of the people, for solid produce and property sold, and they [the banks] formally declare that they will not pay them.... Paper was received on a belief that it was cash [gold], and such scenes are now to take place as will open the eyes of credulity and of insanity itself to the

---

1. Rothbard, *Mystery*, pp. 198–99.
2. *Writings*, Library Edition, Vol. XIV, p. 227.
3. *Writings*, Library Edition, Vol. XIII, p. 364.

dangers of a paper medium abandoned to the discretion of avarice and of swindlers.[1]...

It is a wise rule never to borrow a dollar without laying a tax at the same instant for paying the interest annually and the principal within a given term.[2]... We shall consider ourselves unauthorized to saddle posterity with our debts, and morally bound to pay them ourselves.[3]

... The earth belongs to the living, not the dead.... We may consider each generation as a distinct nation, with a right to ... bind themselves, but not the succeeding generation.[4]...

The modern theory of the perpetuation of debt has drenched the earth with blood, and crushed its inhabitants under burdens ever accumulating.[5]

And *still*, Congress did not listen.

SUMMARY

America had its first central bank even before the Constitution was drafted. It was called the Bank of North America and was chartered by the Continental Congress in 1781. Modeled after the Bank of England, it was authorized to issue more paper promissory notes than it held in deposits. In the beginning, these notes were widely circulated and served as a national currency. Although the bank was essentially a private institution, it was designed for the purpose of creating money to lend to the federal government, which it did from the start.

The Bank of North America was riddled with fraud, and it quickly fell into political disfavor. Its inflated bank notes eventually were rejected by ordinary citizens and ceased to circulate outside of the Bank's home city of Philadelphia. Its charter was allowed to expire and, in 1783, it was converted into a purely commercial bank chartered by the state of Pennsylvania.

The advocates of fiat money did not give up. In 1791, the First Bank of the United States (America's *second* central bank) was created by Congress. The new bank was a replica of the first, including fraud. Private investors in the Bank were among the nation's most wealthy and influential citizens, including some Congressmen and Senators. But the largest investment and the

---

1. Letter to Dr. Thomas Cooper, Sept. 10, 1814, *Writings*, Library Edition, Vol. XIV, pp. 187–89.
2. *Writings*, Library Edition, Vol. XIII, p. 269.
3. *Ibid*, p. 358.
4. *Ibid.*, p. 270.
5. *Ibid.*, p. 272.

most powerful influence in the new Bank came from the Rothschilds in Europe.

The Bank set about immediately to serve its function of creating money for the government. This led to a massive inflation of the money supply and rising prices. In the first five years, 42% of everything people had saved in the form of money was confiscated through the hidden tax called inflation. This was the same phenomenon that had plagued the colonies less than two decades earlier, but instead of being caused by printing-press money, it was now fueled by fractional-reserve bank notes created by a central bank.

As the time for renewal of the Bank's charter approached, two groups with opposite intentions became strange political allies against it: the Jeffersonians who wanted sound money; and the frontier banks, called wildcatters, who wanted unlimited license to steal. On January 24, 1811, the charter was defeated by one vote in the Senate and one in the House. The central bank was gone, but the wildcatters were everywhere.

The War of 1812 was not popular among the American public, and funding would have been impossible through taxes alone. The government chose to fund the war by encouraging wildcat banks to purchase its war-debt bonds and convert them into bank notes which the government then used to purchase war material. Within two years, the nation's money supply had tripled, and so had prices. Once again, the monetary and political scientists had succeeded in fleecing the American public of approximately 66% of all the money they held during that period. And that was on *top* of the 42% fleecing they got a few years earlier by the Bank of the United States.

Chapter Seventeen

A DEN OF VIPERS

The story of the Second Bank of the United States, the nation's third central bank; the election of Andrew Jackson on an anti-bank platform; the battle between President Jackson and the head of the bank, Nicholas Biddle; the deliberate creation of a depression to frighten the public into keeping the bank; Jackson's ultimate victory.

The monetary chaos that existed at the end of the War of 1812, outlined in the previous chapter, was caused by an almost universal fraud within the banking industry. Depositors in good faith placed their gold and silver into banks for safekeeping and for the convenience of using paper money in their everyday transactions. The banks, in turn, promised them they could exchange the paper for their coins whenever they wished. At the same time, however, through the mechanism of fractional-reserve banking, paper money was created far in excess of the value of the coins held in reserve. Since the new money had just as much claim to the coins as the old, the bankers knew that, if a sizable percentage of their customers were to request a withdrawal of their coins, that solemn promise simply could not be kept. This, in fact, is precisely what happened over and over again during that period.

By 1814, Thomas Jefferson had retired to Monticello and had bitterly resigned himself to defeat on the issue of money. In a letter to John Adams he said:

> I have ever been the enemy of banks; not of those discounting for cash [that is, charging interest on loans of *real* money], but of those foisting their own paper into circulation, and thus banishing our cash. My zeal against those institutions was so warm and open at the establishment of the bank of the U.S. that I was derided as a Maniac by the tribe of bank-mongers, who were seeking to filch from the public their swindling and barren gains.... Shall we build an altar to the old paper money of the revolution, which ruined individuals but saved the republic, and burn on that all the bank charters present and future,

and their notes with them? For these are to ruin both republic and individuals. This cannot be done. The Mania is too strong. It has seized by its delusions and corruptions all the members of our governments, general, special, and individual.[1]

Jefferson was right. Congress had neither the wisdom nor the courage to let the free market clean up the mess that remained after the demise of the first bank of the U.S. If it had, the fraud soon would have become understood by the public, the dishonest banks would have folded, the losses would have been taken, and the suffering would have been ended, perhaps forever. Instead, Congress moved to *protect* the banks, to *organize* the fraud, and to *perpetuate* the losses. All of this was accomplished in 1816 when a twenty-year charter was given to the *Second* Bank of the United States.

THE SECOND BANK OF THE UNITED STATES

In every respect the new bank was a carbon copy of the old, with one minor exception. Congress unashamedly extracted from the private investors what amounted to nothing less than a bribe in the form of $1.5 million "in consideration of the exclusive privileges and benefits conferred by this Act."[2] The bankers were glad to pay the fee, not only because it was a modest price for such a profitable enterprise, but also because, as before, they received an immediate government deposit of one-fifth the total capitalization which then was used as the base for manufacturing much of the remaining startup capital. The charter required the Bank to raise a minimum of $7 million in specie, but even in its second year of operation, its specie never rose above $2.5 million.[3] Once again, the monetary and political scientists had carved out their profitable niches, and the gullible taxpayer, his head filled with sweet visions of "banking reform," was left to pick up the tab.

Another important continuity between the old and the new Bank was the concentration of foreign investment. In fact, the largest single block of stock in the new Bank, about one-third in all, was held by this group.[4] It is certainly no exaggeration to say that

---

1. Lester J. Cappon, ed., *The Adams-Jefferson Letters* (New York: Simon and Schuster, 1971), Vol. II, p. 424.
2. Act of 1816, Section 20, 3 Stat. at 191.
3. Rothbard, *Mystery*, p. 203.
4. Krooss, p. 25.

the Second Bank of the United States was rooted as deeply in Britain as it was in America.

The nation's third central bank ran into deep trouble from the start. It had promised to continue the tradition of moderating the other banks by refusing to accept any of their notes unless they were redeemable in specie on demand. But when the other banks returned the gesture and required that the new Bank also pay out specie on *their* demand, it frequently lost its resolve. There was also the tiny matter of corruption. As the Bank's major historian writes: "So many influential people were interested [in the state banks] as stockholders that it was not advisable to give offense by demanding payment in specie, and borrowers were anxious to keep the banks in the humor to lend."[1]

In economics, every policy carries a consequence, and the consequence of the loose monetary policy of the Second Bank of the United States was that America was introduced to her first experience with what now is called the "boom-bust" cycle. Galbraith tells us: "In 1816, the postwar boom was full on; there was especially active speculation in western lands. The new Bank joyously participated."[2]

The Bank had the advantage over its competitors of a federal charter plus the government's agreement to accept its notes in the payment of taxes. But the state banks were by no means left out of the game. It was still within their power to create money through fractional-reserve banking and, thus, to further inflate the amount of the nation's circulating currency. Anxious to get in on this action, Pennsylvania chartered thirty-seven new banks in 1817. That same year, Kentucky followed suit with forty new charters. The total number of banks grew by 46% in just the first two years after the central bank was created. Any spot along the road that had "a church, a tavern, or a blacksmith shop was deemed a suitable place for setting up a bank."[3] In that same time frame, the money supply was expanded by an additional $27.4 million; another taxpayer fleecing of over forty per cent.

---

1. Ralph C.H. Catterall, *The Second Bank of the United States* (Chicago: University of Chicago Press, 1902), p. 36.
2. Galbraith, p. 77.
3. Norman Angell, *The Story of Money* (New York: Frederick A. Stokes Co., 1929), p. 279.

THE FIRST BOOM-BUST CYCLE

In the past, the effect of this inflationary process always had been the gradual evaporation of purchasing power and the continuous transfer of property *from* those who produced it *to* those who controlled the government and ran the banks. This time, however, the process took on a new twist. Gradualism was replaced by catastrophism. The monetary scientists, with their hands firmly on the controls of the money machine, now began to throw the levers, first one way, and then the other. The expansion and then *deliberate contraction* of the money supply literally threw the nation into economic convulsions. Why wait for the apples to fall when the harvest can be hastened simply by shaking the tree?

In 1818, the Bank suddenly began to tighten its requirements for new loans and to call in as many of the old loans as possible. This contraction of the money supply was justified to the public then exactly as it is justified today. It was necessary, they said, *to put the brakes on inflation.* The fact that this was the same inflation the Bank had helped to create in the first place, seems to have gone unnoticed.

There is no doubt that many bankers and politicians act in good faith in their attempt to bring under control the inflation they themselves have caused. Not everyone who benefits from the central-bank mechanism fully understands it. Like Frankenstein, they create a monster without realizing they cannot control it. Their crime is one of stupidity, not malice. But stupidity is not a characteristic of the average banker, especially a *central* banker, and we must conclude that many of the monetary scientists are well aware of the monster's power for destruction. At best, they just don't care as long as *they* are safe. And at worst, they perceive that they are in the apple-harvesting business. They deliberately tease and prod the monster in anticipation of his rampage through the village orchards. In the final analysis, of course, it is of little importance whether the shaking of the trees is out of innocence or malice. The end result is the same. My, how the apples do fall.

The country's first experience with a deliberately created monetary contraction began in 1818 when the Bank became concerned about its own ability to survive. Professor Rothbard says:

> Starting in July 1818, the government and the BUS [Bank of the United States] began to see what dire straits they were in; the

enormous inflation of money and credit, aggravated by the massive fraud, had put the BUS in danger of going under and illegally failing to maintain specie payments. Over the next year, the BUS began a series of enormous contractions, forced curtailment of loans, contractions of credit in the south and west.... The contraction of money and credit swiftly brought to the United States its first widespread economic and financial depression. The first nationwide "boom-bust" cycle had arrived in the United States....

The result of this contraction was a rash of defaults, bankruptcies of business and manufacturers, and a liquidation of unsound investments during the boom.[1]

THE CYCLE IS WORSENED BY GOVERNMENT INTERFERENCE

It is widely believed that panics, boom-bust cycles, and depressions are caused by unbridled competition between banks; thus the need for government regulation. The truth is just the opposite. These disruptions in the free market are the result of government *prevention* of competition by the granting of monopolistic power to a *central* bank. In the absence of a monopoly, individual banks may operate in a fraudulent manner only to a limited extent and for a short period of time. Inevitably, they will be exposed by their more honest competitors and will be forced out of business. Yes, their depositors will be injured by the bankruptcy, but the damage will be limited to a relatively few and will occur only now and then. Even geographical regions may be hard hit on occasion, but it will not be a *national* tragedy with *everyone* brought to their knees. The overall economy will absorb the losses, and commerce at large will continue to prosper. Within an environment of prosperity, even those who have been injured by fraudulent banking would have a good chance for rapid recovery. But, when a central bank is allowed to protect the fraudulent operators and to force *all* banks to function the same, the forces of competition can no longer dampen the effect. The expansion becomes universal and gigantic. And, of course, so does the contraction. Except for the bankers and the politicians, *everyone* is injured at the same time; depression is *everywhere*; and recovery is long delayed.

This is exactly what happened in the so-called panic of 1819. In the *Documentary History of Banking and Currency*, Herman Krooss writes:

---

1. Rothbard, *Mystery*, pp. 204–05. Also see Galbraith, p. 77.

The Bank, as the largest creditor [to the state banks], had two alternatives: it could write off its debts which of course would wipe out the stockholders' equity and result in bankruptcy, or it could force the state banks to meet their obligations which would mean wholesale bankruptcy among state banks. There was no doubt about the choice.... The pressure placed upon state banks deflated the economy drastically, and as the money supply wilted, the country sank into severe depression.[1]

As historian William Gouge observed: "The Bank was saved, and the people were ruined."[2]

Competition between the national Bank and the state banks during this period had been moved from the open field of the free market to the closed arena of politics. Free-market competition had been replaced by government favoritism in the form of charters which granted the right of monopoly. A federal charter was clearly better than one issued by a state, but the states fought back fiercely with what weapons they possessed, and one of those was the power to tax. Several states began to levy a tax on the paper notes issued by any bank doing business within their borders which was not also locally chartered. The intent, although pretended to be the raising of state revenue, was really to put the federal Bank out of business.

THE SUPREME COURT UPHOLDS THE BANK

When the Bank refused to pay such a tax to the state of Maryland, the issue was taken to the Supreme Court in 1819 as the celebrated case of *McCulloch v. Maryland*. The Chief Justice at that time was John Marshall, a leading Federalist and advocate of a strong, centralized federal government. As was expected, the Marshall Court carefully tailored its decision to support the federal government's central bank.

The narrow issue upon which the constitutionality of the Bank was decided was *not* whether Congress had the power to directly or indirectly emit bills of credit or otherwise convert debt into money. If that *had* been the issue, the Court would have been hard pressed to uphold the Bank, for that not only is expressly prohibited by the Constitution, it is precisely what the Bank had been

---

1. Krooss, Vol. I, pp. 190–91.
2. William M. Gouge, *A Short History of Paper Money and Banking in the United States* (New York: Augustus M. Kelly, 1968), p. 110.

doing all along, and everyone knew it. Instead, the Court focused upon the narrow question of whether or not the Bank was a "necessary and proper" means for Congress to execute any *other* constitutional powers it might have. From *that* perspective, it was unanimously held that the Bank was, indeed, constitutional.

Were the Bank's paper notes the same as Bills of Credit? No, because they were backed by the credit of the Bank, not the federal government. True, the Bank created money, and most of it was used by the government. Never mind all that. The Treasury did not print it, therefore, it was not *government* money.

Was not the Bank the same as an agency of government? No, because merely granting it a national monopoly and enforcing that monopoly with the power of the state does not *necessarily* make it "state action."

Furthermore, the states cannot tax the federal government or any of its instruments, including the Bank of the United States, because, as Marshall stated: "The power to tax is the power to destroy."

Here was another end run around the Constitution, executed this time by the very men who were assumed to be its most loyal defenders.

The Supreme Court had spoken, but the Court of Public Opinion had not yet disposed of the case. During the 1820s, popular sentiment shifted back to the laissez-faire and sound-money principles espoused by the Jeffersonian Republicans. But since the Republican Party had by then abandoned those principles, a new coalition was formed, headed by Martin Van Buren and Andrew Jackson, to resurrect them. It was called the Democratic Party, and one of its agenda items was to abolish the Bank of the United States. After Jackson was elected to the Presidency in 1828, he wasted no time in attempting to build Congressional support for that goal.

NICHOLAS BIDDLE

By this time, the Bank had come under the direction of Nicholas Biddle who was a formidable adversary to Jackson, not only because of the power of his position, but because of his strong will and sense of personal destiny. He was the archetype of the new Eastern Establishment: wealthy, arrogant, ruthless, and brilliant. He had graduated from the University of Pennsylvania at the age of only thirteen, and, as a young man entering business, had fully mastered the secret science of money.

With the ability to control the flow of the nation's credit, Biddle soon became one of the most powerful men in America. This was brought out dramatically when he was asked by a Senate Committee if his bank ever took advantage of its superior position over the state banks. He replied: "Never. There are very few banks which might not have been destroyed by an exertion of the powers of the Bank. None has ever been injured."[1] As Jackson publicly noted a few months later, this was an admission that most of the state banks existed only at the pleasure of the Bank of the United States, and that, of course, meant at the pleasure of Mr. Biddle.

The year was 1832. The Bank's charter was good for another four years. But Biddle decided not to wait that long for Jackson to build his forces. He knew that the President was up for reelection, and he reasoned that, as a candidate, he would hesitate to be too controversial. To criticize the Bank is one thing, but to come down squarely for its elimination altogether would surely cost him many votes. So, Biddle requested Congress to grant an *early* renewal of the charter as a means of softening Jackson's campaign against it. The bill was backed by the Republicans led by Senator Henry Clay and was passed into law on July 3, just before the election campaigns began in earnest.

JACKSON OVERRIDES CONGRESS

It was brilliant strategy on Biddle's part but it didn't work. Jackson decided to place his entire political career on the line for this one issue and, with perhaps the most passionate message ever delivered to Congress by any President, before or since, he vetoed the measure. The President's biographer, Robert Remini, says: "The veto message hit the nation like a tornado. For it not only cited constitutional arguments against recharter—supposedly the *only* reason for resorting to a veto—but political, social, economic, and nationalistic reasons as well."[2]

Jackson devoted most of his veto message to three general topics: (1) the injustice that is inherent in granting a government-

---

1. J.D. Richardson, *A Compilation of the Messages and Papers of the Presidents, 1789–1908* (Washington: Bureau of National Literature and Art, 1908), Vol. II, p. 581.
2. Robert V. Remini, *The Life of Andrew Jackson* (New York: Harper & Row, 1988), pp. 227–28.

sponsored monopoly to the Bank; (2) the unconstitutionality of the Bank even if it were not unjust; and (3) the danger to the country in having the Bank heavily dominated by foreign investors.

Regarding the injustice of a government-sponsored monopoly, he pointed out that the stock of the Bank was owned only by the richest citizens of the country and that, since the sale of stock was limited to a chosen few with political influence, the common man, not only is unfairly excluded from an opportunity to participate, but he is forced to pay for his banking services far more than they are worth. Unearned profits are bad enough when they are taken from one class of citizens and given to another, but it is even worse when the people receiving those benefits are not even citizens at all but are, in fact *foreigners*. Jackson said:

> It is not our own citizens only who are to receive the bounty of our Government. More than eight millions of the stock of this bank are held by foreigners. By this act the American Republic proposes virtually to make them a present of some millions of dollars.... It appears that more than a fourth part of the stock is held by foreigners and the residue is held by a few hundred of our own citizens, chiefly of the richest class. For their benefit does this act exclude the whole American people from competition in the purchase of this monopoly and dispose of it for many millions less than it is worth.[1]

Regarding the issue of constitutionality, he said that he was not bound by the previous decision of the Supreme Court, because the President and Congress had just as much right to decide *for themselves* whether or not a particular law is constitutional. This view, incidentally, was not novel at that time. It is only in relatively recent decades that people have begun to think of the Supreme Court as being *specifically* authorized to pass on this question. In fact, as Jackson correctly pointed out in his veto message, the founding fathers created a government with power divided between the executive, legislative, and judicial branches, and that the purpose of this division was, not merely to divvy up the chores, but to *balance* one branch against the other. The goal was not to make government efficient but to deliberately make it *inefficient*. Each President and each legislator is morally bound, even by oath, to uphold the Constitution. If each of them does not have the power to

---

1. Krooss, pp. 22–23.

decide in conscience what *is* constitutional, then taking an oath to uphold it has little meaning.

THE BANK CONTROLLED BY FOREIGN INVESTORS

Regarding the danger to our national security, Jackson returned to the fact that a major portion of the Bank's stockholders were foreigners. Even though foreign investors technically were not allowed to vote their shares, their financial power was so great that the American investors were clearly beholden to them and would likely follow their instructions. Jackson concluded:

> Is there no danger to our liberty and independence in a bank that in its nature has so little to bind it to our country?... [Is there not] cause to tremble for the purity of our elections in peace and for the independence of our country in war?... Of the course which would be pursued by a bank almost wholly owned by the subjects of a foreign power, and managed by those whose interests, if not affections, would run in the same direction there can be no doubt.... Controlling our currency, receiving our public monies, and holding thousands of our citizens in dependence, it would be more formidable and dangerous than a naval and military power of the enemy.[1]

Jackson saved the greatest passion of his argument for the end. Speaking now, not to Congress, but to the voters at large, he said:

> It is to be regretted that the rich and powerful too often bend the acts of government to their selfish purposes. Distinctions in society will always exist under every just government. Equality of talents, of education, or of wealth cannot be produced by human institutions. In the full enjoyment of the gifts of Heaven and the fruits of superior industry, economy, and virtue, every man is equally entitled to protection by law; but when the laws undertake to add to these natural and just advantages artificial distinctions, to grant titles, gratuities, and exclusive privileges, to make the rich richer and the potent more powerful, the humble members of society—the farmers, mechanics, and laborers—who have neither the time nor the means of securing like favors to themselves, have a right to complain of the injustice of their Government. There are no necessary evils in government. Its evils exist only in its abuses. If it would confine itself to equal protection, and, as Heaven does its rains, shower its favor alike on the high and the low, the rich and the poor, it would be an unqualified blessing. In the act before me there seems to be a wide and unnecessary departure from these just principles.[2]

---

1. Krooss, pp. 26–27.
2. *Ibid.*, pp. 36–37.

The veto did not defeat the Bank. It was merely a declaration of war. The major battles were yet to come.

BIDDLE'S CONTROL OVER CONGRESS

As Commanding General of the pro-bank forces, Biddle had one powerful advantage over his adversary. For all practical purposes, Congress was in his pocket. Or, more accurately, the product of his generosity was in the pockets of *Congressmen*. Following the Rothschild Formula, Biddle had been careful to reward compliant politicians with success in the business world. Few of them were willing to bite the hand that fed them. Even the great Senator, Daniel Webster, found himself kneeling at Biddle's throne. Galbraith says:

> Biddle was not without resources. In keeping with his belief that banking was the ultimate source of power, he had regularly advanced funds to members of Congress when delay on appropriations bills had held up their pay. Daniel Webster was, at various times, a director of the Bank and on retainer as its counsel. "I believe my retainer has not been renewed or *refreshed* as usual. If it be wished that my relation to the Bank should be continued, it may be well to send me the usual retainers." Numerous other men of distinction had been accommodated, including members of the press.[1]

Webster is a particularly interesting study in how even so-called "great" men can be compromised by an addiction to wealth. He had always been an advocate of sound money in Congress, yet, as a lawyer on Biddle's payroll, he represented the Bank's position before the Supreme Court in *McCulloch v. Maryland*. Much of the twisted logic that allowed the Court to end-run the Constitution and *destroy* sound money came from his pen.

After Jackson's veto of the Bank's charter, Biddle requested Webster to deliver speeches specifically for the purpose of having the Bank reprint them for mass distribution. In one of those speeches, Webster echoed the old refrain that the Bank served as a moderating influence on the nation's other banks and then piously proclaimed: "Congress can alone coin money;... no State (nor even Congress itself) can make anything a tender but gold and silver, in the payment of debts."[2] In an act of astounding hypocrisy, this speech was distributed widely by the very institution that was

---

1. Galbraith, p. 80.
2. Krooss, p. 2.

designed specifically for creating fractional fiat money, *without* gold or silver backing, to function as tender in the payment of debts. Then, as now, most people did not discern between words and actions and believed that this speech, delivered by such a "great" man, was evidence of the Bank's worthiness. Biddle even distributed 300,000 copies of Jackson's veto message, apparently in the belief that many would not read it. Obviously, if the Bank thought it was so bad as to distribute it, it *must be bad.*[1]

The power of the Bank's money was everywhere. It was as John Randolph, the fiery Old Republican from Virginia, had said: "Every man you meet in this House or out of it, with some rare exceptions, which only serve to prove the rule, is either a stockholder, president, cashier, clerk or doorkeeper, runner, engraver, papermaker, or mechanic in some other way to a bank."[2]

JACKSON APPEALS DIRECTLY TO THE VOTERS

Congress, the banks, speculators, industrialists, and segments of the press; these were the forces commanded by Biddle. But Jackson had a secret weapon which had never been used before in American politics. That weapon was a direct appeal to the electorate. He took his message on the campaign trail and delivered it in words well chosen to make a lasting impression on the voter. He spoke out against a moneyed aristocracy which had invaded the halls of Congress, impaired the morals of the people, threatened their liberty, and subverted the electoral process. The Bank, he said, was a hydra-headed monster eating the flesh of the common man. He swore to do battle with the monster and slay it or be slain by it. He bellowed his position to every crowd he could reach: *Bank and no Jackson, or no bank and Jackson!*[3]

On the subject of paper money, the President was equally emphatic. His biographer describes the campaign:

> On his homeward journey he reportedly paid all his expenses in gold. "No more paper money, you see, fellow citizens," he remarked with each gold payment, "if I can only put down this Nicholas Biddle and his monster bank." Gold, hardly the popular medium of exchange, was held up to the people as the safe and sound currency

---

1. Remini, *Life*, p. 234.
2. *Annals of Congress*, 14 Cong., 1st sess., pp. 1066, 1110 ff.
3. Robert Remini, *Andrew Jackson and the Course of American Freedom, 1822–1832* (New York: Harper & Row, 1981), p. 373.

which Jackson and his administration hoped to restore to regular use. Unlike paper money, gold represented real value and true worth. It was the coin of honest men. Rag money, on the other hand, was the instrument of banks and swindlers to corrupt and cheat an innocent and virtuous public.[1]

Jackson had awakened the indignation of the American people. When the November ballots were cast, he received a mammoth vote of confidence. He received fifty-five per cent of the popular vote (with thirty-seven per cent for Clay, eight per cent for Wirt) and eighty per cent of the vote in the electoral college. But the war *still* was not over. Jackson won the election, but the Bank had four more years to operate, and it intended to use those years to sway public sentiment back to its support. The biggest battles were yet to come.

JACKSON REMOVES FEDERAL DEPOSITS

Jackson did not wait to act. He knew that time would be used as a weapon against him. "The hydra of corruption is only *scotched, not dead*," he said.[2] Soon after the election, he ordered Secretary of the Treasury, William Duane, to place all new deposits of the federal government into various state banks around the country and to pay current expenses out of the funds still held by the Bank of the United States until that account was drained to zero. Without the use of federal money, surely the monster would perish. To Jackson's chagrin, however, Duane balked at the order out of a sincere conviction that, to do so, would be disruptive to the economy.

This was not the first time a Cabinet officer and a President had come to disagreement. In the past, however, the impasse had always been resolved by the resignation of the Secretary. This time was different. Duane refused to resign, and that raised an interesting constitutional question. A President could appoint a member of the executive branch only with the consent of the Senate. The Constitution was silent, however, on the matter of dismissal. Did that, too, require Senate approval? The implication was that it did, but the issue had never been tested.

Jackson had no patience for such theoretical questions. The letter arrived promptly on Duane's desk: "Your further services as

---

1. Remini, *Life*, pp. 234–35.
2. Remini, *Course*, p. 52.

Secretary of the Treasury are no longer required."[1] On October 1, 1833, federal deposits began to move out of the Bank.

Jackson felt that he finally had the monster firmly within his grasp. "I have it chained," he said.[2] With gleeful confidence, he added: "I am ready with the screws to draw every tooth and then the stumps." If I am not mistaken, he went on, we will have "Mr. Biddle and his Bank as quiet and harmless as a *lamb* in six weeks."[3]

BIDDLE DELIBERATELY CREATES MONETARY CHAOS

The President's view of the Bank's meek captivity was premature, to say the least. Biddle responded, not like a lamb, but more like a wounded lion. His plan was to rapidly contract the nation's money supply and create another panic-depression similar to the one the Bank had created thirteen years earlier. This then could be blamed on Jackson's withdrawal of federal deposits, and the resulting backlash surely would cause Congress to override the President's veto. Remini tells us:

> Biddle counterattacked. He initiated a general curtailment of loans throughout the entire banking system.... It marked the beginning of a bone-crushing struggle between a powerful financier and a determined and equally powerful politician. Biddle understood what he was about. He knew that if he brought enough pressure and agony to the money market, only then could he force the President to restore the deposits. He almost gloated. "This worthy President thinks that because he has scalped Indians and imprisoned Judges, he is to have his way with the Bank. He is mistaken."[4]...
>
> "The ties of party allegiance can only be broken," he declared, "by the actual conviction of existing distress in the community." And such distress, of course, would eventually put everything to rights. "Nothing but widespread suffering will produce any effect on Congress.... Our only safety is in pursuing a steady course of firm restriction—and I have no doubt that such a course will ultimately lead to restoration of the currency and the recharter of the Bank.[5]... My

---

1. William J. Duane, *Narrative and Correspondence Concerning the Removal of the Deposits and Occurrences Connected Therewith* (Philadelphia: n.p., 1838), pp. 101–03. Quoted by Remini, *Life*, p. 264.
2. Quoted by Herman J. Viola, *Andrew Jackson* (New York: Chelsea House, 1986), p. 88.
3. A letter from Jackson to Van Buren, November 19, 1833, *Van Buren Papers*, Library of Congress. Quoted by Remini, *Life*, p. 264.
4. Remini, *Life*, p. 265.
5. Remini, *Democracy*, p. 111.

own course is decided. All other banks and all the merchants may break, but the Bank of the United States shall not break."[1]

Biddle, therefore, decided to use the American people as sacrificial pawns in the giant chess match for the Bank's survival. The resulting economic chaos is not difficult to imagine. Biddle's contraction of the money supply was executed at a particularly vulnerable moment. Business had been expanding as a result of the Bank's prior easy credit and now was dependent on it. Also, the tariff came due at precisely this time, placing still more demand for cash and credit. Losses were sustained everywhere, wages and prices sagged, men were put out of work, companies went bankrupt. By the time Congress reconvened in December, in what was called the "Panic Session," the nation was in an uproar. Newspapers editorialized with alarm, and letters of angry protest flooded into Washington.

As the pressure continued to build in Congress, it began to look as though Biddle's plan would work. In the public eye, it was Jackson who was solely responsible for the nation's woes. It was *his* arrogant removal of Secretary Duane; it was *his* foolish insistence on removing the deposits; it was *his* obstinate opposition to Congress.

JACKSON IS CENSURED BY THE SENATE

For one-hundred days, a "phalanx of orators" daily excoriated the President for his arrogant and harmful conduct. At length, a resolution of censure was introduced into the Senate and, on March 28, 1834, it was passed by a vote of 26 to 20. This was the first time that a President had ever been censured by Congress, and it was a savage blow to Jackson's pride. Biddle, at last, had the upper hand.

The President rumbled around the White House in a fit of rage. "You are a den of vipers," he said to a delegation of the Bank's supporters. "I intend to rout you out and by the Eternal God I will rout you out."[2]

The censure was by no means indicative of popular sentiment. Even in the Senate, which was a hotbed of pro-Bank support, a swing of only three votes would have defeated the measure.

---

1. Biddle to William Appleton, January 27, 1834, and to J.G. Watmough, February 8, 1834. Nicholas Biddle, *Correspondence, 1807–1844*, Reginald C. McGrane, ed. (New York: Houghton Mifflin, 1919), pp. 219, 221.
2. Quoted by Viola, p. 86.

During all this time, imperceptibly at first, but quickly growing, the public had been learning the truth. Jackson, of course, was doing everything within his power to hasten the process, but other factors also were at work, not the least of which was Biddle himself. So large was his ego that he could not keep from boasting in public about his plan to deliberately disrupt the economy. People heard these boasts and they *believed* him. The turning point came when Governor George Wolf of Pennsylvania, the Bank's home state, came out publicly with a strong denunciation of both the Bank and Biddle. This was like the starting bell at a horse race. With the Bank's home state turned against it, there was no one left to defend it and, literally within days, the mood of the country and of Congress changed.

The Democrats wasted no time consolidating these unexpected gains. To test their strength on the issue, on April 4, 1834, they called for a vote in the House on a series of resolutions which were aimed at nullifying the censure in the Senate. In essence, the resolutions stated that the House totally approved the President's bank policy. The first resolution, passed by a vote of 134 to 82, declared that the Bank of the United States "ought not to be rechartered." The second, passed by a vote of 118 to 103, agreed that the deposits "ought not to be restored." And the third, passed by an overwhelming vote of 175 to 42, called for the establishment of a special committee of Congress to investigate whether the Bank had deliberately instigated the current economic crisis. It was an overwhelming victory for Jackson which would be culminated a few years later with the passage of a resolution in the Senate which formally rescinded the previous vote of censure.

BIDDLE DEFIES CONGRESS

When the investigating committee arrived at the Bank's doors in Philadelphia armed with a subpoena to examine the books, Biddle flatly refused. Nor would he allow inspection of correspondence with Congressmen relating to their personal loans and advances. And he steadfastly refused to testify before the committee back in Washington. For lesser mortals, such action would have resulted in citations of contempt of Congress and would have carried stiff fines or imprisonment. But not for Nicholas Biddle. Remini explains:

The committeemen demanded a citation for contempt, but many southern Democrats opposed this extreme action, and refused to cooperate. As Biddle bemusedly observed, it would be ironic if he went to prison "by the votes of members of Congress because I would not give up to their enemies their confidential letters." Although Biddle escaped a contempt citation, his outrageous defiance of the House only condemned him still further in the eyes of the American public.[1]

The Bank was still alive but had been mortally wounded. By this time, Jackson had completely paid off the national debt incurred by the War of 1812 and had even run up a surplus. In fact, he ordered the Treasury to *give back to the states* more than $35 million, which was used for the construction of a wide variety of public works.

With these accomplishments close on the heels of his victory over the Bank, the President had earned the undying hatred of monetary scientists, both in America and abroad. It is not surprising, therefore, that on January 30, 1835, an assassination attempt was made against him. Miraculously, both pistols of the assailant misfired, and Jackson was spared by a quirk of fate. It was the first such attempt to be made against the life of a President of the United States. The would-be assassin was Richard Lawrence who either was truly insane or who *pretended* to be insane to escape harsh punishment. At any rate, Lawrence was found not guilty due to insanity.[2] Later, he boasted to friends that he had been in touch with powerful people in Europe who had promised to protect him from punishment should he be caught.[3]

The ending to this saga holds no surprises. The Bank's charter expired in 1836 and it was restructured as a state bank by the Commonwealth of Pennsylvania. After a spree of speculation in cotton, lavish advances to the Bank's officers, and the suspension of payment in specie, Biddle was arrested and charged with fraud. Although not convicted, he was still undergoing civil litigation when he died. Within five years, the establishment was forced to close its doors forever, and America's third experience with central banking came to a close.

---

1. Remini, *Life*, p. 274.
2. Remini, *Democracy*, p. 228–29.
3. Robert J. Donovan, *The Assassins* (New York: Harper & Brothers, 1952), p. 83.

SOME BAD MIXED IN WITH THE GOOD

It is tempting to let the story stop right there and allow Jackson to forever wear the crown of hero and dragon slayer. But a more balanced view of these events leads to the conclusion that the forces of virtue were not without contamination. Jackson represented the position of those who wanted only gold and silver for the nation's money. But this group was not large enough to match the power of the Bank. He was joined in that battle by many groups which hated the Bank for *other*, less admirable reasons. State banks and business interests along the expanding frontier, for example, were not the least interested in Constitutional money. They wanted just the *opposite*. They viewed the modest restraints of the federal Bank as *excessive*. With the federal Bank out of the way, they anticipated no restraints at all. As we shall see in the following section, it is ironic that this is the group that got what it wanted, not the hard-money Jacksonians.

One cannot blame Jackson for accepting the support of these groups in his effort to slay the dragon. In politics, it often is necessary to make temporary alliances with one's opponents to achieve occasional common objectives. But Jackson went further than that. More than any other President before him, and rivalled by only a few since, he changed the character of American politics. He led the nation away from the new concept of diffused powers, carefully worked out by the founding fathers, back toward the Old-World tradition of concentration and monarchy. By strongly challenging the right of the States to secede from the Union, he set into motion a concept that, not only would lead to civil war, but which would put an end forever to the ability of the states to check the expanding power of the federal government. No longer was the Union to be based on the principle of consent of the governed. It was now to be based on force of arms. And through the manipulation of voter passion on the Bank issue, he changed the perception of the role of President from *public servant* to *national leader*.

At the height of the battle against the Bank, when Jackson was making a direct appeal to the voters for support, he declared: "The President is the direct representative of the people." To fully comprehend the significance of that statement, it must be remembered that the plan of the Constitution was for the President to be elected indirectly by the state legislatures, not by the voters at large.

After fighting a war to throw off the rule of King George, III, the founding fathers wanted nothing more to do with kings of any kind, and they went out of their way to make sure that the President of the United States would never be looked upon as such. They realized that an elected ruler, unless his power is carefully limited and diffused, can become just as despotic as an unelected one. Article 2, Section 1, of the Constitution, therefore, established an electoral college to select the President.

Members of the college are to be appointed by the states. Congressmen, Senators, or other officers of the federal government are specifically and wisely excluded. The college is supposed to select a President strictly on the basis of his integrity and executive ability, not his party label, political connections, good looks, charisma, or stirring orations. The people may elect their Congressmen, but the electoral college chooses the President. Thus, it was intended that the President would have a different constituency from Congress, and this difference was important to insure the balance of power that the framers of the Constitution worked so hard to create. As a means of keeping government under control, it was a truly brilliant piece of political engineering.

All of that was changed in the election of 1832. One of the sad facts of history is that good causes often are the occasion for establishing bad precedents. Jackson's fight against the Bank of the United States was one of those events.

SUMMARY

The government had encouraged widespread banking fraud during the War of 1812 as an expedient for paying its bills, and this had left the nation in monetary chaos. At the end of the war, instead of allowing the fraudulent banks to fall and letting the free market heal the damage, Congress decided to protect the banks, to organize the fraud, and to perpetuate the losses. It did this by creating the nation's third central bank called the Second Bank of the United States.

The new bank was almost an exact carbon copy of the previous one. It was authorized to create money for the federal government and to regulate state banks. It influenced larger amounts of capital and was better organized across state lines than the old bank. Consequently its policies had a greater impact on the creation and extinguishing of the nation's money supply. For the first time in our history, the effects began to ricochet across the entire country at once instead of being confined to geographical regions. The age of the boom-bust cycle had at last arrived in America.

In 1820, public opinion began to swing back in favor of the sound-money principles espoused by the Jeffersonian Republicans. But since the Republican Party had by then abandoned those principles, a new coalition was formed, headed by Martin Van Buren and Andrew Jackson, called the Democrat Party. One of its primary platforms was the abolishment of the Bank. After Jackson was elected in 1828, he began in full earnest to bring that about.

The head of the Bank was a formidable adversary by the name of Nicholas Biddle. Biddle, not only possessed great personal abilities, but many members of Congress were indebted to him for business favors. Consequently, the Bank had many political friends.

As Jackson's first term of office neared its end, Biddle asked Congress for an early renewal of the Bank's charter, hoping that Jackson would not risk controversy in a reelection year. The bill was easily passed, but Jackson accepted the challenge and vetoed the measure. Thus, a battle over the Bank's future became the primary presidential campaign issue.

Jackson was reelected by a large margin, and one of his first acts was to remove federal deposits from the Bank and place them into private, regional banks. Biddle counterattacked by contracting credit and calling in loans. This was calculated to shrink the money supply and trigger a national panic-depression, which it did. He publicly blamed the downturn on Jackson's removal of deposits.

The plan almost worked. Biddle's political allies succeeded in having Jackson officially censured in the Senate. However, when the truth about Biddle's strategy finally leaked out, it backfired against him. He was called before a special Congressional investigative committee to explain his actions, the censure against Jackson was rescinded, and the nation's third central bank passed into oblivion.

Chapter Eighteen

LOAVES AND FISHES
AND CIVIL WAR

Attempts to stabilize the banking system by political measures, including regulation of frac-tional-reserve ratios and establishing bank-failure insurance funds; the failure of all such schemes; the resulting economic conditions that led up to the Civil War.

As detailed in the previous chapter, by 1836 the hydra-headed monster had been slain and, true to the President's campaign promise, the nation had *Jackson and no Bank.*

In April of that year, the Administration moved to consolidate its victory and pushed a series of monetary reforms through Congress. One of these required all banks to cease issuing paper notes under five dollars. The figure later was increased to twenty dollars, and its purpose was to compel the nation to return to the use of gold and silver coin for everyday use, leaving bank notes primarily for large commercial transactions. The White House also announced that, in the future, all federal land sales would require full payment in "lawful money," which, of course, meant precious-metal coins.[1]

It must be remembered, however, that even though the Bank of the United States was dead, *banking* was very much alive, and so were Jackson's enemies. Much to the disappointment of the hard-money advocates, these measures were not sufficient to usher in the millennium. Not only were they inadequate by themselves, they were soon circumvented by the development of new banking techniques and eventually were dismantled completely by a fickle Congress.

---

1. Otto Scott, *The Secret Six: The Fool as Martyr,* Vol. III of *The Sacred Fool Quartet* (Columbia, South Carolina: Foundation for American Education, 1979), p. 115.

The prohibition against bank notes of small denomination deserves special notice. It was an excellent concept, but what the legislators failed to understand, or at least *pretended* not to understand, was that banks at this time were increasingly dealing with *checkbook* money, technically called demand deposits. As people gradually became accustomed to this new method of transferring funds, the importance of bank notes declined. Placing a limit on the issuance of bank notes without any restriction on the creation of demand deposits was an exercise in futility.

In 1837, as the Bank of the United States slipped into history, the nation was at the tail end of an economic boom. Professor Rothbard tells us that this expansion and the accompanying inflation had been "fueled by the central bank."[1] Total money in circulation had risen by eighty-four per cent in just four years. Then, as inevitable as the setting sun, that portion of the money supply which had been created by fractional-reserve banking—in other words, the part which was backed by *nothing*—began to contract. Sixteen per cent of all the nation's money totally disappeared in just that first year. Again, men were put out of work, businesses went into bankruptcy, homes and savings were lost. Many banks folded also, but their operators walked away with the spoils. Only the depositors were left holding the empty bag.

There were numerous proposals advanced regarding how to infuse stability into the banking system. But, then as now, none of them dealt with the real problem, which was fractional-reserve banking itself. As Groseclose observed, these proposals were "each according to a particular theory of how to multiply loaves and fishes, or how to make candy wool."[2] Since the proposals presented then are identical to the ones being offered today, and since each of them was actually tried, it would seem appropriate to inquire into the actual results of these experiments.

PROPOSAL TO BASE MONEY ON BANK ASSETS

There were four schools of thought regarding the multiplication of loaves and fishes. The first of these was that the creation of money should be limited to a ratio of the bank's assets. This was the formula that was tried in the New England states. In Massachusetts, for example, the issuance of bank notes was limited to two

---

1. Rothbard, *Mystery*, p. 211.
2. Groseclose, *Money and Man*, p. 184.

times the amount of the bank's capital actually held in the vault. Furthermore, this could not be in the form of paper money, bonds, securities, or other debt instruments; it had to be strictly gold or silver coin. Also, the banks were limited in the number of small-denomination bank notes they could issue and, in this, Massachusetts served as the model for Jackson's attempted reform at the federal level. By previous standards, and certainly by the standards that prevail today, this was an exceptionally conservative policy. In fact, even during the previous stress of the War of 1812, when banks were failing by the hundreds across the country, the Massachusetts banks, and most of the other New England banks as well, were able to maintain full payment in specie.

With the passage of time, however, the limit on bank notes became less important, because the banks now were using *checkbook* money instead. Their paper notes may have been limited to two-hundred per cent of their capital, but there was no effective limit to the numbers they could ink into people's deposit books. So the "fraction" in fractional-reserve banking began to shrink again. Consequently, the monetary contraction of 1837 "was like a scythe over the crop," says Groseclose, and thirty-two Massachusetts banks collapsed between that year and 1844.[1]

The state attempted to patch the system by instituting a network of bank examiners and by increasing the liability of bank stockholders for the lost funds of their depositors, but the underlying problem was *still* ignored. A new crop of banks then sprang into existence and a new wave of speculative mania swept through the economy. By 1862, even though the law still limited bank notes to two times capital, the banks had created $73,685,000 in total money, including checkbook money. This was supported by a base of only $9,595,000 of specie, a reserve of only thirteen per cent. Massachusetts had not solved the problem.

PROPOSAL TO PROTECT DEPOSITS WITH A SAFETY FUND

The second theory about how to have stable banking *and* allow the banks to create money out of nothing was to create a "safety fund." This fund, supported by all the banks, would come to the aid of any member which needed an emergency loan to cover a

---

1. Groseclose, *Money and Man*, p. 185.

sudden drain of its reserves. It was the forerunner of today's Federal Deposit Insurance Corporation and related agencies.

The first safety fund was established in New York in 1829. The law required each bank to contribute annually one-half of one per cent of its capital stock until the total reached three per cent. The fund was first put to the test during the crisis of 1837, and was almost swamped. The only thing that saved it was that the state agreed to accept the worthless notes of all the defunct banks as payment for canal tolls. In other words, the taxpayers were compelled to make up the difference. When the fund was exhausted, the solvent banks were punished by being forced to pay for the deficits of the insolvent ones. Naturally, this impelled *all* banks to act more recklessly. Why not? The up side was that profits would be higher—for a time, at least—and the down side was that, if recklessness got them into trouble, the safety fund would bail them out. The result was that the system provided a penalty for prudence and an incentive for recklessness; a situation with perfect parallel to that which exists in the banking system today. Groseclose says:

> The conservatively managed institutions, lending upon the safer risks, upon which naturally the margins of profit were smaller, found the assessments burdensome, and were compelled to embark upon the more speculative business in order to carry the charges.[1]

Gradually, all banks sank into the quagmire and, in 1857, the Massachusetts safety-fund was abandoned.

Michigan's experience with a safety fund was perhaps more typical of the period. It was established in 1836 and was completely blown away the next year, during the panic of 1837.

PROPOSAL TO BASE MONEY ON SECURITIES

The third proposal for maintaining a stable monetary system while, at the same time, allowing the banks to operate fraudulently was to base the money supply on government securities; in other words, upon paper certificates of government debt. This was the scheme adopted in the 1850s by Illinois, Indiana, Wisconsin and other Midwestern states. It also set the precedent for the Federal Reserve System sixty years later. Groseclose continues:

---

1. Groseclose, *Money and Man*, p. 186.

So rampant was the note-issue mania that the notes came to be called by the appropriate name of "red dog" and "wild cat" currency.... The rising crop of banks created a fictitious demand and a rising market for securities (to be used as capital stock) and a consequent stimulus to the creation of public debt by the issue of securities. This was followed by more bank notes being issued against the securities, demand increasing and the market rising, more securities issues, more bank notes, and so on in an endless chain of debt creation and the inflation of paper wealth. The process was finally brought to a stop by the panic of 1857.[1]

PROPOSAL TO BACK MONEY WITH STATE CREDIT

The fourth proposal for producing something out of nothing was to back the issuance of money by the full faith and credit of the state. This was the method tried by many of the Southern states and it, too, has survived to become one of the cornerstones of our modern-day banking system.

Alabama, for example, in 1835 created a state bank funded by a public bond issue of $13,800,000. Instant money flooded through the economy and people were joyous over the miracle prosperity. The legislators were so intoxicated with the scheme that they completely abolished direct taxation and decided to run the government on bank money instead. In other words, instead of raising state revenue through taxes, they found it easier to raise it through inflation.

Like all the others, this bubble also burst in the panic of 1837. A postmortem examination of the Bank showed that $6,000,000 of its assets were completely worthless. The people who had lent their real money to the venture, backed by the full faith and credit of the state, lost almost all of their investment—in *addition* to what they had paid through inflation.

Mississippi put its full faith and credit behind a state bank in 1838 and issued $15,000,000 in bonds as backing for its bank notes. The bank was belly-up within four years, and the state completely repudiated its obligations on the bonds. This infuriated the bond holders, particularly the *British* financiers who had purchased a large portion of the issue. The devastating effect upon the state and its people is described by Henry Poor:

---

1. Groseclose, *Money and Man*, pp. 188–89.

The $48,000,000 of the bank's loans were never paid; the $23,000,000 of notes and deposits were never redeemed. The whole system fell, a huge and shapeless wreck, leaving the people of the State very much as they came into the world.... Everybody was in debt, without any possible means of payment. Lands became worthless, for the reason that no one had any money to pay for them.... Such numbers of people fled ... from the State that the common return upon legal processes against debtors was in the very abbreviated form "G.T.T."—gone to Texas.[1]

Money, based on the full faith and credit of the state, met similar fates in Illinois, Kentucky, Florida, Tennessee, and Louisiana. When the state bank collapsed in Illinois in 1825, all of the "full-faith" bank notes left in its possession were ceremoniously burned at the public square. Another bank was formed in 1835 and collapsed in 1842. So devastating were these experiences that the Illinois Constitution of 1848 stipulated that, henceforth, the state should never again create a bank or own banking stock.

In Arkansas, even real estate was tried as a magic wand. Subscribers to the state bank, instead of putting up cash, were allowed merely to pledge their real estate holdings as collateral. The bank notes rapidly plummeted in value to only twenty-five per cent of their face amount, and within four years, the bank was gone.

THE MIRAGE OF FREE BANKING

There was a parallel development at this time called "free banking." The name is an insult to truth. What was called free banking was merely the conversion of banks from corporations to private associations. Aside from no longer receiving a charter from the state, practically every other aspect of the system remained the same, including a multitude of government controls, regulations, supports, and other blocks against the free market. George Selgin reminds us that "permission to set up a bank was usually accompanied by numerous restrictions, including especially required loans to the state."[2]

---

1. Henry V. Poor, *Money and Its Laws* (London: Henry S. King and Co., 1877), p. 540.
2. George A. Selgin, *The Theory of Free Banking: Money Supply under Competitive Note Issue* (Totowa, New Jersey: Rowman & Littlefield, 1988), p. 13.

The free banks were no less fraudulent than the chartered banks. The old custom was revived of rushing gold coins from one bank to another just ahead of the bank examiners, and of "putting a ballast of lead, broken glass and (appropriately) ten-penny nails in the box under a thinner covering of gold coins."[1] When one such free bank collapsed in Massachusetts, it was discovered that its bank note circulation of $500,000 was backed by exactly $86.48.[2]

Professor Hans Sennholz writes:

> Although economists disagree on many things, most see eye to eye on their acceptance of political control.... These economists invariably point at American money and banking before the Civil War which, in their judgment, confirms their belief. In particular, they cite the "Free Banking Era" of 1838–1860 as a frightening example of turbulent banking and, therefore, applaud the legislation that strengthened the role of government.
>
> In reality, the instability experienced during the Free Banking Era was not caused by anything inherent in banking, but resulted from extensive political intervention.... "Free banking" acts ... did not repeal burdensome statutory provisions and regulatory directives. In fact they added a few.[3]

For banking to have been truly free, the states would have had to do only two things: (1) enforce banking contracts the same as any other contract, and then (2) step out of the picture. By enforcing banking contracts, the executives of any bank which failed to redeem its currency in specie would have been sent to prison, an eventuality which soon would have put a halt to currency overissue. By stepping out of the picture and dropping the pretense of protecting the public with a barrage of rules, regulations, safety funds, and guarantees, people would have realized that it was *their* responsibility to be cautious and informed. But, instead, the banks continued to enjoy the special privilege of suspending payment without punishment, and the politicians clamored to convince the voters that they were taking care of everything.

In short, throughout this entire period of bank failures, economic chaos, and fleecing of both investors and taxpayers, America

---

1. Galbraith, p. 87.
2. Charles Beard, *The Rise of American Civilization* (New York: Macmillan, 1930), Vol. I, pp. 429–30.
3. "Old Banking Myths," by Hans F. Sennholz, *The Freeman* (Irvington-on-Hudson, New York), May, 1989, pp. 175–76.

tried everything *except* full redemption by gold and silver. As the name of Andrew Jackson faded into history, so did the dream of honest banking.

Not all banks were corrupt, and certainly not all bankers were conspirators against the public. There were many examples of honest men striving to act in an ethical manner in the discharge of their fiduciary responsibilities. But they were severely hampered by the system within which they labored, a system which, as previously illustrated, punished prudence and rewarded reckless-ness. In balance, the prudent banker was pushed aside by the mainstream and became but a footnote to the history of that period.

INDUSTRIAL EXPANSION IN SPITE OF DISHONEST BANKING

Another positive aspect to the picture is that it was during this same time that many business enterprises came into being and greatly prospered, albeit at the expense of those who had no desire to contribute. The great canals were dug, the railroads pushed back the frontier, boom towns sprang up along the way, prairies were turned into agricultural land, and new businesses followed in their wake. Much of this expansion was facilitated by a flood of fraudulent money created by the banks. Apologists for fractional-reserve banking have been prone to look at this development and conclude that, in net balance, it was a good thing. The fact that some people were cheated in order for others to prosper did not seem to be important. America just wouldn't have grown and prospered without funny money. Galbraith, for example, exudes:

> As civilization, or some approximation, came to an Indiana or Michigan crossroads in the 1830s or 1840s, so did a bank. Its notes, when used and loaned to a farmer to buy land, livestock, feed, seed, food or simple equipment, put him into business. If he and others prospered and paid off their loans, the bank survived. If he and others did not so prosper and pay, the bank failed, and someone—perhaps a local creditor, perhaps an eastern supplier—was left holding the worthless notes. But some borrowers from this bank were by now in business. Somewhere, someone holding the notes had made an involuntary contribution to the winning of the West.... The [banking] anarchy served the frontier far better than a more orderly system that kept a tight hand on credit could have done.[1]

---

1. Galbraith, p. 85.

William Greider continues this rationale:

"Reckless, booming anarchy," in short, produced fundamental progress. It was not a stable system, racked as it was with bank failures and collapsed business ventures, outrageous speculation and defaulted loans. Yet it was also energetic and inventive, creating permanent economic growth that endured after the froth had blown away.[1]

This, of course, is a classic example of the failure of liberal economics. When evaluating a policy, it focuses only on *one* beneficial consequence for *one* group of people and ignores the *multitude* of harmful effects which befall *all other groups*. Yes, if we look only at the frontiersmen who acquired new ranches and established new business, the fractional-reserve system looks pretty good. But, if we add in to the equation all the financial losses to all of the people who were victimized by the system—what Galbraith calls "an involuntary contribution" and what Greider lightly dismisses as "froth"—then the product is zero at best and, in terms of morality, is deeply in the negative.

Galbraith, Greider, and other popular economists assume that the West could not possibly have been won with honest banking. Logic does not support such a conclusion. There is every reason to believe that the bank failures and the resulting business failures *on the frontier* all but canceled out the gains that were made by hard work and honest industry. Had these destructive convulsions been absent, as most of them would have been under a less chaotic system, there likely would have been fewer business starts, but a greater number would have *finished*, and it is entirely possible that the West would have been won even faster than it was.

It's too bad the theory has never been tried.

THE UNION IN JEOPARDY

As chronicled in a previous section, economic conflict has always played a major role in fomenting war. There is no time in American history in which there was more economic conflict between segments of the population than there was prior to the Civil War. It is not surprising, therefore, that this period led directly into the nation's bloodiest war, made all the more tragic because it pitted brother against brother.

---

1. Greider, p. 259.

There are many popular myths about the cause of the War Between the States. Just as the Bolshevik Revolution is commonly believed to have been a spontaneous mass uprising against a tyrannical aristocracy, so, too, it is generally accepted that the Civil War was fought over the issue of slavery. That, at best, is a half-truth. Slavery was *an* issue, but the primary force for war was a clash between the economic interests of the North and the South. Even the issue of slavery itself was based on economics. It may have been a moral issue in the North where prosperity was derived from the machines of heavy industry, but in the agrarian South, where fields had to be tended by vast work forces of human labor, the issue was primarily a matter of economics.

The relative unimportance of slavery as a cause for war was made clear by Lincoln himself during his campaign for the Presidency in 1860, and he repeated that message in his first inaugural address:

> Apprehension seems to exist among the people of the Southern States that by the accession of a Republican administration their property and their peace and personal security are to be endangered.... I have no purpose, directly or indirectly, to interfere with the institution of slavery in the states where it now exists. I believe I have no lawful right to do so, and I have no inclination to do so.[1]

Even after the outbreak of war in 1861, Lincoln confirmed his previous stand. He declared:

> My paramount object in this struggle is to save the Union, and it is *not* either to save or destroy slavery. If I could save the Union without freeing any slave, I would do it; and if I could save it by freeing *all* the slaves, I would do it; and if I could do it by freeing some and leaving others alone, I would also do that.[2]

It may come as a surprise to learn that, by strict definition, Abraham Lincoln was a white supremacist. In his fourth debate with Senator Stephen Douglas, he addressed the subject bluntly:

> I am not nor ever have been in favor of bringing about in any way the social and political equality of the white and black races—that I am

---

1. Don E. Fehrenbacher, ed., *Abraham Lincoln: Speeches and Writings, 1859–1865* (New York: Library of America, 1989), p. 215.
2. Quoted by Robert L. Polley, ed., *Lincoln: His Words and His World* (Waukesha, Wisconsin: Country Beautiful Foundation, 1965), p. 54.

not nor ever have been in favor of making voters or jurors of Negroes, nor of qualifying them to hold office, nor to intermarry with white people; and I will say in addition to this that there is a physical difference between the white and black races which I believe will forever forbid the two races living together on terms of social and political equality. And inasmuch as they cannot so live, while they do remain together there must be the position of superior and inferior, and I as much as any other man am in favor of having the superior position assigned to the white race.[1]

This is not to say that Lincoln was indifferent to the institution of slavery, for he felt strongly that it was a violation of personal and national morality, but he also knew that slavery was gradually being swept away all over the world—with the possible exception of Africa itself—and he believed that it would soon disappear in America simply by allowing the natural forces of enlightenment to work their way through the political system. He feared—and rightly so—that to demand immediate and total reform, not only would destroy the Union, it would lead to massive bloodshed and more human suffering than was endured even under slavery itself. He said:

> I have not allowed myself to forget that the abolition of the Slave trade by Great Britain was agitated a hundred years before it was a final success; that the measure had its open fire-eating opponents; its stealthy "don't-care" opponents; its dollar-and-cent opponents; its inferior-race opponents; its Negro-equality opponents; and its religion and good-order opponents; that all these opponents got offices, and their adversaries got none. But I have also remembered that though they blazed like tallow-candles for a century, at last they flickered in the socket, died out, stank in the dark for a brief season, and were remembered no more, even by the smell. School boys know that Wilbeforce and Granville Sharpe helped that cause forward; but who can now name a single man who labored to retard it? Remembering these things I cannot but regard it as possible that the higher object of this contest may not be completely attained within the term of my natural life.[2]

If Lincoln's primary goal in the War was not the abolition of slavery but simply to preserve the Union, the question arises: Why did the Union *need* preserving? Or, more pointedly, why did the Southern states want to secede?

---

1. Fehrenbacher, p. 636.
2. *Ibid.*, p. 438.

LEGAL PLUNDER, NOT SLAVERY, THE CAUSE OF WAR

The South, being predominantly an agricultural region, had to import practically all of its manufactured goods from the Northern states or from Europe, both of which reciprocated by providing a market for the South's cotton. However, many of the textiles and manufactured items were considerably cheaper from Europe, even after the cost of shipping had been added. The Southern states, therefore, often found it to their advantage to purchase these European goods rather than those made in the North. This put considerable competitive pressure on the American manufacturers to lower their prices and operate more efficiently.

The Republicans were not satisfied with that arrangement. They decided to use the power of the federal government to tip the scales of competition in their favor. Claiming that this was in the "national interest," they levied stiff import duties on almost every item coming from Europe that was also manufactured in the North. Not surprisingly, there was no duty applied to cotton which, presumedly, was not a commodity in the national interest. One result was that European countries countered by stopping the purchase of U.S. cotton, which badly hurt the Southern economy. The other result was that manufacturers in the North were able to charge higher prices without fear of competition, and the South was forced to pay more for practically all of its necessities. It was a classic case of legalized plunder in which the law was used to enrich one group of citizens at the expense of another.

Pressure from the North against slavery in the South made matters even more volatile. A fact often overlooked in this episode is that the *cost* of a slave was very high, around $1,500 each. A modest plantation with only forty or fifty slaves, therefore, had a large capital investment which, in terms of today's purchasing power, represented many millions of dollars. To the South, therefore, abolition meant, not only the loss of its ability to produce a cash crop, but the total destruction of an enormous capital base.

Many Southern plantation owners were working toward the day when they could convert their investment to more profitable industrial production as had been done in the North, and others felt that freemen who were paid wages would be more efficient than slaves who had no incentive to work. For the present, however, they were stuck with the system they inherited. They felt that a complete and sudden abolition of slavery with no transition period would destroy their economy and leave many of the former slaves to starve—all of which actually happened in due course.[1] That was the situation that existed at the time of Lincoln's campaign and why, in his speeches, he attempted to calm the fears of the South about his intentions. But his words were mostly political rhetoric. Lincoln *was* a Republican, and he was totally dependent on the Northern industrialists who controlled the Party. Even if he had wanted to—and there is no indication that he did—he could not have reversed the trend of economic favoritism and protectionism that swept him into office.

MEXICO AND THE MONROE DOCTRINE

In addition to the conflicting interests between North and South, there were other forces also working to split the nation in two. Those forces were rooted in Europe and centered around the desire of France, Spain, and England to control the markets of Latin America. Mexico was the prime target. This was the reason the Monroe Doctrine had been formulated thirty-eight years previously. President James Monroe had put the European nations on notice that the United States would not interfere in *their* affairs, and that any interference by them in *American* affairs would not be tolerated. In particular, the proclamation said that the American continents were no longer to be considered as available for colonization.

None of the European powers wanted to put this issue to the test, but they knew that if the United States were to become embroiled in a civil war, it could not also cross swords in Latin America. To encourage war between the states, therefore, was to pave the way for colonial expansion in Mexico. The Americas had become a giant chess board for the game of global politics.

In the *American Heritage Picture History of the Civil War*, we read:

> The war had not progressed very far before it was clear that the ruling classes in each of these two countries [England and France] sympathized strongly with the Confederacy—so strongly that with just a little prodding they might be moved to intervene and bring about Southern independence by force of arms.... Europe's aristocracies had never been happy about the prodigious success of

---

1. See "No Civil War at All; Part One," by William McIlhany, *Journal of Individualist Studies*, Winter, 1992, p. 41.

the Yankee democracy. If the nation now broke into halves, proving that democracy did not contain the stuff of survival, the rulers of Europe would be well pleased.[1]

The global chess match between Lincoln on the one side and England and France on the other was closely watched by the other leaders of Europe. One of the most candid observers at that time was the Chancellor of Germany, Otto von Bismarck. Since Bismarck was, himself, deeply obligated to the power of international finance, his observations are doubly revealing. He said:

> The division of the United States into federations of equal force was decided long before the Civil War by the high financial powers of Europe. These bankers were afraid that the United States, if they remained in one block and as one nation, would attain economic and financial independence, which would upset their financial domination over Europe and the world. Of course, in the "inner circle" of Finance, the voice of the Rothschilds prevailed. They saw an opportunity for prodigious booty if they could substitute two feeble democracies, burdened with debt to the financiers,... in place of a vigorous Republic sufficient unto herself. Therefore, they sent their emissaries into the field to exploit the question of slavery and to drive a wedge between the two parts of the Union.... The rupture between the North and the South became inevitable; the masters of European finance employed all their forces to bring it about and to turn it to their advantage.[2]

The strategy was simple but effective. Within months after the first clash of arms between North and South, France had landed troops in Mexico. By 1864, the Mexicans were subdued, and the French monarch installed Ferdinand Maximilian as the puppet emperor. The Confederacy found a natural ally in Maximilian, and it was anticipated by both groups that, after the successful execution of the War, they would combine into a new nation— dominated by the financial power of Rothschild, of course. At the same time, England moved eleven-thousand troops into Canada,

---

1. Bruce Catton, author; Richard M. Ketchum, ed., *The American Heritage Picture History of the Civil War* (New York: American Heritage Publishing Co., 1960), p. 249.
2. This statement was quoted by Conrad Siem, a German who became a U.S. citizen and who wrote about the life and views of Bismark. It was published in *La Vieille France*, No. 216, March 17–24, 1921, pp. 13–16. The reader should be cautioned that Bismarck was no paragon of virtue and, as the father of modern socialism, his political views should be taken with a healthy degree of caution. All that aside, there is little doubt that this quotation represents an accurate appraisal of the machinations of the European Cabal at that time.

positioned them menacingly along the Union's northern flank, and placed the British fleet onto war-time alert.[1]
The European powers were closing in for a checkmate.

SUMMARY

The Second Bank of the United States was dead, but *banking* was very much alive. Many of the old problems continued, and new ones arrived. The issuance of banknotes had been severely limited, but that was largely offset by the increasing use of checkbook money, which had no limits at all on its issue.

When The Second Bank of the U.S. slipped into history, the nation was nearing the end of the boom phase of a boom/bust cycle. When the inevitable contraction of the money supply came, politicians began to offer proposals on how to infuse stability into the banking system. None dealt with the real problem, which was fractional-reserve banking itself. They concentrated instead on proposals on how to make it work. All of these proposals were tried and they failed.

These years are sometimes described as a period of free banking, which is an insult to truth. All that happened was that banks were converted from corporations to private associations, a change in form, not substance. They continued to be burdened by government controls, regulations, supports, and other blocks against the free market.

The economic chaos and conflict of this period was a major cause of the Civil War. Lincoln made it clear during his public speeches that slavery was *not* the issue. The basic problem was that North and South were dependent on each other for trade. The industrialized North sold its products to the South which sold its cotton to the North. The South also had a similar trade with Europe, and that was an annoyance to the North. Europe was selling many products at lower prices, and the North was losing market share. Northern politicians passed protectionist legislation putting import duties on industrial products. This all but stopped the importation of European goods and forced the South to buy from the North at higher prices. Europe retaliated by curtailing the purchase of American cotton. That hurt the South even more. It was a classic case of legalized plunder, and the South wanted out.

---

1. Catton and Ketchum, p. 250. Also Otto Eisenschiml, *The Hidden Face of the Civil War* (New York: Bobbs-Merril, 1961), p. 25.

Meanwhile, there were powerful forces in Europe that wanted to see America embroiled in civil war. If she could be split into two hostile countries, there would be less obstacle to European expansion on the North American continent. France was eager to capture Mexico and graft it onto a new empire which would include many of the Southern states as well. England, on the other hand, had military forces poised along the Canadian border ready for action. Political agitators, funded and organized from Europe, were active on both sides of the Mason-Dixon line. The issue of slavery was but a ploy. America had become the target in a ruthless game of world economics and politics.

Chapter Nineteen

GREENBACKS AND OTHER CRIMES

The causes of the Civil War shown to be economic and political, not the issue of freedom vs. slavery; the manner in which both sides used fiat money to finance the war; the important role played by foreign powers.

In the previous chapter, we saw how the American continent had become a giant chess board in a game of global politics. The European powers had been anxious to see the United States become embroiled in a civil war and eventually break into two smaller and weaker nations. That would pave the way for their further colonization of Latin America without fear of the Americans being able to enforce the Monroe Doctrine. And so it was that, within a few months after the outbreak of war between North and South, France landed troops in Mexico and, by 1864, had installed Maximilian as her puppet monarch. Negotiations were begun immediately to bring Mexico into the war on the side of the Confederacy. England moved her troops to the Canadian border in a show of strength. America was facing what appeared to be a checkmate from the powers in Europe.

RUSSIA ALIGNS WITH THE NORTH

It was a masterful move that possibly could have won the game had not an unexpected event tipped the scale against it. Tsar Alexander II—who, incidentally, had never allowed a central bank to be established in Russia[1]—notified Lincoln that he stood ready to militarily align with the North. Although the Tsar had recently freed the serfs in his own country, his primary motivation for

---

1. His grandson, Tsar Nicholas, II, did accept loans from J.P. Morgan. In a classic application of the Rothschild Formula, Morgan also funded the Mensheviks and the Bolsheviks. The Mensheviks forced Nicholas to abdicate, and the Bolsheviks executed him. See Chernow, pp. 195, 211.

coming to the aid of the Union undoubtedly had little to do with emancipating the slaves in the South. England and France had been maneuvering to break up the Russian empire by splitting off Finland, Estonia, Latvia, Poland, Crimea, and Georgia. Napoleon III, of France, proposed to Great Britain and Austria that the three nations immediately declare war on Russia to hasten this dismemberment.

Knowing that war was being considered by his enemies, Tsar Alexander decided to play a chess game of his own. In September of 1863, he dispatched his Baltic fleet of war ships to Alexandria, Virginia, and his Asiatic fleet to San Francisco. The significance of this move was explained by Russian-born Carl Wrangell-Rokassowsky:

> No treaty was signed between Russia and the United States, but their mutual interest, and the threat of war to both, unified these two nations at this critical moment. By dispatching his Baltic Fleet to the North American harbors, the Tsar changed his position from a defensive to an offensive one. Paragraph 3 of the instructions given to Admiral Lessovsky by Admiral Krabbe, at that time Russian Secretary of the Navy, dated July 14th, 1863, ordered the Russian Fleet, in case of war, to attack the enemies' commercial shipping and their colonies so as to cause them the greatest possible damage. The same instructions were given to Admiral Popov, Commander of the Russian Asiatic Fleet.[1]

The presence of the Russian Navy helped the Union enforce a devastating naval blockade against the Southern states which denied them access to critical supplies from Europe. It was not that these ships single-handedly kept the French and English vessels at bay. Actually there is no record of them even firing upon each other, but that is the point. The fact that neither France nor England at that time wanted to risk becoming involved in an open war with the United States *and* Russia led them to be extremely cautious with overt military aid to the South. Throughout the entire conflict, they found it expedient to remain officially neutral. Without the inhibiting effect of the presence of the Russian fleet, the course of the war could have been significantly different.

---

1. Carl Wrangell-Rokassowsky, *Before the Storm* (Ventimiglia, Italy: Tipo-Litografia Ligure, 1972), p. 57.

The beginning of the war did not go well for the North, and in the early years, the outcome was far from certain. Not only did the Union army face repeated defeats on the battlefield, but enthusiasm from the people at home was badly sagging. As mentioned previously, at the outset this was not a popular war based on humanitarian principle; it was a war of business interests. That presented two serious problems for the North. The first was how to get people to fight, and the second was how to get them to pay. Both problems were solved by the simple expediency of violating the Constitution.

THE EMANCIPATION PROCLAMATION

To get people to fight, it was decided to convert the war into an anti-slavery crusade. The Emancipation Proclamation was primarily a move on the part of Lincoln to fan the dying embers of support for the "Rich-man's war and the poor-man's fight," as it was commonly called in the North. Furthermore, it was not an amendment to the Constitution nor even an act of Congress. It was issued, totally without constitutional authority, as the solitary order of Lincoln himself, *acting as Commander-in-Chief of the armed forces.*

Preservation of the Union was not enough to fire men's enthusiasm for war. Only the higher issue of freedom could do that. To make the cause of freedom synonymous with the cause of the North, there was no alternative but to officially declare against slavery. After having emphasized over and over again that slavery was not the reason for war, Lincoln later explained why he changed his course and issued the Proclamation:

> Things had gone from bad to worse until I felt we had reached the end of our rope on the plan we were pursuing; that we had about played our last card, and must change our tactics or lose the game. I now determined upon the adoption of the emancipation policy.[1]

The rhetoric of the Proclamation was superb, but the concept left a great deal to be desired. Bruce Catton, writing in the *American Heritage Pictorial History of the Civil War* explains:

> Technically, the proclamation was almost absurd. It proclaimed freedom for all slaves in precisely those areas where the United States could not make its authority effective, and allowed slavery to continue in slave states which remained under Federal control.... But in the end

---

1. Quoted by Charles Adams, *Fight, Flight, Fraud: The Story of Taxation* (Curacao, The Netherlands: Euro-Dutch Publishers, 1982), p. 229.

it changed the whole character of the war and, more than any other single thing, doomed the Confederacy to defeat.[1]

The Proclamation had a profound impact on the European powers as well. As long as the war had been viewed as an attempt on the part of a government to put down rebellion, there was nothing sacred about it, and there was no stigma attached to helping either side. But now that *freedom* was the apparent issue, no government in Europe—least of all England and France—dared to anger its own subjects by taking sides against a country that was trying to destroy slavery. After 1862 the chance that Europe would militarily intervene on behalf of the Confederacy rapidly faded to zero. On the propaganda front, the South had been maneuvered into a position which could not be defended in the modern world.

Converting the war into an antislavery crusade was a brilliant move on Lincoln's part, and it resulted in a surge of voluntary recruits into the Union army. But this did not last. Northerners may have disapproved of slavery in the South but, once the bloodletting began in earnest, their willingness to *die* for that conviction began to wane. At the beginning of the war, enlistments were for only three months and, when that period was over, many of the soldiers declined to renew. Lincoln faced the embarrassing reality that he soon would have no army to carry on the crusade.

RAISING ARMIES ON BOTH SIDES

Historically, men are willing to take up arms to defend their families, their homes, and their country when threatened by a hostile foe. But the only way to get them to fight in a war in which they have no perceived personal interest is either to pay them large bonuses and bounties or to *force* them to do so by conscription. It is not surprising, therefore, that both methods were employed to keep the Union army in the field. Furthermore, although the Constitution specifies that only Congress can declare war and raise an army, Lincoln did so entirely on his own authority.[2]

The Northern states were given an opportunity to fill a specified quota with volunteers before conscription began. To meet these quotas and to avoid the draft, every state, township, and county developed an elaborate bounty system. By 1864, there were

---

1. Catton and Ketchum, p. 252.
2. Congress later ratified Lincoln's actions, but, by that time, it had little choice. The War was underway.

many areas where a man could receive more than $1,000—equivalent to over $50,000 today—just for joining the army. A person of wealth could avoid the draft simply by paying a commutation fee or by hiring someone else to serve in his place.

In the South, the government was even more bold in its approach to conscription. Despite its cherished views on states' rights, the Confederacy immediately gathered into Richmond many of the powers and prerogatives of a centralized, national government. In 1862 it passed a conscription law which placed exclusive control over every male citizen between the ages of eighteen and thirty-five into the hands of the Confederate President. As in the North, there were important loopholes. The owner or overseer of twenty slaves, for example, could not be called into military service.[1] In all fairness, it must be noted that many did not take advantage of this exclusion. In contrast to the North, soldiers perceived that they were fighting for the defense of their families, homes, and property rather than for an abstract cause or for a cash bounty.

REBELLION IN THE NORTH

When conscription was initiated by Lincoln in 1863, people in the North were outraged. In New York's Madison Square, thousands of protesters marched in torch parades and attended anti-Lincoln rallies. Historian James Horan describes the mood: "When caricatures of the President were lifted above the speaker's stand, hisses rose to fill the night with the noise of a million angry bees."[2] Federal troops eventually had to be called in to put down antidraft riots in Ohio and Illinois. In New York City, when the first names of the draft were published in the papers on July 12, mobs stormed the draft offices and set fire to buildings. The riots continued for four days and were suppressed only when the federal Army of the Potomac was ordered to fire into the crowds. Over a thousand civilians were killed or wounded.[3]

After the passage of many years, it is easy to forget that Lincoln had an insurrection on his hands in the North as well as in the South. The shooting of a thousand civilians by soldiers of their *own*

---

1. Catton and Ketchum, pp. 484–85.
2. James D. Horan, *Confederate Agent: A Discovery in History* (New York: Crown, 1954), p. 209.
3. Catton and Ketchum, pp. 486, 511.

government is a tragedy of mammoth proportions and it tells much about the desperate state of the Union at that time. To control that insurrection, Lincoln ignored the Constitution once again by suspending the right of *habeas corpus*, which made it possible for the government to imprison its critics without formal charges and without trial. Thus, under the banner of opposing slavery, American citizens in the North, not only were killed on the streets of their own cities, they were put into military combat against their will and thrown into prison without due process of law. In other words, free men were enslaved so that slaves could be made free. Even if the pretended crusade had been genuine, it was a bad exchange.

How to get people to *pay* for the war was handled in a similar fashion. If the Constitution could be pushed aside on the issue of personal rights and of war itself, it certainly would not stand in the way of mere *funding*.

It has often been said that truth is the first casualty in war. To which we should add: money is the second. During the fiscal year ending in 1861, expenses of the federal government had been $67 million. After the first year of armed conflict they were $475 million and, by 1865, had risen to one *billion*, three-hundred million dollars. On the *income* side of the ledger, taxes covered only about eleven per cent of that figure. By the end of the war, the deficit had risen to $2.61 billion. That money had to come from *somewhere*.

INCOME TAXES AND WAR BONDS

The nation's first experiment with the income tax was tried at this time; another violation of the Constitution. By today's standards it was a small bite, but it was still an extremely unpopular measure, and Congress knew that any additional taxes would further fan the flames of rebellion.

Previously, the traditional source of funding in time of war had been the banks which simply created money under the pretense of lending it. But that method had been severely hampered by the demise of the Bank of the United States. The state banks were anxious to step into that role; but, by this time, most of them had already defaulted in their promise to pay in specie and were in no position to manufacture further money, at least not money which the public would be willing to accept.

American banks may have been unable to supply adequate loans, but the Rothschild consortium in Britain was both able and willing. It was during this time that the Rothschilds were consolidating their new industrial holdings in the United States through their agent, August Belmont. Derek Wilson tells us: "They owned or had major shareholdings in Central American ironworks, North American canal construction companies, and a multiplicity of other concerns. They became the major importers of bullion from the newly discovered goldfields."[1]

Belmont had placed large amounts of Rothschild money into the bonds of state-sponsored banks in the South. Those bonds, of course, had fallen in value to practically zero. As the war shifted in favor of the North, however, he began to buy up as many additional bonds as he could, paying but a few pennies on each dollar of face value. It was his plan to have the Union force the Southern states at the end of the war to honor all of their pre-war debt obligations—in full. That, of course, would have been a source of gigantic speculative profits to the Rothschilds. Meanwhile, on the northern side of the Mason-Dixon Line, Belmont became the chief agent for the sale of Union bonds in England and France. It was rumored that, when Belmont called on President Lincoln and personally offered Rothschild money at 27 ½ per cent interest, he was rudely thrown out of the office. The story is doubtful, but it represents a larger truth. Profiting from war and placing money on both sides of the conflict were exactly the kinds of maneuvers for which the Rothschilds had become famous throughout Europe and were now practicing in America.

In the North, the sale of government bonds was the one measure for raising funds that seemed to work. Even that, however, with the lure of compounded interest to be paid in gold at a future date, failed to raise more than about half the needed amount. So the Union faced a real dilemma. The only options remaining were (1) terminate the war or (2) print fiat money. For Lincoln and the Republicans who controlled Congress, the choice was never seriously in doubt.

The precedent had already been set during the War of 1812. At that time, Secretary of the Treasury, Albert Gallatin, had abrogated the Constitutional ban against "bills of credit" by printing Treasury

---

1. See Derek Wilson, p. 178.

notes, most of which paid interest at 5.4 per cent. The money was never declared legal tender, and that probably was the basis on which it was defended as constitutional.

THE GREENBACKS

By the time of the War Between the States, however, all pretense at constitutionality had been dropped. In 1862, Congress authorized the Treasury to print $150 million worth of bills of credit and put them into circulation as money to pay for its expenses. They were declared as legal tender for all private debts but could not be used for government duties or taxes. The notes were printed with green ink and, thus, became immortalized as "greenbacks." Voters were assured that this was a one-time emergency measure, a promise that was soon broken. By the end of the war, a total of $432 million in greenbacks had been issued.

The pragmatic mood in Washington was that a constitution is nice to have in times of peace, but an unaffordable luxury in war. Salmon P. Chase, for example, as Secretary of the Treasury, strongly endorsed the greenbacks which were issued under his direction. They were, in his words, an "indispensable necessity." Eight years later, as Chief Justice of the Supreme Court, he declared that they were unconstitutional. Had he changed his mind? Not at all. When he endorsed them, the nation was at war. When he declared them unconstitutional, it was at peace. It was merely another example of the universal trait of all governments in time of war. That trait was presented in a previous section as the premise of the Rothschild Formula: "The sanctity of its laws, the prosperity of its citizens, and the solvency of its treasury will be quickly sacrificed by any government in its primal act of self-survival."

The pressure for issuance of greenbacks originated in Congress, but Lincoln was an enthusiastic supporter. His view was that:

> Government, possessing power to create and issue currency and credit as money and enjoying the right to withdraw currency and credit from circulation by taxation and otherwise, need not and should not borrow capital at interest.... The privilege of creating and issuing money is not only the supreme prerogative of the government but it is the government's greatest creative opportunity.[1]

---

1. This is taken from an abstract of Lincoln's monetary policy that was prepared by the Legislative Reference Service of the Library of Congress. Quoted by Owen, p. 91.

It would appear that Lincoln objected to having the govern-ment pay interest to the banks for money they create out of nothing when the *government* can create money out of nothing just as easily and *not* pay interest on it. If one ignores the fact that *both* of these schemes are forbidden by the Constitution and is willing to tolerate the plunder-by-inflation that is the consequence of both, then there is an appealing logic to the argument. The politicians continue to have their fiat money, but at least the *banks* are denied a free ride.

LINCOLN'S MIXED VIEW OF BANKING

It is apparent that Lincoln had undergone a change of heart regarding banks. Early in his political career, he had been a friend of the banking industry and an advocate of easy credit. As a member of the Whig political party in the 1830s—before becoming a Republican in his campaign for the Presidency—he had been a supporter of Biddle's Second Bank of the United States.[1] During his famous debates with Senator Stephen Douglas, one of the points of contention between the two was that Lincoln defended the Bank and advocated its reestablishment. Furthermore, after becoming President, he took the initiative in requesting Congress to reestab-lish central banking.[2]

Lincoln appears to have been inconsistent, and one gets a gnawing feeling that, in his effort to finance an unpopular war, he sometimes found it necessary, like Salmon Chase and other politi-cians of the time, to anesthetize his personal convictions and do whatever was required to meet the exigencies of governmental survival.

One thing, however, is clear. Regardless of Lincoln's personal views on money, the greenbacks were not pleasing to the bankers who were thereby denied their customary override on government debt. They were anxious to have this federal fiat money replaced by *bank* fiat money. For that to be possible, it would be necessary to create a whole new monetary system with government bonds used as backing for the issuance of bank notes; in other words, a return to central banking. And that was precisely what Secretary Chase was preparing to establish.

---

1. See Lincoln's speech on the Sub-Treasury, Fehrenbacher, pp. 56–57.
2. See Lincoln's annual message to Congress, December 1, 1862, Fehrenbacher, p. 398.

In 1862, the basic position of the bankers was outlined in a memo, called *The Hazard Circular*, prepared by an American agent of British financiers and circulated among the country's wealthy businessmen. It said:

> The great debt that capitalists will see to it is made out of the war must be used as a means to control the volume of money. To accomplish this the bonds must be used as a banking basis. We are now waiting for the Secretary of the Treasury to make this recommendation to Congress. It will not do to allow the greenback, as it is called, to circulate as money any length of time, as we cannot control that. But we can control the bonds and through them the bank issues.[1]

THE NATIONAL BANKING ACT

On February 25, 1863, Congress passed the National Banking Act (with major amendments the following year) which established a new system of nationally-chartered banks. The structure was similar to the Bank of the United States with the exception that, instead of one *central* bank with power to influence the activities of the others, there were now to be many *national* banks with control over all of them coming from Washington. Most banking legislation is sold to the public under the attractive label of reform. The National Banking Act was one of the rare exceptions. It was promoted fairly honestly as a wartime emergency scheme to raise money for military expenses by creating a market for government bonds and then transforming those bonds into circulating money. Here is how it worked:

When a national bank purchased government bonds, it did not hold on to them. It turned them back to the Treasury which exchanged them for an equal amount of "United States Bank Notes" with the bank's name engraved on them. The government declared these to be legal tender for taxes and duties, and that status caused them to be generally accepted by the public as money. The bank's net cost for these bonds was zero, because they got their money back immediately. Technically, the bank still owned the bonds and collected interest on them, but they also had the use of an equal amount of newly created bank-note money which also could be lent out at interest. When all the smoke and

---

1. The Hon. Charles A. Lindburgh, *Banking and Currency and the Money Trust* (Washington, D.C.: National Capital Press, 1913), p. 102.

mirrors were moved away, it was merely a variation on the ancient scheme. The monetary and political scientists had simply converted government debt into money, and the bankers were collecting a substantial fee at both ends for their service.

The one shortcoming of the system, at least from the point of view of the manipulators, was that, even though the bank notes were widely circulated, they were not classified as "lawful" money. In other words, they were not legal tender for *all* debts, just for taxes and duties. Precious-metal coins and greenbacks were still the country's official money. It was not until the arrival of the Federal Reserve System fifty years later that government debt in the form of bank notes would be mandated as the nation's official money for *all* transactions—under penalty of law.

The National Banking Act of 1863 required banks to keep a percentage of their notes and deposits in the form of lawful money (gold coins) as a reserve to cover the possibility of a run. That percentage varied depending on the size and location of the bank but, on an average, it was about twelve per cent. That means a bank with $1 million in coin deposits could use approximately $880,000 of that ($1 million less 12%) to purchase government bonds, exchange the bonds for bank notes, lend out the bank notes, and collect interest on *both* the bonds *and* the loans. The bank could now earn interest on $880,000 lent to the *government* in the form of coins plus interest on $880,000 loaned to its *customers* in the form of bank notes.[1] That doubled the bank's income without the inconvenience of having to increase its capital. Needless to say, the bonds were gobbled up just as fast as they could be printed, and the problem of funding the war had been solved.

Another consequence of the national banking system was to make it impossible from that date forward for the federal government ever to get out of debt. Please reread that statement. It is not an exaggeration. Even friends of central-banking are forced to admit this reality. Galbraith says gloomily:

> Rarely has economic circumstance managed more successfully to confound the most prudent in economic foresight. In numerous years

---

1. That represents the theoretical maximum. The actual numbers would have been slightly less due to the fact that banks seldom were able to keep a full 100% of their bank notes circulating in the form of loans. The functional asset leverage probably averaged about 70% rather than 88%.

following the war the Federal government ran a heavy surplus. It could not pay off its debt, retire its securities, because to do so meant there would be no bonds to back the national bank notes. To pay off the debt was to destroy the money supply.[1]

As pointed out in a previous section, that is essentially the situation which exists today. Every dollar of our currency and checkbook money was created by the act of lending. If all debt were repaid, our entire money supply would vanish back into the inkwells and computers. The *national* debt is the principal foundation upon which money is created for *private* debt.[2] To pay off or even greatly reduce the national debt would cripple our monetary system. No politician would dare to advocate that, even if surplus funds were available in the Treasury. The Federal Reserve System, therefore, has virtually locked our nation into perpetual debt.

THE HIDDEN COST OF WAR

The third consequence of the National Banking Act will come as no surprise to anyone who has survived the previous pages of this book. During the war, the purchasing power of the greenbacks fell by 65%. The money supply increased by 138%. Prices more than doubled while wages rose by less than half. By that mechanism, Americans surrendered to the government and to the banks more than half of all the money they earned or held during that period—in *addition* to their taxes.[3]

Financial conditions in the South were even worse. With the exception of the seizure of about $400,000 in gold from the Federal mint at New Orleans, almost all of the war was funded by the printing of fiat money. Confederate notes increased in volume by 214% per year, while the volume of all money, including bank notes and check-book money, rose by over 300% per year. In addition to the Confederate notes, each of the Southern states issued its own fiat money and, by the end of the war, the total of all notes was about a billion dollars. Within the four-year period, prices shot up by 9,100%. After Appomattox, of course, Confederate notes and bonds alike were totally worthless.[4]

---

1. Galbraith, p. 90.
2. See chapter ten, The Mandrake Mechanism.
3. See Paul and Lehrman, pp. 80–81; Groseclose, *Money and Man*, p. 193; Galbraith, pp. 93–94; Rothbard, *Mystery*, p. 222.
4. See Galbraith, p. 94. Also Paul and Lehrman, p. 81.

As usual, the average citizen did not understand that the newly created money represented a hidden tax which he would soon have to pay in the form of higher prices. Voters in the Northern states certainly would not have tolerated an open and honest tax increase of that magnitude. Even in the South where the cause was perceived as one of self defense, it is possible that they would not have done so had they known in advance the true dimension of the assessment. But especially in the North, because they did not understand the secret science of money, Americans not only paid the hidden tax but applauded Congress for creating it.

On June 25, 1863, exactly four months after the National Bank Act was signed into law, a confidential communique was sent from the Rothschild investment house in London to an associate banking firm in New York. It contained an amazingly frank and boastful summary:

> The few who understand the system [bank loans earning interest and also serving as money] will either be so interested in its profits or so dependent upon its favors that there will be no opposition from that class while, on the other hand, the great body of people, mentally incapable of comprehending,... will bear its burdens without complaint.[1]

LINCOLN'S CONCERN FOR THE FUTURE

Lincoln was privately apprehensive about the Bank Act, but loyalty to his Party and the need to maintain unity in time of war compelled him to withhold his veto. His personal view, however, was unequivocal. In a letter to William Elkins the following year he said:

> The money power preys upon the nation in times of peace and conspires against it in times of adversity. It is more despotic than monarchy, more insolent than autocracy, more selfish than bureaucracy. I see in the near future a crisis approaching that unnerves me and causes me to tremble for the safety of my country. Corporations have been enthroned, an era of corruption will follow, and the money power of the country will endeavor to prolong its reign by working upon the prejudices of the people, until the wealth is aggregated in a few hands, and the republic destroyed.[2]

---

1. Quoted by Owen, pp. 99–100.
2. A letter to William F. Elkins, November 21, 1864. Archer H. Shaw, ed., *The Lincoln Encyclopedia: The Spoken and Written Words of A. Lincoln* (New York: Macmillan Co., 1950), p. 40.

In reviewing Lincoln's role throughout this painful chapter of history, it is impossible not to feel ambivalence. On the one hand, he declared war without Congress, suspended the writ of *habeas corpus*, and issued the Emancipation Proclamation, not as an administrative executive carrying out the wishes of Congress, but as the Commander-in-Chief of the armed forces. Furthermore, the Proclamation was *not* issued out of humanitarian motives, as popular history portrays, but as a maneuver to generate popular support for the war. By participating in the issuance of the greenbacks, he violated one of the most clearly written and important sections of the Constitution. And by failing to veto the National Bank Act, he acquiesced in the delivery of the American people back into the hands of the international Cabal, an act which was similar in many ways to the forcible return of captured runaway slaves.

On the positive side, there is no question of Lincoln's patriotism. His concern was in preserving the *Union*, not the Constitution, and his refusal to let the European powers split America into a cluster of warring nation-states was certainly wise. Lincoln believed that he had to violate part of the Constitution in order to save the whole. But that is dangerous reasoning. It can be used in almost any national crisis as the excuse for the expansion of totalitarian power. There is no reason to believe that the only way to save the Union was to scrap the Constitution. In fact, if the Constitution had been meticulously observed from the very beginning, the Southern minority could never have been legally plundered by the Northern majority and there likely would have been no movement for secession in the first place. And, even if there had been, a strict reading of the Constitution at *that* point could have led the way to an honorable and peaceful settlement of differences. The result would have been, not only the preservation of the Union *without* war, but Americans would be enjoying far less government intervention in their daily lives today.

WITH MALICE TOWARD NONE

There is one point that is clearly on Lincoln's side. While his political compatriots were howling for economic vengeance against the South, the President stood firmly against it. "With malice toward none" was more than a slogan with him, and he was willing to risk his political survival on that one issue. The reason he had vetoed the Wade-Davis emancipation bill was because it would have applied a lien against Southern cotton at the end of the war to the benefit of New England textile manufactures. The cotton also would have been taken as security to pay off Southern debt which had been contracted before the war, thus providing the funds to buy back *at face value* all of the bonds which had been purchased at discount by Rothschild's agent, August Belmont. Such defiance of the financiers and speculators undoubtedly required great courage.

But the issue ran deeper than that. Lincoln had offered a general amnesty to any citizen in the South who would agree to take a loyalty oath to the Union. When ten per cent of the voters had taken such an oath, he proposed that they could then elect Congressmen, Senators, and a state government which would be recognized as part of the Union once again. The Republicans, on the other hand, had incorporated into the Wade-Davis bill the provision that each seceded state was to be treated like a conquered country. Political representation was to be denied until fifty-one per cent, not ten per cent, had taken an oath. Former slaves were given the right to vote—although women had not yet gained that right even in the North—but, because of their lack of education and political awareness, no one expected them to play a meaningful role in government for many years to come. Furthermore, those taking the oath had to swear that they had never taken up arms against the Union. Since almost every able-bodied white male had done so, the effect would have been to deny the South political representation for at least two generations.

Under Lincoln's amnesty policy, it would not be long before the Republicans would be overwhelmed in Congress by a large majority of Democrats. The Democrats in the North were already gaining strength on their own and, once they could be joined by the solid block of Democrats from the reunited South, the Republicans' political and economic power would be lost. So, when Lincoln vetoed the bill, his own Party bitterly turned against him.

Running throughout these cross-currents of motives and special interests were two groups which found it increasingly to their advantage to have Lincoln out of the way. One group consisted of the financiers, Northern industrialists, and radical Republicans, all of whom wanted to legally plunder the South at the end of the war. The politicians within that group also looked forward to further consolidating their power and literally establishing a military dictatorship.[1] The other group was smaller in size but equally dangerous. It consisted of hothead Confederate sympathizers— from both South *and* North—who sought revenge. Later events revealed that both of these groups had been involved in a conspiratorial liaison with an organization called the Knights of the Golden Circle.

KNIGHTS OF THE GOLDEN CIRCLE

The Order of the Knights of the Golden Circle was a secret organization dedicated to revolution and conquest. Two of its better known members were Jesse James and John Wilkes Booth. It was organized by George W.L. Bickley who established its first "castle" in Cincinnati in 1854, drawing membership primarily from Masonic lodges. It had close ties with a secret society in France called The Seasons, which itself was a branch of the Illuminati.[2] After the beginning of the war, Bickley was made head of the Confederacy's secret service, and his organization quickly spread throughout the border and Southern states as well.

In the North, the conspirators were seeking "to seize political power and overthrow the Lincoln government."[3] In fact, the Northern anti-draft riots mentioned previously were largely the result of the planning and leadership of this group.[4] In the South "they tried to promote the extension of slavery by the conquest of Mexico."[5] In partnership with Maximilian, the Knights hoped to establish a Mexican-American empire which would be an effective counter force against the North. In fact, the very name of the organization is based on their goal of carving an empire out of North America with geographical boundaries forming a circle with the center in Cuba, and its circumference reaching northward to Pennsylvania, southward to Panama.

---

1. For highly readable accounts of this movement, see Theodore Roscoe, *The Web of Conspiracy: The Complete Story of the Men Who Murdered Abraham Lincoln* (Englewood Cliffs, New Jersey: Prentice-Hall, 1959); also Claude G. Bowers, *The Tragic Era: The Revolution after Lincoln*, (New York: Houghton Mifflin, 1957).
2. "No Civil War at All, Part Two," by William McIlhany, *Journal of Individualist Studies*, Fall, 1992, pp. 18–20.
3. Horan, p. 15.
4. *Ibid.*, pp. 208–23.
5. *Ibid.*, p. 16. Regarding the annexation of Mexico, also see the *Columbia Encyclopedia*, Third Edition, p. 1143.

In 1863 the group was reorganized as the Order of American Knights and, again the following year, as the Order of the Sons of Liberty. Its membership then was estimated at between 200,000 and 300,000. After the war, it went further underground and remnants eventually emerged as the Ku Klux Klan.

JOHN WILKES BOOTH

One of the persistent legends of this period is that John Wilkes Booth was not killed in Garrett's barn, as generally accepted, but was allowed to escape; that the corpse actually was that of an accomplice; and that the government, under the firm control of War Secretary Edwin M. Stanton, moved heaven and earth to cover up the facts. On the face of it, that is an absurd story. But, when the voluminous files of the War Department were finally declassified and put into the public domain in the mid 1930s, historians were shocked to discover that there are many facts in those files which lend credence to the legend. The first to probe these amazing records was Otto Eisenschiml whose *Why Was Lincoln Murdered?* was published by Little, Brown and Company in 1937. The best and most readable compilation of the facts, however, was written twenty years later by Theodore Roscoe. In the preface to this work, he states the startling conclusions which emerge from those long-hidden files:

> Of the immense 19th century literature that exists on Lincoln's assassination, much of the writing treats the tragedy at Ford's theater as though it were Grand Opera.... Only a few have seen the crime as a murder case: Lincoln dying by crass felony, Booth a stalking gunman leading a gang of primed henchmen, the murder plot containing ingredients as base as the profit motive. Seventy years after the crime, writers were garbling it with a dignity it did not deserve: Lincoln, the stereotyped martyr; Booth, the stereotyped villain; the assassination avenged by classic justice; conspiracy strangled; Virtue (in the robes of Government) emerging triumphant, and Lincoln "belonging to the ages."
>
> But the facts of the case are neither so satisfying nor so gratifying. For the facts indicate that the criminals responsible for Lincoln's death got away with murder.[1]

Izola Forrester was the granddaughter of John Wilkes Booth. In her book entitled *This One Mad Act*, she tells of discovering the

---

1. Roscoe, p. vii.

secret records of the Knights of the Golden Circle which had been carefully wrapped and placed in a government vault many decades ago and designated as classified documents by Secretary Stanton. Since the assassination of Lincoln, no one had ever been allowed to examine that package. Because of her lineage to Booth and because of her credentials as a professional writer, she was eventually permitted to become the first person in all those years to examine its contents. Forrester recounts the experience:

> It was five years before I was able to examine the contents of the mysterious old package hidden away in the safe of the room which contained the relics and exhibits used in the Conspiracy Trial.... I would never have seen them, had I not knelt on the floor of the cell five years ago and seen into the back of the old safe where the package lay. It is all part of the odd mystery thrown about the case by the officials of the war period—the concealment of these documents and articles, and the hiding away of the two flakes of bone with the bullet and pistol. What mind ever grouped together such apparently incongruous and macabre exhibits?...
>
> Here at last was a link with my grandfather. I knew that he had been a member of the secret order founded by Bickley, the Knights of the Golden Circle. I have an old photograph of him taken in a group of the brotherhood, in full uniform, one that Harry's daughter had discovered for me in our grandmother's Bible. I knew that the newspapers, directly following the assassination, had denounced the order as having instigated the killing of Lincoln, and had proclaimed Booth to have been its member and tool. And I was reminded again of those words I had heard from my grandmother's lips, that her husband had been "the tool of other men."[1]

An interesting comment. One is compelled to wonder: The tool of *what* other men? Was Forrester's grandmother referring to the leaders of the Knights of the Golden Circle? To agents of European financiers? Or was it to conspirators within Lincoln's own Party? We shall probably never know with certainty the extent to which any of these groups may have been involved in Lincoln's assassination, but we *do* know that there were powerful forces within the federal government, centered around Secretary of War Stanton, which actively concealed evidence and hastily terminated the investigation. *Someone* was protected.

---

1.   Izola Forrester, *This One Mad Act* (Boston: Hale, Cushman & Flint, 1937), p. 359.

SUMMARY

It is time now to leave this tragic episode and move along. So let us summarize. America's bloodiest and most devastating war was fought, not over the issue of freedom versus slavery, but because of clashing economic interests. At the heart of this conflict were questions of legalized plunder, banking monopolies, and even European territorial expansion into Latin America. The boot print of the Rothschild formula is unmistakable across the graves of American soldiers on both sides.

In the North, neither greenbacks, taxes, nor war bonds were enough to finance the war. So a national banking system was created to convert government bonds into fiat money, and the people lost over half of their monetary assets to the hidden tax of inflation. In the South, printing presses accomplished the same effect, and the monetary loss was total.

The issuance of the Emancipation Proclamation by Lincoln and the naval assistance offered by Tsar Alexander, II, were largely responsible for keeping England and France from intervening in the war on the side of the Confederacy. Lincoln was assassinated by a member of the Knights of the Golden Circle, a secret society with rumored ties to American politicians and British financiers. Tsar Alexander was assassinated a few years later by a member of the People's Will, a Nihilist secret society in Russia with rumored ties to financiers in New York City, specifically, Jacob Schiff and the firm of Kuhn, Loeb & Company.

As for the Creature of central banking, there had been some victories and some defeats. The greenbacks had for a while deprived the bankers of their override on a small portion of government debt, but the National Banking Act quickly put a stop to that. Furthermore, by using government bonds as backing for the money supply, it locked the nation into *perpetual* debt. The foundation was firmly in place, but the ultimate structure still needed to be erected. The monetary system was yet to be concentrated into *one* central-bank mechanism, and the control was yet to be taken away from the politicians and placed into the hands of the bankers themselves.

It was time for the Creature to visit Congress.

President Andrew Jackson put his political career on the line in 1832 by vetoing renewal of the charter for the Second Bank of the United States. He called the Bank a monster and declared: "I am ready with the screws to draw every tooth and then the stumps." Voters approved and re-elected him by a large margin.

Nicholas Biddle was head of the Second Bank of the United States. With many Congessmen and Senators financially beholden to him, he wielded great political power. He deliberately created a banking panic and a depression for the purpose of frightening the voters and blaming Jackson's anti-bank policy. Biddle declared: "All other banks and all the merchants may break, but the Bank of the United States shall not break." In the end, he lost the contest. The Bank's charter expired in 1836.

During the Civil War, Lincoln had an insurrection on his hands in the North as well as the South, These two Leslie's engravings depict the 1863 anti-draft riots that occurred in Ohio, Illinois, and New York. In New York, over 1,000 civilians were killed or wounded by federal soldiers. The Civil War was started over economic issues, not slavery. The War was not popular in the North until the issue of slavery was added at a later time to turn it into a moral crusade.

Above and below: New York Historical Society

The crew of the Russian ship, *Osliaba,* posed for this photograph at Alexandri.
Virginia, in 1863. Tsar Alexander II had dispatched his Baltic fleet to Alexandria ar
his Asiatic fleet to San Fransciso where they were committed to assist the Union
blockade against the South. This had little to do with freeing the slaves. France h;
designs on Mexico, and England wanted a divided America. Russia was mere
reacting against France and England who were her enemies. The powers of Europ
were deeply involved in the American Civil War for purposes of their own. Witho
Russia's intervention, the outcome of the War could have been quite different.

Montagu Norman (above) was head of the Bank of England during the first years of the Federal Reserve. He is shown here in 1931 aboard the *Duchess of York* at Southampton. Norman frequently traveled to the U.S. to meet in secret with Benjamin Strong, head of the Federal Reserve. Strong agreed to use the Federal Reserve System to unofficially help Great Britain meet its financial obligations, and billions of dollars subsequently flowed from the U.S. It was that outflow that set the stage for America's great depression of the 1930's.

William Wentworth (right) met Norman aboard ship in 1929. Norman told him in confidence that there soon was going to be a "shake-out" in the U.S. financial markets. The stock-market crashed just a few months later.

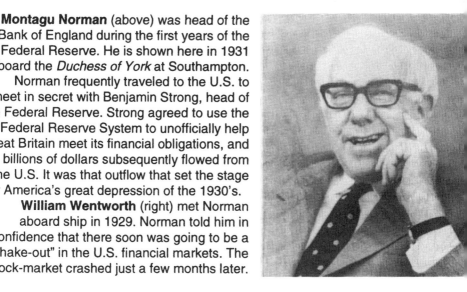

399

John D. Rockefeller, Sr., is shown here giving a dime to a child, while an admiri
crowd looks on. This was one of his favorite publicity stunts. It was conceived by I
public-relations staff as a means of offsetting adverse publicity regarding his busine
dealings. Large-scale philanthropy was an extension of that same technique.

John D. Rockefeller, III (right) presents a check in the amount
of $8,500,000 to Trygve Lie, First Secretary-General of the
United Nations. The date is March 25, 1947. The money is for
buying the land on Manhattan Island which will house the UN
building. Through the Council on Foreign Relations (CFR), the
Rockefellers have been in the forefront of the drive for a world
government which is to be built upon the principles of
socialism and feudalism. They have no doubt that they and
their counterparts in other countries will be in control.

402

William Jennings Bryan (left) was one of the most powerful Democrats in Congress. He opposed the Federal Reserve Act because it would privately issue money rather than through the government. He was fooled into supporting the bill when phony compromises were made which gave the *appearance* of public control and government issue but which, in fact, did neither. Bryan was also rewarded with an appointment as Secretary of State. He became disillusioned by the duplicity of his own government and resigned after Wilson failed to warn the public that the *Lusitania* was carrying munitions. He complained that it was "like putting women and children in front of an army."

Alan Greenspan (above), was an eloquent spokesman for the gold standard and a critic of the System's subservience to the banking cartel. That was in 1966. After he became a director of J.P. Morgan & Company and was appointed Chairman of the Federal Reserve in 1987, he became silent on these issues and did nothing to anger the Creature he now served. Like Bryan, even the best of men can be corrupted by the rewards of politics.

403

The First National Bank in St. Petersburg, Florida experiences a run on June 12, 1930. Angry depositors want their money, but the bank cannot pay them. Their money has been loaned to others. This scene has been repeated thousands of times throughout history and in every country. It is the consequence of fractional-reserve banking.

John Kenneth Galbraith, well-known historian and professor at Harvard, has verified that he was asked to be part of the team that put together *The Report from Iron Mountain*, a think-tank study commissioned by the Defense Department. The purpose of the study was to explore novel ways of keeping the masses in subservience. When a copy of the *Report* was leaked to the press, the government claimed it was a hoax. Galbraith confirmed that it was totally authentic.

Section V

THE HARVEST

Monetary and political scientists continue to expound the theoretical merits of the Federal Reserve System. It has become a modern act of faith that economic life simply could not go on without it. But the time for theory is past. The Creature moved into its final lair in 1913 and has snorted and thrashed about the landscape ever since. If we wish to know if it is a creature of service or a beast of prey, we merely have to look at what it has done. And, after the test of all those years, we can be sure that what it has done, it will continue to do. Or, to use the Biblical axiom, a tree shall be known by the fruit it bears. Let us now examine the harvest.

Chapter Twenty

THE LONDON CONNECTION

> *The rise of the House of Morgan; Morgan's ties with England and the House of Rothschild; the connection between the Federal Reserve System and the Bank of England; the Fed's decision to inflate American dollars to assist the ailing British economy.*

The period between the Civil War and the enactment of the Federal Reserve System was one of great economic volatility and no small measure of chaos. The National Banking Acts of 1863–65 established a system of federally chartered banks which were given significant privilege and power over the monetary system. They were granted a monopoly in the issuance of bank notes, and the government agreed to accept those notes for the payment of taxes and duties. They were allowed to back this money up to ninety per cent with government bonds instead of gold. And they were guaranteed that every bank in the system would have to accept the notes of every other bank at face value, regardless of how shaky their position. The net effect was that the banking system of the United States after the Civil War, far from being free and unregulated as some historians have claimed, was literally a halfway house to central banking.

The notion of being able to generate prosperity simply by creating more money has always fascinated politicians and businessmen, but at no time in our history was it more in vogue than in the second half of the nineteenth century. The nation had gone mad with the Midas complex, a compulsion to turn everything into money through the magic of banking. Personal checks gradually had become accepted in commerce just as readily as bank notes, and the banks obliged their customers by entering into their passbooks just as many little numbers as they cared to "borrow." As Groseclose observed: "The manna of cheap money became the universal cry, and as with the Israelites, the easier the manna was acquired, the louder became the complaint, the less willing the people to struggle for it."[1]

The prevailing philosophy of that time was aptly expressed by Jay Cooke, the famous financier who had marketed the huge Civil War loans of the federal government and who now was raising $100 million for the Northern Pacific Railroad. Cooke had published a pamphlet which was aptly summarized by its own title: *How Our National Debt May Be a National Blessing. The Debt is Public Wealth, Political Union, Protection of Industry, Secure Basis for National Currency.* "Why," asked Cooke, "should this Grand and Glorious country be stunted and dwarfed—its activities chilled and its very life blood curdled by these miserable 'hard coin' theories—the musty theories of a bygone age."[2] As it turned out, however, the chilling and curdling came, not from the musty hard-coin theories of the past, but from the glittering easy-money theories of the present. The Northern Pacific went bankrupt and, as the mountain of imaginary money invested in it collapsed back into nothing, Cooke's giant investment firm disappeared along with it, triggering the panic of 1873 as it went. Matthew Josephson writes:

> "*All about the failure of Jay Cooke!*" newsboys hawked throughout the country....
>
> The largest and most pious bank in the Western world had fallen with the effect of a thunderclap. Soon allied brokers and national banks and 5,000 commercial houses followed it into the abyss of bankruptcy. All day long, in Wall Street, one suspension after another was announced; railroads failed; leading stocks lost 30 to 40 points, or half their value, within the hour; immeasurable waves of fear altered the movement of greed; the exchanges were closed; the stampede, the "greatest" crisis in American history, was on.[3]

AND STILL MORE BOOMS AND BUSTS

Altogether, there were four major contractions of the money supply during this period: the so-called panics of 1873, 1884, 1893, and 1907. Each of them was characterized by inadequate bank reserves and the suspension of specie payment. Congress reacted,

---

1. Groseclose, *Money and Man*, p. 202.
2. Quoted by Rothbard, *Mystery*, p. 231.
3. Matthew Josephson, *The Robber Barons: The Great American Capitalists, 1861–1901* (New York: Harcourt Brace Jovanovich, 1934), p. 170.

not by requiring an increase in reserves which would have improved the safety margin, but by allowing a *decrease*. In June of 1874, legislation was passed which permitted the banks to back their notes entirely with government bonds. That, of course, meant more fiat money for Congress, but it also meant that bank notes no longer had *any* specie backing at all, not even ten per cent. This released over $20 million from bank reserves which then could be used as the basis for pyramiding even more checkbook money into the economy.

It has become accepted mythology that these panics were caused by seasonal demands for farm loans at harvest time. To supply those funds, the country banks had to draw down their cash reserves which generally were deposited with the larger city banks. This thinned out the reserves held in the cities, and the whole system became more vulnerable. Actually that part of the legend is true, but apparently no one is expected to ask questions about the rest of the story. Several of them come to mind. Why wasn't there a panic *every* Autumn instead of just every eleven years or so? Why didn't *all* banks—country or city—maintain adequate reserves to cover their depositor demands? And why didn't they do this in *all* seasons of the year? Why would merely saying no to some loan applicants cause hundreds of banks to fail? The myth falls apart under the weight of these questions.

The truth is that, if it hadn't been seasonal demand by agriculture, the money magicians simply would have found another scapegoat. It would have been "immobile" reserves, lack of "elasticity" in the money supply, "imbalance" of international payments, or some other technocratic smoke screen to cover the real problem which was—and always has been—fractional-reserve banking itself. The bottom line was that, in spite of an elaborate scheme to pool the minuscule reserves of country banks into larger regional banks where they could be rushed from town to town like a keg of coins on the old frontier, it still didn't work. The loaves and fishes stubbornly refused to multiply.

MORGAN PROSPERS WHEN OTHERS FAIL

The monetary expansions and contractions of this period were large waves that capsized thousands of investment ships at sea. But there was one large vessel that, somehow, bobbed up and down with the surges quite well and could be seen throughout the storm salvaging the abandoned cargoes of those that were in distress. This vessel brought back to port untold riches that once had been the property of others but now belonged to the master of the salvage ship in accordance with rules of the high sea. The captain's name was J.P. Morgan.

It will be recalled from a previous section that J.P. Morgan and Company was no small player in the world chess match called World War I. Morgan had been chosen by the French and British governments as the official agent to sell their war bonds in the U.S. When the war began to go badly for them, the Morgan interests began to agitate for American entry into the conflict, a move which was calculated to save the loans. The Morgan firm also was the official U.S. trade agent for Britain. In violation of international treaty, it handled the purchase and shipping to England of all war material, including the enormous cargo of munitions aboard the *Lusitania* when she went down.

The close relationship between the Morgans and Great Britain was no accident. J.P. Morgan, Jr., was the driving force behind the Council on Foreign Relations, the American branch of a secret society established by Cecil Rhodes for the expansion of the British empire. In truth, the Morgans were more British than American.

The reason for this is to be found in the origin of the Morgan dynasty. It all began with an American merchant from Danvers, Massachusetts, by the name of George Peabody. In 1837, Peabody travelled to England as a bond salesman for the Chesapeake and Ohio Canal, hoping to find British investors to replace the missing ranks of Americans who, because of a recession at that time, showed little interest in the project. He routinely was rejected by the large investment houses of London but, eventually, his persistence paid off. Stanley Jackson, in his biography of Morgan, says of Peabody:

> When the panic [in the U.S.] at last started to subside, he called time and again on the big City barons [in London] to assure them that Maryland and other states would honor their bonds. He also continued backing American securities with his personal funds. Buying at almost giveaway levels, he later reaped a rich harvest. He unloaded most of the Chesapeake and Ohio Canal bonds and won acclaim back home for returning his $60,000 commission intact to Maryland's meager treasury.[1]

---

1. Stanley Jackson, *J.P. Morgan* (New York: Stein and Day, 1983), p. 37.

It was during this trip that Peabody opened an import-export business at 22 Old Broad Street in London and began to provide loans and letters of credit to many of his shippers. That moved him into the investment business specializing in transactions between Britain and the United States.

It was fortunate timing. This was the beginning of a period of rapid expansion in the United States, accompanied by an insatiable need for investment capital and a plethora of bond issues offering tantalizing rates of return which were substantially higher than comparable offerings in Europe. Peabody's firm was in an unusual position to exploit this expanding market, and his firm grew rapidly.

Peabody never married and, as he advanced in years, began to look for someone to carry on the business. The qualifications for such a position were difficult. First, the man had to be an American by birth in order to appear authentic as the representative of American investments. Secondly, he had to be British by instinct and preference. This included being well educated and with good breeding in order to be accepted by the aristocracy in London's financial world. Third, he had to have knowledge of Anglo-American finance. And fourth, Peabody had to like him.

JUNIUS MORGAN SELECTED BY PEABODY

When the Boston merchant, Junius Morgan, met George Peabody at a London dinner party in 1850, little did he realize that the elder financier took an immediate liking to him and began to discreetly inquire into his background and reputation. This began an extended period of business and social contact that eventually ended in 1854 when Junius moved his family to London and became a full partner in the firm which, eventually, became known as Peabody, Morgan & Company.

In addition to selling bonds in England for American commercial ventures and state governments, the partnership also became the chief fiscal agent for the Union government during the Civil War, and it was during this period that the firm's great profits pushed it into the top echelons of London's financial fraternity. In 1864, Peabody finally retired and completely turned the business over to Junius who immediately changed the firm's name to J.S. Morgan and Company.

Junius's son, John Pierpont, attended the English High School in Boston but, during much of his youth, was enrolled in European schools and became engulfed in British tradition. He had been born in the United States, however, and that made him ideally suited to carry on the Anglo-American role played so deftly by Peabody and Junius. It was inevitable that the boy would be trained in international finance and groomed to step into his father's shoes. The first move was to find employment for him in 1857 at the New York investment firm of Duncan, Sherman & Company. Seven years later, Junius acquired a competitor New York firm and set his son up as a partner in Dabney, Morgan & Company, which became the New York branch of the London firm. In 1871, with the addition of a third partner, Anthony Drexel from Philadelphia, the firm became Drexel, Morgan & Company. In 1895, following the death of Drexel, there was a final change of name to J.P. Morgan & Company. A branch in Paris became known as Morgan, Harjes & Company.

AMERICANIZING THE NEW YORK BRANCH

After the unexpected death of Junius in a carriage accident a few years later, it was decided by Pierpont to reshape the image of the London firm to be a more British operation. This would allow the New York branch to represent the American side with less suspicion of being essentially the same firm. By that time, his son, J.P. Morgan, Jr.—known as Jack by his friends—had already been brought into the firm as a partner, and he was to play an important role in the creation of that image. Biographer John Forbes tells us:

> J.P. Morgan, Jr., became a partner in the London house of J.S. Morgan & Co. on January 1, 1898, and a fortnight later, with his wife Jessie and their three children,... he left New York and took up residence in England for the next eight years.
>
> Morgan was sent to London to do two specific things. The first was to learn at first hand how the British carried on a banking business under a central banking system dominated by the Bank of England. Morgan, Sr., anticipated the establishment of the Federal Reserve System in the United States and wanted someone who would eventually have authority in the Morgan firms to know how such a system worked. The second was quietly to look about the City and select British partners to convert the elder Morgan's privately owned J.S. Morgan & Co. into a British concern.[1]

---

1. John Douglas Forbes, *J.P. Morgan, Jr.* (Charlottesville: University Press of Virginia, 1981), p. 31.

This eventually was accomplished by the addition of Edward Grenfell, a long-time director of the Bank of England, as the new senior partner of what became Morgan, Grenfell & Company. But none of this window dressing altered the reality that J.P. Morgan & Co. in New York remained more British in orientation than American.[1]

A casual reading of the events of this period would lead to the conclusion that Peabody and Morgan were fierce competitors of the Rothschilds. It is true they often bid against each other for the same business, but it is also true that almost every biographer has told how the American newcomers to London were in awe of the great power of the Rothschilds and how they purposely cultivated their friendship, a friendship that eventually became so intimate that the Americans were received as the personal house guests of the Rothschilds. The Morgan firm often worked closely with the House of Rothschild on large joint ventures, but that was—and still is—common practice among large investment houses. In light of subsequent events, however, it is appropriate to consider the possibility that an arrangement had been worked out in which the Peabody/Morgan firm went one step further and, on occasion, became a secret Rothschild agent.

CONCEALED ALLIANCE WITH ROTHSCHILD?

Some writers have suggested that the clandestine relationship began almost from the beginning. Eustace Mullins, for example, writes:

> Soon after he arrived in London, George Peabody was surprised to be summoned to an audience with the gruff Baron Nathan Mayer Rothschild. Without mincing words, Rothschild revealed to Peabody that much of the London aristocracy openly disliked Rothschild and refused his invitations. He proposed that Peabody, a man of modest means, be established as a lavish host whose entertainments would soon be the talk of London. Rothschild would, of course, pay all the bills. Peabody accepted the offer and soon became known as the most popular host in London. His annual Fourth-of-July dinner, celebrating American Independence, became extremely popular with the English aristocracy, many of whom, while drinking Peabody's wine, regaled each other with jokes about Rothschild's crudities and bad manners,

---

1. This apparently has not diminished over the years. The December 23, 1991, issue of *Business Week* (p. 69) reminds us that the CEO of J.P. Morgan & Co., Dennis Weatherstone who lives in Connecticut, was knighted by Queen Elizabeth II.

without realizing that every drop they drank had been paid for by Rothschild.[1]

Mullins does not give a reference for the source of this story, and one cannot help being skeptical that such details could be proved. Nevertheless, a secret arrangement of this kind is not as absurd as it may sound. There is no question that the Rothschilds were quite capable of such a clandestine relationship and, in fact, this is exactly the kind of deception for which they had become famous. Furthermore, there was ample reason for them to do so. A strong anti-Semitic and anti-Rothschild sentiment had grown up in Europe and the United States, and the family often found it to its advantage to work through agents rather than to deal directly. Derek Wilson tells us: "The name 'Rothschild' was, thus, beginning to be heard in places far removed from sophisticated London and Paris. But the connection with the great bankers was sometimes tenuous."[2]

That tenuous connection was precisely the role to be played by August Belmont in the United States, and the anti-Semitism he found there was undoubtedly the reason he changed his name from Schoenberg to Belmont upon landing in New York in 1837. Prior to that, the Rothschild agent had been the firm of J.L. and S.I. Joseph & Company, about as American sounding as one can get. It was not long, however, before the Belmont-Rothschild connection became common knowledge, and the ploy ceased to be effective.

In 1848, the family decided to send Alphonse Rothschild to the United States to check on Belmont's operations and to evaluate the possibility of replacing him with a *direct* Rothschild representative, perhaps Alphonse himself. After an extended visit, he wrote home:

> In a few years from now America will have attracted to itself the greater part of trade with China and the Indies and will be enthroned between the two oceans.... The country possesses such elements of prosperity that one would have to be blind not to recognize them.... I have no hesitation in saying that a Rothschild house, and not just an agency, should be established in America.... Today we are presented with a fine opportunity. Later on, difficulties will of necessity arise as a result of competition from all sides.[3]

---

1. Eustace Mullins, *Secrets of the Federal Reserve* (Virginia: Bankers Research Institute, 1983), p. 49.
2. Derek Wilson, p. 176.
3. B. Gille, *Histoire de la Maison Rothschild*, Vol. I, 1965–1967, p. 581, cited by Derek Wilson, p. 181.

Some historians have expressed amazement over the fact that the recommendation was never acted upon. Wilson says: "This was the greatest opportunity the Rothschilds ever lost."[1] Those with a more skeptical bent are tempted to wonder if the opportunity really *was* lost or if it was merely taken in a more indirect fashion. It is significant that, precisely at this time, George Peabody was making a name for himself in London and had established a close relationship with Nathan Rothschild. Is it possible that the Peabody firm was given the nod from the Rothschild consortium to represent them in America? And is it possible that the plan included allowing Belmont to operate as a known Rothschild agent while using Peabody & Company as an *unknown* agent, thus, providing their own competition?

John Moody answers: "The Rothschilds were content to remain a close ally of Morgan rather than a competitor as far as the American field was concerned."[2] Gabriel Kolko says: "Morgan's activities in 1895–1896 in selling U.S. gold bonds in Europe were based on his alliance with the House of Rothschild."[3] Sereno Pratt says: "These houses may, like J.P. Morgan & Company ... represent here the great firms and institutions of Europe, just as August Belmont & Company have long represented the Rothschilds."[4] And George Wheeler writes: "Part of the reality of the day was an ugly resurgence of anti-Semitism.... Someone was needed as a cover. Who better than J. Pierpont Morgan, a solid, Protestant exemplar of capitalism able to trace his family back to pre-Revolutionary times?"[5]

RISE OF THE HOUSE OF MORGAN

With these considerations as background, the meteoric rise of Morgan's star over London and Wall Street can be readily understood. It is no longer surprising, for example, that Peabody & Company was the sole American investment firm to receive a gigantic loan from the Bank of England during the U.S. panic of 1857, a loan which not only saved it from sinking, but made it

---

1. Derek Wilson, p. 182.
2. Moody, p. 27.
3. Kolko, *Triumph*, p. 142.
4. Sereno S. Pratt, *The Work of Wall Street* (New York: D. Appleton, 1916; rpt. New York: Arno Press, 1975), p. 349.
5. Wheeler, pp. 17–18, 42.

possible to seize and salvage many other ships that were then cap-sized on Wall Street.

Peabody had become active in the business of discounting acceptances, which is banker language for insuring commercial loans issued for the purchase of goods. This is how it works: The seller issues a bill with a stipulation that he must be paid at a future date, usually ninety days. When the buyer receives the bill, his bank writes the word "accepted" across the face of it and adds the signa-ture of an officer, making it a legally binding contract. In other words, the bank becomes a co-signer on the buyer's credit and guar-antees payment even if the buyer should default.

Naturally, there is a price for this guarantee. That price is stated as a percentage of the total bill and it is either added to the amount paid by the buyer or deducted from the amount received by the seller. Actually there is a fee paid at both ends of the transaction, one to the seller's bank which receives the acceptance and pays out the money, and one to the issuing bank which assumes the liability of guaranteeing payment. The sale is said to be "discounted" by the amount paid to the banks. And so it was that Peabody & Company had been active in the business of discounting acceptances, primar-ily between sellers in England and buyers in the United States.

MORGAN AND THE PANIC OF 1857

In the Wall Street panic of 1857, many U.S. buyers were unable to pay their bills, and Peabody and Morgan were expected to make good on their guarantees. Naturally, they didn't have the money, and the firm was facing certain bankruptcy unless the money could be obtained from *somewhere*. Stanley Jackson provides the details:

> The slump was catastrophic for Peabody & Co. It suddenly found itself committed to acceptances of £2 million and with no hope of discharging even part of a stockpile of depreciating bonds on New York brokers and bankers, themselves now desperately short of ready funds. The firm was soon paying out thousands of pounds a day. Without raising a large temporary loan the partners would be forced to suspend business altogether.[1]

Ron Chernow, in *The House of Morgan*, says: "Rumors raced through London that George Peabody and Company was about to fail, a prospect heartily relished by rivals.... The major London

---

1. Jackson, p. 56.

houses told Morgan they would bail out the firm—but only if Peabody shut down the bank within a year."[1] Jackson continues the narrative:

> The clouds lifted dramatically when the Bank of England announced a loan to Peabody's of £800,000, at very reasonable interest, with the promise of further funds up to a million sterling if and when required. It was a remarkable vote of confidence as Thomas Hankey [governor of the Bank of England] had already rejected similar appeals from various American firms who did not measure up to his standards.... Peabody & Company recovered almost overnight and indeed hoisted its turnover above pre-slump levels.[2]

With an almost unlimited access to cash and credit backed by the Bank of England, Peabody and Morgan were able to wade hip deep through the depreciated stocks and bonds that were sold to them at sacrifice prices on Wall Street. Within only a few years, when sanity had been restored to American markets, the assets of the firm had grown to gigantic proportions.[3]

This event tells us a great deal about relationships. If the Rothschilds truly had been competitors, they would have seized upon this opportunity and used their great influence within the Bank of England and the other investment houses in London to squeeze out Peabody, not to assist him. The Barings, in particular, were already trying to accomplish exactly that. The Rothschilds must have believed that a successful Peabody firm ultimately would be in their own best interest.

ANTI-SEMITISM WAS PROFITABLE

In later years, Jack Morgan (J.P., Jr.) would assume the role of a staunch anti-Semite, and this undoubtedly strengthened his hand at dealing with American investors and borrowers who were loath to have anything to do with Jewish bankers. That, of course, included officials of the U.S. Treasury. It was particularly helpful during the 1896 rescue of the federal government from a decline in its gold reserves. Fearing that it would not be able to honor its promise to exchange paper money for gold coins, the government was forced to borrow $62 million in gold. The House of Rothschild was an obvious source for such a loan, but the Treasury wanted to avoid an

---

1. Chernow, p. 11.
2. Jackson, pp. 56–57.
3. Josephson, p. 60.

anti-Semitic backlash. Everything fell into place, however, when Morgan and Company became the *primary* lender, with Rothschild apparently demoted to the role of a mere participant. Wheeler writes:

> The consummate politicians of the Cleveland administration ... were certainly aware of the dangers inherent in promoting a rescue effort for the United States Treasury that would be financed by those archetypes of "international Jewish financiers," the Rothschilds....
>
> During these developments, Pierpont Morgan took no direct part in the salvage effort. Up to this point it looked as if the aging financier—he would be fifty-eight in two months—would be merely one among many in this and whatever subsequent bond arrangements would be necessary. It seemed as though he would move on into old age with little more to round out his obituary than his awkward attempt to profiteer on the sale of rifles at the start of the Civil War, his minor shorting of the Union in gold trading toward the close, and a bold but largely unsuccessful move in the 1880s to impose an eastern capitalist cease-fire on the country's warring railroads.
>
> But there were steps being taken even now to bring him out of the financial backwaters—and they were not being taken by Pierpont Morgan himself. The first suggestion of his name for a role in the recharging of the reserve originated with the London branch of the House of Rothschild.[1]

The apparent anti-Semitism of J.P. Morgan, Jr., was again extremely profitable during World War I, when it was widely publicized that the Kaiser was funded by German-Jew bankers. To deal with the Morgan group, therefore, as opposed to Kuhn Loeb, for example, was in some circles almost a point of national patriotism.

When J.P. Morgan, Sr., died in 1913, people were shocked to learn that his estate was valued at only $68 million, a paltry sum compared to the fortunes held by the Vanderbilts, Astors, and Rockefellers. It was even more unbelievable when Jack Morgan died in 1943 and left an estate valued at only $16 million. A small amount had been transferred to members of their families prior to their deaths, but that did not account for the vast fortunes which they visibly controlled during their lives. Surely, there had been a bookkeeping sleight-of-hand. On the other hand, it may have been true. When Alphonse Rothschild died in Paris in 1905, it was revealed that *his* estate contained $60 million in American securities.

---

1. Wheeler, pp. 16–17.

The Rothschilds in Britain undoubtedly held an equally large bloc. Furthermore, many of these securities were handled *through* the House of Morgan.[1] The possibilities are obvious that a major portion of the wealth and power of the Morgan firm was, and always had been, merely the wealth and power of the Rothschilds who had raised it up in the beginning and who sustained it through its entire existence.

How much of Morgan's apparent anti-Semitism was real and how much may have been a pragmatic guise is, in the final analysis, of little importance, and we should not give unwarranted emphasis to it here. Regardless of one's interpretation of the nature of the relationship between the Houses of Morgan and Rothschild, the fact remains that it was close, it was ongoing, and it was profitable to both. If Morgan truly did harbor feelings of anti-Semitism, neither he nor the Rothschilds ever allowed them to get in the way of their business.

To put the London connection into proper perspective, it will be necessary once again to abandon a strict chronological sequence of events and jump ahead to the year 1924. So let us put our cast of characters on hold for a moment and, before allowing them to act out the drama of creating the Federal Reserve System, we shall pick up the storyline eleven years after that event had already taken place.

ENGLAND FACES A DILEMMA

At the end of World War I, Britain faced an economic dilemma. She had abandoned the gold standard early in the war in order to remove all limits from the creation of fiat money, and the result had been extreme inflation. But now she wanted to regain her former position of power and prestige in the world's financial markets and decided that, to accomplish this, it would be necessary to return to the gold standard. It was decided, further, to set the exchange value of the pound sterling (the British monetary unit) at exactly $4.86 in U.S. currency, which was approximately what it had been before the war began.

To say that she wanted to return to the gold standard actually is misleading. It was not a pure standard in which every unit of money was totally backed by a stated weight of gold. Rather, it was a

---

1. See "Head of Rothschilds' Paris House Is Dead," *The New York Times*, May 27, 1905, p. 9.

fractional gold standard in which only a certain fraction of all the monetary units were so backed. But, even that was much to be desired over no backing whatsoever for three reasons. First, it created greater consumer confidence in the money system because of the implied promise to redeem all currency in gold—even though such promises are always broken when based on a fractional-reserve.[1] Secondly, it provided an efficient means of settling financial accounts between nations, gold always being the international medium of choice. Thirdly, it applied *some* braking action to the production of fiat money, thus, providing a certain degree of restraint to inflation and the boom-bust cycle.

The decision to return to a fractional gold standard, therefore, while it left much to be desired, was still a step in the right direction. But there were two serious problems with the plan. The first was that the exchange value of gold can never be decided by political decree. It will always be determined by the interplay of supply and demand within the marketplace. Trying to fix the number of dollars which people will be willing to exchange for a pound sterling was like trying to legislate how many baseball cards a schoolboy will give for a purple agate. The international currency market is like a huge auction. If the auctioneer sets the opening bid too high, there will be no takers—which is exactly what happened to the pound.

The other problem was that, during the war, England had adopted a massive welfare program and a strong network of labor unions. The reason this was a problem was that the only way to make the pound acceptable in international trade was to allow its value to drop to a competitive and realistic level, and that would have meant, not only a drastic reduction in welfare benefits, but also a general lowering of prices—including the price of labor which is called wages. Politicians were quite willing to allow prices of commodities to move downward, but they did not have the courage to take any action which would reduce either welfare benefits or wages. To the contrary, they continued to bid for votes with promises of still more socialism and easy credit. Prices continued to rise.

---

1. The government hedged even on this provision. Only bars of gold bullion were available for redemption, not coins. This insured that gold would not circulate as money and that it would be used almost exclusively for large-scale international transactions.

ENGLAND IN DEPRESSION

With the value of the pound set artificially high in order to sustain prices, wages, and profit levels, the cost of British exports also became high, and they ceased to be competitive in world markets. With exports in decline, the amount of money coming into the country also declined. England became a debtor nation, which means that her payments to other countries were larger than her income from those countries.

As pointed out in chapter five, if an individual spends more than his income, he must either increase his income, dip into savings, sell off assets, create counterfeit, or borrow. The same is true of nations. England had already borrowed to the limit of her credit and was rapidly exhausting her savings in order to continue purchasing foreign goods to sustain the high standard of living to which she had grown accustomed. She couldn't counterfeit because payments for these imports had to be settled in gold, which meant that, as her national savings were spent, her gold supply moved out of the country. The handwriting was on the wall. If this process continued, the nation soon would be broke. It was a situation, incidentally, which was amazingly parallel to what has plagued the United States since the end of Word War II, and for mostly the same reasons.

By March of 1919, England's trade was so depressed that she had no choice but to let the value of the pound "float," which means to seek its own level in response to supply and demand. Within a year it had dropped to $3.21, a loss of thirty-four per cent. Since the American dollar was the *de facto* world monetary standard at that time, receiving fewer dollars for each pound sterling meant that the pound was valued lower in all the markets of the world. The result was that the price Britishers had to pay for imported goods was becoming higher while the price she received for the export of her own goods was becoming lower. The British economy was, not only badly anemic, it was experiencing a monetary hangover from the vast inflation of World War I. In other words, it was undergoing a painful but, in the long run, healthy recovery and a return to reality.

Such a condition was intolerable to the monetary and political scientists who were determined to find a quick and painless remedy which would allow the binge to continue. Several emergency therapies were administered. The first was to use the Financial

Committee of the League of Nations—which England dominated—
to require all the other European nations to follow similar inflationary monetary policies. They were also required to establish what
was called the "gold exchange standard," a scheme whereby all
countries based their currency, not on gold, but on the pound sterling. In that way, they could all inflate together without causing a
disruptive flow of gold from one to the other, and England would
act as the regulator and guarantor of the system. In other words,
England used the power of her position within the League of Nations to establish the Bank of England as a master central bank for all
the other central banks of Europe. It was the prototype for what the
Cabal now is doing with Federal Reserve and the World Bank
within the framework of the United Nations.

PROBLEM OF AMERICAN PROSPERITY

Europe was well in hand, but that still left the United States to be
controlled. America had also inflated during the war but not nearly
as much. She also had a fractional gold standard, but the stockpile of
gold was very large and still growing. As long as America continued to exist as the producer of so many commodities that England
needed for import, and as long as the value of the dollar continued
to be high, the anemia of the pound sterling would continue.[1]

The therapy chosen for this problem was simple. Perform a
monetary transfusion from a healthy patient to the unhealthy one.
All the London financiers had to do was find a large and robust
specimen who, without asking too many questions, would be willing to become the donor. The specimen selected, of course, was
Uncle Sam himself. It was the prototype of the *transfer mechanism*,
previously described, which has been the life support keeping alive
the moribund Communist and Socialist countries since World War
II.

There are several ways the life blood of one nation can be trans-
fused to another. The most direct method, of course, is to make an
outright gift, such as the bizarre American ritual called foreign aid.
Another is to make a gift disguised as something else, such as need-
lessly stationing military bases abroad for the sole purpose of bolstering the foreign economy, or granting a loan to a foreign

---

1. For an overview of the foregoing developments, see "The Federal Reserve as A
Cartelization Device," by Murray N. Rothbard, in *Money in Crisis*, Barry N. Siegel,
ed. (New York: Ballinger, 1984), pp. 115–17.

government at below market rates or—worse—with the full expectation that the loan will never be repaid. But the third way is the most ingenious of them all: to have one nation deliberately inflate its currency at a rate greater than the other nation so that real purchasing power, in terms of international trade, moves from the more inflating to the less inflating nation. This is a method truly worthy of the monetary scientists. It is so subtle and so sophisticated that not one in a thousand would even think of it, much less object to it. It was, therefore, the ideal method chosen in 1925 to benefit England at the expense of America. As Professor Rothbard observed:

> In short, the American public was nominated to suffer the burdens of inflation and subsequent collapse [the crash of 1929] in order to maintain the British government and the British trade union movement in the style to which they insisted on becoming accustomed.[1]

At the inception of the Federal Reserve System, there had been a brief struggle for power but, within a few years, the contest was decisively won by the head of the New York Bank, Benjamin Strong. Strong, it will be recalled, previously had been head of Morgan's Bankers Trust Company and was one of the seven participants at the secret meeting on Jekyll Island. Professor Quigley reminds us that "Strong owed his career to the favor of the Morgan bank.... He became Governor of the Federal Reserve Bank of New York as the joint nominee of Morgan and Kuhn, Loeb and Company."[2]

Strong was the ideal choice for the cartel. Not the least of his qualifications was his alliance with the financial powers of London. When Montagu Norman was made the Governor of the Bank of England in 1920, there began a close personal relationship between the two central bankers which lasted until Strong's sudden death in 1928.

Norman was considered by many to be eccentric if not mentally unbalanced. Quigley says:

> Norman was a strange man whose mental outlook was one of successfully suppressed hysteria or even paranoia. He had no use for government and feared democracy. Both of these seemed to him to be threats to private banking, and thus to all that was proper and precious in human life.... When he rebuilt the Bank of England, he

---

1. Rothbard, *Crisis*, pp. 131–32.
2. Quigley, *Tragedy*, p. 326.

constructed it as a fortress prepared to defend itself against any popular revolt, with the sacred gold reserves hidden in deep vaults below the level of underground waters which could be released to cover them by pressing a button on the governor's desk. For much of his life, Norman rushed about the world by fast steamship, covering tens of thousands of miles each year, often travelling incognito, concealed by a black slouch hat and a long black cloak, under the assumed name of "Professor Skinner."...

Norman had a devoted colleague in Benjamin Strong.... In the 1920s, they were determined to use the financial power of Britain and of the United States to force all the major countries of the world to go on the gold standard [with an artificial value set for the benefit of England] and to operate it through central banks free from all political control, with all questions of international finance to be settled by agreements by such central banks without interference from governments.[1]

Strong and Norman spent many holidays together, sometimes in Bar Harbor, Maine, but usually in Southern France, and they crisscrossed the Atlantic on numerous other occasions to consult with each other on their plan for controlling the world economy. Lester Chandler tells us: "Their associations were so frequent and prolonged and their collaboration so close that it is still impossible to determine accurately their relative roles in developing some of the ideas and projects that they shared."[2] The Bank of England provided Strong with an office and a private secretary during his visits, and the two men kept in close contact with each other through the weekly exchange of private cables. All of these meetings and communiques were kept in strict secrecy. When their frequent visits drew inquiries from the press, the standard reply was that they were just friends getting together for recreation or informal chats. By 1926, the heads of the central banks of France and Germany were occasionally included in their meetings which, according to Norman's biographer, were "more secret than any ever held by Royal Arch Masons or by any Rosicrucian Order."[3]

---

1. Quigley, *Tragedy*, p. 326.
2. Lester V. Chandler, *Benjamin Strong, Central Banker* (Washington, D.C.: Brookings Institution, 1958, reprinted by Arno Press, A New York Times Company, 1978), p. 259.
3. John Hargrave, *Montagu Norman* (New York: Greystone Press, 1942), p. 108.

SECRET MEETING OF 1927

The culmination of these discussions took place at a secret meeting in 1927 at which it was agreed that the financial lifeblood of the American people would be donated for a massive transfusion to Great Britain. Galbraith sets the scene:

> On July 1, 1927, the *Mauretania* arrived in New York with two notable passengers, Montagu Norman, Governor of the Bank of England, and Hjalmar Schacht, head of the German Reichsbank.... The secrecy covering the visit was extreme and to a degree ostentatious. The names of neither of the great bankers appeared on the passenger list. Neither, on arriving, met with the press....
>
> In New York the two men were joined by Charles Rist, the Deputy Governor of the Banque de France, and they went into conference with Benjamin Strong, the Governor of the Federal Reserve Bank of New York....
>
> The principle, or in any case the ultimately important, sub· · ʳ discussion was the persistently weak reserve position of the Bank of England. This, the bankers thought, could be helped if the Federal Reserve System would ease interest rates, encourage lending. Holders of gold would then seek the higher returns from keeping their metal in London. And, in time, higher prices in the United States would ease the competitive position of British industry and labor.[1]

Galbraith speaks with soft phrases to cushion a harsh reality. What he is saying is that the purpose of the meeting was to finalize a plan whereby the Governor of the Federal Reserve System was to deliberately create inflation in the U.S. so that American prices would rise, making U.S. goods less competitive in world markets and causing American gold to move to the Bank of England. Governor Strong needed little convincing. That is precisely what he and Norman had planned to do all along and, in fact, he had already begun to implement the plan. The purpose of inviting the Germans and the French to the meeting was to enlist their agreement to create inflation in their countries as well. Schacht and Rist would have no part of it and left the meeting early, leaving Strong and Norman to work out the final details between them.

Strong was more concerned about British fortunes than American. In a letter written in May of 1924 to Secretary of the Treasury Andrew Mellon, he discussed the necessity of lowering American interest rates as a step toward money expansion with the

---

1. Galbraith, pp. 174–75.

objective of raising American prices relative to those in Great Britain. He acknowledged that the goal was to protect England from having to cut back on wages, profits, and welfare. He said:

> At the present time it is probably true that British prices for goods internationally dealt in are as a whole, roughly, in the neighborhood of 10 percent above our prices, and one of the preliminaries to the re-establishment of gold payment by Great Britain will be to facilitate a gradual readjustment of these price levels *before* monetary reform is undertaken. In other words, this means some small advance in prices here and possibly some small decline in their prices....
>
> The burden of this readjustment must fall more largely upon us than upon them. It will be difficult politically and socially for the British Government and the Bank of England to face a price liquidation in England ... in face of the fact that trade is poor and they have over a million unemployed people receiving government aid.[1]

BRINGING DOWN THE DOLLAR

The Mandrake Mechanism of the Federal Reserve went into high gear on behalf of the Bank of England in 1924, several years before the historic meeting between Strong, Norman, and Rist. There were two great surges of monetary expansion. The first came with the monetization of $492 million in bonds plus almost twice as much in banker's acceptances. The second burst of inflation came in the latter half of 1927, immediately following the secret meeting between Strong, Norman, Schacht, and Rist. It involved the funding of $225 million in government bonds plus $220 million in banker's acceptances, for a total increase in bank reserves of $445 million. At the same time, the rediscount rate to member banks (the interest rate they pay to borrow from the Fed) was lowered from 4 to 3.5 per cent, making it easier for those banks to acquire additional "reserves" out of which they could create even more fiat dollars. The amount created on top of that by the commercial banks is about five and a-half times the amount created by the Fed, which means a total money flood in excess of $10 billion in just six years.[2]

---

1. Chandler, pp. 282–84.
2. Approximately $1,328,000,000 in the first burst, including both bonds and acceptances, plus $445,000,000 in the second burst equals $1,773,000,000. This amount multiplied by 5.5 equals $9,751,500,000. Add the original $1,773,000,000 used as a base, and the total is $11,524,500,000. This estimate is reasonably close to the figure of $10,661,000,000 published by the Fed itself, which represents the growth in total deposits and currency in circulation during that period. See "Deposits and Currency," p. 34.

Throughout this period, the demand by the System for government bonds and acceptances pushed interest rates down.[1] As anticipated, people with gold then preferred to send it to London where it could earn a higher yield, and America's gold supply began to move abroad. Furthermore, as inflation began to eat its way into the purchasing power of the dollar, the prices of American-made goods began to rise in world markets making them less competitive; U.S. exports began to decline; unemployment began to rise; low interest rates and easy credit led to speculation in the securities markets; and the system lunged full speed ahead toward the Great Crash of 1929. But that part of the story must wait for another chapter.

The technician who actually drafted the final version of the Federal Reserve Act was H. Parker Willis. After the System was created, he was appointed as First Secretary of the Board of Governors. By 1929, he had become disillusioned with the cartel and, in an article published in *The North American Review*, he wrote:

> In the autumn of 1926 a group of bankers, among whom was one with a world famous name, were sitting at a table in a Washington hotel. One of them raised the question whether the low discount rates of the System were not likely to encourage speculation. "Yes," replied the conspicuous figure referred to, "they will, but that cannot be helped. It is the price we must pay for helping Europe."[2]

There can be little doubt that the banker in question was J.P. (Jack) Morgan, Jr. It was Jack who was imbued with English tradition from the earliest age, whose financial empire had its roots in London, whose family business was saved by the Bank of England, who spent six months out of every year of his later life as a resident of England, who had openly insisted that his junior partners demonstrate a "loyalty to Britain,"[3] and who had directed the Council on Foreign Relations, the American branch of a secret society dedicated to the supremacy of British tradition and political

---

1. When an item is in demand, its price goes up. In the case of bonds and other interest-bearing debt instruments, the price is expressed in *reverse* of its interest yield. The higher the price, the lower the interest. In other words, the higher the price, the more one has to pay to obtain the same dollar return in interest. Therefore, when the Fed creates an artificial demand for bonds or commercial paper, such as acceptances, the interest yield on these items goes down, which makes them more costly as an investment.

2. "The Failure of the Federal Reserve," by H. Parker Willis, *The North American Review*, May, 1929, p. 553.

3. Chernow, p. 167.

power. It is only with that background that one can fully appreciate the willingness to sacrifice American interests. Indeed, "it is the price we must pay for helping Europe."

In spite of the growing signs of crisis in the American economy, Morgan's protégé, Benjamin Strong, was nonetheless pleased with his accomplishment. In a letter written in 1929 to Parker Gilbert, who was the American Agent for Reparations, he said:

> Our policy of the last four years, up to this January, has been effective in accomplishing the purpose for which it was designed. It has enabled monetary reorganization to be completed in Europe, which otherwise would have been impossible. It was undertaken with the well recognized hazard that we were liable to encounter a big speculation and some expansion of credit.... Our course was perfectly obvious. We had to undertake it. The conditions permitted it, and the possibility of damage abroad was at a minimum.[1]

Damage *abroad*? What about damage *at home*? It is clear that Strong saw little difference between the two. He was the forerunner of the internationalists who have operated the Federal Reserve ever since. He viewed the United States as but one piece in a complex world financial structure, and what was good for the world was good for America. And, oh yes, what was good for England was good for the world!

THE BRITISH-AMERICAN UNION

It is one of the least understood realities of modern history that many of America's most prominent political and financial figures—then as now—have been willing to sacrifice the best interests of the United States in order to further their goal of creating a one-world government. The strategy has remained unchanged since the formation of Cecil Rhodes' society and its offspring, the Round Table Groups. It is to merge the English-speaking nations into a single political entity, while at the same time creating similar groupings for other geopolitical regions. After this is accomplished, all of these groupings are to be amalgamated into a global government, the so-called Parliament of Man. And guess who is planning to control that government from behind the scenes.

This strategy was expressed aptly by Andrew Carnegie in his book, *Triumphant Democracy*. Expressing concern that England was in decline as a world power, he said:

---

1. Chandler, p. 458. For additional clarification, also see pp. 459–63.

Reunion with her American children is the only sure way to prevent continued decline.... Whatever obstructs reunion I oppose; whatever promotes reunion I favor. I judge all political questions from this standpoint....

The Parliament of Man and the Federation of the World have already been hailed by the poet, and these mean a step much farther in advance of the proposed reunion of Britain and America.... I say that as surely as the sun in the heavens once shone upon Britain and America united, so surely is it one morning to rise, shine upon, and greet again the reunited state, "The British-American Union."[1]

SUMMARY

After the Civil War, America experienced a series of expansions and contractions of the money supply leading directly to economic booms and busts. This was the result of the creation of fiat money by a banking system which, far from being free and competitive, was a half-way house to central banking. Throughout the chaos, one banking firm, the House of Morgan, was able to prosper out of the failure of others. Morgan had close ties with the financial structure and culture of England and was, in fact, more British than American. Events suggest the possibility that Morgan and Company was in concealed partnership with the House of Rothschild throughout most of this period.

Benjamin Strong was a Morgan man and was appointed as the first Governor of the Federal Reserve Bank of New York which rapidly assumed dominance over the System. Strong immediately entered into close alliance with Montagu Norman, Governor of the Bank of England, to save the English economy from depression. This was accomplished by deliberately creating inflation in the U.S. which caused an outflow of gold, a loss of foreign markets, unemployment, and speculation in the stock market, all of which were factors that propelled America into the crash of 1929 and the great depression of the 30s.

Although not covered in this chapter, it must be remembered that the same forces were responsible for American involvement in both world wars to provide the economic and military resources England needed to survive. Furthermore, the key players in this

---

1. Andrew Carnegie, *Triumphant Democracy* (New York: Charles Scribner's Sons, 1893), pp. 530–49. This is a revised edition of the book which was originally written in 1886. Earlier editions do not contain these words.

action were men who were part of the network of a secret society established by Cecil Rhodes for the expansion of the British empire.

Chapter Twenty-One
COMPETITION IS A SIN

The story of how the New York investment bankers formed a cartel to avoid competition; the drafting of proposed legislation to legalize that cartel; the strategy to camouflage the true nature of the legislation; the failure of the deception and the defeat of the bill.

We have travelled to many points on a large circle of time and now are reapproaching the journey to Jekyll Island where this book began.

In the last chapter, we saw how the expansion and contraction of the money supply following the Civil War led to a series of booms and busts. We saw how the firm of J.P. Morgan & Company, with help from financiers in London, was able to reap great profits from both sides of those cycles but particularly from the recessions. At that point, we jumped ahead in time to examine how J.P. Morgan and other leading American financiers were closely aligned with British interests. We also saw how, in the 1920s, the American dollar was deliberately weakened by Morgan agents within the Federal Reserve System in order to prop up the sagging British economy. Let us return now to the point of departure and allow our cast to resume playing out that most important prior scene: the actual creation of the Federal Reserve System itself.

HALF-WAY HOUSE TO CENTRAL BANKING

Historians seeking to justify governmental control of the monetary system have claimed that the booms and busts that occurred during this period were the result of free and competitive banking. As we have seen, however, these destructive cycles were the direct result of the creation and then extinguishing of fiat money through a system of federally chartered national banks—dominated by a handful of firms on Wall Street—which constituted a half-way house to central banking. None of these banks were truly free of state control nor were they competitive in the traditional sense of the word. They were in fact subsidized by the government and had many monopolistic privileges. From the perspective of bankers on Wall Street, however, there was a great deal more to be desired. For one thing, America still did not have a "lender of last resort." That is banker language for a full-blown central bank with the power to create unlimited amounts of fiat money which can be rushed to the aid of any individual bank that is under siege by its depositors wanting their money back. Having a lender of last resort is the only way a bank can create money out of nothing and still be protected from a potential "run" by its customers. In other words, it is the means by which the public is forced to pay a hidden tax of inflation to cover the shortfall of fractional-reserve banking. That is why the so-called virtue of a lender of last resort is taught with great reverence today in virtually all academic institutions offering degrees in banking and finance. It is one of the means by which the system perpetuates itself.

The banks could now inflate more radically and more in unison than before the war but, when they pushed too far and too fast, their bank-generated booms still collapsed into recessions. While this could be highly profitable to the banks, it was also precarious. As the American economy expanded in size, the magnitude of the booms and busts increased also, and it was becoming more and more difficult for firms like Morgan & Company to safely ride out the storm. There was a growing dread that the *next* collapse might be more than even they could handle.

In addition to these concerns was the fact that many state banks, mostly in the developing Southern and Western states, had elected not to join the national banking system and, consequently, had escaped control by the Wall-Street-Washington axis. As the population expanded south and westward, much of the nation's banking moved likewise, and the new banks were becoming an increasing source of competition to the New York power center. By 1896, the number of non-national banks had grown to sixty-one per cent, and they already held fifty-four per cent of the country's total banking deposits. By 1913, the year in which the Federal Reserve Act was passed, those numbers had swelled to seventy-one per cent non-national banks holding fifty-seven per cent of the nation's deposits.[1] Something had to be done to stop this movement.

---

1. See Kolko, *Triumph*, p. 140.

Additional competition was developing from the trend in industry to finance itself from profits rather than borrowed capital. Between 1900 and 1910, seventy per cent of American corporate growth was funded internally, making industry increasingly independent of the banks. What the bankers wanted—and what many businessmen wanted also—was a more "flexible" or "elastic" money supply which would allow them to create enough of it at any point in time so as to be able to drive interest rates downward at will. That would make loans to businessmen so attractive they would have little choice but to return to the bankers' stable.

TRUSTS AND CARTELS REPLACE COMPETITION

One more problem facing Wall Street was the fact that the biggest investment houses, such as Morgan & Company and Kuhn, Loeb & Company, although they remained as competitors, were by this time so large they had ceased doing serious battle against each other. The concept of trusts and cartels had dawned in America and, to those who already had made it to the top, joint ventures, market sharing, price fixing, and mergers were far more profitable than free-enterprise competition. Ron Chernow explains:

> Wall Street was snowballing into one big, Morgan-dominated institution. In December 1909, Pierpont had bought a majority stake in the Equitable Life Assurance Society from Thomas Fortune Ryan. This gave him strong influence over America's three biggest insurance companies—Mutual Life, Equitable, and New York Life.... His Bankers Trust had taken over three other banks. In 1909, he had gained control of Guaranty Trust, which through a series of mergers he converted into America's largest trust.... The core Money Trust group included J.P. Morgan and Company, First National Bank, and National City Bank....
>
> Wall Street bankers incestuously swapped seats on each others boards. Some banks had so many overlapping directors it was hard to separate them.... The banks also shared large equity stakes in each other....
>
> Why didn't banks just merge instead of carrying out the charade of swapping shares and board members? Most were private partnerships or closely held banks and could have done so. The answer harked back to traditional American antipathy against concentrated financial power. The Morgan-First National-National City trio feared public retribution if it openly declared its allegiance.[1]

---

1. Chernow, pp. 152–53.

Interlocking directorates and other forms of hidden control were far more safe than open consolidation but they, too, had their limitations. For one thing, they could not penetrate the barriers of similar competitive groupings. As these combines became larger and larger, ways were sought to bring *them* together at the top rather than to capture the corporate entities which comprised them. Thus was born the concept of a cartel, a "community of interest" among businessmen in the same field, a mechanism for coming together as partners at a high level and to reduce or eliminate altogether the harsh necessity of competition.

All cartels, however, have an internal self-destruct mechanism. Sooner or later, one of the members inevitably becomes dissatisfied with his agreed-upon piece of the pie. He decides to compete once again and seeks a greater share of the market. It was quickly recognized that the only way to prevent this from happening was to use the police power of government to enforce the cartel agreement. The procedure called for the passage of laws disguised as measures to protect the consumer but which actually worked to ensure the elimination of competition. Henry P. Davison, who was a Morgan partner, put it bluntly when he told a Congressional committee in 1912: "I would rather have regulation and control than free competition."[1] John D. Rockefeller was even more to the point in one of his often repeated comments: "Competition is a sin."[2]

This trend was not unique to the banking industry. Ron Paul and Lewis Lehrman provide the historical perspective:

> After 1896 and 1900, then, America entered a progressive and predominantly Republican era. Compulsory cartelization in the name of "progressivism" began to invade every aspect of American economic life. The railroads had begun the parade with the formation of the ICC in the 1880s, but now field after field was being centralized and cartelized in the name of "efficiency," "stability," "progress," and the general welfare.... In particular, various big business groups, led by the J.P. Morgan interests, often gathered in the National Civic Federation and other think tanks and pressure organizations, saw that the voluntary cartels and the industrial merger movements of the late

---

1. Quoted by Gabriel Kolko, *Main Currents in Modern American History* (New York: Harper & Row, 1976), p. 13.
2. Quoted by William Hoffman, *David: A Report on a Rockefeller* (New York: Lyle Stewart, Inc., 1971), p. 29.

1890s had failed to achieve monopoly prices in industry. Therefore, they decided to turn to governments, state and federal, to curb the winds of competition and to establish forms of compulsory cartels, in the name, of course, of "curbing big business monopoly" and advancing the general welfare.[1]

The challenge no longer was how to overcome one's adversaries, but how to keep new ones from entering the field. When John D. used his enormous profits from Standard Oil to take control of the Chase National Bank, and his brother, William, bought the National City Bank of New York, Wall Street had yet one more gladiator in the financial arena. Morgan found that he had no choice except to allow the Rockefellers into the club but, now that they were in, they all agreed that the influx of competitors had to be stopped. And that was to be the hidden purpose of federal legislation and government control. Gabriel Kolko explains:

> The sheer magnitude of many of the mergers, culminating in U.S. Steel, soon forced him [Morgan] to modify his stand, though at times he would have preferred total control. More important, by 1898 he could not ignore the massive power of new financial competitors and had to treat them with deference. Standard Oil Company, utilizing National City Bank for its investments, had fixed resources substantially larger than Morgan's, and by 1899 was ready to move into the general economy.... The test came, of course, in the Northern Securities battle, which was essentially an expensive draw. Morgan and Standard paid deference to each other thereafter, and mutual toleration among bankers increased sharply.... A benign armed neutrality, rather than positive affection, is as much a reason as any for the high number of interlocks among the five major New York banking houses.[2]

Writing in the year 1919, from the perspective of an inside view of Wall Street at that time, John Moody completes the picture:

> This remarkable welding together of great corporate interests could not, of course, have been accomplished if the "masters of capital" in Wall Street had not themselves during the same period become more closely allied. The rivalry of interests which was so characteristic during the reorganization period a few years before had very largely disappeared. Although the two great groups of financiers, represented on the one hand by Morgan and his allies and on the other by the Standard Oil forces, were still distinguishable, they were now

1. Paul and Lehrman, p. 119.
2. Kolko, *Triumph*, pp. 143–44.

working in practical harmony on the basis of a sort of mutual "community of interest" of their own. Thus the control of capital and credit through banking resources tended to become concentrated in the hands of fewer and fewer men.... Before long it could be said, indeed, that two rival banking groups no longer existed, but that one vast and harmonious banking power had taken their place.[1]

THE ALDRICH-VREELAND ACT

The monetary contractions of 1879 and 1893 were handled by Wall Street fairly easily and without government intervention, but the crisis of 1907 pushed their resources close to the abyss. It became clear that two changes had to be made: all remnants of banking competition now had to be totally eliminated and replaced by a national cartel; and far greater sums of fiat money had to be made available to the banks to protect them from future runs by depositors. There was now no question that Congress would have to be brought in as a partner in order to use the power of government to accomplish these objectives. Kolko continues:

> The crisis of 1907, on the other hand, found the combined banking structure of New York inadequate to meet the challenge, and chastened any obstreperous financial powers who thought they might build their fortunes independently of the entire banking community.... The nation had grown too large, banking had become too complex. Wall Street, humbled and almost alone, turned from its own resources to the national government.[2]

The first step in this direction was openly a stop-gap measure. In 1908, Congress passed the Aldrich-Vreeland Act which, basically, accomplished two objectives. First, it authorized the national banks to issue an emergency currency, called script, to substitute for regular money when they found themselves unable to pay their depositors. Script had been used by the bank clearing houses during the panic of 1907 with partial success, but it had been a bold experiment with no legal foundation. Now Congress made it quite legal and, as Galbraith observed, "The new legislation regularized these arrangements. This could be done against the security of sundry bonds and commercial loans—these could, in effect, be turned into cash without being sold."[3]

---

1. Moody, pp. 117–18, 150
2. Kolko, *Triumph*, p. 144.
3. This legalized script was used only once—in 1914 at the outbreak of World War I. See Galbraith, p. 120.

The second and perhaps most important feature of the Act was to create a National Monetary Commission to study the problems of American banking and then make recommendations to Congress on how to stabilize the monetary system. The commission consisted of nine senators and nine representatives. The Vice-Chairman was Representative Edward Vreeland, a banker from the Buffalo area. The chairman, of course, was Senator Nelson Aldrich. From the start, it was obvious that the Commission was a sham. Aldrich conducted virtually a one-man show. The so-called fact-finding body held no official meetings for almost two years while Aldrich toured Europe consulting with the top central bankers of England, France, and Germany. Three-hundred thousand tax dollars were spent on these junkets, and the only tangible product of the Commission's work was thirty-eight massive volumes of the history of European banking. None of the members of the Commission were ever consulted regarding the official recommendations issued by Aldrich in their name. Actually, these were the work of Aldrich and six men who were not even members of the Commission, and their report was drafted, not in a bare Congressional conference room in Washington, but in a plush private hunting resort in Georgia.

And this event finally brings us back to that cold, blustery night at the New Jersey railway station where seven men, representing one-fourth of the wealth of the world, boarded the Aldrich private car for a clandestine journey to Jekyll Island.

THE JEKYLL ISLAND PLAN

As summarized in the opening chapter of this book, the purpose of that meeting was to work out a plan to achieve five primary objectives:

1. Stop the growing influence of small, rival banks and to insure that control over the nation's financial resources would remain in the hands of those present;
2. Make the money supply more elastic in order to reverse the trend of private capital formation and to recapture the industrial loan market;
3. Pool the meager reserves of all the nation's banks into one large reserve so that at least a few of them could protect themselves from currency drains and bank runs;

4. Shift the inevitable losses from the owners of the banks to the taxpayers;
5. Convince Congress that the scheme was a measure to protect the public.

It was decided that the first two objectives could be achieved simply by drafting the proper technical language into a cartel agreement and then re-working the vocabulary into legislative phraseology. The third and fourth could be achieved by including in that legislation the establishment of a lender of last resort; in other words, a true central bank with the ability to create unlimited amounts of fiat money. These were mostly technical matters and, although there was some disagreement on a few minor points, generally they were content to follow the advice of Paul Warburg, the man who had the most experience in these matters and who was regarded as the group's theoretician. The fifth objective was the critical one, and there was much discussion on how to achieve it.

To convince Congress and the public that the establishment of a banking cartel was, somehow, a measure to protect the public, the Jekyll Island strategists laid down the following plan of action:

1. Do not call it a cartel nor even a central bank.
2. Make it look like a government agency.
3. Establish regional branches to create the appearance of decentralization, not dominated by Wall Street banks.
4. Begin with a conservative structure including many sound banking principles knowing that the provisions can be quietly altered or removed in subsequent years.
5. Use the anger caused by recent panics and bank failures to create popular demand for monetary reform.
6. Offer the Jekyll Island plan as though it were in response to that need.
7. Employ university professors to give the plan the appearance of academic approval.
8. Speak out *against* the plan to convince the public that Wall Street bankers do not want it.

A CENTRAL BANK BY ANY OTHER NAME

Americans would never have accepted the Federal Reserve System if they had known that it was half cartel and half central bank. Even though the concept of government protectionism was rapidly gaining acceptance in business, academic, and political circles, the idea of cartels, trusts, and restraint of free competition was still quite alien to the average voter. And within the halls of Congress, any forthright proposal for either a cartel or a central bank would have been soundly defeated. Congressman Everis Hayes of California warned: "Our people have set their faces like steel against a central bank."[1] Senator John Shafroth of Colorado declared: "The Democratic Party is opposed to a central bank."[2] The monetary scientists on Jekyll Island decided, therefore, to devise a name for their new creature which would avoid the word *bank* altogether and which would conjure the image of the federal government itself. And to create the deception that there would be no concentration of power in the large New York banks, the original plan calling for a central bank was replaced by a proposal for a network of regional institutions which supposedly would share and diffuse that power.

Nathaniel Wright Stephenson, Senator Aldrich's biographer, tells us: "Aldrich entered the discussion at Jekyll Island an ardent convert to the idea of a central bank. His desire was to transplant the system of one of the great European banks, say the Bank of England, bodily to America."[3] Galbraith explains further: "It was his [Senator Aldrich's] thought to outflank the opposition by having not one central bank but many. And the word bank would itself be avoided."[4]

Frank Vanderlip tells us the regional concept was merely window dressing and that the network was always intended to operate as one central bank. He said: "The law as enacted provided for twelve banks instead of one,... but the intent of the law was to coordinate the twelve through the Federal Reserve Board in Washington, so that in effect they would operate as a central bank."[5]

If not using the word *bank* was essential to the Jekyll Island plan, avoiding the word *cartel* was even more so. Yet, the cartel nature of the proposed central bank was obvious to any astute observer. In an address before the American Bankers Association,

---

1. *Congressional Record*, pt. 5, 1913, p. 4655.
2. *Congressional Record*, pt. 6, 1913, p. 6021.
3. Stephenson, p. 378.
4. Galbraith, p. 122.
5. Vanderlip, "From Farm Boy to Financier," p. 72.

Aldrich laid it out plainly. He said: "The organization proposed is not a bank, but a cooperative union of all the banks of the country for definite purposes."[1] Two years later, in a speech before that same group of bankers, A. Barton Hepburn of Chase National Bank was even more candid. He said: "The measure recognizes and adopts the principles of a central bank. Indeed, if it works out as the sponsors of the law hope, it will make all incorporated banks together joint owners of a central dominating power."[2] It would be difficult to find a better definition of the word *cartel* than that.

The plan to structure the Creature conservatively at the start and then to remove the safeguards later was the brainchild of Paul Warburg. The creation of a powerful Federal Reserve Board was also his idea as a means by which the regional branches could be absorbed into a central bank with control safely in New York. Professor Edwin Seligman, a member of the international banking family of J&W Seligman, and head of the Department of Economics at Columbia University, explains and praises the plan:

> It was in my study that Mr. Warburg first conceived the idea of presenting his views to the public.[3]... In its fundamental features the Federal Reserve Act is the work of Mr. Warburg more than any other man in the country.... The existence of a Federal Reserve Board creates, in everything but in name, a real central bank.... Mr. Warburg had a practical object in view.... It was incumbent on him to remember that the education of the country must be gradual and that a large part of the task was to break down prejudices and remove suspicion. His plans therefore contain all sorts of elaborate suggestions designed to guard the public against fancied dangers and to persuade the country that the general scheme was at all practicable. It was the hope of Mr. Warburg that with the lapse of time it may be possible to eliminate

1. Krooss, Vol. III, 1969 edition, p. 1202.
2. Quoted by Kolko, *Triumph*, p. 235.
3. Most historians share Seligman's view regarding Warburg's seminal role in the creation of the Federal Reserve System. Certain participants in the drama, however, apparently eager to capture some of the spotlight of fame for themselves, are in vigorous disagreement. For example, William McAdoo, Secretary of the Treasury at the time, says: "This assertion is so completely erroneous that it must have emanated from ignorance rather than mendacity." See McAdoo, p. 281. Competing egos notwithstanding, an objective reading of the record leads to the conclusion that, while others no doubt provided great input in the areas of technical drafts and political negotiations, the *essence* of the plan, its overall *concept* and the *rationale* that was put forward to sell the plan to Congress was essentially the product of Warburg's twisted genius.

from the law not a few clauses which were inserted largely, at his suggestion, for educational purposes.[1]

THE ALDRICH BILL

The first draft of the Jekyll Island plan was submitted to the Senate by Nelson Aldrich but, due to the Senator's unexpected illness when he returned to Washington, it was actually written by Frank Vanderlip and Benjamin Strong.[2] Although it was co-authored by Congressman Vreeland, it immediately became known as the Aldrich Bill. Vreeland, by his own admission, had little to do with it either, but his willingness to be a team player in the game of national deception was of great value. Writing in the August 25, 1910, issue of *The Independent*, which incidentally was owned by Aldrich himself and was anything *but* independent, Vreeland said: "The bank I propose.... is an ideal method of fighting monopoly. It could not possibly itself become a monopoly and it would prevent other banks combining into monopolies. With earnings limited to four and one-half per cent, there could not be a monopoly."[3]

What an amazing statement. It is brilliantly insidious because of the half truths it contains. It is true that monopolies cannot—or at least *do* not—operate at four and one-half per cent interest. But it is untrue that the Federal Reserve banks were to be held to that lowly rate. It is true that four per cent was the stated amount they would earn on the stock purchased in the System, but it is also true that the real profits were to be made, not from stock dividends, but from the harvesting of interest payments on fiat money. To this was to be added the profits made possible from operating on smaller safety margins yet still being protected from bankruptcy. Furthermore, being on the inside of the nation's central bank would make them privy to the important money-making data and decisions long before their competitors. The profits that could be derived from such an advantage would be equal to or even greater than those from the Mandrake Mechanism. It is true that the Federal Reserve was to be a private institution, but it is certainly not true

---

1. Edwin Seligman, Proceedings of the Academy of Political Science, Vol IV, No. 4 (New York: 1914), pp. 3–6.
2. Vanderlip, "From Farm Boy to Financier," p. 72.
3. "A Better System of Banking and Currency," by Edward B. Vreeland, *The Independent*, August 25, 1910, p. 394.

that this was to mark the disappearance of the government from the banking business. In fact, it was just the opposite, because it marked the *appearance* of the government as a partner with private bankers and as the enforcer of their cartel agreement. Government would now become more deeply involved than ever before in our history.

Half truths and propaganda notwithstanding, the organizational structure proposed by the Aldrich Bill was similar in many ways to the old Bank of the United States. It was to have the right to convert federal debt into money, to lend that money to the government, to control the affairs of regional banks, and to be the depository of government funds. The dissimilarities were in those provisions which gave the Creature *more* privilege and power than the older central bank. The most important of these was the right to create the official money of the United States. For the first time in our history, the paper notes of a banking institution became legal tender, not only for public debts, but for private ones as well. Henceforth, anyone refusing to accept these notes would be sent to prison. The words "The United States of America" were to appear on the face of every note along with the great seal of the United States Treasury. And, of course, the signature of the Treasurer himself would be printed in a conspicuous location. All of this was designed to convince the public that the new institution was surely an agency of the government itself.

TURNING THE OPPOSITION AGAINST ITSELF

Now that the basic strategy was in place and a specific bill had been drafted, the next step was to create popular support for it. This was the critical part of the plan and it required the utmost finesse. The task actually was made easier by the fact that there was a great deal of genuine opposition to the concentration of financial power on Wall Street. Two of the most outspoken critics at that time were Wisconsin Senator Robert LaFollette and Minnesota Congressman Charles Lindbergh. Hardly a week passed without one of them delivering a scathing speech against what they called "the money trust" which was responsible, they said, for deliberately creating economic booms and busts in order to reap the profits of salvaging foreclosed homes, farms and businesses. If anyone doubted that such a trust really existed, their skepticism was abruptly terminated when LaFollette publicly charged that the entire country was controlled by just fifty men. The monetary scientists were not dismayed nor did they even bother to deny it. In fact, when George F. Baker, who was a partner of J.P. Morgan, was asked by reporters for his reaction to LaFollette's claim, he replied that it was totally absurd. He knew from personal knowledge, he said, that the number was not more than eight![1]

The public was, of course, outraged, and the pressure predictably mounted for Congress to do something. The monetary scientists were fully prepared to turn this reaction to their own advantage. The strategy was simple: (1) set up a special Congressional committee to investigate the money trust; (2) make sure the committee is staffed by friends of the trust itself; and (3) conceal the full scope of the trust's operation while revealing just enough to intensify the public clamor for reform. Once the political climate was hot enough, then the Aldrich Bill could be put forward, supposedly as the answer to that need.

This strategy was certainly not new. As Congressman Lindbergh explained:

> Ever since the Civil War, Congress has allowed the bankers to completely control financial legislation. The membership of the Finance Committee in the Senate and the Committee on Banking and Currency in the House, has been made up of bankers, their agents and attorneys. These committees have controlled the nature of the bills to be reported, the extent of them, and the debates that were to be held on them when they were being considered in the Senate and the House. No one, not on the committee, is recognized ... unless someone favorable to the committee has been arranged for.[2]

THE PUJO COMMITTEE

The Pujo Committee was a perfect example of this kind of chicanery. It was a subcommittee of the House Committee on Banking and Currency and it was given the awesome responsibility of conducting the famous "Money Trust" investigation of 1912. Its chairman was Arsene Pujo of Louisiana who, true to form, was regarded by many as a spokesman for the "Oil Trust." The hearings dragged on for eight months producing volumes of dry statistics and self-serving testimony of the great Wall Street bankers themselves. At no time were the financiers asked any questions about

---

1. Mullins, p. 16.
2. Lindbergh, p. 76.

their affairs with foreign investment houses. Nor were they asked about their response to competition from new banks. There were no questions about their plan to protect the speculative banks from currency drains; or their motive for wanting artificially low interest rates; or their formula for passing on their losses to the taxpayer. The public was given the impression that Congress was really prying off the lid of scandal and corruption, but the reality was more like a fireside chat between old friends. No matter what vagaries or absurdities fell from the bankers' lips, it was accepted without contest.

These hearings were conducted largely as a result of the public accusations made by Congressmen Lindbergh and Senator LaFollette. Yet, when they requested to appear before the Committee, both of them were denied access. The only witnesses to testify were the bankers themselves and their friends. Kolko tells us:

> Fortunately for the reformers, the Pujo Committee swung into high gear in its investigation of the Money Trust during the summer of 1912, and for eight months frightened the nation with its awesome, if inconclusive, statistics on the power of Wall Street over the nation's economy.... Five banking firms, the elaborate tables of the committee showed, held 341 directorships in 112 corporations with an aggregate capitalization of over $22 billion. The evidence seemed conclusive, and the nation was suitably frightened into realizing that reform of the banking system was urgent—presumably to bring Wall Street under control....
>
> The orgy of Wall Street was resurrected by the newspapers, who quite ignored the fact that the biggest advocates of banking reform were the bankers themselves, bankers with a somewhat different view of the problem.... Yet it was largely the Pujo hearings that made the topic of banking reform a serious one.[1]

Kolko has touched upon an interesting point. Almost no one put any significance to the fact that some of the biggest bankers on Wall Street were the first marchers to lead the parade for banking reform. The most conspicuous among these was Paul Warburg of Kuhn, Loeb & Company who, for seven years prior to passage of the Federal Reserve Act, travelled around the country doing nothing but giving "reform" speeches and writing scholarly articles for the media, including an eleven-part series for *The New York Times*. Spokesmen from the houses of Morgan and Rockefeller

---

1. Kolko, *Triumph*, p. 220.

joined in and made regular appearances before professional and political bodies echoing the call for reform. Yet no one paid any attention to the unmistakable odor of fish.

ENLISTING THE HELP OF ACADEMIA

The speeches and articles by big-name bankers were never intended to sway the public at large. They served the function of putting forth the basic arguments and the technical details which were to be the starting point for the work of others who could not be accused of having self-serving motives. To carry the message to the voters, it was decided that representatives from the world of academia should be enlisted to provide the necessary aura of respectability and intellectual objectivity. For that purpose, the banks contributed a sum of $5 million to a special "educational" fund, and much of that money found its way into the environs of three universities: Princeton, Harvard, and the University of Chicago, all of which had been recipients of large endowments from the captains of industry and finance.

It was precisely at this time that the study of "economics" was becoming a new and acceptable field, and it was not difficult to find talented but slightly hungry professors who, in return for a grant or a prestigious appointment, were eager to expound the virtues of the Jekyll Island plan. Not only was such academic pursuit financially rewarding, it also provided national recognition for them as pioneers in the new field of economics. Galbraith says:

> Under Aldrich's direction a score or more of studies of monetary institutions in the United States and, more particularly, in other countries were commissioned from the emergent economics profession. It is at least possible that the reverence in which the Federal Reserve System has since been held by economists owes something to the circumstance that so many who pioneered in the profession participated also in its [the System's] birth.[1]

The principal accomplishment of the bank's educational fund was to create an organization called the National Citizens' League. Although it was entirely financed and controlled by the banks under the personal guidance of Paul Warburg, it presented itself merely as a group of concerned citizens seeking banking reform. The function of the organization was to disseminate hundreds of

---

1. Galbraith, p. 121.

thousands of "educational" pamphlets, to organize letter-writing campaigns to Congressmen, to supply quotable material to the news media, and in other ways to create the illusion of grass-roots support for the Jekyll Island plan.

Nathaniel Stephenson, in his biography of Nelson Aldrich, says: "The league was non-partisan. It was careful to abstain from emphasizing Senator Aldrich.... First and last, hundreds of thousands of dollars were spent by the league in popularizing financial science."[1]

The man chosen to head up that effort was an economics professor by the name of J. Laurence Laughlin. Kolko says that "Laughlin, nominally very orthodox in his commitment to laissez faire theory, was nevertheless a leading academic advocate of banking regulation ... and was sensitive to the needs of banking as well as the realities of politics."[2] Did his appointment bring intellectual objectivity to the new organization? Stephenson answers: "Professor Laughlin of the University of Chicago was given charge of the League's propaganda."[3] To which Congressman Lindbergh adds this reminder: "The reader knows that the University of Chicago is an institution endowed by John D. Rockefeller with nearly fifty million dollars. It may truly be said to be the Rockefeller University."[4]

This does not necessarily mean that Laughlin was purchased like so many pounds of hamburger and told by Rockefeller what to say and do. It doesn't work that way. The professor undoubtedly believed in the virtue of the Jekyll Island plan, and the evidence is that he pursued his assignment with enthusiastic sincerity. But there is no doubt that he was selected for his new post precisely because he *did* support the concept of a partnership between banking and government as a healthy substitute for "destructive" competition. In other words, if he didn't honestly agree with John D. that competition was a sin, he probably never even would have been given a professorship in the first place.[5]

---

1. Stephenson, pp. 388–89.
2. Kolko, *Triumph*, p. 187.
3. Stephenson, p. 388.
4. Lindbergh, p. 131.
5. For an excellent overview of the formation and activities of the League, see Kolko, *Triumph*, pp. 186–228.

WILSON AND WALL STREET

Woodrow Wilson was yet another academic who was brought into the national spotlight as a result of his views on banking reform. It will be recalled from a previous chapter that Wilson's name had been put into nomination for President at the Democratic national convention largely due to the influence of Col. Edward Mandell House. But that was 1912. Ten years prior to that, he was relatively unknown. In 1902 he had been elected as the president of Princeton University, a position he could not have held without the concurrence of the University's benefactors among Wall Street bankers. He was particularly close with Andrew Carnegie and had become a trustee of the Carnegie Foundation.

Two of the most generous donors were Cleveland H. Dodge and Cyrus McCormick, directors of Rockefeller's National City Bank. They were part of that Wall Street elite which the Pujo Committee had described as America's "Money Trust." Both men had been Wilson's classmates at Princeton University. When Wilson returned to Princeton as a professor in 1890, Dodge and McCormick were, by reason of their wealth, University trustees, and they took it upon themselves to personally advance his career. Ferdinand Lundberg, in *America's Sixty Families*, says this:

> For nearly twenty years before his nomination Woodrow Wilson had moved in the shadow of Wall Street.... In 1898 Wilson, his salary unsatisfactory, besieged with offers of many university presidencies, threatened to resign. Dodge and McCormick thereupon constituted themselves his financial guardians, and agreed to raise the additional informal stipendium that kept him at Princeton. The contributors to this private fund were Dodge, McCormick, and Moses Taylor Pyne and Percy R. Pyne, of the family that founded the National City Bank. In 1902 this same group arranged Wilson's election as president of the university.[1]

A grateful Wilson often had spoken in glowing terms about the rise of vast corporations and had praised J.P. Morgan as a great American leader. He also had come to acceptable conclusions about the value of a controlled economy. "The old time of individual competition is probably gone by," he said. "It may come back; I don't know; it will not come back within our time, I dare say."[2]

---

1. Lundberg, pp. 114–15.
2. Greider, p. 276.

H.S. Kenan tells us the rest of the story:

> Woodrow Wilson, President of Princeton University, was the first prominent educator to speak in favor of the Aldrich Plan, a gesture which immediately brought him the Governorship of New Jersey and later the Presidency of the United States. During the panic of 1907, Wilson declared that: "all this trouble could be averted if we appointed a committee of six or seven public-spirited men like J.P. Morgan to handle the affairs of our country."[1]

OPPOSITION TO THE ALDRICH BILL

One of the disagreements at the Jekyll Island meeting was over the name to be attached to the proposed legislation. Warburg, being the master psychologist he was, wanted it to be called the National Reserve Bill or the Federal Reserve Bill, something which would conjure up the dual images of government and reserves, both of which were calculated to be subconsciously appealing. Aldrich, on the other hand, acting out of personal ego, insisted that *his* name be attached to the bill. Warburg pointed out that the Aldrich name was associated in the minds of the public with Wall Street interests, and that would be an unnecessary obstacle to achieving their goal. Aldrich said that, since he had been the chairman of the National Monetary Commission which was created specifically to make recommendations for banking reform, people would be confused if his name were not associated with the bill. The debate, we are told, was long and heated. But, in the end, the politician's ego won out over the banker's logic.

Warburg, of course, was right. Aldrich was well known as a Republican spokesman for big business and banking. His loyalties were further publicized by recently sponsored tariff bills to protect the tobacco and rubber trusts. The Aldrich name on a bill for banking reform was an easy target for the opposition. On December 15, 1911, Congressman Lindbergh rose before the House of Representatives and took careful aim:

> The Aldrich Plan is the Wall Street Plan. It is a broad challenge to the government by the champion of the money trust. It means another panic, if necessary, to intimidate the people. Aldrich, paid by the government to represent the people, proposes a plan for the trusts instead.[2]

---

1.   H.S. Kenan, *The Federal Reserve Bank* (Los Angeles: Noontide Press, 1966), p. 105.
2.   Quoted by H.S. Kenan, p. 118.

The Aldrich Bill never came to a vote. When the Republicans lost control of the House in 1910 and then lost the Senate and the Presidency in 1912, any hope there may have been of putting through a Republican bill was lost. Aldrich had been voted out of the Senate by his constituents, and the ball was now squarely in the court of the Democrats and their new president, Woodrow Wilson.

How this came to pass is an interesting lesson on reality politics, and we shall turn to that part of the story next.

SUMMARY

Banking in the period immediately prior to passage of the Federal Reserve Act was subject to a myriad of controls, regulations, subsidies, and privileges at both the federal and state levels. Popular history portrays this period as one of unbridled competition and free banking. It was, in fact, a half-way house to central banking. Wall Street, however, wanted more government participation. The New York bankers particularly wanted a "lender of last resort" to create unlimited amounts of fiat money for their use in the event they were exposed to bank runs or currency drains. They also wanted to force all banks to follow the same inadequate reserve policies so that more cautious ones would not draw down the reserves of the others. An additional objective was to limit the growth of new banks in the South and West.

This was a time of growing enchantment with the idea of trusts and cartels. For those who had already made it to the top, competition was considered chaotic and wasteful. Wall Street was snowballing into two major banking groups: the Morgans and the Rockefellers, and even they had largely ceased competing with each other in favor of cooperative financial structures. But to keep these cartel combines from flying apart, a means of discipline was needed to force the participants to abide by the agreements. The federal government was brought in as a partner to serve that function.

To sell the plan to Congress, the cartel reality had to be hidden and the name "central bank" had to be avoided. The word *Federal* was chosen to make it sound like it was a government operation; the word *Reserve* was chosen to make it appear financially sound; and the word *System* (the first drafts used the word *Association*) was chosen to conceal the fact that it was a central bank. A structure of 12 regional institutions was conceived as a further ploy to create the illusion of decentralization, but the mechanism was designed from the beginning to operate as a central bank closely modeled after the Bank of England.

The first draft of the Federal Reserve Act was called the Aldrich Bill and was co-sponsored by Congressman Vreeland, but it was not the work of either of these politicians. It was the brainchild of banker Paul Warburg and was actually written by bankers Frank Vanderlip and Benjamin Strong.

Aldrich's name attached to a banking bill was bad strategy, because he was known as a Wall Street Senator. His bill was not politically acceptable and was never released from committee. The groundwork had been done, however, and the time had arrived to change labels and political parties. The measure would now undergo minor cosmetic surgery and reappear under the sponsorship of a politician whose name would be associated in the public mind with anti-Wall Street sentiments.

Chapter Twenty-Two

THE CREATURE SWALLOWS CONGRESS

The second attempt to pass legislation to legalize the banking cartel; the bankers' selection of Woodrow Wilson as a Presidential candidate; their strategy to get him elected; the role played by Wilson to promote the cartel's legislation; the final passage of the Federal Reserve Act.

The election of 1912 was a textbook example of power politics and voter deception. The Republican President, William Howard Taft, was up for reelection. Like most Republicans of that era, his political power was based upon the support of big-business and banking interests in the industrial regions. He had been elected to his first term in the expectation that he would continue the protectionist policies of his predecessor, Teddy Roosevelt, particularly in the expansion of cartel markets for sugar, coffee, and fruit from Latin America. Once in office, however, he grew more restrained in these measures and earned the animosity of many powerful Republicans. The ultimate breach occurred when Taft refused to support the Aldrich Plan. He objected, not because it would create a central bank which would impose government control over the economy, but because it would not offer *enough* government control. He recognized that the Jekyll Island formula would place the bankers into the driver's seat with only nominal participation by the government. He did not object to the ancient partnership between monetary and political scientists, he merely wanted a greater share for the political side. The bankers were not adverse to negotiating the balance of power nor were they unwilling to make compromises, but what they really needed at this juncture was a man in the White House who, instead of being lukewarm on the plan, could be counted on to become its champion and who would use his influence as President to garner support from the fence straddlers in Congress. From that moment forward, Taft was marked for political extinction.

This was a period of general prosperity, and Taft was popular with the voters as well as with the rank-and-file Party organization. He had easily won the nomination at the Republican convention, and there was little doubt that he could take the presidential election as well. Wilson had been put forth as the Democratic challenger, but his dry personality and aloof mannerisms had failed to arouse sufficient voter interest to make him a serious contender.

THE BULL MOOSE CANDIDATE

However, when Teddy Roosevelt returned from his latest African safari, he was persuaded by Morgan's deputies, George Perkins and Frank Munsey, to challenge the President for the Party's nomination. When that effort failed, he was then persuaded to run against Taft as the "Bull Moose" candidate on the Progressive Party ticket. It is unclear what motivated him to accept such a proposition, but there is no doubt regarding the intent of his backers. They did not expect Roosevelt to win, but, as a former Republican President, they knew he would split the Party and, by pulling away votes from Taft, put Wilson into the White House.

Presidential campaigns need money and lots of it. The Republican Party was well financed, largely from the same individuals who now wanted to see the defeat of its own candidate. It would not be possible to cut off this funding without causing too many questions. The solution, therefore, was to provide the financial resources for *all three* candidates, with special attention to the needs of Wilson and Roosevelt.

Some historians, while admitting the facts, have scoffed at the conclusion that deception was intended. Ron Chernow says: "By 1924, the House of Morgan was so influential in American politics that conspiracy buffs couldn't tell which presidential candidate was more beholden to the bank."[1] But one does not have to be a conspiracy buff to recognize the evidence of foul play. Ferdinand Lundberg tells us:

---

1. Chernow, p. 254.

J.P. Morgan and Company played the leading role in the national election of 1912.... Roosevelt's preconvention backers were George W. Perkins and Frank Munsey. These two, indeed, encouraged Roosevelt to contest Taft's nomination.... Munsey functioned in the newspaper field for J.P. Morgan and Company—buying, selling, creating, and suppressing newspapers in consonance with J.P. Morgan's shifting needs.... Perkins resigned from J.P. Morgan and Company on January 1, 1911, to assume a larger political role....

The suspicion seems justified that the two were not over-anxious to have Roosevelt win. The notion that Perkins and Munsey may have wanted Wilson to win ... is partly substantiated by the view that Perkins put a good deal of cash behind the Wilson campaign through Cleveland H. Dodge. Dodge and Perkins financed, to the extent of $35,500, the Trenton *True American*, a newspaper that circulated nationally with Wilson propaganda....

Throughout the three-cornered fight, Roosevelt had Munsey and George Perkins constantly at his heels, supplying money, going over his speeches, bringing people from Wall Street in to help, and, in general, carrying the entire burden of the campaign against Taft.... Perkins and J.P. Morgan and Company were the substance of the Progressive Party; everything else was trimming.... Munsey's cash contribution to the Progressive Party brought his total political outlay for 1912 to $229,255.72. Perkins made their joint contribution more than $500,000, and Munsey expended $1,000,000 in cash additionally to acquire from Henry Einstein the New York *Press* so that Roosevelt would have a New York City morning newspaper. Perkins and Munsey, as the Clapp [Senate Privileges and Election] Committee learned from Roosevelt himself, also underwrote the heavy expense of Roosevelt's campaign train. In short, most of Roosevelt's campaign fund was supplied by the two Morgan hatchet men who were seeking Taft's scalp.[1]

Morgan & Company was not the only banking firm on Wall Street to endorse a three-way election as a means of defeating Taft. Within the firm of Kuhn, Loeb & Company, Felix Warburg was dutifully putting money into the Republican campaign as expected, but his brother, Paul Warburg and Jacob Schiff were backing Wilson, while yet another partner, Otto Kahn, supported Roosevelt. Other prominent Republicans who contributed to the Democratic campaign that year were Bernard Baruch, Henry Morgenthau, and Thomas Fortune Ryan.[2] And the Rockefeller

---

1. Lundberg, pp. 106–12.
2. Kolko, *Triumph*, pp. 205–11.

component of the cartel was just as deeply involved. William McAdoo, who was Wilson's national campaign vice chairman, says that Cleveland Dodge of Rockefeller's National City Bank personally contributed $51,300—more than one-fourth the total raised from all other sources. In McAdoo's words, "He was a Godsend."[1] Ferdinand Lundberg describes Dodge as "the financial genius behind Woodrow Wilson." Continuing, he says:

> Wilson's nomination represented a personal triumph for Cleveland H. Dodge, director of the National City Bank, scion of the Dodge copper and munitions fortune.... The nomination represented no less a triumph for Ryan, Harvey, and J.P. Morgan and Company. Sitting with Dodge as co-directors of the National City Bank at the time were the younger J.P. Morgan, now the head of the [Morgan] firm, Jacob Schiff, William Rockefeller, J. Ogden Armour, and James Stillman. In short, except for George F. Baker, everyone whom the Pujo Committee had termed rulers of the "Money Trust" was in this bank.[2]

And so it came to pass that the monetary scientists carefully selected their candidate and set about to clear the way for his victory. The maneuver was brilliant. Who would suspect that Wall Street would support a Democrat, especially when the Party platform contained this plank: "We oppose the so-called Aldrich Bill or the establishment of a central bank; and ... what is known as the money trust."

What irony it was. The Party of the working man, the Party of Thomas Jefferson—formed only a few generations earlier for the specific purpose of opposing a central bank—was now cheering a new leader who was a political captive of Wall Street bankers and who had agreed to the hidden agenda of establishing the Federal Reserve System. As George Harvey later boasted, the financiers "felt no animosity toward Mr. Wilson for such of his utterances as they regarded as radical and menacing to their interests. He had simply played the political game."[3]

William McAdoo, Wilson's national campaign vice chairman, destined to become Secretary of the Treasury, saw what was happening from a ringside seat. He said:

---

1. McAdoo, p. 117.
2. Lundberg, pp. 109, 113.
3. Quoted by Lundberg, p. 120.

The major contributions to any candidate's campaign fund are made by men who have axes to grind—and the campaign chest is the grindstone.... The fact is that there is a serious danger of this country becoming a pluto-democracy; that is, a sham republic with the real government in the hands of a small clique of enormously wealthy men, who speak through their money, and whose influence, even today, radiates to every corner of the United States.

Experience has shown that the most practicable method of getting hold of a political party is to furnish it with money in large quantities. This brings the big money-giver or givers into close communion with the party leaders. Contact and influence do the rest.[1]

THE MONEY TRUST THEY LOVE TO HATE

Roosevelt actually had very little interest in the banking issue, probably because he didn't understand it. Furthermore, in the unlikely event the blustery "trust buster" would actually win the election, the financiers still had little to fear. In spite of his well-publicized stance of opposing big business, his true convictions were quite acceptable to Wall Street. As Chernow observed:

> Although the Roosevelt-Morgan relationship is sometimes caricatured as that of trust buster versus trust king, it was far more complex than that. The public wrangling obscured deeper ideological affinities.... Roosevelt saw trusts as natural, organic outgrowths of economic development. Stopping them, he said, was like trying to dam the Mississippi River. Both TR and Morgan disliked the rugged, individualistic economy of the nineteenth century and favored big business.... In the sparring between Roosevelt and Morgan there was always a certain amount of shadow play, a pretense of greater animosity than actually existed.... Roosevelt and Morgan were secret blood brothers.[2]

It is not surprising, therefore, as Warburg noted in January, 1912—ten months before the election—that Teddy had been "fairly won over to a favorable consideration of the Aldrich Plan."[3]

Inner convictions on these issues notwithstanding, both Wilson and Roosevelt played their roles to the hilt. Privately financed by Wall Street's most powerful bankers, they publicly carried a flaming crusade against the "Money Trust" from one end of the country to the other. Roosevelt bellowed that the "issue of currency

---

1. McAdoo, pp. 165–66.
2. Chernow, pp. 106–12.
3. Warburg, Vol. I, p. 78.

should be lodged with the government and be protected from domination and manipulation by Wall Street."[1] And he quoted over and over again the Bull Moose (Progressive Party) platform which said: "We are opposed to the so-called Aldrich Currency Bill because its provisions would place our currency and credit system in private hands." Meanwhile, at the other end of town, Wilson declared:

> There has come about an extraordinary and very sinister concentration in the control of business in the country.... The growth of our nation, therefore, and all our activities, are in the hands of a few men.... This money trust, or as it should be more properly called, this credit trust ... is no myth.[2]

Throughout the campaign, Taft was portrayed as the champion of big business and Wall Street banks—which, of course, he was. But so were Roosevelt and Wilson. The primary difference was that Taft, judged by his actual performance in office, was *known* to be such, whereas his opponents could only be judged by their words.

The outcome of the election was exactly as the strategists had anticipated. Wilson won with only forty-two per cent of the popular vote, which means, of course, that fifty-eight per cent had been cast against him. Had Roosevelt not entered the race, most of his votes undoubtedly would have gone to Taft, and Wilson would have become a footnote. As Colonel House confided to author George Viereck years later, "Wilson was elected by Teddy Roosevelt."[3]

Now that the Creature had moved into the White House, passage of the Jekyll Island plan went into its final phase. The last bastion of opposition in Congress consisted of the Populist wing of the Democratic Party under the leadership of William Jennings Bryan. The problem with this group was that they had taken their campaign platform seriously. They really *were* opposed to the Money Trust. While it may have been a simple matter to pull the wool over the eyes of voters, it would not be so easy to fool this group of experienced politicians. What was needed now was an

---

1. Henry S. Commager, ed., *Documents of American History* (New York: F.S. Cofts & Co., 1940), pp. 77–79.
2. Quoted by Carter Glass, *Adventures in Constructive Finance* (New York: Doubleday, 1927; rpt. Arno Press, a New York Times Co., 1975), p. 78–79.
3. Viereck, p. 34.

entirely new bill that, on the surface, would appear to contain changes of sufficient magnitude to allow the Bryan wing to change its position. The essential features of the plan, however, must not be abandoned. And, to coordinate this final strategy, the services of someone with great political skill would be essential. Fortunately for the planners, there was exactly such a man residing at the White House. It was not the President of the United States. It was Edward Mandell House.

THE ROLE OF COLONEL HOUSE

Colonel House, who had been educated in England and whose father represented England's merchant interests in the American South, had come into public life through the London Connection. It will be recalled from previous chapters that, perhaps more than any other person in America, he had helped maneuver the United States into World War I on the side of a desperate Britain and, by so doing, had also rescued the massive loans to Britain and France made by the Morgan interests. Not only had he been responsible for Wilson's nomination at the Democratic convention, but had become the President's constant companion, his personal adviser, and in many respects his political superior. It was through House that Wilson was made aware of the wishes of the Money Trust, and it was House who guided the President in every aspect of foreign and economic policy. An admiring biographer, Arthur Smith, writing in the year 1918, says that House "holds a power never wielded before in this country by any man out of office, a power greater than that of any political boss or Cabinet member."[1] A more recent biographer, George Viereck, was not exaggerating when he described House as "Chief Magistracy of the Republic," "Super-ambassador," "The pilot who guided the ship."[2] Continuing, he said:

> For six years two rooms were at his disposal in the North Wing of the White House.... In work and play their thoughts were one. House was the double of Wilson. It was House who made the slate for the Cabinet, formulated the first policies of the Administration and practically directed the foreign affairs of the United States. We had, indeed, two Presidents for one!...

1. Arthur Smith, *The Real Colonel House* (New York: George H. Doran Company, 1918), p. 14.
2. Viereck, p. 4.

The Schiffs, the Warburgs, the Kahns, the Rockefellers, the Morgans put their faith in House. When the Federal Reserve legislation at last assumed definite shape, House was the intermediary between the White House and the financiers.[1]

Daily entries in the personal journal of Colonel House reveal the extent to which his office had become the command post for the Jekyll Island team. The following sample notations are typical:

December 19, 1912. I Talked with Paul Warburg over the telephone regarding the currency reform. I told of my Washington trip and what I had done there to get it in working order.

March 24, 1913. I had an engagement with Carter Glass at five. We drove, in order not to be interrupted.... I spoke to the President about this after dinner and advised that McAdoo and I whip the Glass measure into final shape, which he could endorse and take to Owen [Chairman of the Senate Banking Committee] as his own.

March 27, 1913. Mr. J.P. Morgan, Jr., and Mr. Denny of his firm, came promptly at five. McAdoo came about ten minutes afterwards. Morgan had a currency plan already formulated and printed. We discussed it at some length. I suggested he have it typewritten [so it would not seem too prearranged] and sent to us today.

October 19, 1913. I saw Senator Reed of Missouri in the late afternoon and discussed the currency question with him.

October 19, 1913. Paul Warburg was my first caller, and he came to discuss the currency measure.... Senator Murray Crane followed Warburg. He has been in touch with Senators Weeks and Nelson of the Currency Committee.

November 17, 1913. Paul Warburg telephoned about his trip to Washington. He is much disturbed over the currency situation and requested an interview, along with Jacob Schiff and Cleveland H. Dodge.

January 21, 1914. After dinner we [Wilson and House] went to the President's study as usual and began work on the Federal Reserve Board appointments.[2]

---

1. Viereck, pp. 4, 35, 37.
2. Seymour, Vol. I, pp. 161–68.

As far as the banking issue was concerned, Colonel House *was* the President of the United States, and all interested parties knew it. Wilson made no pretense at knowledge of banking theory. He said: "The greatest embarrassment of my political career has been that active duties seem to deprive me of time for careful investigation. I seem almost obliged to form conclusions from impressions instead of from study.... I wish that I had more knowledge, more thorough acquaintance, with the matters involved."[1] To which Charles Seymour adds: "Colonel House was indefatigable in providing for the President the knowledge that he sought.... The Colonel was the unseen guardian angel of the bill."[2]

DEATH OF THE ALDRICH PLAN

The first task for the Jekyll Island team was to hold a funeral for the Aldrich Plan without actually burying it. Professor Laughlin had come to agree with Warburg regarding the inadvisability of having Aldrich's name attached to any banking bill, especially now that the Democrats were in control of both Congress and the White House, and he was anxious to give it a new identity. Writing in the periodical *Banking Reform*, which was the official publication of the National Citizens' League, Laughlin said: "It is progress that the Aldrich plan came and went. It is progress that the people have been aroused and interested." The League was now free, he said, to "try to help in getting a proper bill adopted by the Democrats," a bill that "in non-essentials ... could be made different from the old plan."[3]

It did not take long for the Democrats to bring forth their own proposal. In fact, that process had begun even before the election of 1912. One of the most outspoken critics of the Aldrich plan was the Democratic Chairman of the House Banking and Currency Committee, Congressman Carter Glass from Virginia. And it was Glass

---

1. Seymour, Vol. I, p. 160.
2. *Ibid.* William McAdoo, Wilson's Secretary of the Treasury, was indignant over the credit generally given to Paul Warburg for his part in the creation of the Federal Reserve because McAdoo felt he should have received the recognition. Later, we find Carter Glass similarly piqued over Seymour's interpretation of House's importance. Glass' book, *Adventures in Constructive Finance*, was written primarily to show that it was he, not House, who rightfully deserved such glory. But neither McAdoo nor Glass were part of the hidden power which is the focus of this study and neither had any inkling of who was really calling the shots.
3. Quoted by Kolko, *Triumph*, p. 222.

who was given the responsibility of developing the new plan. By his own admission, however, he had virtually no technical knowledge of banking. To provide that expertise and to actually write the bill, he hired an economics teacher from Washington and Lee University, Henry Parker Willis. We should not be surprised to learn that Willis had been a former student and protégé of Professor Laughlin and had been retained by the National Citizens' League as a technical writer. Explaining the significance of this relationship, Kolko says:

> Throughout the spring of 1912 Willis wrote Laughlin about his work for the Glass Committee, his relationship to his superior, and Washington gossip. The advice of the old professor was much revered.... "When you arrive," he wrote Laughlin concerning a memorandum he had written, "I should like to show it to you for such criticisms as occur to you." The student-teacher relationship between the two men was still prominent....
>
> Laughlin, Colonel House, and Glass were to frequently consult with major bankers about reform, and provided an important and continuous bridge for their ideas while bills were being drafted.... Colonel House, in addition, was talked to by Frick, Otto Kahn, and others in late February, and the following month also met Vanderlip, J.P. Morgan, Jr., and other bankers to discuss currency reform.... To make sure the reform was more to the liking of bankers, a steady barrage of personal, unobtrusive communications with Glass, House, and Wilson was kept up throughout February and March.... The [Citizens'] league was fulsome in its praise of Glass, and bankers felt greater and greater confidence as Colonel House began visiting Glass and showing interest in his currency measure....
>
> The new President admitted "he knew nothing" about banking theory or practice. Glass made the same confession to Colonel House in November, and this vacuum is of the utmost significance. The entire banking reform movement, at all crucial stages, was centralized in the hands of a few men who for years were linked, ideologically and personally with one another.[1]

THE GLASS–OWEN BILL EMERGES

In his Committee House Report in 1913, Glass objected to the Aldrich Bill on the following grounds: It lacked government control, he said; it concentrated power into the hands of the larger New York banks; it opened the door to inflation; it was dishonest in its estimate of cost to the taxpayer; and it established a banking

---

1. Kolko, *Triumph*, pp. 219–28.

monopoly. All of which was correct. What the country needed, Glass said, was an entirely fresh approach, a genuine reform bill which was not written by agents of the Money Trust and which would truly meet the needs of the common man. That, too, was quite correct. Then he brought forth his own bill, drafted by Willis and inspired by Laughlin, which in every important detail was merely the old corpse of the Aldrich Bill pulled from its casket, freshly perfumed, and dressed in a new suit.

The Glass Bill was soon reconciled with a similar measure sponsored by Senator Robert L. Owen and it emerged as the Glass–Owen Bill. Although there were initially some minor differences between Glass and Owen on the proper degree of government control over banking, Owen was basically of identical mind to Willis and Laughlin. While serving in the Senate, he also was the president of a bank in Oklahoma. Like Aldrich, he had made several trips to Europe to study the central banks of England and Germany, and these were the models for his legislation.

The less technically minded members of the cartel became nervous over the anti-Wall Street rhetoric of the Bill's sponsors. Warburg, in an attempt to quell their fears and, at the same time, strengthen his private boast that he had been the real author, published a side-by-side comparison of the Aldrich and Glass proposals. The analysis showed that, not only were the two bills in agreement on all essential provisions, but they even contained entire sections that were identical in their wording.[1] He wrote: "Brushing aside, then, the external differences affecting the 'shells,' we find the 'kernels' of the two systems very closely resembling and related to one another."[2]

It was important for the success of the Glass Bill to create the impression it was in response to the views of a broad cross section of the financial community. To this end, Glass and his committee staged public hearings for the announced purpose of giving everyone a chance for input to the process. It was, of course, a sham. The first draft of the Bill had already been completed in secret several months before the hearings were held. And, as was customary in such matters, Congressman Lindbergh and other witnesses opposing the Jekyll Island plan were not allowed to

---

1. Warburg, Vol. I, p. 98.
2. *Ibid.*, p. 412.

speak.[1] The hearings were widely reported in the press, and the public was given the impression that the favorable testimony was truly representative of expert opinion. Kolko summarizes:

> Although they were careful to keep the contents of their work confidential, to aid the passage of any bill that might be agreed upon Glass deemed it desirable to hold public hearings on the topic and to make sure the course of these hearings was not left to chance.... The public assumption of the hearing was that no bills had been drafted, and Willis' draft was never mentioned, much less revealed.... The hearings of Glass' subcommittee in January and February, 1913, were nothing less than a love feast.[2]

BANKERS BECOME DIVIDED

The public was not the only victim of deception. The bankers themselves were also targeted—at least the lesser ones who were not part of the Wall Street power center. As early as February, 1911, a group of twenty-two of the country's most powerful bankers met for three days behind closed doors in Atlantic City to work out a strategy for getting the smaller banks to support the concept of using the government to authorize and maintain their own cartel. The objective frankly discussed among those present was that the proposed cartel would bring the smaller banks under control of the larger ones, but that this fact had to be obscured when presenting it to them for endorsement.[3]

The annual meeting of the American Bankers Association was held a few months later, and a resolution endorsing the Aldrich Bill was steam rollered through the plenary session, much to the dismay of many of those present. Andrew Frame was one of them. Representing a group of Western bankers, he testified at the hearings of the Glass subcommittee, mentioned previously, and described the hoax:

> When that monetary bill was given to the country, it was but a few days previous to the meeting of the American Bankers Association in New Orleans in 1911. There was not one banker in a hundred who had read that bill. We had twelve addresses in favor of it. General Hamby of Austin, Texas, wrote a letter to President Watts asking for a hearing against the bill. He did not get a very courteous answer. I refused to

---

1. Lindbergh, p. 129.
2. Kolko, *Triumph*, p. 225.
3. Rothbard, *Crisis*, p. 101. Also Kolko, *Triumph*, p. 186.

vote on it, and a great many other bankers did likewise.... They would not allow anyone on the program who was not in favor of the bill.[1]

It is interesting that, during Frame's testimony, Congressman Glass refrained from commenting on the unfairness of allowing only one side of an issue to be heard in a public forum. He could hardly afford to. That is exactly what he was then doing with his own agenda.

As the Federal Reserve Act moved closer to its birth in the form of the Glass–Owen Bill (Owen was the co-sponsor in the Senate), both Aldrich and Vanderlip threw themselves into a great public display of opposition. No opportunity was overlooked to make a statement to the press—or anyone else of public prominence—expressing their eternal animosity to this monstrous legislation. Vanderlip warned against the evils of fiat money and rampant inflation. Aldrich charged that the Glass–Owen Bill was inimical to sound banking and good government. Vanderlip predicted speculation and instability in the stock market. Aldrich sourly complained that the bill was "revolutionary in its character" (implying Bolshevistic) and "will be the first and most important step toward changing our form of government from a democracy to an autocracy."[2]

THE PRETENSE IS DROPPED

That all of this was merely high-level showmanship was made clear when Vanderlip accepted a debate with Congressman Glass before the New York Economic Society on November 13. There were eleven hundred bankers and businessmen present, and Vanderlip was under pressure to make a good showing before this impressive group. The debate was going badly for him and, in a moment of desperation, he finally dropped the pretense. "For years," he said, "bankers have been almost the sole advocates of just this sort of legislation that it is now hoped we will have, and it is unfair to accuse them of being in opposition to sound legislation."[3] Twenty-two years later, when the need for pretense had long passed, Vanderlip was even more candid. Writing in the

---

1. Quoted by Mullins, p. 13.
2. Aldrich to John A. Sleicher, July 16, 1913; Aldrich to William Howard Taft, Oct. 3, 1913, Nelson Aldrich Papers, Library of Congress.
3. Frank A. Vanderlip, *Address Before the Economics Club of New York, November 13, 1913*, (New York: 1913), pp. 6, 11 ff. Also see Glass, pp. 125, 168–76.

Saturday Evening Post, he said: "Although the Aldrich Federal Reserve Plan was defeated when it bore the name Aldrich, nevertheless its essential points were all contained in the plan that finally was adopted."[1]

In his autobiography, Treasury Secretary William McAdoo offers this view:

> Bankers fought the Federal Reserve legislation—and every provision of the Federal Reserve Act—with the tireless energy of men fighting a forest fire. They said it was populistic, socialistic, half-baked, destructive, infantile, badly conceived, and unworkable....
>
> These interviews with bankers led me to an interesting conclusion. I perceived gradually, through all the haze and smoke of controversy, that the banking world was not really as opposed to the bill as it pretended to be.[2]

That is the key to this entire episode: mass psychology. Since Aldrich was recognized as associated with the Morgan interests and Vanderlip was President of Rockefeller's National City Bank, the public was skillfully led to believe that the "Money Trust" was mortally afraid of the proposed Federal Reserve Act. *The Nation* was the only prominent publication to point out that every one of the horrors described by Aldrich and Vanderlip could have been equally ascribed to the Aldrich Bill as well. But this lone voice was easily drowned by the great cacophony of deception and propaganda.

The Glass Bill was a flexible document which was designed from the beginning to be altered in non-essential matters in order to appear as though compromises were being made to satisfy the various political factions. Since very few understood central-bank technicalities, the ploy was easy to execute. The basic strategy was to focus debate on such relatively unimportant items as the number of regional banks, the structure of the governing board, and the process by which that board was to be selected. When truly crucial matters could not be avoided, the response was to agree to almost anything but to write the provisions in vague language. In that way, the back door would be left ajar for later implementation of

---

1. "From Farm Boy to Financier," by Frank A. Vanderlip, *Saturday Evening Post*, February 9, 1935, p. 72.
2. McAdoo, pp. 213, 225–26.

the original intent. The goal was to get the bill *passed* and perfect it later.

House and Warburg feared that, if they waited until they had everything they wanted, they would get nothing at all or, worse, that opponents of a central bank would be able to muster their forces and pass a reform bill of their own; a *real* one. Willis was quick to agree. In a letter to his former professor, he wrote: "It is much better to take a half a loaf rather than to be absolutely deprived of a chance of getting any bread whatsoever.... The so-called 'progressive' element—such as Lindbergh and his supporters—will be encouraged to enact dangerous legislation."[1] Glass echoed the sentiment. Directing his remarks at those smaller banks which were resisting domination by the New York banks, he said: "Unless the conservative bankers of the country are willing to yield something and get behind the bill, we shall get legislation very much less to be desired, or have nothing done at all."[2]

BRYAN MAKES AN ULTIMATUM

The Populist, William Jennings Bryan, was considered at that time to be the most influential Democrat in Congress, and it was clear from the start that the Federal Reserve Act could never be passed without his approval and support. As Charles Seymour observed: "The Commoner's sense of loyalty [to the Party] had kept him from an attack upon the Federal Reserve Act which, it would appear, he never entirely understood.... With his influence in the Party, he could have destroyed the measure which failed to accord with his personal doctrines."[3]

Bryan had said that he would not support any bill that resulted in *private* money being issued by *private* banks. The money supply, he insisted, must be *government* issue. When he finally saw an actual draft of the bill in midsummer of 1913, he was dismayed to find that, not only was the money to be privately issued, but the entire governing body of the central bank was to be composed of private bankers. His ultimatum was not long in coming. He hotly demanded (1) that the Federal-Reserve notes must be *Treasury* currency, issued and guaranteed by the government; and (2) that

---

1. Letters from Willis to Laughlin, J. Laurence Laughlin Papers, Library of Congress, July 14 & 18, 1912.
2. From a letter to Festus Wade. Quoted by Kolko, *Triumph*, p. 234.
3. Seymour, Vol. I, p. 173.

the governing body must be appointed by the President and approved by the Senate.

Colonel House and the other monetary scientists were reasonably sure that these provisions eventually would be required for final approval of the bill but, being master strategists, they deliberately withheld them from early drafts so they could be used as bargaining points and added later as concessions in a show of compromise. Furthermore, since practically no one really understood the technical aspects of the measure, they knew it would be easy to fool their opponents by creating the *appearance* of compromise when, in actual operation, the originally intended features would remain.

AN AMAZING REVELATION

The nature of this deception was spelled out years later by Carter Glass in his book, *Adventures in Constructive Finance*. From this source we learn that, after Bryan had delivered his ultimatum, Glass was summoned to the White House and told by Wilson that the decision had been made to make the Federal Reserve notes obligations of the United States government. "I was for an instant speechless!" wrote Glass who then explained how he reminded the President that the only backing for the new currency would be a small amount of gold, a large amount of government and commercial debt, and the private assets of the individual banks themselves. "It would be a pretense on its face," he said. "Was there ever a government note based primarily on the property of banking institutions? Was there ever a government issue not one dollar of which could be put out except by demand of a bank? The suggested government obligation is so remote it could never be discovered."

To which the President replied: "Exactly so, Glass. Every word you say is true; the government liability *is* a mere thought. And so, if we can hold the substance of the thing and give the other fellow the shadow, why not do it, if thereby we may save our bill?"[1]

Years later, Paul Warburg would explain further:

> While technically and legally the Federal Reserve note is an obligation of the United States Government, in reality it is an obligation, the sole actual responsibility for which rests on the reserve

---

1. Glass, pp. 124–25.

banks.... The government could only be called upon to take them up after the reserve banks had failed.[1]

Warburg's explanation should be carefully analyzed. It is an incredibly important statement. The man who masterminded the Federal Reserve System is telling us that *Federal Reserve notes constitute privately issued money with the taxpayers standing by to cover the potential losses of those banks which issue it.* One of the more controversial assertions of this book is that the objectives set forth at the Jekyll Island meeting included the shifting of the cartel's losses from the owners of the banks to the taxpayers. Warburg himself has confirmed it.

But let us return to the great deceit of 1913. The second demand made by Bryan—political control over the System, not banker control—was met with an equally beguiling "compromise." In addition to the governing board of regional bankers previously proposed, there now would be a central regulatory commission, to be called the Federal Reserve Board, appointed by the President with the advice and consent of the Senate.[2] Thus, the public was to be protected through a sharing of power, a melding of interests, a system of checks and balances. In this way, said Wilson, "the banks may be instruments, not the masters, of business and of individual enterprise and initiative."[3]

The arrangement was heralded as a bold, new experiment in representative government. In reality, it was but the return of the ancient partnership between the monetary and political scientists. The only thing new was that power was now to be shared *openly* in plain view of the public. But, of course, there would not be much to see. All the deliberations and most of the decisions were to happen behind closed doors. Furthermore, the division of power and responsibility between these groups was left deliberately vague. Without a detailed line of command or even a clear concept of function, it was inevitable that, as with the drafting of the bill itself, real power would gravitate into the hands of those with technical knowledge and Wall Street connections. To the monetary scientists drafting the bill and engineering the compromises, the eventual

---

1. Warburg, Vol. I, p. 409.
2. The original plan called for the Secretary of the Treasury and the Comptroller of the Currency to be on the board also, but this was later dropped.
3. Quoted by Greider, p. 277.

concentration of effective control into their hands was never in serious doubt. And, as we shall see in the next chapter, subsequent events have proved the soundness of that strategy.

BRYAN ENDORSES THE BILL

Bryan was no match for the Jekyll Island strategists and he accepted the "compromises" at face value. Had there been any lingering doubts in his mind, they were swept away by gratitude for his appointment as Wilson's Secretary of State. Now that he was on the team, he declared:

> I appreciate so profoundly the service rendered by the President to the people in the stand he has taken on the fundamental principles involved in currency reform, that I am with him in all the details.... The right of the government to issue money is not surrendered to the banks; the control over the money so issued is not relinquished by the government.... I am glad to endorse earnestly and unreservedly the currency bill as a much better measure than I supposed it possible to secure at this time.... Conflicting opinions have been reconciled with a success hardly to have been expected.[1]

With the conversion of Bryan, there was no longer any doubt about the final outcome. The Federal Reserve Act was released from the joint House and Senate conference committee on December 22, 1913, just as Congress was preoccupied with departure for the Christmas recess and in no mood for debate. It quickly passed by a vote of 282 to 60 in the House and 43 to 23 in the Senate. The President signed it into law the next day.

The Creature had swallowed Congress.

SUMMARY

President Taft, although a Republican spokesman for big business, refused to champion the Aldrich Bill for a central bank. This marked him for political extinction. The Money Trust wanted a President who would aggressively promote the bill, and the man selected was Woodrow Wilson who had already publicly declared his allegiance. Wilson's nomination at the Democratic national convention was secured by Colonel House, a close associate of Morgan and Warburg. To make sure that Taft did not win his bid for reelection, the Money Trust encouraged the former Republican President, Teddy Roosevelt, to run on the Progressive ticket. The

---

1. Glass, pp. 139–42.

result, as planned, was that Roosevelt pulled away Republican support from Taft, and Wilson won the election with less than a majority vote. Wilson and Roosevelt campaigned vigorously against the evils of the Money Trust while, all along, being dependent upon that same Trust for campaign funding.

When Wilson was elected, Colonel House literally moved into the White House and became the unseen President of the United States. Under his guidance, the Aldrich Bill was given cosmetic surgery and emerged as the Glass–Owen Bill. Although sponsored by Democrats, in all essential features it was still the Jekyll Island plan. Aldrich, Vanderlip, and others identified with Wall Street put on a pretense of opposing the Glass–Owen Bill to convince Congress and the public that big bankers were fearful of it. The final bill was written with many sound features which were included to make it palatable during Congressional debate but which were predesigned to be dropped in later years. To win the support of the Populists under the leadership of William Jennings Bryan, the Jekyll Island team also engineered what appeared to be compromises but which in actual operation were, as Wilson called them, mere "shadows" while the "substance" remained. In short, Congress was outflanked, outfoxed, and outclassed by a deceptive, but brilliant, psycho-political attack. The result is that, on December 23, 1913, America once again had a central bank.

Chapter Twenty-Three

THE GREAT
DUCK DINNER

*How Federal-Reserve policies led to the crash of
1929; the expansion of the money supply as a
means of helping the economy of England; the
resulting wave of speculation in stocks and real
estate; evidence that the Federal-Reserve Board
had foreknowledge of the crash and even executed
the events that were designed to trigger it.*

The story is told of a New England farmer with a small pond in
his pasture. Each summer, a group of wild ducks would frequent
that pond but, try as he would, the farmer could never catch one.
No matter how early in the morning he approached, or how
carefully he constructed a blind, or what kind of duck call he tried,
somehow those crafty birds sensed the danger and managed to be
out of range. Of course, when fall arrived, the ducks headed South,
and the farmer's craving for a duck dinner only intensified.

Then he got an idea. Early in the spring, he started scattering
corn along the edge of the pond. The ducks liked the corn and,
since it was always there, they soon gave up dipping and foraging
for food of their own. After a while, they became used to the farmer
and began to trust him. They could see he was their benefactor and
they now walked close to him with no sense of fear. Life was so
easy, they forgot how to fly. But that was unimportant, because
they were now so fat they couldn't have gotten off the water even if
they had tried.

Fall came, and the ducks stayed. Winter came, and the pond
froze. The farmer built a shelter to keep them warm. The ducks
were happy because they didn't have to fly. And the farmer was
especially happy because, each week all winter long, he had a
delicious duck dinner.

That is the story of America's Great Depression of the 1930s.

CONSOLIDATION OF POWER

When the Federal Reserve Act was submitted to Congress, many of its most important features were written in vague language. Some details were omitted entirely. That was a tactical move to avoid debate over fine points and to allow flexibility for future interpretation. The goal was to get the bill *passed* and perfect it later. Since then, the Act has been amended 195 times, expanding the power and scope of the System to the point where, today, it would be almost unrecognizable to the Congressmen and Senators who voted for it.

In 1913, public distaste for concentration of financial power in the hands of a few Wall Street banks helped to fuel the fire for passage of the Federal Reserve Act. To make it appear that the new System would put an end to the New York "money trust," as it was called, the public was told that the Federal Reserve would not represent any one group or one region. Instead, it would have its power diffused over twelve regional Federal Reserve Banks, and none would be able to dominate. As Galbraith pointed out, however, the regional design was "admirable for serving local pride and architectural ambition and for lulling the suspicions of the agrarians."[1] But that was not what the planners had in mind for the long haul.

In the beginning, the regional branches took their autonomy seriously, and that led to conflict with members of the national board. The Board of Governors was composed of political appointees representing diverse segments of the economy. They were outclassed by the heads of the regional branches of the System who were *bankers* with bankers' experience.

RETURN OF THE NEW YORK "MONEY TRUST"

The greatest power struggle arose from the New York Reserve Bank which was headed by Benjamin Strong. Strong had the contacts and the experience. It will be recalled that he was one of the seven who drafted the cartel's structure at Jekyll Island. He had been head of J.P. Morgan's Bankers Trust Company and was closely associated with Edward Mandell House. He had become a personal friend of Montagu Norman, head of the Bank of England, and of Charles Rist, head of the Bank of France. Not least of all, he

---

1. Galbraith, p. 130.

was head of the *New York* branch of the System which represented the nation's largest banks, the "money trust" itself. From the outset, the national board *and* the regional branches were dominated by the New York branch. Strong ruled as an autocrat, determining Fed policy often without even consulting with the Federal Reserve Board in Washington.

The United States entry into World War I provided the impetus for increasing the power of the Fed. The System became the sole fiscal agent of the Treasury, Federal Reserve Notes were issued, virtually all of the gold reserves of the nation's commercial banks were gathered together into the vaults of the Federal System, and many of the legislative restraints placed into the original Act were abandoned. Voters ask fewer questions when their nation is at war.

The concentration of power into the hands of the very "money trust" the Fed was supposed to defeat, is described by Ferdinand Lundberg, author of *America's Sixty Families*:

> In practice, the Federal Reserve Bank of New York became the fountainhead of the system of twelve regional banks, for New York was the money market of the nation. The other eleven banks were so many expensive mausoleums erected to salve the local pride and quell the Jacksonian fears of the hinterland. Benjamin Strong,... president of the Bankers Trust Company [J.P. Morgan] was selected as the first Governor of the New York Reserve Bank. An adept in high finance, Strong for many years manipulated the country's monetary system at the discretion of directors representing the leading New York banks. Under Strong the Reserve System, unsuspected by the nation, was brought into interlocking relations with the Bank of England and the Bank of France.[1]

BAILING OUT EUROPE

It will be recalled from Chapters Twelve and Twenty that it was this interlock during World War I that was responsible for the confiscation from American taxpayers of *billions* of dollars which were given to the central banks of England and France. Much of that money found its way to the associates of J.P. Morgan as interest payments on war bonds and as fees for supplying munitions and other war materials.

Seventy per cent of the cost of World War I was paid by inflation rather than taxes, a process that was orchestrated by the

---

1. Lundberg, p. 122.

Federal Reserve System. This was considered by the Fed's supporters as its first real test, and it passed with flying colors. American
inflation during that period was only slightly less than in England,
which had been more deeply committed to war and for a longer
period of time. That is not surprising inasmuch as a large portion of
Europe's war costs had been transferred to the American taxpayers.

After the war was over, the transfusion of American dollars
continued as part of a plan to pull England out of depression. The
methods chosen for that transfer were artificially low interest rates
and a deliberate inflation of the American money supply. That was
calculated to weaken the value of the dollar relative to the English
pound and cause gold reserves to move from America to England.
Both operations were directed by Benjamin Strong and executed by
the Federal Reserve. It was not hyperbole when President Herbert
Hoover described Strong as "a mental annex to Europe."[1]

Before Alan Greenspan was appointed as Chairman of the
Federal Reserve by President Reagan in 1987, he had served on the
Board of the J.P. Morgan Company. Before that, however, he had
been an outspoken champion of the gold standard and a critic of
the System's subservience to the banking cartel. In 1966 he wrote:

> When business in the United States underwent a mild contraction
> in 1927, the Federal Reserve created more paper reserves in the hope
> of forestalling any possible bank reserve shortage. More disastrous,
> however, was the Federal Reserve's attempt to assist Great Britain
> who had been losing gold to us.... The "Fed" succeeded: it stopped the
> gold loss, but it nearly destroyed the economies of the world in the
> process. The excess credit which the Fed pumped into the economy
> spilled over into the stock market—triggering a fantastic speculative
> boom.... As a result, the American economy collapsed.[2]

After his appointment to the Fed , Greenspan became silent on
these issues and did nothing to anger the Creature he now served.

AGENTS OF A HIGHER POWER

When reviewing this aspect of the Fed's history, questions arise
about the patriotic loyalty of men like Benjamin Strong. How is it
possible for a man who enjoys the best that his nation can
offer—security, wealth, prestige—to conspire to plunder his fellow
citizens in order to assist politicians of other governments to

---

1. Galbraith, p. 180.
2. Greenspan, pp. 99–100.

continue plundering theirs? The first part of the answer was illustrated in earlier sections of this book. International money managers may be citizens of a particular country but, to many of them, that is a meaningless accident of birth. They consider themselves to be citizens of the world first. They speak of affection for all mankind, but their highest loyalty is to themselves and their profession.

That is only half the answer. It must be remembered that the men who pulled the financial levers on this doomsday machine, the governors of the Bank of England and the Federal Reserve, were themselves tied to strings which were pulled by others above them. Their minds were not obsessed with concepts of nationalism or even internationalism. Their loyalties were to *men*. Professor Quigley reminds us:

> It must not be felt that these heads of the world's chief central banks were themselves substantive powers in world finance. They were not. Rather, they were the technicians and agents of the dominant investment bankers of their own countries, who had raised them up and were perfectly capable of throwing them down. The substantive financial powers of the world were in the hands of these investment bankers (also called "international" or "merchant" bankers) who remained largely behind the scenes in their own unincorporated private banks. These formed a system of international cooperation and national dominance which was more private, more powerful, and more secret than that of their agents in the central banks.[1]

So, we are not dealing with the actions of men who perceive themselves as betraying their nation, but technicians who are loyal to the monetary scientists and the political scientists who raised them up. Of the two groups, the financiers are dominant. Politicians come and go, but those who wield the power of money remain to pick their successors.

FARMERS BECOME DUCK DINNER

During the war, prices for agricultural products rose to an all-time high, and so did profits. Farmers had put part of that money into war bonds, but much of it had been placed into savings accounts at banks within the farming communities, which is to say, mostly in the Midwest and South. That was unacceptable to the

---

1. Quigley, *Tragedy*, pp. 326–27.

New York banks which saw their share of the nation's deposits begin to decline. A way had to be devised to reclaim that money. The Federal Reserve System, which by then was the captive of the New York banks, was pressed into service to accomplish the deed.

Few of those country banks had chosen to become members of the Federal Reserve System. That added insult to injury, and it also provided an excuse for the Fed to wage economic war against them. The plan was neither complex nor original; it had been used many times before by central bankers. It was (1) extend easy credit to the farmers to lure them into heavy debt, and then (2) create a recession which would decrease their income to the point where they could not make payments. The country banks then would find themselves holding non-performing loans and foreclosed property which they could not sell without tremendous losses. In the end, both the farmers and the banks would be wiped out. The banks were the target. Too bad about the farmers.

Congressman Charles Lindbergh, Sr., father of the man who made the world's first solo transatlantic flight, explained it this way: "Under the Federal Reserve Act, panics are scientifically created; the present panic is the first scientifically created one, worked out as we figure a mathematical problem."[1]

The details of how this panic was created were explained in 1939 by Senator Robert Owen, Chairman of the Senate Banking and Currency Committee. Owen, a banker himself, had been a co-author of the Federal Reserve Act, a role he later regretted. Owen said:

> In May 1920 ... the farmers were exceedingly prosperous.... They were paying off their mortgages. They had bought a lot of new land, at the instance of the government—had borrowed money to do it—and then they were bankrupted by a sudden contraction of credit and currency, which took place in 1920....
>
> The Federal Reserve Board met in a meeting which was not disclosed to the public—they met on the 18th of May 1920; it was a secret meeting—and they spent all day; the minutes made 60 printed pages, and it appears in Senate Document 310 of February 10, 1923.... Under action taken by the Reserve Board on May 18, 1920, there resulted a violent contraction of credit.... This contraction of credit and currency had the effect, the next year, of diminishing the national

---

1.   Charles A. Lindbergh, Sr. *The Economic Pinch* (1923 rpt. Hawthorne, California: Omni Publications, 1968), p. 95.

production $15,000,000,000; it had the effect of throwing millions of people out of employment; it had the effect of reducing the value of lands and ranches $20,000,000,000.[1]

The contraction of credit had a disastrous effect on the nation as a whole, not just farmers. But the farmers were more deeply involved, because the recently created Federal Farm Loan Board had lured them with easy credit—like ducks at the pond—into extreme debt ratios. Furthermore, the large-city banks which were members of the System were given support by the Fed during the summer of 1920 to enable them to extend credit to manufacturers and merchants. That allowed many of them to ride out the slump. There was no such support for the farmers or the country banks which, by 1921, were falling like dominoes. History books refer to this event as the Agricultural Depression of 1920–21. A better name would have been *Country-Duck Dinner in New York*.

BUILDING THE MANDRAKE MECHANISM

In Chapter Ten, we examined the three methods by which the Federal Reserve is able to create or extinguish money. Of the three, the purchase and sale of debt-related securities in the open market is the one that provides the greatest effect on the money supply. The purchase of securities by the Fed (with checks that have no money to back them) *creates* money; the sale of those securities *extinguishes* money. Although the Fed is authorized to buy and sell almost any kind of security that exists in the world, it is obligated to show preference for bonds and notes of the federal government. That is the way the monetary scientists discharge the commitment to create money for their partners, the political scientists. Without that service, the partnership would dissolve, and Congress would abolish the Fed.

When the System was created in 1913, it was anticipated that the primary way to manipulate the money supply would be to control the "reserve ratios" and the "discount window." That is banker language for setting the level of mandatory bank reserves (as a percentage of deposits) and also setting the interest rate on loans made by the Fed to the banks themselves. The reserve ratio under the old National Bank Act had been 25%. Under the Federal Reserve Act of 1913, it was reduced to 18% for the large New York

---

1. U.S. Cong., Senate, Special Committee on the Investigation of Silver, *Silver*, Part 5, 76th Cong., 1st sess. (Washington, DC: GPO, 1939), April 7, 1939, pp. 196–97.

banks, a drop of 28%. In 1917, just four years later, the reserve requirements for Central Reserve-City Banks were further dropped from 18% to 13% (with slightly lesser reductions for smaller banks). That was an additional 28% cut.[1]

It quickly became apparent that setting reserve ratios was an inefficient tool. The latitude of control was too small, and the amount of public attention too great. The second method, influencing the interest rate on commercial loans, was more useful. Here is how that works:

Under a fractional-reserve banking system, a bank can create new money merely by issuing a loan. The amount it creates is limited by the reserve ratio or "fraction" it is required to maintain to cover its cash-flow needs. If the reserve ratio is 10%, then each $10 it lends includes $9 that never existed before. A commercial bank, therefore, can create a sizable amount of money merely by making loans. But, once the bank is "loaned up," that is to say, once it has already lent $9 for every $1 it holds in reserve, it must stop and wait for some of the old loans to be paid back before it can issue new ones. The only way to expand that process is to make the reserves larger. That can be accomplished in one of four ways: (1) attract more deposits, (2) use some of the bank's profits, (3) sell additional stock to investors, or (4) borrow money from the Fed.

WHEN BANKS BORROW FROM THE FED

The fourth option is the most popular and is called going to the "discount window." When banks go to the Fed's discount window to obtain a loan, they are expected to put up collateral. This can be almost any debt contract held by the bank, including government bonds, but it commonly consists of commercial loans. The Fed then grants credit to the bank in an amount equal to those contracts. In essence, this allows the bank to convert its old loans into new "reserves." Every dollar of those new reserves then can be used as the basis for lending *nine more* dollars in checkbook money!

The process does not stop there. Once the new loans are made, they, too, can be used as collateral at the Fed for still *more* reserves. The music goes 'round and 'round, with each new level of debt

---

1. In 1980, statutory limits on reserve ratios were eliminated altogether. The Federal Reserve Board now has the option to lower the ratio to *zero*, which means the power to create *unlimited* quantities of money. It is the ultimate dream of central bankers.

becoming "reserves" for yet a higher level of loans, until it finally plays itself out at about twenty-eight times.[1] That process is commonly called "discounting commercial paper." It was one of the means by which the Fed was able to flood the nation with new money prior to the Great Dam Rupture of 1929.

But, there is a problem with that method, at least as far as the Fed is concerned. Even though interest rates at the discount window can be made so low that most bankers will line up like ducks looking for free corn, some of them—particularly those "hicks" in the country banks—have been known to resist the temptation. There is no way to force the banks to participate. Furthermore, the banks themselves are dependent upon the whims of their customers who, for reasons known only to themselves, may not want to borrow as much as the bank wants to lend. If the customers stop borrowing, then the banks have no new loans to convert into further reserves.

That left the third mechanism as the preferred option: the purchase and sale of bonds and other debt obligations in the open market. With the discount window, banks have to be enticed to borrow money which later must be repaid, and sometimes they are reluctant to do that. But with the open market, all the Fed has to do is write a fiat check to pay for the securities. When that check is cashed, the new money it created moves directly into the economy without any concurrence required from the recalcitrant banks.

But, there was a problem with this method also. Before World War I, there were few government bonds available on the open market. Even after the war, the supply was limited. Which means the vast inflation that preceded the Crash of 1929 was *not* caused by deficit spending. In each year from 1920 through 1930 there was a surplus of government revenue over expenses. Surprising as it may be, on the eve of the depression, America was getting out of debt.[2] As a consequence, there were few government bonds for the Fed to buy. Without government bonds, the open-market engine was constantly running out of gas.

The solution to all these problems was to create a new market tailor-made to the Fed's needs, a kind of half-way house between

---

1. See chapter ten for details.
2. See Robert T. Patterson, *The Great Boom and Panic; 1921–1929* (Chicago: Henry Regnery Company, 1965), p. 223.

the discount window and the open market. It was called the "acceptance window," and it was through that imagery that the System purchased a unique type of debt-related security called *banker's acceptances.*

BANKER'S ACCEPTANCES

Banker's acceptances are contracts promising payment for commercial goods scheduled for later delivery. They usually involve international trade where delays of three to six months are common. They are a means by which a seller in one country can ship goods to an unknown buyer in another country with confidence that he will be paid upon delivery. That is accomplished through guarantees made by the banks of both buyer and seller. First, the buyer's bank issues a letter of credit guaranteeing payment for the goods, even if the buyer should default. When the seller's bank receives this, one of its officers writes the word "accepted" on the contract and pays the seller the amount of the sale. The accepting bank, therefore, advances the money to the seller in expectation of receiving future payment from the buyer's bank. For this service, both banks charge a fee expressed as a percentage of the contract. Thus, the buyer pays a little more than the amount of the sales contract, and the seller receives a little less.

Historically, these contracts have been safe, because the banks are careful to guarantee payment only for financially sound firms. But, in times of economic panic, even sound firms may be unable to honor their contracts. It was underwriting that kind of business that nearly bankrupted George Peabody and J.P. Morgan in London during the panic of 1857, and would have done so had they not been bailed out by the Bank of England.

Acceptances, like commercial loan contracts, are negotiable instruments that can be traded in the securities market. The accepting banks have a choice of holding them until maturity or selling them. If they hold them, their profit will be realized when the underlying contract is eventually paid off and it will be equal to the amount of its "discount," which is banker language for its fee. Acceptances are said to be "rediscounted" when they are sold by the original discounter, the underwriter. The advantage of doing that is that they do not have to wait three to six months for their profit. They can acquire immediate capital which can be invested to earn interest.

The sale price of an acceptance is always less than the value of the underlying contracts; otherwise no one would buy them. The difference represents the potential profit to the buyer. It is expressed as a percentage and is called the "rate" of discount—or, in this case, rediscount. But the rate given by the seller must be lower than what he expects to earn with the money he receives, otherwise he will be better off not selling.

Although bankers' acceptances were commonly traded in Europe, they were not popular in the United States. Before the Federal Reserve Act was passed, national banks had been prohibited from purchasing them. A market, therefore, had to be created. The Fed accomplished this by setting the discount rate on acceptances so low that underwriters would have been foolish not to take advantage of it. At a very low discount, they could acquire short-term funds which then could be invested at a higher rate of return. Thus, acceptances quickly became plentiful on the open market in the United States.

But who would want to *buy* them at a low return? No one, of course. So, to create that market, not only did the Federal Reserve set the discount rate artificially low, it also pledged to buy all of the acceptances that were offered. The Fed, therefore, became the principal buyer of these securities. Banks also came into the market as buyers, but only because they knew that, at any time they wanted to sell, the Fed was pledged to buy.

Since the money was being created out of nothing, the cost did not really matter, nor did the low profit potential. The Fed's goal was not to make a profit on investment. It was to increase the nation's money supply.

WARBURG AND FRIENDS MAKE A LITTLE PROFIT

The man who benefited most from this artificially created market was none other than Paul Warburg, a partner with Kuhn, Loeb and Co. Warburg was in attendance at the Jekyll Island meeting at which the Federal Reserve System was conceived. He was considered by all to have been the master theoretician who led the others in their deliberations. He was one of the most influential voices in the public debates that followed. He had been appointed as one of the first members of the Federal Reserve Board and later became its Vice Governor until outbreak of war, at which time he resigned because of publicity regarding his connections with

German banking. He was a director of American I.G. Chemical
Corp. and Agfa Ansco, Inc., firms that were controlled by I.G.
Farben, the infamous German cartel that, only a few years later,
would sponsor the rise to power of Adolph Hitler.[1] He was also a
director of the CFR (Council on Foreign Relations). It should not be
surprising, therefore, to learn that he was able to position himself at
the center of the huge cash flow resulting from the Fed's purchase
of acceptances.

Warburg was the founder and Chairman of the International
Acceptance Bank of New York, the world's largest acceptance
bank. He was also a director of several smaller "competitors,"
including the prestigious Westinghouse Acceptance Bank. He was
founder and Chairman of the American Acceptance Council.
Warburg *was* the acceptance market in America. But he was not
without friends who also swam in the river of money. Men who
controlled America's largest financial institutions became directors
or officers of the various acceptance banks. The list of companies
that became part of the interlocking directorate included Kuhn,
Loeb and Co.; New York Trust Co.; Bank of Manhattan Trust Co.;
American Trust Co.; New York Title and Mortgage Co.; Chase
National Bank; Metropolitan Life Insurance Co.; American Express
Co.; the Carnegie Corp.; Guaranty Trust Co.; Mutual Life Insurance
Co.; the Equitable Life Assurance Society of New York; and the
First National Banks of Boston, St. Louis, and Los Angeles, to name
just a few. The world of acceptance banking was the private
domain of the financial elite of Wall Street.

Behind the American image, however, was a full partnership
with investors from Europe. Total capital of the IAB's American
shareholders was $276 million compared with $271 million from
foreign investors. A significant portion of that was divided between
the Warburgs in Germany and the Rothschilds in England.[2]

Just how large and free-flowing was that river of acceptance
money? In 1929, it was 1.7 trillion-dollars wide. Throughout the
1920s, it was *over half* of all the new money created by the Federal
Reserve—greater than all the other purchases on the open market

---

1. For a detailed account of this episode, see Part Two of the author's book, *World
without Cancer: The Story of Vitamin B17* (Westlake Village, California: American
Media, 1974).
2. Larry Schweikart, ed. *The Encyclopedia of American History and Biography* (New
York: Facts on File, 1990), p. 448.

plus all the loans to all the banks standing in line at the discount window.[1]

The monetary scientists who created the Federal Reserve, and their close business associates, were well-rewarded for their efforts. Profit-taking by insiders, however, is not the issue. Far more important is the fact that the *consequence* of this self-serving mechanism was the massive expansion of the money supply that made the Great Depression inevitable. And that is the topic which impelled us to look at acceptances in the first place.

CONGRESS SUSPICIOUS BUT AFRAID TO TINKER

By 1920, suspicions and resentment were growing in the halls of Congress. Politicians were not getting their share. It is possible that many of them failed to realize that, as partners in the scheme, they were *entitled* to a share. Nevertheless, they were dazzled by banker language and accounting tricks and were afraid to tinker with the System lest they accidentally push the wrong button.

Watching with amusement from London was Fabian Socialist John Maynard Keynes. Speaking of the Federal Reserve's manipulation of the value of the dollar, he wrote:

> That is the way by which a rich country is able to combine new wisdom with old prejudice. It can enjoy the latest scientific improvements, devised in the economic laboratory of Harvard, whilst leaving Congress to believe that no rash departure will be permitted.... But there is in all such fictions a certain instability.... The suspicions of Congressmen may be aroused. One cannot be quite certain that some Senator might not read and understand this book.[2]

There was not much danger of that! By then, American politicians had acquired a taste for the heady wine of war funding and stopped asking questions. World War I had created enormous demands for money, and the Fed provided it. By the end of the war, Congressional hostility to the Federal Reserve became history.

PAYING FOR WORLD WAR I

Much of the war debt was absorbed by the public which responded to patriotic instincts and purchased war bonds. The Treasury launched a massive publicity campaign for "Liberty Loans" to reinforce that sentiment. These small-denomination

---

1. *Ibid.*, p. 448; also Murray N. Rothbard, *America's Great Depression* (Kansas City: Sheed and Ward, 1963), p.117.
2. Keynes, *A Tract on Monetary Reform*, pp. 198–99.

bonds did not expand the money supply and did not cause inflation, because the money came from savings. It already existed. However, many people who thought it was their patriotic duty to support the war effort went to their banks and *borrowed* money so they could buy bonds. The bank created most of that money out of nothing, drawing upon credits and bookkeeping entries from the Federal Reserve, so those purchases *did* inflate the money supply. The same result could have been obtained more simply and less expensively by getting the money directly from the Fed, but the government encouraged the trend anyway, because of its psychological value in generating popular support for the war. When people make sacrifices for an endeavor, it reinforces their belief that it *must* be worthy.

Although the war was financed partly by taxes and partly by Liberty Bonds purchased by the public, a significant portion was covered by the sale of Treasury bonds to the Federal Reserve in the open market. Benjamin Strong's biographer, Lester Chandler, explains:

> The Federal Reserve System became an integral part of the war financing machinery. The System's overriding objective, both as a creator of money and as fiscal agent, was to insure that the Treasury would be supplied with all the money it needed, and on terms fixed by Congress and the Treasury.... A grateful nation now hailed it as a major contributor to the winning of the war, an efficient fiscal agent for the Treasury, a great source of currency and reserve funds, and a permanent and indispensable part of the banking system.[1]

THE EMERGENCE OF GOVERNMENT DEBT

The war years were largely a period of testing new strategies and consolidating power. Ironically, it was not until *after* the war—when there was no longer a justification for deficit spending—that government debt became plentiful. Up until World War I, annual federal expenses had been running about $750 million. By the end of the war, it was running $18 and-a-half *billion*, an increase of 2,466%. Approximately 70% of the cost of war had been financed by debt. Murray Rothbard reminds us that, on the eve of depression in 1928, ten years after the end of war, the banking system held more government bonds than during the war itself.[2] That means

---

1. Chandler, pp. 101–102.
2. *Depression*, p. 125.

the government did not pay off those bonds when they came due. Instead, it rolled them over by offering new bonds to replace the old. Why? Was it because Congress needed more money? No. The bonds had become the basis for money in circulation and, if they had been redeemed, the money supply would have decreased. A decrease in the money supply is viewed by politicians and central bankers as a threat to economic stability. Thus, the government found itself unable to get out of debt even when it had the money to do so, a dilemma that continues to this day.

There is an apparent contradiction here. In his book, *The Great Boom and Panic*, Robert Patterson says that, on the eve of depression, America was getting out of debt.[1] Yet, Rothbard tells us there were more government bonds held by the banking system than during the war! The only way both statements can be true is if there were, in fact, more bonds outstanding during the war but they were held by the *public*, not by the banking system. That would make it possible for there to be fewer total bonds in 1928 and yet the System could still hold more of them than previously. That would be the expected result of the Fed's growing role in the open market. As the publicly-held bonds matured, the Treasury rolled them over, and the Fed picked them up. Bonds purchased by the public do not increase the money supply whereas those purchased by banks do. Therefore, conditions in 1928 would have been far more inflationary than during the war—even though the government was getting out of debt.

Before 1922, the Federal Reserve bought Treasury bonds primarily for three purposes: (1) for income to operate the system, (2) to pay for the newly issued Federal Reserve Notes which were replacing silver certificates, and (3) to push down interest rates. The motive for manipulating interest rates was to encourage borrowing from abroad in the United States (where rates were low).[2] It also encouraged investment *from* the United States *into* Europe (where rates were higher). By making it possible to borrow American dollars at one rate and invest them elsewhere at a higher rate, the Fed was deliberately moving money out of the United States, with gold reserves following behind. As President Kennedy had said in

---

1. Page 223.
2. Chandler, p. 211; also Rothbard, *Depression*, p. 127.

his 1963 address at the IMF, the outflow of American gold "did not come about by chance."[1]

THE "DISCOVERY" OF THE OPEN MARKET

It is commonly asserted by writers on this topic that the power of the open-market mechanism to manipulate the money supply was "discovered" by the Fed in the early 1920s and that it came as a total surprise. Martin Mayer, for example, in his book, *The Bankers*, writes:

> Now, through an accident as startling as those which produced the discovery of X-Rays or penicillin, the central bank learned that "open market operations" could have a significant effect on the behavior of the banks.[2]

This makes the story interesting, but it is difficult to believe that Benjamin Strong, Paul Warburg, Montagu Norman, and the other monetary scientists who were pulling the levers at that time were taken by surprise. These men could not possibly have been ignorant of the effect of creating money out of nothing and pouring it into the economy. The open market was merely a different *funnel*. If there was any element of surprise, it likely was only in the ease with which the mechanism could be activated. It is not important whether that part of the story is fact or fiction, except that it perpetuates the "accidental" view of history, the myth that no one is responsible for political or economic chaos: *Things just happen. There was no master plan. No one is to blame. Everything is under control. Relax, pay your taxes, and go back to sleep!*

In any event, by the end of the war, Congress had awakened to the fact that it could use the Federal Reserve System to obtain revenue without taxes. From that point forward, deficit spending became institutionalized. A gradually increasing issuance of Treasury bonds was encouraging to the Fed because it provided still one more source of debt to convert into money, a source that eventually would become far more reliable than either bank loans or banker's acceptances. Best of all, now that Congress was becoming dependent on the free corn, there was little chance it would find its wings and fly away. The more dependent it became, the more secure the System itself became.

---

1. See Chapter six.
2. Mayer, p. 401.

In 1921, the twelve regional Reserve banks were separately buying and selling in the open market. But motives varied. Some merely needed income to cover their operating overhead, while others—notably the New York branch under Benjamin Strong—were more interested in sending American gold to England. Strong began immediately to gather control of all open-market operations into the hands of his own bank. In June of 1922, the "Open-Market Committee" was formed to coordinate activities among the regional Governors. In April of the next year, however, the national board in Washington replaced the Governor's group with one of its own creation, the "Open-Market Investments Committee." Benjamin Strong was its chairman. The powers of that group were enhanced ten years later by legislation which made it mandatory for the regional branches to follow the Open-Market Committee's directives, but that was a mere formality, for the die had been cast much earlier. From 1923 forward, the Fed's open-market operations have been carried out by the New York Federal Reserve Bank. The money trust has always been in control.

DROWNING IN CREDIT

Actions have consequences, and one of the consequences of purchasing Treasury bonds and other debt-related securities in the open market is that the money created to purchase them eventually ends up in the commercial banks where it is used for the expansion of bank credit. "Credit" is another of those weasely words that have different meanings to different people. In banker language, the expansion of credit means the banks have "excess reserves" (bookkeeping entries) which can be multiplied by nine and earn interest for them—if only someone would be kind enough to *borrow*. It is money *waiting* to be created. The message is: "Come on to the bank, folks. Don't be bashful. We've got plenty of money to lend. You have credit you didn't even know you had."

In the 1920s, the greater share of bank credit was bestowed upon business firms, wealthy investors, and other high rollers, but the little man was not ignored. In 1910, consumer credit accounted for only 10% of the nation's retail sales. By 1929, credit transactions were responsible for half of the $60 billion retail market. In his book, *Money and Man*, Elgin Groseclose says: "By 1929 the United States was overwhelmed by a flood of credit. It had covered the land. It was pouring into every nook and cranny of the national economy."[1]

The impact of expanding credit was compounded by artificially low interest rates—the other side of the same coin—which were intended to help the governments of Europe. But they also stimulated borrowing here at home. Since borrowing is what causes money to be created under fractional-reserve banking, the money supply in America began to expand. From 1921 through June of 1929, the quantity of dollars increased by 61.8%, substantially more than the increase in national product. During that same time, the amount of *currency* in circulation remained virtually unchanged. That means the expansion was comprised entirely of money substitutes, such as bonds and loan contracts.

BOOMS AND BUSTS MADE WORSE

The forces of the free market are amazingly flexible. Like the black market, they manage to exert themselves in unexpected ways in spite of political decree. That had been the case throughout most of American history. Prior to the creation of the Federal Reserve, banking had been coddled and hobbled by government. Banks were chartered by government, protected by government, and regulated by government. They had been forced to serve the political agendas of those in power. Consequently, the landscape was strewn with the tombstones of dead banks which had taken to their graves the life savings of their hapless depositors. But these were mostly regional tragedies that were offset by growth and prosperity in other areas. Even within the communities most severely affected, recovery was swift.

Now that the cartel had firm control over the nation's money supply, the pattern began to change. The corrective forces of the free market were more firmly straight-jacketed than ever. All banks in the entire country were in lock step with each other. What happened in one region is what happened in all regions. Banks were not allowed to die, so there could be no adjustments after their demise. Their illness was sustained and carried like a deadly virus to the others.

The expansion of the money supply in the 1920s clearly shows that effect. It was not a steady advance but a series of convulsions.

---

1. Groseclose, *America's Money Machine*, p. 154.

TULIPOMANIA

Easy credit was not the only problem in this period. Equally important was the *effect* that had on the behavior patterns of the populace. Responding to herd instinct and a belief in the possibility of something-for-nothing, men were driven to the most bizarre form of investment speculation.

This was not the first time such hysteria had seized a population. One of the most graphic examples occurred in Holland between the years 1634 and 1636. It came to pass that a new, rare flower, called the tulip, was discovered in the gardens of some of the more wealthy inhabitants of Constantinople, now known as Istanbul. When the root bulbs of these exotic blossoms were brought into Holland, they rapidly became a status symbol among the wealthy—much as race horses or rare breeds of dogs are today in our own society—and those with surplus funds found that an investment in tulips brought them significant social recognition.

The price of tulip bulbs climbed steadily until they became, not merely symbols of status, but speculative investments as well. At one point, prices doubled every few days, and speculators were seen everywhere amassing great fortunes with no input of either labor or service. Many otherwise prudent people found themselves infected by the hysteria. They borrowed against their homes and invested their life savings to get in on the anticipated windfall. This pushed up prices even further and tended to create the fulfillment of its own prophecy. Contracts for the future delivery of tulip bulbs—a form of today's commodity market—became a dominant feature of Holland's stock market.

Tulip bulbs eventually became more precious than gemstones. As new varieties were developed, the market became more complex, requiring experts to certify their origin and their grade. Prices soared, and the herd went insane. One bulb of the species called *Admiral Liefken* was valued at 4,400 florins; a *Semper Augustus*, worth 5,500 florins, was purchased for a new carriage, two gray horses, and a complete set of harnesses. It was recorded that, at one sale, a single *Viceroy* brought two lasts of wheat, four lasts of rye, four fat oxen, eight fat swine, twelve fat sheep, two hogsheads of wine, four casks of butter, one-thousand pounds of cheese, a bed and mattress, a suit of clothes, and a silver drinking cup.

Then, one day without warning, reality returned from her two-year vacation. By that time, everyone knew deep in their hearts that the spiralling prices bore no honest relationship to the value of the tulips and that, sooner or later, someone was going to get hurt. But they continued to speculate for fear of being too quick in their timing and losing out on profits yet to come. Everyone was confident they would sell out precisely at the top of the market. In any herd, however, there are always a few who *will* take the lead and, by 1636, all it took was one or two prominent merchants to sell out their stock. Overnight, there were no buyers whatsoever, at any price. The tulip market vanished, and speculators by the thousands saw their dreams of easy wealth—and, in many cases, their life savings also—disappear with it. Tulipomania, as it was called at the time, had come to an end.[1]

Or did it? As we have seen, the Federal Reserve can create large amounts of money simply by going into the open market and buying debt contracts. But, once it is in the mainstream of the economy, commercial banks can multiply that money by up to a factor of nine, and that is where the real inflationary action is. To protect that privilege is one of the reasons the banks formed this cartel in the first place. Nevertheless, the public still has the final say. If no one wants to borrow their money, the game is over.

That possibility is more theoretical than real. Although men may be hesitant to go into debt for legitimate business ventures in times of economic uncertainty, they can be lured by easy credit to take a long shot. Dreams of instant wealth are powerful motivaters. Gaming casinos, poker parlors, race tracks, lottery windows, and other forms of tulipomania are convincing evidence that the lust for gambling is embedded in genetic code. The public has always been interested in free corn.

TULIPS IN THE STOCK MARKET

During the final phase of America's credit expansion of the 1920s, the rise in prices on the stock market was entirely speculative. Buyers did not care if their stocks were overpriced compared to the dividends they paid. Commonly traded issues were selling for 20 to 50 times their earnings; some traded at 100. Speculators acquired stock merely to hold for a while and then sell at a profit. It

---

1. See Charles Mackay, LL.D., *Extraordinary Popular Delusions and the Madness of Crowds* (1841 rpt. New York: L.C. Page & Company, 1932), pp. 89–97.

was the "Greater-Fool" strategy. No matter how high the price is today, there will be a greater fool tomorrow who will buy at an even higher price. For a while, that strategy seemed to work.

To make the game even more exciting, it was common for investors to purchase their stocks on margin. That means the buyer puts up a small amount of money as a deposit (the margin) and *borrows* the rest from his stockbroker—who gets it from the bank, which gets it from the Fed. In the 1920s, the margin for small investors was as low as 10%. Although the average stock yielded a modest 3% annual dividend, speculators were willing to pay over 12% interest on their loans, meaning their stock had to appreciate about 9% per year just to break even.

These margin accounts are sometimes referred to as "call loans" because the broker has the right to "call them in" on very short notice, often as short as twenty-four hours. If the broker calls the loan, the investor must produce the money immediately. If he cannot, the broker will obtain the money by selling the stock. In theory, the sale of the stock will be sufficient to cover the loan. But, in practice, about the only time brokers call their loans is when the market is tumbling. Under *those* conditions, the stock cannot be sold except at a loss: a *total* loss of the investor's margin; and a *variable* loss to the broker, depending on the severity of the price fall. To obtain even more leverage, investors sometimes use the stocks they already own as collateral for a margin loan on *new* stocks. Therefore, if they cannot cover a margin call on their new stocks, they will lose their old stocks as well.

In any event, such silly concerns were not in vogue in the 1920s. From August of 1921 to September of 1929, the Dow-Jones industrial stock-price average went from 63.9 to 381.17, a rise of 597%. Credit was abundant, loans were cheap, profits were big.

BANKS BECOME SPECULATORS

The commercial banks were the middlemen in this giddy game. By the end of the decade, they were functioning more like speculators than banks. Instead of serving as dependable clearing houses for money, they also had become players in the market. Loans to commercial enterprises for the production of goods and services—which normally are the backbone of sound banking practice—were losing ground to loans for speculating in the stock market and in urban real estate. Between 1921 and 1929, while commercial loans remained constant, total bank loans increased from $24,121 million to $35,711 million. Loans on securities and real estate rose nearly $8 billion. Thus, about 70% of the increase during this period was in speculative investments. And that money was created by the banks.

New York banks and trust companies had over $7 billion on loan to brokers at the New York Stock Exchange for use in margin accounts. Before the war, there were 250 securities dealers. By 1929, the number had grown to 6,500.

The banks not only generated the money for speculation, they became speculators themselves by purchasing large blocks of high-yield bonds, many of which were of dubious quality. Those were the kinds of securities that are difficult to liquidate in a declining market. Borrowing money on short term and investing on long term, the banks were maneuvering themselves into a precarious position.

· Did the Federal Reserve cause the speculation in the stock market? Of course not. *Speculators* did that. The Fed undoubtedly had other objects in mind, but that did not cancel its responsibility. It was acutely aware of the psychological effect of easy credit and had consciously used that knowledge to manipulate public behavior on numerous occasions. Behavioral psychology is a necessary tool of the trade. So it could claim neither ignorance nor innocence. In the unfolding of this tragedy, it was about as innocent as a spider whose web "accidentally" caught the fly.

THE FINAL BUBBLE

In the Spring of 1928, the Federal Reserve expressed concern over speculation in the stock market and raised interest rates to curb the expansion of credit. The growth in the money supply began to slow down, and so did the rise in stock prices. It is conceivable that the soaring economy could have been brought in for a "soft landing"—except that there were other agendas to be considered. Professor Quigley had said that the central bankers were not substantive powers unto themselves but were as marionettes whose strings were pulled by others. Just as the speculation spree appeared to be coming under control, those strings were yanked, and the Federal Reserve flip-flopped once again.

The strings originated in London. Even after seven years of subsidy by the Federal Reserve, the British economy was sagging from the weight of its socialist system, and gold was moving back into the United States. The Fed, in spite of its own public condemnation of excessive speculation, reversed itself at the brink of success and purchased over $300 million of banker's acceptances in the last half of 1928, which caused an increase in the money supply of almost $2 billion. Professor Rothbard says:

> Europe, as we have noted, had found the benefits from the 1927 inflation dissipated, and European opinion now clamored against any tighter money in the U.S. The easing in late 1928 prevented gold inflows into the U.S. from getting very large. Great Britain was again losing gold, and sterling was weak once more. The United States bowed once again to its overriding wish to see Europe avoid the inevitable consequences of its own inflationary policies.[1]

Prior to the Fed's reversal of policy, stock prices had actually declined by five per cent. Now, they went through the roof, rising twenty per cent from July to December. The boom had returned in spades.

Then, in February of 1929, a curious event occurred. Montagu Norman travelled to the United States once again to confer privately with the officers of the Federal Reserve. He also met with Andrew Mellon, Secretary of the Treasury. There is no detailed public record of what transpired at these closed meetings, but we can be certain of three things: it was *important*; it concerned the economies of America and Great Britain; and it was thought best not to tell the public what was going on. It is not unreasonable to surmise that the central bankers had come to the conclusion that the bubble—not only in America, but in Europe—was probably going to rupture very soon. Rather than fight it, as they had in the past, it was time to stand back and let it happen, clear out the speculators, and return the markets to reality. As Galbraith put it: "How much better, as seen from the Federal Reserve, to let nature take its course and thus allow nature to take the blame."[2]

Mellon was even more emphatic. Herbert Hoover described Mellon's views as follows:

> Mr. Mellon had only one formula: "liquidate labor, liquidate stocks, liquidate the farmers, liquidate real estate." He insisted that, when the people get an inflation brainstorm, the only way to get it out

---

1. Rothbard, *Depression*, p. 147.
2. Galbraith, p. 181.

of their blood is to let it collapse. He held that even a panic was not altogether a bad thing. He said: "It will purge the rottenness out of the system. High costs of living and high living will come down. People will work harder, live a moral life. Values will be adjusted, and enterprising people will pick up the wrecks from less competent people."[1]

If this had been the mindset between Mellon and Norman and the Federal Reserve Board, the purpose of their meetings would have been to make sure that, when the implosion happened, the central banks could coordinate their policies. Rather than be overwhelmed by it, they should *direct* it as best they can and turn it ultimately to their advantage. Perhaps we shall never know if that scenario is accurate, but the events that followed strongly support such a view.

ADVANCE WARNING FOR MEMBERS ONLY

Immediately after the meetings, the monetary scientists began to issue warnings to their colleagues in the financial fraternity to *get out of the market*. On February 6, the Federal Reserve issued an advisory to its member banks to liquidate their holdings in the stock market. The following month, Paul Warburg gave the same advice in the annual report to the stockholders of his International Acceptance Bank. He explained the reason for that advice:

> If the orgies of unrestrained speculation are permitted to spread, the ultimate collapse is certain not only to affect the speculators themselves, but to bring about a general depression involving the entire country.[2]

Paul Warburg was a partner with Kuhn, Loeb & Co. which maintained a list of preferred customers. These were fellow bankers, wealthy industrialists, prominent politicians, and high officials in foreign governments. A similar list was maintained at J.P. Morgan Co. It was customary to give these men advance notice on important stock issues and an opportunity to purchase them at two to fifteen points below their price to the public. That was one of the means by which investment bankers maintained influence over the

---

1. Quoted by Burton Hersh, *The Mellon Family: A Fortune in History* (New York: William Morrow and Co., 1978), p. 290.
2. This advice was reprinted in the *Commercial and Financial Chronicle*, March 9, 1929, p. 1444.

affairs of the world. The men on these lists were notified of the coming crash.

John D. Rockefeller, J.P. Morgan, Joseph P. Kennedy, Bernard Baruch, Henry Morganthau, Douglas Dillon—the biographies of all the Wall Street giants at that time boast that these men were "wise" enough to get out of the stock market just before the Crash. And it is true. Virtually all of the inner club was rescued. There is no record of any member of the interlocking directorate between the Federal Reserve, the major New York banks, and their prime customers having been caught by surprise. Wisdom, apparently, was greatly affected by whose list one was on.

A MESSAGE OF COMFORT TO THE PUBLIC

While the crew was abandoning ship, the passengers were told it was a lovely cruise. President Coolidge and Treasury Secretary Mellon had been vociferous in their public utterances that the economy was in better shape than ever. From his socialist perch in London, John Maynard Keynes exclaimed that the management of the dollar by the Federal Reserve Board was a "triumph" of man over money. And, from the plush offices of his New York Federal Reserve Bank, Benjamin Strong boasted:

> The very existence of the Federal Reserve System is a safeguard against anything like a calamity growing out of money rates.... In former days the psychology was different, because the facts of the banking situation were different. Mob panic, and consequently mob disaster, is less likely to arise.[1]

The public was comforted, and the balloon continued to expand. It was now time to sharpen the pin. On April 19, the Fed held an emergency meeting under cloak of great secrecy. The following day, the New York Times reported as follows:

RESERVE COUNCIL CONFERS IN HASTE
Atmosphere of Mystery Is Thrown
about Its Meeting in Washington

An atmosphere of deep mystery was thrown about the proceedings both by the board and the council. No advance announcement had been made that an extraordinary session of the council was contemplated, and the fact that the members were in the city became known only when

---

1. Quoted by Greider, p. 298.

newspaper correspondents happened to see some of them entering the Treasury Department building. Even after that, evasive replies were given.... While the joint meeting was in progress at the Treasury Department, every effort was made to guard the proceedings, and a group of newspaper correspondents were asked to leave the corridor.[1]

Let us return briefly to Montagu Norman. His biographer tells us that, after he became head of the Bank of England, his custom was to journey to the United States several times each year, although his arrival was seldom noted by the press. He travelled in disguise, wearing a long, black cloak and a large, broad-brimmed hat, and he used the pseudonym of Professor Skinner.[2] It was on one of those unpublicized trips that he ran into a young Australian by the name of W.C. Wentworth. Sixty years later, Wentworth wrote a letter to *The Australian*, a newspaper in Sydney, and told of his encounter:

> In 1929 I was a member of the Oxford and Cambridge athletic team, visiting America to run against American Universities. Late in July we split up to return, and I, together with some other members, boarded a smallish passenger vessel in New York. (There were, of course, no aeroplanes in those days.)
>
> A fellow passenger was "Mr. Skinner," and a member of our team recognized him. He was Montagu Norman, returning to London, after a secret visit to the US Central Bank, travelling incognito.
>
> When we told him we knew who he was, he asked us not to blow his cover, because if the details of his movement were made public, it could have serious financial consequences. Naturally, we agreed, and on the days following, as we crossed the Atlantic, he talked to us very frankly.
>
> He said, "In the next few months there is going to be a shake-out. But don't worry—it won't last for long."[3]

On August 9, just a few weeks after that ship-board encounter, the Federal Reserve Board reversed its easy-credit policy and raised the discount rate to six per cent. A few days later, the Bank of England raised its rate also. Bank reserves in both countries began to shrink and, along with them, so did the money supply. Simulta-

---

1. "Reserve Council Confers in Haste," *New York Times*, April 20, 1929, p. 89.
2. Hargrave, p. 1.
3. "Letters to the editor," *The Australian* (GPO Box 4162, Sydney, NSW. 2001), February 7, 1989.

neously, the System began to sell securities in the open market, a maneuver that also contracts the money supply. Call rates on margin loans had jumped to fifteen, then twenty per cent. The pin had been inserted.

THE DUCK DINNER BEGINS

The securities market reached its high point on September 19. Then, it began to slide. The public was not yet aware that the end had arrived. The roller coaster had dipped before. Surely it would shoot upward again. For five more weeks, the public bought heavily on the way down. More than a million shares were traded during that period. Then, on Thursday, October 24, like a giant school of fish suddenly turning direction in response to an unseen signal, thousands of investors stampeded to sell. The ticker tape was hopelessly overloaded. Prices tumbled. Thirteen million shares exchanged hands. Everyone said the bottom had dropped out of the market. They were wrong. Five days later, it did.

On Tuesday, October 29, the exchanges were crushed by an avalanche of selling. At times there were no buyers at all. By the end of the trading session, over sixteen million shares had been dumped, in most cases at *any* price that was offered. Within a single day, millions of investors were wiped out. Within a few weeks of further decline, $3 billion of wealth had disappeared. Within twelve months, $40 billion had vanished. People who had counted their paper profits and thought they were rich suddenly found themselves to be very poor.

The other side of the coin is that, for every seller, there was a buyer. The insiders who had moved their investments into cash and gold were the buyers. It must be remembered that falling stock prices didn't necessarily mean that there was anything wrong with the stocks. Those representing solid companies were still paying dividends and were good investments—at a realistic price. In the panic, prices had tumbled far below their natural levels. Those who had the cash picked them up for a small fraction of their true worth. Giant holding companies were formed for that task, such as Marine Midland Corporation, the Lehman Corporation, and the Equity Corporation. J.P. Morgan set up the food trust called Standard Brands. Like the shark swallowing the mackerel, the big speculators devoured the small.

There is no evidence that the Crash was planned for the purpose of profit taking. There was considerable motivation for the monetary scientists to avert it, and they might have done so had not their higher-priority agendas gotten in the way. Yet, once they realized the inevitability of a collapse in the market, they were not bashful about using their privileged position to take full advantage of it. In that sense, FDR's son-in-law, Curtis Dall, was right when he wrote: "It was the calculated 'shearing' of the public by the World Money Powers."[1]

NATURAL LAW NO. 5

Here is another of those "natural laws" of economics that needs to be added to our list:

LESSON: It is human nature for man to place personal priorities ahead of all others. Even the best of men cannot long resist the temptation to benefit at the expense of their neighbors if the occasion is placed squarely before them. This is especially true when the means by which they benefit is obscure and not likely to be perceived as such. There may be exceptional men from time to time who can resist that temptation, but their numbers are small. The general rule will prevail in the long run.

A managed economy presents men with precisely that kind of opportunity. The power to create and extinguish the nation's money supply provides unlimited potential for personal gain. Throughout history the granting of that power has been justified as being necessary to protect the public, but the results have always been the opposite. It has been used against the public and for the personal gain of those who control. Therefore,

LAW: When men are entrusted with the power to control the money supply, they will eventually use that power to confiscate the wealth of their neighbors.

There is no better illustration of that law than the Crash of 1929 and the lingering depression that followed.

---

1. Curtis B. Dall, *FDR: My Exploited Father-In-Law* (Tulsa, Oklahoma: Christian Crusade Publications, 1967), p. 49.

FROM CRASH TO DEPRESSION

The lingering depression is an important part of the story. The speculators had been ruined, but what they lost was money acquired without effort. There were some unfortunate souls who also lost their life savings, but only because they gambled those savings on call loans. Those who bought stock with money they actually possessed did not have to sell, and they did quite well in the long run. For the most part, something-for-nothing had merely been converted back into nothing. The price of stocks had plummeted, but the companies behind them were still producing products, still employing people, and still paying dividends. No one lost his job just because the market fell. The tulips were gone, but the wheat crop remained.

So, where was the problem? In truth, there was none—at least not yet. The crash, as devastating as it was to the speculators, had little effect on the average American. Unemployment didn't become rampant until the depression years which came later and were caused by continued government restraint of the free market. The drop of prices in the stock market was really a long-overdue and *healthy* adjustment to the economy. The stage was now set for recovery and sound economic growth, as always had happened in the past.

It did not happen this time. The monetary and political scientists who had created the problem now were in full charge of the rescue. They saw the crash as a golden opportunity to justify even more controls than before. Herbert Hoover launched a multitude of government programs to bolster wage rates, prevent prices from dropping, prop up failing firms, stimulate construction, guarantee home loans, protect the depositors, rescue the banks, subsidize the farmers, and provide public works. FDR was swept into office by promising even more of the same under the slogan of a New Deal. And the Federal Reserve launched a series of "banking reforms," all of which were measures to further extend its power over the money supply.

In 1931, fresh money was pumped into the economy to restart the cycle, but this time the rocket would not lift off. The dead weight of new bureaucracies and government regulations and subsidies and taxes and welfare benefits and deficit spending and tinkering with prices had kept it on the launching pad.

Eventually, the productive foundation of the country also began to crumble under the weight. Taxes and regulatory agencies forced companies out of business. Those that remained had to curtail production. Unemployment began to spread. By every economic measure, the economy was no better or worse in 1939 than it was in 1930 when the rescue began. It wasn't until the outbreak of World War II, and the tooling up for war production that followed, that the depression was finally brought to an end.

It was a dubious save. In almost every way, it was a repeat of the drama played out with World War I, even to the names of two of its most important players. FDR and Churchill worked together behind the scenes to bring America into the conflict—Churchill wanting American assistance in a war England was losing and could not afford, FDR wanting a jolt to the economy for political reasons, and the financiers, gathered behind J.P. Morgan, wanting the profits of war. But that is another chapter, and this book is long enough.

What happened *after* World War II was the focus of the first six chapters. That brings us to the end of the historical record. It's time, now, to reset the coordinates on our time machine and return to the present.

SUMMARY

Congress had been assured that the Federal Reserve Act would decentralize banking power away from Wall Street. However, within a few years of its inception, the System was controlled by the New York Reserve Bank under the leadership of Benjamin Strong whose name was synonymous with the Wall Street money trust.

During the nine years before the crash of 1929, the Federal Reserve was responsible for a massive expansion of the money supply. A primary motive for that policy was to assist the government of Great Britain to pay for its socialist programs which, by then, had drained its treasury. By devaluing the dollar and depressing interest rates in America, investors would move their money to England where rates and values were higher. That strategy succeeded in helping Great Britain for a while, but it set in motion the forces that made the stock-market crash inevitable.

The money supply expanded throughout this period, but the trend was interspersed with short spasms of contraction which were the result of attempts to halt the expansions. Each resolve to use restraint was broken by the higher political agenda of helping the governments of Europe. In the long view, the result of plentiful money and easy credit was a wave of speculation in the stock market and urban real estate that intensified with each passing month.

There is circumstantial evidence that the Bank of England and the Federal Reserve had concluded, at a secret meeting in February of 1929, that a collapse in the market was inevitable and that the best action was to let nature take its course. Immediately after that meeting, the financiers sent advisory warnings to lists of preferred customers—wealthy industrialists, prominent politicians, and high officials in foreign governments—to get out of the stock market. Meanwhile, the American people were being assured that the economy was in sound condition.

On August 9, the Federal Reserve applied the pin to the bubble. It increased the bank-loan rate and began to sell securities in the open market. Both actions have the effect of reducing the money supply. Rates on brokers' loans jumped to 20%. On October 29, the stock market collapsed. Thousands of investors were wiped out in a single day. The insiders who were forewarned had converted their stocks into cash while prices were still high. They now became the buyers. Some of the greatest fortunes in America were made in that fashion.

Section VI

TIME TRAVEL INTO THE FUTURE

In the previous sections of this book, we have travelled through time. We began our journey by stepping into the past. As we crisscrossed the centuries, we observed wars, treachery, profiteering, and political deception. That has brought us to the present. Now we are prepared to ride our time machine into the future. It will be a hair-raising trip, and much of what lies ahead will be unpleasant. But it has not yet come to pass. It is merely the projection of present forces. If we do not like what we see, we still have an opportunity to change those forces. The future will be what we choose to make it.

Chapter Twenty-Four

DOOMSDAY MECHANISMS

The decline of American prosperity; the increase in the size of government; the decrease in personal freedom; the growth of taxes; evidence that this is according to plan by an elite ruling group which hopes to merge the United States into world government on the basis of "equality" with less-developed nations; the environmentalist movement shown to be an outgrowth of that plan.

That's enough history for one book. It will soon be time to reset the coordinates on our time machine and jump into the future. Before activating that switch, however, let's take one last look around us. The future is molded by the present. Where we are *now* will greatly affect where we are *going* to be.

MIRED IN DEBT

One of the most obvious characteristics of our present time is the extent to which Americans and their government have become mired in debt. Annual federal deficits have grown steadily since 1950, and the rate of growth now is in a vertical climb. It took 198 years for the government to borrow the first trillion dollars. Then, in just twelve years—mostly under the Reagan Administration—it borrowed another *three* trillion. By the first year of the George W. Bush Administration, even before the terrorist attack on September 11, the federal debt had risen to over $5.8 trillion. By 2007, it had risen to $59.1 trillion when all government liabilities are included.

It is difficult to comprehend numbers of that size or to translate them into their effect upon each of us. $59.1 trillion represents more than all the goods sold and all the services rendered in America throughout the entire year. If you had a stack of $100 bills 40 inches high, you would be a millionaire. $59.1 trillion would rise over thirty-five miles into space.

By 2006, gross interest payments on the national debt were running $406 billion per year. That consumed about 17% of all federal revenue.[1] It now represents the government's largest single expense; greater than defense; larger than the combined cost of the departments of Agriculture, Education, Energy, Housing and Urban Development, Interior, Justice, Labor, State, Transportation, and Veterans' Affairs.

These charges are *not* paid by the government; they are paid by *you*. You provide the money through taxes and inflation. The cost currently is about $5,000 for each family of four. All families pay through inflation but not all pay taxes. The cost to each *taxpaying* family, therefore, is higher. On average, over $5,000 is extracted from your family each year, *not* to provide government services or even to pay off previous debt. Nothing is produced by it, not even roads or government buildings. No welfare or medical benefits come out of it. No salaries are paid by it. The nation's standard of living is not raised by it. It does nothing except pay interest.

Furthermore, the interest is compounded, which means, even if the government were to completely stop its deficit spending, the total debt would continue to grow as a result of interest on that portion which already exists. In 2006, interest on the national debt was already consuming 39% of all the revenue collected by personal income taxes.[2]

Amazing, isn't it? Without interest on the national debt, we would save enough to cut our personal income taxes by a third and we could reduce corporate taxes as well. Unfortunately, under present policies and programs, that is not going to happen, because Congress does not live within its income. Many expenses are paid, not from taxes, but from selling government bonds and going deeper into debt each year. So, even though we could save enough to slash personal income taxes, it would not be enough. The

1. The Treasury claims that we should look only at the *net* interest which, in 2001, was "only" $206 billion. That is because some of the interest was paid to various federal agencies which hold part of the debt—such as the Social Security Fund. Theoretically, this is a case of the government merely paying itself. However, the so-called interest received is not received as cash payments but as more IOUs(!) which is to say that it is not received at all. Forget the mirage of *net* gross interest. It is merely an accounting trick to hide the true cost of the national debt.
2. See "Historical Tables," *Budget of the United States; Fiscal Year 2008.*
Also: *Interest Expense on the Debt Outstanding*, www.treasurydirect.gov/reports/ir/ir_expense.htm.

government would still go into the red to keep up its present life style. However, if a reduction in the size and scope of the bureaucracy were accomplished at the same time, then personal *and* corporate income taxes *could* be entirely eliminated, and the government would have an annual surplus.[1]

THE DOOMSDAY MECHANISM

Unfortunately, the locomotive is running in the opposite direction. Government is growing larger, not smaller. By 2008, outlays of the federal government were one-fourth the economy of the entire nation. More people now work for government than for all manufacturing companies in the private sector. There are more bank regulators than bankers, more farm-bureau workers than farmers, more welfare administrators than recipients. More citizens receive government checks than those who pay income taxes.

By 1996, welfare benefits in 29 states were higher than the average secretary's wage; and in 6 states, they were more than the entry-level wage for computer programmers. When people can vote on issues involving the transfer of wealth to themselves from others, the ballot box becomes a weapon with which the majority plunders the minority. That is the point of no return, the point where the doomsday mechanism begins to accelerate until the system self-destructs. The plundered grow weary of carrying the load and eventually join the plunderers. The productive base of the economy diminishes further until only the state remains.

The doomsday mechanism is also operating within government itself. By 1992, more than half of all federal outlays went for what are called entitlements. Those are expenses—such as Medicare, Social Security, and government retirement programs—which are based on promises of *future* payments. Many of them are contractual obligations, and millions of people depend on them.

That does not mean they cannot be eliminated. For example, entitlements include $24 billion per year for food stamps. There is no contractual obligation to continue those, only political expediency. By now, most Americans have stood in grocery lines and

---

1. The federal government derives substantial revenue from sources other than income taxes, such as excise taxes and import taxes. These, plus occasional assessments to the states, were the only taxes which the founding fathers intended for the federal government. The arrangement worked well for 135 years until the income-tax was adopted in 1913.

watched the well-dressed customer in front of them use food stamps for ice cream and pretzels, pay cash for two bottles of wine. and then drive away in a late-model car. The political function of the food stamp program is not to help the hungry but to buy votes.

The programs that do involve contractual obligations—such as Social Security and Medicare—could be turned over to private firms which would not only operate them more efficiently but also would pay out higher benefits. Congress, however, does not dare to touch any of these entitlements for fear of losing votes.

Normally, with contracts for future obligations of this kind, the issuer is required by law to accumulate money into a fund to make sure that there will be enough available when future payments become due. The federal government does not abide by those laws. The funds exist on paper only. The money that comes in for future obligations is immediately spent and replaced by a government IOU. So, as those future payments come due, *all* of the money must come from revenue being collected at that time.

Herein lies the doomsday mechanism. These obligations *will* be paid out of future taxes or inflation. Entitlements currently represent 52% of all federal outlays, and they are growing at the rate of 12% each year. When this is added to the 14% that is now being spent for interest payments on the national debt, we come to the startling conclusion that two-thirds of all federal expenses are now entirely automatic, and that percentage is growing each month.

Even if Congress were to stop all of the spending programs in the normal budget—dismantle the armed forces, close down all of its agencies and bureaus, stop all of its subsidies, and board up all of its buildings, including the White House—it would be able to reduce its present spending by only one-third. And even that small amount is shrinking by 10 to 12% per year. That is a best-case scenario. The real-case is that Congress is accelerating its discretionary spending, not canceling it. One does not have to be a statistical analyst to figure out where this trend is headed.

The biggest doomsday mechanism of all, however, is the Federal Reserve System. It will be recalled that every cent of our money supply—including coins, currency, and checkbook money—came into being for the purpose of being lent to someone. All of those dollars will disappear when the loans are paid back. They will exist only so long as the debt behind them exists. Underneath the pyramid of money, supporting the entire structure, are the so-called reserves which represent the Fed's monetization of debt. If we tried to pay off the national debt, those reserves would also start to disappear, and our money supply would be undermined. The Federal Reserve would have to scramble into the money markets of the world and replace U.S. securities with bonds from corporations and other countries. Technically, that can be done, but the transition could be devastating. Under the Federal Reserve System, therefore, Congress would be fearful to eliminate the national debt even if it wanted to.

These are the doomsday mechanisms already in operation. If we do not understand how they function, we will not be prepared for our trip into the future. The scenes that will unfold there will appear too bizarre, the events too shocking. We would be convinced that something surely had gone wrong with our time machine.

WHO OWNS THE NATIONAL DEBT?

It has been said that we need not worry about interest on the national debt because "We owe it to ourselves." Let's take a look at who owes what to whom.

It may come as a surprise to learn that the Federal Reserve holds but a small portion of the national debt, only about 9%. Agencies of the federal government have 28% (this constitutes an IOU for money taken from various "reserve" funds, such as Social Security, and spent for other purposes). Foreign investors own approximately 43% (2002 figures), and private-sector investors in the U.S. hold the balance. It is partly true, therefore, that "We owe it to ourselves" but it is more accurate to say that *all* of us owe it to *some* of us. The *some* of us who receive the interest are private investors seeking income that is exempt from state income taxes, and large institutions such as banks, corporations, insurance companies, and investment funds. With institutions, the money represents pooled assets belonging to thousands of small investors. So, a major portion of the interest on the national debt does, indeed, accrue to the benefit of a large sector of the American people.

That's the good news. The bad news is that the government obtains every cent of the money it pays to us by confiscating it from us in the first place. If it is true that we owe it to ourselves, then it is also true that we *pay* it to ourselves. The money goes out of one pocket back into the other—minus a handling fee. The government takes $1,000 from us in taxes and inflation and gives us back $350. The so-called "benefit" to the public is but a giant scam.

And more bad news: When people purchase government bonds, there is less money available for investment in private industry. It is well known that government credit "crowds out" private credit. The result is that the productive side of the nation is handicapped by unfair competition for investment capital. To obtain new money for growth, private companies must pay higher interest rates. These are passed on to the consumer in the form of higher prices. Many companies are forced to curtail their plans for expansion, and potentially new jobs are never created. Some companies are forced out of business altogether, and their employees are put out of work. The economy is always retarded by government debt. The larger the debt, the greater the damage.

The 43% portion of the national debt held by foreign investors is a huge bite. One-trillion, three-hundred-million dollars cannot be ignored. These bonds could become a serious problem down the line as they mature. So far, they have been a partial blessing because they were purchased with money that already existed. Therefore, they were not inflationary. But it is not difficult to imagine future conditions under which bond holders would decide not to renew. What would happen if the stability of the government were to be questioned, or if the productive capacity of the United States were to be challenged by massive terrorist attacks? In order to pay off those bonds on maturity, the Treasury would have to issue new ones. The Federal Reserve would have to purchase the new bonds with fiat money. Therefore, foreign-held federal debt is a ticking time bomb. If it should ever have to be picked up by the Fed, the inflationary impact on our country would be staggering.

WHAT DIFFERENCE DOES IT MAKE?

There is a tendency to read about these trends with a kind of detached fascination: Isn't that *interesting*! But where is the relevance? Why get excited over such technicalities and abstractions? So what if the government is mired in debt? Who cares if the interest will never be paid? What of it if we have a world currency or a world government? What difference will any of it make to *me*?

The first step toward answering those questions is to see what difference it already has made. Our upcoming trip into the future will merely extend those lines.

Based on doomsday predictions of environmental disaster, government has saddled private companies with such burdensome expenses for eliminating waste products that heavy industry, once the mainstay of American prosperity, has fled our shores. Because of concern over the habitat of the spotted owl and the desert kangaroo rat, millions of acres of timber and agricultural land have been taken out of production. High taxes, unrealistic rules for safety devices in the work place, so-called fair-employment practices, and mandatory health insurance are rapidly destroying what is left of America's private industry. The result is unemployment and dislocation for millions of American workers.

Federal taxes, including Social-Security, now take more than 40% of our private incomes. State, county, and local taxes are on top of that. Inflation feeds on what is left. We spend half of each year working for the government.

A study by the AFL-CIO in 1977 revealed that, in spite of wage increases in terms of dollars, the *real* wages of the average American—in terms of what he can buy with those dollars—were going down. That trend was confirmed in 1980 by the U.S. Census Bureau. In 1992, the Consumers' Union analyzed how many hours one had to work to buy common items compared to thirty years previously. The report concluded:

> The average U.S. household has maintained its living standard largely because families are working more hours. Millions of women entered the work force in the past 25 years. In 1970, about 21 million women worked full time. Now that figure is over 36 million. That has helped to keep family buying power fairly stable. But for many families, it now represents the labor of two earners rather than one.[1]

In 1999, a report published by The Economic Policy Institute revealed that the average middle-class American family was working an average of six weeks more each year than when the study began in 1989. Yet, this was still not enough. To maintain their old life style, these families were consuming the last of their savings and going into debt. In 1999, the average personal savings rate finally became a *negative* one percent, which means that the facade of prosperity is now being paid for with borrowed money.

The message here is that real wages in America have declined. Young couples with a single income now have a lower standard of

---

1. "Has Our Living Standard Stalled?" *Consumer Reports*, June, 1992, p. 392.

living than their parents did. In spite of two incomes, the net worth of the average household is falling. For many it has become negative. The percentage of Americans who own their homes is dropping. The age at which a family acquires a first home is rising. Mortgage foreclosures are increasing. The number of families in the middle class is falling. Savings accounts are smaller. Family debt is greater. The number of people below the officially defined poverty level is rising. The percentage of people working beyond age 65 is also rising. The rate of personal bankruptcy is quadruple what it was in the 1960s. More and more Americans are broke at age 65.

THE NEW WORLD ORDER

None of this is happening by accident. Chapters five and six documented the currently unfolding plan to create a functional world government within the framework of the United Nations. Often referred to as *The New World Order* by its advocates, the proposed global government is designed upon the principles of collectivism. It is the dream-come-true for the world's socialist theoreticians, politicians, and technicians who see it as the ultimate laboratory for their social experiments upon mankind.

There are two mechanisms of power being readied at the UN. One is a military command to eventually control all national armies and super weapons. That is being accomplished under the slogans of peace and disarmament. The other is a world central bank, now called the IMF/World Bank, with the ability to issue a common money which all nations must accept. That is being accomplished under the slogans of international trade and economic growth.

Of the two mechanisms, monetary control is the more important. The use of military force is viewed as a crude weapon in the arsenal of world government to be used only as a last resort. The effect of monetary control is more powerful than mega-tons of atomic energy. It reaches into every shop and home, a feat that could never be accomplished by standing armies. It can be used with precision against a nation, a group, or even one person while sparing or benefiting all others. Military force may be irresistible but it causes resentment and political unrest that can smolder for decades. Since monetary manipulation is seldom understood by its victims, it does not incur their wrath. In fact, the manipulators enjoy high social status and financial reward. For these reasons, monetary control is the weapon of choice in The New World Order.

A future world parliament based upon the concept of minimum coercion and maximum freedom could be a wonderful advent for mankind. Without trying to cram all nations into a centrally-directed beehive, it would welcome cultural and religious variety. Instead of trying to place the world into a collectivist straight-jacket of rules, regulations, quotas, and subsidies, it would encourage diversity and freedom-to-choose. Instead of levying ever-larger taxes on every conceivable economic activity and destroying human incentive in the process, it would encourage member nations to reduce the taxes that already exist and thereby stimulate production and creativity.

A world parliament, dedicated to the concept of freedom, would have to withhold membership from any government that violated the basic rights of its citizens. It could be the means by which totalitarian governments would be encouraged to abandon their oppressive policies in order to obtain the economic and political advantages of acceptance in the world body. It could become the greatest force for peace and prosperity and freedom we have ever known.

But The New World Order that is now incubating at the United Nations is an entirely different creature. Its members represent just about every dictator and warlord in the world. Its philosophy is built upon the socialist doctrine that all good flows from the state. Those who do not conform must be bent to the government's will or be eliminated. It cannot oppose totalitarianism for the simple reason that it *is* totalitarianism.

AMERICA IS THE TARGET

The New World Order cannot become a functional reality so long as the United States remains able to go it alone. America is viewed as a potential bull in the china shop. Right now, it is safely under control, but the world planners are worried it might break loose in the future. If the American people were to awaken to the realities of world politics and regain control over their government, they still would have the military and economic power to break away. Among the world planners, therefore, it has become the *prime directive* to weaken the United States both militarily and economically. And this directive has come from *American* leaders, not those of other countries. CFR members sitting in the White House, the State Department, the Defense Department, and the

Treasury are now working to finalize that part of the plan. It is yet one more doomsday mechanism that, once it gains sufficient momentum, will pass the critical point of no return.

The Korean War was the first time American soldiers fought under UN authority. That trend has accelerated and now includes military actions in Iraq, Yugoslavia, Bosnia, Somalia, and Haiti. While the American military is being absorbed into the UN, steps are also underway to hand over American atomic weapons. When that happens, the doomsday mechanism will become activated. It will be too late to escape.

Likewise, the IMF/World Bank is already functioning—in conjunction with the Federal Reserve System—as a world central bank. The American economy is being deliberately exhausted through foreign giveaways, endless wars, and domestic boondoggles. The object is, not to help those in need or to defend freedom or preserve the environment, but to *bring the system down*. When once-proud and independent Americans are standing in soup lines, they will be ready to accept the carefully arranged "rescue" by the world bank. The Euro is already in place as a regional currency. The Amero is next. These are but transitions to a planned world currency. From these, also, there will be no escape.

THE REPORT FROM IRON MOUNTAIN

The substance of these stratagems can be traced to a think-tank study released in 1966 called the *Report from Iron Mountain*. Although the origin of the report is highly debated, the document itself hints that it was commissioned by the Department of Defense under Defense Secretary, Robert McNamara, and was produced by the Hudson Institute located at the base of Iron Mountain in Croton-on-Hudson, New York. The Hudson Institute was founded and directed by Herman Kahn, formerly of the Rand Corporation. Both McNamara and Kahn were members of the CFR.

The self-proclaimed purpose of the study was to explore various ways to "stabilize society." Praiseworthy as that may sound, a reading of the *Report* soon reveals that the word *society* is used synonymously with the word *government*. Furthermore, the word *stabilize* is used as meaning to *preserve* and to *perpetuate*. It is clear from the start that the nature of the study was to analyze the different ways a government can perpetuate itself in power, ways to control its citizens and prevent them from rebelling.

It was stated at the beginning of the report that morality was not an issue. The study did not address questions of right or wrong; nor did it deal with such concepts as freedom or human rights. Ideology was not an issue, nor patriotism, nor religious precepts. Its sole concern was how to perpetuate the existing government. The report said:

> Previous studies have taken the desirability of peace, the importance of human life, the superiority of democratic institutions, the greatest "good" for the greatest number, the "dignity" of the individual, the desirability of maximum health and longevity, and other such wishful premises as axiomatic values necessary for the justification of a study of peace issues. We have not found them so. We have attempted to apply the standards of physical science to our thinking, the principal characteristic of which is not quantification, as is popularly believed, but that, in Whitehead's words, "... it ignores all judgments of value; for instance, all esthetic and moral judgments."[1]

The major conclusion of the report was that, in the past, war has been the only reliable means to achieve that goal. It contends that only during times of war or the threat of war are the masses compliant enough to carry the yoke of government without complaint. Fear of conquest and pillage by an enemy can make almost any burden seem acceptable by comparison. War can be used to arouse human passion and patriotic feelings of loyalty to the nation's leaders. No amount of sacrifice in the name of victory will be rejected. Resistance is viewed as treason. But, in times of peace, people become resentful of high taxes, shortages, and bureaucratic intervention. When they become disrespectful of their leaders, they become dangerous. No government has long survived without enemies and armed conflict. War, therefore, has been an indispensable condition for "stabilizing society." These are the report's exact words:

> The war system not only has been essential to the existence of nations as independent political entities, but has been equally indispensable to their stable political structure. Without it, no government has ever been able to obtain acquiescence in its "legitimacy," or right to rule its society. The possibility of war provides the sense of external necessity without which no government can long remain in power. The historical record reveals one instance

---

1. Leonard Lewin, ed., *Report from Iron Mountain on the Possibility and Desirability of Peace* (New York: Dell Publishing, 1967), pp. 13–14.

after another where the failure of a regime to maintain the credibility of a war threat led to its dissolution, by the forces of private interest, of reactions to social injustice, or of other disintegrative elements. The organization of society for the possibility of war is its principal political stabilizer.... It has enabled societies to maintain necessary class distinctions, and it has insured the subordination of the citizens to the state by virtue of the residual war powers inherent in the concept of nationhood.[1]

A NEW DEFINITION OF PEACE

The report then explains that we are approaching a point in history where the old formulas may no longer work. Why? Because it may now be possible to create a world government in which all nations will be disarmed and disciplined by a world army, a condition which will be called peace. The report says: "The word *peace,* as we have used it in the following pages,... implies total and general disarmament."[2] Under that scenario, independent nations will no longer exist and governments will not have the capability to wage war. There could be military action by the world army against renegade political subdivisions, but these would be called peace-keeping operations, and soldiers would be called peace keepers. No matter how much property is destroyed or how much blood is spilled, the bullets will be "peaceful" bullets and the bombs—even atomic bombs, if necessary—will be "peaceful" bombs.

The report then raises the question of whether there can ever be a suitable *substitute* for war? What *else* could the regional governments use—and what could the *world* government itself use—to legitimize and perpetuate itself? To provide an answer to that question was the stated purpose of the study.

The *Report from Iron Mountain* concludes that there can be no substitute for war unless it possesses three properties. It must (1) be economically wasteful, (2) represent a credible threat of great magnitude, and (3) provide a logical excuse for compulsory service to the government.

A SOPHISTICATED FORM OF SLAVERY

On the subject of compulsory service, the report explains that one of the advantages of standing armies is that they provide a

---

1. *Ibid.,* pp. 39, 81.
2. *Ibid.,* p. 9.

place for the government to put antisocial and dissident elements of society. In the absence of war, these forced-labor battalions would be told they are fighting poverty or cleaning up the planet or bolstering the economy or serving the common good in some other fashion. Every teenager would be required to serve—especially during those years in which young people are most rebellious against authority. Older people, too, would be drafted as a means of working off tax payments and fines. Dissidents would face heavy fines for "hate crimes" and politically incorrect attitudes so, eventually, they would all be in the forced-labor battalions. The report says:

> We will examine ... the time-honored use of military institutions to provide anti-social elements with an acceptable role in the social structure.... The current euphemistic clichés—"juvenile delinquency" and "alienation"—have had their counterparts in every age. In earlier days these conditions were dealt with directly by the military without the complications of due process, usually through press gangs or outright enslavement....
>
> Most proposals that address themselves, explicitly or otherwise, to the postwar problem of controlling the socially alienated turn to some variant of the Peace Corps or the so-called Job Corps for a solution. The socially disaffected, the economically unprepared, the psychologically uncomfortable, the hard-core "delinquents," the incorrigible "subversives," and the rest of the unemployable are seen as somehow transformed by the disciplines of a service modeled on military precedent into more or less dedicated social service workers....
>
> Another possible surrogate for the control of potential enemies of society is the reintroduction, in some form consistent with modern technology and political processes, of slavery.... It is entirely possible that the development of a sophisticated form of slavery may be an absolute prerequisite for social control in a world at peace. As a practical matter, conversion of the code of military discipline to a euphemized form of enslavement would entail surprisingly little revision; the logical first step would be the adoption of some form of "universal" military service.[1]

BLOOD GAMES

The report considered ways in which the public could be preoccupied with non-important activities so that it would not have time to participate in political debate or resistance. Recreation,

---

1. *Ibid.*, pp. 41–42, 68, 70.

trivial game shows, pornography, and situation comedies could play an important role, but blood games were considered to be the most promising of all the options. Blood games are competitive events between individuals or teams that are sufficiently violent in nature to enable the spectators to vicariously work off their frustrations. As a minimum, these events must evoke a passionate team loyalty on the part of the fans and must include the expectation of pain and injury on the part of the players. Even better for their purpose is the spilling of blood and the possibility of death. The common man has a morbid fascination for violence and blood. Crowds gather to chant "Jump! Jump!" at the suicidal figure on the hotel roof. Cars slow to a near stop on the highway to gawk at broken bodies next to a collision. A schoolyard fight instantly draws a circle of spectators. Boxing matches and football games and hockey games and automobile races are telecast daily, attracting millions of cheering fans who give rapt attention to each moment of danger, each angry blow to the face, each broken bone, each knockout, each carrying away of the unconscious or possibly dying contestant. In this fashion, their anger at "society" is defused and focused, instead, on the opposing team. The emperors of Rome devised the Circuses and gladiator contests and public executions by wild beasts for precisely that purpose.

Before jumping to the conclusion that such concepts are absurd in modern times, recall that during the 1985 European soccer championship in Belgium, the spectators became so emotionally involved in the contest that a bloody riot broke out in the bleachers leaving behind 38 dead and more that 400 injured. *U.S. News & World Report* gives this account:

> The root of the trouble: A tribal loyalty to home teams that surpasses an obsession and, say some experts, has become a substitute religion for many. The worst offenders include members of gangs such as Chelsea's Anti-Personnel Firm, made up of ill-educated young males who find in soccer rivalry an escape from boredom.
>
> Still, the British do not have a patent on soccer violence. On May 26, eight people were killed and more than 50 injured in Mexico City,... a 1964 stadium riot in Lima, Peru, killed more than 300—and a hotly disputed 1969 match between El Salvador and Honduras led to a week-long shooting war between the two countries, causing hundreds of casualties.
>
> The U.S. is criticized for the gridiron violence of its favorite sport, football, but outbursts in the bleachers are rare because loyalties are

spread among many sports and national pride is not at stake. Said Thomas Tutko, professor of psychology at California's San Jose State University: "In these other countries, it used to be their armies. Now it's their competitive teams that stir passions."[1]

Having considered all the ramifications of blood games, the *Report from Iron Mountain* concluded that they were not an adequate substitute for war. It is true that violent sports are useful distracters and do, in fact, allow an outlet for boredom and fierce group loyalty, but their effect on the nation's psyche could not match the intensity of war hysteria. Until a better alternative could be found, world government would have to be postponed so that nations could continue to wage war.

FINDING A CREDIBLE GLOBAL THREAT

In time of war, most citizens uncomplainingly accept their low quality of life and remain fiercely loyal to their leaders. If a suitable substitute for war is to be found, then it must also elicit that same reaction. Therefore, a new enemy must be found that threatens the entire world, and the prospects of being overcome by that enemy must be just as terrifying as war itself. The report is emphatic on that point:

> Allegiance requires a cause; a cause requires an enemy. This much is obvious; the critical point is that the enemy that defines the cause must seem genuinely formidable. Roughly speaking, the presumed power of the "enemy" sufficient to warrant an individual sense of allegiance to a society must be proportionate to the size and complexity of the society. Today, of course, that power must be one of unprecedented magnitude and frightfulness.[2]

The first consideration in finding a suitable threat to serve as a global enemy was that it did not have to be real. A real one would be better, of course, but an invented one would work just as well, provided the masses could be *convinced* it was real. The public will more readily believe some fictions than others. Credibility would be more important than truth.

Poverty was examined as a potential global enemy but rejected as not fearful enough. Most of the world was already *in* poverty. Only those who had never experienced poverty would see it as a global threat. For the rest, it was simply a fact of everyday life.

---

1. "British Soccer's Day of Shame," *U.S. News & World Report*, June 10, 1985, p. 11.
2. Lewin, *Report*, p. 44.

An invasion by aliens from outer space was given serious consideration. The report said that experiments along those lines already may have been tried. Public reaction, however, was not sufficiently predictable, because the threat was not "credible." Here is what the report had to say:

> Credibility, in fact, lies at the heart of the problem of developing a political substitute for war. This is where the space-race proposals, in many ways so well suited as economic substitutes for war, fall short. The most ambitious and unrealistic space project cannot of itself generate a believable external menace. It has been hotly argued that such a menace would offer the "last best hope of peace," etc., by uniting mankind against the danger of destruction by "creatures" from other planets or from outer space. Experiments have been proposed to test the credibility of an out-of-our-world invasion threat; it is possible that a few of the more difficult-to-explain "flying saucer" incidents of recent years were in fact early experiments of this kind. If so, they could hardly have been judged encouraging.[1]

This report was released in 1966 when the idea of an alien presence seemed far fetched to the average person. In the ensuing years, however, that perception has changed. A growing segment of the population now believes that intelligent life forms may exist beyond our planet and could be monitoring our own civilization. Whether that belief is right or wrong is not the issue here. The point is that a dramatic encounter with aliens shown on network television—even if it were to be entirely fabricated by high-tech computer graphics or laser shows in the sky—could be used to stampede all nations into world government supposedly to defend the Earth from invasion. On the other hand, if the aliens were perceived to have peaceful intent, an alternative scenario would be to form world government to represent a unified human species speaking with a single voice in some kind of galactic federation. Either scenario would be far more credible today than in 1966.

THE ENVIRONMENTAL-POLLUTION MODEL

The final candidate for a useful global threat was pollution of the environment. This was viewed as the most likely to succeed because it could be related to observable conditions such as smog and water pollution—in other words, it would be based partly on fact and, therefore, be credible. Predictions could be made showing

---

1. *Ibid.*, p. 66.

end-of-earth scenarios just as horrible as atomic warfare. Accuracy in these predictions would not be important. Their purpose would be to frighten, not to inform. It might even be necessary to *deliberately* poison the environment to make the predictions more convincing and to focus the public mind on fighting a new enemy, more fearful than any invader from another nation—or even from outer space. The masses would more willingly accept a falling standard of living, tax increases, and bureaucratic intervention in their lives as simply "the price we must pay to save Mother Earth." A massive battle against death and destruction from global pollution possibly could replace war as justification for social control.

Did the *Report from Iron Mountain* really say that? It certainly did—and much more. Here are just a few of the pertinent passages:

> When it comes to postulating a credible substitute for war ... the "alternate enemy" must imply a more immediate, tangible, and directly felt threat of destruction. It must justify the need for taking and paying a "blood price" in wide areas of human concern. In this respect, the possible substitute enemies noted earlier would be insufficient. One exception might be the environmental-pollution model, if the danger to society it posed was genuinely imminent. The fictive models would have to carry the weight of extraordinary conviction, underscored with a not inconsiderable actual sacrifice of life.... It may be, for instance, that gross pollution of the environment can eventually replace the possibility of mass destruction by nuclear weapons as the principal apparent threat to the survival of the species. Poisoning of the air, and of the principal sources of food and water supply, is already well advanced, and at first glance would seem promising in this respect; it constitutes a threat that can be dealt with only through social organization and political power....
>
> It is true that the rate of pollution could be increased selectively for this purpose.... But the pollution problem has been so widely publicized in recent years that it seems highly improbable that a program of deliberate environmental poisoning could be implemented in a politically acceptable manner.
>
> However unlikely some of the possible alternative enemies we have mentioned may seem, we must emphasize that one *must* be found of credible quality and magnitude, if a transition to peace is ever to come about without social disintegration. It is more probable, in our judgment, that such a threat will have to be invented.[1]

---

1. *Ibid.*, pp. 66–67, 70–71. When the *Report* was written, terrorism had not yet been considered as a substitute for war. Since then, it has become the most useful of them all. Do not expect it to be defeated by Fabians. It serves their purpose too well.

AUTHENTICITY OF THE REPORT

The Report from Iron Mountain states that it was produced by a Special Study Group of fifteen men whose identities were to remain secret and that it was not intended to be made public. One member of the group, however, felt the report was too important to be kept under wraps. He was not in disagreement with its conclusions. He merely believed that more people should read it. He delivered his personal copy to Leonard Lewin, a well-known author and columnist who, in turn, negotiated its publication by Dial Press. It was then reprinted by Dell Publishing.

This was during the Johnson Administration, and the President's Special Assistant for National Security Affairs was CFR member Walt Rostow. Rostow was quick to announce that the report was a spurious work. Herman Kahn, CFR director of the Hudson Institute, said it was not authentic. The *Washington Post*—which is owned and run by CFR member Katharine Graham—called it "a delightful satire." *Time* magazine, founded by CFR-member Henry Luce, said it was a skillful hoax. Then, on November 26, 1967, the report was reviewed in the book section of the *Washington Post* by Herschel McLandress, which was the pen name for Harvard professor John Kenneth Galbraith. Galbraith, who also had been a member of the CFR, said that he knew firsthand of the report's authenticity because he had been invited to participate in it. Although he was unable to be part of the official group, he *was* consulted from time to time and had been asked to keep the project a secret. Furthermore, while he doubted the wisdom of letting the public know about the report, he agreed totally with its conclusions. He wrote:

> As I would put my personal repute behind the authenticity of this document, so would I testify to the validity of its conclusions. My reservations relate only to the wisdom of releasing it to an obviously unconditioned public.[1]

Six weeks later, in an Associated Press dispatch from London, Galbraith went even further and jokingly admitted that he was "a member of the conspiracy."[2]

---

1. "News of War and Peace You're Not Ready For," by Herschel McLandress, *Book World*, in *The Washington Post*, November 26, 1967, p. 5.
2. "The Times Diary," *London Times*, February 5, 1968, p. 8.

That, however, did not settle the issue. The following day, Galbraith backed off. When asked about his "conspiracy" statement, he replied: "For the first time since Charles II *The Times* has been guilty of a misquotation.... Nothing shakes my conviction that it was written by either Dean Rusk or Mrs. Clare Booth Luce."[1]

The reporter who conducted the original interview was embarrassed by the allegation and did further research. Six days later, this is what he reported:

> Misquoting seems to be a hazard to which Professor Galbraith is prone. The latest edition of the Cambridge newspaper *Varsity* quotes the following (tape recorded) interchange:
>
> Interviewer: "Are you aware of the identity of the author of *Report from Iron Mountain?*"
>
> Galbraith: "I was in general a member of the conspiracy but I was not the author. I have always assumed that it was the man who wrote the foreword—Mr. Lewin."[2]

So, on at least three occasions, Galbraith publicly endorsed the authenticity of the report but denied that he wrote it. Then who did? Was it Leonard Lewin, after all? In 1967 he said he did not. In 1972 he said that he did. Writing in the *New York Times Book Review* Lewin explained: "I wrote the 'Report,' all of it.... What I intended was simply to pose the issues of war and peace in a provocative way."[3]

But wait! A few years before that, columnist William F. Buckley told the *New York Times* that *he* was the author. That statement was undoubtedly made tongue-in-cheek, but who and what are we to believe? Was it written by Herman Kahn, John Kenneth Galbraith, Dean Rusk, Clare Booth Luce, Leonard Lewin, or William F. Buckley?

In the final analysis, it makes little difference. The important point is that *The Report from Iron Mountain*, whether written as a think-tank study or a political satire, explains the reality that surrounds us. Regardless of its origin, the concepts presented in it are now being implemented in almost every detail. All one has to do is hold the *Report* in one hand and the daily newspaper in the other to realize that every major trend in American life is conform-

---

1. "Galbraith Says He Was Misquoted,"*London Times*, February 6, 1968, p. 3.
2. "Touche, Professor,"*London Times*, February 12, 1968, p. 8.
3. "Report from Iron Mountain,"*New York Times*, March 19, 1968, p. 8.

ing to the blueprint. So many things that otherwise are incomprehensible suddenly become clear: foreign aid, wasteful spending, the destruction of American industry, a job corps, gun control, a national police force, the apparent demise of Soviet power, a UN army, disarmament, a world bank, a world money, the surrender of national independence through treaties, and the ecology hysteria. *The Report from Iron Mountain* is an accurate summary of the plan that has already created our present. It is now shaping our future.

ENVIRONMENTALISM A SUBSTITUTE FOR WAR

It is beyond the scope of this study to prove that currently accepted predictions of environmental doom are based on exaggerated and fraudulent "scientific studies." But such proof is easily found if one is willing to look at the raw data and the assumptions upon which the projections are based. More important, however, is the question of why end-of-world scenarios based on phony scientific studies—or no studies at all—are uncritically publicized by the CFR-controlled media; or why radical environmental groups advocating socialist doctrine and anti-business programs are lavishly funded by CFR-dominated foundations, banks, and corporations, the very groups that would appear to have the most to lose. *The Report from Iron Mountain* answers those questions.

As the *Report* pointed out, truth is not important in these matters. It's what people can be made to *believe* that counts. "Credibility" is the key, not reality. There is just enough truth in the fact of environmental pollution to make predictions of planetary doom in the year two-thousand-something seem believable. All that is required is media cooperation and repetition. The plan has apparently worked. People of the industrialized nations have been subjected to a barrage of documentaries, dramas, feature films, ballads, poems, bumper stickers, posters, marches, speeches, seminars, conferences, and concerts. The result has been phenomenal. Politicians are now elected to office on platforms consisting of nothing more than an expressed concern for the environment and a promise to clamp down on those nasty industries. No one questions the damage done to the economy or the nation. It makes no difference when the very planet on which we live is sick and dying. Not one in a thousand will question that underlying premise. How could it be false? Look at all the movie celebrities and rock stars who have joined the movement.

While the *followers* of the environmental movement are preoccupied with visions of planetary doom, let us see what the *leaders* are thinking. The first Earth Day was proclaimed on April 22, 1970, at a "Summit" meeting in Rio de Janeiro, attended by environmentalists and politicians from all over the world. A publication widely circulated at that meeting was entitled the *Environmental Handbook*. The main theme of the book was summarized by a quotation from Princeton Professor Richard A. Falk, a member of the CFR. Falk wrote that there are four interconnected threats to the planet—wars of mass destruction, overpopulation, pollution, and the depletion of resources. Then he said: "The basis of all four problems is the inadequacy of the sovereign states to manage the affairs of mankind in the twentieth century."[1] The *Handbook* continued the CFR line by asking these rhetorical questions: "Are nation-states actually feasible, now that they have power to destroy each other in a single afternoon?... What price would most people be willing to pay for a more durable kind of human organization—more taxes, giving up national flags, perhaps the sacrifice of some of our hard-won liberties?"[2]

In 1989, the CFR-owned *Washington Post* published an article written by CFR member George Kennan in which he said: "We must prepare instead for ... an age where the great enemy is not the Soviet Union, but the rapid deterioration of our planet as a supporting structure for civilized life."[3]

On March 27, 1990, in the CFR-controlled *New York Times*, CFR member Michael Oppenheimer wrote: "Global warming, ozone depletion, deforestation and overpopulation are the four horsemen of a looming 21st century apocalypse.... As the cold war recedes, the environment is becoming the No. 1 international security concern."[4]

---

1. Garrett de Bell, ed., *The Environmental Handbook* (New York: Ballantine/Friends of the Earth, 1970), p. 138.
2. *Ibid.*, p. 145.
3. "A Europe Now Free from A Confining Cold War Vision," by George Kennan, *Washington Post* syndication, *Sacramento Bee*, November 14, 1989, p. B7.
4. The *New York Times* has been one of the principal means by which CFR policies are inserted into the mainstream of public opinion. The paper was purchased in 1896 by Alfred Ochs, with financial backing from CFR pioneer J.P. Morgan, Rothschild agent August Belmont, and Jacob Schiff, a partner in Kuhn, Loeb & Co. It is now owned by CFR member Arthur Sulzberger, who is also the publisher, and it is staffed by numerous CFR editors and columnists. See Perloff, p. 181.

CFR member, Lester Brown, heads up another think tank called the Worldwatch Institute. In the Institute's annual report, entitled *State of the World 1991*, Brown said that "the battle to save the planet will replace the battle over ideology as the organizing theme of the new world order."[1]

In the official publication of the 1992 Earth Summit, we find this: "The world community now faces together greater risks to our common security through our impacts on the environment than from traditional military conflicts with one another."

How many times does it have to be explained? The environmental movement was *created* by the CFR. It is a substitute for war that they hope will become the emotional and psychological foundation for world government.

HUMANITY ITSELF IS THE TARGET

The Club of Rome is a group of global planners who annually release end-of-world scenarios based on predictions of overpopulation and famine. Their membership is international, but the American roster includes such well-known CFR members as Jimmy Carter, Harlan Cleveland, Claiburne Pell, and Sol Linowitz. Their solution to overpopulation? A world government to control birth rates and, if necessary, apply euthanasia. That is a gentle word for the deliberate killing of the old, the weak, and of course the uncooperative. Following the same reasoning advanced at Iron Mountain, the Club of Rome has concluded that fear of environmental disaster could be used as a substitute enemy for the purpose of unifying the masses behind its program. In its 1991 book entitled *The First Global Revolution*, we find this:

> In searching for a new enemy to unite us, we came up with the idea that pollution, the threat of global warming, water shortages, famine and the like would fit the bill.... All these dangers are caused by human intervention.... The real enemy, then, is humanity itself.[2]

Socialist theoreticians have always been fascinated by the possibility of controlling population growth. It excites their imagination because it is the ultimate bureaucratic plan. If the real enemy

1. Lester R. Brown, "The New World Order," in Lester R. Brown et al., *State of the World 1991: A Worldwatch Institute Report on Progress Toward a Sustainable Society* (New York: W.W. Norton, 1991), p. 3.
2. Alexander King and Bertrand Schneider, *The First Global Revolution*, A Report by the Council of the Club of Rome (New York: Pantheon Books, 1991), p. 115.

is humanity itself, as the Club of Rome says, then humanity itself must become the target. Fabian Socialist Bertrand Russell[1] expressed it thus:

> I do not pretend that birth control is the only way in which population can be kept from increasing.... War, as I remarked a moment ago, has hitherto been disappointing in this respect, but perhaps bacteriological war may prove more effective. If a Black Death could be spread throughout the world once in every generation, survivors could procreate freely without making the world too full....
>
> A scientific world society cannot be stable unless there is world government.... It will be necessary to find ways of preventing an increase in world population. If this is to be done otherwise than by wars, pestilences and famines, it will demand a powerful international authority. This authority should deal out the world's food to the various nations in proportion to their population at the time of the establishments of the authority. If any nation subsequently increased its population, it should not on that account receive any more food. The motive for not increasing population would therefore be very compelling.[2]

Very compelling, indeed. These quiet-spoken collectivists are not kidding around. For example, one of the most visible "environmentalists" and advocate of population control is Jacques Cousteau. Interviewed by the United Nations *UNESCO Courier* in November of 1991, Cousteau spelled it out. He said:

> What should we do to eliminate suffering and disease? It is a wonderful idea but perhaps not altogether a beneficial one in the long run. If we try to implement it we may jeopardize the future of our species. It's terrible to have to say this. World population must be stabilized, and to do that we must eliminate 350,000 people per day. This is so horrible to contemplate that we shouldn't even say it, but it is just as bad not to say it.[3]

GORBACHEV BECOMES AN ECOLOGY WARRIOR

We can now understand how Mikhail Gorbachev, formerly the leader of one of the most repressive governments the world has known, became head of a new organization called the International Green Cross, which supposedly is dedicated to environmental

1. See Martin, pp. 171, 325, 463–69.
2. Bertrand Arthur William Russell, *The Impact of Science on Society* (New York: Simon and Schuster, 1953), pp. 103–104, 111.
3. Interviewed by Bahgat Eluadi and Adel Rifaat, *Courrier de l'Unesco*, November 1991, p. 13.

issues. Gorbachev has never denounced collectivism, only the *label* of a particular *brand* of collectivism called Communism. His real interest is not ecology but world government with himself assured a major position in the power structure. In a public appearance in Fulton, Missouri, he praised the Club of Rome, of which he is a member, for its position on population control. Then he said:

> One of the worst of the new dangers is ecological.... Today, global climatic shifts; the greenhouse effect; the "ozone hole"; acid rain; contamination of the atmosphere, soil and water by industrial and household waste; the destruction of the forests; etc. all threaten the stability of the planet.[1]

Gorbachev proclaimed that global government was the answer to these threats and that the use of government force was essential. He said: "I believe that the new world order will not be fully realized unless the United Nations and its Security Council create structures ... authorized to impose sanctions and make use of other measures of compulsion."[2]

Here is an arch criminal who fought his way up through the ranks of the Soviet Communist Party, became the protégé of Yuri Andropov, head of the dreaded KGB, was a member of the USSR's ruling Politburo throughout the Soviet invasion of Afghanistan, and who was selected by the Politburo in 1985 as the supreme leader of world Communism. All of this was during one of the Soviet's most dismal periods of human-rights violations and subversive activities against the free world. Furthermore, he ruled over a nation with one of the worst possible records of environmental destruction. At no time while he was in power did he ever say or do anything to show concern over planet Earth.

All that is now forgotten. Gorbachev has been transformed by the CFR-dominated media into an ecology warrior. He is calling for world government and telling us that such a government will use environmental issues as justification for sanctions and other "measures of compulsion." We cannot say that we were not warned.

1. Michail Gorbachev, "The River of Time and the Necessity of Action," 46th John Findley Green Foundation Lecture, Westminster College, Fulton, Missouri, May 6, 1992, transcript from Westminster College Department of Press Relations, p. 6.
2. *Ibid.*, p. 9.

U.S. BRANDED AS ECOLOGICAL AGGRESSOR

The use of compulsion is an important point in these plans. People in the industrialized nations are not expected to cooperate in their own demise. They will have to be forced. They will not like it when their food is taken for global distribution. They will not approve when they are taxed by a world authority to finance foreign political projects. They will not voluntarily give up their cars or resettle into smaller houses or communal barracks to satisfy the resource-allocation quotas of a UN agency. Club-of-Rome member Maurice Strong states the problem:

> In effect, the United States is committing environmental aggression against the rest of the world.... At the military level, the United States is the custodian. At the environmental level, the United States is clearly the greatest risk.... One of the worst problems in the United States is energy prices—they're too low....
>
> It is clear that current lifestyles and consumption patterns of the affluent middle class ... involving high meat intake, consumption of large amounts of frozen and 'convenience' foods, ownership of motor-vehicles, numerous electric household appliances, home and work-place air-conditioning ... expansive suburban housing ... are not sustainable.[1]

Mr. Strong's remarks were enthusiastically received by world environmental leaders, but they prompted this angry editorial response in the *Arizona Republic*:

> Translated from eco-speak, this means two things: (1) a reduction in the standard of living in Western nations through massive new taxes and regulations, and (2) a wholesale transfer of wealth from industrialized to under-developed countries. The dubious premise here is that if the U.S. economy could be reduced to, say, the size of Malaysia's, the world would be a better place.... Most Americans probably would balk at the idea of the U.N. banning automobiles in the U.S.[2]

Who is this Maurice Strong who sees the United States as the environmental aggressor against the world? Does he live in poverty? Does he come from a backward country that is resentful of American prosperity? Does he himself live in modest circum-

---

1. "Ecology Remedy Costly," (AP), *Sacramento Bee*, March 12, 1992, p. A8. Also Maurice Strong, Introduction to Jim MacNeil, Pieter Winsemius, and Taizo Yakushiji, *Beyond Interdependence* (New York: Oxford University Press, 1991), p. ix.
2. "Road to Ruin," *Arizona Republic*, March 26, 1992.

stances, avoiding consumption in order to preserve our natural resources? None of the above. He is one of the wealthiest men in the world. He lives and travels in great comfort. He is a lavish entertainer. In addition to having great personal wealth derived from the oil industry in Canada—which he helped nationalize— Maurice Strong was the Secretary-General of the 1992 Earth Summit in Rio; head of the 1972 UN Conference on Human Environment in Stockholm; the first Secretary-General of the UN Environment Program; president of the World Federation of United Nations; co-chairman of the World Economic Forum; member of the Club of Rome; trustee of the Aspen Institute; and a director of the World Future Society. That is probably more than you wanted to know about this man, but it is necessary in order to appreciate the importance of what follows.

A PLOT FOR ECONOMIC CRISIS

Maurice Strong believes—or *says* that he believes—the world's ecosystems can be preserved only if the affluent nations of the world can be disciplined into lowering their standard of living. Production and consumption must be curtailed. To bring that about, those nations must submit to rationing, taxation, and political domination by world government. They will probably not do that voluntarily, he says, so they will have to be forced. To accomplish that, it will be necessary to engineer a global monetary crisis which will destroy their economic systems. Then they will have no choice but to accept assistance and control from the UN.

This strategy was revealed in the May, 1990, issue of *West* magazine, published in Canada. In an article entitled "The Wizard of Baca Grande," journalist Daniel Wood described his week-long experience at Strong's private ranch in southern Colorado. This ranch has been visited by such CFR notables as David Rockefeller, Secretary-of-State Henry Kissinger, founder of the World Bank Robert McNamara, and the presidents of such organizations as IBM, Pan Am, and Harvard.

During Wood's stay at the ranch, the tycoon talked freely about environmentalism and politics. To express his own world view, he said he was planning to write a novel about a group of world leaders who decided to save the planet. As the plot unfolded, it became obvious that it was based on real people and real events. Wood continues the story:

Each year, he explains as background to the telling of the novel's plot, the World Economic Forum convenes in Davos, Switzerland. Over a thousand CEOs, prime ministers, finance ministers, and leading academics gather in February to attend meetings and set economic agendas for the year ahead. With this as a setting, he then says: "What if a small group of these world leaders were to conclude that the principal risk to the earth comes from the actions of the rich countries? And if the world is to survive, those rich countries would have to sign an agreement reducing their impact on the environment. Will they do it?... The group's conclusion is 'no.' the rich countries won't do it. They won't change. So, in order to save the planet, the group decides: Isn't the *only* hope for the planet that the industrialized civilizations collapse? Isn't it our responsibility to bring that about?."

"This group of world leaders," he continues, "form a secret society to bring about an economic collapse. It's February. They're all at Davos. These aren't terrorists. They're *world leaders*. They have positioned themselves in the world's commodity and stock markets. They've engineered, using their access to stock exchanges and computers and gold supplies, a panic. Then, they prevent the world's stock markets from closing. They jam the gears. They hire mercenaries who hold the rest of the world leaders at Davos as hostages. The markets *can't close*. The rich countries..." And Strong makes a slight motion with his fingers as if he were flicking a cigarette butt out the window.

I sit there spellbound. This is not *any* storyteller talking, this is Maurice Strong. He knows these world leaders. He is, in fact, co-chairman of the Council of the World Economic Forum. He sits at the fulcrum of power. He is in a position to *do it*.

"I probably shouldn't be saying things like this," he says.[1]

Maurice Strong's fanciful plot probably shouldn't be taken too seriously, at least in terms of a *literal* reading of future events. It is unlikely they will unfold in exactly that manner—although it is not impossible. For one thing, it would not be necessary to hold the leaders of the industrialized nations at gun point. *They* would be the ones engineering this plot. Leaders from Third-World countries do not have the means to cause a global crisis. That would have to come from the money centers in New York, London, or Tokyo. Furthermore, the masterminds behind this thrust for global government have always resided in the industrialized nations. They have come from the ranks of the CFR in America and from other

---

1. "The Wizard of Baca Grande," by Daniel Wood, *West* magazine, May, 1990, p. 35.

branches of the International Roundtable in England, France, Belgium, Canada, Japan, and elsewhere. They are the ideological descendants of Cecil Rhodes and they are fulfilling his dream.

It is not important whether or not Maurice Strong's plot for global economic collapse is to be taken literally. What is important is that men like him are *thinking* along those lines. As Wood pointed out, they are in a position to *do it*. Or something *like* it. If it is not this scenario, they will consider another one with similar consequences. If history has proven anything, it is that men with financial and political power are quite capable of heinous plots against their fellow men. They have launched wars, caused depressions, and created famines to suit their personal agendas. We have little reason to believe that the world leaders of today are more saintly than their predecessors.

Furthermore, we must not be fooled by pretended concern for Mother Earth. The call-to-arms for saving the planet is a gigantic ruse. There is just enough truth to environmental pollution to make the show "credible," as *The Report from Iron Mountain* phrased it, but the end-of-earth scenarios which drive the movement forward are bogus. The real objective in all of this is world government, the ultimate doomsday mechanism from which there can be no escape. Destruction of the economic strength of the industrialized nations is merely a necessary prerequisite for ensnaring them into the global web. The thrust of the current ecology movement is directed totally to that end.

SUMMARY

The United States government is mired in a 5.8-trillion-dollar debt. By 2001, interest payments on that debt were running $360 billion per year. That consumes about 19% of all federal revenue and costs the average family over $5,000 each year. Nothing is purchased by it. It merely pays interest. It represents the government's largest single expense. Interest on the national debt is already consuming more than 36% of all the revenue collected from personal income taxes. If the long-term trend continues, there is nothing to prevent it from eventually consuming all of it.

By 1992, there were more people working for government than for manufacturing companies in the private sector. There are more citizens receiving government checks than there are paying income taxes. When it is possible for people to vote on issues involving the transfer of wealth to themselves from others, the ballot box becomes a weapon whereby the majority plunders the minority. That is the point of no return. It is a doomsday mechanism.

By 1992, more than half of all federal outlays went for what are called entitlements. Here is another doomsday mechanism. Entitlements are expenses—such as Social Security and Medicare—which are based on promises of *future* payments. Entitlements represent 52% of federal outlays. When this is added to the 14% that is now being spent for interest payments on the national debt, we come to the startling conclusion that two-thirds of all federal expenses are now entirely automatic, and that percentage is growing each month.

The biggest doomsday mechanism of all is the Federal Reserve System. Every cent of our money supply came into being for the purpose of being loaned to someone. Those dollars will disappear when the loans are paid back. If we tried to pay off the national debt, our money supply would be undermined. Under the Federal Reserve System, therefore, Congress would be fearful to eliminate the national debt even if it wanted to.

Political environmentalism has caused millions of acres of timber and agricultural land to be taken out of production. Heavy industry has been chased from our shores by our own government. High taxes, rules beyond reason for safety devices in the work place, so-called fair-employment practices, and mandatory health insurance are rapidly destroying what is left of the private sector. The result is unemployment and dislocation for millions of American workers. Government moves in to fill the void it creates, and bureaucracy grows by the hour.

Federal taxes now take more than 40% of our private incomes. State, county, and local taxes are on top of that. Inflation feeds on what is left. We spend half of each year working for the government. Real wages in America have declined. Young couples with a single income have a lower standard of living than their parents did. The net worth of the average household is falling. The amount of leisure time is shrinking. The percentage of Americans who own their homes is dropping. The age at which a family acquires a first home is rising. The number of families counted among the middle class is falling. The number of people living below the officially defined poverty level is rising. More and more Americans are broke at age 65.

None of this is accidental. It is the fulfillment of a plan by members of the CFR who comprise the hidden government of the United States. Their goal is the deliberate weakening of the industrialized nations as a prerequisite to bringing them into a world government built upon the principles of socialism, with themselves in control.

The origin of many of the stratagems in this plan can be traced to a government-sponsored think-tank study released in 1966 called the *Report from Iron Mountain*. The purpose of the study was to analyze methods by which a government can perpetuate itself in power—ways to control its citizens and prevent them from rebelling. The conclusion of the report was that, in the past, war has been the only reliable means to achieve that goal. Under world government, however, war technically would be impossible. So the main purpose of the study was to explore other methods for controlling populations and keeping them loyal to their leaders. It was concluded that a suitable substitute for war would require a new enemy which posed a frightful threat to survival. Neither the threat nor the enemy had to be real. They merely had to be believable.

Several surrogates for war were considered, but the only one holding real promise was the environmental-pollution model. This was viewed as the most likely to succeed because (1) it could be related to observable conditions such as smog and water pollution—in other words, it would be based partly on fact and, therefore, believable—and (2) predictions could be made showing end-of-earth scenarios just as horrible as atomic warfare. Accuracy in these predictions would not be important. Their purpose would be to frighten, not to inform.

While the *followers* of the current environmental movement are preoccupied with visions of planetary doom, the *leaders* have an entirely different agenda. It is world government.

Chapter Twenty-Five

A PESSIMISTIC
SCENARIO

This chapter remains exactly as first published in 1994. The original whimsical look into the future has become an incredibly accurate portrayal of many real events since then. A banking crisis and massive bailouts have already come to pass. The still unfolding scenario includes hyperinflation, collapse of the economy, a new global currency, domestic violence, U.N. "Peacekeeping" forces in the U.S., and the arrival of high-tech feudalism.

We are ready now for the final trip in our time machine. On the control panel in front of us are several selector switches. The one on the left indicates *Direction of Time*. Set it to *Future*. The switch on the right indicates *Primary Assumptions*. Set it to the first notch which reads: *Present trends unaltered*. Leave the *Secondary-Assumption* switch where it is. The lever in the center is a throttle to determine speed of travel. Nudge it forward—and hang on tight!

A BANKING CRISIS

It is 4:05 in the morning. While New York City sleeps, the computers on the fourth floor at Citibank are aware that a full-blown crisis is underway. It started in London—five hours ahead of the East coast—and within minutes had spread like an electronic virus to Tokyo and Hong Kong. That was an hour ago. Alarms are now sounding on computer terminals in all the trading centers of the world, and automatic dialing devices are summoning money managers to their board rooms.

The panic started from rumors that one of the large U.S. banks was in trouble because of the simultaneous default of its loan to Mexico and the bankruptcy of its second-largest corporate borrower. Yesterday afternoon, the bank's president held a press conference and denied that these were serious problems. To reinforce his optimism, he announced that, on Friday, the bank will be paying a higher-than-usual quarterly dividend. The professional money managers were not convinced. They knew that writing off these loans would wipe out the bank's entire net worth.

By 5 A.M., the money-center banks are facing heavy withdrawals from overseas depositors. By the time the sun peeks between the New York skyscrapers, Americans are also taking their money. These are not small transactions. They involve other banks, insurance companies, and investment funds. The average withdrawal is over $3 million. The reservoir is draining fast.

It is now 7:45. The banks will soon be opening their doors, and already newspaper reporters and TV crews are arriving outside. A plan of unified action must be made quickly.

The Chairman of the Federal Reserve has arranged an emergency conference call with the CEOs of all the major banks, including one who was located at great effort at his fishing lodge in northern Canada. The President is also tied into the telephone network but on a "silent-monitor" basis. Other than the Chairman, no one else knows he is listening.

TO SAVE THE BANKS IS TO SAVE THE WORLD

The CEO at Citibank quickly summarizes the problem. None of the banks will be able to sustain withdrawals of this magnitude for more than about forty-eight hours. Perhaps less. The money is not in their vaults. It has been put into interest-bearing loans. Even if the loans were performing, they would not have the money. Now that some of the larger loans are in default, the problem is even worse. If the Fed doesn't provide the money, the banks will have no choice but to close their doors and go out of business. That would cause a collapse of the economy and untold suffering would follow. Americans would be thrown out of work; families would go hungry; national security would be weakened. And it would undoubtedly spread to the entire world. Who knows what dire consequences would follow—chaos, famine, and riots here at home? Revolution abroad? The return of a militaristic regime in Russia? Atomic war?

The Chairman cuts the monologue short. He is well aware that the banks must not be allowed to fail. That, after all, was one of the reasons the Federal Reserve was created. He wants to get on with the details of how to do it.

Yes, the FDIC is already broke, but don't worry about that. Congress will authorize a "loan" or some other mechanism for the Fed to create whatever amount of new money the FDIC might need. If Congress moves too slowly, the Fed has other technical means to accomplish the same result. In the meantime, unlimited funding will be available at the Fed's discount window by 8 A.M., Eastern Standard time. The printing presses are already running at full capacity to provide the currency. Fleets of airplanes and armored cars are standing by to deliver it. Furthermore, don't give up on those defaulted loans. Congress will probably bail out the bankrupt American corporations. And the President has said he will ask for additional funding for the IMF/World Bank. That money will be created by the Fed and carry the stipulation that it must be used by Mexico and other defaulting countries to resume interest payments on their loans.

The bankers are told to open their doors to the public and act calm. The press already knows that something is going on but not the seriousness of it. So tell them only what they already know. Nothing more. If people want to withdraw their money, give it to them. If lines should develop, call the police to maintain order, but continue paying out. Offer to stay open after closing hours, if necessary, to accommodate everyone. Above all, have the tellers take their time. Check and double check each transaction. Move the lines slowly.

The armored trucks will arrive at the busiest hours so the guards can carry sacks of money past the customers for visual confirmation that there is enough for everyone. A bank officer then should tell the crowd that a fresh delivery of money has just been made from the Federal Reserve System and that there is plenty more where that came from. Once people become convinced that the bank is able to pay, most of them will tire of the wait and go home.

PANIC AVERTED

It is now 6 P.M. of the following day. The plan was successful. Lines of anxious depositors had formed yesterday morning, mostly in the larger cities, and resumed again this morning. But there has been enough money for everyone. The news media treated the story lightly, making sure to include sound bites from various experts that banks can no longer fail, thanks to the FDIC and the

Federal Reserve System. More than half the video time is devoted to armored trucks and guards carrying sacks of money. The banks closed on schedule today, and there were no more lines.

While everything appears calm to the passengers on deck, the fire still rages out of control in the boiler room. Over a billion dollars has already fled, mostly overseas, and the hemorrhage continues. The Fed is pumping in fresh money to replace it. Two of the banks have instructed their computer technicians to activate an automatic two-hour delay on all incoming transactions. There is talk of deliberately disabling the entire network and blaming the breakdown on overload, but the idea is abandoned. There are too many people in the system. Someone surely would leak the truth to the press.

The danger of a run on the banks by private depositors used to be the nightmare of the Federal Reserve. Now it is nothing compared to the electronic run that is taking place involving institutional depositors around the world. These are professionals who are not impressed by armed guards carrying bags of currency. They want their money now—and they are getting it. Although they are receiving it in the form of electronic credits, they are immediately exchanging that for something more dependable, such as stocks, other currencies, and bullion.

This is the Fed's finest hour. It is exercising its many powers, carefully accumulated over the years, to create money out of whatever is at hand: U.S. Treasury bonds, bonds from other governments, corporate debt obligations, even direct loans to individuals and partnerships. Billions of new dollars are springing into existence. They are spreading around the globe to fulfill the banks' obligation to give people back their money.

A REAL RUN ON THE BANKS

It is now seven weeks later. Something happened, but no one knows what. Like a spark igniting a twig, spreading to a branch, and then engulfing the entire forest, the public has panicked. Responding to a primitive herd instinct, they are descending on the banks and the thrifts. They want their money. They want their savings.

Perhaps it was the newly released statistics showing higher unemployment, or the continued rise in bankruptcies, or the Congressional vote to increase the national debt again, or the jump in Social-Security taxes, or the loss of another 140,000 jobs to Mexico, or the riots in Chicago and Detroit for more food stamps and government housing, or the presence of UN "Peacekeeping" troops to augment the National Guard, or the rumor that the Bank of America was technically insolvent, or the UN World Court ruling that the number of American automobiles had to be cut by 30% by December 31st, or the skeptical tone in the voice of the CBS news anchor as he quoted the latest prediction of renewed prosperity.

Whatever it was, there are now long lines of sober-faced depositors outside every bank. There is not enough cash in the vaults to meet the demand. Most money is checkbook money, which means it consists merely of magnetic impulses in a computer. Only about five per cent of the monetary supply is in the form of coins or currency. Most of that is already outside the banks in cash registers, wallets, and mattresses. The amount inside the banks is only about one-half of one per cent. The Fed's emergency supply of currency—a large quantity warehoused for exactly this kind of crisis—is inadequate. This time, the printing presses cannot keep up.

Spokesmen from the Treasury and the Federal Reserve appear on TV and assure the nation that there is no need for panic. Everything is under control. The only problem is the irrational behavior of alarmists who have no faith in their country.

No one believes them. The lines grow longer, and the people become angry. Bank employees are jeered on their way to work. Bomb threats are made. Sporadic violence breaks out, and bank windows are smashed. The International Guard is called up. The President declares a bank holiday.

Since people cannot close out their bank accounts by withdrawing currency, they rush through the stores on checkbook-spending sprees. If they cannot get their money back, at least they can buy things with it. Garages and basements are filling up with canned goods, shoes, liquor, tires, ammunition. Goods are becoming scarce, pushing prices upward. The Dow Jones is going through the roof as investors empty their checking accounts to buy anything for sale. The Securities and Exchange Commission finally suspends trading.

Nine months have now passed. The crisis has been a blessing for politicians. They have thrived upon it and grown in stature because of it. It has given them an excuse to swarm through the country on fact-finding trips, to appear in shirt sleeves at town-hall meetings, to give speeches, and to be seen on television—all the time expressing grave concern and appearing to take charge. It has legitimized their role and somehow made them seem more necessary than before. They have been converted in the public eye from oafs and bumpkins to serious-minded statesmen.

The party in power said it inherited the mess. The previous party blamed the current one for dropping the ball. Both parties, however, agreed on the solution: more of exactly the same policies that created the crisis: expanded power to the Federal Reserve, more government control over the economy, more subsidies and benefits, and more international commitments. These were called "emergency reforms" and became law. The same men who created the problem prescribed the solution. The public was grateful to have leaders of such vision and wisdom.

BANK BAILOUT AND MORE INFLATION

The most important emergency reform was to bail out the banks with taxpayers' dollars. Defaulted foreign loans were taken over by the IMF/World Bank, and the failing corporate borrowers were given government grants disguised as loans—loans which everyone knew would never be paid back.

Next, the banks were nationalized, at least in part. In return for the bailout money, they gave large blocks of stock to the government which now operates as an official business partner. This was not a drastic change. The banks were already heavily regulated by government, even to the point of determining their profits, dividends, and executive salaries. That is the way the cartel wanted it. It was the means by which competition was avoided and profits assured. Monetary scientists and political scientists have always worked as a hidden partnership. This merely made the relationship more visible.

Technically, no bank was allowed to fail. The Fed kept its promise on that. When the troubled banks were taken over, all depositors with $100,000 or less were fully protected. If they wanted their money and the bank didn't have it, the Fed simply manufactured it. No one was worried about the value of those dollars. They were just happy to have them.

Ten more months have now passed. Those new dollars are flooding throughout the system. The money supply has increased by the amount of the bailout plus the amount of new spending for welfare, health care, interest on the national debt, and foreign aid, all of which are in a vertical climb. Inflation has become institutionalized.

The dollar has been dethroned as the world's de facto currency. Foreign investors and central banks no longer have any use for dollars. They have sent them back to the United States whence they came. Trillions of them have returned to our shores like a huge flock of homing pigeons that fills the sky from horizon to horizon. They are buying our refrigerators, automobiles, computers, airplanes, cargo ships, armored tanks, office buildings, factories, real estate—pushing prices to levels that would have seemed impossible a year ago. A single postage stamp costs as many dollars as once would have purchased a new TV set.

Most stores have stopped accepting checks and credit cards. Workers are paid daily with bundles of paper money. People rush to the stores to purchase groceries before prices rise even further. Commerce is paralyzed. Bank loans and mortgages are unobtainable. Savings accounts have been destroyed, including the cash values of insurance policies. Factories are shutting down. Businesses are closing their doors. Barter is commonplace. Old silver coins come out of private hoards and a hundred-dollar bill is exchanged for one silver dime.

Following the crash of 1929, the supply of paper money was limited because it was backed by silver, and the amount of silver itself was limited. Those who had money were able to buy up the assets of those who did not. Since prices were falling, the longer they held on to their dollars, the more they could buy. Now, things are exactly the opposite. There is nothing to back the money supply except politics. There is no limit to the amount of currency that can be created. It is just a question of printing and delivering it. Money is abundant, and prices are rising. Those who have money are spending it as soon as possible to prevent further loss of purchasing power. In the 1930s, everyone wanted dollars. Now, everyone wants to get rid of them.

The Emergency Banking Regulation No. 1, originally issued in 1961, empowered the Secretary of the Treasury—*without* consent of Congress—to seize anyone's bank account, savings account, or safe-deposit box. It also gave him the power to fix rents, prices, salaries, and hourly wages, and to impose rationing. This was to be done "in the event of attack on the United States." That phrase now has been changed to read: "in the event of national emergency." The Federal Emergency Management Agency (FEMA) has been expanded to administer the directives of the Treasury. FEMA also has the power to detain and forcibly relocate any citizen "in the event of a national emergency."

NEW MONEY

Three more months have passed, and the President has declared a state of national emergency. Today, the Secretary of the Treasury announced that the nations of the world had ratified a multilateral treaty that would solve the inflationary problems of the United States. This will be accomplished through the issuance of a new world-wide monetary unit called the Bancor, the name proposed by John Maynard Keynes at the Bretton Woods Conference in 1944. This new money will restore our commerce and put a stop to inflation. At last, said the Treasury Secretary, man will have total control over his economic destiny. Money will now become his servant instead of his master.

The United States, he said, has agreed to accept the Bancor as legal tender for all debts, public and private. The old money will still be honored but will be phased out over a three-month period. After that date, Federal Reserve Notes will no longer be valid. During the transition period, the old money may be exchanged at any bank at the ratio of one Bancor for five-hundred dollars. All existing contracts expressed in dollars—including home mortgages—are now converted to Bancors in that same ratio.

In the same announcement, the Secretary advised that the IMF/World Bank was backing this new money with something far more precious than gold. Instead, it will be backed by the assets of the world. These include bonds from the participating governments plus millions of acres of wilderness lands that have been deposited into the UN "Environmental Bank."[1] The National Parks

---

1. "Debt-for-nature" swaps were proposed at the 4th World Wilderness Conference held in Denver, Colorado, in 1987 and they are being implemented right now. Costa Rica, Bolivia, and Ecuador have already agreed to swap their debt in exchange for a commitment to prevent wilderness areas from being developed. UN control over those lands is inevitable.

and forests of the United States have been added to those reserves, and they will now be under the supervision of the UN Wilderness Asset Preservation and Enhancement Agency (WAPEA). From this date forward, the Federal Reserve System will operate as a subdivision of the IMF which is now the central bank of the world.

Although the Secretary did not mention it in his public appearance, the UN treaty also obligated the government to put restrictions on the use of cash. Every citizen is to be issued an international ID card. The primary purpose of these machine-readable cards is to provide positive identification for all citizens at transportation depots and military checkpoints. They also can be used by the banks and stores to access checking accounts, which are now called *debit* accounts.

Every citizen is being issued an account in a bank near his place of residence. All payments by employers or government agencies will be made by electronic transfer. Cash transactions larger than five Bancors will be illegal in three months. Most expenditures will be paid by debit card. That is the only way in which the UN Monetary Transaction Tracking Agency (MTTA) can combat counterfeiting and prevent money laundering by organized crime. That, of course, is camouflage. The government complex issuing the new money is the greatest perpetrator of counterfeiting and organized crime the world has ever seen.[1] The real targets are political dissidents and those escaping taxes in the underground economy.

No one will be allowed to earn or buy or sell without this ID card, nor will they be allowed to leave the country or even to migrate to another city. If any government agency has reason to red-flag an individual, his card will not clear, and he will be blocked from virtually all economic transactions and geographical movements. It is the ultimate control.

The new money offers the Cabal yet one more benefit. There can never be another run on the banks, because it is now illegal to demand currency.

---

1. That is not hyperbole. All fiat money is counterfeit. Furthermore, there is evidence that the CIA and the DEA have been deeply involved in the smuggling of illicit drugs. The money derived from those drugs was apparently laundered through Panamanian branches of U.S. banks and used to finance covert operations in Nicaragua and elsewhere. Virtually all governments have been involved in activities that would be criminal offenses if committed by ordinary citizens.

THE RISE OF REVOLUTIONARY MOVEMENTS

Hyperinflation is fertile ground for the seeds of revolution. Economic despair led the masses to grasp at the promises of Lenin in Russia, Hitler in Germany, Mussolini in Italy, and Mao in China. It has now been three years since that fateful run on the banks in New York, and inflation has not abated, even with the introduction of the Bancor. Now we are witnessing massive public demonstrations in every major city for higher wages, more jobs, larger government benefits, and more stringent price controls. Since there are practically no goods in the stores at *any* price, the demonstrators are also calling for higher output from government factories. The demonstrations have been organized by radical organizations advocating the overthrow of the "decadent capitalist" system and the enthronement of socialism in its place. The participants in the street do not understand the words they chant. They are unaware that capitalism has been dead in America for many years and that it is socialism they already have.

Nevertheless, there are tens of thousands of desperate people who are attracted to the rhetoric of revolution. Terrorism and revolutionary insurgency have become common occurrences in the major urban areas. The ranks of the revolutionaries are swelled by those who come solely for the looting that always follows.

People are frightened by these violent events and demand the restoration of law and order. They are relieved when martial law is declared. They are happy to see the International Guard patrolling their neighborhoods. They are not resentful of being confined in their homes or arbitrarily detained by soldiers. They are actually grateful for the omni-presence of the police state.

It is curious that the revolutionary groups behind this violence have not been inhibited by the government. To the contrary, they have been given grants from CFR organizations, and their leaders have been treated courteously by CFR politicians. The CFR media have given them extended coverage in the news and has presented their cause with sympathy. A few dissidents have begun to wonder if the revolutionaries are but the unknowing pawns of those in power and that their primary function is to frighten the population into accepting the constraints of a police state.

Such voices, however, are quickly silenced. Those who question the government or the media are branded as extremists at the lunatic fringe. Authorities say that they are the cause of our present woes. They are remnants of the old system based on profit-seeking and race-hating. They are guilty of politically-incorrect attitudes and hate crimes. They are sentenced to attitude-correction centers for psychological treatment and rehabilitation. Those who do not immediately recant are never seen again.

HOMES ARE NATIONALIZED

One of the first industries to feel the raw power of "emergency measures" was the home industry. During the early stages of inflation, people were applying their increasingly worthless dollars to pay down their mortgages. That was devastating to the lenders. They were being paid back in dollars that were worth only a fraction of the ones they had lent out. The banking crisis had caused the disappearance of savings and investment capital, so they were unable to issue new loans to replace the old. Besides, people were afraid to sell their homes under such chaotic times and, if they did, very few were willing to buy with interest rates that high. Old loans were being paid off, and new loans were not replacing them. The S&Ls, which in the 1980s had been in trouble because home prices were falling, now were going broke because prices were rising.

Congress applied the expected political fix by bailing them out and taking them over. But that did not stop the losses. It merely transferred them to the taxpayers. To put an end to the losses, Congress passed the Housing Fairness and Reform Act (HFRA). It converted all Bancor-denominated contracts to a new unit of value—called the "Fairness Value"— which is determined by the National Average Price Index (NAPI) on Fridays of the preceding week. This has nothing to do with interest rates. It relates to Bancor values. For the purpose of illustration, let us convert Bancors back to dollars. A $50,000 loan on Friday became a $920,000 loan on Monday. Few people could afford the payments. Thousands of angry voters stormed the Capitol building in protest. While the mob shouted obscenities outside, Congress hastily voted to declare a moratorium on all mortgage payments. By the end of the day, no one had to pay anything! The people returned to their homes with satisfaction and gratitude for their wise and generous leaders.

That was only an "emergency" measure to be handled on a more sound basis later on. Many months have now passed, and

Congress has not dared to tamper with the arrangement. The voters would throw them out of office if they tried. Millions of people have been living in their homes at no cost, except for county taxes, which were also beyond the ability of anyone to pay. Following the lead of Congress, the counties also declared a moratorium on their taxes—but not until the federal government agreed to make up their losses under terms of the newly passed Aid to Local Governments Act (ALGA).

Renters are now in the same position, because virtually all rental property has been nationalized, even that which had been totally paid for by their owners. Under HFRA, it is not "fair" for those who are buying their homes to have an advantage over those who are renting. Rent controls made it impossible for apartment owners to keep pace with the rising costs of maintenance and especially their rising taxes. Virtually all rental units have been seized by county governments for back taxes. And since the counties themselves are now dependent on the federal government for most of their revenue, their real estate has been transferred to federal agencies in return for federal aid.

All of this was pleasing to the voters who were gratified that their leaders were "doing something" to solve their problems. It gradually became clear, however, that the federal government was now the owner of all their homes and apartments. The reality is that people are living in them only at the pleasure of the government. They can be relocated to other quarters if that is what the government wants.

WAGE–PRICE CONTROLS AND WORK ARMIES

Meanwhile, the UN Wage and Price Stabilization Agency (WPSA) has instituted wage and price controls to combat inflation. What few businesses were able to survive the ravages of inflation are knocked out by these measures. Vital industries have been seized by the WPSA and prevented from closing. When employees refuse to work for low, fixed wages or to take the jobs assigned to them, they are placed under arrest and convicted of anti-democratic activities. Given a choice between prison or "volunteering" for the UN Full Employment and Environmental Restoration Army (FEERA), most of them chose the army. They are now doing the work prescribed for them in return for food and shelter. Many have been reassigned to new jobs, new cities, even new countries, depending on the employment quotas established by the UN International Human Resource Allocation Agency (IHRAA). Their families have been given living quarters which are appropriate to their work status and their willingness to cooperate.

Automobiles are now used only by the ruling elite who hold government positions of authority. To the extent possible, workers have been relocated to barracks which were constructed within walking distance of major industries. Others use rapid-transit systems, which have been greatly expanded by FEERA. For middle management and the more skilled workers who are allowed to live in the suburbs, there are "Peoples' Van Pools" (PVPs) that shuttle them to and from assigned boarding areas.

Last week, Maurice Strong, who is now the Director of IHRAA, toured the fifteen regional subdivisions that have been carved out of the North-American continent—including the former United States and Canada—and expressed gratification that America, at last, has ceased to be an aggressor against the world.

Another twenty years have slipped by, and we now find ourselves in The New World Order. No one around us is sure exactly when it began. In fact, there was no official starting date, no announcement in the media, no ceremony with blaring of trumpets. Sometime during the past ten or fifteen years, it became obvious that it just *was*, and everyone accepted it as the natural evolution of political trends and necessities. Now, a whole generation is in place that has no memory of another way of life. Many of the older folks have all but forgotten the details of their previous existence. And, of course, many of them have been eliminated. Schools and textbooks speak of the bygone era as one of unbridled competition, selfishness, and injustice. Previously commonplace possessions such as automobiles and private homes and three pairs of shoes are hardly mentioned, and when they are, they are derided as wasteful artifacts of a decadent society that, fortunately, has ceased to exist.

NO TAXES OR INFLATION OR DEPRESSIONS

The public is no longer concerned over high taxes. For the most part, there are none. Everyone works for the government—directly or indirectly—and is paid by electronic transfer to a government-regulated bank which controls all spending accounts. Even those large corporations which have been allowed to maintain the appearance of private ownership are merely junior partners of government. They are totally regulated and, at the same time, totally protected from failure. The amount each citizen receives for his labor is determined by his technical usefulness and his political rank. His taxes are pleasantly low or non-existent. The cost of government now is derived almost totally from expansion of the money supply—and from the economic value of the work battalions.

Each regional government of the world determines its spending needs and then offers to sell bonds in the open market to raise the money. The IMF/World Bank, acting as the UN's central bank, is the primary buyer. The Bank determines how much money to allow each regional government and then "purchases" that amount of bonds. It accomplishes that by making an electronic transfer of "credits" to one of its correspondent banks within the region receiving the money. Once that has happened, the local government can draw upon those credits to pay its bills. Not a single tax dollar is needed for any of that. The IMF/World bank simply creates the money and the regional governments spend it.

In days gone by, this increase in the money supply would have caused prices and wages to go up almost immediately. Not anymore. Prices and wages are controlled. What does happen, however, is that the government is caught in its own trap. It needs to keep the workers happy by giving them wage increases, but it also needs to keep its factories functioning by allowing price increases as well. The wage-price spiral, therefore, is not eliminated. It is merely delayed a few months. And, instead of happening in response to the interplay of supply and demand in a free market, it is directed by bureaucratic formula. The end result is the same either way. The people of the world are still paying the cost of their international and local governments through the hidden taxation called inflation.

In the chaotic past, the industrialized nations of the world went through phases of disruptive inflation often exceeding 1000% per year. That served a purpose in helping to destroy public faith in their existing national governments. It softened them up and made them more willing to accept drastic changes in their life styles and their political institutions. It paved the way to The New World Order. But now we have arrived, and extreme inflation rates—at least in the absence of war—would cause public dissatisfaction and be counterproductive. Inflation, therefore, has now been institutionalized at about 5% per year. That has been determined to be the optimum level for generating the most revenue without causing public alarm. Five per cent, everyone agrees, is "moderate." We can live with that, but we tend to forget it is 5% per year, *forever*.

A 5% devaluation applies, not only to the money earned this year, but to all that is left over from previous years. At the end of the first year, the original dollar is worth 95 cents. At the end of the second year, it is reduced again by 5% leaving its worth at 90 cents, and so on. After 20 years, the government will have confiscated 64% of every dollar we saved at the beginning of our careers. After working 45 years, the hidden tax on those first-year dollars will be 90%. The government will take virtually all of them over our lifetime. Current income and earned interest will partially offset this effect but it will not alter the underlying reality of government confiscation.

EFFECT OF "MODEST" 5% INFLATION

For the past fifty years, all the published charts illustrating the decline of the dollar from such-and-such a date to the "present" show the following type of curve.

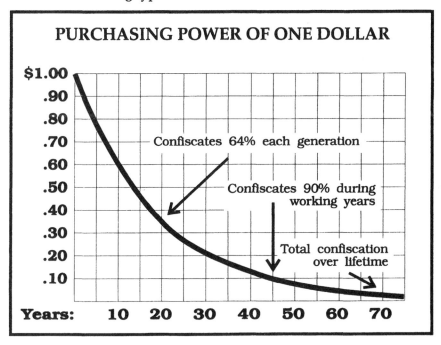

These, of course, are averages. A few people in the middle class of the bureaucracy will have managed to place some of their dollars into tangible assets or income-producing securities—what few remain—where they are somewhat protected from the effects of inflation. For the vast majority, however, inflation hedges constitute but a tiny fraction of all they have earned over a lifetime.

And so we find that, in The New World Order, inflation has been institutionalized at a "modest" level of five per cent. Once in every five or six generations—as prices climb higher and higher—a new monetary unit can be issued to replace the old in order to eliminate some of the zeros. But no one will live long enough to experience more than one devaluation. Each generation is unconcerned about the loss of the previous one. Young people come into the process without realizing it is circular instead of linear. They cannot comprehend the total because they were not alive at the beginning and will not be alive at the end. In fact, there need not even be an end. The process can be continued forever.

By this mechanism—and with the output of work battalions—government can operate entirely without taxes. The lifetime output of every human being is at its disposal. Workers are allowed a color TV, state-subsidized alcohol and recreational drugs, and violent sports to amuse them, but they have no other options. They cannot escape their class. Society is divided into the rulers and the ruled, with an administrative bureaucracy in between. Privilege is now largely a right of birth. The worker class and even most of the administrators serve masters whom they do not know by name. But serve they do. Their new lords are the monetary and political scientists who created and who now control The New World Order. All of mankind is in a condition of high-tech feudalism.

HIGH-TECH FEUDALISM

Inflation is not the only aspect of economic chaos that is now under control. Booms and busts in the business cycle are also a thing of the past. Like direct taxes, there *are* no business cycles any more. Now that the government has firm control over every economic check point, business cycles simply are not allowed. There is no speculation in the market, because no one has funds with which to speculate. There are no expansions of inventories or capital goods in order to maximize future profits, because inventories now are determined by formula. Besides, profits are also determined by formula and, although they are just large enough to keep pace with inflation, they are guaranteed.

Chaos in the economy is now impossible because it is not tolerated. Neither is a depression. Yes, there are hundreds of millions of human beings living under conditions of extreme hardship, and thousands die of starvation every day, but depressions are outlawed. No politician, no author, no one in the media would dare to suggest that the system was a failure. Each month the government releases new statistics showing in some obscure way or another that the economy is steadily improving. Although people are starving everywhere, hunger does not exist anymore. Although work battalions are crammed into flimsy barracks and tents, and although older homes and apartment buildings are falling down for lack of maintenance, forcing more and more families to share their tiny, unheated dwellings—nevertheless, the housing shortage is officially being eliminated. There are no more problems in the economy, because they now are illegal.

VOICES FROM THE PAST

There is a message flashing on the front panel of our time machine. It reads: *Duplicate sequence in memory bank. Check years 1816, 1831, 1904, and 1949.* That tells us that the on-board computer has found a similarity between what we are now viewing in the future and something that was recorded in the past. We had better check it out. On your keyboard, type: *Send data to printer* and press the key labelled *Execute*.

The first item is coming out of the printer now. It is a warning. In the year 1816, Thomas Jefferson wrote a letter to Sam Kercheval in which he said:

> We must make our election between *economy and liberty, or profusion and servitude.* If we run into such debts as that we must be taxed in our meat and in our drink, in our necessities and our comforts, in our labors and our amusements,... our people ... must come to labor sixteen hours in the twenty-four, give our earnings of fifteen of these to the government,... have no time to think, no means of calling our mis-managers to account; but be glad to obtain sustenance by hiring ourselves out to rivet their chains on the necks of our fellow-sufferers.... And this is the tendency of all human governments ... till the bulk of society is reduced to be mere automatons of misery.... And the forehorse of this frightful team is

public debt. Taxation follows that, and in its train wretchedness and oppression.[1]

Here is the second printout. It is a political commentary and a prophesy. In the year 1831, a young Frenchman, named Alexis de Tocqueville, toured the United States to prepare an official report to his government on the American prison system. His real interest, however, was the social and political environment in the New World. He found much to admire in America but he also observed what he thought were the seeds of its destruction. Upon his return to France the following year, he began work on a four-volume analysis of the strengths and weaknesses he found. His perceptivity was remarkable, and his work, entitled *Democracy in America*, has remained as one of the world's classic works in political science. This is the part that our computer recognized:

> The Americans hold that in every state the supreme power ought to emanate from the people; but when once that power is constituted, they can conceive, as it were, no limits to it, and they are ready to admit that it has the right to do whatever it pleases.... The idea of rights inherent in certain individuals is rapidly disappearing from the minds of men; the idea of the omnipotence and sole authority of society at large rises to fill its place....
>
> The first thing that strikes the observation is an innumerable multitude of men, all equal and alike, incessantly endeavoring to procure the petty and paltry pleasures with which they glut their lives. Each of them, living apart, is a stranger to the fate of all the rest; his children and his private friends constitute to him the whole of mankind....
>
> Above this race of men stands an immense and tutelary power, which takes upon itself alone to secure their gratifications and to watch over their fate. That power is absolute, minute, regular, provident, and mild. It would be like the authority of a parent if, like that authority, its object was to prepare men for manhood; but it seeks, on the contrary, to keep them in perpetual childhood: it is well content that the people should rejoice, provided they think of nothing but rejoicing....
>
> After having thus successively taken each member of the community in its powerful grasp and fashioned him at will, the supreme power then extends its arm over the whole community. It covers the surface of society with a network of small, complicated rules, minute and uniform, through which the most original minds

---

1. *Basic Writings* (New York: Willey Book Co., 1944), pp. 749–50.

and the most energetic characters cannot penetrate, to rise above the crowd. The will of man is not shattered, but softened, bent, and guided; men are seldom forced by it to act, but they are constantly restrained from acting. Such a power does not destroy, but it prevents existence; it does not tyrannize, but it compresses, enervates, extinguishes, and stupefies a people, till each nation is reduced to nothing better than a flock of timid and industrious animals, of which the government is the shepherd....

Our contemporaries are constantly excited by two conflicting passions: they want to be led, and they wish to remain free. As they cannot destroy either the one or the other of these contrary propensities, they strive to satisfy them both at once. They devise a sole, tutelary, and all-powerful form of government, but elected by the people. They combine the principle of centralization and that of popular sovereignty; this gives them a respite: they console themselves for being in tutelage by the reflection that they have chosen their own guardians. Every man allows himself to be put in leading-strings, because he sees that it is not a person or a class of persons, but the people at large who hold the end of his chain. By this system the people shake off their state of dependence just long enough to select their master and then relapse into it again.[1]

EDUCATION AS A TOOL FOR HUMAN ENGINEERING

The third printout is dated 1904 and is a report issued by the General Education Board, one of the first foundations established by John D. Rockefeller, Sr.. The purpose of the foundation was to use the power of money, not to *raise* the level of education in America, as was widely believed at the time, but to influence the *direction* of that education. Specifically, it was to promote the ideology of collectivism and internationalism. The object was to use the classroom to teach attitudes that encourage people to be passive and submissive to their rulers. The goal was—and is—to create citizens who are educated enough for productive work under supervision but not enough to question authority or seek to rise above their class. True education was to be restricted to the sons and daughters of the elite. For the rest, it would be better to produce skilled workers with no particular aspirations other than to enjoy life. It was enough, as de Tocqueville phrased it, "that the people should rejoice, provided they think of nothing but rejoicing."

---

1. Alexis de Tocqueville, *Democracy in America*, Vol. II (New York: Alfred Knopf, 1945), pp. 290–91, 318–19.

In the first publication of the General Education Board, Fred Gates explained the plan:

> In our dreams we have limitless resources, and the people yield themselves with perfect docility to our molding hands. The present educational conventions fade from our minds, and unhampered by tradition, we work our own good upon a grateful and responsive rural folk. We shall not try to make these people or any of their children into philosophers of mental learning or of science. We have not to raise from among them authors, editors, poets, or men of letters. We shall not search for embryo great artists, painters, musicians, nor lawyers, doctors, preachers, politicians, statesmen of whom we have ample supply. The task we set before ourselves is very simple as well as a very beautiful one: To train these people as we find them to a perfectly ideal life just where they are.... in the homes, in the shop, and on the farm.[1]

BACK TO THE FUTURE

Here is the fourth computer printout from the past. It is a satire—and a warning. In the year 1949, George Orwell wrote his classic novel entitled *1984*. In it, he portrayed the same "futuristic" scenes that now lie before us as we sit in our time machine. His only error appears to have been the date that became the title of his book. If he were writing it today, it is likely he would call it *2054*.

Orwell described the world of our future as being divided into three regions called Oceania, Eurasia, and Eastasia. Oceania consists of the Americas plus England, Australia, and the Pacific Islands; Eurasia is Russia and continental Europe; Eastasia comprises China, Japan, Southeast Asia, & India. These superstates are constantly at war with each other. The wars are not fought to conquer the enemy, they are waged for the primary purpose of controlling the population. The people in all three territories tolerate their misery and oppression because sacrifices are necessary in time of war. Most of the stratagems outlined in *The Report from Iron Mountain* are to be found in Orwell's narrative, but Orwell described them first. The think-tank was even willing to credit Orwell as the source of some of its concepts. For example, on the subject of establishing a modern, sophisticated form of slavery, the group at Iron Mountain said:

---

1. "Occasional Paper No. 1," General Education Board, 1904.

Up to now, this has been suggested only in fiction, notably in the works of Wells, Huxley, Orwell, and others engaged in the imaginative anticipation of the sociology of the future. But the fantasies projected in *Brave New World* and *1984* have seemed less and less implausible over the years since their publication. The traditional association of slavery with ancient preindustrial cultures should not blind us to its adaptability to advanced forms of social organization.[1]

From this we see that Orwell's work is far more than an entertaining novel. It is relevant to our present journey in time. Our would-be masters have studied him carefully. So should we. This is what he wrote:

These three superstates are permanently at war, and have been so for the past twenty-five years. War, however, is no longer the desperate, annihilating struggle that it was in the early decades of the twentieth century.... This is not to say that either the conduct of the war, or the prevailing attitude toward it, has become less bloodthirsty or more chivalrous. On the contrary, war hysteria is continuous and universal in all countries, and such acts as raping, looting, the slaughter of children, the reduction of whole populations to slavery, and reprisals against prisoners which extend even to boiling and burying alive, are looked upon as normal....

The primary aim of modern warfare ... is to use up the products of the machine without raising the general standard of living. [The "machine" is society's technical and industrial capacity to produce goods.] ... From the moment when the machine first made its appearance it was clear to all thinking people that the need for human drudgery, and therefore to a great extent for human inequality, had disappeared. If the machine were used deliberately for that end, hunger, overwork, dirt, illiteracy, and disease could be eliminated within a few generations....

But it was also clear that an all-around increase in wealth threatened the destruction—indeed in some cases was the destruction—of a hierarchical society. In a world in which everyone worked short hours, had enough to eat, lived in a house with a bathroom and a refrigerator, and possessed a motorcar or even an airplane, the most obvious and perhaps the most important form of inequality would already have disappeared. If it once became general, wealth would confer no distinction.... Such a society could not long remain stable. For if leisure and security were enjoyed by all alike, the great mass of human beings who are normally stupefied by poverty would become literate and would learn to think for themselves; and

---

1. Lewin, *Report*, p. 70.

when once they had done this, they would sooner or later realize that the privileged minority had no function, and they would sweep it away. In the long run, a hierarchical society was only possible on a basis of poverty and ignorance....

The essential act of war is destruction, not necessarily of human lives, but of the products of human labor. War is a way of shattering to pieces, or pouring into the stratosphere, or sinking into the depths of the sea, materials which might otherwise be used to make the masses too comfortable, and hence, in the long run, too intelligent....

In practice the needs of the population are always underestimated, with the result that there is a chronic shortage of half the necessities of life; but this is looked on as an advantage. It is deliberate policy to keep even the favored groups somewhere near the brink of hardship, because a general state of scarcity increases the importance of small privileges and thus magnifies the distinction between one group and another.... The social atmosphere is that of a besieged city, where the possession of a lump of horseflesh makes the difference between wealth and poverty. And at the same time the consequences of being at war, and therefore in danger, makes the handing over of all power to a small caste seem the natural, unavoidable condition of survival....

War, it will be seen, not only accomplishes the necessary destruction, but accomplishes it in a psychologically acceptable way. In principle it would be quite simple to waste the surplus labor of the world by building temples and pyramids, by digging holes and filling them up again, or even by producing vast quantities of goods and then setting fire to them. But this would provide only the economic and not the emotional basis for a hierarchical society....

War, it will be seen, is now a purely internal affair.... waged by each ruling group against its own subjects, and the object of the war is not to make or prevent conquests of territory, but to keep the structure of society intact.[1]

THE FUNCTION OF WASTE IN MODERN TOTALITARIANISM

Once again, it is clear that Orwell's grim narrative was a primary model for *The Report from Iron Mountain*. The authors of that blueprint for *our* future spoke at length about the value of planned waste as a means of preventing the masses from improving their standard of living. They wrote:

The production of weapons of mass destruction has always been associated with economic "waste." The term is pejorative, since it

1. George Orwell, *1984* (New York: New American Library/Signet, 1949), pp. 153–164.

implies a failure of function. But no human activity can properly be considered wasteful if it achieves its contextual objective....

In the case of military "waste," there is indeed a larger social utility.... In advanced modern democratic societies, the war system ... has served as the last great safeguard against the elimination of necessary social classes. As economic productivity increases to a level further and further above that of minimum subsistence, it becomes more and more difficult for a society to maintain distribution patterns insuring the existence of "hewers of wood and drawers of water."...

The arbitrary nature of war expenditures and of other military activities make them ideally suited to control these essential class relationships.... The continuance of the war system must be assured, if for no other reason, among others, than to preserve whatever quality and degree of poverty a society requires as an incentive, as well as to maintain the stability of its internal organization of power.[1]

These documents from the real past and the imagined future can help us to better understand our present. The spectacle of wasteful government spending suddenly becomes logical. It is not stupidity that pays farmers to destroy their crops, or that purchases trillion-dollar weapons systems that are never deployed or in some cases not even completed, or that provides funding for studies of the sex life of the tse-tse fly, or that gives grants to pornographers posing as artists. The overriding object behind most of these boondoggles is to waste the resources of the nation. It is obvious by now that the decline in living standards in the Western world is associated with a widening gap between the haves and the have-nots. What is not so obvious, however, is that this is according to plan. To that end, massive waste in government spending is not an unfortunate by-product, it is the *goal*.

That brings us back to the question of finding an acceptable substitute for war. War is not only the ultimate waste, it is also the ultimate motivation for human action. As Orwell said, waste in the absence of war "would provide only the economic and not the emotional basis for a hierarchical society." Will the environmental-pollution model be able to sufficiently motivate human action to be a substitute for war?

That is not a safe assumption. The possibility of war in our future cannot be ruled out. The environmental-pollution model is not yet thoroughly proven. It is working well for limited purposes

---

1. Lewin, *Report*, pp. 34–35, 40–41.

and on a limited scale, but it is still doubtful that it will ever equal the hysteria potential of a physical war. The world planners will not abandon the use of war until the new model has been proven over many years. On that point, the *Report from Iron Mountain* was emphatic:

> When asked how best to prepare for the advent of peace, we must first reply, as strongly as we can, that the war system cannot responsibly be allowed to disappear until 1) we know exactly what it is we plan to put in its place, and 2) we are certain, beyond reasonable doubt, that these substitute institutions will serve their purposes in terms of the survival and stability of society…. It is uncertain, at this time, whether peace will ever be possible. It is far more questionable … that it would be desirable even if it were demonstrably attainable.[1]

REGIONALISM AS A TRANSITION TO WORLD GOVERNMENT

The coalescing of the world's nations into three regional superstates was already visible even before we activated our time machine. The first steps had been strictly economic but were soon followed by political and military consolidation. The European Union (EU), including Russia, began with the issuance of a common money and eventually merged into a functional regional government. It was Orwell's Eurasia, even though it avoided calling itself by that name. Treaties binding Canada, the United States, Mexico, and South America formed the basic outline of Oceania, built around the Federal-Reserve Note as the regional money. Japan eventually became hostile to the West when trading was no longer to her sole advantage and, along with China which had been built up by Western aid and technology, and with India which had been given atomic technology by the West, became the political center of Eastasia. Even as far back as the 1980s, it was known as the "Greater East Asia Co-Prosperity Sphere." Its monetary system was to be based upon the Yen.

The people of the former nations were not yet ready for a giant leap into world government. They had to be led to that goal by a series of shorter and less frightening steps. They were more willing to surrender their economic and military independence to regional groupings of people who were closer in ethnic and cultural origin and who shared common borders. Only after several decades of

---

1. *Ibid.*, pp. 88–90.

transition was it possible to make the final merger. In the mean-time, the world was plunged alternately between war and peace. After each cycle of war, the population was more frightened, impoverished, and collectivised. In the end, world government was irresistible. By that time, the environmental-pollution model and the alien-invasion model had been perfected to provide high levels of human motivation. But, even then, regional uprisings were occasionally engineered when necessary to justify massive "peacekeeping" operations. War was never fully abandoned. It remained, as it always had been, a necessity for the stabilization of society.

HOW FIXED IS THE FUTURE?

Let us return now to the present from which we departed and reflect upon our journey. The first thing that strikes us is that we cannot be certain the future will unfold exactly as we have seen it. There are too many variables. When we originally set our *Primary-Assumption* selector to *Present trends unaltered*, we left the *Secondary-Assumption* selector where it was. It was pointing to *Banking Crisis*. Had we chosen the next position, *No Banking Crisis*, our journey would have been different. We would not have seen long lines of depositors or panic-buying in the stores or closing of the stock market. But we would still have witnessed the same scenes of despair in the more distant future. We merely would have travelled a different path of events to get there.

The forces driving our society into global totalitarianism would not change one iota. We still would have the doomsday mecha-nisms at work. We would have the CFR in control of the power centers of government and the media. And we would have an electorate which is unaware of what is being done to them and, therefore, unable to resist. Through environmental and economic treaties and through military disarmament to the UN, we would witness the same emergence of a world central bank, a world government, and a world army to enforce its dictates. Inflation and wage/price controls would have progressed more or less the same, driving consumer goods out of existence and men into bondage. Instead of moving toward The New World Order in a series of economic spasms, we merely would have travelled a less violent path and arrived at exactly the same destination.

There is little doubt that the master planners would prefer to follow the more tranquil route. Patient gradualism is less risky. But not everything is within their control. Events can get out of hand, and powerful economic forces can become suddenly unleashed. Banking crises *can* occur even without being deliberately caused.

On the other hand, the Cabal also knows that crises are useful in driving the masses into the corral faster than they would otherwise move. Therefore, the application of *some* kind of scientifically engineered crisis cannot be ruled out. It could take many forms: Ethnic violence, terrorism, plague, even war itself. But none of that makes any difference. It will not alter our direction of travel through time. It will only determine our specific route. Like a flowing river, it may be diverted this way or that by natural barriers or even by man-made channels, dikes, and dams, but it eventually will reach the sea. Our concluding reflection, therefore, is that it is relatively unimportant whether there will be a banking crisis or any other cataclysmic event. These are all secondary assumptions which are meaningless. Our only real hope for averting the new feudalism of the future is to change the *Primary* assumption. We must change it to read: *Present Trends Reversed.*

SUMMARY

A pessimistic scenario of future events includes a banking crisis, followed by a government bailout and the eventual nationalization of all banks. The final cost is staggering and is paid with money created by the Federal Reserve. It is passed on to the public in the form of inflation.

Further inflation is caused by the continual expansion of welfare programs, socialized medicine, entitlement programs, and interest on the national debt. The dollar is finally abandoned as the de facto currency of the world. Trillions of dollars are sent back to the United States by foreign investors to be converted as quickly as possible into tangible assets. That causes even greater inflation than before. So massive is the inflationary pressure that industry and commerce come to a halt. Barter becomes the means of exchange. America takes her place among the depressed nations of South America, Africa, and Asia—mired together in economic equality.

Politicians seize upon the opportunity and offer bold reforms. The reforms are more of exactly what created the problem in the first place: expanded governmental power, new regulatory agencies, and more restrictions on freedom. But this time, the programs begin to take on an international flavor. The American dollar is replaced by a new UN money, and the Federal Reserve System becomes a branch operation of the IMF/World Bank.

Electronic transfers gradually replace cash and checking accounts. This permits UN agencies to monitor the financial activities of every person. A machine-readable ID card is used for that purpose. If an individual is red flagged by any government agency, the card does not clear, and he is cut off from all economic transactions and travel. It is the ultimate control.

Increasing violence in the streets from revolutionary movements and ethnic clashes provide an excuse for martial law. The public is happy to see UN soldiers checking ID cards. The police-state arrives in the name of public safety.

Eventually all private dwellings are taken over by the government as a result of bailing out the home-mortgage industry. Rental property is also taken, as former landlords are unable to pay property taxes. People are allowed to live in these dwellings at reasonable cost, or no cost at all. It gradually becomes clear, however, that the government is now the owner of all homes and apartments. People are living in them only at the pleasure of the government. They can be reassigned at any time.

Wages and prices are controlled. Dissidents are placed into work armies. There are no more autos except for the ruling elite. Public transportation is provided for the masses, and those with limited skills live in government housing within walking distance of their assigned jobs. Men have been reduced to the level of serfs who are subservient to their masters. Their condition of life can only be described as high-tech feudalism.

There is no certainty that the future will unfold in exactly that manner, because there are too many variables. For example, if we had assumed that there will *not* be a banking crisis, then our journey would be different. We would not see long lines of depositors or panic-buying in the stores or closing of the stock market. But we would still witness the same scenes of despair in the more distant future. We merely would have travelled a different path of events to get there. That is because the forces driving our society into global totalitarianism would not have changed one iota. We still would have the doomsday mechanisms at work. We would have the CFR in control of the power centers of government and the media. We would have an electorate which is unaware of what is being done to them and, therefore, unable to resist. Through environmental and economic treaties and through military disarmament to the UN, we would witness the same emergence of a world central bank, a world government, and a world army to enforce its dictates. Inflation and wage/price controls would have progressed more or less the same, driving consumer goods out of existence and men into bondage. Instead of moving toward The New World Order in a series of economic spasms, we merely would have travelled a less violent path and arrived at exactly the same destination.

Chapter Twenty-Six

A REALISTIC
SCENARIO

What must be done if we are to avert the pessimistic scenario; a list of specific measures that must be taken to stop the monetary binge; an appraisal of how severe the economic hangover will be; a checklist for personal survival—and beyond.

The pessimistic scenario presented in the previous chapter is the kind of narrative that turns people off. No one wants to hear those things, even if they are true—or we should say *especially* if they are true. As Adlai Stevenson said when he was a candidate for President: "The contest between agreeable fancy and disagreeable fact is unequal. Americans are suckers for good news."

So, where is the *optimistic* scenario in which everything turns out all right, in which prosperity is restored and freedom is preserved after all? Actually, it is not hard to locate. You can find it every day somewhere in your newspaper. It is the shared faith of almost all politicians, experts, and commentators. If that is what you want to hear, you have just wasted a lot of time reading this book.

There is no optimistic scenario. Events have progressed too far for that. Even if we begin to turn things around by forcing Congress to cut spending, reduce the debt, and disentangle from UN treaties, the Cabal will not let go without a ferocious fight. When the Second Bank of the United States was struggling for its life in 1834, Nicholas Biddle, who controlled it, set about to cause as much havoc in the economy as possible and then to blame it on President Jackson's anti-bank policies. By suddenly tightening credit and withdrawing money from circulation, he triggered a full-scale national depression. At the height of his attack, he declared: "All other banks and all the merchants may break, but the

Bank of the United States shall not break."[1] The amount of devastation that could be caused by today's Federal Reserve is infinitely greater than what Biddle was able to unleash. It would be pure self-deception to think that the Cabal would quietly give up its power without exercising that option. We must conclude that no one is going to get out of this one unscathed. There is hell to pay, and it is we who are going to pay it.

SEVENTH REASON TO ABOLISH THE FED

What has any of this to do with the Federal Reserve System? The answer is that the Federal Reserve is the *starting point* of the pessimistic scenario. The chain of events begins with fiat money created by a central bank, which leads to government debt, which causes inflation, which destroys the economy, which impoverishes the people, which provides an excuse for increasing government power, which is an on-going process culminating in totalitarianism. Eliminate the Federal Reserve from this equation, and the pessimistic scenario ceases to exist. *That* is the seventh and final reason to abolish the Fed: *It is an instrument of totalitarianism.*

If the optimistic scenario is too optimistic and the pessimistic scenario is too pessimistic, then what is the scenario that we should hope lies in our future?

There is a middle course that lies between optimism and pessimism. It is called realism. Calling it a *realistic* scenario is not meant to imply that it is predetermined to happen, nor that it is even likely to happen. It is realistic only in the sense that it *can* happen if certain conditions are met. The balance of this chapter will be devoted to an analysis of those conditions.

Let us begin by allowing our opponent, Cynicism, to state the problem we face: "Is it realistic to believe that the current trends can actually be reversed? Isn't it just fantasy to think that anything can be done at this late date to break the CFR's hold over government, media, and education? Do we really expect the gum-chewing public to go upstream against the indoctrination of newspapers, magazines, television, and movies?"

Apathy joins in: "Forget it. There's nothing you can do. The bankers and politicians have all the money and all the power. The

---

1. See chapter seventeen.

game is already over. Make the most of it, and enjoy life while you can."

Do not listen to Cynicism and Apathy. They are agents of your enemy. They want you to quietly get in line and submit without a struggle. However, they do make a point that must not be overlooked. The battle has progressed far, and our position is not good. If we are to reverse the present trends, we must be prepared to make a herculean effort. That does not mean "Write your Congressman" or "Vote on Tuesday" or "Sign a petition" or "Send in a donation." That is far too easy. Those measures still play an important role in the battle plan but they fall far short of the need. Armchair campaigns will no longer do it.

Before turning to the question of what kind of effort *will* be required, let us first be clear on *what* it is we want to accomplish.

WHAT MUST NOT BE DONE

Let us begin with the negatives: what must *not* be done. The most obvious item in this category is that we must not turn to government for more of the same "cures" that have made us ill. We do not want more power granted to the Fed or the Treasury or the President, nor do we need another government agency. We probably don't even need any new laws, with the possible exception of those legislative acts which repeal some of the old laws now on the books. Our goal is the reduction of government, not its expansion.

We do *not* want to merely abolish the Fed and turn over its operation to the Treasury. That is a popular proposal among those who know there is a problem but who have not studied the history of central banking. It is a recurrent theme of the Populist movement and those advocating what they call Social Credit. Their argument is that the Federal Reserve is privately owned and is independent of political control. Only Congress is authorized to issue the nation's money, not a group of private bankers. Let the Treasury issue paper money and bank credit, they say, and we can have all the money we need without having to pay one penny in interest to the bankers.

It is an appealing argument, but it contains serious flaws. First, the concept that the Fed is privately owned is a legal fiction. The member banks hold stock, but it carries no voting weight. No matter how large the bank or how much capital is paid in, each bank has one vote. The stock cannot be sold or traded. Stockholders have none of the usual elements of control that come with ownership and, in fact, they are subservient to the central board. The seven members of the Board of Governors are appointed by the President and confirmed by the Senate. It is true that the Fed is independent of *direct* political control, but it must never be forgotten that it was created by Congress and it can be extinguished by Congress. In truth, the Federal Reserve is neither an arm of government nor is it private. It is a hybrid. It is an association of the large commercial banks which has been granted special privileges by Congress. A more accurate description would be simply that it is a *cartel* protected by federal law.

But the more important point is that it makes no difference whether the Fed is government or private. Even if it were entirely private, merely turning it over to the government would not alter its function. The same people undoubtedly would run it, and they would continue to create money for political purposes. The Bank of England is the granddaddy of central banks. It was privately owned at its inception but became an official arm of the British government in more recent times. It continues to operate as a central bank, and nothing of substance has changed. The central banks of all the other industrialized nations are direct arms of their respective governments. They are indistinguishable in function from the Federal Reserve. The technicalities of structure and ownership are not as important as function. Turning the Federal Reserve over to the Treasury without at the same time denuding it of its function as a central bank—that is, its ability to manipulate the money supply—would be a colossal waste of time.

The proposal of having the Treasury issue the nation's money is another question and has nothing to do with who owns the Fed. There is nothing wrong with the federal government issuing money so long as it abides by the Constitution and adheres to the principle of honesty. Both of these restraints forbid Congress from issuing paper money that is not 100% backed by gold or silver. If you are in doubt about the reasoning behind that statement, it would be a good idea to review chapter fifteen before continuing.

It is true that, if Congress had the power to create as much money as it needs *without* the Federal Reserve System, interest would not have to be paid on the national debt. But the Fed holds only a small percentage of the debt. Over 90% of those bonds are held by individuals and institutions in the private sector. Terminating interest payments would not hurt those big, bad bankers nearly as much as it would the millions of people who would lose their insurance policies, investments, and retirement plans. The Social Credit scheme would wipe out the economy in one fell swoop.

And we still would not have solved the deeper problem. The bankers would be cut out of the scam, but the politicians would remain. Congress would now be acting as its own central bank, the money supply would continue to expand, inflation would continue to roar, and the nation would continue to die. Besides, issuing money without gold or silver backing violates the Constitution.

THE JFK RUMOR

In 1981, a rumor was circulated that President Kennedy had been assassinated by agents of the hidden money power because he had signed Executive Order #11110 instructing the Treasury to print more than $4 billion in United States Notes. That is precisely the kind of money we are discussing: paper currency without gold or silver backing issued by the government, not the Federal Reserve. According to the rumor, the bankers were furious because they would lose interest payments on the money supply. When the Order was tracked down, however, it involved *Silver Certificates*, not United States Notes. Silver Certificates are backed by silver, which means they are real money, so the rumor was wrong on that point. But there is no interest paid on Silver Certificates either, so the rumor held up on that point. There was a third point, however, which everyone seemed to overlook. The Executive Order did not instruct the Treasury to issue Silver Certificates. It merely *authorized* it to do so if the occasion should arise. The occasion never arose. The last issuance of Silver Certificates was in 1957, and that was six years *before* the Kennedy executive order. In 1987, the order was rescinded by Executive Order 12608 signed by President Reagan.

The government did print some U.S. Notes in 1963, but these were in response to an 1868 act of Congress which directed the Treasury to maintain the amount of U.S. Notes outstanding at a fixed level. That required worn or damaged specimens of older Notes to be replaced by new ones. Some of these new Notes did get into circulation but were quickly snapped up by private collectors. They never became a significant part of the money supply and were not intended to. This printing was not ordered by JFK and, in fact, there was no reason for him even to have had knowledge of it.

The persistent rumor regarding the bankers' role in JFK's death was reinforced by several books circulated in conservative circles. They contained an ominous passage from Kennedy's speech at Columbia University, just ten days before his assassination. He is quoted as saying: "The high office of President has been used to foment a plot to destroy the Americans' freedom, and before I leave office I must inform the citizen of his plight."[1] However, when Columbia University was contacted to provide a transcript of the speech, it was learned that Kennedy never spoke there—neither ten days before his assassination *nor at any other time!* Ronald Whealan, head librarian at the John Fitzgerald Kennedy Library in Boston, provides this additional information: "Ten days prior to the assassination he was at the White House meeting with, among others, the ambassador to the United States from Portugal."[2]

It is possible that the President did make the remarks attributed to him on a different date before a different audience. Even so, it is a cryptic message which could have several meanings. That he intended to expose the Fed is the *least* likely of them all. Kennedy had been a life-long socialist and internationalist. He had attended the Fabian London School of Economics; participated in the destruction of the American money supply; and engineered the transfer of American wealth to foreign nations. (See page 109.) There is little reason to believe that he had suddenly "seen the light" and was reversing his life-long beliefs and commitments.[3]

MONETARISTS VS SUPPLY-SIDERS

But we are off the topic. Let us return to those unworkable theories regarding monetary reform. Prominent in this category are the Monetarists and the Supply-Siders. The Monetarists, adhering to the theories of Milton Friedman, believe that money should continue to be created by the Mandrake Mechanism of the Federal Reserve, but that the supply should be determined by a strict formula established by Congress, not the Fed. The Supply-siders, represented by Arthur Laffer and Charles Kadlec, believe in

---

1. Quoted by M.J. "Red" Beckman, *Born Again Republic* (Billings, Montana: Freedom Church, 1981), p. 23; also by Lindsey Williams, *To Seduce A Nation* (Kasilof, Arkansas: Worth Publishing, 1984), p. 26.
2. Letter to Hollee Haswell, Curator at the Low Memorial Library, Columbia University, October 13, 1987.
3. For a more comprehensive analysis of the "JFK Myth," visit the web site, www.realityzone.com, and see the Update section for *The Creature from Jekyll Island.*

formulas also, but they have a different one. They want the quantity of money to be determined by the current demand for gold. They are not talking about a true gold standard in which paper money is fully backed. By following what they call a "gold-price rule," they would simply observe the price of gold in the free market and then tinker with the dollar by expanding or contracting the money supply to keep its relative value, compared to gold, fairly constant.

These groups share the same underlying philosophy. Each has a different formula, but they agree on method: manipulation of the money supply. They share the same conviction that the free market will not work without assistance; the same faith in the wisdom and integrity of politically-created formulas, bureaus, and agencies. The Fed remains unscathed throughout all these debates because it is the ultimate mechanism for intervention. These people don't really want to change it. They just want their turn at running it.

Occasionally a truly original proposal appears that captures one's attention. Addressing a prestigious gathering of conservative monetary theorists in 1989, Jerry Jordan suggested that the monetary base could be expanded by holding a national lottery. The government would pay out more dollars in prize money than it received in ticket sales. The excess would represent the amount by which the monetary base would expand. Presumably, if they wanted to contract the money supply, they would pay out fewer dollars than taken in. It was an intriguing thought, but Mr. Jordan was quick to add: "The problem, of course, is that there would not be any effective institutional restraint on the growth of the monetary base."[1] Indeed, that is the problem with *all* schemes involving monetary control by men.

BALANCED-BUDGET AMENDMENT

A so-called balanced-budget amendment to the Constitution is not the answer either. In fact, it is an illusion and a fraud. Some of the biggest spenders in Congress are supporters. They know that it is popular with the voters but would not cramp their spending style in the least. If they were not permitted to spend more than they receive in taxes, they would have a perfect excuse for raising taxes. It would be a way of punishing the voters for placing limits

---

1. "The Future of Price Stability in A Fiat Money World," by Jerry L. Jordan, *Durell Journal of Money and Banking*, August, 1989, p. 24.

on them. The voters, on the other hand, would collapse under the burden of higher taxes and demand that their Congressmen circumvent the very amendment they previously supported. And that would be easy. Most versions of the balanced-budget amendment have an escape hatch built for just that purpose. Congress shall balance its budget *"except in cases of emergency."* Who decides what constitutes an emergency? Congress, of course. In other words, Congress shall balance its budget except when it doesn't want to. So what else is new?

A serious amendment would have to tackle, not balancing the budget, but *limiting the spending.* If that were done, the budget would take care of itself. But even that would be a waste of time considering the present composition of Congress. Instead of generating political pressure for a Constitutional amendment, we would be better off directing that same effort toward throwing the big spenders out of office. As long as the spenders are allowed to stay in there, they will find a way to get around any law—including the Constitution itself.

Another flaw in most versions of the balanced-budget amendment is that it would not affect the off-budget expenditures called entitlements. They now represent 52% of all federal outlays and are growing by 12% each year. A strategy that ignores that back-breaking load is not worth even considering. Even if Congress could be forced to stop deficit spending, the balanced-budget amendment would not solve the problem of inflation or paying off the national debt. The Federal Reserve can now inflate our money supply by using literally any debt in the world. It does not have to come from Congress. Unless we zero in on the Fed itself, we will just be playing political games with no chance of winning.

Every year, a few concerned Congressmen submit a bill to investigate or audit the Federal Reserve System. They are to be commended for their effort, but the process has been an exercise in futility. Their bills receive little or no publicity and never get out of committee for a vote. Even if they did receive serious attention, however, they could actually be counterproductive.

On the surface, it would appear that there is nothing wrong with a Congressional investigation or an audit, but what is there to investigate? We must assume the Fed is doing exactly what it says and is in total compliance with the law. A few minor improprieties probably would be discovered involving personal abuse of funds or insider profiteering, but that would be minor compared to the gigantic fraud that already is out in the open for all to see. The Federal Reserve is the world's largest and most successful scam. Anyone who understands the nature of money can see that without a team of investigators and auditors.

The danger in a proposal to audit the Fed is that it would delay serious action for years while the audit is going on. It would give the false impression that Congress is *doing something*. It also would give the monetary technicians an opportunity to lay down a smoke screen of verbiage and confusing statistics. The public would expect that all the answers will be forthcoming from the investigation, but the very groups and combines that need to be investigated would be conducting, or at least confounding, the investigation. By the time fourteen volumes of testimony, charts, tables, and exhibits finally appear, the public would be intimidated and fatigued. We do not need a bill to audit the Fed. We need one to *abolish* it.

A PLAN FOR ELIMINATING THE FED

So much for things *not* to do. All that would be required to abolish the Federal Reserve System is an act of Congress consisting of one sentence: *The Federal Reserve Act and all of its amendments are hereby rescinded.* But that would wipe out our monetary system overnight and create such havoc in the economy that it would play right into the hands of the globalists. They would use the resulting chaos as evidence that such a move was a mistake, and the American people then likely would welcome a rescue from the IMF/World Bank. We would find ourselves back in the Pessimistic Scenario even though we had done the right thing.

There are certain steps that must precede the abandonment of the Fed if we are to have a safe passage. The first step is to convert our present fiat money into real money. That means we must create an entirely new money supply which is 100% backed by precious metal—and we must do so within a reasonably short period of time.[1] To that end, we also must establish the true value of our present fiat money so it can be exchanged for new money on a

---

1. Most money is issued by governments, but there are many examples of private money that has functioned better than politically created money. A recent example in the U.S. was The Liberty Dollar, a privately issued currency 100% backed by silver and gold. In November 2007 its assets were seized by the government on the absurd claim that people might mistake it for worthless federal reserve notes.

realistic basis and phased out of circulation. Here is how it can be done:

1. **Repeal the legal-tender laws.** The federal government will continue accepting Federal Reserve Notes in the payment of taxes, but everyone else will be free to accept them, reject them, or discount them as they wish. There is no need to force people to accept honest money. Only fiat money needs the threat of imprisonment to back it up. Private institutions should be free to innovate and to compete. If people want to use Green Stamps or Disney-ride coupons or Bank-of-America Notes as a medium of exchange, they should be free to do so. The only requirement should be faithful fulfillment of contract. If the Green-Stamp company says it will give a crystal lamp for seven books of stamps, then it should be compelled to do so. Disney should be required to accept the coupon in exactly the manner printed on the back. And, if Bank of America tells its depositors they can have their dollars back *any time they want*, it should be required to keep 100% backing (coins or Treasury Certificates) in its vault at all times. In the transition to a new money, it is anticipated that the old Federal Reserve Notes will continue to be widely used.

2. **Freeze the present supply of Federal Reserve Notes,** except for what will be needed in step number six.

3. **Define the "real" dollar in terms of precious-metal content,** preferably what it was in the past: 371.25 grains of silver. It could be another weight of silver or even another metal, but the old silver dollar is a proven winner.

4. **Establish gold as an auxiliary monetary reserve** which can be substituted for silver, not at a fixed-price ratio, but at whatever ratio is set by the free market. Fixed ratios always become unfair over time as the prices of gold and silver drift relative to each other. Although gold may be substituted for silver at this ratio, it is only silver that is the foundation for the dollar.

5. **Restore free coinage at the U.S. Mint** and issue silver "dollars" as well as gold "pieces." Both dollars and pieces will be defined by metal content, but only coins with silver content can be called dollars, half-dollars, quarter-dollars, or tenth-dollars (dimes). At first, these coins will be derived only from metal brought into

the Mint by private parties. They must not be drawn from the Treasury's supply which is reserved for use in step number six.

6. **Pay off the national debt with Federal Reserve Notes** created for that purpose. Creating money without backing is forbidden by the Constitution; however, when no one is forced by law to accept Federal Reserve Notes as legal tender, they will no longer be the official money of the United States. They will be merely a kind of government script which no one is required to accept. Their utility will be determined by their usefulness in payment of taxes and by the public's anticipation of having them exchanged for real money at a later date. The creation of Federal Reserve Notes, with the understanding that they are not the official money of the United States, would therefore not be a violation of the Constitution. In any event, the deed is already done. The decision to redeem government bonds with Federal Reserve Notes is not ours. Congress decided that long ago, and the course was set at the instant those bonds were issued. We are merely playing out the hand. The money *will* be created for that purpose. Our only choice is *when*: now or later. If we allow the bonds to stand, the national debt will be repudiated by inflation. The value of the original dollars will gradually be reduced to zero while only the interest remains. Everyone's purchasing power will be destroyed, and the nation will die. But if we want *not* to repudiate the national debt and decide to pay it off *now*, we will be released from the burden of interest payments and, at the same time, prepare the way for a sound monetary system.

7. **Pledge the government's hoard of gold and silver** (except the military stockpile) to be used as backing for all the Federal Reserve Notes in circulation. The denationalization of these assets is long overdue. At various times in recent history, it was illegal for Americans to own gold, and their private holdings were confiscated. The amount which was taken should be returned to the private sector as a matter of principle. The rest of the gold supply also belongs to the people, because they paid for it through taxes and inflation. The government has no use for gold or silver except to support the money supply. The time has come to give it back to the people and use it for that purpose.

8. **Determine the weight of all the gold and silver** owned by the U.S. government and then calculate the total value of that supply in terms of real (silver) dollars.

9. **Determine the number of all the Federal Reserve Notes** in circulation and then calculate the real-dollar value of each one by dividing the value of the precious metals by the number of Notes.

10. **Retire all Federal Reserve Notes from circulation** by offering to exchange them for dollars at the calculated ratio. There will be enough gold or silver to redeem every Federal Reserve Note in circulation.[1]

11. **Convert all contracts based on Federal Reserve Notes to dollars** using the same exchange ratio. That includes the contracts called mortgages and government bonds. In that way, monetary values expressed within debt obligations will be converted on the same basis and at the same time as currency.

12. **Issue Silver Certificates.** As the Treasury redeems Federal Reserve Notes for dollars, recipients will have the option of taking coins or Treasury Certificates which are 100% backed. These Certificates will become the new paper currency.

13. **Abolish the Federal Reserve System.** It would be possible to allow the System to continue as a check clearing-house so long as it did not function as a central bank. A check clearing-house will be needed, and the banks that presently own the Fed should be allowed to continue performing that service. However, they must no longer receive tax subsidies to operate, and competition must be allowed. However, the Federal Reserve System, as presently chartered by Congress, must be abolished.

14. **Introduce free banking.** Banks should be deregulated and, at the same time, cut loose from protection at taxpayers' expense. No more bailouts. The FDIC and other government "insurance" agencies should be phased out, and their functions turned over to real insurance companies in the private sector. Banks should be required to keep 100% reserves for demand deposits, because that is a contractual obligation. All forms of time deposits should be presented to the public exactly as CDs are today. In other words, the depositor should be fully informed that his

---

1. Since the value of FRNs would be firmly established in terms of real dollars, there would be no compelling reason to exchange them, and it is possible that people would continue to use them in daily commerce. Therefore, to retire the FRNs and make the transition as quickly as possible, it would be necessary to have the banks automatically exchange them for real dollars whenever they are deposited. In short order, they would become collectors' items and historical curiosities.

money is invested and he will have to wait a specified time before he can have it back. Competition will insure that those institutions that best serve their customers' needs will prosper. Those that do not will fall by the wayside—without the need of an army of bank regulators.

15. **Reduce the size and scope of government.** No solution to our economic problems is possible under socialism. It is the author's view that the government should be limited to the protection of life, liberty, and property—nothing more. That means the elimination of almost all of the socialist-oriented programs that now infest the federal bureaucracy. If we hope to retain—or perhaps to regain—our freedom, they simply have to go. To that end, the federal government should sell all assets not directly related to its primary function of protection; it should privately sub-contract as many of its services as possible; and it should greatly reduce and simplify its taxes.

16. **Restore national independence.** A similar restraint must be applied at the international level. We must reverse all programs leading to disarmament and economic interdependence. The most significant step in that direction will be to *Get us out of the UN and the UN out of the US*, but that will be just the beginning. There are hundreds of treaties and administrative agreements that must be rescinded. There may be a few that are constructive and mutually beneficial to us and other nations, but the great majority of them will have to go. That is not because we are isolationist. It is simply because we want to avoid being engulfed in global tyranny.

Some will say that paying off the national debt with Federal Reserve Notes amounts to a repudiation of the debt. Not so. Accepting the old Notes for payment of taxes is not repudiation. Exchanging them for their appropriate share of the nation's gold or silver is not repudiation. Converting them straight across to a sound money with little or no loss of purchasing power is not repudiation. The only thing that would be repudiated is the old monetary system, but that was *designed* to be repudiated. The monetary and political scientists who created and sustained the Federal Reserve System never intended to repay the national debt. It has been their ticket to profit and power. Inflation is repudiation on the installment plan. The present system is a political trick, an accounting gimmick. We are merely acknowledging what it is. We are simply refusing to pretend we don't understand what they are doing to us. We are refusing to play the game any longer.

MEASURING THE SIZE OF THE HANGOVER

So those are the sixteen steps, but what are their effects? It should come as no surprise that there is a price to pay for a return to monetary sobriety. A hangover cannot be avoided, except by continuing the binge, which is the road to death. Let's take a look at what this binge has already cost us. We will measure that by calculating how much each Federal Reserve Note will be worth when the new money appears.

The following figures are presented for illustrative purposes only. The data are drawn from public sources and from the Federal Reserve itself, but there is no way to know how accurate they really are. In addition to the question of accuracy, there are some statistical items which are so obscure that not even the experts at the Fed are certain what they mean. When the time comes to apply this program, it will be necessary to assemble a task force of experts who can audit the books and assay the metals. Nevertheless, based on the best information available to the public, this is what we get:

> The total quantity of silver held by the government on September 30, 1993, was 30,200,000 troy ounces. If we assume the new dollar will be defined as 371.25 grains of silver (which equals .77344 troy ounces), then that supply is valued at $39,046,338.[1]
> The price of gold on that date was 384.95 Federal-Reserve notes per ounce. Silver was 4.99 fiat dollars per ounce. The ratio between them, therefore, was 77-to-1.
> The supply of gold was 261,900,000 ounces. The value of the gold supply, therefore, (at 77 times its weight in ounces) was $26,073,517,000.
> The value of silver and gold combined would be $26,112,563,338.

---

1. Although the weight of the silver-dollar is 412.5 grains (.8594 troy ounces), it is only 90% pure. Its silver content, however, is exactly 371.25 grains (.77344 troy ounces).

The number of Federal-Reserve notes this supply would have to redeem would be the combined total of the M1 money supply (currency and demand deposits) plus the additional number of notes needed to pay off the national debt. M1 on September 27, 1993, was 1,103,700,000,000 FRNs.[1] The national debt stood at 4,395,700,000,000 FRNs. The total amount to be redeemed, therefore, would be 5,499,400,000,000 FRNs.

The bottom line of this calculation is that the value of each Federal-Reserve note will be equal to .0047 silver dollar. One silver dollar would be worth 213 Federal-Reserve notes!

BAD, BUT NOT THAT BAD

That will be a bitter pill to swallow, but it sounds worse than it really is. Remember that the new dollars will have more purchasing power than the old. Coins will play a larger role in everyday transactions. The nickel phone call and the ten-cent cigar will have returned. In the beginning at least, the price of these items probably will be less than that. As explained in chapter seven, *any* quantity of gold or silver will work as the foundation for a monetary system. If the quantity is low—as certainly will be the case at the time of transition—it merely means the value of each unit of measure will be high. In that case, coins will solve the problem. Pennies would be used for a cup of coffee; one mill (a tenth of a cent) would pay for a phone call, and so on. New, small-denomination tokens would fill that need. In a relatively short period of time, however, the monetary supply of gold and silver would increase in response to free-market demand. When the supply increases, the relative value will decrease until a natural equilibrium is reached—as always has happened in the past. At that point, the tokens will no longer be needed and can be phased out.

An inconvenience? Yes. Vending machines will have to be retrofitted for the new coins, but that would be no more difficult than retrofitting them to take paper bills or plastic debit cards, which is what will be required if we do *not* adopt these measures. It is a small price to pay for an orderly return to real money.

---

1. For those who feel that M2 or M3 would be a more logical figure, see "Is M1 Subtractive or Accumulative?" in the Appendix, containing the author's notes and correspondence with the Federal Reserve.

Another possible solution would be to redefine the new dollar to contain a smaller quantity of silver. The advantage would be that we could continue to use our present coinage. On the negative side, however, is the fact that it would create headaches *after* the transition, because coinage then would be too cheap. Instead of changing over *now*, we would merely be postponing the task for *later*. Now is the time to do it—and do it right. The original value of a silver dollar was determined after centuries of trial and error. We don't have to reinvent the wheel. We *know* that it will work in the long run.

In the past, the banks have enjoyed a bountiful cash flow from interest on money created out of nothing. That will change. They will have to make a clear distinction between demand deposits and time deposits. Customers will be informed that, if they want the privilege of receiving their money back *on demand*, their deposit of coins or Treasury Certificates will be kept in the vault and not lent to others. Therefore, it will not earn interest for the bank. If the bank cannot make money on the deposit, then it must charge the depositor a fee for safeguarding his money and for checking services. If the customer wants to earn interest on his deposit, then he will be informed that it will be invested or lent out, in which case he cannot expect to get it back any time he wants. He will knowingly put his money into a *time* deposit with the agreement that a specified amount of time must pass before the investment matures.

The effect of this practice on banking will be enormous. Banks will have to pay higher interest rates to attract investment capital. They will have to trim their overhead expenses and eliminate some of the plush. Profit margins will be tightened. Efficiency will improve. They used to offer "free" services which actually were paid out of interest earned on their customers' demand deposits. Now they will charge for those services, such as checking and safe storage of deposits. Customers probably will grumble at first at having to pay for those things, and there will be no more free toasters.

Electronic transfer systems will probably become popular for their convenience, but they will be optional. Cash and check transactions will continue to play an important role. Government monitoring will be illegal. Although there will be fewer dollars in circulation than there were Federal Reserve Notes, the value of each one will be correspondingly greater. Each person will end up with the same purchasing power he had before the conversion. For a short period, both the old and the new money will circulate together, and some people will have difficulty making the necessary calculations to determine their relative values. But that is a routine operation for people who live in Europe or for anyone who travels to a foreign country. There is no reason to think that Americans are too stupid to handle it.

SOME BAD NEWS AND SOME GOOD

We should not delude ourselves into thinking that this will be an easy transition. It will be a very difficult period, and people will have to get used to a whole new way of thinking and doing. The freeze on the current money supply may trigger panic in the stock market and the business community. Stock prices could tumble, causing paper fortunes to disappear back into the computers from which they came. Some businesses may fold for a lack of easy credit. Weak banks will be allowed to close rather than be bailed out with taxes. Unemployment may worsen for a while. Those who have been used to a free ride will now have to walk or push or pay their way. The masses on welfare will not give up their checks and food stamps quietly. The media will fan the flames of discontent. The Cabal will be at every switch to derail the train.

This will be the moment of our greatest danger, the moment when the people could tire of their hard journey in the desert and lose interest in the promised land. This is the time when they may long for a return to captivity and head back to the slave pits of Pharaoh.

The important point, however, is that most of these problems would be temporary. They would be present only during the period of transition to a new money. As soon as free coinage is available at the Mint, and as soon as people see how much demand there is for silver and gold coins, there will be a steady stream of miners and jewelers who will add great new stores of precious metal to the nation's monetary stock. Foreigners undoubtedly will add to the inflow. Old silver and gold coins will also reappear in the market place. Very quickly, as the stores of precious metal respond to supply and demand, the quantity of money will increase and its per-unit value will drop to its natural equilibrium.

Won't that be inflation? Yes it will, but it will be significantly different from inflation by fiat money on four counts: (1) instead of being caused by politicians and bankers attempting to manipulate the economy to enhance their personal agendas, it will be caused by natural economic forces seeking an equilibrium of supply and demand; (2) instead of being harmful to the nation, leading to the destruction of the economy, it will be part of a healing process, leading to prosperity; (3) it will be less severe than what we will experience if we do *not* make the transition; and (4), instead of being part of a continuum that is designed to go on forever, it will have a built-in termination point: the point of natural equilibrium where the human effort to mine gold and silver equals the effort to create those things which gold and silver can buy. When that point is reached, the money supply will cease to expand, and inflation will stop—once and for all. The hangover will be gone. From that point forward, prices will begin a gradual descent as advances in technology allow improved efficiency in production. With the arrival of lower prices, better job opportunities, and increasing prosperity, the voices of discontent will gradually fade. After the storm is over, America will have an honest money supply, a government with no national debt, and an economy without inflation.

No matter what scenario unfolds in the future, there is white water ahead. We had better tighten our straps and prepare for the rapids. We owe it to ourselves and our families to take measures which will increase our chances of coming out at the other side. If the pessimistic scenario is played out, it will make little difference what we do, because there will *be* no other side. But in the realistic scenario, there are certain precautions that will make a big difference in our economic well being.

To fully appreciate the wisdom of some of these measures, it is well for us to pause and consider the possibility that a transition to economic safety and sanity will not be orderly. Another variant of the realistic scenario is that our entire system could collapse, including the international structure being assembled at the UN. If that should happen, we won't have to worry about an orderly transition to a sound monetary system, because it won't happen. Our primary concern will be basic survival.

Economic chaos and civil disorder would not *necessarily* have to be the prelude to world government. If a sufficient number of people were well enough informed to know in advance what the enemy's game plan is, and especially if they were in the right places within the system, they might be able to provide leadership at the critical moment. If there is blood in the streets and long periods of anarchy, it is theoretically possible that groups of enlightened individuals who have prepared in advance could move into the power vacuum and take charge. That may sound like another pessimistic scenario, but it is not. In the final analysis, it may be the most realistic one of all. But we should not hope for it. All we can do is prepare for it should it come to pass.

HOW TO PREPARE

What can we do to prepare financially? To avoid making this a lengthy dissertation, let's use the outline form. Elaboration should not be necessary.

1. **Get out of debt.** A mortgage on one's home is a logical exception, provided the price is right. Borrowing for one's business is also an exception if based on a sound business plan. Speculative investments are not a good idea in these times unless they are made with money you can afford to lose.

2. **Pick a sound bank.** Maintain accounts at several institutions. Do not keep over $100,000 in any one bank. Remember that not all types of accounts are covered by FDIC. Some institutions now offer private insurance. Make sure you know to what extent you are at risk.[1]

3. **Diversify your investments** among blue chip, over-the- counter, growth, income, large, small, mutuals, bonds, real estate, bullion coins, mining stock, tangibles, and even currencies. Industries that do well in hard times are gambling, alcohol, and escapist entertainment. Study the fields and companies in which you invest. Personal knowledge is indispensable.

4. **Avoid the most recent "best" performers.** Their great track records are historical. They have no bearing on future performance. To the contrary, they may now be overpriced and

---

1. That is not an easy assignment. It helps to have professional assistance from an independent source which is able to analyze asset quality, loan ratios, equity ratios, loan-loss reserves, and the like. One of the best sources of this kind of information is Veribanc. For a nominal fee, this bank-rating service will provide you with detailed reports on any bank or saving & loan in America. If you want their brochure, write to them at P.O. Box 461, Wakefield, MA 01880.

poised for a fall. See how an investment fared over the long run—at least fifteen years—and particularly how it performed during periods of economic downturn.

5. **When investing in coins,** avoid those with high numismatic value—unless you are prepared to become an expert. As with other types of investments, seek advice but don't depend on it. The same is true for diamonds, art pieces, and other collectibles. Stay with what you know. Otherwise, you will be vulnerable in shark-infested waters where even the most experienced traders can lose money.

6. **Maintain a stash of cash,** including some old silver coins. The currency should be enough to provide your family with necessities for about two months. The coins are for more severe and prolonged conditions. There is no "correct" quantity. It is a matter of personal judgment and financial ability.

PROFITING FROM DISASTER

All of this is aimed at surviving the storm and preparing ourselves to offer leadership in troubled times ahead. That is a rather negative view. There is a more positive outlook for those who are looking for good news, as Adlai Stevenson said. It is the exciting prospect that we can turn this calamity to our advantage. We can actually profit from the coming collapse. That thought has spawned hundreds of books and newsletters offering advice on how to get rich while others are being destroyed. There is even one that gives advice on how to cash in on the environmental-industry boom. The pitch is how to make a fortune on the downfall of America.

There is no doubt that opportunities exist to profit from investment decisions based on a realistic appraisal of current trends. Most of those opportunities, however, depend on making market-timing decisions. One must know precisely when to buy, when to sell, and at what price. To know all that, the investor must become expert on the nature of the industries involved and must monitor the daily shifts in market forces. He must attempt to complete his analysis and reach his conclusions in advance of the crowd. And, of course, he must be right. Most investors are not prepared to do that, so they must depend on the services of professionals, usually the same experts who are encouraging them to invest in these kinds of enterprises. If the investment is profitable, the analyst receives an income. If the investment turns sour, the analyst *still* receives an income.

That relationship is not unique to the "profit-from-crash" group. It is to be found at every level of the investment business as well as within the legal and medical professions. The customer pays for the advice regardless of its quality. What is disturbing about this investment concept is that it actually may help to make matters worse. By focusing on finding clever ways to avoid the effects of inflation or of making a profit from it, we are doing nothing to stop it and, thereby, encouraging its continuation. Those who are gaining from inflation are not likely to offer serious resistance to it. As they watch their profits pile up, they may become its most ardent supporters—even though they know deep in their hearts that it will destroy them in the end.

There is nothing wrong with trying to preserve one's capital in hard times, but the only real solution is to *use* one's capital to *stop* the present trends. In the long run, there is no way to profit from a destroyed America. There is no refuge from a collapse. There is no way to protect your assets, your home, your job, your family, your freedom. As Henry Hazlitt phrased it, "There is no safe hedge against inflation except to stop it."

A PRO-ACTIVE CRUSADE

It is clear from the facts presented in this book that much more needs to be done than abolishing the Federal Reserve. Although that would be a great victory for economic and personal freedom, unfortunately, the creature has siblings, and they hunt and feed together. There is an income tax designed to eliminate the middle class, a school system more concerned with politically correct attitudes than with education, a controlled media that corrupts the news, controlled political parties that create the illusion of participating in our political destiny, and the UN rapidly absorbing our military and economic sovereignty. We are not likely to slay one of these creatures without the others. We must eradicate the species.

The species is *collectivism*. Collectivism is the concept that the group is more important than the individual and that government is justified in any act so long as it is claimed to be for the greater good of the greater number. That is the foundation upon which the Federal Reserve is built and it is the foundation for literally every other modern assault against our liberty. Collectivism is the enemy of freedom, and we must launch a pro-active crusade against it. Not to do so is to surrender without a fight.

The first step in this crusade is to spread the word. Americans have allowed their nation to be stolen from right under their noses because they did not understand what was happening. This is not just an American phenomenon. The same theft has occurred with minor variations in every advanced nation of the world. There is no hope for the future as long as that condition remains. Therefore, the starting point for any realistic plan for survival *and beyond* is an awakening of America—and the world.

Unfortunately, that will not be enough. Education is important, but it makes little difference what we know if we don't do anything with that knowledge. It has been said that knowledge is power, but that is one of the greatest myths of all time. Men with great knowledge are easily enslaved if they do nothing to defend their freedom. Knowledge by itself is not power, but it holds the *potential* for power if we use it as a guide for action. Truth will always be defeated by tyranny unless people are willing to step forward and put their lives into the battle. The future belongs, not to ideas, but to people who act on those ideas.

WHAT WILL BE REQUIRED FOR VICTORY

Defeating the global powers of collectivism is a big order, and we must be very clear on what will be required. Here are the realities.

1. There is not much that can be done by one person alone. We need lots of help, and it will have to be international in scope. National efforts will continue to be important, but collectivism is entrenched globally. The whole world is now our theater of conflict.

2. We need a corps of dedicated men and women who are prepared to devote a major portion of their lives to this mission. Much more will be required than merely supporting a political party, or subscribing to a periodical, or writing letters to politicians. The time for armchair patriotism is over.

3. We need a comprehensive training program to expose the tactics used by agents of collectivism and to show how we can ethically counter them.

4. We need the same support mechanisms that our foes have long enjoyed: coordination, strategy, training, communications. Any plan without these elements is doomed to failure.

5. We need an organizational structure that cannot be subverted by our opponents. It must be designed, not as a pyramid with all control at the top, but as a hologram with each of the smallest units able to create the entire movement from the bottom up.

6. We need dependable funding to support the many services needed for organizational activities.

7. We need a clear statement of positive principle. It is not enough to know what we are against. We must also know what we are for.

8. We need a strategy, not for petitioning leaders, but for *becoming* leaders within our respective countries.

9. We need the long view of history, realizing that our mission may not be completed in our lifetime. What we set in motion must be larger than ourselves and it must have momentum into the future.[1]

CONCLUSIONS AND SUMMARY

We have finally come to the end of this book. It was not a textbook on banking theory. It was a who-dunnit, and by now you know the answer.

We have covered a vast expanse of history and have wandered far afield from our main topic. It was necessary. Without the larger view, the case against the Federal Reserve System would have been weak. It would have omitted the elements of war, revolution, depression, and fraud. Without that long journey, we would be limited to a sterile discussion of interest rates, discount policies, and reserve ratios. That is not where the body is hidden.

In the foreword, it was stated that there were seven reasons to abolish the Federal Reserve System. It is time to repeat them:

---

1. All of these attributes have been incorporated into an organization called Freedom Force International. Additional information is located at the end of this chapter.

- It is incapable of accomplishing its stated objectives.
- It is a cartel operating against the public interest.
- It is the supreme instrument of usury.
- It generates our most unfair tax.
- It encourages war.
- It destabilizes the economy.
- It is an instrument of totalitarianism.

The purpose of this book has been to demonstrate the accuracy of those assertions.

A plan for recovery was finally presented which involves sixteen steps, each based upon lessons which emerged from history. These lessons were mingled with a large amount of theory which is traceable only to the mind of the author himself. Which is to say there is no guarantee the plan will work. But it *is* a plan. It is better to fail trying than to do nothing. Like men on a sinking ship, we must risk the water. We cannot stay where we are.

There undoubtedly are technical flaws in these proposals, for the mechanism is merely a prototype. Someone surely will discover a gear that will not mesh or a lever that is disconnected. It will need the additional work of specialists in many diverse fields. Even then, the job will not be complete, for it must finally be handed over to those who are skilled in drafting legislation. Their task will be two-fold. First, they must make it workable in the real world of politics. Secondly, they must prevent loopholes and vagaries which could eventually subvert the plan.

But none of these considerations should deter us from beginning the process. We may not have answers to all the technical questions, but we *do* have an answer to the big question. We *do* know that the Federal Reserve System must be abolished. Let us, therefore, begin.

The Creature has grown large and powerful since its conception on Jekyll Island. It now roams across every continent and compels the masses to serve it, feed it, obey it, worship it. If it is not slain, it will become our eternal lord and master.

Can it be slain? Yes it can.

How will it be slain? By piercing it with a million lances of truth.

Who will slay it? A million crusaders with determination and courage.

The crusade has already begun.

AN INVITATION
from G. Edward Griffin

Since writing the first edition of this book, it has become increasingly obvious that much more needs to be done than abolishing the Fed. Although that would be a great victory in the battle for economic and personal freedom, unfortunately, the creature has siblings. There are many other fronts and issues that also need our attention. It is for that reason I have launched an aggressive action program based largely on the ideals advocated in this book. It is called Freedom Force International and its mission is nothing less than to change the world.

If you are motivated to do more than merely be informed, I urge you to visit the Freedom Force web site and examine its goals, strategy, and principles. The fact that you have made it all the way to the end of this long book means you probably are the kind of person who will want to be part of this movement. If you really want to make a difference in the world and are willing to commit a portion of your life to that end, I would be pleased to welcome you as a member of Freedom Force.

For additional information, visit our web site:
www.freedom-force.org

If you are looking for reliable books, audio, and video programs relating to freedom issues, visit the web site of the publisher of this book:
www.realityzone.com

(A.) STRUCTURE AND FUNCTION
OF THE FEDERAL RESERVE SYSTEM

The three main components of the Fed are: (1) the national Board of Governors, (2) the regional Reserve Banks, and (3) the Federal Open Market Committee. Lesser components include: (4) the commercial banks which hold the stock, and (5) the advisory councils.

The function of the national Board of Governors is to determine the system's monetary policy. The Board consists of seven members who are appointed by the President and confirmed by the Senate. Their terms of office are fourteen years and are staggered so that they do not coincide with the presidential term of office. The purpose of this is to insure that no single President can dominate Fed policy by stacking the Board with his appointments. One Board member is appointed as the Chairman for four years and another as Vice Chairman for four years. The Chairman controls the staff and is the single most powerful influence within the system.

Control is exercised by the Board and a handful of top staff employees. The Federal Reserve Act mandated that the President, when selecting Governors "shall have due regard to a fair representation of the financial, agricultural, industrial and commercial interests, and geographical divisions of the country." This mandate is now almost completely ignored, and the men come primarily from the fields of banking and finance.

The function of the regional Reserve Banks is to hold cash reserves of the system, supply currency to member banks, clear checks, and act as fiscal agent for the government.

The twelve regional Reserve Banks are located in Atlanta, Boston, Chicago, Cleveland, Dallas, Kansas City, Minneapolis, New York, Philadelphia, Richmond, San Francisco, and St. Louis. They are corporations with stock held by the commercial banks which are members of the system. Member banks elect the directors of the regional Reserve Banks of which they are a part. The larger banks hold more shares but they have only one vote in the selection of the Directors.

Within each regional-bank system there are nine Directors. The member banks elect three Class-A directors who represent the banking industry and three Class-B directors who represent the general public. The remaining three Class-C directors are appointed by the national Board. The Chairman and Vice Chairman of each regional Reserve Bank must be Class-C directors. The selection of President and other officers is subject to veto by the national Board of Governors. In this way, the national Board is able to exercise control over the regional branches of the system.

The function of the Federal Open Market Committee is to implement the monetary policy set by national Board, although it exercises considerable autonomy in setting its own policy. It manipulates the money supply and interest rates primarily by purchasing or selling government securities—although it also accomplishes that through the purchase or sale of foreign currencies and the securities of other governments as well. Money is created and interest rates go down when it purchases. Money is extinguished and interest rates go up when it sells. Policy is formulated on a daily basis. In fact, it is monitored by the minute and the Committee often intervenes in the market to affect immediate changes.

The Open Market Committee is composed of the national Board of Governors plus five of the twelve regional Presidents who serve on a rotating basis. The exception to this is the President of the New York regional Bank who is always on the Committee. Thus, once again, the System is firmly in control of the national Board with the President of the New York regional Bank being more powerful than the others.

Twenty-four bond dealers handle all sales of government securities. Government agencies cannot exchange with each other without going through dealers who earn commissions on each transaction.

Decisions are made at secret meetings. Interest rate changes are announced immediately afterward and the minutes are released three weeks later. Transcripts of the deliberations are destroyed. That policy was begun in 1970 when the Freedom-of-Information Act was passed.

The function of the member banks is to conduct the nation's banking business and to implement the System's monetary policy in terms of putting money into or drawing it out of the system at the point of contact with individual or corporate borrowers.

This leads to the troublesome question of ownership. The federal government does not own any stock in the System. In that sense, the Fed is privately owned. That, however, is misleading in that it implies a typical private-ownership relationship in which the stockholders own and control. Nothing could be further from the truth. In this case, the stock carries no proprietary interest, cannot be sold or pledged as collateral, and does not carry ordinary voting rights. Each bank is entitled to but one vote regardless of the amount of stock it holds. In reality, the stock is not evidence of "ownership" but simply certificates showing how much operating capital each bank has put into the System. It is not a government agency and it is not a private corporation in the normal sense of the word. It is subject to political control yet, because of its tremendous power over politicians and the elective process, it has managed to remain independent of political oversight. Simply stated, it is a cartel, and its organizational structure is uniquely structured to serve that end.

(B.) NATURAL LAWS
OF HUMAN BEHAVIOR IN ECONOMICS

NATURAL LAW NO. 1

LESSON: When gold (or silver) is used as money and when the forces of supply and demand are not thwarted by government intervention, the amount of new metal added to the money supply will always be closely proportional to the expanding services and goods which can be purchased with it. Long-term stability of prices is the dependable result of these forces. This process is automatic and impartial. Any attempt by politicians to intervene will destroy the benefit for all. Therefore,

LAW: Long-term price stability is possible only when the money supply is based upon the gold (or silver) supply without government interference.

NATURAL LAW NO. 2

LESSON: Whenever government sets out to manipulate the money supply, regardless of the intelligence or good intentions of those who attempt to direct the process, the result is inflation, economic chaos, and political upheaval. By contrast, whenever government is limited in its monetary power to only the maintenance of honest weights and measures of precious metals, the result is price stability, economic prosperity, and political tranquility. Therefore,

LAW: For a nation to enjoy economic prosperity and political tranquility, the monetary power of its politicians must be limited solely to the maintenance of honest weights and measures of precious metals.

NATURAL LAW NO. 3

LESSON: Fiat money is paper money without precious-metal backing and which people are required by law to accept. It allows politicians to increase spending without raising taxes. Fiat money is the cause of inflation, and the amount which people lose in purchasing power is exactly the amount which was taken from them and transferred to their government by this process. Inflation, therefore, is a hidden tax. This tax is the most unfair of all because it falls most heavily on those who are least able to pay: the small wage earner and those on fixed incomes. It also punishes the thrifty by eroding the value of their savings. This creates resentment among the people, leading always to political unrest and national disunity. Therefore,

LAW: A nation that resorts to the use of fiat money has doomed itself to economic hardship and political disunity.

NATURAL LAW NO. 4

LESSON: Fractional money is paper money which is backed by precious metals up to only a portion of the face amount. It is a hybrid, being part receipt money and part fiat money. Generally, the public is unaware of this fact and believes that fractional money can be redeemed in full at any time. When the truth is discovered, as periodically happens, there are runs on the bank, and only the first few depositors in line can be paid. Since fractional money earns just as much interest for the bankers as does gold or silver, the temptation is great for them to create as much of it as possible. As this happens, the fraction which represents the reserve becomes smaller and smaller until, eventually, it is reduced to zero. Therefore,

LAW: Fractional money will always degenerate into fiat money. It is but fiat money in transition.

NATURAL LAW NO. 5

LESSON: It is human nature for man to place personal priorities ahead of all others. Even the best of men cannot long resist the temptation to benefit at the expense of their neighbors if the occasion is placed squarely before them. This is especially true when the means by which they benefit is obscure and not likely to be perceived as such. There may be exceptional men from time to time who can resist that temptation, but their numbers are small. The general rule will prevail in the long run.

A managed economy presents men with precisely that kind of opportunity. The power to create and extinguish the nation's money supply provides unlimited potential for personal gain. Throughout history the granting of that power has been justified as being necessary to protect the public, but the results have always been the opposite. It has been used against the public and for the personal gain of those who control. Therefore,

LAW: When men are entrusted with the power to control the money supply, they will eventually use that power to confiscate the wealth of their neighbors.

(C.) IS M-1 SUBTRACTIVE OR ACCUMULATIVE?

Below is a copy of the author's letter to Mike Dubrow at the Public Information department of the Federal Reserve System. In a telephone conversation on February 14, 1994, Mr. Dubrow said that the assumption stated in the letter would be correct if it were not for the fact that the system is under the control of a central bank. The Federal Reserve, he said, would not allow that to happen, because it would be inflationary. The Fed would reduce the money supply to offset the effect of monetary expansion as dollars moved from M-1 to M-2 and back to M-1 again. In other words, the assumption is correct, but the Fed has the power to offset it—if it wants to. The bottom line is that M-1 is *accumulative*. As such, it is the most meaningful measure of the money supply.

G. Edward Griffin
Box 4646, Westlake Village CA 91359

January 19, 1994

MikeDubrow
FAX # (202) 452-2707
FederalReserveSystem
Washington,DC

DearMr.Dubrow,

As we discussed during our phone conversation this morning, I am preparing a paper on the Federal Reserve System, and an interesting question has arisen. It is so fundamental that almost everyone with whom I have spoken *thought* they knew the answer but, upon analysis, have concluded they were not so sure after all. **IS M1 SUBTRACTIVE OR ACCUMULATIVE?** It is my understanding that there are three optional definitions of the money supply:

M1 = currency + short-term deposits.
M2 = M1 + short-term time deposits.
M3 = M2 + institutional long-term deposits.

It is clear that, when money is paid out of a checking account and put into a savings account, it increases M2, but the question is: Does it remain as part of M1 or is it subtracted from it? Herbert Mayo, in his book *Investments* (Chicago: Dryden Press, 1983), says "If individuals shift funds from savings accounts to checking accounts, the money supply is increased under the narrow definition (M-1) but is unaffected if the broader definition (M-2) is employed." This implies that, when money is moved from a checking account to a savings account, it is subtracted from M1. Otherwise, it would not increase M1 when it is moved back again from savings to checking. When we spoke on the phone, you confirmed that his interpretation is correct.

But how can that be? The money moved from checking to savings or any other investment does not disappear into a vault. It is spent in fulfillment of the investment project. It is given to a vendor or a contractor or an employee and reappears in their checking accounts where it becomes part of M1 once again. It would seem, therefore, that it doesn't really leave M1 at all. It merely increases M2.

I have hypothesized one possible explanation. It is that the money *does*, in fact, disappear into a vault, or at least into a bookkeeping ledger, *for a short period of time*. That would be the time between its deposit into the savings account and its subsequent transfer to the checking accounts of borrowers. The time period might be short—perhaps less than thirty days on the average—but it still needs to be considered when calculating the money aggregates. Therefore, M1 *is* reduced when money is transferred from checking to savings, but that is only a temporary effect. M1 will be increased once again just as soon as the new M2 money is redirected to borrowers. Is that a correct explanation?

Thank you for your help with these puzzling items.

Sincerely,

G. Edward Griffin
(805)496-1649

Adams, Charles. *Fight, Flight, Fraud: The Story of Taxation*. Curacao, The Netherlands: Euro-Dutch Publishers, 1982.

Aldrich, Nelson W. Letters to John A. Sleicher, July 16, 1913; to William Howard Taft, Oct. 3, 1913. Nelson Aldrich Papers. Library of Congress.

Angell, Norman. *The Story of Money*. New York: Frederick A. Stokes Co., 1929.

Attali, Jacques. Translated by Barbara Ellis. *A Man of Influence: Sir Siegmund Warburg, 1902–82*. London: Weidenfeld, & Nicolson, 1986.

Atwood, Harry. *The Constitution Explained*. Merrimac, Massachusetts: Destiny Publishers, 1927; 2nd ed. 1962

Bagwell, Tyler E. *Images of America: The Jekyll Island Club*. Charlston, SC: Arcadia, 1998.

Ballard, Robert. "Riddle of the Lusitania." *National Geographic*. April, 1994, p. 68.

Balsiger, David, & Charles Sellier. *The Lincoln Conspiracy*. LA: Schick Sunn Classic, 1977.

Bancroft, George. *A Plea for the Constitution*. New York: Harpers, 1886; rpt. Sewanee, Tennessee: Spencer Judd Publishers, 1982.

Barnes, Harry Elmer. *In Quest of Truth and Justice: De-Bunking the War Guilt Myth*. Chicago: National Historical Society, 1928. Rpt. New York: Arno Press, 1972.

Barron, Clarence W. *They Told Barron; Notes of Clarence Walker Barron*. Edited by Arthur Pound and Samuel Taylor Moore. New York: Harper and Brothers, 1930.

Basso, Louis. *A Treatise on Monetary Reform*. St. Louis, Missouri: Monetary Realist Society, 1982.

Bentley, Elizabeth. *Out of Bondage*. New York: Devin-Adair, 1951.

Beard, Charles. *The Rise of American Civilization*. New York: Macmillan, 1930. Vol. I.

Bell, Garrett de, ed. *The Environmental Handbook*. New York: Ballantine/Friends of the Earth, 1970.

Biddle, Nicholas. *Correspondence, 1807–1844*. Reginald C. McGrane, ed. New York: Houghton Mifflin, 1919.

Birmingham, Stephen. *"Our Crowd": The Great Jewish Families of New York*. New York: Harper & Row, 1986.

Bogart, Ernest Ludlow. *Economic History of the American People*. New York: Longmans, Green & Co., 1930.

Bolles, Albert S. *The Financial History of the United States*, 4th ed. New York: D. Appleton, 1896. Vol. I.

Bovard, James. *The World Bank vs. The World's Poor*. Cato Policy Analysis. Washington, D.C.: Cato Institute, 1987.

Bowers, Claude G. *The Tragic Era: The Revolution after Lincoln*. New York: Houghton Mifflin, 1957.

Bryan, William Jennings and Mary Baird. *The Memoirs of William Jennings Bryan*. New York: Kennikat Press, 1925.

Brzezinski, Zbigniew. *Between Two Ages: America's Role in the Technetronic Era*. Westport, Connecticut: Greenwood Press, 1970.

Budenz, Louis F. *The Techniques of Communism*. Chicago: Henry Regnery, 1954.

Burnham, James. *The Web of Subversion: Underground Networks in the U.S. Government*. New York: The John Day Co., 1954.

Cappon, Lester J., ed. *The Adams-Jefferson Letters*. New York: Simon and Schuster, 1971.

Carnegie, Andrew. *Triumphant Democracy*. New York: Charles Scribner's Sons, 1893.

Catterall, Ralph C.H. *The Second Bank of the United States*. Chicago: University of Chicago Press, 1902.

Catton, Bruce, author. Richard M. Ketchum, ed. *The American Heritage Picture History of the Civil War*. New York: American Heritage Publishing Co., 1960.

Chambers, Whittaker. *Witness*. New York: Random House, 1952.

Chandler, Lester V. *Benjamin Strong, Central Banker*. Washington, D.C.: Brookings Institution, 1958; rpt. New York: Arno Press, 1978.

Chernow, Ron. *The House of Morgan: An American Banking Dynasty and the Rise of Modern Finance*. New York: Atlantic Monthly Press, 1990.

Churchill, Winston. *The World Crisis.* New York: Scribner's Sons, 1949.

Clark, Kenneth. *Ruskin Today.* New York: Holt, Reinhart & Winston, 1964.

Commager, Henry S., ed. *Documents of American History.* New York: F.S. Cofts & Co., 1940.

Cooper, Richard N. "A Monetary System for the Future." *Foreign Affairs.* Fall, 1984.

Crane, Philip M. *Surrender in Panama.* Ottawa, Illinois: Caroline House Books, 1978.

Crozier, Michael; Huntington, Samuael P.; and Watanuki, Joji. *The Crisis of Democracy.* New York: New York University Press, 1975.

Davidson, James Dale, and Rees-Mogg, Lord William. *The Great Reckoning.* New York: Summit Books, 1991.

Dall, Curtis B. *FDR: My Exploited Father-In-Law.* Tulsa, Oklahoma: Christian Crusade Publications, 1967.

Diggins, John P. *Mussolini and Fascism: The View from America.* Princeton, New Jersey: Princeton University Press, 1972.

Disraeli, Benjamin. *Coningsby.* New York & London: Alfred A. Knopf, 1844.

Dobbs, Zygmund. *The Great Deceit: Social Pseudo-Sciences.* West Sayville, New York: Veritas Foundation, 1964.

Donovan, Robert J. *The Assassins.* New York: Harper & Brothers, 1952.

Eisenschiml, Otto. *The Hidden Face of the Civil War.* New York: Bobbs-Merril, 1961.

———. *Why Was Lincoln Murdered?* Boston: Little, Brown and Company, 1937.

Ewert, Ken S. "The International Monetary Fund." *The Freeman.* April, 1989.

Federal Reserve Bank of Chicago. *Modern Money Mechanics.* Revised October 1982

Federal Reserve Bank of St. Louis. "Money, Credit and Velocity." *Review.* May, 1982, Vol. 64, No. 5, p. 25.

Federal Reserve Bulletin. October, 1988.

Fehrenbacher, Don E., ed. *Abraham Lincoln: Speeches and Writings, 1859–1865.* New York: Library of America, 1989.

Ferrell, Robert H. *Woodrow Wilson and World War I.* New York: Harper & Row, 1985.

Figgie, Jr., Harry. *Bankruptcy 1995: The Coming Collapse of America and How to Stop It.* Boston: Little, Brown and Company, 1992.

Finder, Joseph. *Red Carpet.* New York: Holt, Rinehart and Winston, 1983.

Fisher, Irving. *100% Money.* New York: Adelphi, 1936.

Forbes, John Douglas. *J.P. Morgan, Jr.* Charlottesville: University Press of Virginia, 1981.

Forrester, Izola. *This One Mad Act.* Boston: Hale, Cushman & Flint, 1937.

Galbraith, John Kenneth. *Money: Whence It Came, Where It Went.* Boston: Houghton Mifflin, 1975.

Gardner, Richard. "The Hard Road to World Order." *Foreign Affairs,* April, 1974.

Glass, Carter. *Adventures in Constructive Finance.* New York: Doubleday, 1927; rpt. New York: Arno Press, 1975.

Gouge, William M. *A Short History of Paper Money and Banking in the United States.* Philadelphia: T.W. Ustick, 1833; rpt. New York: Augustus M. Kelly, 1968.

Goulevitch, Arsene de. *Czarism and Revolution.* Hawthorne, California: Omni Publications, n.d., rpt. from 1962 French edition.

Gyohten, Toyoo, and Morrison, Charles E. *Regionalism in A Converging World.* New York: Trilateral Commission, 1992.

Green, Timothy. *The New World of Gold.* New York: Walker & Co., 1981.

Greenspan, Alan. "Gold and Economic Freedom." In *Capitalism: The Unknown Ideal.* Ed. Ayn Rand. New York: Signet Books, 1967.

Greider, William. *Secrets of the Temple.* New York: Simon and Schuster, 1987.

Groseclose, Elgin. *America's Money Machine: The Story of the Federal Reserve.* Westport, Connecticut: Arlington House, 1966.

———. *Money and Man: A survey of Monetary Experience,* 4th ed. Oklahoma: University of Oklahoma Press, 1976.

Hacker, Louis M. *American Capitalism*. New York: Anvil, 1957.

Hagedorn, Hermann. *The Magnate: William Boyce Thompson and His Time*. New York: Reynal & Hitchcock, 1935.

Hancock, Graham. *Lords of Poverty*. New York: Atlantic Monthly Press, 1989.

Hargrave, John. *Montagu Norman*. New York: Greystone Press, 1942.

Hersh, Burton. *The Mellon Family: A Fortune in History*. New York: William Morrow and Co., 1978.

Hoffman, William. *David: A Report on a Rockefeller*. New York: Lyle Stewart, Inc., 1971.

Horan, James D. *Confederate Agent: A Discovery in History*. New York: Crown, 1954.

Jackson, Stanley. *J.P. Morgan*. New York: Stein and Day, 1983.

Jasper, William F. *Global Tyranny*. Appleton, Wisconsin: Western Islands, 1992.

Jastram, Roy W. *The Golden Constant*. New York: Wiley, 1977.

Jefferson, Thomas. *The Basic Writings of Thomas Jefferson*. New York: Willey Book Company, 1944.

———. *The Writings of Thomas Jefferson*. New York: G.P. Putnam's Sons, 1894. Vols. 4, 10.

———. *The Writings of Thomas Jefferson*. Library Edition. Washington: Jefferson Memorial Association, 1903. Vols. XIII, XIV.

Jensen, Merrill. *The New Nation*. New York: Vintage Books, 1950.

Josephson, Matthew. *The Robber Barons: The Great American Capitalists, 1861–1901*. New York: Harcourt Brace Jovanovich, 1934.

Jud, G. Donald and Woelfel, Charles J. *The Desktop Encyclopedia of Banking*. Chicago: Probus Publishing Co., 1988.

Kellock, Harold. "Warburg, the Revolutionist." *The Century Magazine*. May 1915, p. 79.

Kenan, H.S. *The Federal Reserve Bank*. Los Angeles: Noontide Press, 1966.

Kennan, George F. *The Decision to Intervene: Soviet-American Relations, 1917–1920*. Princeton, New Jersey: Princeton University Press, 1958.

———. *Russia Leaves the War: Soviet-American Relations, 1917–1920*. Princeton, New Jersey: Princeton University Press, 1956.

———. *Russia and the West under Lenin and Stalin*. Boston: Little, Brown and Company, 1961.

Kenworthy, Joseph M., and George Young. *The Freedom of the Seas*. New York: Ayer Company, 1929.

Keynes, John Maynard. *Collected Writings*, Vol V. 1930 rpt. New York: Macmillan, 1971.

———. *A Tract on Monetary Reform*. London: MacMillan and Co., 1923.

———. *Economic Consequences of The Peace*. New York: Harcourt, Brace, & Howe, 1919.

Kitchel, Denison. *The Truth About the Panama Canal*. New Rochelle, New York: Arlington House, 1978.

Kolko, Gabriel. *Main Currents in Modern American History*. New York: Harper & Row, 1976.

———. *The Triumph of Conservatism*. New York: The Free Press of Glencoe, a division of the MacMillan Co., 1963.

Krooss, Herman E., ed. *Documentary History of Banking and Currency in the Unites States*. New York: Chelsea House, 1983. Vol. III. Also 1969 edition. Vol. III.

Labaree, Leonard W., ed. *The Papers of Benjamin Franklin*. New Haven: Yale University Press, 1960. Vol. II.

Larson, Martin A. *The Continuing Tax Rebellion*. Old Greenwich, Connecticut: Devin-Adair, 1979.

Laughlin, J. Lawrence. *The Federal Reserve Act: Its Origin and Problems*. New York: Macmillan, 1933.

Lewin, Leonard, ed. *Report from Iron Mountain on the Possibility and Desirability of Peace*. New York: Dell Publishing, 1967.

Lewinsohn, Richard. *The Profits of War through the Ages*. New York: E.P. Dutton, 1937.

Lindbergh, Charles A., Sr. *Banking and Currency and the Money Trust.* Washington, D.C.: National Capital Press, 1913.

———. *The Economic Pinch.* 1923 rpt. Hawthorne, California: Omni Publications, 1968.

Lockhart, R.H. Bruce. *British Agent.* New York and London: G.P. Putnam's Sons, 1933.

Lundberg, Ferdinand. *America's Sixty Families.* New York: Vanguard Press, 1937.

Lyons, Eugene. *Workers' Paradise Lost.* New York: Funk & Wagnalls, 1967.

Mackay, LL.D.,Charles. *Extraordinary Popular Delusions and the Madness of Crowds.* 1841 rpt. New York: L.C. Page & Company, 1932.

Makin, John H. *The Global Debt Crisis: America's Growing Involvement.* New York: Basic Books, 1984.

Martin, Rose L. *Fabian Freeway: High Road to Socialism in the U.S.A.* Boston: Western Islands, 1966.

Mayer, Martin. *The Bankers.* New York: Weybright & Talley, 1974.

McAdoo, William G. *Crowded Years.* New York: Houghton Mifflin, 1931. Rpt. New York: Kennikat Press, 1971.

McIlhany, William H. "No Civil War at All." *Journal of Individualist Studies.* Fall and Winter, 1992.

McLaughlin, Andrew C. *The Confederation and the Constitution.* New York: Collier Books, 1962.

Moody, John. *The Masters of Capital.* New Haven: Yale University Press, 1919.

Morton, Frederic. *The Rothschilds: A Family Portrait.* New York: Atheneum, 1962.

Mullins, Eustace. *Secrets of the Federal Reserve.* Staunton, Virginia, Bankers Research Institute, 1983.

Myers, C.V. *Money and Energy: Weathering the Storm.* Darien, Connecticut: Soundview Books, 1980.

Myers, Gustavus. *History of the Great American Fortunes.* New York: Random House, 1936.

North, Douglass C. *The Economic Growth of the United States.* New York: W.W. Norton, 1966.

Orwell, George. *1984.* New York: New American Library/Signet, 1949.

Owen, Robert L. *National Economy and the Banking System.* Washington, D.C.: U.S. Government Printing Office, 1939.

Paul, Ron, and Lewis Lehrman. *The Case for Gold.* Washington, D.C.: Cato Institute, 1982.

Perloff, James. *Shadows of Power.* Appleton, Wisconsin: Western Islands, 1988.

Pike, Henry R. *A History of Communism in South Africa.* Germiston, South Africa: Christian Mission International of South Africa, 1985.

Polley, Robert L., ed. *Lincoln: His Words and His World.* Waukesha, Wisconsin: Country Beautiful Foundation, 1965.

Poor, Henry V. *Money and Its Laws.* London: Henry S. King and Co., 1877.

Pratt, Sereno S. *The Work of Wall Street.* New York: D. Appleton, 1916; rpt. New York: Arno Press, 1975.

Quigley, Carroll. *The Anglo-American Establishment: From Rhodes to Cliveden.* New York: Books in Focus, 1981.

———. *Tragedy and Hope: A History of the World in Our Time.* New York: MacMillan, 1966.

Ramsay, David. *History of the American Revolution.* London: Johnson and Stockdale, 1791. Vol. II.

Rees, David. *Harry Dexter White: A Study in Paradox.* New York: Coward, McCann & Geoghegan, 1973.

Remini, Robert V. *Andrew Jackson and the Course of American Democracy, 1833–1845.* New York: Harper & Row, 1984.

———. *Andrew Jackson and the Course of American Freedom, 1822–1832.* New York: Harper & Row, 1981.

———. *The Life of Andrew Jackson*. New York: Harper & Row, 1988.

Ricardo, David. *The Works and Correspondence of David Ricardo: Pamphlets 1815–1823*. Piero Sraffa, ed. Cambridge: Cambridge University Press, 1951. Vol. IV.

Richards, R.D. *The Early History of Banking in England*. New York: Augustus M. Kelley, 1929; rpt. 1965.

Richardson, J.D. *A Compilation of the Messages and Papers of the Presidents, 1789–1908*. Washington: Bureau of National Literature and Art, 1908. Vol. II.

Ritter, Lawrence S., ed. *Money and Economic Activity*. Boston: Houghton Mifflin, 1967.

Roscoe, Theodore. *The Web of Conspiracy: The Complete Story of the Men Who Murdered Abraham Lincoln*. Englewood Cliffs, New Jersey: Prentice-Hall, 1959.

Rothbard, Murray N. *America's Great Depression*. Kansas City: Sheed and Ward, 1963.

———. *Conceived in Liberty: The Revolutionary War, 1775–1784*. New Rochelle, New York: Arlington House, 1979. Vol. IV.

———. "The Federal Reserve as A Cartelization Device." *Money in Crisis*. Barry N. Siegel, ed. New York: Ballinger, 1984, pp. 89 ff.

———. *The Mystery of Banking*. New York: Richardson & Snyder, 1983.

———. *What Has Government Done to Our Money?* Larkspur, Colorado: Pine Tree Press, 1964.

Ruml, Beardsley. "Taxes for Revenue Are Obsolete." *American Affairs*. January, 1946, p. 35.

Russell, Bertrand Arthur William. *The Impact of Science on Society*. New York: Simon and Schuster, 1953.

Samuelson, Paul A. *Economics*, 8th ed. New York: McGraw-Hill, 1970.

Saussy, F. Tupper. *The Miracle on Mainstreet*. Sewanee, Tennessee: Spencer Judd, 1980.

Schrader, Del. *Jesse James Was One of His Names*. Arcadia, California: Santa Anita Press, 1975.

Schlesinger, Jr., Arthur M. *The Age of Jackson*. New York: Mentor Books, 1945.

Schweikart, Larry, ed. *The Encyclopedia of American History and Biography*. New York: Facts on File, 1990.

Scott, Otto. *The Secret Six: The Fool as Martyr*. Vol. III of *The Sacred Fool Quartet*. Columbus, South Carolina: Foundation for American Education, 1979.

Selgin, George A. *The Theory of Free Banking: Money Supply under Competitive Note Issue*. Totowa, New Jersey: Rowman & Littlefield, 1988.

Seligman, Edwin. Proceedings of the Academy of Political Science. Vol IV, No. 4. New York: 1914. pp. 3–6.

Sennholz, Hans F. "The Great Banking Scandal." *The Freeman*. Nov., 1990, p. 404.

———. "The Great Depression." *The Freeman*. Irvington-on-Hudson. March, 1988, p. 90.

———. *Money and Freedom*. Spring Mills, Pennsylvania: Libertarian Press, 1985.

———. "Old Banking Myths." *The Freeman*. Irvington-on-Hudson, New York. May, 1989, pp. 175–76.

Seymour, Charles. *The Intimate Papers of Colonel House*. 4 vols. New York: Houghton Mifflin Co., 1926.

Shapiro, Leonard. *The Russian Revolutions of 1917*. New York: Basic Books, 1984.

Shaw, Archer H., ed. *The Lincoln Encyclopedia: The Spoken and Written Words of A. Lincoln*. New York: Macmillan Co., 1950.

Shaw, W.A. *Theory and Principles of Central Banking*. London & New York: Sir I. Pitman & Sons, Ltd., 1930.

Siegel, Barry. *Money in Crisis: The Federal Reserve, the Economy, and Monetary Reform*. Cambridge, Massachusetts: Ballinger, 1984

Simpson, Colin. *The Lusitania*. Boston: Little, Brown & Co., 1972.

Smith, Arthur. *The Real Colonel House*. New York: George H. Doran Company, 1918.

Smith, Vera C. *The Rationale of Central Banking*. London: P.S. King & Son, 1936.

Smyth, Albert Henry, ed. *The Writings of Benjamin Franklin*. New York: Macmillan, 1906. Vol. VII.

Sprague, Irvine H. *Bailout: An Insider's Account of Bank Failures and Rescues*. New York: Basic Books, 1986.

Steffens, Lincoln. *The Letters of Lincoln Steffens*. New York: Harcourt, Brace, 1941.

Stephenson, Nathaniel Wright. *Nelson W. Aldrich in American Politics*. New York: Scribners, 1930; rpt. New York: Kennikat Press, 1971.

Sumner, William Graham. *A History of American Currency*. New York: Holt, 1884.

Sutton, Antony C. *The Best Enemy Money Can Buy*. Billings, Montana: Liberty House Press, 1986.

————. *National Suicide: Military Aid to the Soviet Union*. New Rochelle. New York: Arlington House, 1973.

————. *Wall Street and the Bolshevik Revolution*. New Rochelle, New York: Arlington House, 1974.

————. *Wall Street and FDR*. New Rochelle, New York: Arlington House, 1975.

————. *Wall Street and the Rise of Hitler*. Seal Beach, California: '76 Press, 1976.

————. *The War on Gold*. Seal Beach, California: '76 Press, 1977.

Tocqueville, Alexis de. *Democracy in America*, Vol. II. New York: Alfred Knopf, 1945.

Trotsky, Leon. *My Life*. New York: Scribner's, 1930.

Turner, Dennis. *When Your Bank Fails*. Princeton, New Jersey: Amwell Publishing, Inc., 1983.

United Nations. *1985 Report on the World Social Situation*. New York: United Nations, 1985. Publication E/CN.5/1985/Rev.1, p. 14.

Vanderlip, Frank A. "From Farm Boy to Financier: Stories of Railroad Moguls." *The Saturday Evening Post*. Feb. 9, 1935, p. 24.

————. *From Farm Boy to Financier*. New York: D. Appleton–Century Company, 1935.

Vieira, Jr., Edwin. *Pieces of Eight: The Monetary Powers and Disabilities of the United States Constitution*. New Jersey: Sound Dollar Committee, 1983.

Viereck, George Sylvester. *The Strangest Friendship in History: Woodrow Wilson and Colonel House*. New York: Liveright Publishers, 1932.

Viola, Herman J. *Andrew Jackson*. New York: Chelsea House, 1986.

Warburg, James. *The Long Road Home*. New York: Doubleday, 1964.

Warburg, Paul. *The Federal Reserve System: Its Origin and Growth*. New York: Macmillan, 1930. Vol. I.

Watt, James G. *The Courage of A Conservative*. New York: Simon and Schuster, 1985.

Weinstein, Allen. *Perjury: The Hiss-Chambers Case*. New York: Vintage Books, 1978.

Weiss, Roger W. "The Colonial Monetary Standard of Massachusetts." *Economic History Review*, No. 27, November, 1974, p. 589.

Welles, Chris. *The Last Days of the Club*. New York: E.P. Dutton, 1975.

Wheeler, George. *Pierpont Morgan and Friends: The Anatomy of a Myth*. Englewood Cliffs, New Jersey: Prentice Hall, 1973.

"Why Did We Let Trotsky Go? How Canada Lost an Opportunity to Shorten the War." *MacLeans* magazine. Canada, June, 1919.

Willis, H. Parker. "The Failure of the Federal Reserve." *The North American Review*. May, 1929, pp. 547–56.

————. Letters from Henry Parker Willis to J. Laurence Laughlin. July 14, 18, 1912. J. Laurence Laughlin Papers, Library of Congress, July 14 & 18, 1912.

Wilson, Derek. *Rothschild: The Wealth and Power of A Dynasty*. New York: Charles Scribner's Sons, 1988.

Wilson, R. McNair. *Monarchy or Money Power*. London: Eyre and Spottiswoode, Ltd., 1933.

Wrangell-Rokassowsky, Carl. *Before the Storm*. Ventimiglia, Italy: Tipo-Litografia Ligure, 1972.

Yago, Glenn. *Junk Bonds: How High Yield Securities Restructured Corporate America*. New York: Oxford University Press, 1991.